SEA AND LAND

SEA AND LAND:

AN ILLUSTRATED HISTORY OF

THE WONDERFUL AND CURIOUS THINGS OF NATURE EXISTING BEFORE AND SINCE THE DELUGE

BEING

A NATURAL HISTORY OF THE SEA

JAMES W. BUEL

GYAN

Published by

Gyan Publishing House
5, Ansari Road
Daryaganj, New Delhi-110002
Phone: 011-47034999, 9811692060
E-mail: books@gyanbooks.com

Distribution Network
gyanbooks.com
India, USA, Canada, UK, Australia

ISBN: 978-93-6920-024-5 (PB)

First Published, 1887

2nd Impression 2025

Printed at: Gyan Press, Delhi.

SEA AND LAND
Author: JAMES W. BUEL

SEA AND LAND

AN ILLUSTRATED HISTORY

The Wonderful and Curious Things of Nature Existing before and since the Deluge.

EMBODYING DESCRIPTIONS OF THE MIGHTY WORLD OF WATERS, AND OF THE MARVELOUS CREATURES WHICH COMPRISE ITS INHABITANTS.

BEING

A NATURAL HISTORY OF THE SEA.

Illustrated by Stirring Adventures with Whales, Devil-Fish, Giant Polypi, Sharks, Sword-Fish, Dog-Fish, Stinging-Fish, Crocodiles, etc.; to which are added Descriptions of all the Phenomenal Creatures and Things that are Found in the Deep Sea, together with a Full Account of the Remarkable Legends and Superstitions so Prevalent among Sailors.

INCLUDING

A HISTORY OF THE WORLD ASHORE, THE SURPRISES THAT ARE TO BE MET WITH IN ALL THE REGIONS OF THE EARTH, IN THE KINGDOMS OF ANIMAL, INSECT AND VEGETABLE CREATION.

ALSO,

A NATURAL HISTORY OF LAND-CREATURES

Such as Lions, Tigers, Elephants, Rhinoceri, Hippopotami, Gorillas, Chimpanzees, Mandrills, Bears, Wild Dogs, etc., with Hundreds of Thrilling Escapades illustrating their Character and Disposition.

TO WHICH IS APPENDED A DESCRIPTION OF

THE CANNIBALS AND WILD RACES OF THE WORLD,

Their Customs, Habits, Ferocity and Curious Ways.

BY J. W. BUEL,

Author of "The World's Wonders," "Heroes of the Plains," "Exile Life in Siberia," etc., etc.

ILLUSTRATED WITH 300 ENGRAVINGS, REPRESENTING THE WONDERFUL CREATURES OF THE WORLD IN THEIR NATURAL CONDITION, AND

SUPERB EMBLEMATIC COLORED PLATES.

SOLD BY SUBSCRIPTION ONLY.

Published by

J. S. ROBERTSON & BROS.

TORONTO, ONT.

INTRODUCTORY.

THE work of preparing the following pages has been a peculiarly pleasant one, prompted as it was by a passionate love for the wonderful in nature, and the valuable study it permitted in the most fruitful fields of literature and observation. Before commencing to harvest in the field of nature's wonders, or to glean behind the reapers who have preceded me in the unfolding of the curiosities of sea and land, I had utterly failed to appreciate how prodigal nature is; how illimitable her resources, how marvelous the diversity of her creative power. As I proceeded, gathering interesting facts, each new wonder became the parent of a host of rarer marvels, until I became fairly bewildered by a sabbaoth of natural phenomena, and a multiplicity of animate organisms of which I had before formed no conception.

It has been my purpose, and, indeed, the chief idea that prompted this compilation, to bring to the attention of my readers only those things which are best calculated to inspire the loftiest conceptions of Deity, and a profound admiration for the wondrous works by which we are surrounded and associated; to incite a desire in both young and old to become better acquainted with the evolutions in nature, and the curious species of life with which we are least familiar; to exalt the study of Natural History, Geography, Mankind, and those branches of science which bring us into a closer relation with, and a better understanding and appreciation of, the mysterious and infinite wisdom of nature's God.

Though I have been somewhat of a traveler, my own observations find place in comparatively few of the following pages, having confined myself principally to discoveries made by more noted investigators. In so doing I have spared nothing to become familiar with the works of the greatest travelers and scientists, and to glean from them their most valuable and interesting revelations, by which we are brought into familiar acquaintanceship with every portion of the globe, and the wonderfully diversified vegetable and animal life thereon. To attain this end more perfectly, I have consulted more than a thousand standard books of Natural History, and have carefully endeavored to transfer the best thought of each to this work; to these several good authors I therefore desire to extend my acknowledgments, and to give them the larger credit, reserving to myself only whatever merit I may deserve for gathering their ideas and discoveries from out so large a library and condensing them into a single book, to which I have given the comprehensive title, "SEA AND LAND."

J. W. B.

LIST OF ILLUSTRATIONS.

TABLE OF CONTENTS.

MYSTERIES OF THE DEEP SEA.

CHAPTER XI.

THE WORLD DOWN UNDER THE SEA.

CHAPTER XII.

MODERN MONSTERS OF THE OCEAN WORLD.

CHAPTER XIII.

TITANIC CREATURES OF THE SEA—WHALES.

CHAPTER XIV.

THE VORACIOUS SHARK.

CHAPTER XV.

THE SWORD-FISH AND SAW-FISH.

CHAPTER XVI.

MARINE MEN.

WILD RACES OF THE WORLD.

MYSTERIES OF THE DEEP SEA.

CHAPTER I

WHO has not longed to gaze upon the ocean, or to ride upon its mighty bosom, a world unto itself? Yet, to see it, or plough its sky-tinted waves, fringed by the horizon on every side, is but the threshold of interest, over which we may pass into mysterious labyrinths, the abode of marvels which the landsman has hardly dreamed of. All the wonders of land have their counterpart in the sea, whether animals, birds or reptiles, monstrosities, or sun-hued beauties, gigantic forests, or gardens of floral loveliness. There, too, are mighty cities, peopled by myriads of active and ingenious creatures, living in houses resplendent with richest colors, and more bewitching than was Solomon's Temple, or the floating gardens of Ancient Babylon. Wild and uncouth forms, dreadful as the Cyclopean Polyphemus, ravage the sea-world, while about the Madripore caverns, unmindful of croaking monsters, flit, with lambent wings, gay-plumaged humming-birds, whose iris-decked scales are more gorgeous than was ever painted feather.

It is the purpose of this book to describe the ocean-world, its phenomena and inhabitants, that those who have never had the opportunity of crossing the sea, as well, also, those whose opportunities have been wasted by want of observation or time for study, may know how truly wonderful, if not mysterious, are the creatures that move in that buoyant sphere — where man is hardly permitted to enter — in a world distinctively their own.

BEGINNING OF THE WORLD.

We are told that the world is composed of one-fourth land and three-fourths water, but to be scientifically exact we must say the world is about nineteen-twentieths water, for there are many times more water than solids in all animal life, while the earth is filled with unremitting streams of the life-giving liquid. Superficially, however, the geographical assertion is correct; but, considering even this to be so, the mind pauses in contemplating this vast disproportion, since, as land animals, we are apt to consider the soil and its principles in their essential uses for the support of animal life, and regard the sea as a medium for international communication. How selfish this conception is, must appear when we reflect that God's creatures make up the sum of life, and that He is as regardful for the smallest insect as of the intellectual giants of mankind. The proportion of life in the sea compared with that on the land is much greater than the difference which we find in the proportion of land and water, for while the land teems with swarms of life, the ocean has its myriads in nearly every drop.

VITALIZING EFFECTS OF RAIN.

Science teaches us that primarily our planet was a molten mass; some say it was a fragment thrown off by centrifugal force from the sun, while others attempt to describe its cosmos. We will leave the scientists to their theories, pipes and beer, making no attempt to follow where they lead, and confine ourselves to established facts. If a basin of water is left long exposed to the sun we find that it disappears, and we know that the disappearance is due to evaporation; the sun is continually lifting up water, which becomes condensed into clouds, and after being charged heavily enough with moisture it is precipitated again in the form of rain. This process of lifting up and discharging again, subserves one of the most beneficent effects of creation, because it acts the double part of purifying and vitalizing. It purifies by causing the ocean to continue in motion, for as the discharge of rain is variable so the ocean level is variable, and as it is ever seeking to maintain a level it is always at unrest, and can therefore never stagnate. The vitalizing effect of rain is in the nourishment it supplies to vegetation. Like the human body, all vegetable forms continually throw off a secretion through their pores, and this effete matter needs removal; this the rain does, while at the same time it furnishes food for the roots, and needful nourishment for the branches. In lifting water from the ocean the sun's beams do not decompose the salt, but leave it, as it is too heavy for carriage, and thus only fresh water is raised and precipitated. This fact is of great service to sailing vessels, for sometimes voyages are so long that the supply of fresh water taken on board becomes exhausted, in which event a canvass is spread over the vessel in such manner as the rain falling thereon runs off into barrels and is thus collected.

Evidences, which cannot be misinterpreted, show us that at one time the world was covered with water, and there is every reason also to believe that previous to the era of universal ocean, the world was enveloped with fire. It is asserted that when the earth was in a cooling state, only fairly solidified, the first precipitation of aqueous vapors, coming in contact with certain metals, they were decomposed, and the result was the earth became enveloped in flames, which raged fiercely until the metals themselves were decomposed.

Sir Humphrey Davy suggested a very beautiful and easy experiment showing the probability of such a catastrophe having occurred.

EVOLUTION OF WATER OUT OF FLAMES.

But the sea of flame gradually retired as vapors continued condensing, until at length the ocean of water took its place and creation developed the majesty of life. Though deep waters covered the earth, the sea of flame did not die out in the cavernous depths where Pluto held his reign, and the fierce fire-belching volcanoes continued to disturb the "landscape of the sea." Mangin says:

"Imagination not unwillingly pictures to itself the strange and superb spectacle of a limitless ocean seething over its volcanic bed, and heaving in every direction its contending billows, kindled here and there by the blood-red lustre of a glowing sky, struggling through a dense and stifling mist; while in its waves myriads of invisible beings, embryos of future organisms, fighting for life, and rising to the surface in quest of inspiring light, wait expectant, amidst the throes of the terrible stir and tumult all around them, the dawn of a true day upon a completed world."

During the period of universal fire we may safely assert that there was no life, but as the earth became covered with water animated creatures came into existence, so that the ocean was really the origin of life; but here we have a singular proof of the theory of evolution, for we find nature advancing from the simple to the complex, and that the lower species of plants and animals preceded the creation of the higher. In truth, a series of concurrent facts and testimonies prove quite conclusively that man was preceded by nearly all other forms of life, he being apparently reserved for the capsheaf of creation's handiwork.

We may very properly assume that, among the first, and as far as human interests are concerned, the most important creatures that existed, were the *Madreporidæ* or coral Zoophytes, which have ever been so industrious in their work, that some of our largest islands are the result of their labors. Leopold Von Buch asserts that the whole formation of Jura mountains consists of huge banks of antidiluvian corallines, which surround at a certain distance the ancient mountain-chains.

PHENOMENA OF THE SEA—THE TIDES.

Before proceeding to a description of the animal life of the sea, let us cursorily examine some of the most important phenomena which distinguish it. First of these are the tides—omitting the currents, which are to the sea what the circulation of blood is to the animal system:

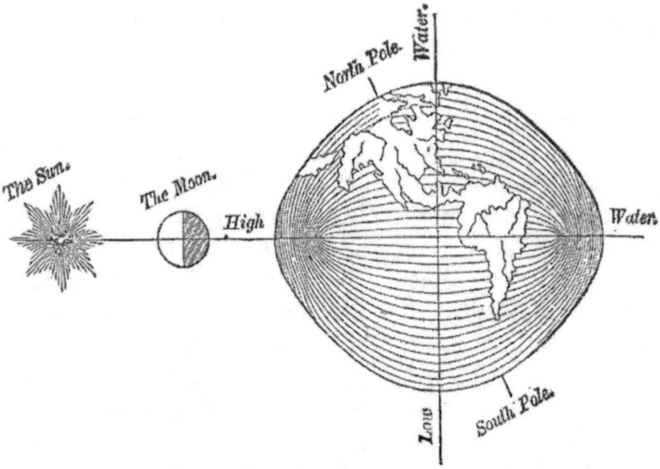

ILLUSTRATING THE SOLAR-LUNAR TIDES.

The tides are produced by the joint action of the sun and moon, and may be briefly explained as follows: It being known by every person that the planets are held in their several orbits by the forces of attraction and gravitation, it must follow that there is a reciprocal influence, and all are inter-dependent. The moon is governed by the sun because the latter is her center of gravitation, while the moon is similarly governed by the earth. As the earth, therefore, revolves, it is subjected to the attractive force of the sun and moon, but while the crust preserves at all times its exact configuration, owing to the cohesion of its molecules, the liquid, readily responding to all influences, is raised or depressed, as it were, by the solar or lunar attraction. In fact, under the influence of this attraction the ocean waters are periodically upraised, and assume the shape of a liquid mountain, which follows the apparent motion of the sun, and consequently moves in an opposite direction to that of our planet. But, as Mangin says: "These first oscillations of the ocean, which are *solar* tides, are not to be compared with the *lunar* tides, and, in fact, only become perceptible when combined with them; for, though the attractive force of the sun is incomparably greater than that of the moon, yet, owing to the more remote distance of the former, the difference of effect on our globe is very much less." Thus, then, the moon, the earth's handmaid, plays the principal part in the production of tides. As between bodies attraction is always reciprocal; as the stronger — that whose density is greater — always controls the weaker, the moon is compelled to obey the earth and gravitate round her; but the seas, boundless as they appear to us, represent only a minimum fraction of the terrestrial mass, and our satellite is strong enough and sufficiently near us to draw in her train a portion of the waters of our ocean round the planet from which it cannot separate them. The tides usually happen twice in twenty-four hours, because the rotation of the globe brings the same point of the ocean twice under the meridian of the moon.

The winds exercise a very remarkable influence upon the tide, even to its partial suppression. Such is particularly the case in the Gulf of Vera Cruz, where, instead of two tides daily, there is often but one in three or four days, when the wind blows violently in a direction contrary to the wave. If the force of an adverse wind can stay the approaching tides, we can conceive how greatly it will increase their rush in a formidable degree when it blows in the same direction. The sea then falls with fury upon the shores, often carrying frightful destruction.

DREADFUL DEVASTATION BY THE TIDES.

The low coasts of Denmark and Holland are frequently exposed to the fury of devastating tides, and some of the most appalling disasters which history records have been caused by tides pushed onward by high winds. A few of these may here be given as illustrating the direful consequences as explained.

In the fall of 1634, a tempestuous tide broke upon the Isle of Nordstrand, and in the space of a few hours destroyed no less than thirteen hundred houses, six thousand people and fifty thousand head of cattle.

In the year 1280, a similar disaster occurred at Winchelsea, on the coast of Sussex, where three hundred houses and more than a thousand people were overwhelmed.

In 1446, the coast of Holland was overtaken by a tide that destroyed seventy-two villages and one hundred thousand persons.

In 1483, a rushing tide overflowed the banks of the Severn River for a period of ten days, and so devastated the country that the highest hills were covered, and thousands of persons lost their lives.

In 1530, more than four hundred thousand people were drowned by the breaking of the dikes on the Holland coast.

In 1617, Catalonia was overwhelmed by a tide that destroyed fifty thousand human beings.

In 1717, a tidal inundation devastated a portion of New Zealand, causing the loss of thirteen hundred people.

Dublin suffered from a similar disaster in 1787, by the sudden rising of the Liffey, but the number of lives lost has not been estimated.

In 1829, the Vistula was suddenly overflowed, destroying four thousand houses, ten thousand head of cattle, and so many men, women and children, that when the waters subsided the territory appeared to be covered with corpses.

In 1780, a dreadful devastation of Barbadoes Island occurred, in which an immense amount of property was destroyed, and thousands of persons lost their lives; but stranger still was the fact that after a subsidence of the storm there were several old guns found on the shore, which had been washed up from the bottom of the sea by the tempest's fury.

Figuier says, if the waves in their reflux meet with obstacles, whirlwinds and whirlpools are the result. Such are the whirlpools in the Straits of Messina, between the rocks of Scylla and Charybdis. Another celebrated whirlpool is that of Euripus, near the island of Eubœa, and another of yet greater importance exists in the Gulf of Bothnia. But the most dangerous of all is the mælstrom off the coast of Norway, which, at certain intervals, is so powerful as to draw into its vortex and destroy vessels of no inconsiderable size.

Tides and whirlpools sometimes combine, and in their effects produce hurricanes, so dreadful to navigators. The Indian Ocean is chiefly the scene of these devastating winds, which are almost powerful enough to blow vessels out of the water, striking their keels with such a force as to throw them about in the most helpless manner.

TIDAL INUNDATION ON THE DANISH COAST.

STORMS AND WATER-SPOUTS.

Storms are phenomena with which we are all familiar. The lowering or green-crested clouds, followed by the inky pall of rolling cumulus, through which vivid flashes from heaven's artillery split their way and roar with deafening resonance; then comes the wind, a fitful gust at first, playing with light atoms, which are lifted in a whirl, then dropped again; soon the trees begin to nod and we hear a sullen rattle which now rapidly increases until the storm bursts full upon us, perhaps a cyclone clearing its way through forest or town, like a fell monster with Titanic arm, wielding the axe of devastation, uprooting and tearing down with a rage that subsides only when desolation is complete.

For the storm we all feel awe, foreseeing or prophesying calamity as its legitimate spoil, but the storm on land is but a lamb compared with the storm-lion on the sea. Once only in my life have I been a witness to the fury which the elements of sea and air sometimes exhibit to the luckless mariner. It was during my second voyage across the Atlantic, fortunately on a staunch steamer built to withstand the fiercest onslaughts of wind and wave; but never can I forget the terror of my experience. It was in the evening, at the close of a lovely day, when the saloon became an inviting place for social pastimes. A game was in progress and none had a thought of impending danger, until the captain appeared and said: "A storm is brewing; better get below."

Hardly had the words been uttered when a crash, loud as a columbiad at our very side, thundered at the saloon door and blanched every face inside. So surprised were all, that none at first could tell what caused the report, though the tremor which went through the ship told that something had struck her. It was a wave, that, with the force of a falling mountain, had plunged against the vessel's broadside and broke over the decks and saloon as well. It was only a storm, but I was spell-bound with interest; we quickly went below, and the hatches being put down we were entombed in the ship, though there were not wanting sky-lights and port-holes through which we could witness the furious display which now followed. Though the night had now come on and darkness brooded over the desolate waste, by the lightning's incessant flashes the panorama of lashing waves and a laboring vessel were distinctly visible. How dreadfully calamitous looked the boiling clouds that hung down like

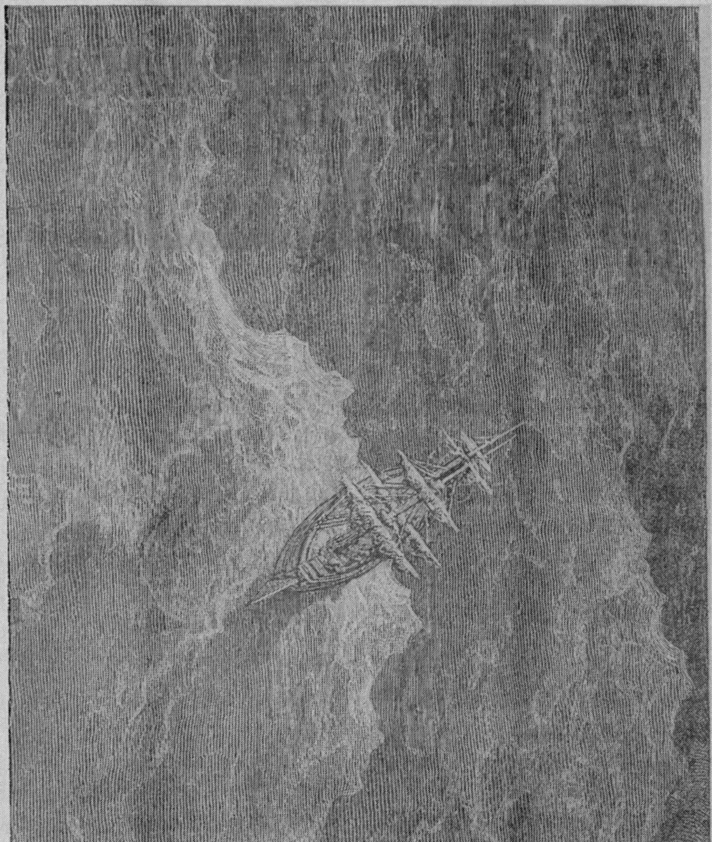

A VESSEL IN A STORM, BY DORE.

the hand of Satan, pronged and hooked, grasping for the live freight of the assaulted ship! The masts were bare of canvass, and yet, they curved and tossed under the wind-pressure while the ropes rattled like hail on a window pane. The waves rolled up in beetling craigs, then went down again into gorges as cavernous as ocean caves, while one after another they covered our good ship with their shrouds of spray. Onward we sped, the unceasing throbbing of the screw barely audible above the storm's ravings, but it kept the vessel's head on, though billowy waves would rise before her, and so powerful that the impact would be like striking a rock. Nobly would she dive through the liquid barrier, then vault up again and toss the water like a monster creature shaking the brine from its mane, and bidding defiance to Neptune's anger. Surrounding her with vengeance and fell purpose, the on-rushing billows would strike the vessel's side with such a force as to heel her over until her very keel would be visible, and only a miracle, it would appear, could prevent her from capsizing. Thus wave-swept and buffeted like a cork, the ship steamed on, but groaning at every rivet in her iron sides and plunging like a mortally wounded bull blinded by his own blood. On the decks a scene of wild commotion had been enacted, which, had I seen, would have increased my solicitude, for nearly all the life-boats had been either stove-in or broken away, while the saloon was fairly smashed into kindling-wood by the irresistible waves. The thought was constantly occurring, what if our ship should spring a leak; if the rivets should be drawn, as seemed always threatening; or, if she should capsize, take fire, or even her engines become disabled? In the wake of these thoughts arose the spectre of three hundred frantic passengers crying for help when there could be no help save that of God alone, for in the dark pall of that tumultuous night, out on that wide, tempestuous sea, there was naught but a melancholy waste of woe and elemental vengeance; nothing but the dashing, wild surges growling with maniacal anger; no beacon, harbor, aid; none, save God's omnipresence. The petrels, gulls and other tireless wings were on the shore or flown to some spot where the raging winds were not. I thought, should calamity befall, what if the life-boats are launched, or what friend would a light spar be; for the curling waves would fill the best life-boat before it could receive a load, and lashed on a wave-washed spar would be like embracing death. I thought again, if this thin barrier which separates us from eternity should be ruptured, how our ship will be reported overdue; then suspicions of disaster will follow, while the papers will tell stories of how some were passengers against their will, while others were providentially prevented from embarking; and then, as the months went by and still no news of our foundered vessel, her name would be added to the list of mysterious disappearances at sea, and thus our eventful lives would end in ocean's grimy catacombs. These thoughts were not the creatures of fear, for I had implicit confidence in the ship and crew, never doubt-

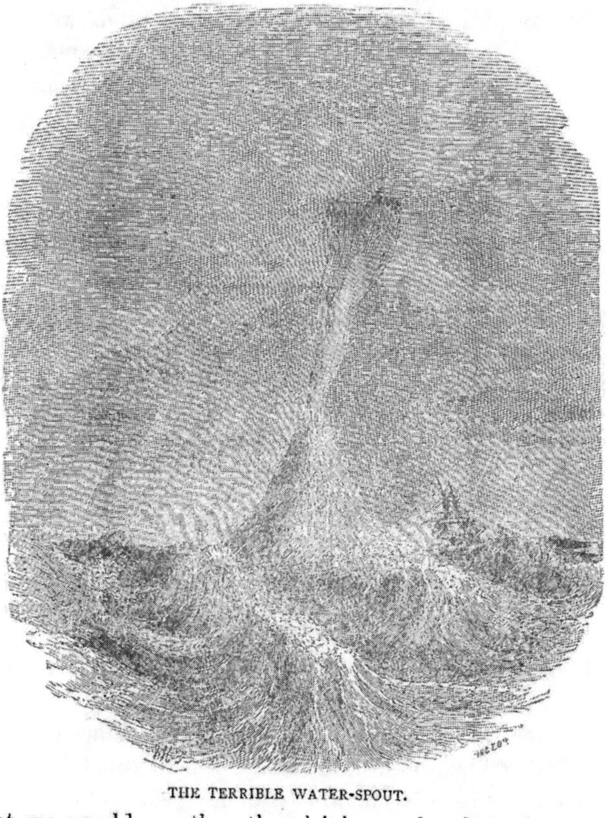

THE TERRIBLE WATER-SPOUT.

ing that we would weather the driving gale, but they were the spontaneous emanations of the mind then brought into the presence of a contemplated disaster, and are common to all persons under like circumstances.

THE DANGEROUS WATER-SPOUT.

But more dangerous than the storm is a water-spout at sea, though so small is the space which it affects, that it is seldom vessels fall within its power. Our modern definition of water-spout is a dense cloud, highly charged with electricity, moving irregularly and with amazing rapidity, with inclination to dip. This cloud, owing to an apparent tendency to fall while gyrating with extraordinary velocity, inwardly assumes the shape of a reversed cone, or funnel. Its color, as described by Maury, is a deep gray, its aspect frightful beyond expression, and no less so are the elemental displays which precede it. The sky becomes dreadfully lowering, an unnatural darkness prevails, caused by a sickly, yellowish sunlight, and the atmosphere is often impregnated with sulphurous fumes. A hurricane or, more properly, cyclone, sweeps over the breaking waves with ominous screechings, and a dull, monotous roar. It seems as if a volcano were pouring forth from the deep bowels of the earth, while the lightning darts in blinding flashes, and terriffic crashes of thunder swiftly follow each other; then the water-spout falls nearer and nearer the water, which becomes violently agitated underneath, until, rising into a cone, the lowering, twisting cloud reaches the swirling cone of water, and the two are united in a roar so terrible as to be fairly deafening. The cyclone on land is the water-spout at sea, and woe to the luckless vessel that chances to be within its influence, for it would almost certainly dismantle and swallow her up, however strong she might be.

CHAPTER II.

CURIOSITIES OF THE OCEAN.

BEFORE proceeding to describe the wonderful life that crowds the sea, let us explain one of the most remarkable facts in nature, viz.: Why is the ocean salt? This question has interested civilization for ages, and for an equal length of time scientists have had to make answer by quoting some idle fable. It was formerly believed that the saline properties of the sea were due to the fact that during the early period of maritime industry, ships were charged to throw into it large pyramids of salt; what for, no one pretended to know. The strictly scientific maintained that salt was engendered spontaneously at the bottom of the sea. The scientists were never satisfied that this was the case, but for want of a better explanation, they encouraged the belief of immense salt-beds in the ocean, and looked wise, as usual.

L. Figuier, borrowing somewhat from the theories of Maury, has given us, at length, the true cause of the ocean's salt, and so perfectly consistent is his theory with well-established natural laws, that it is, I believe, now universally accepted. From his explanation I therefore quote:

"In the first stage of our planet, before the watery vapors contained in the primitive atmosphere were condensed, and before they had begun to fall on the earth in the form of boiling rain, the shell of the earth contained an infinite variety of heterogeneous mineral substances, some soluble in water, others not. When rain fell on the burning surface for the first time, the waters became charged with all the soluble substances, which were reunited, and afterwards deposited, accumulating in the large depressions of the soil. The seas of the primitive globe were thus formed of rain-water, holding in solution all that the earth had given up, collected in large basins. Chloride of sodium, sulphates of soda, magnesia, potassium, lime, and silicium, in the form of soluble silicate; in a word, every soluble matter that the primitive globe contained formed part of the mineral contingent of this water. If we reflect that through all time, up to the present day, none of the general laws of nature have changed; if we consider that the soluble substances contained in the water of the primitive seas have remained there, and that the fresh waters of the rivers constantly replace the water which disappears by evaporation, we have the true explanation of the saltness of sea water."

In the saline properties of sea water, Maury discovers one of the principal forces from which currents in the ocean proceed. "The brine of the ocean is the ley of the earth," he says, "from it the sea derives dynamical powers, and its currents their main strength. Why is the sea made salt? It is the salts of the sea that impart to its waters those curious anomalies in the law of freezing and of thermal dilitation (expansion by heat). It is the salts of the sea that assist the rays of the sun to penetrate its bosom. The circulation of the ocean is indispensable to the distribution of temperature—to the maintenance of the meteorological and climatic conditions which rule the development of life; and this circulation could not exist—at least, the character of its waters would be completely changed—if they were fresh, in place of salt."

THE WORLD DOWN UNDER THE SEA.

Jules Verne, in his "Twenty Thousand Leagues Under the Sea," has given us a beautiful, though imaginative, description of the cities and marvels which exist under the waves, yet his industrious fancy has hardly succeeded in reaching even the boundary of existing facts. So deep are the oceans — sometimes exceeding three miles — that we can never explore, save with plummets, the recesses which are so well guarded by the extraordinary pressure which there prevails. While beyond our immediate observation, we know that even these dark-darkling caves are the abodes of life, teeming, in fact, with an eye-less *infusoria* whose skeletons have been heaped into mountains, and helped to make the continents. In the ocean is displayed a marvelous mechanism and distributed force, which prevents our planet from becoming a lifeless, frigid body. The ocean life might continue even were there no islands or continents, for land is hardly essential to marine animals. Yet naught on land could survive the drying up of the ocean. The womb of life is in the sea, and therefore it is the ocean and not the earth that is our mother. So infinitely great is the life in the sea, that if we take a portion of ocean water and enclose it in a bottle it almost immediately becomes noisome and corrupt. It can neither be transported nor preserved, and this is due to the fact that its every drop is alive with invisible animalculæ, which die the moment they are separated from the great body that nourishes them. The variable color of the ocean often, though not always, is caused by the minute animals which swarm upon its surface. The Black Sea derives its name from the frequent storms which convulse it. Around the Maldine Islands the ocean is really black; in the Persian Gulf a beautiful pure green; in the Gulf of Guinea white, and in the Polar Sea an olive green. The Vermillion Sea is so called on account of its color, produced by microscopic animalculæ; the Red Sea, however, is colored, at certain periods, by a species of *frog-spittle*, a kind of water-plant that has its roots barely below the water surface. But the most remarkable effect produced by the infusoria is seen in the luminosity which their infinitely numerous bodies impart to large areas of the sea. Of this phenomenon, Mangin writes:

GLEAMING LIGHTS OF THE SEA.

"That those infusoria should tint the sea is, undoubtedly, a marvelous phenomenon; but they do more — they brighten and enkindle it. The phosphorescence of ocean was long a mystery, before which man's reason stood confounded, and which inspired him with mingled feelings of admiration and terror. Luminous water! The sea on fire, yet harmless, and still preserving its cold or warm temperature. How extraordinary a mirage! How strange an anomaly! * * * In our temperate climates, and in that region which extends between the English and French coasts, we see the ocean phosphorescent only in summer, and in seasons of great tranquility. The foam of the waves, which die upon the ribbed sand, the spray which is churned up by the boatman's oar, or the steamer's paddle-wheel, the wake of the vessel, all seem composed of a luminous snow with keen steel-blue reflections. But this spectacle may not be compared with the scenes presented by the great tropical sea, hot and electric, and teeming with life. There the phenomenon occurs both in fair and bad weather. In the former case, the waves seem to dart lightnings, like a storm-cloud. Cook, and several other navigators, have observed the phosphorescence in these regions in misty weather and on a billowy sea."

I may also add that I once witnessed the same phenomenon during the severe winter of 1881–'82, while making a trip by sea from Portland to Boston.

WHAT MAKES THE SEA LUMINOUS?

The luminosity of the sea has been attributed to various causes, but it was not until 1854 that the real cause was discovered, and settled beyond dispute for all time. In a letter written by Captain Klingman, of the American clipper *Shooting Star*, to Captain Maury, the facts of this interesting discovery are set forth, as follows:

"At forty-five minutes past 7 P. M., my attention was attracted by the color of the sea, which rapidly became whiter and whiter. We were in a very frequented track, and unable to account for what I saw. I dropped the sounding lead without finding bottom at sixty fathoms. I then resumed my course. The temperature of the water was 77° 14′ F., as at 8 A. M. We filled with this water a jug, holding about six gallons, and discovered that it was full of small, luminous bodies, which, when the water was disturbed, presented the appearance of insects and worms in motion; some of them seemed one-fourth of an inch in length. We could take them up in our hands, and they preserved their splendor until within a few feet of a lamp; but if we placed them nearer they became invisible; under a magnifying glass, their appearance was that of a colorless, gelatinous substance. One of the specimens was about an inch and a half long;

its thickness was that of a coarse hair, with a kind of head at each extremity. The surface of the sea thus covered was about twenty-

THE LUMINOUS SEA.

three miles from north to south ; I do not know its extent from east to west. In the middle stretched an irregular band, of a deep color, and about half a mile in breadth. * * *

"While the ship made nine knots an hour, it glided through the water without making any noise. Ocean seemed a plain covered with snow; and so great was its phosphorescent brightness that the sky, despite its purity, scarcely showed stars of the first magnitude."

But phosphorescence in the sea is not always due to animalculæ, for it is an equally well-attested fact, that under certain conditions unknown to science the ocean becomes luminous. Dead fish render salt water luminous, while shoals of herring and other fishes often leave behind them a kind of secretion which is luminous.

CHAPTER III.

PRE-HISTORIC MONSTERS OF THE DEEP.

THE ocean, while apparently changeless, is nevertheless subject to disturbances no less consequential than those which rive the earth, rise up and crumble away mountains, overwhelm cities and desolate vast tracts of land. Where islands now are, once were continents, and where cities once stood, inhabited by a vast world of industrious and opulent people, now the sea sweeps in deep and sullen roar. Not only do wonderful physical changes occur in the ocean-bed, but the life therein is marked by mutations equally remarkable, and still the equilibrium of creation is maintained.

"When we contemplate," writes Captain Maury, "the works of nature, we are struck by the admirable system of compensation which presides therein, and by the accuracy with which everything is balanced. A thousand different agents accomplish distinct and closely defined functions, and yet the equilibrium of all these agents is so perfect that the utmost harmony reigns throughout the whole."

If we examine the progressive character of creation we find that the appearance of each species was preceded by preparations for its maintenance; in other words, that the lower orders of creation preceded the higher. The super-imposed strata of rocks and earth-crusts are to the geologists the chronicles of cosmogony, in which he reads as easily as he would the printed lines in a book, the history of all those wonderful things which lived and moved freely upon the earth or waters before man crowned the work of creation.

BEGINNING OF LIFE.

The first life, which teemed in the sea before any land had appeared, was the zoophytes, creatures which partake of both the vegetable and

FISHES OF THE SILURIAN AGE.

animal life, and are therefore called plant-animals. Of these we still have examples in the sea-stars, sea-hedgehogs, venus-girdle, jelly-fish, etc. Some of these—for there are many different orders of zoophytes—had the appearance of beautiful flowers, and covered the bed of the ocean with forests and gardens as picturesque as eye ever beheld. They possessed solid bodies, generally, which bore some resemblance to the skeletons of superior animals.

Next to the zoophytes, and of a higher order of creation, are the molluscs, which are protected by hard shells. Of this order, the ammonites now exist only in a fossil state, but the nautili still survive in abundance. The order of molluscs comprehends such an immense variety (200) that it would weary the patience of any ordinary reader to describe them here, so we will proceed merely to mention the various orders as they came into being.

Fish of two species, one of which resembled our modern perch, the other having irregular teeth and exceedingly small fins, followed the molluscs. Remains of these are found in the Silurian * stage. The shark and lias were nearly contemporaneous with the first fishes, being found in carboniferous formations, which immediately followed the Devonian or age of fishes.

SAURIAN MONSTERS.

We now come to the saurian (fish-lizard) order of creation, which made its appearance at the same time as the crustacean (shell-fish) and the huge scorpion. It was now that the great paleosaurus, ichthyosaurus, and many species of the nothosauri haunted the marshy and reed-fringed shores of the desolate world, limiting the seas' population by their voracious appetites. Cuvier, the renowned naturalist, whose studies in comparative anatomy created and raised that branch of science to a pre-eminent position, has given us a complete and and accurate description of these once mighty monsters, so fantastic and yet so terrible in aspect as to make it appear almost impossible that creation could suffer such things to mar her handiwork.

In the ichthyosaurus there is the anomalous combination of crocodile teeth, the head and breast of a lizard, snout of a dolphin, the vertebræ of a fish, and four fins of the whale—certainly a most ghoulish creature. But in the plesiosaurus, we have a yet more horrid creature, for to an equally grisly body there is the long neck of a serpent, terminating in the head of a lizard. The fossil remains of these animals have only been found in banks of marly stone, of the second

* This word is derived from Silurus, an ancient portion of Wales, where many remains of extinct animals have been discovered. Silurian belongs to the older Paleozoic age, the oldest of geologic time.

period, and chiefly in England, where they must have been at one time quite abundant. Such large quantities of their remains have

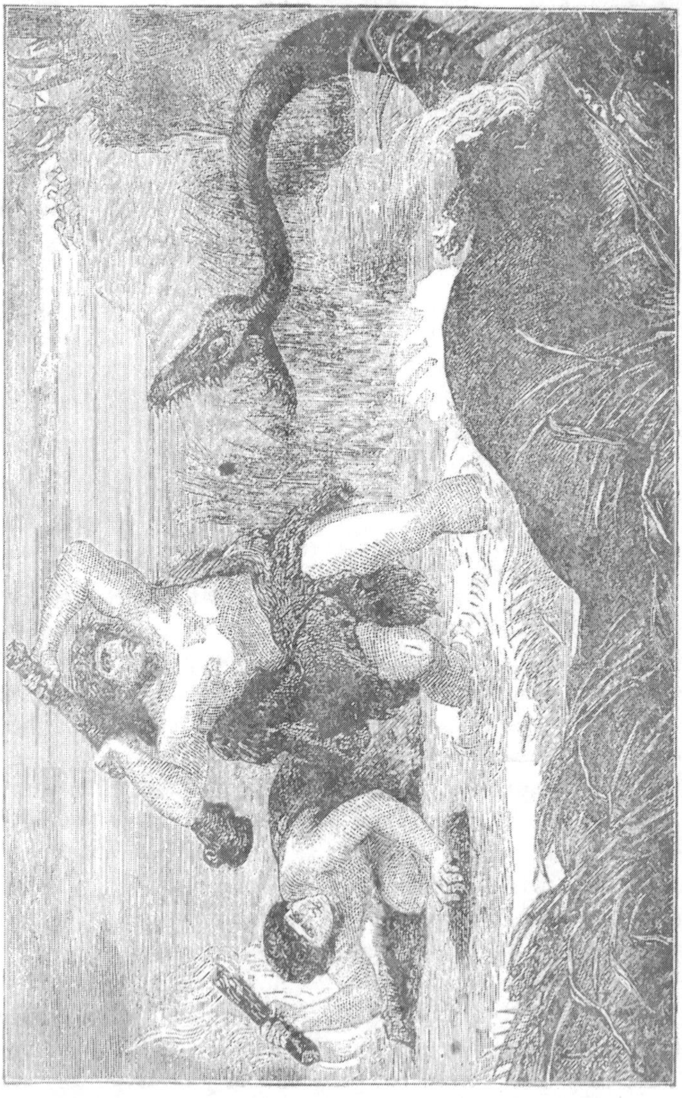

EARLY MAN CONTENDING WITH THE PLESIOSAURUS.

been gathered that several entire skeletons have been reconstructed, and are now to be seen in the British Museum. Professor Owen, one of the greatest paleontologists of the century, has grouped these several saurians into one family, which he calls *Enaliosauridœ* — quite a large word, but it is only the Greek for sea-lizard. Some of these lizards have been found measuring more than thirty feet in length, with heads six feet long.

SERVICES TO NATURE RENDERED BY THE SEA MONSTERS.

Mangin says: "It is supposed that these monstrous amphibians discharged at the Jurassic (middle secondary) epoch the function which now-a-days devolves upon the cetaceans, viz.: that of checking the excessive multiplication in the ocean of the molluscs and fish. The ichthyosauri were specially designed for this destruction; their eyes were of extraordinary magnitude, while their powerful vision enabled them both to discover their prey at great distances, and to remove it during the night to the obscurest depths of the sea. The skulls of the ichthyosauri have been discovered, whose orbital cavities measured from ten to twelve inches in diameter. In the largest species the jaws, armed with sharp teeth, yawned for a width of nearly seven feet. The voracity of these animals exposed them to the frequent loss of their teeth; but these, as is the case with the crocodile, were quickly replaced. * * *

"As for the plesiosaurus, the small dimensions of its head, and its thin, elongated neck, would seem to indicate that its appetite resembled those of our huge serpents. * * * It is probable that this strange creature, whose extraordinary long neck would prevent it from moving rapidly through the water, swam upon the surface, or kept close to the shore in shallow water, where, concealed among the algæ (sea-weed), it might both ensnare its prey and hide itself from the piercing gaze of the ichthyosauri, its most formidable enemies."

THE MIGHTY MEGALOSAURUS.

Buckland, the great naturalist, who has done so much for science, while pursuing his researches in West England discovered the remains of a marine crocodile, to which he gave the name *Megalosaurus* (great lizard). This animal is the most remarkable of any that is known to have existed. Its form was somewhat like a crocodile, particularly the Nile monitor, its teeth being almost identical in appearance to those of the monitor, but it was so very large, in proportion to the crocodile, that it must have exceeded seventy feet in length — a lizard large as a whale. Owen, however, thinks it did not exceed thirty feet.

The celebrated gravel-pits in the St. Pierre mountains, near Maestricht, have furnished us with wonders scarcely less marvelous, such

THE FLYING PTERODACTAL.

as skeletons of monstrous sea-turtles, an infinity of shells, and with a genus of lizard but little inferior in size to the megalosaurus. This gigantic species, which Professor Conybeare calls *Mosaosaurus*, (monitor-lizard), was upwards of twenty-five feet in length. Its monster jaws were furnished with strong teeth, conical in shape, arched and raised into a ridge, while several were strongly attached to the palate, like the shark's. In the specimen that was uncovered, the spine contained one hundred and thirty vertebræ.

Dr. Mantell, another enthusiastic paleontologist, discovered the remains of an animal which evidently belongs to the same family as the megalosaurus, but its material differences entitle it to the distinct name which has been given it, viz: *Iguandon*. It was an herbiverous lizard, and its teeth and toes particularly so closely resembled the iguana, that hence the name. Its stature was about twenty-eight feet, and it is believed to have been the tallest of all creatures on the eastern continent; its length was nearly thirty feet. A splendid plaster specimen of this remarkable reptile may be seen in the Smithsonian Institute at Washington City.

A HORRIBLE CREATURE.

We have next to describe the most grotesque and horrifying creature that inhabited the ancient ocean, a wild phantasm of nature, more terrible in its appearance than a nightmare conception. Its hybridity was so remarkable that it was reptile, bird and bat all at once, having the characteristics and semblance of each. The scientific appellation of this mongrel monstrosity is *Pterodactylus*, which is a Greek word that implies wing-toed. This name was given it because the fifth toe of its anterior limbs was enormously elongated into a ribbed stem, intended to support a membrane which made the wing. This wing very much resembled the bat's, except that the phalanges were much stronger in proportion, as were also the muscles, so that its flight was very much swifter. The nose was prolonged into a beak which was severely armed with teeth.

Dr. Buckland, in his "Bridgewater Treatise," expresses the opinion that the pterodactyl possessed the faculty of swimming, and also that it fed on fishes, which it caught by dashing down upon them after the manner of various fish-catching sea-birds. Cuvier judged it to be nocturnal from the extraordinary size of its eyes, and this probability is increased by its other bat-like characteristics. Mangin says:

"The size and shape of the feet prove that these animals could stand erect with firmness, their wings folded, and that they thus possessed a mode of progression analogous to that of birds; like them, also, they could perch upon trees, while, at the same time, they had

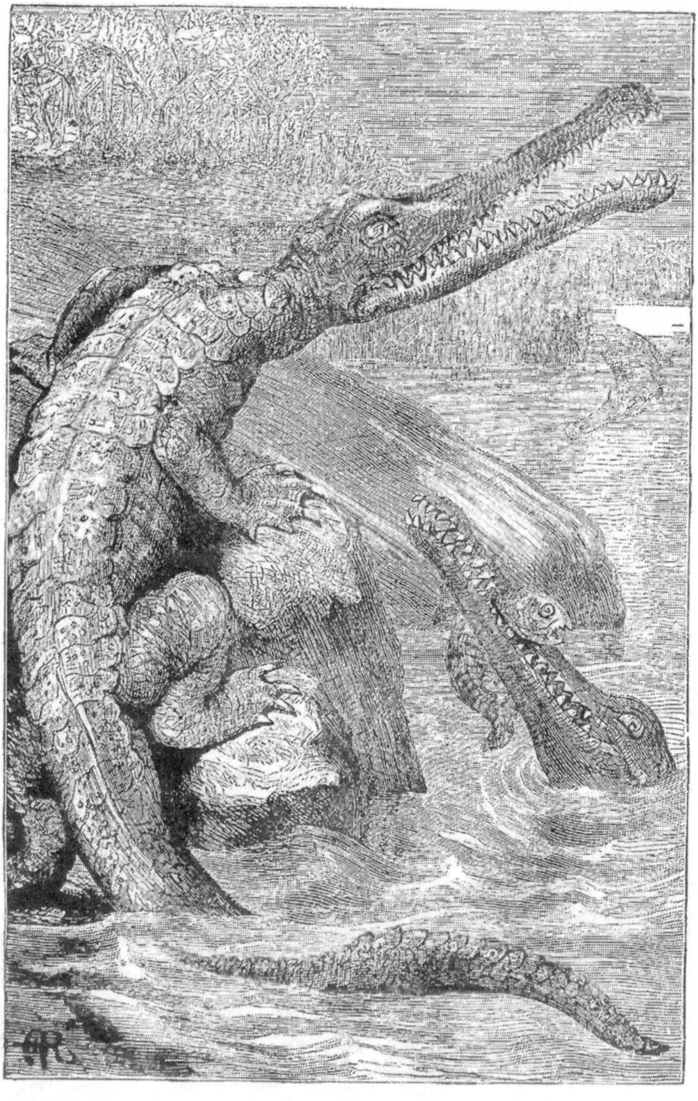

THE TELEOSAURUS.

the faculty of climbing along rocks and cliffs, assisting themselves with their feet and hands like our modern bats and lizards."

"The most striking peculiarity of this animal," says Dr. Hoefer, "is the curious assemblage of vigorous wings, joined to a reptile's body; the imagination of poets alone has hitherto framed anything resembling it. Hence the description of those dragons, which fable represents to us as having, in the early ages of the world, disputed with man the sovereignty of the earth, and whose destruction was one of the glorious attributes of the mythic heroes, gods and demi-gods."

THE INVULNERABLE TELEOSAURUS.

But there was one other monster which I must not omit to mention, since its importance among the antediluvian inhabitants of the deep can hardly be over-estimated. I refer to the *Teleosaurus* or perfect lizard, *teleo* being the Greek word for complete, perfect. The plesiosaurus and ichthyosaurus were destitute of scaly covering, but the teleosaurus was clothed with an adamantine coat of mail, which would have been impervious to the heaviest rifle-ball of to-day. It was also armed with tremendous teeth, and its massive jaws, which it could open to a distance of six feet, made it capable of swallowing the largest ox. This fearful animal was thirty feet in length, and is supposed to have been the most destructive monster of the mighty deep.

Dr. Buckland also mentions another saurian, which he calls the *Dicynodon*, the meaning of which I do not now recall. Fossil remains of this animal were discovered by a Mr. Bain in South-eastern Africa, and described by Professor Owen soon after (1845). In shape it resembled the lizard, tortoise and crocodile, being scarcely less hybrid than the pterodactyl. Its size was equal to the modern walrus, which it also resembled in being armed with two tusks; while, like the tortoise, the anterior part of the jaw was sheathed with horn.

CHAPTER IV.

THE PRE-HISTORIC AMERICAN OCEAN.

THAT our globe was at one time covered with water, without a vestige of land appearing anywhere above the surface, is a fact attested by many evidences; and that the oceans, seas, lakes, etc., which are now known, are not as they were left after the evaporation of waters, and the appearance of land which first prescribed their limits, is equally well proved. Erosions and accretions, eruptions, climatic changes, storms, earthquakes, the earth's movements, particularly those which occur once in 21,000 years, which will hereafter be explained, and deluges, have evolved and dried up, or displaced oceans, as will be done again in the earth's ever active life.

The evidences that there was at one time a great sea, covering the vast region which now comprises our western plains, are indubitable and interesting. Not only do the remains of ocean animals found scattered over the West prove the existence of a sea, but the agglomeration of saurian bones which lie heaped in singular confusion, as found in Kansas, attest the fact that in the subsidence of waters, from whatever cause, the last water remaining must have been a lake or pool, in the region where the fossil remains of the prehistoric animals are now found; for there they evidently perished.

The ancient ocean-bed to which I refer, is easily traced in the State of Kansas, and the last struggles of the monsters in the slime and stagnant waters of that expiring sea were evidently made in a lake, whose limits are seen in the *mauvaise terres*, or Bad Lands, of the State, a region of country that has been recently examined by a party of scientists. A description of this wonderful territory, the graveyard of gigantic creatures more formidable than the eye of modern man ever looked upon, is thrilling in the extreme.

WONDERS OF THE KANSAS PLAINS.

From elevated points the plains appear to be dotted with ruined villages and towns, with avenues lined with painted walls of fortifications, churches and towers, while side alleys pass beneath natural bridges or expand into small pockets and caverns, smoothed by the action of the wind, carrying hard mineral particles. If the explorer searches the bottoms of the rain-washes and ravines, he will doubtless come upon the fragment of a tooth or jaw, and will generally find a line of such pieces leading to an elevated position on the bank or bluff where lies the skeleton of some monster of the ancient sea. He may find the vertebral column running far into the limestone, or a paddle extending on the slope, as though entreating aid; or a pair of jaws lined with horrid teeth; or he may find a conic mound with bleached bones on the apex. Sometimes a pile of huge remains will be discovered, which the dissolution of the rock has deposited on the lower level, the force of rain and wash having been insufficient to carry them away. The descriptions of these wonderful creatures savor of the exaggerations of Verne, yet are facts. The fabulous monsters that were believed in in the olden times, the dragons, serpents, etc., are thrown in the shade by these truly ancient monsters that once swam in the ocean that finally became land-locked, and the bottom of which is now raised high above the water level. The shore line of that old ocean is distinctly marked. Imagine the water between New York and London a dry plain, its whales and fishes stranded in the mud, on the sides of the great hills, and on the plateaus that we know exist, and an idea can be formed of the *mauvaise terres*. Professor Marsh says that in one place he counted from his horse the remains of five huge monsters spread upon the plain. One of the largest of these, a reptile called the *Liodon*, exceeded in size the largest whale, and of its discovery Lieutenant Whitten, of the army, says: "A part of the face, with teeth, was observed projecting from the side of a bluff, and we at once proceeded to follow up the indication with knives and picks. Soon the lower jaws were uncovered, with their glistening teeth, and then the vertebræ and ribs. Our delight was at its height when the bones of the pelvis and part of the hind limbs were laid bare, for they had never been seen before in the species, and scarcely in the order. While lying on the bottom of the cretaceous sea, the carcass had been dragged hither and thither by the sharks and other rapacious animals, and the parts of the skeleton were displaced and gathered into a small area. The massive tail stretched away into the bluff, and after much laborious excavation, we left a portion of it to more persevering explorers."

A GIGANTIC TURTLE.

One of the most remarkable discoveries was a turtle, the maximum length of which may not have been far from thirty feet, with a corresponding width of twenty feet. The discovery of a medium-sized one is thus referred to by the finder: "The fragments of the *Protostega* were seen by one of the men projecting from a ledge of a low bluff. Their thinness, and the distance to which they were traced, excited my curiosity, and I straightway attacked the bank with the pick. After several square feet of rock had been removed, we cleared up the floor, and found ourselves well repaid. Many long, slender pieces of two inches in width lay upon the ledge. They were evidently ribs, with the usual heads, but behind each head was a plate like the flattened bowl of a huge spoon, placed crosswise. Beneath these stretched two broad plates, two feet in width, and no thicker than binders' board. The edges were fingered, and the surface hard and smooth. All this was quite new among fully grown animals, and we at once determined that more ground must be explored for further light. After picking away the bank and carving the soft rock, new masses of strange forms were disclosed. Some bones of a large paddle were recognized, and a leg bone. The shoulder-blade of a huge tortoise came next, and further examination showed that we had stumbled on the burial place of the largest species of sea turtle yet known. The single bones of the paddle were eight inches long, giving the spread of the expanded flippers as con-

THE PROTOSTEGE, OR GREAT TURTLE.

siderably over fifteen feet. But the ribs were those of an ordinary turtle just hatched, and the great plates represented the bony deposit in the skin, which, commencing independently in modern turtles, unite with each other at an early day. But it was incredible that the largest of known turtles should be but just hatched, and for this and other reasons it has been concluded that this 'ancient mariner' is one of those forms not uncommon in old days, whose incompleteness in some respects points to the truth of the belief that animals have assumed their modern perfections by growth from more simple beginnings."

Other specimens were found that had evidently been torn by sharks, that were on a scale equally gigantic, had attained a length of one hundred and fifty feet, and could easily have taken a horse and cart in their mouths. Dr. John Hunter, of the College of Physicians and Surgeons, London, in describing a specimen of medium size, says: "The length of the base of this tooth, from the *Carcharodon megalodon* (Agassiz), is four inches eight lines; that of the longest of its sides, five inches ten lines; with it is placed a tooth of an unusually large specimen of the largest known living species of *Carcharais*, the length of the base of which is one inch eight lines, and that of the longest of its sides two inches three lines. This tooth is from a shark twenty feet long. The fossil shark, if bearing the same proportion to the teeth, must have been over sixty feet long." The fossil tooth used in Sir John's comparison, was from the miocene tertiary formations of Malta, and was a third smaller than the largest found in America. Professor Agassiz made similar comparisons with like results. The teeth, although having lain untold ages under ground, still in many cases retain their beautiful polish, and the fine serrations of the trenchant edges are as perfect as when first deposited.

FLYING REPTILES OF ASTOUNDING SIZE.

Though the Bad Lands of Kansas furnish many fossil remains of marvelous extinct animals, other sections of our country are rich with equally wonderful specimens which have been exhumed during the last few years.

Near Charleston, S. C., in the beds of the Ashley and Cooper rivers, was recently found several teeth of a species of land tortoise which are larger on the grinding surface than the outspread palm of a man's hand. Let imagination determine the size of the mouth of this creature! In the same region have been discovered the remains of one of the largest reptiles of that ancient period, a veritable flying dragon, which has been named by scientists the *Pterodactyl umbrasus*, very similar in appearance to the pterodactyl, already described, but many times larger. It measured when found, twenty-nine feet from finger to finger, and when alive and spread in the air, the gigantic creature was one of the most terrible flyers of the border of this ancient sea. It derived its powers of flight, not by a membrane stretched over four elongated fingers, with a rudimentary thumb, like the bat's, nor by a wing without distinct fingers, as on birds, but by a wing sustained principally on a very elongated toe, while the other members possessed their normal shortness, and were

COMBAT BETWEEN THE ICHTHYOSAURUS AND PLESIOSAURUS.

armed with claws. With this remarkable conformation were associated a long neck and beak. It could fly in the air, remain on the wing a long time, and suspend itself to trees and rocks by its short toes. Another wonder discovered was the *Hesperornis* (night-bird), a large water bird seven feet in height, and having knife-like teeth. The teeth were set in grooves, the wings were rudimentary and useless, while the legs were like those of a duck. A study of its skeleton shows it to have been closely related to the ostrich. Another wonder was a flying bird, the *Ichthyornis* (fish-bird), having still more reptilian characteristics. Its teeth, like the alligator's, were in distinct sockets, and, stranger yet, its vertebræ is bi-concave, a peculiarity only found in the fishes and a few reptiles. One of the most gigantic reptiles discovered was the *Amphicœlias* (a name given to express the peculiarity of its having both the fore and hinder ends concave). The thigh bone was so heavy that the finders were forced to harness a mule to it to drag it out of the hole. It measured more than eleven feet in length. A section of the vertebræ, from the dorsal portion, was a heavy lift for four men, and when placed on the ground in the position assumed by the animal, it towered above the tallest of the party, being more than six feet in height. To appreciate this, the reader must remember that the corresponding bone of the nearest living representative of this animal can be lifted by the little finger. Other fossil saurians, the thigh bones of which are six feet in length, have been given a length of more than one hundred and fifty feet. If they increased in proportion to the size of this bone, we should have a creature more than two hundred feet in length, but of course this is merely a supposition, though quite a probable one. A thigh bone of an allied genus more than six feet in length can be seen in the Museum of Natural History, Central Park. It is in a case in Geographical Hall, and side by side with the same bone of the nearest allied form. Near by are other creatures, representing the same age. Some of the whales of this and later times were one hundred and fifty feet in length, and the State of Alabama was once their roaming ground.

THE LARGEST ANIMAL CAPABLE OF MOTION ON LAND.

In the Bad Lands of Colorado an animal has been found which is by far the largest animal supposed to be capable of moving on dry land. It fed on the forests of the time, a fact proved by the remains found with it. It was called the *Titanosaurus* (the giant lizard, evidently a misnomer), a huge animal, seventy feet in length and eighty in height. That age abounded in flying reptiles and turtles, besides the monster saurians already mentioned. Some of the land turtles were nine feet in length, and proportionately high. One specimen now extinct would easily hide or cover two men, being about four feet high. At that period a great revolution was culminating, and a perceptible change is noticed, that gives indications of a new era. The body was elevated, instead of being dragged along; the limbs were lengthened, and in animal life at that period the iguanodon takes a prominent position. The thigh, when full grown, was more than four and a half feet in length, and the circumference around the head was four and a half feet. The teeth were obtusely conical, and laterally compressed, so as to present a cutting edge, which was serrated like the teeth of the Mexican iguana, from which it was named. As restored by Mr. Hawkins, it has a slight resemblance to an immense tiger. Mr. Hawkins says, to give an idea of the size of that animal, that the iguanodon, as it now stands in the Crystal Palace, is composed of four iron columns, nine feet in length by seven inches in diameter, six hundred bricks, one thousand five hundred and fifty tiles, thirty-eight casks of cement, ninety casks of broken stone, with one hundred feet of iron hooping, and twenty feet of cubic inch bar. The specimen was modeled after the great Horsham specimen, and to show more clearly the size, the mold was afterward converted into a "*salle a manger*," in which Professors Forbes, Owen and twenty other gentlemen sat down to dinner.

The great cretaceous ocean of the West, that is now only known to us by its arid deserts and chalky plains, was no less remarkable for its fishes than its reptiles, and swarmed with large forms related to the salmon and saury. Vertebræ and other fragments of those species project from the worn limestone in many places, and one of them attracts attention by its formidable appearance. The density and hardness of the bones had shed the rain off on either side, so that the radiating gutters and ravines finally isolated the stony monster. The head was some inches longer than that of a fully-grown grizzly bear, and the jaws were deeper in proportion to their length. The muzzle was shorter and deeper than that of a bulldog. The teeth were all sharp, cylindric fangs, smooth and glistening, and of irregular size. At certain points in each jaw, they projected three inches above the gum, and were sunk one inch into deep pits, being thus as long as the fangs of a tiger, but more slender. Two pairs of such fangs crossed each other on each side of the end of the snout. That fish is known as *Portheus Molossus* (Cope). Besides the smaller fishes, the reptiles, no doubt, supplied the demands of their appetite. The ocean in which flourished this abundant and vigorous life, was at

MONSTERS OF THE KANSAS PLAINS IN THEIR LAST STRUGGLES.

last completely enclosed on the west by elevations of sea bottom, so that it only communicated with the Atlantic and Pacific at the Gulf of Mexico and the Arctic Sea. The continued elevation of both eastern and western shores, contracted its area, and when ridges of the sea bottom reached the surface, forming long, low bars, parts of the water area were enclosed, and connection with salt water prevented. Thus were the living beings imprisoned, and subjected to many new risks. The stronger could more readily capture the weaker, while the fishes would gradually perish through the constant freshening of the water. With the death of any considerable class, the balance of food supply would be lost, and many larger species would disappear from the scene. The most enduring would longest resist the approach of starvation, but would finally yield to inexorable fate; the last one being caught by the shifting bottom among the shallow pools, from which his exhausted energies could not extricate him.

CHAPTER V.

APPEARANCE OF LAND ANIMALS.

WE now approach the epoch of great change, when the waters began to subside, and continents were upheaved from the desolate waste of waters, calling into being new forms of life, and radically changing, by metamorphosing or destroying, the creatures of the primitive sea. These changes were the product of violent eruptions, coral-builders, great cataclysms, modifications of ocean temperature, and the voracity of certain species, which brought about an annihilation of themselves. Monster saurians, finding their nourishment curtailed, fell upon their own species and thus made way for other and superior animals like the mammalia of the sea, such as whales, sea-cows, dolphins, etc.

The cetacea, or mammiferous sea animals, evidently existed before the present age, but how long before is not known. They are placed in the period immediately preceding the quaternary epoch, which bordered on our present age, but so few and imperfect fossils have been found that we know little of them. It is well ascertained, however, that whales which existed in the ancient seas were very different from our present species, in that they were more active, while the structure of their jaws and strength of teeth prove that they subsisted, not on small animals, as now, but on large prey, and thus they, too, helped to bring about that great change which constitutes an epoch in the sea.

EVOLUTION OF LIFE IN THE SEA.

The lowest order of life in the sea is the zoophyte or plant-animal, in which the boundary between the animal and vegetable is so difficult to discover that, like the bat, they are a part of two kingdoms, if I may be permitted to speak thus generally. Of these semi-animals

NEPTUNE'S CUP.

the sponge is most difficult to classify, notwithstanding the fact that even at as early a day as Pliny lived, they were pronounced animals, and the males and females distinguished from each other. But in modern times the sponge has been looked upon as vegetable up to a very recent period, when it has again been placed in the animal kingdom, though at the very lowest place. Grant has even undertaken to prove that the sponge is oviparous, and describes its mode of reproduction as follows:

"At certain periods of the year small spheroidal bodies are developed in the interior of the sponges, drop into the lacunæ (air-cell), with which they are pierced, and are expelled along with the water which pours through them. These corpuscles—the reproductive germs of the sponges—are accordingly armed with hair or filaments, by means of which they move in the water with tolerable rapidity, and succeed in fixing themselves upon some object, whence they do not stir. Ordinarily, they choose in preference the rocks and calcareous stones, and even excavate a kind of lodging, which at first serves them for an asylum, and then insures them, while expanding, a more solid support."

The test which admitted the sponge into the animal kingdom was subjecting it to fire, in which it emanates an odor very like burning horn, thus proving that its component parts are horn, silicate and carbonate of lime, which resemble the bones and cartilage of a zoophyte. The sponge while living secretes a gelatinous substance, from which chemists have extracted a fatty matter, thus again demonstrating its animal life; though of organs there is no trace, nor do we know how it dies.

THE SPONGE AN ANIMAL.

Says Pouchet: "Sponges are the most truly manifold in form of any animals; they are met with of all shapes, sizes and colors. Some branch out like trees, many resemble a funnel or a trumpet; others are divided into lobes, like great fingers; for instance, *Neptune's Glove;* and there are some which are known by the name of *sea-muffs* and *sea-tapers*, on account of their form.

"A closely allied variety produces regular sponge monuments, which grow from three to six feet high, on the submarine rocks. They have a narrow stalk which, at a certain height, expands considerably, and gives the structure the look of a cup symmetrically hollowed out, and exactly like an immense drinking goblet. To such a colossal the imagination of the sailor could only give one name, that of the redoubtable god of the sea; this living vase is the *Cup of Neptune.*"

51 SPONGE GATHERING IN THE MEDITERRANEAN.

MARVELOUS ARTISANS OF THE SEA.

But a single degree above the sponge, is an order called *Anthozoas*, meaning flower animal, which are rich in coloring, delicate in texture, and of the most elaborate designs, composing, at times, large and gorgeously beautiful flower gardens, and at others, stately and fantastic forests. There is a classification of the anthozoas, called *Zoantharia*, and having the same meaning, which comprise the most interesting features of sea-life. This last branch is again divided into two further divisions, viz.: the fleshy and the stony zoantharia. Of the former, the sea anemones are the more popular examples, as they may be seen in nearly all public aquaria. Their body bears some resemblance to a bag, adhering at one end to the sea-bed, while the other lies free and open for the reception of food. This opening is armed with tentacles, by which the flower animal seizes its prey and holds it until devoured. Singular enough, though the anemones present to the superficial eye nothing but a sluggish stem of apparent vegetation, yet they are not only carnivorous, but actually catch fish and feed upon them. So voracious are they that it is hardly safe to introduce them into an aquarium with small fishes.

CORAL WONDERS.

The stony zoantharia, also called madrepore and lithophytes (stone-animals), is beyond compare the most wonderful inhabitant of the ocean, as you must agree after reading even the following short description of its habits and mighty labors. In speaking of this animal, we will use the name by which it is most generally known, *Coral*, and thereby avoid possible confusion. The coral with which we are best acquainted has a pinkish-red color, but coral is also frequently found bearing a dozen different shades of red, so that it is classified technically among the divers and traders as "blood foam," "flower of blood," "first," "second" and "third" blood.

Sages of antiquity were never agreed as to their opinions respecting the nature of coral, some maintaining that it was a vegetable, others as strongly asseverating that it was mineral. In 1750, Peyssonnel demonstrated that all the old wiseacres were wrong, and that coral is the direct result of a polyp (many-footed) animal, which builds its fairy grottoes by secreting a calcareous matter. These singular creatures bear no small resemblance to other flower animals, and are sometimes mistaken for sea flowers.

Dr. Chenu, in his admirable description of the coral, says:

"The tubulose substance by which they are connected in one mass, is filled with a spiculæ somewhat resembling chalky needles, and fur-

ARCHITECTURAL WONDERS OF THE CORAL WORM.

rowed, as it were, by a great quantity of channels, which communicate with the different digestive cavities; carbonate of lime, mingled with a blood-red coloring matter, and abundantly secreted by the animal, unites together the different masses of polyps, and produces a stem whose size is increased by the addition of new layers, and whose elongation is effected by means of the development of new animals at the extremity of the aggregation."

The whole presents the appearance of a tangled, branchy shrub, destitute of leaves and twigs. The diameter of the trunk never exceeds eight inches, produced entirely by a calcareous secretion deposited in concentric layers by the polyps. The exterior layer, or bark, is usually of a light gray color, covered with tubercles, while at the summit there is a pierced aperture divided into eight compartments,

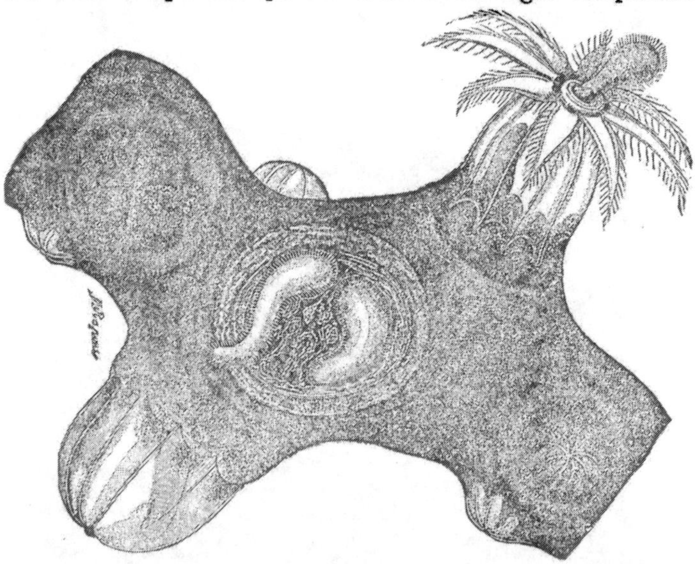

BIRTH OF THE CORAL WORM.

to provide means for the issue of as many tentacles of the polyps.

These curious creatures are remarkable for their fecundity, but are very much more wonderful for their admirable workmanship, skillful engineering and illimitable industry, building up, as they do, with the materials extracted from their own bodies, such massive citadels that the most gigantic monuments of ancient or modern people are dwarfed by comparison.

Cuvier, in his "Discourse on the Surface Revolutions of the Globe," says: "In the torrid zone, where the lithophytes (coral) are numerous in species and propagate abundantly, their stony trunks intertwine themselves into rocks and reefs which, rising to the surface of the water, close up the mouths of harbors, and lay the most terrible snares for navigators. The sea, throwing up sand and mud on the summit of these reefs, sometimes raises their surface above its own level, and forms them into level islands, which in due time a rich vegetation vivifies."

The tropical districts of the Pacific Ocean particularly abound with prodigious quantities of coral, which have become veritable palaces of the sea, as gorgeous as ever fairy raised in the creative mind of youth.

"Plants of fibre fine as silkworm's thread,
Yea, beautiful as Mermaid's golden hair
Upon the waves dispread;
Others that, like the broad banana growing,
Raised their long wrinkled leaves of purple hue,
Like streamers wide out-flowing.

"Trees of the deep, and shrubs and fruits and flowers
As fair as ours,
Wherewith the sea-nymphs love their locks to braid,
When to their father's hall, at festival
Repairing, they, in emulous array,
Their charms display,
To grace the banquet and the solemn day." *

CURIOSITIES OF THE CORAL WORM.

Captain Hall has written a very excellent account of the coral and its habits, from which the following is extracted: "The examination of a coral reef during the different stages of one tide, is particularly interesting. When the sea has left it for some time it becomes dry, and appears to be a compact rock, exceedingly hard and ragged; but no sooner does the tide rise again, and the waves begin to wash over it, than millions of coral worms protrude themselves from holes on the surface, which were before quite invisible.

"These animals are of a great variety of shapes and sizes, and in such prodigious numbers that in a short time the whole surface of the rock appears to be alive and in motion. The most common of the worms at Loo Choo was in the form of a star, with arms from four to six inches in length, which are moved about with a rapid motion in all directions, probably in search of food. Others were so sluggish that they were often mistaken for pieces of rock; these were gen-

* Southey: "Curse of Kehama."

erally of a dark color, from four to five inches long, and two or three round. When the rock was broken from a spot near the level of high water, it was found to be a hard, solid stone; but if any part of it were detached at a level to which the tide reached every day, it was discovered to be full of worms of all different lengths and colors, some being as fine as a thread and several feet long, generally of a bright yellow, and sometimes of a blue color; while others resembled snails, and some were not unlike lobsters and prawns in shape, but soft, and not above two inches long.

"The growth of coral ceases when the worm which creates it is no longer exposed to the washing of the tide. Thus a reef rises in the form of a gigantic cauliflower, till its top has gained the level of the highest tides, above which the worm has no power to carry its operations, and the reef, consequently, no longer extends itself upwards. * * * The reef, however, continually increases, and being prevented from going higher, must extend itself laterally in all directions; and this growth being probably as rapid at the upper edge as it is lower down, the steepness of the face of the reef is preserved; and it is this circumstance which renders this species of rock so dangerous to navigation. In the first place, they are seldom seen above water; and in the next, their sides are so abrupt that a ship's bow may strike against the rock before any change of soundings indicates the approach of danger."

ISLANDS BUILT BY CORAL WORMS.

Chamisso, another learned investigator, has given us the result of his observations among the coral, in a very interesting work, in which he says, that after the reef is extended to the surface of the water the animals cease their work, and it would perhaps remain in this shape but for the fact that below the line they have traced is a continuous stony mass, composed of shells, molluscs, etc., and fragments of coral connected by calcareous sand. It often happens that the heat of the sun penetrates this calcareous mass when it is dry, and causes it to split open in many places; the waves then possess sufficient force to break up the coral into blocks about six feet long and three or four broad, which are piled up on the reef. Thus the reef is crested by these accumulations until the waves can no longer break over. The calcareous sands which now accumulate offer to the seeds brought thither by the waves or winds a soil wherein vegetation strikes root and soon covers it with a luxurious growth. Whole trunks of trees, transported from remote distances, find here a resting place; next, small animals, such as lizards or insects, are conveyed by some inscrutable means to the artificial island and thus

ISLAND BUILT BY CORAL WORMS.

become the first inhabitants of the reefs. Even before the woods grow dense, sea-birds build their nests in the copses, and finally, long after the industrious and patient coral-builders have completed their work, man appears and rears his habitation on the fertile soil.

It is principally in the South Sea and the Red Sea that the coral-builders abound. At the approaches to the Maldive Islands they form extraordinary masses, of no less extent than the Alps. After describing the process by which the coral animals raise their dangerous reefs, Owen thus refers to the gigantic character of their labors: "The prodigious surface over which the combined and ceaseless toil of the little architects extends ought to be taken into consideration in order to understand the important part they play in nature. They have built a barrier of reefs four hundred miles long round New Caledonia, and another which extends along the north-east coast of Australia, one thousand miles in length. This represents a mass in comparison with which the walls of Babylon and the Pyramids of Egypt are child's toys. And these edifices of the polyps have been reared in the midst of the ocean-waves, and in defiance of tempests which so rapidly annihilate the strongest works constructed by man."

OTHER ARCHITECTS OF THE SEA.

The coral builders represent the most perfect workmanship in construction and up-rearing, but we have other marine animals that are almost as skillful architects, besides being true miners, hewing their way through stone, cleaving even adamantine marble, and often so seriously attacking ships as to send the strongest wooden hull to the bottom of the sea. The most renowned stone-borers scientists have called *Pholades*, meaning, literally, lurking in a hole; they are bivalved molluscs, with thin, white, elongated shells open at both ends. At one opening is situated the respiratory tubes that pump up the sea-water, from which it extracts the infusoria (animalculæ), on which it feeds. At the other, or front opening, projects the foot, so-called, being a thick, powerful sole, which it uses to rasp the rock, and thus, at the expense of the greatest labor it gradually works its way into the stone by using the foot alone. Stone which lies long in the sea is much softened by the water, and if we but rub our finger briskly on the surface while wet, we find it easily indented. It is this same rubbing process which the pholades employ, and by this means finally burrow into the stone out of sight.

One of these marble cutters has acquired great distinction in geology, by reason of its having attacked the temple of Jupiter Serapis, situated on the borders of the Mediterranean, and almost on a level with its waves. It has cut numerous excavations in the beautiful columns of this sanctuary several feet above the present water line.

THE DESTRUCTIVE SHIP-WORM.

But there are other workmen in the sea more injurious and no less industrious than the pholades. I refer to the *Taredo* (from the Greek, to rub) *navalis*, or ship-worm. These animals are vermiform molluscs, which live in the interior of wood that is submerged in the sea. It is continually gnawing, and thus cuts numerous tortuous galleries, until the wood which it attacks is reduced to the frailest shell. The head of this animal is armed with a little shell, projecting beyond its soft body with which it does the cutting; hence the Greek word by which it is known is hardly applicable, since it certainly does not cleave its way in the wood by rubbing.

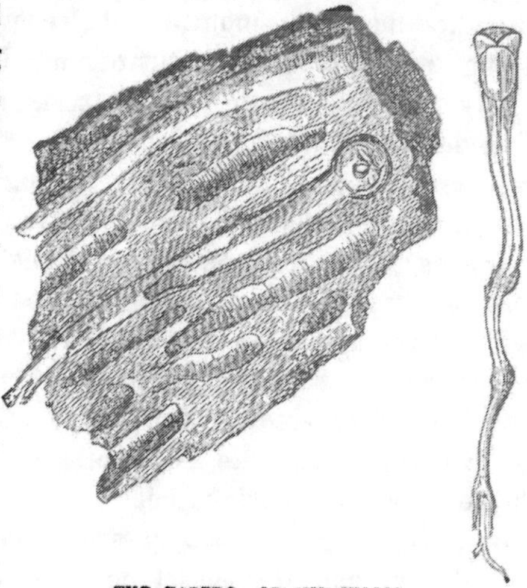

THE TAREDO, OR SHIP-WORM.

The ravages of the taredo, when it attacks ships, is something terrible, since in a short space of time they reduce the strongest beams and timbers to a state of fragile sponge. In 1731 these animals came very near occasioning the submerging of Holland, having devoured a greater part of the Zealand dykes before their mischievous work was discovered.

Working always in the interior of the wood, the ravages they perpetrate are not easily detected until the whole is ready to collapse from weakness; hence, to preserve vessels from these dreadful wood devourers, their bottoms are carefully lined with copper.

CHAPTER VI.

ARMOR-CLAD SEA WARRIORS.

THE infinite life which pervades the ocean requires an encyclopedia for its description; hence, it will be necessary to pass over many interesting things in order to give space to the most important. I should have liked to mention the medusa, or jelly-fish, which are so curious, and which have afforded me many hours of amusement; also, the sea hedgehog, venus-girdle and a score of other plant-animals, as they are called, but I must forego my wishes, else this work must necessarily "be stretched out to the crack of doom:" for no one book could contain it all.

Mangin has well said: "To restrain the infinite multiplication of inferior beings, and to cleanse the shores from the refuse of dead or dying animals accumulated thereon by the ebbing tides, ocean nourishes numerous monsters, hideously ugly and voracious, but strong, invulnerable, admirably organized, armed with a view to their deadly mission — death and destruction. These animals are the *Crustaceæ* — should they not rather be called the cuirassiers? — lobsters, crabs, and especially those horrible sea-spectres, with sidelong march, crooked claws, disproportionately long in some species, with enormous talons of extraordinary strength, a squat body encased in a hard, thick shell, ingeniously composed of pieces which present no point of vantage to an enemy, and yet preserve perfect liberty of movement. In the infernal regions of crabs, monsters two feet long have been discovered." I may also add that upon one occasion I saw a live lobster, quite as large as an ordinary dog. It was kept chained, and well it might be, for it was as ferocious as a bull-dog and equally dangerous; a grip of its huge claw would have destroyed a man's arm, and so vengeful did it always appear, that no one dared to approach within its reach.

Michelet has observed: "If, in the first place, one visits a rich collection of mediæval armor, and after having contemplated the heavy masses of iron which immured our knights, one flies immediately to a museum of natural history, and inspects the arms and mail of the crustaceæ, one feels a sincere compassion for the arts of man. The former are but a carnival of absurd disguises, heavy and cumbrous, well adapted to suffocate the warrior and render him helpless and harmless. The others, and especially those of the terrible decapodo, (having ten feet) are so frightful, that if these animals were enlarged only to man's size, no one could endure their aspect; the bravest would be overwhelmed, magnetized with terror."

The crustaceæ (shell-covered) are nearly all arrayed, in their attitudes of combat, under that formidable offensive and defensive arsenal which they carry so lightly; strong pincers, sharpened lances, mandibles which could eat through iron, bucklers bristling with darts which have but to clasp you close, and pierce you with a thousand stabs. We give thanks to Nature that she made them of no larger dimensions, otherwise we could not have contended with them, as nothing short of large cannon balls could penetrate their armor. The elephant must have sought a hiding place, and the tiger have climbed into tall trees; the rhinoceros even, would have found no protection in his thick hide.

A FUNNY EXPERIENCE WITH SAND FIDDLERS.

The smallest crab, the *Talitre*, is a cunning little fellow that appears to spring spontaneously from the sand, together with millions of his fellow-countrymen, as soon as some carcass is washed up on the beach. My first experience with these little creatures was a very comical one. Previous to the building of the jetties at the mouth of the Mississippi River, I was sent to the delta in a reportorial capacity in the interest of Captain Eads, the subsequent builder. One day, having occasion to go out upon a board foot-path which had been made across a sedgy peninsula, at the terminus of Pass l'Outre, I came suddenly upon a large number of talitres, generally called "sand fiddlers," and having in my mind's eye visions of deadly tarantula, I immediately concluded that I was beset by a colony of these dreadful spiders, and must certainly be bitten before escape was possible. The manner in which I sought to avoid the little crabs must have been extremely amusing, and when I made the last desperate jump, clearing the patch of insects, the limit of ludicrousness was evidently reached. I had been sorely frightened by a number of very harmless and exceedingly timid creatures, that would have quickly disappeared had I attempted to approach them closely. When walking they apparently touch only their toes to the ground, and progress sideways very slowly, until alarmed, when they dart off suddenly. They are great scavengers, and so numerous that they keep the beach cleansed of all animal matter.

THE FORMIDABLE CANCER-CRAB.

The largest and most terrible of the family of crustaceæ is the cancer-crab, a creature of great power and armed with all natural weapons to make his power dreadful. When two males meet they immediately begin to battle, but the manner in which they approach each other is martial in the extreme. Lifting their heads high as possible, they walk on tip-toe, with their huge claws elevated, which they clash together most savagely, evidently with the intent of terrifying, and the sounds they produce, coupled with their ferocious appearance, is dreadfu. enough. They fight like gladiators of old, leaving some of their lances (claws) always on the ground. But the loss of a claw or leg to the crab is of little consequence, for the lost members are speedily reproduced.

A SHIP-WRECKED CREW DEVOURED BY CRABS.

The food of the cancer-crab is decaying animal matter, but they are not averse to fresh meat and have been known even to attack disabled mariners. It is said that several of Drake's seamen, having been cast by shipwreck upon a desert island in a helpless condition, were set upon by a legion of these terrible creatures and devoured.

The species most popularly known on our shores are the hermit, the soldier, and the cenobite crab, each receiving its name from a peculiar characteristic of the animal.

The hermit crab is a veritable cuckold, that despoils a mollusc of its shell and then occupies it itself. But it does not always shelter itself at the expense of another's home, for more commonly it seeks among the empty shells which strew the beach, turning them over and trying them with great fastidiousness until it finds one to suit. At other times they despoil each other, not, however, until a long struggle determines which is the stronger. As the hermit grows he must change his shell to accommodate his body. He is a voracious fellow, living chiefly on molluscs, but in an hour of scarcity he does not hesitate to act the cannibal.

MARVELOUS EXHIBITION OF CANNIBALISM.

But I cannot charge the hermit with greater sins than are committed by his fellows, for all crabs are cannibals, the weaker always succumbing to the stronger. Mr. Rymer Jones relates a singular story, the facts of which must make us harbor more or less dislike for the voracious crustacean. Says Mr. Jones:

"On one occasion I introduced six crabs of different sizes into my aquarium. One of them venturing toward the middle of the reservoir was immediately accosted by another a little larger, which took it with its claws as it might have taken a biscuit, and set about breaking its shell, and so found a way to its flesh. It dug its crooked claws into it with voluptuous enjoyment, appearing to pay no attention to the anger and jealousy of another of its companions, which was still stronger and as cruel, that advanced toward them. Our ferocious crustacean quietly continued its repast, when its companion seized it exactly as it had seized its prey, broke and tore it in the

COCOANUT-EATING CRABS

same fashion, penetrating to its middle, and tearing out its entrails in the same savage manner. In the meantime the victim, singularly enough, did not disturb itself for a moment, but continued to eat the first crab bit by bit, until it was itself entirely torn to pieces by its own executioner—a remarkable instance at once of insensibility to pain and of cruel infliction under the *lex talionis* (the law of retaliation). To eat and to be eaten, seems to be one of the great laws of nature."

CRABS THAT BREAK COCOANUTS.

Though essentially carnivorous, the crustaceans sometimes eat marine vegetables. Many even seem to prefer fruit to animal food. Such is the tree-crab of the Polynesian Isles, which feeds almost exclusively on the cocoanut. This crab has thick and strong claws; the others are comparatively weak. At first glance it seems impossible that it could penetrate a hard cocoanut surrounded by a thick bed of fibre and protected by its strong shell, yet it is a common circumstance, witnessed by many travelers. The crab begins by tearing off the fibre at the extremity where the fruit is, always choosing the right end. When this is removed, it strikes it with its great claws until it has broken an opening through the shell; then, by the aid of its slender claws, and by turning itself round, it extracts the whole substance of the nut.

MONSTER SEA-SPIDERS.

From an article in a recent number of *St. Nicholas*, I condense the following interesting information about crabs:

Among the most remarkable, and the largest of crabs, is the Japanese sea-spider, highly esteemed in the Orient as an excellent article of food. Its principal claws are each five feet in length, measuring from ten to twelve feet between the tips of the nippers, and presenting an astonishing spectacle when entangled in the nets and hauled aboard the boats. With their slow, measured movements and powerful weapons of defense, these crabs are the giants of the spiders of the sea. Professor Ward, who has collected them in Japan, states that they have a remarkable habit of leaving the water at night and crawling up the banks presumably to feed, and that there they are sought by the crab-hunters. A story is told of a party of fishermen who had camped out on a river bank, and one of whom aroused the others in the night by yells and screams. Running to the spot they found that one of these monster crabs, in wandering over the flats, had accidentally crawled over him with his great claws, frightening him almost to death.

Surpassing the spider-crab in strength is the robber-crab of the India coast. It is also found on the Spice Island, where it is fatted like pigs for the table. It chiefly haunts the thick branches of the cocoanut palm tree and makes its nest of the husk of the fruit.

The robber-crab, peculiar to the Samoan Islands, is also a cocoanut-eater, and lives principally in the branches of the cocoanut tree. It

THE JAPANESE, OR SPIDER CRAB.

exercises no little intelligence in getting at the fruit, which it accomplishes by carrying the nut to the very top of the tree, and then dashing it down with force enough to break the shell. A gentleman relates that upon an occasion, while he was walking in a Samoan forest, he saw a robber-crab reach down its claws from a thick palm branch and seize a goat by the ears that was passing underneath. So powerful was the crab that it lifted the goat almost clear from the ground.

The pirate-crab is a voracious creature and adopts many strange devices to procure its food. They are very numerous about Florida Keys and are very destructive of young birds, which they seize in their nests. A propensity for fowl flesh is also exhibited by other species, as the following from *St. Nicholas* will show: "I have often watched the hermit-crabs of Bird Key during the breeding season of a sea-bird called the noddy, when a continual struggle for food is carried on between them and the young birds. The noddy builds its nest upon the low bay cedars, the nest being merely a mass of dried twigs dropped upon the tree in the rudest manner possible.

"When the young bird is hatched it is kept well supplied with small fishes by the parent noddy; but the arrival of these luxuries is carefully watched by a horde of pirate-crabs. The large purple-backed land-crab crawls from holes in the sand; the red-tinted fellow, known as the *Grapsus*, appears as if by magic, while innumerable hermit-crabs, with shells of every conceivable pattern, move onward toward the nest. Some climb neighboring bushes or low trees, and drop down upon the baby-bird; others ascend the trunk of the tree, until finally every branch and twig about the nest is occupied by a robber-crab, while the young bird, with wings erect, vainly endeavors to retain the fish. It is soon in the claws of the advancing throng, that, closing in from all sides, unites in a general battle in which the piratical crabs fall in a shower to the ground, where the combat is renewed, and the largest crab finally carries away the game." It is not infrequently the case that the young bird itself is carried off and eaten. The *Grapsus* has been seen by many persons to catch birds that frequent the beach, to accomplish which it is very cat-like, approaching with great stealth until within a couple of feet of the bird, when it jumps and seizes the prey, which it proceeds to eat without first killing.

The purple, or land-crab, is found in nearly every portion of the tropics, and in the West Indies they commit great ravages upon the sugar-cane plantations. On some of the more unfrequented islands in May or June these crabs make a remarkable pilgrimage. They live for the greater part of the year upon the high lands several miles from the sea; but once a year they leave their holes, and move at night in vast columns, often three miles long and two hundred and fifty feet broad, to the sea, where they deposit their eggs. Nothing seems to deter this great army, the march being kept up with an undaunted perseverance that overcomes all obstacles. At this time they are caught in large numbers for the table, as on the return march to the hills they are in poor condition and soon shed their shells

CURIOUS CRABS.

The mask-crab is a curious specimen of the quaint in nature, its back being so singularly marked as to strikingly resemble a human face, and particularly a mask, from whence it takes its name. The glass-crab is another curiosity, since its body is so transparent that print may be easily read through it, a precaution nature has taken to protect it from hungry fishes whose eyes fail to discover it.

CRAB LIFTING A GOAT.

"In the selection of their homes the crabs show curious characteristics. Some of the hermits burrow in the sand, arranging the opening so that the large claw fits it perfectly, forming an animated door that rises up to grasp any intruder that seeks entrance. Certain crabs travel about on the backs of turtles; there is one kind that lives in the interior of the sea-cucumber, while another crab is found living within the large Brazilian star-fish. One little fellow of the crab family lives in the folds of the jelly-fish, while another clings to the feathers of a certain sea-bird. In the deep sea some crabs are blind, while others have wonderful phosphorescent eyes, and are veritable lamps of that silent world. Many crabs are famous swimmers, and the one known as Henslow's swimming crab, often seen many miles from land, will dart into a school of herrings, seize a fish in its knife-like claws, and cling to it until its victim floats dead upon the surface."

CHAPTER VII.

HORRIBLE MONSTERS OF THE DEEP.

ONE of the most beautiful creatures of the sea is the *Nautilus*, or *Argonauta*, though it has a family alliance with the horrible of horrors, the great polypus, which we will soon describe. There is in reality a slight difference between the nautilus and the argonauta, but so generally are they confounded that they will here be treated as the same. Its body is oval in shape and

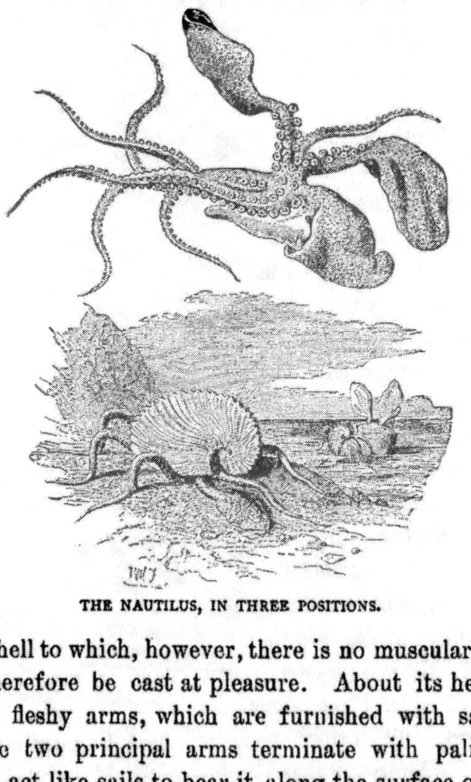

THE NAUTILUS, IN THREE POSITIONS.

reposes in a shell to which, however, there is no muscular attachment, and it may therefore be cast at pleasure. About its head are eight tentaculæ, or fleshy arms, which are furnished with saucer-shaped suckers. The two principal arms terminate with palmated membranes, which act like sails to bear it along the surface of the water. Its shell is shaped like a fairy vessel, and when on the surface presents a very beautiful appearance; but the argonauta not only sails, but swims as well, by driving water through a locomotive tube called the *siphuncle*. Sometimes he crawls on the bottom, and at other times swims in mid-air with great rapidity. So nicely adjusted is his vessel that when alarmed he hides himself completely within his shell and, turning over, sinks quickly to the bottom.

Nearly allied to the argonaut are the cuttle-fish, calamary and the really formidable polypus, or octopus, sometimes, but improperly, called the devil-fish, though it is quite horrible enough to deserve that figurative appellation. Like the argonauta, these animals are supplied with powerful retractile arms, along which are several suckers, which enable them to hold on to rocks with great tenacity; they also have a hard, bony beak, very closely resembling that of the parrot; their body has the form of a bag enveloped by a hood, in which is a pocket secreting a substance that they can eject at will, and which is so intensely black that they can hide themselves entirely from view by discoloring the water with it. This ink is well known to painters under the name of *sepia*. The *calamary* borrows its name from the Latin *calamarium*, formerly applied to writing-cases and their necessary utensils, and very closely resembles the cuttle-fish. Its flesh is sometimes used for food, but is never considered a delicacy, though it is a most excellent bait for fish.

THE FRIGHTFUL POLYPUS.

The polypus has no external bony skeleton, though in its organization it differs but little from other cephalopods. The body seems to be contained in a kind of bag, from whence issues the very large head terminated by eight long tentacles or arms. Just below the base, from which the arms radiate, is situated the mouth, partly covered by a large and extremely hard beak, with which the animal crushes the shell-fish that constitute its principal food.

The formidable tentacles fulfill the double office of locomotion and the means by which it seizes and holds its prey. On the inner side of these are a great many valves for suction, which are used, not as formerly supposed, to draw the blood from the animals it attacks, but to enable it to cling tenaciously to the rocks or whatever prey it may attack.

Generally the polypi are sedentary and solitary, though they may sometimes be seen migrating in groups. They usually lurk in some dark crevice of the rocks, from whence it is exceedingly difficult to dislodge them. At all times carniverous, they wage an unceasing warfare on certain kinds of fish and molluscs, which they often kill merely for the gratification of destroying. The common species rarely exceed twelve feet in length, of which the tentacles occupy more than two-thirds, but there are exceptional monsters, of which I will speak presently. Old mariners, in whom the spirit of exaggeration is predominant, tell marvelous tales of their experience, or reports they have heard, concerning gigantic polypi both in the Polar and Tropical seas. It is said that these monsters not infrequently attack the largest whales, which they kill speedily and glut themselves on the carcass, while many and many are the stories told of unfortunate persons who have fallen victims to their voracity.

THE GREATEST MONSTER OF ANTE-DILUVIAN TIMES.

Michelet gives us a fine description of the ancestry as well as the present character of the polypi, in the following: "In the more ancient formations of the old world we find the murderous beast an eater and a sucker. The first is revealed to us by the imprint of the trilobite, a species now lost, the most destructive of extinct beings (in the paleozoic period). The second subsists in one fearful fragment, a beak nearly two feet in length, which was that of a great sucker or cuttle-fish (*Sepia*). If we may judge from such a beak, this monster, if the other parts of the body were in proportion, must have been enormous; its ventrose, invincible arms, of perhaps twenty or thirty feet, like those of some monstrous spider. The sucker of the world, soft and gelatinous! it is himself. In making war on the molluscs he remains mollusc also; that is to say, always an embryo. He presents the strange, almost ridiculous, if it were not also terrible, appearance of an embryo going to war; of a fœtus furious and cruel, soft and transparent, but tenacious, breathing with a murderous breath, for it is not for food alone that it makes war; it has the wish to destroy. Satiated and even bursting, it still destroys. Without defensive armor, under its threatening murmurs there is no peace; its safety is to attack. It regards all creatures as a possible enemy. It throws about its long arms, or rather thongs, armed with suckers, at random."

ATTACKED BY A HORRID SQUID.

The following incident has been abbreviated from Mr. Beale's "Natural History and Fishery of the Sperm Whale." Mr. Beale had been searching for shells among the rocks in Bonin Island, and was much astonished to see at his feet a most extraordinary looking animal, crawling back toward the surf which it had just left. It was creeping on its eight legs, which, from their soft and flexible nature, bent considerably under the weight of its body, so that it was just lifted by an effort above the rocks. It appeared much alarmed, and

A GIANT ROCK SQUID.

made every attempt to escape. Mr. Beale endeavored to detain it by placing his feet on one of the tentacles, but despite his exertions the animal continually liberated itself. Finally he seized one of the tentacles with his hand and, bracing himself against a rock, held on until it appeared the limb would be parted by the strain. Thus for a while the two pulled with all their strength, neither apparently being the stronger, until suddenly the enraged animal released its hold on the rocks and sprang on to Mr. Beale's arm, which was bared to the shoulder. A more dreadful struggle now ensued, for from captive the cephalopod had become captor and was in the act of making a meal off Mr. Beale's arm. Despite all he could do, the animal clung by its suckers to his arm and tried to tear the flesh with its horrid beak, in which it would certainly have succeeded but for timely assistance from some sailors, who killed it with a boat-hook; yet, to free the animal's tentacles from the arm it was necessary to cut them away bit by bit. Mr. Beale describes its cold, slimy grasp as terribly sickening, and expressed the belief that he would have speedily fainted had assistance been deferred a moment longer.

TERRIBLE ADVENTURE WITH AN OCTOPUS.

The following adventure was related by a gentleman who, previous to the great civil war, was a well-known sponge-gatherer in the South, having at one time hundreds of divers in his employ, and supplying nearly all the sponges used in this country. Said he:

"We were off the Florida coast gathering sponges. In those days—and the practice is still pursued by the poorer classes of sponge-gatherers—we got our sponges by anchoring our small sloop or schooner over the bed, and then diving from her rail to the bottom of the sea, carrying a weight along to sink us the faster. A good pair of lungs and years of practice finally enabled me to reach bottom in thirty or thirty-five feet of water and come up with more or less of a haul.

"On that warm coast the shark and the octopus and other horrible things belonging to the fish or reptile species are present, and often lying in wait. The diver has a horror of them at first, but the feeling soon wears away, and some men become perfectly reckless. During the first year I never went down without a sharp knife in my belt to give any prowling shark a thrust, but later on I would take a header off the rail when a shark's dorsal fin was cutting the water not a hundred yards away.

"During the second season we lost two men by sharks, but I took no precautions and had no narrow escapes. In the beginning of the third season we anchored over a splendid bed, in a location well sheltered from storm and swell, and we had reason to anticipate a profitable catch.

"There were four of us on that trip, and the first man off the rail was an old diver named Peterson. This was about seven o'clock in the morning, and although we had been up for two hours the bay had been clear of sharks. We watched Peterson go over, but we watched in vain for him to come up. Twenty seconds passed—then thirty—then forty, and the captain leaned over the rail and cried out:

"'Boys, the old man has got fast down there and is a goner.'

"We waited ten seconds longer and then felt sure that we should never see the old man alive again. We were in twenty-eight feet of water, and the trawl showed the bottom to be clear of weeds and made up of rock and sand. It was hard to guess what had happened. He might have bumped his head against a rock, or had his foot caught in a crevice; he might have burst a blood-vessel or been taken with cramps. None of us thought of an octopus in connection with his sad fate. We had seen a small one three days before, and we knew that the creatures lurked in the still waters, but somehow we speculated on all other theories but this.

"As you may imagine, the loss of old Peterson upset us, and it was a good half-hour before any of us had rallied our courage. It was my next turn down, and as I finally got ready to go the Captain handed me a long, keen shark-knife on which he had just put an edge. I accepted it, more in hopes that it might be useful in enabling me to send up the dead body than through any bodily fear. If Peterson had been caught in a crevice, or was held fast by a marine plant, the knife would loosen him.

"Well, over I went at last, and it was only a few seconds before I struck bottom close to a large rock. Sponges were growing all around me, and as I reached out for the nearest I felt something whip across my bare shoulders. All the dress I had on was a pair of trunks, leaving legs, shoulders, arms and most of the body naked. That "something" stung and burned and blistered, but in two seconds the feeling had passed from shoulders to waist, and in another second it was in my legs. It was not until I tried to spring away that I realized my situation. At the first move I was jerked in the most violent manner towards the rock, and the burning increased tenfold. An octopus had gripped me. He had three of his terrible arms

FATAL ADVENTURE WITH AN OCTOPUS

around me, and was drawing me to the rock. How his suckers burned and blistered! How the hairy arms gripped and twisted!

"I tell you I was a frightened man, and for several seconds forgot that I had a knife in my belt. When I finally reached for it the octopus had dragged me into the shadow of the rock, and there I saw old Peterson's body. Two of the creature's arms were around it and I was to make a second victim.

"As I drew the knife I caught sight of the body of the reptile. In fact, the arms were drawing me within reach of its beak. I did not slash at the arms, but struck straight at the jelly-like body. I had then been down so long that my ears were roaring and I realized that I had only a few seconds to spare. Luck guided my blows and I slashed at the creature until pieces of the body floated around me and the arms let up their grip. Then I started for the surface, and I reached it about as near dead as a man could be and have any life left. They pulled me inboard, and with me came the three terrible arms which had been cut from the body. Not a sucker would loosen its grip, and they had to cut them off with knives, one by one, close to my flesh.

"Well, that was the last dive I ever made, for I was in bed for months. I can show you thirty spots on my body where the flesh looks like a fire-burn, and the remembrance of the situation down there will start a chill over me in the hottest day."

ADVENTURES WITH THE FRIGHTFUL SQUID.

In olden times sailors were harassed by many groundless fears, superstitions being abundant and ignorance general. The early Spanish poetic chroniclers, who delighted in telling the story of Columbus' voyages, invariably disfigured their narratives with miracles and wonders. In those days Jack, looking over the side of his vessel, was prepared to see anything, and to this willing disposition may be attributed the creation of mermaids, sea-serpents, grinning or winking monsters, and leviathans big enough to swallow a ship. There was the squid which, as the sepia octopus, we know in these days to be an extremely large and most diabolically unpleasant beast; but in the olden times this animal was reckoned to be larger than a cathedral, in proof of which the following story is recited:

"A big ship was on the West African coast; the men were getting the anchor, when a squid arose and wreathed its fearful snake-like limbs around the vessel's spars. The tips of these limbs soared quiveringly high above the mastheads, and the weight of the cuttle hove the ship down on to her beam ends. Here now was a lively sit-

THE KRAKEN SINKING A SHIP.

uation. The crew plied axes and knives, but in vain, whereupon they invoked the aid of their patron saint, Thomas. Eventually the wounded monster grew alarmed and sank, and the crew afterward, to commemorate their deliverance, marched in a body to the Church of St. Thomas, where subsequently there was hung up a painting, representing the unparalleled conflict."

As Figuier says, it is no easy task to separate the real from the fabulous history of the cephalopods (a Greek word, which implies that the position of the feet is in the anterior part of the head). Pliny, the ancient, relates the history of an enormous cuttle-fish that haunted the coast of Spain and destroyed the fishing ground. He asserts that this creature was finally captured, and weighed seven hundred pounds, and that its arms were thirty feet in length. As the cuttle-fish was esteemed by the ancients a most savory dish, the head of this formidable monster was given to Lucullas, to whom it belonged rightfully by reason of his exalted rank.

FACTS ABOUT GIGANTIC CALAMARS.

It is an undisputed fact that there exists in the Mediterranean and other seas, cuttle-fish of extraordinary size; to deny this would be to dispute the assertions of hundreds of responsible persons, as well also to deny the evidences which are contained in several museums, where specimens of this huge creature are preserved. A calamar was caught some years ago near Nice, which weighed upwards of thirty pounds. Less than forty years ago an individual of the same genus was caught in the same place, that measured six feet in length, and its body is now preserved in the Museum of Natural History at Montpelier. Peron, the distinguished naturalist, asserts that he met with one off the coast of Australia that was nearly eight feet long. Two travelers, Quoy and Gaimard, picked up the skeleton of a cuttle-fish in the Atlantic Ocean, near the equator, which, when living, must have weighed at least two hundred pounds. M. Rung found in the Atlantic the body of another, which he describes as being as large as a tun cask. In this instance the tentacles were quite short, and the body of a reddish color. He secured one of its mandibles, which is still preserved in the Museum of the College of Surgeons in Paris, and is the size of a man's hand.

In 1853 a gigantic cephalopod was cast ashore on the coast of Jutland, where it perished. Some fishermen dismembered the body and bore it away in several wheelbarrow loads. The back part of the mouth of this animal is said to have been as large as the head of an infant. Another, equally great, was taken in the Atlantic in 1858, while it was engaged in a deadly combat with a whale, specimens of which may been seen in the museum at Copenhagen.

MONSTERS IN THE GREAT DEPTHS OF THE SEA.

Dr. Walsh, naturalist to the expedition sent out by the English Government to make deep sea soundings off the coast of Greenland in the ship Bull-dog, expressed the opinion that the ophicoma (small serpents), drawn up alive by the sounding lead, inhabit the deeps. This opinion strikingly accords with the old legends that tell of marine monsters living at the bottom of the sea, and enveloping with their arms all things that approached them. Dr. Walsh says: "We cannot, therefore, doubt that the depths of the sea, where vegetables flourish eight hundred feet in length, like the colossal fucus of Forster, are also peopled with monstrous animals, whose organism is adapted to these unknown regions, whence they but rarely emerge. Their very real appearances have formed the basis of the mysterious traditions, which, for more than two thousand years, have been transmitted from generation to generation of mariners, and which have given birth to the fantastic creation of the Kraken and the sea serpent.

"While the masses of small gelatinous medusas floating at the surface provide food for the enormous whales, there is also at the bottom of the sea an abundant prey for these prodigious animals."

But the most important, if not conclusive, evidence yet supplied to sustain the oft-asserted belief that there are mightier monsters in the deep than modern naturalists have yet described, or are willing to admit, is found in an account given by M. Sabin Berthelot, the French consul at Teneriffe, of an encounter with a polypus, as follows:

CAPTURE OF A GIGANTIC CUTTLE-FISH.

"On the 2d of December, 1861, the steam dispatch-boat *Alecto*, commanded by Lieutenant Bouyer, dropped anchor in our roads on her voyage to Cayenne. The ship had encountered at sea, between Madeira and Teneriffe, a monstrous polypus swimming on the surface of the water. This animal measured from sixteen to eighteen feet in length, without counting the eight formidable arms covered with air-holes, that encircled its head. Its color was a brick-red; its eyes, placed level with the top of its head, were prodigiously developed, and glared with a frightful fixity. Its mouth, like a parrot's beak, was nearly a foot and a half in width. Its body fusiform, but much swollen toward the center, presented an enormous mass whose

THE GREAT CUTTLE-FISH AS SEEN FROM THE SHIP ALECTO.

weight might be computed at four thousand four hundred pounds. Its fins, situated at its posterior extremity, were rounded into fleshy lobes of a very great size.

"It was on the 30th of November, about half an hour after noon, that the crew of the *Alecto* descried this terrible cephalopod swimming along-side. The commandant immediately stopped his vessel, and despite the animal's dimensions, manœuvered to catch it. A slip-knot was made ready, muskets were loaded and harpoons prepared in all haste. But at the first balls fired the monster dived underneath the vessel, quickly appearing on the other side. Attacked anew with the harpoons, and after receiving several discharges of musketry, he disappeared twice or thrice, each time showing himself a few moments afterwards at the surface, agitating his long arms. But the ship continued to follow him, or rather checked her course according to the animal's movements. This chase lasted for two or three hours.

"The captain of the *Alecto* grew anxious, at all risks, to capture this novel kind of foe. Nevertheless, he dared not hazard the lives of his sailors by lowering a boat, which this monster would have readily capsized by seizing it with one of its formidable arms. The harpoons aimed at it penetrated its soft flesh and flew back without inflicting any mortal injury. Several balls had hit it in vain. At length it received a shot which seemed to wound it seriously, for it immediately vomited a great quantity of froth and blood mixed with glutinous matter, which diffused a strong odor of musk. It was at this crisis that the sailors contrived to catch it with a running-knot, but the rope glided along the mollusc's elastic body, and only stopped when near the extremity at the junction of the two fins. They attempted to haul it on board, and already the greater portion of its body was clear of the water, when its enormous weight drew the rope right through its flesh, and separated the hinder portion from the remainder of the animal. Then the monster, released from its bonds, fell back into the sea and disappeared."

Berthelot closes this very interesting account with the assertion that he himself saw the posterior parts of this marvelously strange monster, and he also sent a drawing of the polypus, made by a sailor witness, to the Minister of Marine. Lieutenant Bouyer submitted an equally elaborate report of the encounter to the Academy of Sciences, where it was received without any evidences of incredulity.

A MONSTER THAT DESTROYS SHIPS—THE KRAKEN.

The visitor to the coast of Norway, even to-day, is certain to hear stories of the *kraken*, which, according to ancient legend, is a voracious and colossal animal of deformed shape, with arms as long as the

ATTACK ON THE GREAT CUTTLE-FISH.

longest serpent, and covered with innumerable suckers. This monster is malignantly carnivorous, not content with the food which it finds in its natural element, but it is ever lusting after human flesh and blood. It is always at night, and especially during the fury of a storm, that he rises from his lair in the abyss of the deep, to search for the helpless voyagers who are overtaken by the whirlwind. To secure his prey he wraps his mighty arms about the masts of the ship and drags the vessel and its living freight down under the waves. It is said that the sole means of escape for the crew thus attacked is by severing the tentacles of the animal with an axe; but often new members grow again so quickly that even this means of escape is quite uncertain.

Denis de Monfort gives a scientific description and representation of this *kraken*, which he calls the *Colossal Poulpe*, in which the creature is made to embrace a three-masted vessel in its vast arms Delighted with the success which his representation met with, he laughed at the credulity of his contemporaries. "If my kraken takes with them," he said, "I shall make it extend its arms to both shores of the Straits of Gibraltar; if my entangled ship is accepted I will make my poulpe overthrow a whole fleet."

Pontoffian, the holy bishop of Bergen, not to be outdone by Montfort, declared that he had seen the kraken, and that it was so large that a whole regiment of soldiers could easily maneuver on its back.

A SEA MONSTROSITY.

In 1834, Captain Neill, of the ship *Robertson*, who is reputed a sensible and cool-headed man, gives us an account of a monster which he met in mid-ocean, quite as formidable as anything in fable. His attention was first called to an object some distance off, which very much resembled a ship lying on her beam ends, but upon approaching nearer he discovered, so he says, a monster fish swimming to windward. Its head, which he affirmed was only partly out of water, showed twelve feet of its length, and was at least twenty-five feet broad. As the eye was barely out of water, and "showed like a large, deep hole," he calculates that the entire length of the head must have exceeded fifty feet, as the portion seen was the snout.

In considering these stories we must make no small allowance for the well-known disposition of sailors to exaggerate, yet from the numerous and apparently well attested statements of so-called eye-witnesses, it is not unreasonable to suppose that there are rare specimens of ocean monsters which only occasionally show themselves upon the surface of the deep. We know that for a long time naturalists doubted the existence of such animals as the hippopotamus and the gorilla. Since explorations in Central Africa have revealed the existence of at least one of these creatures, and thereby proved a fact which was long looked upon as idle tradition, who can say that there are not as great monsters in the deep as those which are described in numerous legends?

BATTLE WITH THE OCTOPUS.

Jules Verne has given us a wonderfully realistic description of a battle with an octopus, in his great novel, "Twenty Thousand Leagues Under the Sea." He relates that the horrid creature attacked a vessel and seized one of the crew in its monster tentacles, by which he was raised high in the air, and held suspended while it fought his would-be rescuers with its other seven mighty arms. The battle raged furiously for a considerable time and the dreadful creature was not vanquished until the man who had been seized was nearly killed, and the frightful animal had six of its tentacles severed.

CHAPTER VIII.

THE SEA-SERPENT.

STORIES of the gigantic cuttle-fish, whether true or not, naturally lead to a consideration of other marvelous wonders of the sea, most prominent of which is the traditional sea-serpent. I say traditional, because, though thousands declare its existence, and scores have testified to having seen it, yet science does not accept it as a veritable fact, and even denies that such a creature ever habited the mighty and mysterious ocean. Without coming in conflict with the asseverations of naturalists, I may introduce the evidence upon which those who claim that the sea-serpent is a veritable flesh and blood reality, support their belief.

We may note as a curious fact that the leviathan of the Scriptures, ordinarily supposed to be a whale, is put on record as a serpent, Isaiah alluding to it as "leviathan, the piercing serpent; even leviathan, that crooked serpent." And the prophet Amos had evidently heard of sea-snakes or he would not have been moved in denouncing his enemies to declare: "Though they be hid from my sight in the bottom of the sea, thence will I command the serpent, and he shall bite them." It is probable that the prophet had in mind some legend of a voracious beast like the great Egyptian sea-serpent, which, according to Diodorus Siculus, flourished during the reign of Ptolemy II. It was wont to leave the water and devour the inhabitants and cattle on the shore, and being captured after a severe contest and brought to Alexandria, was there put to death to save the expense of boarding him at the public cost. We need not credit this story unless we wish to, or even those described by Olaus Magnus in the sixteenth century, of snakes two hundred feet long and twenty feet thick, which preyed upon the seashore neighborhoods. But when we reach the following century, we find information regarding these nautical phenomena losing its extravagant character and becoming more deserving of attention.

CAPTURE OF A SEA-SERPENT.

In 1629 Thomas Johnson, one of the earliest naturalists, tells of a sea-snake stranded in the shoal water off Sandwich, where it was captured by two fisherman. It was fifty feet long and of a red color, and its captors killed it, ate its flesh and stuffed its skin.

In 1639 we find the sea-serpent paying its first recorded visit to the shores of New England. It was seen by some Englishmen and Indians lying coiled upon a rock at Cape Ann. The Englishmen wanted to shoot it, but the Indians told them that if their shots did not kill it instantly it would attack and destroy the boat, whereupon they wisely let it alone. This story is told by a traveler named Jasselyn, who did not himself see the monster, but who was told of its appearance. In 1687 a sea-snake was seen at Dramoflordan, Norway. In 1720 one came into a creek near Koppenwig, and the following year one was found dead between the rocks at Amudevaagen, in Nordfiord, also in Norway. These mere mentions are simply noteworthy as localizing the creature. Such, also, is a statement founded on the evidence of a broad-sheet, or poster, printed in 1704, that an immense dead serpent was washed ashore at Spitalfields, and was put on exhibition there, exciting much public curiosity.

CIRCUMSTANTIAL ACCOUNTS OF SEA-SERPENTS.

We now come to circumstantial accounts of the appearance of this remarkable phenomenon. Hans Egidius, a missionary to Greenland in 1734, describes a monster seen in 64° north latitude, which was "of so huge a size that, coming out of the water, its head reached as high as the mainmast, its body was as bulky as the ship and three or four times as large." The detailed description of this animal gives the idea of an enormous saurian rather than that of a snake; indeed, one is greatly confused, in going over these many accounts, by the fact that several very different creatures seem to be described.

Bishop Pontroppidan, in his "Natural History of Norway," certainly mentions several different monsters. Of one of these, the kraken, which later investigation has identified with the cuttle-fish, we shall not take space to give accounts here. The good bishop is inclined to be credulous, but we do not think that he gives too much importance to the fact that the concurrent testimony of navigators for centuries had demonstrated the existence of sea-monsters in the Northern ocean. One of the instances which he records was attested by an officer of his acquaintance, Captain DeFerry, commander of the old Castle of Bergen, and confirmed by affidavits of his crew. The length of this monster was declared to be about six hundred feet—obviously an exaggeration—and its back was said to resemble a row of hogsheads floating in line at some distance from each other. The crew pursued this animal and wounded it, but it escaped further injury by diving to the bottom. This was in 1746. In 1757, one Capt. Joseph Kent saw a sea-serpent in Broad (Penobscot) bay. Its length he estimated at one hundred and twenty feet. This creature was seen in 1778 in the same locality by Eleazar Crabtree, who mentions that many others have seen it there also, and again in 1780 by Capt. Geo. Little. Commodore E. Preble also saw a sea-serpent off the

MAGNUS' SEA-SERPENT—FROM A DRAWING IN THE SIXTEENTH CENTURY.

New England coast in 1779. He estimates its length at one hundred and fifty feet and its head as the size of a barrel. Captain Little's serpent was much smaller, being not more than fifty or sixty feet in length and its diameter about fifteen inches. In July, 1802, the Rev. Abraham Cumming testified that he saw a sea-serpent again in Penobscot bay, and he states in his account that within eighteen years six distinct appearances of the creature have been recorded. In 1809 he gives an account of seeing the creature again. Both of his statements are fully attested by other witnesses.

It may be remarked that the favorite haunts of the sea-serpent for more than two centuries have been the bays of New England and those of Norway. If one of the creatures could only be marked in some way, so that it could be known whether they made annual or biennial trips between these localities, science would be duly grateful.

About the opening of the present century the scientific importance of these appearances began to be recognized. In 1808 we find a report made to the Wernerian Society of England, by the Rev. Mr. MacLean, of a sea-serpent which appeared off the coast of Coll. He described it as having a broad head, a somewhat smaller neck, below which the body widened, then tapered to the tail. It seemed to move by undulation, up and down, and to be about seventy or eighty feet long. This creature was seen by the crews of thirteen fishing boats, who were greatly terrified, expecting that it would attack them, so near was it at hand. But it drew away from them and gradually sunk from sight. It may be here noted that this monster, enormous and fear-inspiring as it is, has no affinity with surging and storm-tossed seas. Its appearance is never recorded except in still water, and on the least agitation of the surface by wind or otherwise it instantly retires to the depths below.

SEA-SERPENTS INCREASING.

Were the sea-serpent wholly a myth we would not expect that the increase in the number of observers, and also of the habit of careful observation characteristic of our own century, would be attended by an increase of its appearances. But such has certainly been the case. We have had during the last seventy-five years at least one-third as many well-attested instances in which the sea-serpent has been seen, not by single observers usually, but by numbers of persons with leisure to take full and accurate observations.

A sea-serpent was seen outside the harbor of Gloucester, Mass., in June, 1815, which seems to have lingered on the New England coast, for it was seen there frequently during the year following. In the month of August, 1817, a great snake near Gloucester was seen by so many persons, fishermen and others, that the Linnean society of New England took the matter in hand and took down the testimony of a number of reliable witnesses on oath. Sometimes the serpent was in sight from an hour and a half to two hours, lying in the still water of the harbor. One witness deposed as to its rapid movement when going out to sea, which he thought was about a mile in three minutes. Another described its head as shaped like that of a rattle-snake, but as large as that of a horse. Some had approached within forty or fifty yards of it, and found it to be of a dark color above and light below. Its length was variously estimated at from forty to eighty feet. Finally, the Hon. Lonson Nash, the magistrate before whom the testimony had been taken, himself made oath that August 14, 1817, he saw the strange animal both with eye and spy-glass; that it was about seventy feet long, its color black, and its motion vertical.

PROCFS OF THE SERPENT MULTIPLIED.

In August, 1818, the sea-serpent was again seen frequently, both near Gloucester and in the vicinity of Nahant. Great multitudes of spectators assembled to watch it as it moved swiftly through the water, holding its head high above the surface. In June, July and August of the following year it again returned to this locality, and sworn testimonials of its appearance from such persons as Mr. James Prince, marshal of the district; the Rev. C. Finch, chaplain in the United States Navy, and many captains and officers were presented in the Boston papers of that date. Its subsequent appearances on the New England coast may be briefly summed up, as follows: Off Swampscott in 1820; again at Nahant in 1826; near Kennebunk, Me., in 1830, and in 1833 off Nahant again; in 1849 near Swampscott again, and no more until 1875 and 1877, when its frequent appearance in its favorite haunt near Nahant and at other points gives us, in the opinion of the Rev. J. G. Wood, who pursues eagerly the trail of this "serpent-snake" through the valuable pages of the *Atlantic Monthly*, the most valuable and accurate testimony offered in the whole volume of sea-serpent lore. The testimony was very carefully taken, a paper containing thirty-four questions concerning the animal, its appearance, size, place, when seen, etc., being sent out by the Boston Society of Natural History, to be filled up by the persons claiming to have seen his snakeship. It was also seen by persons off the New Jersey coast, and the remarkable uniformity of detailed description in the different accounts not only shows that the creature seen was the same, but preclude the suspicion that imagination may have constructed a sea-serpent out of a string of buoys or a mass of sea-weed, as is often alleged.

EFFORTS OF NATURALISTS TO PROVE ITS EXISTENCE.

Of appearances seen elsewhere during the past forty years one or two deserve mention. In 1840 Dr. Hooker, assistant surgeon of Captain Ross' Arctic expedition, sent to Dr. Brewster's *Journal of*

Science an account of an enormous serpent seen by him on the American coast. He describes it as nearly one hundred feet long, and as showing the line of humps on its back so often noticed. In 1845, at the request of the English Society of Natural History, the Rev. P. Deinboll, a Norwegian minister, undertook to investigate this monster in its habitat in the northern ocean. He received and recorded the testimony of a large number of persons who had seen

THE SEA-SERPENT OF ANCIENT LEGEND.

the creature at various times. In only one instance was it seen during that year, July 28, in Ronsdale fiord. It is a curious fact that most of these Norwegian stories agree in giving the serpent a mane, which is not noted on the New England phenomenon. This may have been, however, only the effect of spray on its ridged back. In 1848 a captain and three officers on a British man-of-war on the coast of Nova Scotia, saw an eighty-foot serpent, and sent their sworn affidavits to that effect to the Zoological Society of London. August 6, 1849, Captain McInhae of the British navy, while at anchor in latitude 20° 44′ south, and longitude 9° 22′ east, saw a creature with a head like a snake, raised some distance above the water, and a body apparently sixty feet long, pass under the lee quarter of his ship. He made a sketch of the head of the animal, which bears a remarkable likeness to that made by Mr. F. W. Lawrence of Stockbridge, Mass., of the serpent of 1875. Captain McInhae sent a carefully detailed account of the creature he had seen to the British Zoological Society, which gave rise to much discussion in that body, and Professor Owen delivered a long speech to prove that no such thing as a sea-serpent ever existed, and that the object seen by Captain McInhae was probably a seal borne southward on a submarine iceberg, thus causing the eddy supposed to be occasioned by a long body under the water. The Captain replied to this speech by a letter, showing how impossible it was for him to be deluded in the matter, but probably this letter produced little impression upon the preconceived opinion of the wise men of the society.

Leconturier, who has given much attention to traditions respecting the sea-serpent, says that everywhere in Scandinavia there is an implicit belief in the serpent's existence. Scandinavian writers, he says, attribute to it a length of six hundred feet, having a head closely resembling that of the horse, black eyes and a long mane of a light gray color. According to them it is only met with in the ocean, where it suddenly rears itself up to the height of a ship's mast, giving vent to such a horrid hissing noise that can only be compared to the roar of the tempest.

A SEA-SERPENT SIX HUNDRED FEET LONG.

Hans Egidius relates, that on his second voyage to Greenland in the month of July, he descried a sea-serpent so near that he was afforded a perfect sight of it. He affirms that the animal reared its head to a distance of thirty or more feet out of the water, and that it ejected volumes of water through a single vent placed at the summit of its long-pointed muzzle. Instead of fins the monster had two immense ears, comparable to those of an elephant, which it agitated like wings to keep the upper portion of its body above the surface. After sporting for some time on the waves, the gigantic animal dived by flinging itself backward and so exposed several successive folds of its body, which were covered with scales.

There appeared in the *United Service Journal* of August, 1819, a

SEA SERPENT OF HANS EGIDIUS.

letter written by an eye-witness of the great sea-serpent off the coast of Nahant, which contained, among other statements, the following: "I had with me an excellent telescope. When I reached the strand I found many persons assembled, and soon afterward I saw appear at a short distance from the shore, an animal whose body formed a series of blackish curves, of which I counted thirteen; other persons estimated the number at fifteen. The monster passed thrice at a moderate speed, traversing the bay, whose waters writhed in foam under its huge bulk. We could easily calculate that its length could not be less than fifty or sixty feet. * * * This at least I can affirm, without presuming to say to what species belongs the animal which I have just seen, that, at least, it was neither a whale nor cachalot, nor any strong souffleur, nor any other enormous cetacean. None of those gigantic animals have such an undulating back."

A SEA-SERPENT RESEMBLING A CHAIN OF HOGSHEADS.

In addition to this letter describing the sea-serpent, there followed the statement of a sea-captain made in the form of a deposition before the officials of Essex County, Massachusetts. It read as follows:

"I, the undersigned, Gresham Bennett, second master, declare that on the 6th of June at 7 A. M., while navigating on board the sloop *Concord*, on her way from New York to Salem, the vessel being about fifteen miles from Race Point, in sight of Cape St. Anne, I heard the helmsman cry out and call me, saying that there was something close to the ship well worth looking at. I ran immediately to the side he pointed out and saw a serpent of enormous magnitude floating on the water. Its head rose about seven feet above the surface; the weather was clear and the sea calm. The color of the animal in all its visible parts was black, and the skin appeared smooth and free from scales. Its head was about as long as that of a horse, but was the perfect head of a serpent, terminating on the upper part in a flattened surface. We could not distinguish its eyes. I saw it clearly from seven to eight minutes; it swam in the same direction as the sloop and nearly as quickly. Its back consisted of humps or rings the size of a large barrel, separated by intervals of about three feet. These rings appeared fixed and resembled a chain of hogsheads fastened together; the tail was beneath the water. The part of the animal which I actually saw measured about fifteen feet in length; the movement of its rings seemed undulatory."

CAPTAIN HARRINGTON'S MONSTER SEA-SERPENT.

Mangin says that in 1857 the question of the sea-serpent was again brought before the world by an English seaman of recognized ability, Captain Harrington, commanding the ship *Castilian*. There ensued in the scientific journals and societies, especially in London, a very animated discussion, but one of novel character, in which everybody took a side for or against the great sea-serpent; only its opponents, instead of denying purely and simply its existence, maintained that what had been taken for an animal was nothing else than an enormous vegetable waif.

Captain Harrington declared that he saw the serpent quite distinctly, and described it as having a monstrous head shaped like a barrel, whose greatest diameter was between two and three feet. On the apex of the head was a wrinkled crest. For nearly one hundred feet about the animal the sea was agitated and discolored, so that his first impression, he says, was that his ship had gotten into what sailors call "broken water," and which is attributed to some volcanic influence. Closer examination, however, convinced him that before his eyes was a living creature of extraordinary length, apparently directing its slow course toward the land. At the time his ship was sailing too swiftly for him to measure the animal's dimensions, but according to such calculations as he was able to make, it appeared to be more than two hundred feet long. "I am convinced," says Captain Harrington, "that this animal belonged to the serpent species; it was of a sombre color and covered with white spots." In concluding his narrative to the Admiralty, the Captain writes: "As a seaman, I could not be deceived, and I should be as capable of mistaking an eel for a whale, as algæ or any other marine production for a living animal. If it had been some distance off I should have thought myself mistaken, but I saw it pass within twenty yards of my vessel. A score of persons saw it as well as myself, and my two officers, and I can assure you that I saw it as distinctly as I see at this moment the jet of gas in whose light I write to you this description."

CAPTAIN ROBERTS' SEA-SERPENT.

The evidence of the existence of a gigantic sea-serpent seems to be almost endless and of a trustworthy character, but it is a striking fact that seamen do not discover it so frequently in latter years as they did formerly, while those who continue to doubt its reality construe into an argument that sailors, being less inclined to superstition, and our knowledge of natural history being far greater than in previous years, they are not so given to deception and therefore much less frequently see in the billows or floating vegetation the monsters we so like to read about. But occasionally we still find confirmation of the stories about the sea-serpent, a very interesting one being related of how it was distinctly seen as recent as August 5, 1885, which I may repeat here, as follows:

Captain Roberts, of the ship *Emblem*, after putting into the harbor of Queenstown, August 31, made his report in which, among other things, he says: "I was walking on the poop deck at ten o'clock on the morning of the 5th, the wind being light and the sea as smooth as I ever saw it. Suddenly I heard the mate shout, 'Good Heavens! Captain, what can that be?' at the same moment pointing to a long object lying motionless on the surface of the water some yards ahead on the starboard side. The vessel was moving very slowly, scarcely four knots an hour, so that we had ample time and an excellent opportunity to view the object. It remained motionless until we ran almost upon it, and until the wash of the vessel disturbed it, when the monster, for such it proved to be, raised its head, as big as that of a calf's, and gazed fixedly at the ship as if critically surveying it, exhibiting more of curiosity than anger. As we fairly skirted it the creature became excited and, opening its horrid mouth, disclosed two fangs apparently four inchs in length. The body was extended so near the surface and we brushed by it so very close, that the entire crew of twenty-one being called had time and opportunity to view it perfectly. The carpenter suggested that we should harpoon the monster, but the crew objected, and I must confess that I shared their fears, lest the mad animal might plunge against the ship's side and do it serious injury. The length of the creature, which I could estimate with considerable accuracy as it lay along the ship's length as we passed, was about sixty feet."

The Captain's statement was confirmed by Mr. Fletcher, chief mate, and also by all the crew, who added that the apparent girth of the serpent was seven feet near the head, and somewhat greater about the middle. The point of the tail was not visible, as it seemed to curl downward, the head, however, was seen perfectly, and it was the head of a serpent, rather long, like those of the non-poisonous species, but without mane, rings, or other embellishments frequently described as being noticeable on other sea-serpents.

A SEA PRODUCT WHICH RESEMBLES A SERPENT.

We have now to call attention to a peculiar production of the sea which so admirably counterfeits a living monster sea-serpent that thousands have been deceived and went to their graves believing they had seen a veritable gigantic ocean-snake, when in reality they had witnessed only a floating sea-weed. Let us here introduce the experience (as recorded by himself) of a Mr. Smith, who in 1848 was making a voyage in his father's ship *Pekin*. "When near Moulmein, in calm weather I saw at a certain distance something extraordinary, balancing itself on the waves, and which appeared to be an animal of immeasurable length. With our telescopes we could perfectly distinguish an enormous head, and a neck of monstrous size covered with a mane, which alternately appeared and disappeared. This appearance was likewise seen by all our crew, and everybody agreed that it must be the great sea-serpent. I took the resolution of making a closer acquaintance of this celebrated monster, and immediately ordered a boat to be lowered with an officer and four men on board, furnished with arms and a few fathoms of rope. I watched them attentively. The monster did not seem to be disturbed by their approach. At length they arrived quite close to its head. They appeared to me to hesitate; then I saw them busily uncoiling the rope with which they were provided, while the monster continued to raise its head and unfold its enormous length. Suddenly the boat began her course to regain the vessel, followed by the formidable monster. In less than half an hour the latter was hauled on board. The body appeared to be endowed with a certain suppleness so long as it remained suspended. But it was so covered with marine parasites of every species that it was not until some time had elapsed we arrived at the discovery that this terrible animal was neither more nor less than a monstrous algæ, upwards of one hundred feet long and four feet in diameter, whose root at a distance had represented its head, while the motion communicated to it by the waves had given it the semblance of life.

"In a few days this curious algæ, growing dry, spread through the ship such an infectious odor that I was compelled to have it cast into the sea. Immediately after my arrival in London, the *Dœdalus* reported its encounter with the great serpent in nearly the same parts, and I cannot doubt but that it was only the floating wreck of the algæ whose history I have just related. Nevertheless, the illusion is ren-

THE GIGANTIC ALGÆ OR SEA-WEED.

dered so justifiable by the appearance of the object, that if I had been unable to dispatch the boat at the moment I did, I should have remained all my life in the conviction that I had seen the great serpent of the sea."

REASON FOR DOUBTING THERE IS SUCH A CREATURE.

The experience of Mr. Smith certainly throws some doubt on the probability of sea-serpents having been so frequently seen, besides admonishing us to be careful how we accept testimony concerning this phenomenal monster. There are, besides Mr. Smith's suggestions and experience, other grounds for doubting the existence of a gigantic sea-serpent. It is claimed that if such a creature exists it must exist in numbers and reproduce itself at intervals. If it propagated even less rapidly than the whale, which gives birth to young about every three years, it would certainly, in course of centuries, have so increased its numbers that there could no longer be any doubt of its existence and its nature. It is the fact of this doubt, caused by its infrequent appearance, which gives place to the idea of individual delusion. But on the supposition that numbers may exist in the unexplored depths of the sea, "where never plummet sounded," this objection loses its weight. It is also claimed that were such strange animals in existence their dead bodies or bones would be more frequently found. But the bones of a dead whale are very seldom found except where the animal has been known to be killed, common as this creature is. Numbers of elephants must die every year, and yet no explorer ever found the bones of one that had died a natural death. No cast-off horns of the deer are ever found, though these are shed yearly; and of the scores of small birds which must perish in the course of nature annually not a trace is ever found in our woods. It is one of the unsolved mysteries of science how wild creatures dispose of their dead. Besides, some curious specimens supposed to belong to this species have been found. In 1809 a creature in a partially decomposed condition was washed ashore on Stronsay, one of the Orkney Isles. It was said to be fifty-six feet long and twelve feet in circumference. Some parts of the skeleton of this creature are now in the Edinburgh museum, and scientists have never fully decided what was the character of the original body. In September, 1817, a small serpent was killed off Cape Ann, Mass. It was three feet long, and on its back was a series of humps, forty in number, and the spinal column bent vertically, which is impossible to the common snake. There seems no good reason to doubt that this was a young sea-serpent. In 1860 a dead serpent, sixteen feet seven inches long, was washed ashore on the coast of the Bermudas. No scientific person seeing it, no description of its structure was made.

The exaggerated size accredited to most specimens of the sea-serpent casts a doubt upon the accounts given of them, it may be admitted; but it does not prove these accounts false. There are abnormal developments in all species of created creatures. Men are found eight feet high sometimes, and a Jumbo appears occasionally even among elephants. Sperm whales have been seen seventy-one feet long, and walruses thirty-five feet. There is hardly a species of animal which does not occasionally show an individual of unusual size.

CHAPTER IX.

THE DEVIL-FISH AND ITS INFERNAL KIN.

THE octopus, or polypus, is dreadful enough in its appearance to suggest a name indicative of its horrid aspect, and the word meaning eight-armed clearly points it out as a most formidable creature. But we are acquainted with another animal of the deep sea, which, if possible, is more monstrously horrible than the polypus, to which some discriminating naturalist has given the name devil-fish or sea devil, and certainly a more suitable appellation could not be applied; sailors, however, generally call it "sea-bat." Like a grisly spectre, it is dreadful only in appearance, having neither the power nor disposition to do great harm. It belongs to the skate family, but with the exception of being broad and flat it hardly resembles that genus, bearing quite as close resemblance to the sting-ray. A general description gives it eight long arms attached to a broad, flat body, in the center of which are its leering eyes and cavernous mouth, around which are several horny spines. Some singular stories are told of this monster, a few of which I must relate in order to give an idea of its habits, size and immense strength.

Fishers around Tampa Bay, Florida, sometimes meet with the devil-fish while fishing for the tarpon, which is itself a most difficult creature to land. A gentleman while recreating in the South, thus describes his experience with one of these satanic monsters.

"Next to tarpon fishing, in point of excitement, comes the chase of the devil-fish. Up around Tampa and all along the Gulf coast you will find them, and if they do not remind you of their namesake then I am mistaken. They look like great bats, and some call them the bat-fish. You can form some idea of how they look if you imagine a bat overboard measuring, say, twenty feet across from tip to tip, with a tail perhaps ten feet long, shaped like a cowboy's whip. Give it two hornlike claspers at the head, and you have the sea-devil in all its glory. Green hands often strike them, not knowing what they are, and are generally jerked overboard for their pains, or have to cut the line. Some years ago one appeared in a harbor where several schooners were lying and the sailors, who were Swedes, and had never seen one of the fish before, saw them playing around in the harbor and thought it would be a good joke to spear one. So they took a light skiff and a pair of old whale harpoons and ropes that belonged to the schooner and started out, and were joined by the other boats. In a short time one of the boats got alongside of a sea-bat, and a rouser it was, too. When they struck it you would have thought the whole bottom had been hit, and a second later that boat was rushing up the harbor at a rate she never went before. It was a blind lead, though, and the fish had to turn, and the skiff was jerked around so quickly that she half filled, and one man was tumbled overboard. Up the channel they went, some yelling for the other boat and others to cut the line, as it was evident that she would fill in a moment; but it happened that the only man who had a knife had been dropped overboard, and as they could not get the line untied they had to let it go. They said afterward they were about to jump overboard and let everything go, when the fish changed its course and headed right for one of the schooners. They had to jump then, anyhow, and as they went overboard, the fish dived under the vessel and the skiff struck her side with a crash, and was knocked all to pieces. The end plank, as they found out later, to which the line was made fast, went off with the fish. The men were picked up, and two days later the devil-fish floated ashore. It measured about eighteen feet across, and it was estimated to weigh a ton."

LIEUTENANT LAMONT'S EXCITING ADVENTURE.

Kingston harbor is also a favorite spot for devil-fish, where they are quite frequently seen floating on the surface. Lieutenant Lamont, of the United States Navy, tried to catch one which he thus perceived floating, but with what success will be seen in the following:

The Lieutenant's attention was called to a crowd which he saw assembled on the beach at Kingston, intently gazing out at sea. Closer examination revealed to his astonished gaze an animate object flopping on the surface; so large did it appear that he could not make out what it was, but being of an adventurous disposition he ordered the boats lowered, and with several men started for the monster.

As it lay less than one hundred yards from his ship he soon came up with it, and one of the men threw a harpoon into its body, but the moment it was struck the monster, which he now perceived was a

LIEUT. LAMONT'S ADVENTURE WITH A DEVIL-FISH.

sea-devil, made off at the most amazing speed, drawing the boat with equal velocity after it. As it swam around, the other boats came up and harpoon after harpoon was discharged into its body without giving it any fatal wounds or impairing its strength. Thus the battle continued until the boats were drawn more than ten miles out at sea. At length, however, as night was coming on, the impish fish struggled with greatly increased violence and broke loose, carrying with it a dozen harpoons.

A short time after this interesting event, the Lieutenant had another adventure with a larger devil-fish than the first one encountered, and in the same harbor. He attacked it in the same manner, but so rapidly did the fish carry his boat through the water that it was impossible for the other boats to come up with it until, somewhat tired, it sank to the bottom and lay there as if to rest. The other boats now gathered around, and every man lent his aid to draw the creature up, but in vain. After the lapse of nearly half an hour the grisly monster rose again to the surface, when it was dispatched by a dozen musket-balls. When brought ashore it measured fifteen feet in width, and its mouth two and one-half feet, large enough to admit a man with ease, while its weight was so great that the combined strength of forty men was required to drag it.

Hon. Richard Hill describes a devil-fish which he harpooned that drew the boat he was in so rapidly that waves were raised several feet higher than the boat, while the water was beaten with such fury that spray was thrown thirty or more feet high. When killed it measured eighteen feet across. Le Vaillant asserts that he saw a devil-fish in the Atlantic once which would have measured from fifty to sixty feet in breadth, in which event its length would have been nearly one hundred feet. The truth of this story may, with safety, be doubted.

Colonel Elliott, in an admirable little work which he wrote and entitled "Carolina Sports," has given us an excellent description of the physical peculiarities and habits of the devil-fish, and also relates several adventures he has had with the Plutonian monster. He describes an attack once made on one of these creatures, in which it was harpooned and made fast to three large boats; but so great was its strength that the boats, despite the efforts of a dozen strong rowers, were towed rapidly out to sea, and to save themselves from disaster the men had to cut the harpoon lines and let the creature go.

This queer fish has a habit, peculiar to the tentacular family, of rubbing itself against the anchors and hawsers of boats, with which they sometimes become entangled, and clasping the object with their mighty arms, start off with the boat to the great consternation of the occupants.

OFF-SHOOTS OF SATAN.

If the devil-fish is the true satanic representative of the deep, as its name implies, there are numerous other fishes which may well be regarded as minor luminaries of the nether kingdom, for they have about them the very inspiration of horror. Foremost among these children, or near kin of the devil-fish, is the sea-frog or angler, a monstrosity of frightful aspect and voracious disposition. In size it equals the porpoise, but in shape it equals the—devil himself. More than one-half the fish is head, and such a head! The eyes are near the top, and have a dreadful wicked look in them. The mouth, however, is its most repulsive feature, extending, as it does, far beyond the width of its body, and with an armament of teeth more terrible than the shark. When distended, the mouth is capacious enough to take in an animal its own size, while the jaws, palate, tongue and fauces are fairly lined with hooked but mobile teeth,

THE ANGLER, OR FROG-FISH.

from which no prey, when once caught, can possibly escape. All over the body are small fleshy excrescences which look like horrid worms that had fastened their heads into the fish's body. From the nose grows a feeler that terminates in a palm-shaped excrescence of a metallic lustre, which it uses as a bait to attract its prey. Burrowing in the mud until only a small portion of its head is visible, the frog-fish angles with its long feeler, playing it so as to attract the attention of small fishes, which rush toward the bait expecting a sweet morsel, only to be grabbed by the ferocious jaws in waiting. It is this queer habit which has given the fish its very appropriate name, the angler.

The sea-frog, or angler, can live for a long time out of water, and not infrequently makes excursions on dry land in quest of large game. A gentleman traveling on the Mediterranean coast once came upon a sea-frog that had caught and was devouring a fox.

GENUINE SEA-SERPENTS.

The *Stomias-Boa*, though undoubtedly a fish, is apparently a very close connecting link between an eel and a snake, as the accompanying illustration would alone serve to prove. The name is derived from the tentacular appendages corresponding with feet and which it uses as such when moving on the bottom. Its size is never great, fortunately, else, as its appearance indicates, it would undoubtedly be a most formidable creature. Nature has placed a gracefully beautiful body on

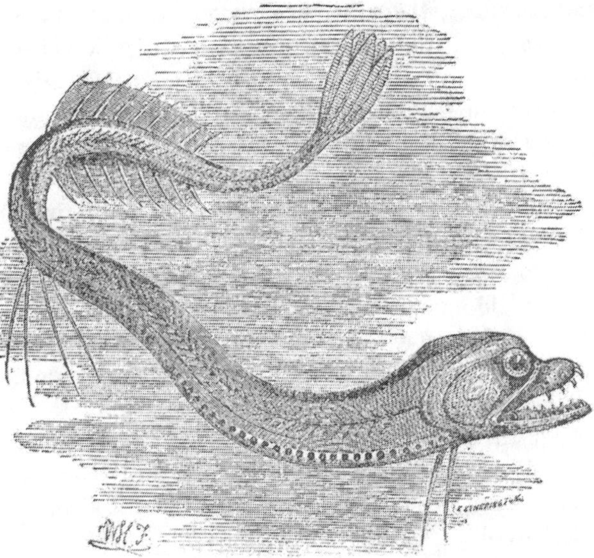

THE STOMIAS BOA, OR SERPENT-FISH.

the stomias but has given it a villainous head; the terminal of its tail, however, is wondrous, very closely resembling a water lily just opening.

Another fish, called by naturalists *Ophisura* (serpent-eater) and by sailors a sea-serpent, is a wonderful animal, which attains a length of six feet and the thickness of a man's arm. Its body is brown on the upper and silvery white on the lower parts, and has but two fins, the dorsal extending its entire length and the ventral more than half its length. The head is more pointed than a serpent's and its mouth is well supplied with teeth, while the body is beautifully mottled. Altogether it is an uncommonly handsome animal.

EELS THAT WERE FED ON HUMAN FLESH.

Living in the Mediterranean with the two species just named, is the *Murœna*, another species of the eel, which the Romans esteemed above all other delicacies. They were bred in large ponds made for the purpose, so connected with the sea that fresh water was always supplied them. For a time all Rome became actually crazy over these fish. At one of Julius Cæsar's banquets celebrating a great victory, he distributed six thousand of these eels to his officers and friends. The craze became so great that some one finally suggested that the murænas should be fed on human flesh in order to render them more tender and succulent, whereupon everybody seized upon the idea, and the great fish ponds were kept supplied with fresh bodies of slaves who were daily thrown in alive to feed the voracious eels. It is related that a certain Vedius Pollio, a rich patrician who owned large numbers of slaves, acquired great reputation by the liberal manner in which he gave his slaves to feed the ponds. The evil became so great that Augustus recognized the importance of bringing the people back to their senses, and to this end he accepted an invitation to dine with Pollio, knowing full well that an opportunity would be offered whereby he could impress upon his host the evil of this human sacrifice. The occasion came soon enough, for a man who was serving them accidentally let fall a crystal goblet, whereat Pollio was so enraged that he immediately ordered the slave to be thrown to the fishes. Augustus interceded for the servant's life, but finding Pollio determined, dismissed the slave himself, then ordered all the goblets broken and the fish-ponds filled up. Thus was the atrocious custom forever destroyed.

Associated with the muræna as a rare gastronomical dish among the ancients was the lamprey, which is somewhat allied to the muræna, having the same eel-like form, and was also similar in size, both measuring about four feet in length. Its main point of difference is in having a mouth for suction that is provided with numerous sharp teeth, while the tongue acts as a piston-rod. The lamprey feeds by attaching its mouth to the largest fishes, where it gnaws the flesh or scarifies it, and then sucks out the blood. On each side are seven holes corresponding to gill orifices, through which the water is drawn or expelled; hence the German name for the fish, *Neun Augen*, "nine-eyed."

Formerly the lamprey was esteemed a royal dish, so that the city of Gloucester, by an old law, was compelled to provide a lamprey pie for the sovereign once a year. Henry I. is said to have died from eating too inordinately of this favorite fish, and the death of Pope, the poet, Johnson asserts, was caused by gorging himself on the same food.

A FALLEN ANGEL.

As we have a prototype of satan in the sea with numerous satel-

THE ANGEL, OR MONK-FISH.

lites of almost equally frightful aspect, so also have we a representation of the celestial empire, but if we are to judge by appearances it must be a Lucifer. I refer to the *Squatina*, or angel-fish. It is also frequently called monk-fish on account of its rounded head, which seems to be enveloped in a hood, and also because of a habit it has of rolling its eyes in a kind of reverential and supplicatory manner. The angel-fish is the antithesis of the devil-fish only in name, for an uglier creature can scarcely be conceived. The head is disproportionately large, the mouth very wide and eyes quite small. Behind each eye is an orifice shaped like a crescent, which seems to be for no other purpose than to increase its horrible aspect. Mangin describes it as resembling a grotesque mask, such as a country boy might fashion out of a hollow pumpkin.

The extraordinary appearance of this "fallen" angel-fish is in thorough accord with its disposition, in which respect it may again

THE PEGASUS DRAGON.

be compared with Lucifer. It has two wings corresponding to pectoral fins, which not only add to its homeliness, but which are very serviceable in propelling it rapidly through the water, and enabling it to swoop down upon its prey in "true angelic fashion." There is nothing that swims that has a more fierce and voracious disposition than the angel-fish, and since it grows to a length of seven or eight feet, it is a dangerous adversary even to man.

FLYING MONSTERS.

Speaking of angel-fish, leads us directly to a consideration of flying-fish, especially since we are mentioning some of the horrid creatures which cleave the deep, and know that there are two or three species of flying-fish that are ugly as Caliban. The *Exocetus Volitaus* (flying beach-sleeper) is a singular specimen of the grotesque in nature. It takes its name from a habit which is ascribed to it, of coming out upon the beach to sleep. Whether it really does leave the water for the purpose of sleeping, is not a well-established fact, but the Greeks evidently thought so, by giving it the name by which it is still known. By means of its extremely large pectoral fins it is enabled to spring from the crest of a wave and maintain a brief flight. They are surely the most unfortunate of God's creatures, since they are continually pursued by dolphins and other predaceous fishes, to escape which nature has given them wings to rise in air that they may fall victims to aquatic birds. The greatest flight they

THE SEA-HORSE.

ever attain is two hundred and fifty yards, and even this distance they can make only by dashing through wave-crests to moisten their fins.

The *Pegasus Dragon*, or flying horse, is another quaint species, but since it hardly exceeds four inches in length, it does not receive the attention which its appearance would otherwise inspire. Beneath its snout is a mouth which is movable like that of the sturgeon or sucker-fish. Its body, which is flattened, is as well armatured as a knight, being fairly encased in radiated shields, while the posterior part has somewhat the appearance of a crocodile's tail. While the pegasus is a flying-fish, its tuberculated body and crustaceous tail give it close kinship to the *Hippocampus*, or sea-horse, a singular little animal having a prehensile tail which it uses like a hand to grasp any object it may choose to fix itself upon. The head, especially when dried, bears a very unique resemblance to that of a horse, from whence its name is derived. Among the ancients, who were given so completely to mythology, there were fabled monsters which they called *Hippo-Centaurs*, half-man and half-horse. These queer creatures were said to inhabit Thessaly, and were represented as fierce warriors. The idea is said to have sprung from the supposed fact that the Thessalonians were first to ride upon horseback; but it may also be reasonably conjectured that the sea-horse, which abounds in the Mediterranean, partly, at least, inspired the mythologic idea of a duplex animal of which the horse was part

The male sea-horse is provided with pouches on its tail in which the female deposits her eggs, and these are carried by the male until they are hatched. They swim always in a vertical position and dart about with such extraordinary rapidity that the eye can scarcely follow them. The beautiful fable of Posidon driving his chariot drawn by sea-horses through the coral halls of the deep, is no doubt derived from the then known existence of these strange little animals.

CHAPTER X.

BEAUTIFUL AND CURIOUS FISH.

HAVING mentioned a few of the most uncouth fish that inhabit the sea, let us turn to a contemplation of those species which are to the ocean what the birds of paradise are to the land, for in the living infinite of the deep there are fish of such iridescent hues that they may be well compared with the most gorgeous plumage that nature ever invested bird with.

The mackerel family includes several species, remarkable for their wonderful beauty, but the most splendid of them all is the King Fish, a habitat of the Northern seas, which grows to a length of six feet and of nearly two hundred pounds in weight. The colors of this fish are exquisitely rich and marvelously blended. The back is of a steel blue gradually shading to a brilliant green toward the tail and a rich rose color on the belly. These well defined colors are variegated by numerous oval spots, some of which are pure white and others reflect the lustre of burnished silver, while the fins are generally ver-

THE BEAUTIFUL AND CURIOUS.

million. This exquisite combination is blended into indescribable beauty when the fish darts through the water.

The John (yellow) Dory is another very beautiful fish habiting the shores of the Mediterranean. It is frequently called St. Peter's fish on account of a legend which is related to the effect that it was from this fish St. Peter obtained the tribute money. The superstitious declare that the two spots which are on its back are the finger-marks of the Apostle. They neglect to tell us why Peter took the fish into his hands, and also why the haddock is identically marked.

The body of the John Dory is a deep olive, flecked with yellow. When taken from the water, as it dries, the fish rapidly changes color into a succession of gold, blue and white.

ANCIENT BARBARITIES PRACTICED ON THE MULLET.

The Red Mullet is delicately colored with rose tints and yellow stripes, which change like the colors on the John Dory when taken from the water, and in its expiring throes nothing can be more beautiful than the kaleidoscopic succession of brilliant colors it undergoes. The ancients esteemed its flesh so greatly that enormous sums were paid for them. According to Pliny, Asinius Celer gave as much as four hundred dollars for a single mullet. These fish were not only estimated for their savory flesh, but also for the beauty of their body, especially during their expiring moments. To gratify this morbid cruelty, the fish were raised in large aquariums, and taken out before guests of the rich in order that the dying fish might afford them amusement by its agonizing death throes.

The Sea-Perch has a scaly coat of gray streaked with blue, shading underneath to silvery white. Another perch called the *Enoplessus* is of a lovely silver-gray, and striped with eight narrow black bands, while the fins are a rich yellow — a very beautiful combination. The *Apognon* of the Mediterranean is even more gorgeously bedecked than the last named, the body being of a delicate crimson on the back, growing paler toward the belly, while the entire fish is gracefully dotted with black spots, while three black stripes cross it perpendicularly. The *Lettered Seranus* has a coat of deep orange, over which pass several brown bands. About the head there are lines of brilliant blue, which at a distance somewhat resemble letters; hence its name. The *Spined Seranus* is still more beautifully marked, its back being of a deep scarlet, changing to a golden hue on its sides, and to silver on the belly. On the head are three stripes of golden

ROMANS WATCHING THE EXPIRING THROES OF A RED MULLET.

yellow, while the nose is decorated by two bands of bright green. Add to this fins that are tinted with yellow and red, and we have here a fish that can scarcely be exceeded for extraordinary beauty.

THE MARVELOUS RIBAND FISH.

We might mention dozens of other fish of equal loveliness, but since attempted description can give hardly an idea of the gorgeous coloring which they really exhibit, it were an idle waste of space to name them all. I cannot afford, however, to omit mention of the Riband Fish, since it is not only phenominally beautiful, but also extremely rare. The body of this strange fish is shaped like a ribbon, being so thin that it is almost transparent, but it is the color of burnished silver, and in the water gives off a sheen of remarkable beauty. Its natural home is at the greatest depths of the sea, from whence it is sometimes dislodged by volcanic disturbance and thrown upon the shore.

The Rainbow and Parrot-fish are also species so exquisite in dainty coloring that they have been rightfully named. The Rabbit-fish, called by the Norwegians the Sea-rat, on account of its rat-shaped tail, is very beautiful, and wears a tuft or thread-like appendage on its head, something like a crown; hence it is also called King-fish. In fact, we discover in the ocean an *alter ego* of all that is on land, that coincidence which marks the brotherhood of land and sea, and the identity that illustrates and imputes the single origin of universal life.

WARRIORS OF THE DEEP.

The piously inclined have dreamed of and conceived a millenium, the superstitious have fortold its coming, but Nature herself has declared that peace on earth is impossible. Not only has she made different dispositions among men whereby differences and disturbances must become our common lot, but she has implanted warring elements throughout earth, sea and air, so that peace is impossible. Nowhere else can we observe with such interest the singular warlike provisions made by nature as in the sea. While inventive art has given to man gunpowder, nature has drawn the lightning and made a store-house of it in many of her ocean children. How wonderful, because it exhibits the care taken by her of the otherwise helpless, which would soon become extinct but for the power thus mysteriously implanted. Let us examine some of these creatures.

The Torpedo Fish, which exists in several different species, is a natural electric battery always charged, and capable of doing immense mischief. Water being an excellent conductor of electricity the torpedo can shock its enemies at a surprising distance. Very frequently when drawing in their nets fishermen receive shocks from the torpedo transmitted to them from their lines; so violent sometimes are these shocks that the fishermen are compelled to let go the lines, thus losing their entire haul. Dr. Walsh was the first one to demonstrate that the power of the torpedo was electrical, and also that it was sufficient to kill small animals.

The electrical eel has also the power of discharging a battery that is capable of producing violent shocks, sometimes attended by painful consequences. Both the torpedo and electrical eel use their physical properties chiefly to catch their prey, which usually swims better than they; by discharging their battery their intended prey is suddenly paralyzed and rendered unconscious of the fate that overtakes them. But the electricity thus stored up is not only used to kill lawful prey, for it is also a means for attack and defense, as we shall presently see.

The electrical eel is found principally along the South American coast and especially at the mouths of rivers debouching into the Atlantic.

Humboldt was the first to give a precise account of this curious fish, in which, however, he gives not his own, but the French traveler, Bonplaud's experience. Briefly the account is as follows:

SINGULAR MANNER IN WHICH ELECTRICAL EELS ARE CAUGHT.

"In traversing the Llanas of the province of Caracas, in order to embark at San Fernando de Apure on his voyage up the Orinoco, M. Bonplaud stopped at Calabozo. The object of this sojourn was to investigate the history of the *gymnotus* (electrical eel), great numbers of which are found in the neighborhood. After three days' residence in Calabozo some Indians conducted them to the Cano de Bera, a muddy and stagnant basin, but surrounded by rich vegetation. They were much surprised when informed that it would be necessary to take thirty half-wild horses from the neighboring savannas in order to fish for the gymnotus.

The idea of this fishing, called in the language of the country *embarboscar con caballos* (intoxicating by means of horses), is very odd. The word *barbosco* indicates the roots of the lacquinia, or any other poisonous plant, by contact with which a body of water acquires the property of killing, or, at least, of intoxicating or stupefying the fishes. These come to the surface when they have been poisoned in

FISHING FOR ELECTRICAL EELS BY THE AID OF HORSES.

this manner. The horses chasing them here and there in a marsh has, it seems, the same effect on the alarmed fishes. While our hosts were explaining to us this strange mode of fishing, the troop of horses and mules had arrived and the Indians had made a sort of battue, pressing the horses on all sides and forcing them into the marsh. The Indians, armed with long canes and harpoons, placed themselves round the basin, some of them mounting the trees whose branches hung over the water, and by their cries, and still more by their canes, preventing the horses from coming ashore. The eels, confused by the noise, defended themselves by repeated discharges of their batteries. For a long time it seemed as if they would be victorious over the horses. Some of the mules especially being almost stifled by the frequency and force of the shocks, disappeared under the water, and some of the horses, in spite of the watchfulness of the Indians, regained the bank where, overcome by the shocks they had undergone, they stretched themselves at their whole length. The picture now presented was indescribable. Groups of Indians surrounded the basin; the horses with bristling manes, terror and grief in their eyes, trying to escape from the storm which had surprised them; the eels, yellow and livid, looking like great aquatic serpents swimming on the surface of the water and chasing their enemies, were objects at once appalling and picturesque. In less than five minutes two horses were drowned. An eel, more than five feet long, glided under one horse, discharged its apparatus through its whole extent, attacking at once the heart, the viscera and the plexus of the nerves of the animal, probably benumbing and finally drowning it.

"When the struggle had endured a quarter of an hour the mules and horses appeared less frightened, the manes became less erect, the eyes expressed less terror, the eels shunned instead of attacking them, at the same time approaching the bank where they were easily taken by throwing little harpoons at them attached to long cords, the harpoon sometimes hooking two at a time, they being landed by means of the long cord. They were thus drawn ashore without being able to communicate any shock."

STINGING FISH.

Electricity is the most powerful and subtle influence in nature, and fishes armed with this mysterious fluid are dangerous to approach, but there is another species of fish that, though comparatively small and weak, are armed with such a trenchant weapon that they are much more to be dreaded than the torpedo fish or electrical eel. The Sting-ray is the most conspicuous specimen of the species to which I refer, and they are almost as dangerous as the man-eating shark. This fish, which is peculiar to the Mediterranean and the Florida coast, attains a considerable size, but hardly in proportion to its power of doing harm. Its pectoral fins are so large that they resemble wings wide spread and grow up close to the creature's head It has a snout somewat like a beak that gives the fish a villainous countenance, which is by no means relieved by two piercing black eyes that always look murderous. The weapon with which it is so deadly armed is the tail; this is at once

THE STING-RAY.

sword and saw, and terrible enough to appall the bravest. The tail is armed with rows of serrated teeth which are so ragged that when the animal strikes it not only punctures but frightfully lacerates the flesh. Being long and flexible, when about to attack, the sting-ray winds almost instantly about its victim and darts its tail so rapidly that no eye can detect the strokes it is making. Fishermen frequently become victims to these attacks despite extraordinary precautions, and before help can arrive their thighs are torn in the most frightful manner.

The sting-bull and little weaver are quite small but hardly so powerless as they appear. They are common along the English coast, where they lie in the sand with dorsal spine erected ready for any emergency. If trod upon they use this weapon most effectively, and woe to the barefoot boy who comes in contact with them.

The lancet-fish is armed with strong and sharp-pointed spines on each side of its tail, which it darts into a victim like a lance. Careless handling of this fish is certain to result in a painful wound. Our common catfish, as all small boys know, are not altogether harmless, for the points of their pectoral fins are capable of inflicting lance-like wounds which do not heal readily, being evidently poisoned.

FLOATING NETTLES.

The most wonderful of all the stinging species that inhabit the ocean, is what sailors call the "Portugese man-of-war," but which scientists have named *Physalia utriculus*, from the Greek, meaning "stinging bubble." Of this strange creature, several species of which exist, Figuier says:

"Let us imagine a great cylindrical bladder dilated in the middle, attenuated and rounded at its extremities, of eleven or twelve inches in length and from one to three broad. Its appearance is glassy and transparent; its color an imperfect purple passing to a violet, then to an azure blue. It is surmounted by a crest, limpid and pure as crystal, veined with purple and violet in decreasing tints. Under the vesicle float the fleshy filaments, waving and contorted into a spiral form, which sometimes descend perpendicularly like so many threads of celestial blue. Sailors believe that the crest which surmounts the vesicle performs the office of a sail, and that they tell the navigator how the wind blows."

When the vesicles are filled with air they are almost projected out of the water. In order to descend it is necessary to expel the air. The floating appendages beneath the body are of divers kinds and serve several different purposes. Some are the organs of reproduction, others nurses, and some tentacles for feeding or grasping food; there are still others called *Soudes* by naturalists, which are probes and suckers, forming offensive and defensive arms truly formidable, for these beautiful and graceful animals, though but one remove above plant-life, are terrible antagonists. Dutertre, the French naturalist, relates the following:

"This galley (our physalia), however agreeable to the sight, is most dangerous to the body, for I can assert that it is freighted with the worst merchandise which floats on the sea. I speak as a natural-

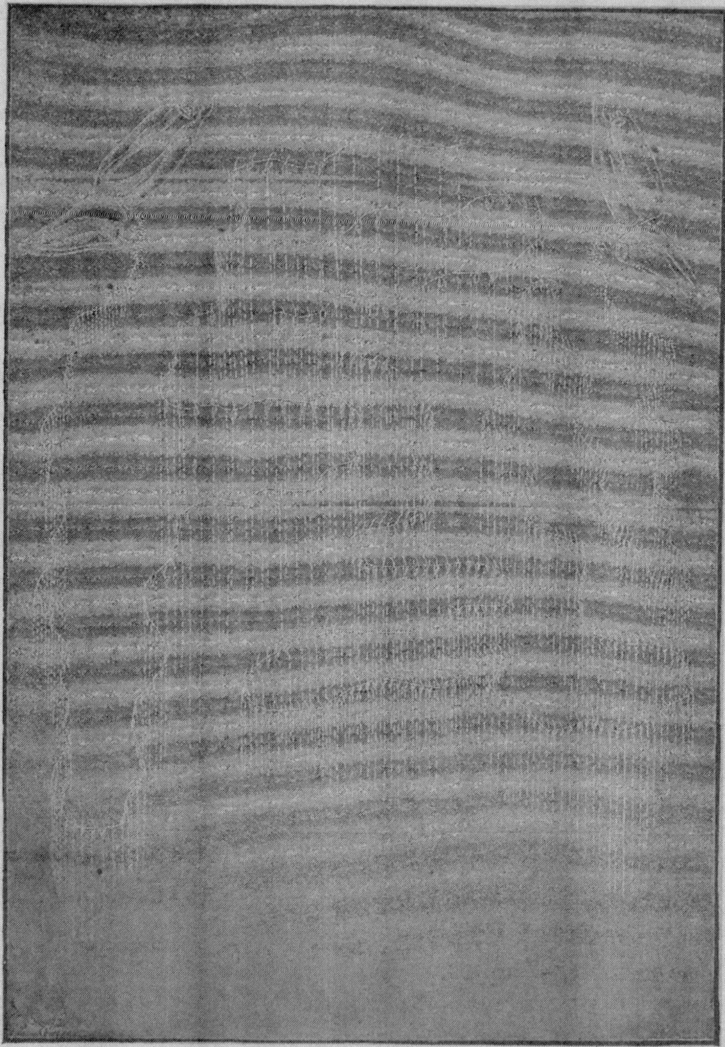

THE PORTUGUESE MAN-OF-WAR.

ist, and as having made experiments at my own personal cost. One day when sailing at sea in a small boat, I perceived one of these little 'galleys,' and was curious to see the form of the animal; but I had scarcely seized it when all its fibres seemed to clasp my hand, covering it as with birdlime, and scarcely had I felt it in all its freshness (for it is very cold to the touch) when it seemed as if I had plunged my arm up to the shoulder in a cauldron of boiling water. This was accompanied with a pain so strange that it was only with a violent effort I could restrain myself from crying aloud."

A NATURALIST BADLY STUNG.

Leblond, another voyager, in his work "Voyage aux Antilles," says: "One day I was bathing with some friends in a bay in front of the house where I dwelt. While my friends fished for sardines for breakfast, I amused myself by diving in the manner of the native Carribeans, under the wave about to break; having reached the other side of one great wave, I had gained the open sea and was returning on the top of the next wave toward the shore. My rashness nearly cost me my life. A physalia, many of which were stranded upon the beach, fixed itself upon my left shoulder at the moment the wave landed me upon the beach. I promptly detached it, but many of its filaments remained glued to my skin, and the pain I experienced immediately was so intense that I nearly fainted. I seized an oil flask that was at hand and swallowed one-half while I rubbed my arm with the other; this restored me to myself and I returned to the house, where two hours of repose relieved the pain, which disappeared altogether during the night."

The physalia are often gregarious, gathering in vast herds in the shoals. Floating along in large numbers near the tropics in both oceans, they may be seen carried by currents or driven by trade winds, dragging behind them their long tentacular appendages, and conspicuous by their rich and varied coloring, from pale crimson to ultramarine. When a fish has the misfortune to come in contact with one of these stinging creatures, each tentacle, by an instantaneous movement, seizes and benumbs it, winding about its body in true boa-constrictor style. A physalia whose body is no larger than a walnut will kill a fish larger than a herring; in fact, the common flying-fish is its habitual prey.

Mr. Bennett describes the physalia as seizing fishes by means of the tentacles, which are alternately contracted to half an inch and then

THE STINGING SEA-NETTLE.

shot out with amazing velocity to the length of several feet, dragging the helpless and entangled prey to its sucker-like mouths and stomach-like cavities concealed among the tentacles, which he saw filled while he looked on.

NEST-BUILDING AND SHOOTING-FISHES.

Birds and fowls are not single in their habits of nidification (nest-building), for, as we have fishes with coats brilliant as the grandest plumage that ever decorated the feathered tribe, so have we fish that fly, and others that lay their eggs in nests built after the manner of

STICKLEBACK IN ITS NEST.

birds, and incubate them in the same way. There are four different species of fish that are called nest-builders, but in reality there is but one that imitates the birds. This curious little creature is the Stickleback, common in English aquariums, and more common along the English coast and in the harbors.

Albert Hancock has given us an excellent description of the habits of the stickleback in an issue of the *Magazine of Natural History*, from which I quote:

"I had the pleasure of seeing the nest built from the very commencement and through all its stages. The place selected for the nest was the bare, flat top of a piece of oolite (small grains of limestone), where it formed a right-angle by resting against the glass partition which separated two ponds (in a tank), in one of which were kept four minnows and two small eels, and in the second the sticklebacks. Now he (the male fish) arrives with a large fibre in his mouth, deposits it, rearranges the whole of the materials already accumulated with his mouth; removing one fibre to this place and another to that, and departs in his search for more. Now he returns, carrying a small piece of gravel which is carefully placed on part of the fibres, as it were, to keep them down; he then draws himself slowly over the whole, and is off again. Now he brings another fibre, which he dibs in with his snout, so as to make it interlace with the others. Now he is busy poking a circular hole in the middle of the accumulated materials with his snout; thus he conveys without cessation, decayed rootlets, gravel, sand and whatever he can find that will answer his purpose.

"But I must observe that the specific gravity of his materials is continually tested; for having found what appears a suitable fibre it is carried a little way, then projected to a short distance from his mouth and watched as it falls; if it falls rapidly it is tried again in the same manner, and if it then proves too light it is abandoned altogether and another selected. If there should be any strong fibre, which he has a difficulty in causing to remain in the position he requires, a small quantity of sand is brought in his mouth and adroitly placed on top of the fibre to keep it down. If this does not effect the purpose so as to please him, the refractory piece is taken out and rejected altogether. At the same time he hangs or hovers close over the surface of the nest and throws his whole body into a curious and rapid vibratory motion, by which he causes a rapid current of water to be projected on the materials as though to prove their stability. Another very curious operation is the action of drawing his body slowly over the materials which compose the nest. I believe that at the time he secretes a glutinous matter which acts as a cement to bind the whole together, at the same time the pressure of his body may render them more compact; or, it may be that the whole surface of the nest is by this action charged with the milt, and thus the impregnation of the eggs more perfectly insured."

The male stickleback, in the breeding season, is really a beautiful fish. His skin is quite iridescent with magnificent red and green colors blended together. These colors, as is the case with most fish, are very evanescent, and soon fade away after death. A peculiarity with the stickleback, however, is its chameleon character of adapting its color to its surroundings, the most remarkable changes occurring as it is transferred from one kind of water to another, having different

THE ARCHER-FISH.

degrees of clearness; they will also adapt themselves to the colors of flowers if placed close to them. The male stickleback is a ferocious warrior, and when two of them engage in a combat, which they are certain to do if circumscribed in their quarters, the battle is continued to the death, for one is almost sure to be ripped up by the sharp spines of the other.

THE SHOOTING-FISH.

Does the reader believe that there is a fish that goes out hunting and shoots its prey in true sportsman's style? Well, the Archer fish may not exactly be termed a sportsman, but it is certainly true that he feeds off the bugs and flies that he shoots. What a funny creature the archer is, and quite small, too, for he rarely exceeds eight inches in length. His range is near the surface of the water and along the shore, where he watches with a sharp eye and voracious stomach. Discovering a fly hovering over the water, or an insect browsing on a leaflet near the surface, the archer takes deliberate aim and propels a small stream of water with almost unerring certainty against the prey, and always brings it tumbling down to its wide-open and waiting mouth. There are three well-known species of the archer fish, two of the largest being peculiar to the Chinese and East India seas. A leading sport among the Javanese is the catching of these fish and confining them in aquaria to watch them shoot flies. The largest species of archer fish can propel a stream of water four feet with wonderful certainty.

MUSICAL FISH.

All professions and trades are represented in the sea, and musical culture is not overlooked. The flying Gurnard has been called the Lyre-fish because some people long ago imagined they were musical. They might more appropriately be called pyrotechnic fish, because at night as they fly from the crest of one wave to another they emit so brilliant a phosphorescent light as to resemble streams of fire. So far as their music is concerned it is very crude, since about the only sound they make is a deep-seated grunt. The *Maigre* is a drummer and wakes the dull, cold ear of the Mediterranean almost constantly. The Roman *Umbrina* go in vast shoals bellowing like long-fasting lions, their coarse notes being plainly heard as the fish swim nearly two hundred feet below the surface.

There is a fish found in the Chinese seas which may be fairly called musical, since it has a voice peculiarly melodious, ranging nearly the entire gamut. Lieutenant White, in a work published in 1824, describing his voyage round the world, relates that upon an occasion while his vessel was lying at the mouth of Cambodia River, his attention was directed toward a strange sound which seemed to proceed from the bottom and sides of his ship. Gradually the noise increased

QUEER FISHES OF THE MEDITERRANEAN.

until there was a great chorus, as of organs, bells, harps and sharp croaking of frogs. The sounds he describes as being quite melodious as well as mysterious, calling to mind the fabled music of mermaids. It was not until some time had elapsed that the Lieutenant discovered his serenaders were rather small fish belonging to the *Maigre* family.

Humboldt has described a similar occurrence to which he was witness during a voyage in the South Sea. He says that at seven o'clock in the evening an extraordinary noise startled the entire crew, none of whom had ever heard anything like it before. The sound was very much like the beating of numerous drums in mid-air, and so mystified the sailors that all the superstition in their natures was at once excited. As the vessel proceeded the noise grew louder, and finally appeared to be in her hold, so that it was thought a leak had been sprung. Humboldt calmed all fears by proving to the crew that it was a school of drum-fish making the noise. Some of these fish exceeded one hundred pounds in weight, and are said to be of splendid flavor when properly cooked.

Sir James Tennant, while traveling in Ceylon, heard strange musical sounds emanating from the sea, which he explored and describes as follows: "In the evening, when the moon had risen, I took a boat and accompanied the fishermen to the spot where musical sounds were said to be heard issuing from the bottom of a lake, and which the natives supposed to proceed from some fish peculiar to the locality. I distinctly heard the sounds in question. They came up from the water like the gentle thrills of a musical chord, or the faint vibrations of a wine-glass when its rim is rubbed with a wet finger. It was not one sustained note, but a multitude of tiny sounds, each clear and distinct in itself, the sweetest treble mingling with the deepest bass. They came evidently and sensibly from the depths of the lake, and appeared to be produced by mollusca, and not by fish."

THE JUMPING FISH OF BORNEO.

As there are many well-known species of warm-blooded animals living almost wholly in the water, so may we expect and do find, not a few fishes that spend most of their time on land, where they obtain their food and find greatest enjoyment. In the foregoing pages I have described some of the very ugly inhabitants of the sea, but we now come to one which not only transcends all others in excessive hideousness, but which also presents more anomalous characteristics than the spectre-headed ornithorhynchus — the bird-beast of Australia. This marvelous creature is called the Jumping Fish of Borneo.

Though not its discoverer, Hornaday is the first person that I remember having given any satisfactory description of this finny curiosity. While traveling in a canoe along the Selangore sea-coast, in quest of crocodiles and other specimens of the natural history of Borneo, he came upon the jumping fish, which he describes as follows:

"The most interesting animals we found on the mud flats were some fishes whose actions were really remarkable. Although apparently stranded there, they seemed to feel perfectly at home, and went jumping round over the mud in every direction with the greatest indifference to their sudden change of element. In reality they were feeding upon the tiny crustaceans left on the bank by the receding

THE JUMPING FISH OF BORNEO.

tide. They were very lively considering the nature of their playground, and when I tried to beguile my Malay boatmen into catching some specimens for me, they declared it would be impossible to catch them on account of the deep mud and the swiftness of the fish. Neither was my young man Francis to be tempted into such a muddy enterprise, and as I make it a rule never to ask a servant or assistant to do anything I would not be willing to do myself, I saw that I would have to lead the attack in person.

"The Malays were thunderstruck when I pulled off my shoes and told them to put me ashore. Seeing that I was really going, Francis, like a good boy, did not hesitate to follow, and we stepped out of the sampan into mud and water hip deep.

"We will never know the actual depth of the mud on that bank, but we sank into it to our knees at every step, and were fortunate enough to stop sinking at that point. What a circus it must have been for those who looked on. But, in for a penny in for a pound, and bidding Francis choose the largest fish when possible, we went for them. There were probably a dozen in sight hopping spasmodically about, or lying at rest on the mud, but when we selected the nearest large specimens and made for them, they developed surprising energy and speed, and made straight for their burrows. They progressed by a series of short but rapidly repeated jumps, accomplished by bending the hinder third of the body sharply around to the left, then straightening it very suddenly, and at the same instant lifting the front half of the body clear of the ground by means of the armlike pectoral fins which act like the front flippers of a sea-lion. These fins are almost like arms in their structure and use, the bones being of great length, and thus giving the member great freedom of movement. Owing to the soft and yielding nature of the mud the leaps were short, about six inches being the distance gained each time, but they were so rapid, the mud so very deep and our progress so slow, the fish always succeeded in getting into their holes before we could reach them. Their burrows were simply mud-holes, going straight down to a depth of three to four feet, large enough in diameter to admit a man's arm easily, and, of course, full of water. Although the mud was soft it was not sticky, and we were able to use our hands for spades very effectually. By digging a big hole two feet deep, and standing on one's head in the bottom of it we were able to reach an arm down two feet further and seize our fish at the bottom of the burrow. Lucky it was for us that they had no sharp and poisonous spines like the mud-laff which stung me in Singapore and paralyzed my right hand for some hours.

"My first fish was hard to get and hard to hold, but, in the immortal words of 'The Shaughraun,' 'begorra, 'twas worth it.'

"As I remarked before, our living specimens were hard to hold. When I was trying to pass a string through the gills of my first fish, he struggled out of my grasp, and the moment he touched the mud started at his best speed for the water twenty yards distant.

"I was horrified at the thought of his getting away, and instantly falling upon my hands and knees I pursued him frantically 'on all fours.' It must have been a sight fit for the gods, for even my stolid and ever respectful Malays actually shouted with laughter to see the 'tuan' go over the mud like a 'buaya' (crocodile). My change of base was successful, however, for I was able to go over the mud instead of through it, and I overhauled my fish in fine style. A few minutes later I saw Francis execute the same brilliant manœuver for the same cause, and it certainly was a most laughable spectacle."

Wallace and Albertii both mention having met the jumping-fish on the coast of New Guinea, but instead of finding it haunting muddy

THE WALKING FISH.

banks and burrowing in holes, they both describe it as being a frequenter of the rocky shore. Attempts to catch the jumping fish, made repeatedly by both explorers, were always unsuccessful, owing to the fact of its very rapid progress over slippery stones as it leaped from one to another, but would rarely take to the water. The habits of the jumping-fish may, therefore, be likened to those of our common bull-frog.

WALKING FISHES.

From jumping to walking is a natural transition, and finding fish that progress by one of these means, we may reasonably suppose that there are species which also employ the other. The walking fish of the Indian Ocean is almost as hideous and uncouth in appearance as is the jumping-fish just described. Wood pronounces it "one of the strange and wild forms that sometimes occur in nature, and which are so entirely opposed to all pre-conceived ideas that they appear rather to be the composition of human ingenuity than beings actually existing. The traveler who first discovered this remarkable fish would certainly have been disbelieved if he had contented himself with making a drawing of it, and had not satisfied the rigid scrutiny of scientific men by bringing home a preserved specimen."

In the walking-fish the carpal bones, *i. e.*, those bones which represent the wrist in man, are very much lengthened, and at their extremity are placed the pectoral fins, which are short and stiff, very closely resembling claws. The body is flat and greatly elevated, so that in walking it looks almost like a sheet of paper going about on legs. This queer creature rarely strays any distance from the sea, generally confining itself to the shallow water of the coast, where it seeks its prey on the sand.

THE WONDERFUL CLIMBING PERCH.

But the jumping and walking-fishes are both exceeded in curiosity, so far as habits are concerned, by the climbing-perch of Asiatic waters, which is the very antithesis of what we might expect a fish to be. Several species of fish have the power of voluntarily leaving failing streams and ponds and making their way across dry tracts in search of water, which their unerring instincts invariably enable them to find. Even the common eel has been frequently observed crossing fields in its passage from one stream to another, but the tracts of land thus crossed, though devoid of water, are at least moist.

The climbing-perch, scientifically known as the *Anabas Scandens*, not only passes from one stream to another, but travels over vast tracts of land, including dusty roads and parched fields, under the full glare of a summer's sun, and feels no inconvenience from the dry transit.

Respecting the singular habits of the anabas, Mr. Morris, the British Government agent at Trincomalee, India, thus writes most interestingly:

"I was lately on duty inspecting the bund of a large tank at Nadecadua, which being out of repair, the remaining water was confined in a small hollow in the otherwise dry bed. While there heavy rains came on, and as we stood on the high grounds we observed a pelican on the margin of the shallow pool gorging itself. Our people went toward him and raised a cry of 'fish! fish!' We hurried down and found numbers of fish struggling upward through the grass, in the rills formed by the trickling of the rain. There was scarcely water to cover them, but nevertheless they made rapid progress up the bank, on which our followers collected about two baskets of them at a distance of forty yards from the tank. They were forcing their way up the knoll, and had they not been interrupted, first by the pelican and afterward by ourselves, they would in a few minutes have gained the highest point, and descended on the other side into a pool which formed another portion of the tank.

THE LAND-TRAVELLING PERCH.

"* * * As the tanks dry up, the fish congregate in the little pools, till at last you find them in thousands in the moistest parts of the beds rolling in the blue mud, which is at that time about the consistence of thick gruel.

"As the moisture further evaporates, the surface fish are left uncovered, and they crawl away in search of fresh pools. In one place I saw hundreds diverging in every direction from the tank they had just abandoned, to a distance of fifty or sixty yards and still traveling onward. In going this distance, however, they must have used muscular exertion enough to have taken them half a mile on level ground, for at these places all the cattle and wild animals of the neighborhood had latterly come to drink, so that the surface was everywhere indented with footmarks in addition to the cracks in the surrounding baked mud, into which the fish tumbled in their progress. In those holes, which were deep and the sides perpendicular, they remained to die, and were carried off by kites and crows.

"My impression is that this migration must take place at night or before sunrise, for it was only early in the morning that I have seen them traveling, and I found that those I brought away with me in the chatties appeared quiet by day, but a large proportion managed to get out of the chatties by night; some escaped altogether while others were trodden on and killed.

"One peculiarity is the large size of the vertebral column, quite disproportioned to the bulk of the fish. I particularly noticed that all in the act of migrating had their gills expanded."

Mr. Morris' description of the fish is accurate enough so far as it goes, but he does not mention the still more singular climbing habit in which it occasionally indulges, to-wit: the climbing of palm trees. Wood, the naturalist, says the fact of its climbing trees is not authenticated, but in this he is certainly mistaken. Several gentlemen of my acquaintance who are perfectly trustworthy, and who have seen great numbers of the fish along the Ganges, assure me that, time and again, they have knocked down these perch from high branches of palm trees, while another gentleman declared to me that on one occasion he saw an anabas climbing up the body of a palm and watched it until it reached the branches.

So well attested are the climbing habits of this curious fish that in the Tomoule language (of India) it is called Paneiri, which means tree-climber. Besides the anabas there is another tree-climbing perch found in Brazil, and which is quite plentiful along the Amazon River.

HOW IT SUSTAINS LIFE WHILE ON LAND.

The natural appearance of the anabas, the utter absence of abnormal developments or appendages to detract from its very common fish-like character, leads us to wonder what means nature has provided to enable it to live for periods of five and six days at a time out of water. This inquiry is answered by the following explanation: What the lungs are to man the gills are to fishes; dry gills will produce suffocation in a fish just as the want of air suffocates a man. If the gills can be kept constantly wet, a fish will live out of water for a long time;

only in some species the gills must be submerged fairly in order to give them enough water for respiration, while in others simple moisture suffices.

If we open the head of a climbing perch the wonderful structure which enables it to live so long out of water is at once seen. Just within the sides of the head the bones which support the orifice between the mouth and the gullet are much enlarged and modified into a series of labyrinthine cells, each of which is a natural reservoir filled

THE CLIMBING PERCH OF SOUTH AMERICA.

with water when the creature begins its dry land journeys. The opening of all these reservoirs is directly over the gill membranes, and as these become dry or require more moisture, the door of the outlet opens and allows a drop of water at a time to fall on the gills, which freshens them thus continually. So soon as the reservoirs become exhausted signs of suffocation follow the drying of the gills, and the fish dies exactly as other species do when taken out of water.

A SUMMARY OF CURIOUS FISHES.

We have seen in the preceding descriptions of inhabitants of the sea such wonderful curiosities as may well excite our surprise and cause us to doubt if the limit to the phenomena of nature as manifested in the ocean has yet been defined by naturalists, for the possibilities of creation appear to be endless.

We have seen fishes clothed with almost invulnerable armature, while, side by side in the water wilderness, roam the most gigantic and tiniest of creatures in all creation; some, that in appearance are more horrible than the most gruesome spectres of a diseased imagination, while in the same element disport species that rival the beauties of the prisms, or the sun-hued plumage of the gorgeous birds of paradise.

But if the marvelous contrarieties and astounding aspects seen in fishes excite our wonder, what shall we say of the effect produced by an understanding of their remarkable habits? We are accustomed to regard the inhabitants of the water as common creatures well understood, and as presenting few, if any, characteristics worthy of our special concern or study. The fact, however, is that no where in nature is what we call phenomenal life so abundant as in the sea. By examining species peculiar to the ocean, and those, too, which belong to the order of fishes proper, we find that some are flyers as well as swimmers; others that progress by walking with perfect naturalness; some that are amphibious and carry their supply of water with them while journeying over land; some that climb trees and spend days among the branches; others that burrow deep in the mud and require only moisture; some that progress entirely by jumping and others by creeping. Then we have some species that are admirable archers, shooting their prey with astonishing precision, while others possess powerful electric batteries, by means of which they disable their enemies and secure their sustenance. Singularly enough, there is at least one species that spends its time in angling, nature having provided it with a pole, line and bait, while for hook its teeth serve the purpose excellently. Then again several kinds of fish possess stings, some like the scorpion and others like the cornworm, with nettles all over its body. Others again have telescopic lips which they can shoot out a distance nearly twice the entire length of the head, by which they secure their prey. Some fish require the coldest water, while others can maintain life only in water that is a few degrees below the boiling point. There are fish which are almost entirely destitute of the power of locomotion, while others are provided with organs which enable them to dart through the water with a speed unequalled by any land animal.

Though there is perhaps little need for artificial light down in the deep sea, still wandering suns, moons and lanterns are found moving through the waters and attracting swarms of small water-creatures, like the electric light attracts willow-flies and beetles. Most of fishes spawn, but others lay their eggs in carefully-built nests and incubate them in excellent imitation of the fowl. Some are possessed of the most acute vision, while others are destitute of the sense of sight, and depend entirely upon an exaggerated sense of feeling or perception.

In short, there is no limit to the curiosities found in fishes, for the ocean is a field of mysteries, many of which are not given us to explore, since the great depths can never be reached save by the sounding-line alone.

CHAPTER XI.

THE WORLD DOWN UNDER THE SEA.

WE have described some of the curious living things which come under the observation of travelers most frequently, and these serve to give us an idea of the intimate connection existing between life on land and in the sea; that the dissimilarity of elements does not necessarily break the harmony and resemblance between sea and land life. We will now descend into the mighty depths of dark ocean's caves, where opalescent rays which beautify the surface never penetrate, and where the deep bellowings of furious tempests are never heard. There is a mystery in nature laid away in the still and pulseless bed of the sea, which the eye or hand of man can never explore; down among dead men's bones, the skeletons of ships and treasure galore.

The wonderful sea in its composition shows a remarkable affinity for the earth, for its liquid bosom carries in solution, besides oxygen and hydrogen, chlorine, iodine, carbon, nitrogen, bromine, potassium, silicon, sodium, flourine, sulphur, phosphorus, barium, strontium, calcium, boron, aluminum, magnesia, copper, lead, zinc, nickel, cobalt, manganese, iron and gold and silver. Of gold, it has been estimated that there is the value of five cents worth in every ton of salt water, and of silver there is said to be two million tons held in solution by ocean water. You will doubtless say, "How surprising and wonderful!" but the greatest surprise is yet to come when we consider the marvels of the ocean bed.

A REGION OF FAIRY SPLENDORS.

Of the world under the sea, Schleiden says: "We dive into the liquid crystal of the Indian Ocean, and it opens to us the most wondrous enchantments, reminding us of fairy tales in childhood's dreams. The strangely branching thickets bear living flowers, the coloring, beauty and variety of which surpass everything. The clear sand of the bottom is covered with the thousand strange forms and tints of sea-urchins and star-fishes. The leaf-like flustras and escharus adhere like mosses and lichens to the branches of the corals; the yellow, green and purple-striped limpets cling like monstrous cochineal insects upon their trunks. Like gigantic cactus blossoms, sparkling in the most ardent colors, the sea anemones expand their crowns of tentacles upon the broken rocks, or more modestly embellish the flat bottom. Around the blossoms of coral shrubs play the humming-birds of the ocean, like fish sparkling with red or blue metallic glitter, or gleaming in golden green or the brightest silvery lustre. Softly, like spirits of the deep, the delicate milk-white or bluish belles of the jelly-fishes float through this charming world. Here the gleaming violets and gold-green Isabelle, and the flaming yellow, black and vermillion-striped coquette choose their prey; there the band-fish shoots, snake-like, through the thicket, like a silver ribbon, glittering with rosy and azure hues. Then comes the famous cuttle-fish decked in all colors of the rainbow, but marked by definite outlines, appearing and disappearing, inter-crossing, joining company and parting again in most fantastic ways; and all this in the most rapid change, and amid the most wonderful plays of light and shade, altered by every breath of wind and every slight curling surface of the ocean. When day declines, and the shades of night lay hold upon the deep, this fantastic garden is lighted up with a new splendor. Millions of glowing sparks, little microscopic medusas and crustaceans dance like glow-worms through the gloom. The sea-feather, which by daylight is vermillion-colored, waves in a green phosphorescent light. Every corner of it is lustrous.

"Parts which by day were perhaps dull and brown, and retreated from the sight amid the universal brilliancy of color, are now radiant in the most wonderful play of light; and to complete the wonders of the enchanted night, the silver disc, six feet across, of the moon-fish, moves, slightly luminous, among the clouds of little sparkling stars. The most luxuriant vegetation of a tropical landscape cannot unfold as great wealth of form, while in the variety and splendor of color it would stand far behind this garden-landscape, which is strangely composed exclusively of animals, and not of plants; for, characteristic as the luxuriant development of vegetation of the temperate zones is of the sea-bottom, the fullness and multiplicity of the marine fauna is just as prominent in the regions of the tropics. Whatever is beautiful, wondrous or uncommon in the great classes of fish and Echinoderus, jelly-fishes and polypus, and the molluscs of all kinds, is crowded into the warm and crystal waters of the tropical ocean, rests in the white sands, clothes the rough cliffs, clings when the room is already occupied, like a parasite, upon the first comers, or swims through the shallows and depths of the elements, while the mass of vegetation is of a far inferior magnitude."

MARVELS IN THE MIGHTY DEEP.

The sea presents all the inequalities that are observed on land; it has its mountains, valleys, hills, plains and caverns. Until within the last fifty years no one had measured its depths nor discovered the formation and character of the sea-bed. Dr. Maury, the eminent savant and navigator, to whom the world is indebted for its most important information concerning the ocean, has explored many of the greatest secrets of its depths, and also the laws by which the ocean-world is governed. The average depth of the Atlantic is two miles, but frequent soundings have been made in both the Atlantic and Pacific of five and even six miles. How wonderful the darkling depths, where sound nor sight nor motion ever disturb the pulseless waste of ocean; where even the fish cannot swim, the waves break or the tempest murmur. Down upon the deep sea-bed, most remarkable to relate, decay is arrested, and but for the infusorial life which alone finds existence there, dead bodies might remain for all time resting as still and perfectly in this water-world as though embalmed in a block of ice. Nor does the temperature change, but maintains a uniformity of 36° F. through all seasons, while never a current or wave wakes the dull, echoless and tomb-like cradle of the billowy deep.

How marvelous is this bed of the sea, for reposing therein is the embryo of continents, of mountain chains, of meadow and field. Figuier states that among the fragments brought up from the dead and currentless depths of the Pacific by Brooks' apparatus, Ehrenburg found one hundred and thirty-five different forms of infusoria, among which were twenty-two species never before met with. Of the infusoria of the Pacific the composition is generally silicious, while those in the Atlantic are calcareous. These animalculæ draw from the sea the mineral matter with which it is charged—that is, the lime or silica which forms their shells. These shells accumulate after the death of the animal and form the bottom of the ocean. Living near the surface, as they die their bodies are consumed by others of their genus, while their carapaces, or shells, descend like snow-flakes to the bottom. This snow-like fall is continuous all over the sea, and the countless myriads gradually raise the bottom of the ocean until islands and vast bodies of land are formed. The horizontal beds of marine deposits, which are called *sedimentary* rocks, and especially the cretaceous rocks and calcareous beds of the Jurassic and Tertiary periods, all result from such remains. The whole of France, England and most of continental Europe were evidently thus formed.

RESTFUL WATERS ALONE PREVENT THE EARTH FROM BEING CUT IN TWAIN.

Down at the great depths where these carapaces first fall the sea is at such complete rest that not the slightest traces of sand are discovered. Did the currents of the ocean extend to these depths the weight of water would be so tremendous that, instead of gentle erosion, as we see on the coast, there would be an abrasion so great as to cut the very globe in twain. The pressure at five miles below the surface is sufficient to collapse an empty bomb, and yet nature, with her illimitable means at command, has created minute animals that live and move freely through this ponderous element that would crush the life out of all other created things. The diver, in his copper helmet and heavy encasement of body, can not go below one hundred and fifty feet on account of pressure; think, then, what the pressure must be five miles below the surface.

A writer has said: "The tooth of running water is very sharp. See how the Hudson has eaten through the highlands, and the Niagara has cut its way through layer after layer of solid rock. But what are the Hudson and Niagara with all the fresh water courses of the world by the side of the Gulf Stream and other great currents in the ocean?

And what is the pressure of fresh water upon river-beds in comparison with the pressure of ocean water upon the bed of the deep sea? It is not so great in contrast as the gutters of the street are to the cataracts. Then why have not the currents of the sea worn its bottom away? Simply because they are not permitted to get down to it."

CHAPTER XII.

MODERN MONSTERS OF THE OCEAN WORLD.

THE changes by extinction or evolution of species is more remarkable in the sea than on the land, and so wonderfully fruitful of marvelous things is the ocean that we can even note the unfoldings of creation in a glass of salt-water. We marvel and exclaim, "How came man upon the stage of life except from progenitors of similar conformation and organization?" We cannot answer this question better, or explain the evolution of all created things more clearly, than by referring the physicist and inquirer to the following experiment: Take a glass of crystal water—especially salt water—so pure that the most powerful microscope cannot detect the existence of any animalcular life; seal it, if you like, to prevent the possible admission of atomic dust or life, and then note the development that transpires. After a period of stagnation, or decomposition, infusorial life is certain to appear; first, infinitesimal, microscopic animals, then the development of larger animalculæ, which will sustain themselves by feeding upon the former until a third species appears, and so on until the water that remains becomes animated by millions of animals, each new species being larger than its predecessor. Is not this the proof of development by evolution? Who, then, can undertake to assert that primitive man, or the essential out of which he grew, was a completely formed man, whose brain was a vast store-house of reason, and whose hands had the cunning to originate and fashion?

The development which marks the sea is wonderfully pronounced; no longer the ichthyosaurus, plesiosaurus, macrocephalus, mosasaurus, and many other frightful monsters, plough the ocean main, but in their stead are other mighty creatures, fierce, powerful and useful, whose origin may be traced back to the antediluvian sea animals.

The links are somewhat broken through the lapse of countless years, whose chronicles are distorted drifts and layers, but the generic marks of species discovered give a connection which is sufficiently understood to furnish a proof of the theory of development of species into ultimately distinct genera.

LEGENDS OF THE TIME OF COLUMBUS.

When Columbus crossed the sea nearly four hundred years ago, the civilized world believed as implicitly in the existence of frightful sea monsters as they did in the virtue of saintly bones, shrines and Calvarean relics. It was almost sacrilegious to dispute the legends which had come down to them from the days of Plato. Some of the enemies of Columbus cried out against his undertaking by declaring that

SEA GRYPHON OF PHILOPONUS.—(AN OLD PRINT.)

he and his crew would certaily fall victims to voracious sea gryphons and other imaginary creatures that guarded the sea-realm from human intrusion.

Singularly enough, there accompanied Columbus on his voyage a priest who was evidently so firmly attached to the superstitions of his times that he felt it his divine duty to perpetuate them, and consequently he wrote a book describing his adventures at sea, which for rank and indefensible lying, is a record that far transcends Baron Munchausen. This priest's true name is in doubt, nor is it to be wondered that he employed means to render it so, considering that the occasion was great. The name by which he was known among his associates was Caspar Plautus, but he wrote under the name of Padre Buel, which is a sad reflection on the present writer, since there is at least an implication that there might possibly be a genealogical weakness transmitted to render the Buels untrustworthy of statement. But he was best known as Philoponus, as this name is the one he used most frequently in his writings.

Philoponus, which I prefer to call him, was a refractory insubordinate, who almost continually quarreled with Columbus and at one time well near influenced the crew to mutiny. Notwithstanding his several weaknesses, Philoponus was a man not without piety and of considerable learning and was created First Patriarch of the West Indies, an honor of no small importance. In his book, which he wrote directly after his return with Columbus to Spain, he records some wonderful adventures to which he called God and man witnesses, that all he wrote was the whole truth, not deviating one jot or tittle from the facts, nor exaggerating the things that he saw and did. One of these adventures he relates as follows:

DREADFUL ADVENTURE OF A PRIEST.

"It was a bright sunny day," says Philoponus, "that we were sailing along pleasantly upon a smooth sea, and not far from home, either, that we suddenly experienced a peculiar shock, and after the vessel had swayed to the right and to the left, insomuch that we thought we had grounded upon a rock, but while we were all in prayers and anxiety we began to feel that our vessel, which was one of the largest in the Armada, began to rise out of the water. This strange phenomenon lasted for quite a considerable time, and we could plainly see the ribs of the vessel from over the bulwarks becoming more and more visible, but still nothing to explain the mystery thereof. When lo! suddenly up from the trembling waters came, it seemed to me, a huge continent, rough and ugly to look upon, and some distance to the right of us two great columns of water were spouting themselves into the air, the volume of which was tremendous. And while with horror-stricken eyes we were beholding all this and the other ships each moment getting further away, we saw a great head projecting from the water, and away some leagues to its rear we saw an enormous tail slashing furiously the water, and making a great splash and splurge. Some of the more frightened immediately said it was a whale, but I, who felt the great power within me, calmed their fears, knowing that nothing could happen as long as there was such an one on board as myself. And then this monster began to swim away from the other vessels, making head toward Spain. Everything was done in our power to make the monster descend, but all the back-proggings that he received did not seem at all to disconcert him, and it is no telling where we should have been carried, until it occurred to me that only through divine interposition could we be saved from shipwreck, and possibly a more horrible death. So I ordered those of the priests who were on board to prepare themselves for the performance of high mass, and to get ready the altar, and the sailors to put over the side of the vessel the long ladder, so that I and the priests, and those who were bold, might, upon the back of this foul monster, say mass.

"Now," continues Padre Philoponus, "we began with strong hearts our service at the altar. We went through the whole mass, but when we came to the *Agnus Dei* we felt a peculiar trembling beneath our feet. The waters on either side began at first to recede from us and then to surge up, while the spoutings began to increase in their violence, and we heard strange noises. I then knew that our prayers were answered, and that this terrible beast was beginning to descend to its depths. But I finished the services, and when we were again all safely on board and had cheered those therein by our manner and speech, the whale began to descend still more quickly, and suddenly took itself from our sight; and the ship again rested on the bosom of the placid ocean. Thus were we alone saved by prayer and through my medium. After this the vessel rejoined her consorts, and the voyage was performed without any too serious an occurrence worthy to be recorded or painted."

A MONSTER TEN-FOLD WORSE THAN THE DEVIL.

Having started his imagination to working, he did not withold oils and stimulants that it might continue with smoothness and alacrity. He relates that coming to one island they found it occupied by a marvelous tribe of Indians, who maintained supremacy not only over the land, but over the ocean monsters as well. A deputation of five of these strange men came to visit the Spaniards on one occasion; not as one would suppose, on foot, horseback or in palanquin, but, surprising to relate, "seated upon the back of a sea-gryphon, an immense animal having a scaly back, fringed collar, a lashing tail and a hog's head. It was also furnished with four huge paws, each paw having three fingers; it also had tremendous wings and fins—a very savage looking monster to behold, and one that struck terror to the nearts of even the bravest of the Spaniards.'' The pious priest further declares that the Indians were armed with breast-plate and buckler, and were as formidable as the dragon they rode. Other Indians were perceived at the same time in many canoes indulging in the sport of lassoing similar monsters.

Philoponus, who should have been a poet before taking orders, foreseeing that his spiritual omnipotence, as illustrated by his celebrating mass on a whale's back, must render him forever famous, saw proper to further impress his importance upon the world by describing a fight with sea-dogs which he asseverates he witnessed on this same voyage off Cape Verde. Several of the small boats of the Spaniards were simultaneously attacked by the apocryphal canines,

COOKING A DINNER ON LEVIATHAN'S BACK—(AN OLD PRINT.)

which, with snorts and growls terrible to hear, overturned the boats and devoured the luckless Spaniards as though they had been fresh beefsteaks the size of a man's hand.

This learned priest concludes his interesting narrative with a declaration that he was told—and he implicitly believed the statement—that during a short period, when he was so badly indisposed by seasickness as to be unable to appear on deck, that his ship was anchored for several hours to a great sea monster having a hog's head and a bear's claws, and that two of the more venturesome of the crew got out upon the leviathan's back and built a fire whereon they cooked a dinner, which in no wise disconcerted the great animal. Montfort. another equally distinguished romancer in the earlier centuries, tells a story very like this, nor did any one rise to offer objection or question.

CHAPTER XIII.

TITANIC CREATURES OF THE OCEAN.

DESCENDING from the lofty and wondrous sphere into which Father Philoponus would fain keep us, and taking up our places again among the realities of life, we will find the sea no less interesting nor the life therein less wonderful when we come to view some of the marvelous facts of nature as they actually exist.

Job has said, writing for the nineteenth century as well as for those long anterior to the first:

"Canst thou draw out leviathan with an hook? or his tongue with a cord thou lettest down? * * * He maketh the deep to boil like a pot; he maketh the sea like a pot of ointment; he maketh a path to shine after him."

From this biblical allusion we understand that the whale was well known to the ancients, and that possibly no means had then been devised by which leviathan could be captured, nor was there any incentive then to hazard battle with him.

Under the name *Cetacea*, naturalists include all fishes having warm blood, venous and arterial, and that are viviparous. These are the whale, black-fish, dolphin, narwhal, porpoise, dugong, manatee and nearly fifty others. If we examine the skeleton of a whale we are amazed to find it formed of articulated bones like those of the feet and hands of terrestrial mammals. Moreover we will detect the principal parts of the skeleton of a terrestrial animal. An examination of the whale's organism discloses yet stronger ties connecting them with land animals. We find that they have warm blood, and breathe by means of lungs through the direct absorption of the air; the digestive system is identical, and finally, they bring forth their young and suckle them in the same manner as animals living on land. An observer who has several times drunk whale's milk declares that there is scarcely a perceptible difference between it and cow's milk.

VARIOUS SPECIES OF WHALES.

The sea has the honor of being the home of the largest of all created living things, which is very proper and as we might expect, considering the disparity between land and water. The Greenland whale not infrequently attains a length of seventy-five feet, which presupposes a weight of as many tons, and of more than forty feet in circumference. The pectoral fins of such a monster are not less than ten or twelve feet long, while the tail, or caudal fin, is nearly twenty-five feet broad. The Northern Rorqual is sometimes found exceeding one hundred feet in length, but it is much smaller of body than the Greenland whale. Some travelers have declared that the *Culammok* and *Umgullik*, found chiefly about the Alutian Islands, grow to a length of one hundred and seventy feet, but we have no record of such a whale ever having been taken. The Sperm whale, generally called Cachelot, peculiar to extreme Southern latitudes, is the largest of all Cetacea, being quite as large of body as the Greenland whale, and often measuring ninety feet in length.

Whales are all provided with a singular apparatus which enables them to take their food without swallowing any of the water. The liquid passes through the nostrils by means of a peculiar disposition of the membrane of the palate, and collects in a bag placed at the external orifice of the nasal cavity; thence, compressed by powerful muscles, the water is expelled through one or two ducts (according to the species) pierced in the upper part of the head, and called blow-holes. It is a matter of much dispute whether the expulsion through the blow-holes is water or vapor; a great majority claim that it is the water taken into the mouth while feeding which is expelled in two powerful jets. Scoresby, a very excellent authority, and several others maintain that it is only the vapor of water, which coming into contact with cold air, immediately condenses, at first in a white cloud and afterwards in a small, fine rain.

During the month of August, 1882, while making the passage from Europe homeward on the maiden trip of the Cunard steamer *Cephalonia*, I had an uncommonly fine opportunity to observe the spouting of whales and to form an opinion upon the disputed point mentioned. When a few hundred miles from Boston I, in common with other passengers, sighted two whales some distance ahead. They appeared to be gamboling, for their disappearance under water was never more than half a minute, and upon coming to the surface they would throw themselves almost entirely out of the sea. As we approached, the number of whales increased from two to nearly a dozen, and apparently so interested were they in their sport that they gave us no heed whatever, and allowed the vessel to come directly into their midst.

So near were we that several times I could have struck them with a stone as they raised their enormous heads or moved their ponderous flukes high in the air as they descended. I do not think they were feeding, for during this period they swim in a direct line with mouths open, whereas upon this occasion all their movements appeared to be sportive gambols. As the whales rose they almost invariably spouted, and I was struck at the time with the very peculiar character the water assumed as it left the blow-holes. Instead of being a vertical column, or stream of water—though it was thrown to a height of thirty or forty feet—it appeared more like steam issuing violently from an

THE SPERM WHALE.

escape-pipe, and as it gained its greatest height floated off very much like steam does. As I had never heard of this peculiarity and had supposed, according to common report, that whales spouted solid columns of water, I was very much surprised at what I saw. I incline to the belief, from what I witnessed, that whales spout as much from sport as they do to relieve their mouths from the water taken in while feeding. It is only reasonable to suppose that the simple process of closing the mouth, with a possible action of the tongue, would expel all the water as thoroughly as though it were driven backward into a reservoir surrounded by muscles that would then expel it by contraction.

Cetaceans are divided into two classes, the larger of which are the whales which feed on small fish, cephaloids, infusoria and other animals, and the other, including lamatins, dugongs, stelleres, etc., which are entirely herbiverous, these latter being confined generally to tropical seas, while whales are chiefly found in colder latitudes. But in both species the blow-holes are present and used similarly.

Mangin says: "A profound instinct of sociability seems one of the characteristic traits of the whale's nature, and this instinct manifests itself in several species, by the powerful and reciprocal affection of the mother and her young. The same attachment exists between the male and his mate, and like the maternal sentiment of affection, reveals a touching character, since it almost always prevails over that instinct which in most animals keeps down every other — too frequently even in man himself — the mean, cowardly instinct of self-preservation.

"The habits of the cetacea differ very much according to their genera. The herbiverous cetacea are of a gentle, kindly nature, and the instinct of family affection is also very strongly developed in them. The same may be said of the gigantic whale, which, in spite of its formidable appearance, is a very inoffensive and usually a very timid animal, ready to fly at the slightest intimation of danger. Yet an intrepid courage is kindled in the breast of this ocean-giant when he sees one of his young attacked or wounded; but his sole object is to draw it from its peril, to expose himself in its place to the assaults of the enemy, and if it dies, to perish with it, for the poor beast will never abandon it. Unprovided with weapons, he can in no wise defend himself; nor does he ever make the attempt, for he is wholly deficient in the instinct of combat. He can suffer, but he cannot fight."

A WHALE SINKS A SHIP.

To Mangin's latter observations I must except, as one or two incidents, involving much exciting adventure, will serve to show. Captain Pollard, of the whale-ship *Essex*, relates, upon an occasion while fishing in the Pacific Ocean, the man in the crow's-nest sighting a family of sperm-whales, three boats were immediately put off in pursuit. Coming up with the monsters, an attempt to cast the harpoon was made by a man in the first boat, but while he was in the act of poising the weapon a whale, whether in anger or by accident, struck the boat a violent blow with its tail, crushing it badly and throwing the harpooner into the water. A return to the vessel was now made to repair damages, but just as the boats reached the ship another very large sperm-whale appeared hardly twenty yards from the ship on the weather-bow. The monster cetacean was swimming at a rapid pace directly toward the vessel, and in an instant struck it nearly amidships, producing a collision so violent that several sailors

SMASHING OF THE SHIP ESSEX BY A WHALE.

were thrown to the deck. The whale then passed under the keel and came up directly thrashing the sea into foam; so great were its contortions that it was at once apparent the animal had been severely hurt and was moved by intense agony and anger. In a few moments the whale ceased lashing the sea, moved deliberately off a hundred yards or more, then turned and made with all possible speed for the ship again. During this exciting interval discovery was made that the vessel was filling, the planking having been sprung by the whale's first attack, and perceiving now that the attack was to be renewed, terror seized the entire crew, one of whom exclaimed: "May God have mercy on us; he is coming again!"

The whale came rushing through the water with incredible swiftness, leaving a foamy track behind him full of swirls and deep waves, and struck the now laboring ship in the starboard bow with the force of a hundred battering rams. There was a loud report, followed by the crashing of heavy timbers, and a spasmodic jerk to the vessel as if she had been gathered up by some Titanic hand and hurled back upon a mighty rock. The whale now disappeared, leaving the sea covered with foam and blood, and ten minutes thereafter the vessel raised high her stern and plunged headlong out of sight. Barely time was given the sailors to cut loose the boats, into which they fortunately managed to escape to a small island called Ducies. This land proved such a barren spot that all of the crew save three embarked again in three boats and set out for the island of Juan Fernandez, two thousand miles distant. Ninety-three days after their embarkation the mate's boat was picked up by a vessel from London with only three survivors in it; the captain's boat, which was come up with by the Dauphin, contained only two survivors, and the third boat nor the three men left on Ducies Island were ever heard of again. Out of a crew of twenty only five remained to tell the terrible story as we have related it here.

A DUTCHMAN RIDES A WHALE.

We have all heard of Neptune's chariot, in which the ancients believed he rode over his tempestuous domain drawn by fierce horses having webbed feet and bifurcated fish-tails. Imagination may have pictured some adventurous sea-dog bestriding a dolphin, but we have to mention the fact of a Dutchman actually riding a whale; nor is there any fable connected with the story, which is as follows:

James Vienke was a Dutch harpooner long engaged in the whale fishery in the beginning of the present century. Upon one occasion, while leading an attack upon a Greenland whale, Vienke's boat was struck by the head of the monster and dashed to pieces. By extraordinary fortune Vienke was hurled high into the air, and in falling lighted so squarely upon the whale's back that he maintained his position. The harpoon, which he still managed to hold on to, served him well now, for, burying it into the monster's back, he held to it and thus avoided slipping off. Instead of sounding, as is usual, the whale kept on the surface, and thus Vienke and his ocean steed cleft the blue sea in truly magnificent style. Great concern was felt for his safety as the crew saw him galloping away at more than double the speed they were able to make in their boats, and Vienke was so overcome with fright that he forgot to let go of the harpoon, by which means he might have easily been at once rescued, but held on as a drowning man will catch at a straw, until he was nearly a mile from the nearest boat. Being at last somewhat accustomed to his novel vehicle, Vienke's presence of mind returned and he no longer hesitated, but cast himself into the sea, very much as a man might fall off a runaway horse. Being an excellent swimmer he managed to keep afloat until picked up by the boat that was after him.

INCIDENTS OF FATALITY IN THE WHALE FISHERY.

Scoresby, in his "History of the Northern Whale Fishery," published in 1820, a copy of which lies before me, gives a number of incidents illustrating the perils of the fishery, a few of which I will here repeat:

"On the 3d of June, 1811, a boat from the ship *Resolution*, commanded at the time by myself, put off in pursuit of a whale and was rowed upon its back. At the moment that it was harpooned it struck the side of the boat a violent blow with its tail, the shock of which threw the boat steerer some distance into the water. A repetition of the blow projected the harpooner and line-manager in a similar manner, and completely drenched the part of the crew remaining in the boat with spray. One of the men regained the boat, but as the fish immediately sank and drew the boat away from the place, his two companions in misfortune were soon left far behind the reach of assistance. The harpooner, though a practiced swimmer, felt himself so bruised and enervated by the blow he had received on the chest that he was totally incapacitated from giving the least support to his fellow sufferer. The ship being happily near, a boat which had been lowered on the first alarm arrived to the succor at the moment when the line-manager, who was unacquainted with the art of swimming, was on the point of sinking to rise no more. Both the line manager and harpooner were preserved, and the fish, after a few hours' close pursuit, was subdued."

THE FORCE OF A WHALE'S TAIL.

"A large whale, harpooned from a boat belonging to the same ship, became the subject of a general chase on the 23d of June, 1809. Being myself in the first boat which approached the fish, I struck my harpoon at arm's length, by which we fortunately evaded a blow that appeared to be aimed at the boat. Another boat then advanced, and another harpoon was struck, but not with the same result; for the stroke was immediately returned by a tremendous blow from the fish's tail. The boat was sunk by the shock, and at the same time whirled around with such velocity that the boat-steerer was precipitated into the water on the side next to the fish, and was actually carried down to a considerable depth by its tail. After a minute or so he arose to the surface and was taken up, along with his companion, into my boat. A similar attack was made on the next boat which came up; but the harpooner being warned of the prior conduct of the fish, used such precautions that the blow, though equal in strength, took effect only in an inferior degree. The boat was slightly stove."

Another somewhat similar incident is related by the same author, though with more serious results:

"While the ship *Resolution* navigated an open lake of water in the eighty-first degree of north latitude, during a keen frost and strong north wind, a whale appeared, and a boat put off in pursuit. On its second visit to the surface of the sea it was harpooned. A convulsive heave of the tail, which succeeded the wound, struck the boat at the stern, and its reaction threw the boat-steerer overboard. As the line in a moment dragged the boat beyond his reach, the crew threw some of their oars toward him for his support, one of which he fortunately seized. The ship and boats being at a considerable distance, and the fast-boat being rapidly drawn away from him, the harpooner cut the line with the view of rescuing him from his dangerous situation. But no sooner was this act performed than, to their extreme mortification, they discovered, that in consequence of some oars being thrown toward their floating comrade, and others being broken or unshipped by the blow from the fish, one oar only remained, with which, owing to the force of the wind, they in vain tried to reach him. A considerable period elapsed before any boat from the ship could afford him assistance, though the men strained every nerve for the purpose. At length, when they reached him, he was found with his arms stretched over an oar almost deprived of sensation. On his arrival at the ship he was in a deplorable condition. His clothes were frozen like mail, and his hair constituted a helmet of ice. He was immediately conveyed into the cabin, his clothes taken off, his limbs and body dried and well rubbed, and a cordial administered. A dry shirt and stockings were then put on him and he was laid in the Captain's bed. After a few hours' sleep he awoke and appeared considerably restored, but complained of a painful sensation of cold. He was, therefore, removed to his own state-room and his messmates ordered to lie on each side of him, whereby the diminished circulation was accelerated, and the animal-heat restored. The shock on his constitution, however, was greater than anticipated and it was with difficulty he was finally restored, his reason for some time threatening to give way."

DASHED TO PIECES BY A WHALE.

A dreadful accident happened to a boat crew belonging to the *Aimwell*, by which three men from a single boat were drowned, though help was near at hand. A large whale being sighted in a Greenland sea, a boat containing seven men was put off and the whale was soon struck. But instead of sinking immediately, as is usual when receiving a wound, the whale only dived for a moment and then rose again beneath the boat, struck it a vicious blow with its tail, dashing it several feet into the air, and then disappeared. The wrecked crew clambered onto the bottom of the boat, which was now upturned, but the lines became fouled, so that as the whale swam off it rolled the boat repeatedly over, throwing the men time and again into the water. Four of them, after each immersion, recovered themselves and clung to the boat, but the other three were less fortunate, and drowned before the assistance that was fast approaching reached them. The four men being rescued and conveyed to the ship, the attack on the whale was renewed, and two more harpoons were stuck into it. But the whale manifested the most furious disposition, churning the sea into foam by terrific lashings of its tail, apparently feeling for the boat, which, however, escaped the blows. The crew, fearing for their lives, abandoned the attack, only too glad that the whale did not follow up its advantage and destroy the boat.

A similar accident happened to a boat crew of the *Henrietta*. A fish which was struck very near the ship, by a blow of its tail stove a small hole in the boat's bow. Every one of the crew, in trying to escape the blows, rushed onto one side of the boat and upset it. They all clung to it while it was bottom-side up, but the line having become entangled in the thwarts, suddenly drew the boat under water, and with it a part of the crew, so that when assistance reached the spot four out of the six that were in the boat were drowned.

During a fresh gale of wind, hardly a favorable time for the sport, a harpooner struck a sucking calf with the hope of luring the mother to her destruction. They were not disappointed, for the old whale soon appeared and began swimming around her cub so rapidly that

A WHALE-BOAT KNOCKED SKYWARD.

the boats were unable to keep pace with her. Scoresby was himself harpooner on this occasion, and finding that the whale was moving in the same circle all the time, he rowed to the edge to intercept her, but instead of getting a favorable opportunity to cast his harpoon, he was soon put to it to save himself. The whale spied the boat, and with a malicious flaunt of her tail, drove it skyward and broke out fifteen square feet of the bottom, so that it speedily sunk and the crew were left struggling in the water. Fortunately, assistance was near at hand, and none were drowned, but the whale made good its escape.

FEROCITY OF THE WHALE.

Scoresby relates another incident of a whale attacking a ship's boat as follows:

"A remarkable instance of the power which the whale possesses in its tail, was exhibited within my own observation in the year 1807. On the 29th of May a whale was harpooned by an officer belonging to the *Resolution*. It descended to a considerable depth, and on its reappearance evinced an uncommon degree of irritation. It made such a display of its fins and tail that few of the crew had courage to approach it. The captain (my father) observing their timidity, called a boat, and himself struck a harpoon. Another boat immediately followed, and unfortunately advanced too far. The tail was again reared into the air in a terrific attitude, the impending blow was evident; the harpooner, who was directly underneath, leaped overboard, and the next moment the threatened stroke was impressed on the center of the boat, which buried it in the water. Happily no one was injured. The harpooner who leaped overboard, escaped certain death by the act, the tail having struck the very spot on which he stood. The effects of the blow were astonishing. The keel was broken, the gunwales and every plank, excepting two, were broken through, and it was evident that the boat would have been completely divided had not the tail struck directly upon a coil of lines. The boat was rendered useless."

Captain Lyons, of the *Roith*, while engaged in the whale fishery off the Labrador coast discovered a large whale spouting at some distance from the ship. Four boats were immediately lowered in pursuit, two of which kept so closely together that they both reached the whale at the same time and cast their harpoons simultaneously. The fish sounded, but soon raised directly beneath one of the approaching boats, striking it so violently with its head that the boat, men and tackle were thrown fully fifteen feet into the air. It was inverted by the stroke and fell back bottom upward. Fortune favored all the men save one, who became entangled in the lines in the boat and was drowned, all the others were picked up by the fourth boat uninjured.

DASHING OF WHALE-BOATS IN PIECES.

An old whaler, who delights to dwell upon the many wild adventures which he has participated in, relates the following, merely as an illustration of the great perils attending the pursuit of whale hunting:

"In one of my earliest voyages I remarked a circumstance which excited my highest astonishment. One of the harpooners struck a whale; it dived, and all the assisting boats had collected round the first boat before it rose to the surface again. The first boat, following the harpoon-line, approached the vertical position without observing the least caution. Suddenly the whale rose with unlooked-for violence directly beneath the boat, which was hurled, together with its crew, nearly a dozen yards high. The boat fell upon its side, projecting the men into the water, but fortunately only one of them was injured, and all were rescued."

It is related that in 1804 the ship *Adonis* and three other vessels engaged a large sperm-whale off the coast of New Zealand, in which the animal became so angered that he set upon and destroyed nine boats, several of the men being drowned.

The few incidents here given, I believe, will be conclusive evidence that, though destitute of weapons, the whale is not destitute of courage, but that, appreciating the power of its momentum and dreadful tail, it not infrequently boldly attacks boats and ships with disastrous results.

PHYSICAL CURIOSITIES OF THE WHALE.

The Greenland whale is destitute of teeth in either jaw, but nature has provided them with numerous horny laminæ, attached to the upper jaw, which is very narrow, by which means it strains out the water taken in with its food; and herein lies another proof that the whale does not spout merely to discharge the water that is engulfed with food.

The laminæ, baleen, or whale-bone, as it is most generally called, is a most wonderful provision of nature, considering the service in which it is employed by the animal. Though of colossal size, the whale feeds upon very small fish, as heretofore described, its throat capacity being hardly large enough to admit a man's fist. So large an animal must needs consume a great quantity of food, which it would be utterly unable to secure but for the baleen with which its mouth is provided. This whalebone—so called, though incorrectly—is attached to the upper jaw and is of a variable length, to conform

THE RIGHT, OR GREENLAND WHALE.

to the mouth when open, filling the sides so completely, with extremely small interstices between the plates, that when a shoal of herrings, or other food, is taken into the mouth the water is strained out and the small fish retained. We have, therefore, in the baleen fringe of the mouth a practical proof that the engulfed water does not pass out of the whale's blow-holes while feeding. The probable use of the blow-holes is for respiration. All whales, however, are not provided with baleen; in fact, the Geenland whale alone has it, the reason for which is not thoroughly understood.

An ordinary-sized Greenland whale will yield about twenty tuns of oil, and being the most valuable commercially, it is pursued most persistently. The sperm-whale is really more valuable than any other species, but its scarcity makes it least profitable for whalers to hunt, the number killed each year now being quite small, and its extinction, it is prophesied, will soon occur.

The sperm-whale, in addition to supplying the best oil and spermaceti, furnishes also that most delicate and valuable of all perfumes, termed ambergris. This substance is found secreted in the animal's intestines, and is of the consistency of wax. It is often found floating in the Indian Ocean in masses of more than two hundred pounds weight, but its origin is attributed by all naturalists to the sperm-whale. Many distinguished persons maintain that ambergris is a morbid secretion, the product of a disease that ultimately kills the whale, but this must ever continue in doubt. One fact, however, remains to throw a shadow of unbelief upon the assertion, viz.: that whales killed secreting large quantities of ambergris have not been noticed to manifest any outward signs of disease, being equally active, strong and courageous with other whales.

HOW THE WHALE IS KILLED.

A large, nearly triangular cavity in the right side of the head, called by whalers the *case*, is lined with a beautiful, silver-like membrane, and covered by a thick layer of muscular fibres. This cavity contains a secretion of an oily fluid which, after the death of the animal, congeals into a granulated, yellowish-hued substance called spermaceti. Its size may be estimated from the fact that in a large whale it frequently contains a tun, or ten barrels, of spermaceti.

In calm weather whalers often experience great difficulty in approaching the whale, on account of the acuteness of its sight and hearing. Under these circumstances they have recourse to paddles instead of oars, by which means they quietly come near enough to use the harpoon. When first struck, a whale almost invariably "sounds," or descends perpendicularly to an astonishing depth, taking out sometimes five thousand feet of line. But he must come to the surface in half an hour to breathe, when he is again harpooned, only to sound again. This he continues to do until his strength is wasted by fatigue and loss of blood, when he no longer goes down, but swims rapidly along the surface, towing the boats that may be fast to him. If the whale does not turn, the boats are brought gradually nearer by drawing in the line, until they come within striking distance with a lance, when he is soon killed.

These animals generally traverse the seas in numerous herds, sometimes as many as two or three hundred being together. Old whalers affirm that they acknowledge a leader, always a patriarchal bull, who swims some distance in advance and gives the signal of flight or combat by uttering a noise something like a muffled great bell. According to Mr. Beale, the sperm-whale can remain under water for an hour and a quarter, and can move at a velocity of five miles an hour, his ordinary speed being half that. When swimming at its greatest velocity, it rapidly rises and depresses its enormous tail, which is lateral with the body; the body following this motion, alternately emerges from and plunges into the sea. At each impulsion it rises from twenty to thirty-five feet out of the water.

Unlike the Greenland whale, the sperm-whale has a throat with capacity sufficient to admit a man, and its lower jaw is armed with forty-two powerful teeth of conical shape, which fit into depressions in the upper jaw. Notwithstanding its large throat and formidable teeth, the sperm-whale finds its food among small fishes, though it may, occasionally, devour some larger flesh, particularly the dead bodies of considerable sized habitats of its element.

THRILLING ADVENTURES WITH WHALES.

Captain Bellair, of the ship *Independence*, tells the following story of a serious adventure which befel him and some of his crew while whaling in the South Pacific: The custom in pursuing whales is to keep a look-out in the crow's-nest—a scaffold erected at the first splicing of the mainmast—where, being considerably elevated, a whale can be seen, when spouting, several miles distant. On the occasion referred to the lookout sighted a sperm-whale, and two boats were sent out to effect its capture. While these boats were absent another whale blowed very near the vessel, and in his eagerness the Captain ordered the remaining boats lowered and the others of the crew to pursue it. The weather being delightful and no trouble anticipated, Captain Bellair joined his men, leaving only a boy and the cook in charge of the vessel. No difficulty was experienced in coming up with the whale and fixing a harpoon, but instead of sounding the whale started with great speed along the surface, and thus towed the boat for a distance of fully fifteen miles, where they could not be seen from the vessel; the whale being now somewhat fatigued descended to a great depth and remained there for several minutes. Gazing down in the crystal depth, where objects were visible nearly one hundred feet below the surface, the Captain was appalled by seeing the whale rising with great rapidity, its mouth widely distended, evidently bent upon destroying his enemies. By a skillful manœuver the boat was shifted just in time to avoid the monster's jaws; the whale then sounded again and repeated the performance of trying to crush the boat, but was again foiled. A third time, however, the whale attacked the boat, and catching it in his powerful jaws crushed it as he would an egg-shell, leaving the men nothing but the small fragments to cling to. It was now drawing late in the evening and little hope was entertained by any of the unfortunates that their companions could find and rescue them. Pieces of the boat were allotted to the men very much as small rations of bread are issued in times of threatened starvation; on these they rode the waters, which chanced to be mild, shouting to their utmost with the very faint hope they might be heard, until nearly half the night was passed. In the meantime the other boats had returned to the ship, and the crew finding their captain and other companions missing, surmised the cause and set out in search of them. Fifteen miles at sea is not a great distance, but owing to the convexity of the water a low-lying boat is not visible above a few miles, and therefore very difficult to find. It was for this reason the search was prosecuted until far into the morning hours before the wrecked men were discovered, nearly half dead from exposure so long in the water. When taken on board the vessel again not one of the unfortunate crew was able to resume his duties until several days had elapsed.

A DREADFUL DEATH.

In "paying out" the line after the harpoon has been struck into a whale the utmost care must be exercised, and it may almost be said

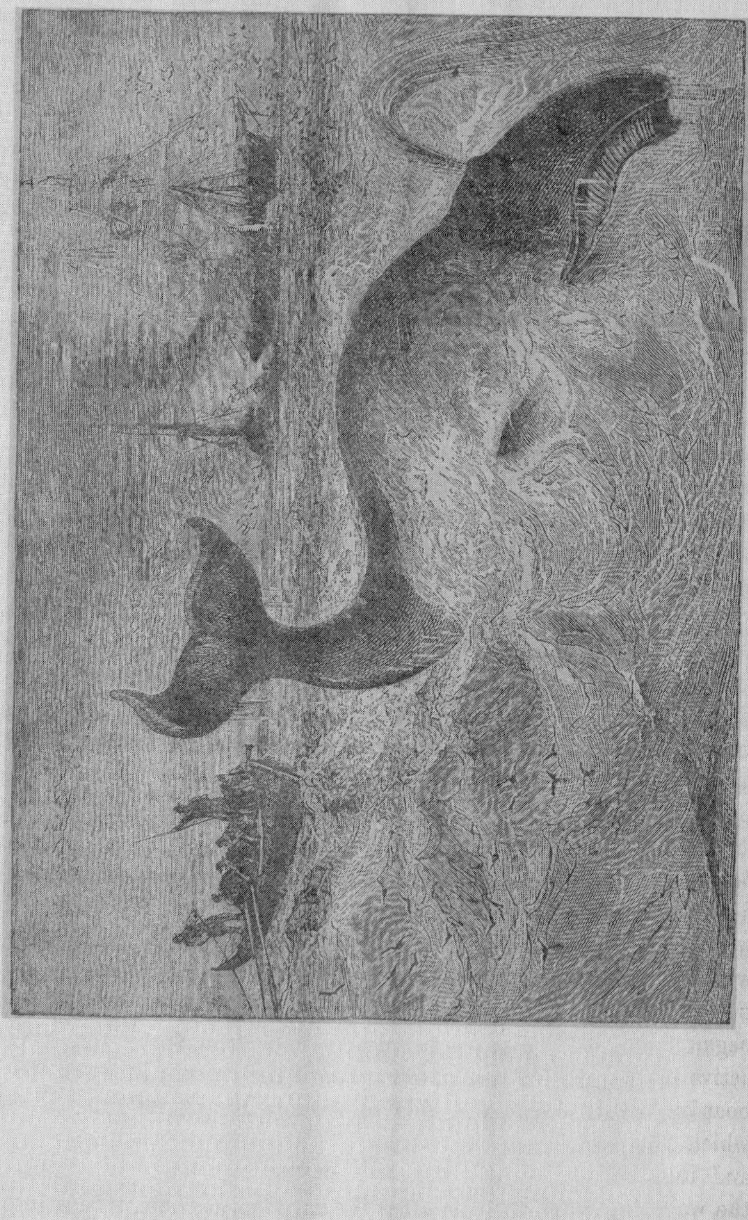

PURSUING A WHALE.

that the lives of a boat crew are in the hands of the man who attends to this most responsible of all duties. Should the line become kinked and catch so as to quit running out the boat would be swamped in an instant; so, if the line is all gone it must be cut on the instant to avoid a like consequence. Captain Scoresby, the most famous of whalers, and a great Arctic explorer, relates the following instance of a fatal accident that occurred to one of the crew that was whaling with him in the North Atlantic:

"As soon as the boats came within hailing distance, my anxiety induced me to call out and inquire what had happened. 'We have lost Carr!' This awful intelligence, for which we were altogether unprepared, shocked me exceedingly, and it was some time before I was able to inquire into the particulars of the accident which had deprived us of one of our shipmates. As far as could be collected from the confused accounts of the crew of the boat of which he went out in charge, the circumstances were as follows: The two boats that had long been absent on the outset, became separated from their companions and, allured by the chase of a whale and the fineness of the weather, they proceeded until far out of sight of the ship. The whale they pursued led them into a vast shoal of the species. They were, indeed, so numerous that their blowing was incessant, and there could not have been less than one hundred. Fearful of alarming them without striking any, the crews in the boats remained for some time motionless, watching a favorable opportunity for commencing the attack. A whale at length arose so near the boat of which William Carr was harpooner, that he ventured to pull toward it, though it was meeting him, and afforded an indifferent chance of success. He, however, fatally for himself, succeeded in harpooning it; the boat and fish, passing each other with great rapidity after the stroke, the line was jerked out of its place, and instead of running over the stern, was thrown over the gunwale. Its pressure in this unfavorable position so careened the boat that the side sank below the water and it began to fill. In this emergency the harpooner, who was a fine, active fellow, seized the bight of the line and attempted to relieve the boat by restoring it to its place; but by some singular circumstance which could not be accounted for, a turn of the line flew over his arm and in an instant dragged him overboard, and plunged him under the water to rise no more! So sudden was the accident that only one man, who had his eye on him at the time, was aware of what had happened; so that when the boat righted — which it immediately did — though half full of water, they all at once, on looking round at the exclamation of the man who had seen him launched overboard, inquired, 'What has got Carr?' It is scarcely possible to imagine a death more awfully sudden and unexpected."

A MAD WHALE.

Captain Deblois, of the ship *Alexander*, relates that while whaling off the coast of Australia, he lost three members of his crew under the following distressing circumstances: The look-out reported a whale nearly two miles from the ship, which one of the large boats and eight of the crew were sent out to dispatch. The weather was very fine and the animal in no wise timid, so that the boat soon came up with the whale and a harpoon was speedily struck into it. But no sooner did he feel the keen instrument in his back than he turned, without sounding, and made at the boat with the viciousness of a bull-dog, seized it in his ponderous jaws and crushed nearly every plank in it, at the same time almost instantly killing three of the men. A second boat, which was started directly after the first, met with the same fate, though none of its crew were injured. Being apparently maddened, or realizing his power to destroy his enemies, the whale next attacked the ship by striking her in the weather-bow, and so powerful was the blow that the vessel sank within an hour. Fortunately the struggling crews that had been thrown into the water, were picked up by their companions in three other boats, and they all made their way to the coast in safety. Four months after this sad disaster the crew of the ship *Rebecca Sims* captured a disabled whale in the same waters. Upon cutting it up they found its head badly damaged with a large ship-plank buried in its flesh, while from the body they took two harpoons, which were marked, "Ann Alexander." The proof was thus established that Captain Deblois' desperate antagonist had met its fate.

ASTONISHING STRENGTH AND ENDURANCE OF A WHALE.

An old whaler, in a book now seldom met with, relates the following interesting account of how he worried a whale and how the whale worried his crew, making one of the fiercest battles ever engaged in between man and a cetacean:

"One of the harpooners belonging to the *Resolution*, of Whitley, under my command, struck a whale by the edge of a small floe of ice. Assistance being promptly afforded, a second boat's lines were attached to those of the fast-boat in a few moments after the harpoon was discharged. The remainder of the boats proceeded to some distance in the direction the fish seemed to have taken. In about a quarter of an hour the fast-boat, to my surprise, again made a signal for lines. As the ship was then within five minutes sail, we instantly steered toward the boat, with the view of affording assistance by means of a spare boat we still had on board. Before we reached the place, however, we observed four oars displayed in signal order, which, by their number, indicated a most urgent necessity for assistance. Two or three men were at the same time seen seated close by the stern, which was considerably elevated, for the purpose of keeping it down, while the bow of the boat, by the force of the line, was drawn down to the level of the sea, and the harpooner, by the friction of the line round the bollard, was enveloped in smoky obscurity. At length, when the ship was scarcely one hundred yards distant, we perceived preparations for quitting the boat. The sailors' pea-jackets were cast upon the adjoining ice, the oars were thrown down, the crew leaped overboard, the bow of the boat was buried in the water, the stern rose perpendicularly and then disappeared under water. The harpooner having caused the end of the line to be fastened to the iron ring at the boat's stern, was the means of its loss; and a tongue of ice on which was a depth of several feet of water, kept the boat. by the pressure of the line against it, at such a considerable distance as prevented the crew from leaping upon the floe. Some of them were, therefore, put to the necessity of swimming for their preservation, but all of them succeeded in scrambling onto the ice, from whence they were taken on board the ship soon after.

"I may here observe, that it is an uncommon circumstance for a fish to require more than two boats' lines in such a situation; none of our harpooners, therefore, had any scruple in leaving the fast boat, never suspecting, after it had received the assistance of one boat with six lines or upwards, that it would need any more.

THE PURSUIT

"Several ships being about us, there was a possibility that some person might attack and make a prize of the whale, when it had so far escaped from us that we no longer retained any hold of it; owing to this we set all the sail the ship could safely sustain, and worked through several narrow and intricate channels in the ice, in the direction I observed the fish had retreated. After a little time it was descried by the people in the boats at a considerable distance to the eastward; a general chase immediately commenced, and within the space of an hour three harpoons were struck. We now imagined the fish was secure, but our expectations were premature. The whale resolutely pushed beneath a large floe that had recently been broken to pieces by the swell, and soon drew all the lines out of the second fast boat, the officer of which, not being able to get any assistance, tied the end of his line to a hummock of ice, and broke it. Soon afterward, the other two boats, still *fast*, were dragged against the broken floe, when one of the harpoons drew out. The lines of one boat, therefore, remained fast to the fish, and this, with six or eight lines out, was dragged forward into the shattered floe with astonishing force. Pieces of ice, each of which was sufficiently large to have answered the purpose of a mooring for a ship, were wheeled around by the strength of the whale; and such was the tension and elasticity of the line, that whenever it slipped clear of any mass of ice, after turning it round into the space between any two adjoining pieces, the boat and its crew flew forward through the crack with the velocity of an arrow, and never failed to launch several feet upon the first mass of ice it encountered.

"While we scoured the sea around the broken floe, the whale continued to press forward in an easterly direction toward the sea. At length, when fourteen lines (10,080 feet), were drawn from the fourth fast boat, a slight entanglement of the line broke it at the stem. The fish then again made its escape, taking along with it a boat and twenty-eight lines, of 720 feet each, the united length being 6,720 yards, or upwards of 3¾ miles; value, with the boat, $750. The obstruction of the sunken boat to the progress of the fish must have been immense, and that of the lines also considerable, the weight of these latter alone being thirty-five hundred pounds.

"So long as the fourth fast boat, through the medium of its lines, retained its hold of the fish, we searched the adjoining sea with the ship in vain; but in a short time after the line was divided, we got sight of the object of our pursuit at the distance of near two miles to the eastward of the ice and boats, in the open sea. One boat only with lines and two empty boats were reserved by the ship. Having, however, fortunately fine weather and a fresh breeze, we immediately gave chase under all sail; though, it must be confessed, with small hope of success, considering the distance of the fish and the rapidity of its flight. At length, after pursuing five or six miles, being at least nine miles from the place it was struck, we came up with it, and it seemed inclined to rest after its extraordinary exertions. The two dismantled or empty boats, having been furnished with two lines each — a very inadequate supply — they, together with one in a good state of equipment, now made an attack upon the whale. One of the harpooners made a blunder; the fish saw the boat, took alarm and again fled. I now supposed it would be seen no more; nevertheless, we chased nearly a mile in the direction I imagined it had taken, and placed the boats to the best of my judgment in the most advantage-

AN EXCITING PURSUIT.

ous situations. In this case we were extremely fortunate. The fish rose near one of the boats, and was immediately harpooned. In a few moments two more harpoons entered its back, and lances were applied against it with vigor and success. Exhausted by its amazing efforts to escape, it yielded itself at length to its fate, received the piercing wounds of the lances without resistance, and finally died without a struggle. Thus terminated with success an attack upon a whale which exhibited the most uncommon determination to escape from its pursuers, seconded by the most astounding strength of any individual I ever witnessed. The quantity of line withdrawn from the different boats engaged in the capture was singularly great. It amounted, altogether, to 10,440 yards, or nearly six English miles. Of these, thirteen lines were lost, together with the sunken boat."

AN EXTRAORDINARY INCIDENT IN THE CAPTURE OF A WHALE.

Scoresby relates the following incident, which I prefer to give in his own words, without comment:

"It is very generally believed by whalers that fish have occasionally been struck which, by a sudden extension or heave of the body, have instantly disengaged themselves from the harpoon. This case usually happens when the whale is struck with a 'slack back,' as that position of the fish is denominated in which the back, being depressed, the flesh is relaxed. A harpoon then struck, occasions an uncommon wound. Hence, if the fish suddenly extends itself, and elevates its back, the wound appears twice the size of the harpoon, and consequently the weapon is capable of being thrown out by a jerk of the body. Under such circumstances as these, a large whale was struck by a harpooner belonging to the ship *Howe*, of Shields. On the fish extending and lifting its back with uncommon violence, the harpoon was disengaged and projected high into the air, when, at the same moment, the fish rolled over upon its back, and received the point of the falling weapon in its belly, whereby it was entangled and caught! This circumstance, romantic as it may appear, is so well authenticated by the person who struck the fish, together with others who were in the boat at the time and were witnesses of the fact, that I have no scruple in introducing it here."

KNOCKING A BOAT SKY-HIGH—THRILLING INCIDENT.

Sir Samuel Baker, who seems to have had a passion for the sea almost equal to his love for wild and unexplored lands, has given a very excellent description of a whale-hunt in which he participated, which is worthy of transcription here, as follows:

"It was not long before the *Sophia* entered upon her promised hunting-grounds. During a calm night a sound of 'blowing' had been heard in various directions, and at sunrise upon the following morning the ship found herself in water of a light green color, which suggested shallows. The deep-sea lead was at once hove, and the soundings gave a depth of six hundred and seventy fathoms—four thousand and twenty feet. The peculiar color of the sea was occasioned by the presence of innumerable living organisms which form the favorite food for whales, and there could be no doubt of their presence.

"The boats' crews were in readiness, and a bright look-out was kept from the mast-head. Suddenly the joyful cry of 'a fall! a fall!' directed the attention of all hands to a jet of steam, about a mile distant upon the starboard quarter; this was quickly followed by several other jets in various positions, and from the continuous issue of watery vapor without a break, there was no doubt of the character of the species—it was a large shoal of sperm-whales. Six boats were lowered without a moment's delay, and hardly had the last boat pushed off from the water when an enormous head protruded from the ship's side, almost touching the copper below the quarter, and blew a dense mass of spray high in air, which fell upon the poop-deck. The next instant the whale, which must have mistaken the bottom of the vessel for one of its own species, inverted itself suddenly and dived perpendicularly, its enormous tail flourishing in the air as it descended. This was a startling challenge to the boats that had just been launched in pursuit, and for about a minute the crews rested upon their oars and anxiously watched the surface. They had not long to wait before one of those peculiar scenes was presented which, although perhaps of frequent occurrence in the gambols of the sperm-whale, are seldom witnessed by human beings. The sea was in good order for whale-fishing, as the surface, without being calm, was unbroken by the crest of waves, therefore any disturbance upon the water could be immediately detected. Without any previous warning, except the sudden appearance of the whale's head just described, an immense sperm-whale shot upward from the surface with an extraordinary velocity, which carried him high into the air, so that the tail appeared to be quite ten or twelve feet clear of the water. This was within three hundred yards of the vessel, and from the great size of the monster, the distance was apparently less than this computation. So great was the exertion, and so unwieldy was the carcass when in mid-air, that the whale had no power to turn head foremost in its descent, but fell flat upon its side into the water, creating a splash that might have been heard two miles.

* * * * * * * * * * * *

"In a short time the leading boat was within a hundred yards of the whale, which, having ceased blowing, was floating with a small portion of its back above the surface, apparently unconscious of the approach of an enemy. The swell was sufficient to conceal both the approaching boat and the whale alternately, thus rendering the conditions of attack most favorable. The crew, at a signal from the steersman, rowed cautiously, and just dipped their oars noiselessly in the water. The harpooner stood up in the bow and slowly raised his arm. He was a powerful man, with broad, muscular shoulders, and his up-lifted hand grasped the harpoon and prepared for a deadly cast.

"The boat was now within fifteen yards of the whale's back; it was evidently one of the largest size. One steady, long, but quiet stroke had given the boat sufficient momentum to complete the approach, and she glided noiselessly but swiftly through the water, while the crew rested on their oars, ready to back-water immediately upon the order being given, when the harpooner should have delivered his harpoon. Every breath was held; the whale's back was not more than ten feet distant, when the weapon flew from the harpooner's hand just as the whale, having discerned the enemy, gave a convulsive plunge downward.

BACK! FOR YOUR LIVES!

"'Back water, all!' shouted the steersman, but hardly had the oars obeyed the command when a tremendous blow from the whale's tail struck it from beneath, and the next instant the boat, with its entire crew, was dashed completely out of the water and fell half inverted, split from end to end, while oars, lines, harpoons, lances and all the numerous appliances were scattered here and there, together with the men, some of whom were swimming, while others clung for safety to their oars.

"The third boat had lost no time in pulling with all the might of her powerful and excited crew in the direction which it was supposed the whale had taken, while the boat which had picked up the disabled crew immediately hoisted the flag as a signal that a whale was 'fast.' The addition of eight men hampered the action of the boat, but some sat down in the bottom, while others assisted at the oars as they best could, and endeavored to save all the floating debris of their damaged boat, which was bottom uppermost. This was quickly effected, and they were considering whether they should right the inverted boat and take it in tow, or whether they should join in the pursuit with the advanced boats, and afterwards return to save their wreck, when it suddenly disappeared with a jerk and was seen no more. The whale had been traveling during the last few minutes at a furious rate, and the line which had remained within the boat had run out to a great length until it became tangled in the thwarts; the boat was then at once dragged beneath the surface. This was a satisfactory proof that the harpoon was holding fast, and accordingly the double crew exerted every effort to continue the chase.

"The leading boat was now a quarter of a mile ahead, and it was expected that the whale would quickly reappear, as the resistance of the water to the sunken boat that was now dragging would cause great exhaustion.

STRUCK, BUT ONLY MADDENED.

"Upon looking toward the advanced boat they perceived an alteration in its course, and almost immediately after they observed the spouting of a whale upon the right, toward which the boat was steer-

SOUNDING.

ing. The accident having been descried from the *Sophia*, another boat had been immediately lowered, which was hurrying to their assistance. The chase was now at its height, and the excitement was intense. It was impossible for the boat with fifteen men to arrive in time to assist in striking the whale, toward which the advance boat was pushing with all possible haste, but they might still be of service. In the meantime the leading boat had arrived within harpooning distance; presently her flag was hoisted, which announced a successful cast; the whale had once more dived, having two harpoons fixed.

"The direction of the whale was uncertain, as it had 'plumbed' the instant it had received the last harpoon. The fast boat accordingly waited in the hope of descrying that peculiar oily streak upon the sea which denotes the track of a wounded whale, resembling the wake of a vessel in calm weather. In the meantime the crowded boat's crew were pulling hard to close with their more fortunate companions. Suddenly they observed the wreck of their own boat floating at a couple of hundred yards distance; steering toward it they shortly arrived, and felt beneath it with a boat-hook to discover whether the line was still fast or had become detached. * * * The line was there; but it was supposed that the harpoon had retracted, or that in some manner the whale had broken loose. The experienced harpooner at once made fast another line before he cut the entangled end adrift from the wrecked boat. Fortunately he had taken this precaution, for almost at the same moment the line became taut and commenced running out at the rate of about six miles an hour. There was no longer any doubt that the whale was still fast, but its first impulsive rush had been expended, and it was now traveling at a slower rate. They signaled to the other boat, which immediately pulled toward them, and shortly arrived within speaking distance. The whale was 'plumbing' steadily into a profound depth. A third line was made fast, and the enormous creature seemed to sink like a leaden plummet, as though determined upon reaching the deepest bottom of the ocean.

"By this time the extra boat had arrived from the *Sophia*, and the crew were ordered to pull far ahead in a direction where it was expected that the whale would emerge when it should be forced to once more seek the surface. The line ceased to run, and for a few minutes an inexperienced person would have imagined that nothing alive was attached. Presently it again moved, but slowly, and at a distance of about half a mile a long, greasy lane or track was plainly discernible. Upon this track the foremost boat was pulling at best speed, the harpooner standing in the bow in expectation of a rise. At once the fast boats began to coil in slack line as they pulled toward the leading boat. A jet of spray suddenly burst from the sea only a few yards ahead; almost at the same instant the harpoon was dexterously thrown, and once more the whale was struck and forced to dive before it had inhaled a sufficient volume of fresh air."

THE BATTLE CONTINUES.

The boats now closed together and followed cautiously in the direction which the whale had taken. The line was run out to its extreme length, and another had been added; this also was insufficient, and a third had been made fast when, after about twenty minutes' interval, the whale rose once more and emitted a long jet of spray tinged with blood. The boats now shot swiftly forward, the men straining every nerve in the exciting race, as the whale was evidently exhausted, and they hoped to arrive sufficiently near to attack it with their lances. The boat that had been dispatched from the *Sophia* was the first to reach the spot, but just as the harpooner prepared to deliver his cast, the whale again headed downward, and the broad-fluked tail dashed the water into the air and descended upon the surface with a smack that narrowly missed the boat, which had fortunately backed water and escaped by only a few feet. The sea around was tinged with blood, and the bleeding would be increased at the depth to which the whale had 'plumbed,' owing to the great pressure of the water.

"The exhausted creature did not appear to be traveling forward, but had merely dived vertically to an enormous depth as though seeking for safety below from its enemies upon the water. Upward of four hundred fathoms of line were hanging almost perpendicularly as though the deep-sea lead was suspended at the bottom. * * * Half an hour had passed and no movement had been perceptible in the lines, which were now hauled taut, as it was supposed that the whale had died in the profound depth to which it had retreated. The crews of each boat hauled away upon the lines until the bows of their boats dipped low upon the water, but no movement responded to the strain, and it seemed as though they were fast to a mass of rock. Suddenly the lines slackened at the same moment, and in a few minutes an immense whale emerged from the sea about two hundred yards in advance; after blowing the usual jet of spray it commenced the most violent lashings with its tail, driving the water into foam and creating a series of loud reports that could be heard at a great distance. The boats now pushed ahead and quickly reached the whale, which still convulsively thrashed the water in a manner that rendered an approach exceedingly dangerous. Another harpoon was thrown and imbedded its barbed head more than a foot deep in the yielding blubber, but this time the exhausted monster remained upon the surface instead of taking the usual plunge. The boats now attacked upon either side and, keeping just behind the head, and well forward of the dangerous tail, which was spasmodically thrashing the water into breaking waves, the crew drove their long lances deep into the vitals of the vanquished sperm, and repeated their thrusts until the action of the whale became fainter by degrees. At length all was still; the whale was dead.

"It was a splendid specimen of a bull sperm-whale, measuring about seventy-two feet in length, and the hunt had lasted upward of four hours from the time the first harpoon was fixed until the death."

CUTTING UP A WHALE.

THE WORK OF BUTCHERING A WHALE.

The death struggles of a whale are something awful to see, for the great leviathan fights death with a power no other living thing can equal. Its mad plunges, wild lashing of its immense tail, the flapping and thrashing of its great fins, the rolling contortions of its monstrous body, and furious gnashing of its mighty jaws, while torrents of blood dye the ocean to a crimson deep, and swirling eddies gather vast quantities of foam, all attest the immeasurable power of the monster. When its energies are finally expended the whale turns over on its back displaying a very mountain of silver white, and the men fix ropes to its tail and tow it along side the ship for the process of cutting up. The first operation, if it be a Greenland whale, is to secure the baleen, which is a very difficult job, owing to the thick, hard, horny substance which has to be separated from the jaw, and which even the heaviest and sharpest instruments can cut but slowly. The next work, called flensing, though not so hard, is very much more disagreeable. A number of sailors, having sharp spikes on their shoes to prevent slipping, descend onto the body, and with sharp instruments like spades, begin cutting through the blubber and separating it into great squares of a half-ton weight each. These pieces are then hoisted on deck by means of pulleys, and there cut into smaller pieces preparatory to stowing away in casks, or rendering the oil out. Formerly the blubber was packed in casks and taken to English or American ports and sold to dealers who rendered it, but during later years whalers usually do their own rendering and return to port with the pure oil. It is also customary now to take the jaw bones on deck and there detach the baleen, instead of breaking or cutting it out before flensing, as was formerly practiced.

The amount of oil yielded by the whale is most surprising; a whale of seventy tons gross weight will yield nearly thirty-five tons of oil, or one-half its weight. In this, however, we behold a wonderful provision of nature, for his thick coat of blubber enables the whale to descend to greater depths of the sea than any other ocean habitat, where pressure of the water would crush any animal not thus protected. Although the whale is monstrous in size it is not without enemies, which pursue it to the death only to eat its tongue; such an enemy is the grampus, and the only means of escape left the whale is by descending to depths where this fish cannot approach.

The whale does not attain its maximum of growth under twenty-five years, and naturalists believe it lives two hundred years. If we are to estimate the whale's longevity by its size, a rule which applies, with some exceptions, to animal creation, it must reach an age of five hundred, or more, years, but as they cannot be kept in captivity, it will probably never be known what age they attain.

The flesh of the whale is red, like a salmon's, and nearly as firm, but very coarse. To those who first eat it the taste is nauseating, not wholly unlike cod-liver-oil, and I doubt that any but an Esquimau can acquire a liking for it. The Esquimaux not only eat whale-flesh with a keen relish, but drink the oil with avidity. Whale-tongue, however, is said to be very palatable; indeed, at one time it was regarded as a royal dish, fit only for kings to dine on.

Tromholt, in his late work on Lapland and the customs of the people of that country, describes the manner in which Lapps pursue the whale as follows:

"The whaling steamers are specially constructed, and measure from eighty to one hundred feet in length, with powerful engines, but their most interesting feature is the gun by which the whales are harpooned and killed. It is mounted on a platform right in the stem, so that it can be turned in all directions. To this novel piece of artillery belongs a shaft, which is inserted into the gun, leaving a small portion outside the muzzle, carrying four movable hooks pointing to the gun and placed crosswise, each about eight inches long. In front of these a large iron ball, or shell, with steel point, is affixed, which is filled with an explosive. On the shaft runs an iron ring, to which a cable is attached about the thickness of an arm, which, when the shaft is inserted in the gun, is run up close to the muzzle end, where it is secured by a cord. When sufficiently near the animal the gun is pointed at one of the softer parts of the body, the fuse lighted, and the terrible projectile launched into the whale. The tremendous jerk of the rope is diminished somewhat by the cord holding the ring breaking, which thus runs up to the top of the shaft. As soon as the wounded animal makes the first pull at the cable, the hooks on the shaft spring into a horizontal position, by which action, through an ingenious mechanism, the shell is fired and explodes with such force that death is almost instantaneous.

CUTTING UP A WHALE.

"When the whale is stranded," says Tromholt, "the process of cutting up begins, by means of large knives fixed on long sticks. When the fin is cut out and detached, the blubber is cut through to the flesh, in strips about a foot wide, running from head to tail, and one end of a chain being fastened to the tail-end, each one is torn off in turn by the steam-engine, the knives assisting in the process. The next stage is the removal of the thin, beautiful layer of muscles which lie on the belly between the blubber and the flesh, which is done by the same agency. The fleshy parts in the jaw are then cut away and the tongue falls out, which is so soft that it trembles at the slightest touch, and if one steps on it, the boots sink to the ankles. The mouth is now open and one can see the baleen plates in the upper jaw. Finally, the breast and belly are opened. During the time this latter operation lasts it is not safe to remain near the whale, as it becomes a kind of animal volcano; dreadful smells rush violently through every fissure, while columns of blood and dirt are thrown out like intermittent geysers. It roars and wheezes in the carcass as if a steam-engine were at work inside, while jets of steam ascend from the blood and entrails. In spite of its being thirty hours since the whale was killed, the internal parts have retained their natural warmth. The entrails are now taken out through the enormous throat, the blood rushes down the breach in veritable torrents, and the whale, which a few hours before impressed the spectator by its noble giant proportions, is reduced to a miserable ruin. The whole operation finished, the trunk of the animal is removed, the flesh separated from the body, cut to pieces, and the fat removed by boiling. The remains are then dried and pulverized and sold as guano, while the blubber and fat are melted to oil. I consider that the flesh of the whale, the least productive part, ought to be put to a better use than guano. At my request one of the men cut me a large piece; it looked like beef, but with a coarser grain, which I had cooked at the hotel as a steak, and although, of course, it could not be compared to the best English beef, I, as well as my friends who tasted it, agreed that we had tasted worse. Dried, pulverized and preserved in tins, it is far superior to the American pemmican, and when it is considered what enormous quantities of this excellent flesh are to be had and its low price, it is to be wished that the population in these parts would overcome their silly prejudice against it and not scorn a food that is to be had for the asking."

The means employed by Esquimaux to capture the whale is thus described by Captain McClure: "A woman's boat is *manned* by ladies, having as harpooner a chosen man of the tribe, and a shoal of small fry in the form of kayaks, or single men canoes, are in attendance. The harpooner singles out a whale, and drives his weapon into the flesh. To the harpoon an inflated seal-skin is attached by means of a walrus-hide thong. The wounded fish is then incessantly harrassed by men in the *kayaks* with harpoons, a number of which, when attached to the whale, baffle its efforts to escape, and wear out its strength until, in the course of a day, the whale dies of sheer exhaustion and loss of blood.

"The harpooner, after a successful day's sport, is a very great personage, and is invariably decorated with the Esquimau order of the blue ribbon, that is, he has a blue line drawn down his face over the bridge of his nose."

FIGHT BETWEEN A WHALE AND GRAMPUS.

Commodore Wilkes gives the following description of a fight he witnessed between a grampus and a whale: "At a distance from the ship a whale was seen floundering in a most extraordinary manner, lashing the smooth sea into a perfect foam, and endeavoring apparedtly to extricate himself from some annoyance. As he approached the ship, the struggle continuing and growing more violent, it was perceived that a fish, seemingly about twenty feet long, held him by the jaws, his contortions, spouting, and throes, all betokening the agony of the huge monster. The whale now threw himself at full length from the water with open mouth, his pursuer still hanging to the jaw, the blood issuing from the wound and dyeing the sea to a distance around; but all his flounderings were of no avail, his pertinacious enemy still maintaining his hold and evidently getting the better of him. Much alarm seemed to be felt by the other whales around.

"These 'killers,' as they are called, are of a brownish color on the back, and white on the belly with a white dorsal fin. They attack a whale in the same manner as dogs bait a bull, and worry him to death. They are armed with strong, sharp teeth, and generally seize the whale by the lower jaw. It is said that the only part of the huge monster they eat is the tongue. The whalers give wonderful accounts of these 'killers' and affirm that they have been known to drag a whale from several boats which were towing it to the ship."

A WHALE'S DEVOTION TO ITS YOUNG.

As an illustration of the whale's well-known devotion to its young, Captain Scoresby relates the following: "In 1811, one of my harpooners struck a sucker (a whale's young) with the hope of leading to the capture of the mother. Presently she arose close to the fast boat, and, seizing the young one, dragged about six hundred feet of line out of the boat with remarkable velocity. Again she rose to the surface, darted furiously to and fro, frequently stopped short, or suddenly changed her direction, and gave every possible intimation of extreme agony. For a length of time she continued thus to act, though pursued closely by the boats, and, inspired with courage and resolution by her concern for her young, seemed regardless of the dangers around her. At length one of the boats approached so near that a harpoon was hove at her; it hit, but did not attach itself. A second harpoon was struck, but she refused to leave her young, and staid by it until three harpoons had hit her vitals, when she yielded up her life in a vain effort to save her young."

The most serious enemies the whale has are the grampus, sword-fish, saw-fish, fox-sharks and man, and so rapidly are these depopulating the sea of its great cetacean that we may predict the day when the skeleton of a whale will be marked with the curiosity which is now excited by the fossil remains of pre-historic sea monsters.

Fox-sharks (thrashers) have been known to combine with saw-fishes in an attack upon a whale. The thrasher is not capable of doing any great harm by its bite, but being extremely active and pertinacious, it can worry a whale almost to the point of death, as it frequently does. When aided by the saw-fish this result is speedily obtained, for while the whale is distracted by the assaults of the smaller enemy, it leaves its body exposed to the fatal thrusts of the greater, and thus soon succumbs.

Previous to the discovery of petroleum whale oil was used most extensively for illuminating purposes, but the introduction of that excellent and cheap illuminator has greatly diminished the demand for whale oil, consequently the increasing scarcity of the animal is not so seriously felt.

CHAPTER XIV.

THE VORACIOUS SHARK.

THE whale, though the largest of all animals, and armed, as some species are, with extraordinary teeth and a tail capable of destroying a ship, yet they are fairly harmless compared with that monarch of the ocean and terror of the sea, the Shark. The lion, tiger, elephant and gorrilla combined are not nearly so dangerous on land as the shark is in the sea, for all land animals flee before man, being terrified by his very presence, but the shark is undaunted before any foe, and will attack man as quickly as any beast will its prey.

The shark has an elongated body, sometimes measuring as much as thirty-five feet in length, this being the greatest size it attains. Its large, cavernous mouth is located below the snout and is armed with six rows above and four rows below, of bristling, compressed and sharp pointed teeth, which are movable at the creature's will. When the animal is undisturbed these teeth lay flat upon the palate directed backward; or, in other words, remain shut up like a jack-knife; but at the moment he pounces upon his prey they are erected, filling the mouth with weapons that are the very inspiration of terror. A singular power is exhibited in the shark in his ability to erect one or more rows of teeth at a time as occasion requires; thus if he attacks a puny prey only the front row of teeth is used, while a larger may call for two rows, and for a strong or fierce antagonist his mouth is made to bristle with teeth from which nothing once caught can possibly escape. The rough skin of the shark is covered with a multitude of bony tubercles; but in some species these lumps are small and can be easily reduced by abrading with sand-paper or pumice-stone, and the skin makes a beautiful shagreen for opera-glass cases and other similar purposes.

FEROCITY OF THE SHARK.

The white shark often grows to a length of thirty feet; but it is rather uncommon to meet with them more than twenty feet long. The head is broad and somewhat depressed, terminating in a dull pointed snout. The mouth is fairly huge, capable of admitting the body of a man and still allow room for its large cartilaginous tongue.

The eyes are the very personification of cruelty, craftiness and rapacity, being of a greenish cast and peculiarly stony glare. The stomach is not only large, but dilatable to an extraordinary degree, almost like that of a snake; the brain, however, is very small, as are all the vital parts, and on this account it is very hard to kill.

The French name for shark is *requin*, a derivative from the Latin *requiem*, so named from a significant fact; if a man falls into the sea in the presence of this voracious animal, his comrades may at once begin the requiem, or recite prayers for the dead. So swiftly can the

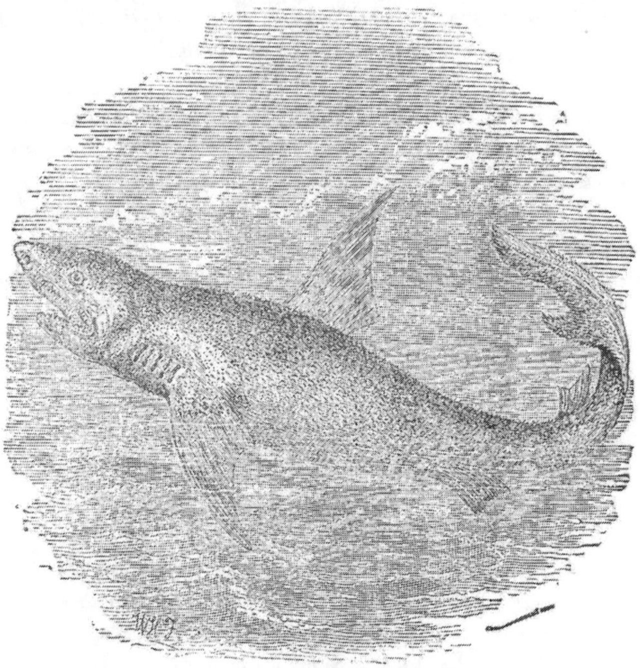

THE WHITE, OR BASKING SHARK.

shark swim through the water that no steamer can keep pace with him, and in strength he has no equal save alone the whale. With a single snap of his powerful jaws he can cut a man in two; we may not, therefore, wonder that he is more dreaded by sailors than any other monster of the monster-haunted deep.

"Frequently," says Mangin, "in the West Indian seas, the negro crew of a boat will cease rowing, and with a significant air indicate to the voyager the hideous form of a shark following in the rear, and apparently waiting for some false movement or sudden accident, which, by capsizing the frail skiff, may provide his ravenous maw with food. Frequently, too, on tempestuous nights, when the wind and the sea seem to howl a funeral dirge, the shark appears in the midst of the heaving billows; the seamen recognize his presence by the phosphorescence — the elfish light — that glints from his shining scales, and know that he lusts after a human victim. In tropical waters he follows the ship with indefatigable patience, ready to swallow the unfortunate who may fall overboard, or the dead mariner whose body is committed to the deep; for to this voracious creature the dead and living are equally satisfactory prey."

ADVENTURES WITH SHARKS.

The shark is met with in all climates, but it is in the torrid seas that his ferocity renders him most formidable. With all his power and valor he has two enemies to dread, though it is doubtful if he really fears either; these are the great cachelot or sperm-whale, which wages against him a murderous war, and man, the enemy of all other created things. The cachelot is carnivorous, but does not make prey of the shark, its motive for attacking it apparently being no other than a desire to rid itself of a rival. The two fight furiously and always to the death.

So ferocious and fearless is the shark that it never considers consequences, and though it might easily avoid its enemy, being much the swifter swimmer, yet it bears every savage assault of the whale and yields only when torn and mangled so that it can fight no more. But it must not be supposed that the shark is incapable of inflicting injury upon the whale, for it really bites out great chunks of blubber from its monstrous assailant; but the whale's vitals are so protected by its fat, which is several feet in thickness, that the shark cannot possibly reach them, and thus the fight is invariably one-sided, in favor of the whale.

The fierce joy of a difficult and even dangerous struggle, the intense gratification of conquering a great destroyer, would be sufficient motives to animate man in hunting the shark; but, besides, several useful products are obtained from the monster. His thick, hard skin is susceptible of a fine polish, and is largely employed in the manufacture of sheaths and instrument cases. His liver yields a large quantity of oil almost identical with that of the cod's, and is a splendid dressing for skins. The flesh of the shark is tough and cannot be boiled to tenderness, yet those who have eaten it in extremities say that its flavor is not at all unpleasant.

THE CAPTURE OF A SHARK.

M. C. Platt, in the "Museum of Sciences," thus describes the capture of a shark in which he was a participant:

"A shark of great size, certainly not less than thirty-five feet in length, had ventured to draw near our vessel. As we were then becalmed and had nothing to do, we hailed the pleasant burst of excitement, the agreeable relief to our monotonous occupations, which he was likely to afford us. By way of precaution, and to keep him occupied, we flung to him a pair of old boots, which he conscientiously swallowed. However, he required as yet no enticement; for while the calm lasted, and so long as our ship did not make more than three or four knots per hour, the shark never stirred from the wake of our floating palace, where he always expected to see something regal allotted to him.

"While he amuses himself in plunging and diving in the wake of the ship, everybody is in a state of tumult upon deck. We arrange our warlike engines and make ready for the battle. An enormous fish-hook is attached by means of a bit of iron chain to the extremity of a long and stout cable. The bait is a large piece of pork, just such another piece as the monster has already swallowed, while it lay soaking in the sea water in readiness for the crew's dinner.

"At length all is ready. The captain holds in his grasp a well-greased harpoon; the slip-knots of the cable glide with complete ease and are disposed within reach of the hand. Everybody has collected on the quarter-deck. A sailor flings the hook into the sea and the fishing begins.

"The shark now ceases to plunge and wheel about the ship; he smells the bait and lazily swims toward the floating piece of pork. He learned years ago that so small a prey cannot escape him. Immediately that he touches it with his snout, he turns on his side, opens his huge mouth and swallows it. But at this moment the cable is violently jerked, forcing the fish-hook into one of his jaws; two hands catch firm hold of the rope and begin to tighten it, while the shark plunges about in wrath and pain, churning the water into foam. Sometimes the hook breaks; in such cases the fishing must be recommenced. The shark, with torn and bleeding throat, nevertheless, swallows a second bait with equal avidity.

"As soon as we are satisfied that the hook is securely fixed, we draw the animal alongside. The man placed at the post of honor—generally, as in the present case, the captain—vigorously darts the harpoon into the shark's body. It is necessary that the iron should so far penetrate into the flesh that the movable portion form a cross with the axis of the lance. We have then two points of attachment, and raise the shark out of the water by means of the cable of the fish-

SHARK FISHING.

hook and the rope of the harpoon, drawing upon both simultaneously. The animal once lifted from the sea, loses a part of his strength; his fins and tail have no longer any point of support. Nothing is easier, while he hangs by the ship's side, than to pass a slip-knot around his tail. The three ropes which now hold him fast run quickly over pulleys fixed to the yard arms, and the shark is speedily landed upon the quarter-deck.

"The prisoner is captured and his punishment not long delayed. In vain are all his struggles; in vain the repeated and heavy blows of his tail, which threaten to crush through the planks. A sailor plunges a hand-spike into his throat to hold him down, while another severs his tail with an axe. In this mutilated condition he is completely harmless and powerless; though a blow from his tail would kill a man, or, at all events, break his thigh. The monster rendered defenseless, we cut open the belly and extract the heart, which is immediately flung overboard. Sometimes a portion of the stomach is put aside to be eaten; sometimes the animal is stripped of his skin, which is dried, while the dorsal spine is fashioned into a handsome walking-stick."

DREADFUL CASUALTIES FROM MAN-EATING SHARKS.

It is related that as the ship *Karnok* was leaving the port of Nassau a pilot fell overboard from her boat in which he was being towed. His position was immediately discovered, and the utmost means were taken for his rescue; two life buoys were at once thrown to him, the vessel stopped and a boat put out to pick him up. The boat drew near enough for the unfortunate pilot to grab hold of one of the oars, at which moment he gave a desperate cry, "For God's sake, save me!" On the very instant the words escaped the poor fellow's mouth, a shark grabbed him and disappeared, leaving only a tinge of blood to indicate his dreadful mission. It was only a few days after this fatal accident when a shark was captured off Nassau, and upon being cut open there were found inside the monster's stomach the pilot's wrist and a portion of his clothing, besides a goat's head, with horns attached nine inches long.

A SINGULAR WAY TO KILL SHARKS.

A gentleman traveling from Calcutta to Batavia witnessed the killing of a shark in a very singular manner, which he relates as follows: "Looking over the bulwarks of the schooner, I saw one of these watchful monsters winding lazily backward and forward, like a long meteor; sometimes rising till his nose disturbed the surface, and a gushing sound, like a deep breath, rose through the breakers; or at others, resting motionless on the water, as if listening to our voices and thirsting for our blood. As we were watching the motions of this monster, Bruce, a lively little negro, suggested the possibility of destroying it. This was, briefly, to heat a fire-brick in the stove, wrap it up hastily in some old greasy cloth as a sort of disguise, and then to heave it overboard. This was the work of a few minutes, and the effect was triumphant. The monster followed after the hissing prey; we saw it dart at the brick like a flash of lightning, and gorge it instanter. The shark rose to the surface almost immediately, and his uneasy motions soon betrayed the success of the manœuvre. His agonies became terrible; the water appeared as if disturbed by a violent squall, and the spray was driven over the taffrail where we stood, while the gleaming body of the fish repeatedly burst through the dark waves, as if writhing with fierce and terrible convulsions. Sometimes, also, we thought we heard a shrill, bellowing cry, as if indicative of anguish and rage, rising through the gurgling waters. His fury was, however, soon exhausted; in a short time the sounds broke away in the distance, and the agitation of the sea subsided. The shark had given himself up to the tides, as unable longer to struggle against the approach of death, and they were carrying his body unresistingly toward the beach."

A COMPANY OF MEN DEVOURED BY SHARKS.

It is related that upon an occasion, a large double canoe containing thirty-two natives of Tahiti Island, while making a crossing to an adjoining land, were wrecked by a sudden squall and all but three of the number were eaten by sharks. The singular part of this account is this: After being thrown into the water, the men, all of whom were expert swimmers, not being able to right the canoe that was overturned, contrived to make a kind of raft, on which they scrambled. Their combined weight, however, sunk it nearly to a level with the water, and while thus awaiting relief a school of sharks appeared. The men tried to frighten the voracious monsters away by kicks and shouts, but it was of no avail. The sharks swam to the very edge of the raft and soon one of them leaped up and caught a man, who was speedily torn into pieces and eaten. The success thus obtained emboldened the other sharks, and one after another of the men were seized and eaten until only three remained. Relieved of so much weight the raft rose so high above the surface that the sharks were unable to spring out of the water far enough to reach the last three, who thus fortunately escaped the horrid death that had befallen their companions.

A SHIPWRECKED CREW ATTACKED BY SHARKS.

Some years ago there appeared in a popular magazine the story of the sufferings experienced by the crew of the schooner *Magpie* while cruising among the West Indies in search of pirates. As the article was contributed by one of the survivors who was well and favorably known, we have no reason to doubt its truthfulness. The story, very much abbreviated, is about as follows:

The *Magpie* was upset by a squall and sunk in a hundred fathoms of water, carrying down two of the crew with her; the others, twenty-two in number, were on deck when the squall struck her and were left struggling in the water; by a piece of good fortune one of the boats became detached from the vessel as she sank, and floated upright in convenient reach of the men, but they all reached her so nearly together that in their efforts to get into her she was overturned, and thus afforded the slimmest chance for escape. Some of the men climbed on her bottom while others clung to the sides, and thus they drifted with a hope that some vessel might pass by and pick them up. Lieutenant Smith, a brave and resolute man, explained to the men how impossible it was to remain long in such a position, and exhorted them to right the boat and bail her out so that they might hoist sail and save themselves. His advice and orders moved the men to action, but before half their labors were accomplished a shark was discovered in their immediate vicinity. This discovery threw all the men into confusion and would have caused a second overturning of the boat had not Smith appealed so fervently to them; their fears somewhat subsided when the shark disappeared and four men bailing the water with their hats had almost relieved the boat when a dozen or more sharks rushed in among the struggling men. The excitement was so intense that the boat was upset and their last hope of rescue now abandoned. In another moment a leg of one of the men was bitten entirely off; the poor fellow raised himself far enough up the sides of the boat to show the bleeding stump, and then fell back and was seized by another shark. Cries of terrible distress arose as one after another of the men were caught by the voracious monsters and drawn down to be devoured. In the midst of all this direful massacre Smith preserved his presence of mind and besought the men to right the boat again, as in that lay the only possible means for their escape. Strange enough, his orders were obeyed, though nearly half the crew had been destroyed. Smith clung to the boat and directed his men with a composure most phenomenal, kicking the water as violently as possible to frighten away the sharks. Presently he became so quiet that the attention of the men was attracted to him; he was pale but still exhorted the men to renewed endeavor; the heroism of the man was almost without parallel, but, despite his resolution, a groan escaped his lips and his now enfeebled hands loosed their hold upon the boat; a shark had bitten off both his legs above the knees. At this most painful of sights the remaining crew felt that to preserve their own lives was no more their duty than to minister to the man who was so willing to sacrifice himself for their safety. He was caught while sinking and laid in the boat, which was now floating half full of water. In all his agony Smith continued to give orders, thinking rather of the men than of himself, until the savage attack of a shark, which caught a man who had a death-like grip upon the edge of the boat, turned it over for a third time, when the heroic sufferer rolled out and sank forever.

All the harrowing scenes which characterized the second overturning of the boat were re-enacted at her third upsetting, and one after another of the men were torn and eaten until only two remained, who righted the boat and got into her. Though still full of water, the boat sustained them, and by dint of superhuman exertion they bailed her fairly dry, so that they could lie down, when exhaustion came, on the bottom, safe at last from the sharks.

It was eight o'clock in the morning when the *Magpie* went down, and an hour afterward all of her crew, except two, had died the most horrible of deaths and become food for the real "pirates of the ocean." These two, so singularly preserved at the expense of all their comrades, were picked up the next day and taken to New Orleans, where they were tried before a court-martial and not only acquitted, but afterward appointed warrant officers.

VORACITY AND TENACITY OF LIFE IN THE SHARK.

There are several species of sharks which come under the class name *Squalidæ*, from the Latin *squalidus*, to be foul or filthy. This term, however, is given more in reproach than as a designation to characterize the habits of the animal. It is true, a shark, like an ostrich, will eat anything, but he is not specially offensive, being quite as cleanly as other carnivora of the deep.

A shark found in the fossil state measured seventy feet in length, a monster altogether more terrible than its saurian contemporaries, since its mouth had a capacity of nearly twenty-five feet, while its great teeth were four inches in their projection above the jaw. Is it possible to conceive of a more formidable monster, considering its ferocious character?

The species of which I have been writing is known as the white, or man-eating, shark. As a further illustration of its voracity, it may be mentioned that in the stomach of one dispatched near Nassau was found a lady's work-box, some ship's papers, remains of two ducks, three chickens, some shavings, pieces of cordage, and a buffalo robe. All these articles had been thrown into the sea from the ship *Alceste* during a storm. It is also related that a sealed tin canister filled with gold coins was found in the stomach of another shark. Not only will it swallow almost anything thrown overboard from the ship, but the shark does not hesitate to devour his own species, like the wolf. Experiments have been frequently tried of wounding sharks when in schools, and in every instance the wounded animal was set upon by the others, torn into pieces and devoured. Large sharks have also been frequently known to seize those not considerably smaller than themselves and eat them.

The vitality of a shark is extraordinary, exceeding that even of the turtle. They have been known to not only live, but swim actively in their element several hours after the head was cut off. Several instances are reported of a shark pursuing and gorging upon its prey after having been cut open and all its entrails removed, including the heart and liver.

TERRIBLE SUFFERINGS OF A SHIPWRECKED CREW.

No calamity can equal the burning of a vessel at sea, the supreme horror of which bursts upon the senses of the crew when the flames roll up in savage frenzy and like a very fiend of malice and destruction drives the victims foot by foot, from quarter to quarter, until there is no longer left a refuge between fire and water; the cry of despair, falling masts, hurried orders, splashing of life-boats cut loose from their davits, and lastly, a smoking hulk that lends its light to the crowded boats as they move off under the pitiless guidance of fate. I cannot picture the unutterable agony of such an event, and must leave to my readers to conjure up in their own imaginations the horrors of a burning ship freighted with human beings, far from shore or a helping hand.

Such a calamity befell the whaling ship *Larking*, in 1862, in the Indian Ocean, and since some of the incidents which followed are directly in the line of the subject I am now treating—sharks—I will give a brief desciption of the sad event.

After a very successful cruise, the *Larking* was on the return home laden with several thousand gallons of whale-oil, when, by some accident, never fully understood, but presumably by the carelessness of a boy sent into the hold with a lighted candle, the ship took fire. The captain was an uncommonly cautious man and cool-headed, as few men are, but despite his exertions the fire gained so rapidly that he soon saw the vessel was doomed and ordered the boats lowered. Everything was done in a quiet way, not the least confusion occurring, and the ship was abandoned only when it was no longer safe to be near her. There were seven boats which carried the entire crew of fifty-six men quite comfortably, but the supply of water and provisions which they had been able to take was alarmingly small, since they were more than a thousand miles from Mauritius, the nearest land.

For five days the boasts were rowed toward the island, the weather being fine and their progress excellent, and the men, though compelled to subsist on raw salt pork, began to treat their misfortune lightly, feeling that the remainder of their voyage would prove auspicious. On the evening of the sixth day, however, the wind rose and soon freshened into a gale, while the sea grew angry, and its increasing billows portended grave danger. The men threw the heads of their boats to the waves, and rowed with all their might against the storm; darkness only added to the danger; it brought no subsidence of the wind, and when morning broke, only one boat, the largest that was launched, containing fourteen men, remained upon the surface, the others and their precious freight having been engulfed.

Although the large boat had weathered the gale and was still in good condition, the surviving crew were but little better off than their companions who were now done with sufferings and fears, for the fresh water was exhausted, and even the last piece of raw pork consumed. To ease their raging thirst, some of the men foolishly drank salt water, and on the following day were raving mad, and in their delirium three of them jumped overboard and were drowned. On the same evening another died, but his body was not cast overboard until some hours after, and when at last it was committed to the sea, the body had become so inflated by gases that it would not sink, but floated around the boat, blackened and distorted, seemingly to remind those yet living of the certain fate that awaited them. Thirst and hunger had well nigh robbed them of their senses, except the sense of suffering, and being now too weak to use their oars, they drifted about utterly destitute of hope.

SAVED BY A SHARK.

"Suddenly," says the account, "a long, dark-brown fin, like a scimeter, protruded from the surface about ten yards distant, and was followed almost immediately by the appearance of a shark, who swam up leisurely to the floating body and then around, as though uncertain whether to seize the prey. Without a moment's hesitation the captain seized a harpoon and made it fast to a line, but the shark had disappeared. 'Keep quiet,' he whispered to the expectant crew, who had been stimulated from their stupor by this unexpected visitor. 'Keep silent, and ship your oars; he'll be here again presently.' The nervous system is a mysterious paradox; the men who were half dead a few minutes before now recovered their spirits at the chance so surprisingly presented, and exhibited a keen interest in sport which was their special calling.

"The captain stood in the bow of the boat with the harpoon ready, watching intently the dead body of their late comrade, which floated only a few yards distant. Some minutes elapsed, and hope began to sink; it was thought the shark had been scared off by the boat and would not return again. The captain's arm slowly raised the harpoon as he gazed almost perpendicularly into the blue water. The next instant there was a dash and quick commotion; the dead body whirled rapidly as though in a sharp eddy, and a flash of white in a long streak was seen beneath, at the same time that the harpoon sped from the captain's hand, and the line whizzed over the gunwale. The shark was struck! It had evidently risen from a considerable depth to attack the body by a sudden dash from below.

"Although the excitement of the moment had added new life to the weary and famished crew, their muscles were weak, and it was with painful difficulty that they managed to play the shark to which they were attached. Having allowed it to run out fifty fathoms of line, they hauled steadily upon it, and shortened the length to twenty yards, then they made fast the line by a round turn about the bow thwart, and the fish towed the boat at discretion until tired. The crew then hauled away until the shark was alongside, when a shot from a musket, in the spine, at the junction with the head, killed it. All hands were then employed in cutting the flesh into long, thin strips that would dry in the hot sun and afford a lasting supply of food. The men drank the shark's blood, and ate the meat raw, as they prepared it, and found it wonderfully refreshing. Their good luck was further increased by a copious shower, which set in directly after the animal was cut up, and by spreading the canvas so as to catch the rain, a good supply of water was soon obtained and their sufferings were at an end, for three days later they reached Mauritius in safety.

SHIPWRECKED, AND EATEN BY SHARKS.

A horrifying accident occurred in July, 1885, off the coast of Hawaii, near the Kau district, by which not only a vessel was lost, but no less than five persons that were on board fell victims to the voracity of sharks. The newspaper accounts of the casualty are to the effect that the schooner *Poholiki*, owned by Mark Robinson, the captain, who had his wife and son on board at the time, was caught in a gale and so seriously injured that she could not be controlled, and running for a lee was capsized. The captain's wife and child were almost instantly seized by sharks, and their piercing cries were hushed in a moment as they disappeared forever. A boat that was being towed astern of the capsized vessel was secured by two of the crew, who got into it and endeavored to rescue the three others that were in the water. The sharks in the meantime attacked the captain, pulling him under the water and tearing his right leg in a shocking manner. He managed to get loose from his tormentors for the time, however, but as the men were pulling him into the boat they were horrified to see another of the voracious creatures fasten onto the left leg of the unfortunate, and for some minutes there was a tugging at the suffering man between the sharks and the men who would fain save him. The Captain was finally drawn into the boat, but not until his legs were so terribly lacerated that he died in less than an hour.

The two sailors that were in the water were attacked simultaneously with the captain, one having a great piece of flesh taken from his left side, while the other lost his left arm, but they were both rescued and taken in the boat to Kaawaloa, where Dr. B. G. Baker attended them and managed to save their lives. The woman and child were devoured so speedily that from the moment they were drawn under water not a vestige of either was again seen.

A MAN TORN TO PIECES BY A SHARK.

John Duncan, of the Firth Life Guards, writing of his travels through the kingdom of Dahomy, in alluding to the traffic of slaves on the Wydah coast, records the following incident: "I forgot to mention the circumstance of a Spaniard, who was employed as a hand on board the *Medóra* schooner, from London. Upon perceiving the slaves put on board the American brig, anchored at a short distance, he jumped overboard to swim to her, but had only been in the water a few seconds before a large shark approached him. The poor fellow kicked with his feet toward the shark, endeavoring to keep it off, but it darted on him and tore his arm. A boat was immediately lowered, but before it reached him the shark made a second attack, and the unfortunate man, who was now swimming with one hand, was again seized on the back of the shoulders and dragged under water, the tail of the shark remaining in sight. When the boat reached the spot, the shark appeared on the surface still holding the man. One of the men in the boat struck the shark's head with a boat-hook, when he relinquished his hold; the poor fellow's flesh was completely torn from the bone. A small rope was fastened around his back, and he was got into the boat, and after being taken on board the *Medora* died in half an hour."

A LAD BITTEN IN TWO BY A SHARK.

Sir Samuel Baker, in his "Eight Years' Wanderings in Ceylon," relates the particulars of a singularly distressing accident which occurred in the harbor of Trincomalee, a beautiful indentation of the shore of Ceylon, in 1845, shortly after the British occupation of the island. He writes:

"The fort stands upon a projecting point of land, which rises to about seventy feet above the level of the race-course, which faces it. Thus it commands the land approach across this flat plain on one side and the sea on the other. This same fort is one of the hottest corners of Ceylon, and forms a desirable residence for those who delight in a temperature of from 90° to 104° in the shade. Bathing is the great enjoyment, but the pleasure in such a country is destroyed by the knowledge that sharks are looking out for you in the sea, and crocodiles in the rivers; thus a man is nothing more than a live bait when he once quits *terra firma*. Accidents must necessarily happen, but they are not so frequent as persons would suppose from the great number of carnivorous monsters that exist. Still, I am convinced that a white man would run greater risk than a black; he is more enticing bait, being bright and easily distinguished in the water. Thus in places where the natives are in the habit of bathing with impunity, it would be most dangerous for a white man to enter. There was a lamentable instance of this some few years ago at Trincomalee. In a sheltered nook among the rocks below the fort, where the natives

BOY BITTEN IN TWAIN BY A SHARK.

were always in the habit of bathing, a party of soldiers of the regiment then in garrison went down one sultry afternoon for a swim. It was a lovely spot for bathing; the water was blue, clear and calm, as the reef that stretched far out to sea served as a break-water to the heavy surf, and preserved the inner water as smooth as a lake. Here were a fine lot of English soldiers stripped to bathe; and although the ruddy hue of British health had long since departed in the languid climate of the East, nevertheless their spirits were as high as those of Englishmen usually are, no matter where or under what circumstances. However, one after the other took a run, and then a 'header' off the dock into the deep blue water beneath. In the long line of bathers was a fine lad of fifteen, the son of one of the sergeants of the regiment; and with the emulation of his age he ranked himself among the men, and on arriving at the edge he plunged himself head foremost into the water and disappeared. A crowd of men were on the margin watching the bathers; the boy rose to the surface within a few feet of them, but as he shook the water from his hair, a cloudy shadow seemed to rise from the deep beneath him, and in another moment the distinct outline of a large shark was visible as his white belly flashed below. At the same instant there was a scream of despair; the water was crimsoned, and a bloody foam rose to the surface—the boy was gone! Before the first shock of horror was felt by those around, a gallant fellow of the same regiment shot head-first into the bloody spot, and presently reappeared from his devoted plunge, bearing in his arms *one-half* of the poor boy. The body was bitten off at the waist, and the lower portion was the prize of the ground shark.

"For several days the soldiers were busily employed in fishing for this monster, while the distracted mother sat in the burning sun, watching in heart-broken eagerness, in the hope of recovering some trace of her lost son. This, however, was not to be; the shark was never seen again."

TERRIBLE ADVENTURE OF A DIVER.

No other people live in such constant fear of the shark as pearl-divers. Every year we hear of divers being lost, who have become the prey of voracious sharks. The sponge-fishers about the Bahamas and Florida coast furnish numerous victims, though they never descend into the water without a large knife with which they defend themselves against such attacks. It is a singular fact that armor-dressed divers are seldom attacked by sharks, not always because their appearance inspires fear, for often the dreaded monster will approach within a few feet of the diver and look at him with every evidence of curiosity and astonishment, yet show no disposition to do him harm. Sometimes, however, perilous adventures befall these sea-inspectors,

COURAGEOUS ATTACK ON A SHARK.

and many forfeit their lives by tempting fortune in the shark's domain.

The pearl-divers are a tempting bait for sharks because they descend to great depths, armed, it is true, with large knives, but their body is naked and thus makes a feast of flesh to the ever-hungry scourge of the sea. In pursuing their dangerous calling, in order to make their descent rapid as possible, the diver grasps a rope to the end of which a large stone is fastened. He goes overboard with this stone, which carries him to a depth of thirty or forty feet almost on the instant. Retaining his hold on the rope, or making it fast to his body, he collects together as many oysters as possible in the time he is able to remain under water, and at a signal is drawn up by the rope.

On one occasion, so it is related, an American visited the coast of India with the purpose of introducing his diving armor to be used in the pearl fishery. A great many natives were engaged in their usual occupation of diving, as above described, and to show them the utility of his armor our American encased himself in it and descended among them. It happened that at this time one of the native divers was attacked by a shark, which, failing to catch him in its dreadful jaws, struck him such a violent blow with its tail as to render him unconscious. The American diver immediately went to the rescue of the stricken native, and was in turn attacked by the shark, but he skillfully avoided its deadly mouth and as it shot by him and snapped its jaws together he plunged his long knife to the hilt into its body, making so large a gash that the entrails protruded; he next seized the prostrate native, who was still unconscious, and at least thirty feet under water, and, signaling to those above, was quickly drawn up. The injured man was nearly dead when brought out of the water, but proper manipulation finally restored him and he recovered. The dead body of the shark, which measured twenty feet in length, was cast on shore a few days afterward.

A SCOURGE FROM BIRTH.

The shark, when scarcely born, says Figuier, becomes the scourge of the sea. He seizes all that comes near him. He eats the cuttle-fish, molluscs, and fishes; among others, flounders and cod-fish. But the prey which has the greatest charm for him is man; the shark loves him dearly, but it is with the affection of the gourmand. It even manifests, according to some authors, a preference for certain races. If we may believe some travelers, when several varieties of human food comes in its way, the shark prefers the European to the Asiatic, and both to the negro. Still, whatever may be the color, he seeks eagerly for human flesh, and haunts the neighborhood where he hopes to find the precious morsel. He follows the ship in which his instinct tells him it is to be found, and makes extraordinary efforts to reach it. He has been known to leap into a boat in order to seize the frightened fishermen; he throws himself upon the ship, cleaving the waves at full speed to snap up some unhappy sailor who has shown himself beyond the bulwarks. He follows the course of the slaver, watching for the horrors of the middle passage, ready to engulf the negroes' corpses as they are thrown into the sea. Cummerson relates a significant fact bearing on the subject. The corpse of a negro had been suspended from a yard-arm twenty feet from the level of the sea. A shark perceived the body and made the most prodigious leaps in his efforts to seize it. After many vain attempts the shark changed his tactics and waited until the bow of the vessel sank lowest in its motion with the waves, and then leaping, seized first the legs, then the body, and thus took it piece-meal until not a vestige remained. The crew viewed with much interest this horrifying spectacle, since the vessel was a slaver and no feelings of humanity had any place among the crew.

The mouth of the shark being placed much below and back of the snout it is necessary for the animal to turn over in the water when seizing its prey. This well-known peculiarity is taken advantage of by natives on the African coast and also of the Malay Archipelago. These bold adventurers, who seem to be at home in the water, do not hesitate to invite the shark to attack them, in which event they watch for an opportunity when the shark turns over and, leaping aside, they plunge a long knife in the creature's abdomen.

SHARK FISHING.

Many persons engage in fishing for sharks, not only for the amusement which it affords, but also for the double purpose of destroying the destructive monster and to possess themselves of its hide and teeth, the latter being extensively used for ornaments. Shark fishing is especially good about Nassau and off the Florida coast, where, we might say, thousands are taken annually, yet their number does not appear to diminish. The fishing is conducted somewhat as follows: A dark night is preferable, though there is no time when sharks will not feed, but the advantage of darkness is in approaching it more readily, and its suspicions are not nearly so great as in daylight. A hook is prepared of steel, having a curve of from five to six inches, and to this is attached a chain instead of rope, since the latter would

EXCITEMENT OF SHARK FISHING.

be quickly bitten in two. A piece of salt pork is generally used for bait, but fresh meat is nearly as good. The bait, which must be well hooked, is thrown overboard; it is soon seen by a shark, which will invariably, unless extremely hungry, swim up to the bait, smell of it, and then move away again; but he quickly returns and makes another inspection, repeating the performance two or three times if the bait be left still; but in order to urge the shark to take it quickly, the bait is pulled over the surface, and the shark, suspecting it to be about to escape, rushes swiftly on and swallows it gluttonously. The fun now begins in earnest. The moment he swallows the bait the shark starts downward, and is only stopped by a strong pull on the line, to which he is now fast. He is as game as a bass or pickerel, and will not give up until he has lashed the sea into foam, leaped a dozen times entirely out of the water, and becomes completely exhausted from his frantic efforts. The line is then drawn in until the shark's head is above water, when a noose is thrown so as to fall over the pectoral fins and run down the body till it rests round the tail; it is then drawn taut, and, heaving at both lines, the men draw the great creature from his element, and make quick work of him, by first lopping off the tail with an axe, and then cutting off the head.

WORSHIP OF THE SHARK.

Says Figuier: "Man worships force; he knows the hand which crushes, the teeth which rend. He respects the master or the king who strikes, and he venerates the shark. The inhabitants of several parts of Africa worship the shark; they call it their *joujou*, and consider its stomach the road to heaven. Three or four times in the year they celebrate the festival of the shark, which is done in this wise: They all move in their boats to the middle of the river, where they invoke, with the strangest ceremonies, the protection of the great shark. They offer to him poultry and goats in order to satisfy his sacred appetite. But this is nothing; an infant, which has been reared for the purpose from its birth, is every year sacrificed to the monster, ; it is feted and nourished for the sacrifice from its birth to the age of ten. On the day of the fete it is bound to a post on a sandy point at low water; as the tide rises the child may utter cries of horror, but it is abandoned to the waves, and the sharks arrive. The mother is not far off; perhaps she weeps, but she dries her tears and thinks that her child has entered heaven through this horrible gate.

MEMBERS OF THE VORACIOUS FAMILY.

The Hammerhead shark is distinguished by the singular conformation of its head, which is flattened horizontally, truncate in front, and the sides prolonged transversely, giving an appearance very much resembling the head of a hammer. The eyes of this fish are placed at the extremities of these lateral prolongations; their color is gray, but the iris is like that of a tiger's; when the animal is excited the iris flashes very flames, so bright is its golden color. Beneath the head and very near the junction of the body, is the mouth, which is semi-

THE HAMMER-HEAD SHARK.

circular, and the jaws are armed with four rows of dagger-like teeth, barbed on two sides. The most common species, found especially numerous in the Carribbean Sea and Bay of Panama, is slender of body, which is grayish, and head of a color between a brown and black. Its greatest length is fifteen feet, which is very seldom attained, ten or twelve feet being the usual size, and the weight about five hundred pounds.

The hammer-head, though smaller than its man-eating congener, is yet its equal in boldness, voracity and blood-craving propensities; it knows no fear, pursuing its prey to the very limit of audacity and encroachment upon man's domain. Its appearance is very frequent in roadsteads, where it swims about ships, ready to pounce upon any eatable thing, from a cracker to a sailor, prefering very much the latter and not infrequently obtaining its choice.

The Greenland shark attains a length of fifteen feet, and is equally voracious as the blue shark or hammer-head, but it is not so dangerous to man; its ravages, however, as a sea-pirate, are very extensive, and it is of the greatest annoyance to whalers. Almost the moment that a whale is killed its body is surrounded by Greenland sharks, which proceed to devour the blubber more rapidly than the sailors can sometimes remove it, and thus get the greater share. It is almost impossible to either kill or drive them away from the feast; harpoon after harpoon, and lance after lance may be driven into their bodies without apparently producing the slightest injury, and even large pieces may be cut out of their bodies without affecting their appetite. Examination of the body of a Greenland shark discloses the fact that they have the least nervous organization of anything in the sea superior to the zoophytes, and the brain is so very small that it is only on the rarest occasion that harpooners are able to strike it.

The flesh of this shark is eaten with much relish by Esquimaux, who consider it next to the walrus, and they also use the skin for making lines, for which purpose it is extremely serviceable. Many persons claim that the Greenland shark pursues and worries the whale to death for the purpose of feasting off its body, but this statement lacks confirmation, and is not probable. Their food is chiefly small fish and crustacæ, but it is a great scavenger and will eat any flesh that it may find.

The basking shark grows to a length of thirty feet, and is equally formidable as the white or man-eating shark; in fact, man-eater may be applied to three or four species, including the basking shark, but this latter is not nearly so voracious as the hammer-head, white or blue shark, and is not much dreaded by sailors.

The spinous shark is not a large fish, seldom reaching more than eight feet in length, but his appearance is horrid in the extreme, covered as he is with prickles like lion-claws. To swim rapidly against a person in the water, a spinous shark would tear the body most frightfully, but whether it is guilty of such practices or not I have not seen stated.

The blue shark, which sometimes measures eight feet in length, is the most graceful and beautiful of this hideous tribe; his back is a blue-green, and the belly is a silver-white. Though comparatively small, he is not wanting in courage, and will attack a person in the water as ferociously as the white shark, about which I have already written enough to show the horror in which he is held. The blue shark feeds principally on pilchards, tunnies and herrings, but he lusts for warm-blooded animals also.

The thrasher, or fox-shark, has two distinguishing characteristics:

THE GREAT PILGRIM SHARK.

the immense development of the upper lobe of the caudal fin, or tail, which enables him to thrash the waters violently till they boil and seethe for some distance around, and the fox-like head, with its small mouth and large eye. In my remarks about whales I have alluded to the habit of the fox-shark combining with the grampus in attacks upon the whale, which they kill. The fox-shark is not only a formidable antagonist of the whale, but it also ferociously attacks other monsters of the deep, such as seals, porpoises, lamantins, etc., and has killed many a shipwrecked sailor by the wild lashings of its terrible tail, out of pure wantonness, for it is not known to eat man.

The picked shark and sand shark are both small and harmless. The former is caught on the Scottish coast, to be split, dried and eaten by the poorer classes. The latter furnishes no little sport to anglers at the sea-coast summer resorts about New Jersey, Long Island and Massachusetts.

The great pilgrim belongs to the shark family, though beyond appearance it has none of the formidable characteristics of its congeners. It has been represented as one of the most implacable persecutors of the whale, but this is only an idle story, utterly destitute of fact. Although carnivorous, like all *squalidæ* (sharks), it confines its diet to small fish and never attacks man. It sometimes reaches a length of thirty-five feet and a weight of over two thousand pounds; it is armed with powerful teeth, and is capable of doing as great mischief as the white shark, but nature has given it a mild temperament compared with all the other members of the shark family, and it therefore escapes persecution from the hand of man.

SATELLITES AND PARASITES OF THE SHARK.

Mangin says, according to a well-known marine superstition, the shark has a satellite, or diminutive companion, that follows him faithfully wherever he goes. This is the Pilot-fish, so called because supposed to guide the shark toward an appetizing meal, and to warn him of any threatening danger. "The truth is, he *follows*, not *pilots*, the voracious animal, to feed upon his ordure and on such morsels as may be disregarded by him." In this opinion Mangin is opposed by many persons well acquainted with the habits of the pilot-fish, as we shall presently see.

In size and shape the pilot-fish resembles the mackerel, to which family it undoubtedly belongs, and is easily recognized by the five conspicuous bands surrounding its body. These stripes are transversal and of dark-blue color, showing very plainly on a general ground color of silvery grayish blue. The head is small; the scales are small and oval; the ventral fins attached to the abdomen by a membrane through one-third of their length; the pectoral fins are clouded with blue and white shades, while the ventrals are nearly black. Altogether, it is a very beautiful and graceful fish, about one foot in length, and exceedingly active in its movements.

A voyager in the East Indies, writing of the sharks he had seen, says: "These have waiting on them six or seven small fishes which never depart, with bands, blue and green, round their bodies, like comely serving men, and they go two and three before them and some on every side." This same traveler further relates that in three instances he saw the shark led certainly by the pilot. When the great creature swam near the ship the pilot kept close to his nose or under one of his breast-fins; occasionally it would dart forward, as if to make a careful survey of what lay ahead, and then return again, as if to make report of its findings. When a hook was thrown overboard baited with a large piece of pork, the pilot-fish swam quickly to the bait, smelt of it and then returned to the shark, which had as yet failed to discover the morsel flung over to tempt him. Again and again the pilot swam to the bait and back again to his great companion, as if to tell him a dainty bit of food lay just ahead, drawing him gradually toward the bait, until at last the shark saw and seized it ravenously.

FIDELITY OF THE PILOT-FISH.

Another instance is reported by the well-known naturalist, Dr. Bennett, as follows: "I have observed that if several sharks swim together, the pilot-fishes are generally absent; whereas, on a solitary shark being seen, it is equally rare to find it unaccompanied by one or more of these reputed guides. The only method by which I could procure this fish was, that when capturing a shark, I was aware that these faithful little creatures would not forsake him until he was taken on board; therefore, by keeping the shark, when hooked, in the water until he was exhausted, or, as the sailors term it, 'drowned,' the pilot-fish kept close to the surface of the water over the shark, and, by the aid of a dipping-net, fixed to the end of a long stick, I was enabled to secure it with great facility."

It is a difficult matter to decide positively the real object of the pilot-fish, but the probability is that, recognizing the power of the shark to seize and mangle large prey, the pilot-fish does really direct him, in a measure at least, knowing that in the death of the prey some remnants will fall to its share. The rhinoceros bird, none will dispute, guards with fidelity its giant companion, giving warning of impending danger like a faithful soldier on picket duty; may we not therefore reasonably suppose that, since all things on land have their counterpart in the sea, the pilot-fish solemnly guards the shark and feeds upon the remains of his feast?

THE WONDERFUL REMORA-FISH.

A parasite of the shark, which is also found frequently adherent to rocks and ships' keels, is a small fish called by scientists the *Remora*, and by the general people *sucking-fish*. Like the pilot-fish, the remora resembles a herring, and is about eighteen inches in length. The ancients indulged their imaginations with wonderful fictions concerning its power of adhesion. Thus it was said that Antony's ship, at the battle of Actium, was prevented from moving through the resistance of remora fish, although several hundred strong sailors were at the oars. It is also told that Caligula's galley was detained for several days between Actium and Astura by a single remora clinging to the helm.

Pliny, who has written many excellent lines, and not a few pleasing

THE REMORA, OR SUCKER-FISH.

fictions, referring to the remora, inquires: "Why should our fleets and armadas at sea make such turrets on the walls and forecastles, when one little fish (see the vanity of man!) is able to arrest and stay, perforce, our goodly and tall ships?" The same author seems to have discovered another extraordinary quality in the fish, for he observes, that if the remora be preserved in salt and then placed at the mouth of any pit wherein valuables lie concealed, that it will draw up the treasure. Greater even than this in drawing properties was this most extraordinary of fishes when dried, pulverized and used as a love filter; it was recommended by the ancients to draw the loveliest women to the homeliest men, its power being irresistible.

These stories have an extremely small foundation to rest on, but they were implicitly believed at one time. The facts are, that owing to a peculiar weakness of its fins, the remora is induced to attach itself to any foreign body that offers a means of support; and this it does with such great tenacity, that unless the effort of separation be applied in a particular direction, the disunion cannot be accomplished without tearing the flesh apart.

The adhesive apparatus of the remora consists of an oval area on the top of the head, transversed by numerous partitions, each of which is bordered by a margin of small and very numerous teeth or bony filaments, while the entire oval space is strengthened by a longitudinal septum passing up the center of the head, on either side of which lie the cavities. These cavities act like an exhaust pump from which the air is forced at will, when they adhere like the half of a rubber ball pressed down upon the flesh. The remora derives its name from the Latin *remorare*, to delay or retard. It is principally an inhabitant of the Mediterranean and Atlantic Seas; is of a uniformly brown color, with a smooth, scaleless skin, a large mouth bristling with many small teeth, little yellowish eyes and a slightly forked tail.

It is very seldom that a shark is seen to the body of which is not attached one or more sucking-fish; the motive in selecting the shark rather than other large fishes is no doubt two-fold. First, the shark, being monarch of the liquid domain, his presence affords protection to the remora; second, the remora being carnivorous and yet without the ability to swim rapidly, or catch its prey, he naturally seeks the shark, which is a ravenous feeder, and thus he thrives upon the small bits which fall from the monarch's feast, in the same manner as the pilot-fish.

The remora does not confine its attachment exclusively to the shark, for its disposition is to adhere to nearly anything that may come in the way, only to remain a short time, however, while with the shark it remains for days, or possibly for weeks, without once relinquishing its hold. The natives about Mozambique employ it in fishing for large turtles. A ring is fastened round its tail, to which a strong cord is fastened. When the fishermen have rowed their boat close to a sleeping turtle, according to the custom of its kind, on the surface of the water, they fling the remora in the sea and it speedily attaches itself to the animal, when both are drawn into the boat.

CHAPTER XV.

THE SWORD-FISH AND SAW-FISH.

NEXT to the shark in ferocity and voraciousness is the Sword-fish, a habitat of nearly all the seas, but most populous in the Mediterranean. It grows to a length of twenty feet, but the powerful, keen, heavy, dentilated blade is one-third its entire length. Like the shark, nature has equipped the sword-fish with so dreadful a weapon, that its province seems to be war, though, strange enough, it is comparatively innocent and extremely timid before man, confining its ravages to its fellow-denizens of the deep. Cuvier classifies it among the mackerel family, but there is room for doubting the correctness of this classification. The dorsal fin is very like a shark's, while the tail and pectoral fins resemble the mackerel, and the steel-blue color of the body is very nearly identical in the two. But mackerel are gregarious, while sword-fish are usually solitary, or in pairs, except at certain seasons, when four or five may sometimes be seen together.

Though timid in the presence of man, the sword-fish is full of courage before the most powerful monsters of his element; he frequently attacks the whale, and gives him a mortal thrust with his inflexible and adamantine beak.

The Sicilian fishermen are accustomed to pursue the sword-fish in boats, and chiefly use the harpoon in effecting its capture; this instrument is light, but a practiced hand can hurl it to a surprising distance. Dr. Wood says the Sicilians, when hunting the sword-fish, chant a kind of song, set to words which no one can understand. The song is thought by some writers to be a corruption of some old Greek verses, and the fishermen believe the sword-fish is so fond of this song that it follows the boat in which it is sung. They will not venture to speak one word of Italian, thinking that the sword-fish would understand them, learn that they contemplated its death, and then make its escape. No bait of any kind is employed, the unintelligible chant being thought to be far more efficacious than any material aid.

The flesh of the sword-fish is always eatable and nourishing, and in small specimens is white and well flavored. Though it is in considerable demand for food, and its skin makes an excellent leather, though rather thick, few of the Mediterranean people, except Sicilians, engage in hunting it. These go in small boats, in the center of which is a heavy mast about twelve feet high; up this mast one of the men climbs, and securing himself to the top, keeps a look-out for the fish. Though the sword-fish does not make its presence conspicuous by gambols or spouting, as does the whale, he has the shark-like habit of lying close to the surface, from which his long dorsal fin protrudes like the main-royal of a sunken ship; this directs the fisherman, and by cautious approaches he gets near enough to cast the harpoon effectively.

SICILIANS HUNTING THE SWORD-FISH.

The killing of sword-fish is a lucrative industry among New England fishermen, who capture great numbers annually for the flesh and oil which they yield. In a recent number of Frank Leslie's Illustrated Monthly, Mr. C. F. Holder gave a very interesting description of the manner in which sword-fish are killed, interspersing his narrative with some interesting incidents as related to him by the captain of the yacht *Laughing Dolly*. Preserving the vernacular of his informant, Mr. Holder repeats the story of the captain as follows:

"So'dfishin' ain't all fun," said the red-faced skipper, who was holding on to the wheel with one leg over the spokes. "There comes a time what makes things look master foggy an' unsartin. Haow so? Why, just this: Afore I took up so'dfishin' for a livin,' I used to trawl it off shore. Ever see a trawl? Wall, it's a line a mile or mebby a mile an' a half long, with abaout three thousand hooks onto it, and a sinker and float at each end. Yaou hev the hull thing coiled up in a basket, and sink one end and sail away, payin' aout as ye go; and when the hull lot's over yaou lay on an' by for two hours or so, and then haul her in. Ye see, ye cover over two miles o' ground, an' if there's any cod or haddock abaout ye're sure to get 'em.

"Wall, as I was goin' to say, I was aout one mornin', I reckon afore sunrise, an' was payin' aout my trawl, when the first thing I knew, blim! came somethin' what give the boat a tip, and I felt somethin' strike my foot, an' a kind o' hot feelin' up along my leg, an' lookin' daown, there was a so'dfish — so'd a-stickin aout o' my ileskins jest at the knee. Wal, if I didn't buckle on to that so'd it's a caution, an' it was pull, haul, yank an' tug for half an hour. But I got the painter araound it with a couple o' turns, an' hailed a mate that was fishin' close by, an' we broke off the so'd an' got the critter aboard. Ye see, the cuss had took me or the boat for a whale or blackfish, an' come rammin' up like a shot; the so'd goin' complete through the bottom o' the dory, strikin' jest alongside my boot, passin' up through the leg o' my ile-skin pants, an' comin' aout at the knee. I tell ye I never was so took back afore except once, an' that was off Nantucket, a year or so ago, when a so'dfish kem near cleanin' us all aout. We got into him all right, an nothin' else bein' in sight, me an' the boys jumped into the dory, an' soon had the keg aboard; but as soon as we touched the rope to take in slack, he started off, an' you'd a thought we'd got foul of a whale. It was an hour afore we got the fish alongside, the schooner keepin' along, but we were afraid o' passin' the rope, thinkin' it might pull aout the iron. Wal, we gradually hauled in, an' I stood up, holdin' an oar up ready to hit the brute on the head, when it gave a kind o' lunge or side cut, takin' the oar right between my hands, an' knockin' me head over heels down in the bottom o' the boat. In the confusion, the man in the bow slacked the rope, and the next minute, crunch came the fish, and up it's so'd came through the plankin', stickin' about a foot into the boat, not three feet from me. I had sense enough to grab it, an' while I hung on, an' lashed it with the painter, the boys pulled alongside, an' we got him aboard. He measured fourteen foot — a pretty big fellow.

"In fair weather they lie mostly on the surface, an' whether they're asleep or jest sunnin' themselves, it's hard to tell. It's a great sight to see 'em in among the bony fish; they go just like a cavalryman, strikin' up and down, right an' left, killin' hundreds o' 'em, an' I've seen 'em keep a-doin' it, which shows they kind o' like the fun of it. I see once——"

But here there came a cry from aloft, and in a moment all hands were on their feet.

"Where away?" shouted the skipper, jumping into the rigging, and following the direction of the topman's arm we soon saw about one hundred yards distant, cutting through the water and flashing in the sun, the sharp fin of a great fish.

"Luff a little," cried the skipper to the man who had taken the

FEROCIOUS ATTACK OF SWORD-FISH.

wheel, and the vessel hauled on the wind and toward the fish we were evidently to meet shortly if each held its course.

The sword-fish was making fair time, and as we neared it the sharp outlines could be plainly seen as it dashed away like a privateer in search of its prey.

"Luff a little," whispered the mate, who now took the deck while the skipper walked out on to the jibboom, unlashed the iron, and took his place in the pulpit, ready for the fray. The line was cleared, and one of the hands took the gayly-colored keg and stood ready to toss it over. Gradually the schooner and fish drew nearer, and finally, by a sign from the mate, the helmsman put the wheel hard down, and the vessel rushed up into the wind, bringing the great fish fairly across the bows.

For a moment the skipper's arms were raised; a gleam of steel, a rush of rope, and the metallic lily was buried in the fish, that, hurling its scythe-like tail in the air, covered the harpooner with spray as it dashed away. Another harpoon being lashed on the pulpit, the skipper stepped aboard.

"Stand clear!" shouted the man with the keg, and with a final hiss the last coil leaped from the tub, the keg going over with a jerk, and rushing away over the sea to tire out the gamy fish.

The vessel now set a big balloon-jib in hot pursuit, but another hail from aloft changed the course, and soon the *Laughing Dolly* was falling away sharp to cross the path of another fish; that, however, was found to be asleep.

"I never could make aout," said the skipper, making way for the mate who was to try his hand, "whether they're asleep or what; but most every so'dfish we get is lyin' still on the surface, and I reckon if fish *do* sleep, they're a-doin' it."

In a few moments the big balloon-jib was flapping and thundering in the wind; sail was shortened, and we were well aboard the second fish, the harpoon soon sent hissing into the luckless victim, and soon two kegs were in sight to be followed.

"I've had half a dozen over at one time," said the skipper, "an' I tell ye it makes a man look alive to keep his glimmers on 'em."

A hail from the top now told that we were gaining on the first fish, and it was soon evident from the deck that the powers of the gamy fish were on the wane, and in half an hour the barrel, now stationary, was alongside. The dory that was tossing astern was hauled alongside, and into it tumbled two of the hands, and the writer as volunteer, and, casting off, we pulled for the keg.

"Look out!" yelled the man in the bow, as he grasped the keg and tossed it into the boat, taking a turn with the line.

But the warning was too late. The fish feeling the haul, started off, throwing the writer down among the oars and bailers, and amid the shouts of the lookers-on we rushed away as if shot out of a gun,

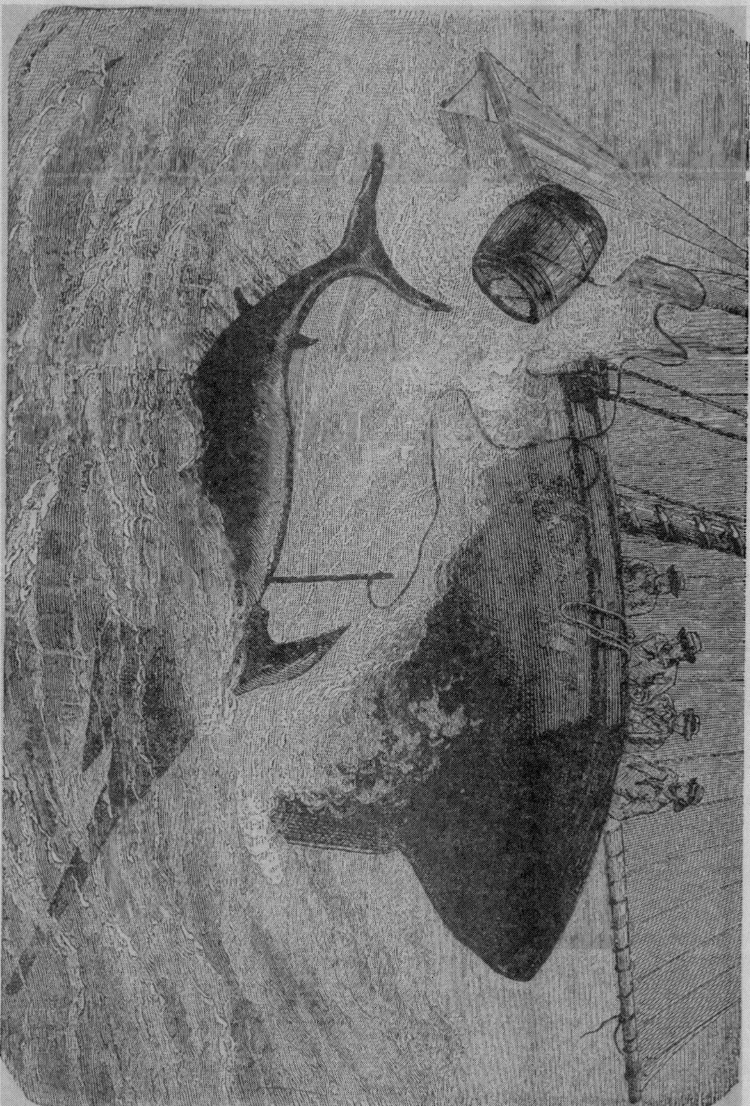

HARPOONING A SWORD-FISH.

huddled in the stern that was high in the air, the bow being buried in foam by the maddened fish.

Under this spurt the schooner was left far astern, and as the speed diminished the men laid hold of the rope and endeavored to take in the slack. Every movement, however, caused a renewal of the terrific burst of speed; but, as there is an end to all things, we finally gained slowly on the fish, and before long had it alongside and lashed. The writer incautiously looked over the side and attempted to grasp the creature's tail, when, with a tremendous effort, the fish doubled up, cutting a vicious blow over the boat that would have been hard to parry, but the men skillfully caught the sword and lashed it while we awaited the arrival of the schooner, that in the meantime had secured the other fish. Once alongside, a block and tackle were rigged, and the struggling yet helpless monster, that was fourteen feet long and must have weighed seven hundred pounds, was hoisted aboard, and the vessel was soon on her course for other fields to conquer.

"If yaou ever get hold of their so'd, yaou've got 'em," said the skipper, as we watched the dismemberment of the swordsman. "I've seen 'em sleepin'—if they do sleep—and grabbed hold of the so'd and held 'em and brought 'em in shore. Bite? Not often; but I've seen 'em bite at a line; but it's rare. They like to run into a school of bony fish or mackerel and do their own killin'. Some folks say they don't use their so'ds to kill fish, but I've seen 'em do it, an' what's more, I've caught a heap o' fish wid their so'd broke off agin the bottom, ships an' whales, and every one of 'em was so poor they didn't amaount to nothin'. No, I never see a young one, and what's more, they don't come araound the coast. I've got a standin' offer of a hundred dollars for the first so'd-fish under a foot long; but it's a safe one, as I say they don't breed here."

This is one of the most interesting facts concerning the sword-fish. They do not breed on our shores, evidently crossing the ocean for that purpose, like the tunny and several others. The young have never been nearer our coast than the mid-Atlantic, and then would scarcely be recognized as sword-fish, so unlike the parent are they in form.

The adult fish of the genus *Xiphias* is extremely common upon our eastern shores, and attains a length of fifteen or sixteen feet, and a weight of over one thousand pounds, their fishery forming an important industry from Maine to Long Island, and hundreds of men and vessels being employed. The fish finds a ready market, the meat somewhat resembling mackerel, to which family they are indeed allied. The sword is a prolongation of the upper jaw, and used to cut

SWORD-FISH STABBING A TUNNY.

up its prey, a proceeding they would be unable to accomplish without this, as they have no teeth for the purpose.

From the earliest times sword-fishing is mentioned, the sport being described by Strabo and many authorities and naturalists of the early days. Ælian described it as entering rivers, and Southey records one that pierced and killed a man while bathing in the Severn near Worcester.

The use of the "sword," says Wood, is not clearly ascertained. In all probability the fish employs this curious weapon in gaining its subsistence, but the precise mode of so doing is not known. It is an ascertained fact that the sword-fish will sometimes attack whales and seals and stab them mortally with its dreadful weapon. It is also known that this fish has several times driven its beak so deeply into a ship's heavy bottom timbers, that it was broken off by the shock. The following may be related in confirmation of this well established fact.

ATTACKED BY A SWORD-FISH.

In the year 1868, the Clyde built merchant vessel, *Dreadnaught*, while passing through the Mediterranean, was struck by a sword-fish with such terrific force that her bottom was pierced and timbers sprung below the water-line. The shock was at first supposed to be caused by the vessel striking, though the sounding lead showed no bottom. Directly after a monster was seen floundering on the sea, and hooks were speedily prepared with the hope of capturing it, but all effort was without avail, and in turning their attention finally from the fish, the crew discovered that the vessel was leaking badly; further examination showed that her hull had been perforated, but while the captain was now convinced that his vessel was suffering from the thrust of a sword-fish, the beak had not been broken off in the timbers, and the proof was therefore only circumstantial. The vessel was put into harbor as soon as possible and claims for insurance made. The insurance company, however, resisted the claim, under the plea that the risk did not cover such a casualty, and a protracted suit in the English courts followed. The final result, I am sorry to say, I have never been able to learn. Professor Owen, the well-known naturalist, was made a witness in the case on the probability of such an accident, and his testimony was conclusive. He related a number of instances of the prodigious power of the sword-fish, stating that it could strike with the force of an artillery projectile, the fish being perhaps the swiftest swimmer in the sea, while his "sword" is almost as hard and strong as steel.

The whaling vessel *Fortune* was also struck by a sword-fish, and examination showed that its weapon had gone through the copper sheathing, next through an inch board, then through three inches of oak board lining, and then through one foot of solid white-oak timber and struck into an oil cask, altogether perforating a sheet of copper

SAVAGE BATTLE WITH A SWORD-FISH.

and seventeen inches of hard timber. It is doubtful if a solid shot from a twenty-four pound gun would have the same penetrability. The "sword" from this fish, which was broken off by the attack, is still preserved in the British Museum. Hundreds of similar incidents are on record and might be quoted but for their want of interest.

The food of the sword-fish is rather varied, consisting of cuttle-fish, especially the squid, and of small fishes, neither of which animals would in any way fall victims to the sword. It certainly has been said that the weapon is used for transfixing the flat-fish as they lie on the bed of the sea, but this assertion does not appear to be worthy of credit.

ADVENTURE OF THREE DIVERS WITH A SWORD-FISH.

The bold character of the sword-fish is in striking contrast with the general timidity of fishes, and it not infrequently occurs that this well-armed warrior exhibits a bravery and savageness which goes far to prove him to be the most fearless, as well as dangerous, enemy that lives in the bounding waves. The following case in point may serve to illustrate this assertion:

In the spring of 1886, a sloop, with valuable cargo, was lost off the coast of Martha Vineyard Island. The vessel lay in only nine fathoms of water, and the owners resolved to recover the freight, and, if possible, to also raise the sloop. In pursuance of this resolve, they employed three expert divers, who, on a comparatively still day, repaired to the spot and descended to the wreck. They had been down only a few minutes when one of them was much alarmed by the sudden appearance of a dark shadow, which hung above him like a cloud, and which he thought was a man-eating shark. He lost no time in communicating his fears to his companions, and the three at once prepared to fight for their lives.

The experience of ocean-divers is a hard one, and teaches them the necessity of being always well-armed when visiting the haunts of ocean monsters, for there is constant dread of fateful adventure with some shark, sword-fish, octopus or dog-fish.

After a few moments of suspense the divers were thoroughly enlightened as to the kind of enemy that was threatening them, for, with a graceful sweep of its broad tail, which made a swirl that nearly raised them off their feet, a great sword-fish swooped down and thrust its powerful weapon between the men, knocking one of them down, but fortunately doing little damage. That the design of the fish was to fight, or drive the invaders from his briny realm, was apparent from the first attack, but he emphasized this purpose by turning and again rushing with savage impetuosity at one of the divers, who would certainly have been impaled but for the thick copper helmet he wore, and which was the object of the fish's attack. The shock was, nevertheless, terrific, and knocked him flat and almost senseless. At this juncture another diver had the rare presence of mind to seize the creature by its sword, and as the fish is comparatively helpless when its weapon is fast, the men soon dispatched it with their long dirk-knives, with which they were happily armed. The adventure had a most fortunate outcome, for it was the greatest luck that one or more of the divers was not killed in waging battle

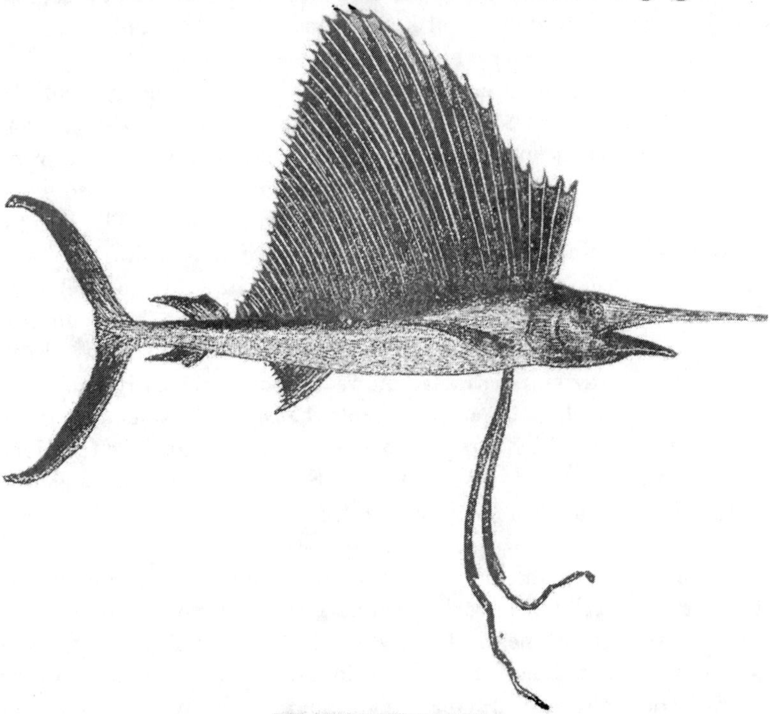

THE SAILOR SWORD-FISH.

with one of the best armed, savage and most dangerous fish that ravages the sea for prey.

THE SAILOR SWORD-FISH.

The sailor sword-fish is sometimes called the Fan, or Sail-fish, and is said to possess the power of raising and lowering its enormous dorsal fin, just as a lady opens or closes her fan. Sir J. Emerson Tennent mentions this singular fish in the following terms: "In the seas around Ceylon, sword-fishes sometimes attain to the length of twenty feet, and are distinguished by the unusual height of the dorsal fin. Those both of the Atlantic and Mediterranean possess this fin in its full proportions only during the earlier stages of their growth. Its dimensions even then are much smaller than in the Indian species; and it is a curious fact, that it gradually decreases as the fish approaches to maturity; whereas, in the seas around Ceylon, it retains its full size throughout the entire period of life. They raise it above the water while dashing along the surface in their rapid course, and there is no reason to doubt that it occasionally acts as a sail."

ADVENTURES WITH THE SAW-FISH.

Somewhat resembling, and yet entirely different in habits and disposition from the sword-fish, is the Saw-fish, which though carnivorous is a most inoffensive creature everywhere except among its prey. The sword-fish has possibly been misrepresented, for all it does occasionally attack vessels with apparently wicked intent. The fact is, the sword-fish sometimes becomes infested with a parasite, a crustacean of the Lernæ family, which burrows into its flesh and bites so viciously that the poor fish grows fairly delirious with pain; in this most unhappy condition, from which there is no relief, the sword-fish strikes maddening and distracted blows which occasionally fall upon the hull of a vessel. It is most probable that all such attacks are made out of frenzy caused by worrying parasites, and not due to a ferocious disposition to harm the vessel or man. For this reason I have chosen to regard the sword-fish as an innocent creature.

CHARACTER OF THE SAW-FISH.

The saw-fish is found throughout a wide range of seas, and is one of the most terrible appearing animals that cleave the ocean. It grows to a length of nearly twenty feet, and in addition to its saw-like beak it has a dreadfully wicked-looking eye, appearances which utterly belie its true character. The snout of the saw-fish is a prolonged beak flattened like a sword, six feet long, and the edges are armed with a row of powerful teeth deeply imbedded in the bone. The tip of the saw, as if specially tempered by nature for severe service, is covered with extremely hard granular scales. Like the sword-fish, it has an antipathy for the whale, and frequently attacks the huge cetacean, thrusting its saw into the thick blubber and causing dreadful wounds; being very agile, it easily avoids the blows directed by the whale, and seldom suffers injury from its monstrous enemy. Captain Drayson says he has frequently seen saw-fish charge into a shoal of herring and mackerel, and by vigorously striking right and left with its serrated weapon, kill large numbers, upon which it afterward fed. This fact explains the purpose designed by nature in giving to the saw-fish such a formidable weapon.

Captain Wilson, commanding the *Halifax*, relates the following adventure which he had with a saw-fish some years ago:

BATTLE WITH A SAW-FISH.

"Being in the Gulf of Paria, in the ship's cutter, I fell in with a Spanish canoe manned by two men, then in great distress, who begged me to assist them to save their lines and canoe. Going to their relief

THE SAW-FISH.

and coming alongside their boat, I discovered that they had got a large saw-fish entangled in their turtle-net, which was towing them out to sea, and but for my assistance they must have lost their net or canoe, and perhaps both, which were their only means of subsistence. Having only two boys with me at the time in the boat, I desired them to cut away the fish, which, however, they refused to do. I then took the bight of the net from them, and with the joint endeavors of themselves and my boat's crew, we succeeded in hauling up the net, and to our astonishment, after great exertions, we raised the saw of the fish about eight feet above the surface of the water. It was a fortunate thing the fish came up with the belly toward the boat, or it might have cut it in two.

"I had abandoned all idea of taking the fish until, by great good luck, it made toward the land, when I made another attempt, and having about three hundred feet of rope in the boat, we succeeded in making a running bowline round the saw of the fish, and this we fortunately made fast on shore. When the fish found itself secured, it plunged so violently that I could not prevail on any one to go near it; the appearance it presented was truly awful. I immediately went alongside the Lima packet, Captain Singleton, and got the assistance of all his ship's crew, but by the time they arrived the fish was less violent. We hauled upon the net again, in which it was still entangled, and got another three hundred feet of line made fast to the saw, and attempted to haul it toward the shore; but, although mustering *thirty hands*, we could not move it an inch. By this time the negroes belonging to Mr. Danglad's estate came flocking to our assistance, making together about one hundred in number, with the Spaniards. We then hauled on both ropes for nearly the day before the fish became exhausted. On endeavoring to raise the fish it became most desperate, sweeping with its saw from side to side, so that we were compelled to get strong ropes to prevent it from cutting us to pieces. After that one of the Spaniards got on its back, and at great risk cut through the joint of the tail, when animation was at once suspended. It was then measured, and found to be twenty-two feet long and eight feet broad, and weighed nearly five tons."

ENCOUNTER WITH A SAW-FISH.

Dr. Quackenbush, the port physician at Mayport, Florida, an inveterate hunter and fisherman, related to me the particulars of a savage fight he had in the summer of 1883 with a gigantic saw-fish, near the mouth of St. John's river. The Doctor stated that he was in a small row-boat with his little daughter, nine years of age, fishing for sea-bass, when a sudden jerk of his line admonished him that some large creature had attacked the bait. Instead of responding to the pull given, the fish made off at a moderate speed and was so heavy that the angler knew at once his quarry was not a bass. The fish took out all the line, but so slowly that it gave time for another one to be added, and continued swimming away from the boat until four lines, of one hundred feet each, had been nearly taken out, and it looked as if he would get away without further ceremony. The strain which the line allowed — it being a quarter of an inch plaited silk — at length caused the fish to turn and make straight toward the boat; as it came within a few yards distance the creature, which up to this time had not shown itself, suddenly shot up a saw-bill four feet in length, and began striking, apparently blindly, from side to side until it reached the boat, when, with one terrific stroke, it tore away two feet of the stern down to the water's edge. The Doctor had now to run

A TERRIBLE FIGHT WITH A SAW-FISH.

toward the bow to keep the craft from taking water, but with admirable presence of mind he seized an oar and continued to thrust it into the infuriated fish's mouth with such force as to repel the vicious attack. The fish now swam away a short distance but soon returned to the boat, though the injury inflicted by the Doctor driving the oar so forcibly into its throat, caused the fish to act abstractedly, and the Doctor succeeded in making a noose of a long rope he had on board and throwing it over the creature's formidable saw. He now jumped to the oars and pulled with all his might toward the shore, which he succeeded in reaching only after two hours of the hardest labor, the fish in the meantime being itself much exhausted by a long continued effort to get away. As the Doctor reached the bank some men, who had watched the contest, but having no boat were unable to render any assistance, ran down and four of them seized the rope by which the saw-fish was made fast, and attempted to draw it ashore; the desperate throes of the creature rendered the effort vain, so that three others, seven men in all, were required to land it. When drawn on land it was measured and proved to be sixteen feet in length.

I was shown the saw-bill of this great fish, which the Doctor had cut off and preserved as a trophy of his queer adventure. It was nearly four inches broad at the base and two inches at the point, and was armed with twenty-two murderous-looking bony daggers on each side, none of which had been broken by its savage attack on the boat.

A FRIENDLY VISITOR.

The pearl-fishers about the coast of North Australia regard the saw-fish with kindly feelings, and cultivate a friendliness with it under the belief that its presence gives them good luck. Frequently, as the diver descends, he carries with him a bit of meat as an offering to the fish, and so tame do the creatures become under this treatment, that they will often follow the pearl-fisher and remain in the closest proximity to him for hours at a time.

THE FEROCIOUS DOG-FISH.

There are several species of the Dog-fish, including the little dog-fish, small-spotted dog-fish, lesser-spotted shark, picked dog-fish, morgay, and Robin Huss. Though none of the species attain to the size of the shark, they are scarcely less ferocious, and are the greatest evils with which fishermen have to contend. The Picked Dog-fish possesses a formidable weapon situated in front of its two dorsal fins, from whence the name. These weapons are sharp spines which the fish is enabled to direct with great precision in striking at its enemies. Mr. Couch says he has known the picked dog-fish to pierce a finger laid upon its head. When about to strike, it curves its body in a bow-shape and suddenly launches out its spears in the intended direction. Fortunately this species does not grow to any considerable size, and is not capable of doing any serious damage.

The spotted dog-fish might be called the wolf-fish with perfect propriety, since its disposition is ferocious, and besides, it is a great glutton. During one of my voyages across the Atlantic I saw a spotted-dog-fish, fully twelve feet long, swimming with easy grace along beside the vessel, scarcely twice its length from me. As the sea was quite calm and the sun shining, I could see the creature with a distinctness almost perfect, and as it showed no signs of temerity, I watched it for a space of several minutes. In all my life I never saw a more beautiful or graceful thing than this fish, which was spotted like a leopard and seemed to feel a pleasure in exhibiting itself in the most fantastic and symmetrical motion. Time and again it would whirl round and, then turning half over, would look at me with a mirthful eye so cunning that my admiration was unbounded. I regretted very much that I had no food at hand to give it, for the familiarity it displayed only needed to be encouraged to make the creature a pet, but I had no desire to get closer.

Dog-fish are a dreaded pest to fishermen, on account of their exceeding great numbers, which frequently get into the nets and destroy an entire catch of herring, haddock, and other useful fish. They have also a habit of taking all the bait, in which event they seldom leave the hooks either, and thus sadly annoy the poor fishers. When they become so numerous, there is nothing left for the fisherman to do but quit fishing for his favorite game, and turn his attention to destroying his despoilers. Great nets, specially strong for the purpose, are then shot around the school of dog-fish, and sometimes drag in as many as two thousand at a single haul.

A BOY AND MAN EATEN BY DOG-FISH.

A fisherman on the coast of Maine relates, that in the summer of 1885, a gentleman and his wife, who were spending the heated term at Town's End, came to him for a row-boat, in which they desired to ride around the bay. The little boat was anchored out a short distance

tance from shore, and the man undressed and swam out to get it, but he had gone only a few yards, his wife sitting on the shore watching him, when he gave a scream and leaped up half out of water, but in the next moment he disappeared, and nothing was seen of him again. The fisherman procured a boat, from some distance up the shore, and rowed back to the scene where the distressing accident occurred, but he could discover no signs of the unfortunate man, but saw a school of spotted dog-fish, that were so ravenous they even bit his oars. The mystery was thus explained.

An accident somewhat similar occurred the year before up the Georges. A schooner came into the bay having on board only three men and the ten year old boy of the skipper. On the evening of the schooner's arrival, by some unlucky chance, the little boy fell overboard. His father was standing near him at the time of the accident, but before he could act the little fellow was seized by a school of dog-fish and torn to pieces; so numerous were the fish that, as they attacked the boy, they appeared like an animated ball, tangled up like a thousand angle worms.

Though the flesh of the dog-fish is said to be not unpalatable, there is a prejudice against eating it, and those that are caught are used principally for fertilizing purposes. From the heart, however, is extracted a very excellent oil, and the skin is valuable for sword-handles and instrument cases.

A NOTED SWIMMER ATTACKED BY A DOG-FISH.

Few persons have not heard of Paul Boynton, who has floated down nearly all the great streams of the world in his peculiar rubber suit, and given aquatic exhibitions in the harbors of Europe, Asia, South America and the United States. Having spent so much of his time in the water it is not strange that he should have met with many adventures, dangerous as well as amusing. During one of his visits to St. Louis he related to the writer the particulars of an exciting incident which befell him while passing through the Straits of Messina, near the Italian coast, in 1882.

Boynton was passing from the town of Messina, in Sicily, to the neighboring shore of Italy, and when near the latter coast he noticed following behind, keeping pace with his own movement in the water, a fish which he thought at first was a shark, though he remarked the absence of a high dorsal fin, which is usually the first thing seen of the shark when it approaches the surface. At all times, when in salt water, the swimmer is well armed to meet the attacks which may at any time be made by some monster of the sea. On this occa-

CAPT. PAUL BOYNTON ATTACKED BY A DOG-FISH.

sion he was provided with a very large saber-like knife, which now stood him well in need.

The pursuing fish did not make itself clearly seen for some time, keeping well under water, but watchful and persistent, evidently seeking for a favorable opportunity to catch his prey at a disadvantage. Boynton placed his knife between his teeth, where it could be most readily seized, and then plied his double-bladed oar with greater vigor in the hope of shaking off his pursuer. The fish, however, was determined, and growing every moment bolder, at length swam beside him and kept a steady pace less than five yards distant. Boynton was now made acquainted with the character of his visitor, for it plainly showed itself, and he saw that the creature was a monster dog-fish, in whose green eyes was the devilish look that makes the shark so dreaded. The purpose of the flesh-loving fish was soon after exhibited, for ceasing its movements for a moment, as if gathering greater strength for the exertion, it gave a tremendous spring toward the swimmer, with horrid gaping jaws, in which gleamed several rows of dagger-like teeth. Boynton was so well prepared for the attack, however, that he received the desperate creature with a swift thrust of his knife that struck it in the head, so that its mouth closed with a loud snap short of its intended prey. Following up his advantage, Boynton plied his weapon vigorously and succeeded in not only beating off the enemy, but also in inflicting upon it such deep wounds that the fish retreated, no doubt fatally injured, for the surrounding water was dyed with blood. and the movements of the fish indicated that it was badly hurt.

TWO BOYS BESIEGED BY DOG-FISH.

In the spring of 1885, a pilot-boat was sunk off the coast of Maine, about two miles from Portland, and, lodging upon the banks, a considerable portion of the mast remained above water. One Sunday, when the sea was still, two boys rowed out to the wreck, and finding the mast solid, they got out upon it, where they fell to playing with each other until, in some manner, their boat became loosened and floated off, to their great horror. Intensely alarmed at their perilous position, they shouted in vain and waved their handkerchiefs with the hope of attracting the attention of passing vessels or some one from shore. Two hours or more were spent in this vain endeavor, when suddenly their attention was attracted to the green, shining body of a large dog-fish that swept by underneath their dangerous perch, casting up its wicked eyes as if whetting its appetite for a contemplated feast. It swam off and disappeared, but soon came back again, bringing with it a school of its horrid fellows, which now began frantic efforts to reach the terribly affrighted youths. The fish appeared to exercise the greatest reason, for, backing off, they would dart for-

PERILOUS POSITION OF TWO BOYS.

ward and leap entirely out of the water in their mad struggles to strike the boys, coming at each time within a few inches of their feet. This continued for another hour, while each minute added to the number of fish, until more than five hundred were at length besieging the boys, and their savage leaps became so terrifying that the lads could scarcely retain their position for fright.

After the adventurers had been on their perch for nearly five hours, they were discovered by a steam-vessel, that first put into port and reported the circumstance, when several row-boats were sent to their assistance. As the boats came into the school of dog-fish, they were set upon and could only be beaten off by vigorous blows from the oars wielded by the several men that came to the rescue, while two of the boats were struck so hard that their planks were sprung and they could only be kept afloat by constant bailing.

THE STURGEON.

In the Sturgeon we have a fish that possesses a cuirass almost equal to that of the alligator, and an appearance as forbidding as the shark, which it nearly rivals in size, yet it is destitute of the power or disposition to do harm. The great sturgeon, which frequently attains the length of twelve feet and a weight of one thousand pounds, is found in all the rivers that flow into the Caspian and Black Seas; and on account of its highly esteemed flesh, the caviare which is made of its eggs, and the isinglass which is made from its air-bladder, it is hunted with great persistency by Russian fishermen. The manner of taking this great fish may be described as follows:

Stakes are driven into the river-bed so as to close the stream entirely, except at one place, where an opening is left barely sufficient to let the sturgeon pass. Toward this center gate-way the dike forms an angle opposed to the current, and the opening leads into an inclosure consisting of fillets, if the time be winter, or of osier-hurdles if it be summer, and over the gate-way a scaffold is erected, on which the fish-men station themselves to look out for the fish. When it enters the opening a gate is dropped so as to prevent its return, and the bottom of the inclosure, which is movable, is raised, and the fish easily taken.

The fishermen are informed during the day of the approach of sturgeons to the inclosure by the movement they communicate to cords suspended to floating corks on the water. During the night the fish enter the inclosure, agitating by their movements other cords arranged round the hurdles. The agitation communicated to the cords is sufficient to shut the gates behind; they are thus imprisoned by the

RUSSIAN MODE OF CAPTURING THE STURGEON.

dropping of the gate, which in falling, causes a bell to ring to wake the watching fisherman on the scaffold, should he be sleeping.

Another plan of capturing sturgeons is employed in various parts of Southern Russia. A great number of fishermen assemble in their boats, and proceed abreast toward retreats of the fish, nets being spread as they row forward, until the sturgeons are completely surrounded, then by a violent beating of the water the fish are excited, and dart about until they are all fast in the nets.

Caviare is made from the roe of the sturgeon, as much as eight hundred pounds of which having been taken from a single fish. It is made by removing all the membranes, and then washing the roe in vinegar or white wine. It is next dried thoroughly, well salted, and then subjected to a strong pressure in order to force out all moisture caused by the wet-absorbing properties of the salt, and is afterward packed in kegs for sale.

In making isinglass the air-bladder is removed from the fish, washed carefully in fresh water, and then hung up for a day or two to stiffen. The outer coat of membrane then becomes separable and is peeled off, while the remainder is cut up into strips. These strips afford so large a quantity of gelatinous matter, that one part of isinglass dissolved in a hundred parts of boiling water. will form a stiff jelly when cold.

In former times the sturgeon was considered a royal dish, both in England and Rome, and in Russia to-day it is more highly esteemed than any other fish, but my opinion of it, judging by a dish of sturgeon which I ate in Moscow, is anything but favorable, and I believe it is not now eaten anywhere out of Russia.

STORIES OF THE DOLPHIN AND ITS KIN.

Having considered some of the ferocious and dangerous subjects of old ocean's melancholy dominion, let us now turn to the more placid characters, in which the spirit of revenge and the power of destruction is either wanting or of comparatively slight development. First of these, because best known and most celebrated in history, embalmed in the most beautiful legends and apothessized by the greatest of ancient poets, is the Dolphin, first cousin to the fanciful mermaid and the genius of loving devotion. By the ancients the dolphin was dedicated to Apollo, who was worshipped with extravagant ceremonials at Delphi, where he was represented as sitting upon a throne supported by dolphins, and sometimes as riding a dolphin. The name is doubtless derived, first, from Delphi, where the oracles were delivered; and second, from Dauphin, the heir apparent to the throne of France, or rather from the province of Dauphiny, from whence the title of Dauphin arose.

Dolphins are always seen in large schools, and they have a habit, not thoroughly understood, of gamboling, in which they throw themselves, by a slow plunge, so as tc show only their curved backs above the water. When thus tumbling of a clear day, they present a beautiful sight, their lustrous bodies reflecting the sheen of burnished gold, mingled with iridescent colors of bewildering splendor. There are two species, the "sea-peacock" and the "blue-fish," receiving their appellations from the variety of their gorgeous decorations. Though covered with only a slick skin, the light is decomposed when striking their bodies, almost as if it were a prism.

THE DOLPHIN.

A beautiful fish and full of grace, yet the dolphin is a most voracious creature, rarely hesitating to gratify its ravenous appetite even upon its own species, but its principal prey is the flying-fish, which it pursues with such constancy as leads to the belief that its hunger is never entirely satisfied. Captain Hall has given an excellent description of the manner in which they take the flying-fish, in the following language:

CHASED AY A DOLPHIN.

"Shortly after observing a cluster of flying-fish rise out of the water, we discovered two or three dolphins ranging past the ship in all their beauty, and watched with some anxiety to see one of those aquatic chases of which our friends, the Indiamen, had been telling us such wonderful stories. We had not long to wait, for the ship, in her progress through the water, soon put up another shoal of these little things, which, as the others had done, took their flight directly to windward. A large dolphin, which had been keeping company with us, abreast of the weather gangway, at the depth of two or three fathoms, and, as usual, glistening most beautifully in the sun, no sooner detected our poor, dear little friends take wings, than he turned his head toward them and, darting to the surface, leaped from the water with a velocity little short, it seemed, of a cannon-ball. But, although the impetus with which he shot himself into the air gave him an initial velocity greatly exceeding that of the flying-fish, the start which his fated prey had got, enabled them to keep ahead of him for a considerable time.

APOLLO RIDING THE FABLED DOLPHIN.

"The length of the dolphin's first spring could not be less than ten yards, and after he fell we could see him gliding like lightning through the water for a moment, when he again arose and shot forward with a considerably greater force than at first, and of course, to a greater distance. In this manner the merciless pursuer seemed to stride along with fearful rapidity, while his brilliant coat sparkled and flashed in the sun quite splendidly. As he fell headlong on the water at the end of each huge leap, a series of circles were sent far over the surface, which lay as smooth as a mirror.

"The group of wretched flying-fish, thus hotly pursued, at length dropped into the sea; but we were rejoiced to observe that they merely touched the top of the swell, and scarcely sank in it; at least, they instantly set off again in a fresh and more vigorous flight. It was particularly interesting to observe that the direction they now took was quite different from the one in which they had set out, implying, but too obviously, that they had detected their fierce enemy, who was following them with giant steps on the waves, and now gaining on them rapidly. His terrific pace was, indeed, two or three times as swift as theirs, poor little things.

"The greedy dolphin, however, was fully as quick-sighted as the flying-fish, which were trying to elude him, for whenever they varied their flight in the smallest degree, he lost not the tenth part of a second in shaping a new course, so as to cut off the chase; while they, in a manner not really unlike the hare, doubled back more than once on their pursuer. But it was soon too plainly to be seen that the strength and confidence of the flying-fish were fast ebbing. Their flights became shorter and shorter, and their course more fluttering and uncertain, while the enormous leaps of the dolphin appeared to grow more vigorous at each bound. Eventually, indeed, we could see, or fancied we could see, that this skillful sea-sportsman arranged all his springs with such an assurance of success, that he contrived to fall at the end of each just under the very spot on which the exhausted flying-fish was about to drop. Sometimes this catastrophe took place at too great a distance for us to see from the deck exactly what happened; but on our mounting high into the rigging, we may be said to have been in at the death, for then we could discover that the unfortunate little creatures, one after another, either popped right into the dolphin's jaws as they lighted on the water, or were snapped up instantly afterward.

"It was impossible not to take an active interest in our little friends of the weaker side, and accordingly we very speedily had our revenge. The middies and the sailors, delighted with the chance, rigged out a dozen or twenty lines from the jibboom-end and spritsail-yard-arms, with hooks baited merely with bits of tin, the glitter of which resembles so much the body and wings of the flying-fish, many a proud dolphin, making sure of a delicious morsel, leaped in rapture at the glittering prize."

THE EYED PTERACLIS.

Very closely allied to the flying-fish, and with a beauty which rivals that of any other creature of the sea, is the strange looking fish illustrated below, and known by the name of *Eyed Pteraclis*, so called on account of the dark-blue round spot found near the edge of its expansive dorsal fin. This peculiar species is found in great

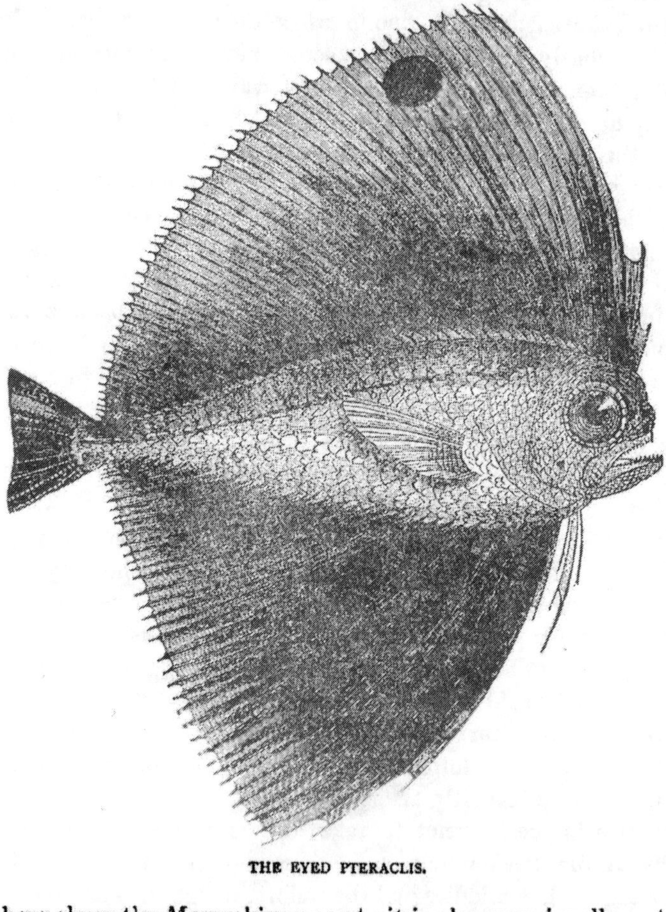

THE EYED PTERACLIS.

numbers along the Mozambique coast; it is also occasionally met with along the American shores, but not so often as to make it a well-known fish to people of our coast. In color it is somewhat like the tarpon, with beautiful, burnished sides, and a golden gleam upon the pectoral and tail fins, while its other fins are tinted with dark-blue.

LEGENDS OF THE DOLPHIN.

The reputed friendship of the Dolphin for mankind is only a sailor's fancy, and no doubt grew out of the fact that dolphins are attracted to ships just as sharks are, to feed off the refuse, or rather, the dolphin feeds off the small fishes that always follow a ship for the sweepings. The sailors were quick to notice that the shark fed equally voraciously on men or fishes, while the dolphin did not offer to molest any one who might unfortunately fall overboard; hence they regarded the dolphin as their friend and told their stories accordingly, with the *penchant* of Munchausen.

Among the authors who have sought to establish the assertion that dolphins court human society, Pausanias is conspicuous. He claims

THE CORYPHENE.

to have been an eye-witness to many of the wonderful things which he records. In one instance he says:

"I have myself seen, at Proselena, a dolphin which, wounded by a fisherman and healed by a child, display a lively gratitude; I have seen it come at the child's call, and when the latter willed, served him for a steed to go to any place he desired."

It is evident, says Mangin, that if this fact be true, the animal was not a dolphin, but perhaps a seal. "If Pausanias," remarks Boitard, "has mistaken a seal for a dolphin, his story explains itself perfectly, and may be true in every point." It might also be possible, if it related to one of the herbivorous cetacea, such as the manatee or dugong.

The name, "Sirenida," which has been bestowed upon them,

reminds us of those fabulous beings, half human, half fish, so frequently celebrated in ancient mythology. Many modern naturalists have identified with the manatee and dugong, those tritons with their wreathed shell horns, those melodious and fatally fascinating sirens, and those charmingly beautiful nereids, who have been immortalized by the poets of Greece and Rome.

Mangin remarks: "The ugly creatures which we now call the *sirenidæ* are very far apart, and inhabit very different seas from those fair creatures with loose-flowing, amber-colored tresses, azure eyes, and voice of enchanting melody, who figure so attractively in the ancient poesy. Nor may they be compared with the merman and mermaids of the Gothic fancy, the mediæval successors of the ancient tritons and sirens."

> "At night I would wander away, away;
> I would fling on each side my low flowing locks,
> And lightly vault from the throne and play
> With the mermen in and out of the rocks;
> We would run to and fro, and hide and seek,
> On the broad sea-wolds in the crimson shells,
> Whose silvery spikes are nearest the sea."

These lines of Tennyson are decidedly poetic, but if we use them to describe the dugong, the comparison destroys all the romance and very beauty of the verse.

THE CORYPHENE.

Partaking of the same nature as the dolphin, with which it is frequently confounded, is the Coryphene, a somewhat larger fish and also more beautiful; in fact, our description of the changing colors and magnificent splendor of the dolphin, applies more appropriately to the coryphene. The porpoise is also quite frequently mistaken for the dolphin, owing to the fact that their gamboling movements in the water are almost identical. One particular difference between the two is found in the fact that while the dolphin is purely carnivorous and, we may say, cleanly in its habits, the porpoise is something of a scavenger, and roots in the mud like a hog, feeding at times on worms, snails and burrowing molluscs, though it also commits great ravages among the fish. They are very sociable and are the most familiar objects one beholds at sea. During a stay of some weeks at the mouth of the Mississippi, I made several short voyages in a tug out on the Gulf of Mexico; on each trip I met great schools of porpoises and amused myself with the somewhat cruel sport of lying in the prow of the boat and shooting the animals as they rolled by within a few feet of me. But in every instance where I succeeded in hitting one—I used only a small pistol—the creature would give voice to a kind of grunt and immediately the herd would cease rising and not another would be seen until a new school appeared. The grunt was evidently a note of warning.

The manatus, dugong and lamantin are all herbivorous and their flesh is excellent food, not inferior to beef or veal. In the Malay Archi-

THE MANATUS AT HOME.

pelago the dugong principally abounds, and on account of the affection which the mother bears for its young, it is there called the "water-mother." Not only does it exhibit rare maternal devotion, but while suckling its young the mother holds it to her breast by means of her flippers in the most loving way. When attacked she covers her young with her body and will invariably sacrifice her life in its defense rather than abandon it. The three species are quite similar in their habits though confined to widely separated districts the lamantins being peculiar to the South American coast, the manatees to Africa, and the dugong to the Malay coasts. The stellar, found chiefly in the Kamtschatka seas, also resembles the dugong, but it is comparatively unknown. It is also called sea-calf, sea-cow and sea-bull, and its flesh is highly esteemed by the Kamtschatdalers, while its hide is employed for many useful purposes.

CHAPTER XVI.

MARINE MEN.

FROM a brief notice of those marine mammalia about which cluster so many wondrous stories, connecting them with the human race, we turn to a consideration of what Mangin felicitously terms *marine men*, though they are known popularly by the name *seal*, and scientifically under the classification *Phocæ*. Though we cannot truthfully picture the seal as a man winding his horn as he rushes through the water on a shell for a carriage, and dolphins for locomotion; nor as a bewitching siren chanting Orphic hymns, or combing sea-weeds out of her tangled tresses, while men looked on and died of love's raptures; but we may describe the species as a type of rare development, the amphibious carnivora of the deep, with frequent expression of countenance very like, and intelligence more strikingly, human. Writers on natural history have not failed to point out that the seal, like the dolphin and dugong, gave rise of old, and in the middle ages, to those fables which represented certain regions as inhabited by fantastic creatures, half human, half fish, or haunted by the shades of shipwrecked mariners. The fact is, that the belief in marine men and women, a belief the origin of which is lost in the night of time, has been maintained down to our own days; this not only among ignorant and superstitious fishermen, but even among very enlightened persons, whom a keen fancy for the marvelous has induced to incline a willing ear to the fables related on this subject, just as others have accredited the stories told in reference to the sea-serpent; but I shall have occasion to speak more specifically on this subject hereafter when I come to relate the superstitions of the sea.

CATCHING A MONK AT SEA.

As an evidence of the imagination, superstition and ignorance of the people of the sixteenth century, whose knowledge of natural history must have been unaccountably limited, Rondelet, a writer of that period says: "In our time there has been caught in Norway, after a great tempest, an ocean monster, to which all who saw it incontinently affixed the name 'Monk,' for it had a man's face, rustic and ungraceful, with a bald, shining head, on whose shoulders, like a monk's hood, were two winglets instead of arms; the extremity of the body terminated in a broad tail. The drawing from which I have taken the present description was given me by the very illustrious lady, Margaret of Valois, Queen of Navarre, and she received it from a gentle-

THE BEAUTIFUL CRESTED SEAL.

man who conveyed a similar one to the Emperor Charles V, then of Spain. The gentleman asserted that he had seen the monster, just as its portrait represented it, in Norway, cast on the shore by the floods and agitation of the sea, at a place named Diezes, near the town of Donelopock. I have seen a similar drawing in Rome, differing in no respect from mine. Among the marine beasts, Pliny makes mention of the marine man and the triton, as things not feigned. Pausauias also refers to the triton. I have seen the portrait of another marine monster at Rome, whither it had been sent, accompanied by letters asserting, as an indubitable fact, that such a monster, habited like a bishop, as in the portrait, had been found in Poland in the year 1331, and conveyed to the king of that county, making certain signs indicative of its great longing to return to the sea; and being carried thither, it immediately flung itself into the waves."

Even the smallest school-boy of our day could have told Rondelet that the animal which he thought so monstrous, was only a crested seal, and yet so ignorant were the people of the time that, though there were vessels crossing every sea and there was every opportunity of seeing all the different species of seals, this writer leaves us to understand that there was no man wise enough at the courts of Navarre or Spain, or among the ecclesiastical pundits of Rome, to know one of the most common of animals when they saw it.

A STRANGE VARIETY AND DOMESTIC CHARACTER OF SEALS.

The Phocæ family is divided into several species, presenting the most remarkable differences, which will be seen hereafter. Among the important species are the common seal, crested seal, sea-lion or bearded seal, marbled or leopard seal, trumpet or elephant-seal, the otary and walrus. They are familiarly called by sailors, sea-calf, sea-cow, sea-dog, sea-horse and sea-lion, being general applications without regard to species.

The entire seal family is very closely allied to our domestic animals in the development of their instincts and intelligence, and under domestication manifest the most gentle and sociable disposition. Dr. Chenu, an excellent authority, says:

"Seals live in great herds in all parts of the globe; yet it appears that most of their species vary, according as they belong to the waters of one or the other pole; for it is remarkable that they prefer cold or temperate countries to the warm climates of the Torrid Zone. It is in general among the rocks and reefs which fringe every sea, and even among the Polar ices, that we must seek for the larger species. They are skillful swimmers, though in this respect are surpassed by the cetaceans. It is a curious, but seemingly indisputable fact, that these animals, when they put to sea, ballast themselves, as is done with a ship, by swallowing a certain quantity of pebbles, which they discharge on returning to the shore. Some prefer sandy and sheltered beeches; others, rocks exposed to the action of the waters; others love to hide among the thick, tufted herbage which flourishes on the shore. On land the phocæ do not eat; therefore, if they remain for some time they grow very thin. In confinement they habitually plunge into the water to devour the food allotted to them; and they will never eat on dry ground unless accustomed to it from their earliest youth, or constrained by excessive hunger. In a state of freedom and in the sea, the seal spends nearly the whole day swimming and hunting for its prey, which principally consists of fish, molluscs and crustaceans.

"In one of his voyages, the naturalist Lesson saw a seal, which was swimming near the ship, seize upon a tern flying close to the surface of the water in company with a great number of gulls. These birds skimmed the waves, and rushed headlong upon one another to catch the *debris* of the fish which the seal devoured; the latter, quickly raising his head from the water, succeeded each time in snapping one of the birds."

MATERNAL LOVE AND SINGULAR HABITS OF THE SEAL.

From Buffon's Natural History I gather many of the following interesting facts concerning the seal:

The females produce their young in the winter, either on a sand-bank, or rock, or some small islet remote from the mainland. They suckle them for twelve or fifteen days in the place where they are born; after which the mother conducts her little ones to the sea, where she teaches them to swim and to seek their food, taking them upon her back when they become tired, where it is very amusing to see them in their clumsy efforts to maintain their places. As she rarely gives birth to more than two at a time, her cares are not overly burdensome, and she soon gives them the education which enables them to provide for themselves. Seals are naturally endowed with much sentiment and intelligence; they understand and assist each other; the young can distinguish their mother with unfailing certainty in the midst of a numerous herd; they recognize her voice, and when she calls, fly to her side with prompt obedience.

Thunder and lightning, so far from intimidating the seal, seems to have the very opposite effect, for at such times they affect the greatest exuberance of spirit. Upon the approach of a storm they leave the sea and avoid the ice-floes, where they must be uncomfortably tossed, and seek the land; here they gambol in mad antics, disporting in many clumsy ways while the rain pours down upon them They possess a prodigious quantity of blood, and as they are loaded

SEAL AND WALRUS HUNTING IN THE FROZEN SEA.

with fat from two to four inches in thickness, they are very heavy and unwieldy, and sleep much and very soundly. Their favorite basking places are the ice-floes or rocks, where the sun is strongest, and it is here that the hunters seek them. The shooting of seals is a most unprofitable means to effect their capture, for so tenacious of life are they, that in nine cases out of ten a seal will make off to the water even with a musket ball in the head. The hunter, therefore, prefers to approach them while sleeping and cut off their retreat from the water. As seals make their way on shore with great difficulty, hunters intercepting their retreat, easily knock them over with clubs.

SQUATTER SOVEREIGNTY AMONG SEALS.

"The corner or mossy rock," says an old seal hunter, "on which a phoca and his family is accustomed to repose, becomes his property as far as regards other individuals of his species, which are strangers to him. Although in the sea these animals live in numerous herds, and protect and valiantly defend each other, once emerged from their favorite element, they regard themselves on their particular rock as in a sacred domicile, where no comrade has a right to intrude upon their domestic tranquility. If one of them approach this family center, the chief—or, shall we say father?—prepares to expel by force, what he considers a foreign aggression; and there invariably takes place a terrible combat, which only ends in the death of the lord of the rock, or in the compulsory retreat of the indiscreet stranger.

"But a family never seizes upon a tract of greater extent than it absolutely requires, and lives on peaceable terms with neighborly families, that are separated from them by an interval of forty or fifty paces. If compelled by necessity, they will even dwell amicably at much narrower intervals; three or four families will share a rock, a cavern, or ice-floe; but each occupies the place allotted to it at the original partition, and shuts itself up in it, so to speak, without ever meddling with individuals of another family."

A GIGANTIC LEAP AND TERRIBLE COMBATS.

On several occasions, during the visits I have made to San Francisco, I amused myself by watching the great number of seals which disport and bask themselves on the rocks opposite what is known as the "cliffs:" I know of no other place in the world where these intelligent creatures may be better viewed than at the "San Francisco

Seal-Rocks." I have seen hundreds of seals in every condition of size, character and disposition, at one time on the three rocks which

THE GREAT SEAL ROCKS, OFF SAN FRANCISCO.

rise up out of the ocean nearly one hundred feet, and have been delightfully entertained by their variable moods and ludicrous actions.

On one occasion I remember having seen a seal, evidently an imitator of Sam Patch, climb with no little exertion to the very apex of the loftiest of the three rocks referred to, and raising his head in an imperious, look-at-me manner, he barked loudly, and then flung himself into the sea, a sheer descent of one hundred feet. The object of this queer antic I could not understand, especially since there was no collection taken up for his benefit, but must still suppose that he was prompted by a spirit of bravado to attempt so remarkable a feat.

That seals are extremely sociable in their relations to each other, is beyond contradiction, but they are quick to resent an insult, and know well how to use the weapons nature has given them. Those who delight in the barbaric sport of fighting, may, any clear day of summer or fall, witness the bloodiest of combats on the seal-rocks. I have watched, with reprehensible interest, such battle between seals as I never saw take place among other animals; a fight between great lions is hardly more terrific than an engagement between large seals. They advance with eyes flashing fire and heads reared to the utmost, and coming together, they worry each other like dogs with their powerful teeth, nor give the lightest blows with their flippers, giving voice all the while to a kind of growling bark, which seems to come from the stomach, deep and awful. This applies more appropriately to the sea-lions, the seal proper being a very much smaller animal, and much less disposed to angry disputations, and it is also more easily domesticated.

While passing through the Baltic sea, on a voyage from Hull to St. Petersburg, one beautiful day, my attention was attracted to several objects in the water some distance ahead of our steamer. As we approached nearer I was fairly beside myself with astonishment at what I verily believed to be, at first, a party of men in bathing, so far from shore that no land was visible. The idea that they were seals did not occur to me, and the illusion was most perfect. The sea was unruffled by a single wave, and the seals, perhaps a dozen, were moving slowly, their heads only above water, looking, at the distance I was from them, exactly like men. At the first suggestion of seals I immediately saw my mistake, but their resemblance to human beings was not lost even when we came up within a hundred yards of them, and I then perceived how naturally the supersition of mermen and mermaids originated.

ADVENTURES IN HUNTING THE SEAL.

The marbled or crested seal, sometimes also called the Greenland seal, and by the Esquimaux, "Neitsersoak," is the most valuable animal the Arctic natives hunt; its flesh affords them excellent food; its fur provides them with the warmest of clothing, and is also used to cover the little kayaks, or boats, which they dexterously use even in tempestuous seas; of the stomach air-buoys are made, which the Esquimau fastens to his lance to float it after it is struck into his prey, and even the teeth are not valueless, for with them the Greenlander heads his spears, and the females sometimes use them for decorating their persons.

There are two methods employed by the natives of the far north in capturing the crested seal, both popular and yet so radically different in the spirit and result, that it is to be wondered why one has not long since superseded the other; they may be briefly described as follows:

Seals are in the habit of excavating considerable cavities in the thick ice, and leaving a kind of shelf upon which to repose; by moving their bodies, in some manner not yet explained, these excavations are made quite round and smooth and are sometimes four and even five feet above the surface of the water. Notwithstanding this slippery doorway, the seal bobs up and climbs the walls without any difficulty. Many of these seal-holes are covered with an incrustation of snow, and this fact is a great aid to the hunter, who can approach without detection, and taking up his position over the hole he waits with unexampled patience the coming of his prey. A seal may leave its hole and remain away for twelve hours or more at a time, but the patient hunter knows it will return, and is contented to cover up his feet and legs and bundle himself for a twelve-hour wait. During all this time he must remain perfectly quiet and hold his lance constantly in position for a blow; the least noise will frighten the animal away, for it is wary almost beyond belief. Its presence at the hole is detected by a slight scratching noise, hearing which the hunter drives his lance through the crust and into the seal, usually striking its head.

The second mode, which seems to be altogether more superior to the first, though it is not more popular, is as follows: Proceeding on the hunt with sledge and dogs, the Esquimau approaches the basking-grounds with great circumspection, and the moment he comes in sight of seals, leaves his sledge and creeps along with the greatest possible care toward his game, moving not only very slowly, but in a position as nearly prostrate as possible. The moment he perceives the animal betray signs of suspicion he lies flat upon the ice until the seal becomes quiet again and reposes itself. The man cannot thereafter crawl as he did before, but must imitate the actions of a seal, which the Greenlanders manage to do with wonderful fidelity; he tumbles and shifts himself like a seal moving its position, but by each movement he continues to approach a little closer, or rather, between the animal and its hole, from which it never strays far. If the hunter succeeds in cutting off the seal's retreat, his success is certain, for the poor animal cannot make fast progress on the ice, nor has it any weapons with which to defend itself against the hunter's clubs and spears.

ANECDOTES OF THE SEAL'S SAGACITY.

Seals are persevering hunters of fish, and their depredations among the salmon fisheries are terrible. Not only are they the most expert of swimmers and catch their prey in a fair chase, but they haunt the fishing-nets and sometimes devour nearly all the catch. These crafty animals have been known to remain by the fishing-nets an entire season, rarely taking a fish outside the meshes, and at the conclusion of the season leave the locality with the business-like characteristics of the fishermen themselves.

Wood says there is a curious tradition among the inhabitants of the Irish coast respecting the seal, which constantly haunts the same spot through a series of years. They think that the animal is supernaturally protected from harm of any kind — that bullets will not strike him however well the gun be aimed; that steel will not enter his body, however keen the blade or strong the arm that wields it; and that the long array of nets are powerless to retain so puissant a being in their manifold meshes. So after a while a seal, if it be only bold and wary, may lead a luxurious life at the fisherman's cost, for no one will venture to attack an animal that has a charmed life.

Fortunately for the seals in general, they are not often visited by the wrath of those they rob, for there is a feeling prevalent among fishermen, that to kill a seal brings misfortune upon the slayer. This idea does not find acceptance beyond the fishermen, for no animal is more remorselessly pursued than the seal, whose soft fur constitutes a source of such infinite delight and envy among ladies.

HOW SEALS ARE CAPTURED.

The customary manner of taking the fur-bearing seal is for the hunters to land quietly, cut off the seals from the water, and then dispatch them with blows from a bludgeon across their nose When driven to desperation they fight savagely but fruitlessly among experienced seal hunters. The animal has a very awkward and no less singular habit when trying to effect its escape, of lying partially on its side and scratching furiously with its fore paws, when, if rushed upon, it tries to fling itself upon the intruder and bear him down. Should the land upon which it is reposing be covered with pebbles, the hunter had better keep well in front of the animal, for in its leaping, caterpillar motion, it flings the stones behind it with great violence, capable of doing serious injury to a man.

Much sea-craft is required for the chase of the seal, as well as considerable knowledge of its habits. It is a remarkable fact, that if the seal be disturbed while the tide is ebbing, it will always make its way seaward, but if alarmed while the tide is flowing, it will direct its course landward. The seal is also a good barometer, and by its movements indicates to the practiced eye the forthcoming changes in the weather. Whenever an old seal is seen rolling and tumbling along a bank, a storm of wind and rain is sure to ensue before many hours are passed.

Nearly every species of seal is fond of musical sounds, and it has been frequently known to follow boats in which musical instruments were being played. Some persons have gone so far in their opinions of the seal's love for music as to seriously recommend that hunters employ pipers to go with them and lure the animal, asserting, at the same time, that the bag-pipe is more seductive to seals than any other instrument. Those who throw out such suggestions are evidently Highlanders, or else they wilfully design to traduce a helpless animal against which they have no right to hold such malice.

The common seal is, as before stated, easily tamed, and quickly becomes one of the most docile of creatures, exhibiting marked affection for its human friends, and a loving and gentle disposition, equally as great as the dog or cat. Many of these animals have been captured when young, and so thoroughly domesticated that they regarded themselves as members of the household, and would lie beside the fireside with the easy indifference of a tabby. An interesting account of the taming of a seal is given as follows:

A PET SEAL.

"When a boy I was presented by some fishermen with a young seal, perhaps not more than a fortnight old. In a few weeks it became so perfectly tame and domesticated that it would follow me about, eat from my hand, and showed unmistakable signs of recognition and attachment whenever I approached. It was fond of warmth, and would lie for hours at the kitchen fire, raising its head to look at every newcomer, but never attempted to bite, and would nestle quite close to the dogs, who soon became quite reconciled to their new friend.

"Unfortunately, the winter after I obtained it, the weather was unusually rough and stormy. Upon that wild coast boats could seldom put to sea, and the supply of fish became scanty and precarious. We were obliged to substitute milk in its place, of which the seal consumed large quantities, and as the scarcity of other food still continued, it was determined in a family council that it should be consigned to its own element, to shift for itself. Accompanied by a clergyman, who took great interest in my pet, I rowed out for a couple of miles to sea, and dropped it quickly overboard. Very much to our astonishment, however, we found that it was not easy to shake off. Fast as we pulled away it swam still faster after the boat, crying so loudly all the time that it might easily have been heard a mile away, and so pitifully that we were obliged to take it in again and bring it home, where, after this new proof of attachment, it lived in clover for several months. It might still be in existence but for the untimely fate which most pets are doomed sooner or later to experience, and to which this one was no exception."

Another story, very similar to the above, is related in "Maxwell's Wild Sports," where a young seal was taken and tamed by a lady who had a great love for pets. It is told that the seal lived in the family for many years, until its familiarity became unpleasant, when, to get rid of it, a man was engaged to take it far out to sea with the hope that it might again make its home in the ocean; what was the family's surprise to see the seal next morning lying peacefully beside the fireplace, having effected an entrance into the house through an open window. Some months after, during the winter season, the seal was again taken off, this time several miles distant, and thrown into the sea. The following night was wild and stormy, but the poor seal contrived to find its way through the driving waves and blinding snow back to its beloved home. It searched in vain for some hole through which to reach its sleeping place again, but finding none, it returned to the door, and there laid and cried, unheard by its mistress, until the bitter cold froze out its affectionate life.

A FIGHT WITH A MOTHER SEAL.

A story is also told in the same work somewhat as follows: A number of men had gone in a boat to the Sound of Achil, and having seen a seal and her young one reposing on the sand, had borrowed an old musket and set off to attack them. They succeeded in securing the cub before it could reach the sea, and tossed it into their boat. The mother seal, however, inspired by maternal love, swam after the boat that contained her offspring, and could not be deterred from following the captors, in the hope of rescuing her child. The men attempted several times to shoot the poor creature, but their rusty weapon would not explode until it had been snapped a number of times; the weapon was finally discharged, and the bullet lodged in the creature's head. Life being apparently extinct, the mother was lifted into the boat, but at this moment she recovered from the stunning effects of the shot and made a furious attack upon her enemies, floundering about so violently as to threaten to upset the boat, and snapping savagely at the men. At such close quarters, and several in the boat, the seal had a decided advantage, which she was pressing, and would have no doubt killed one or more of her assailants had not aid from a neighboring boat reached them when it did.

The Harp or Atak-seal, so-called from the singular coloring of the fur on its back, is most common along the Greenland coast, and on account of the very rich oil it yields is regarded as being most valuable, commercially, of all the species. Two harp-seals were placed in the zoological garden of Paris, where they soon left off their shyness and manifested the greatest docility, allowing even strangers to caress them, and showing much pleasure at having their heads rubbed. Two small dogs were put in the pen with them, and it was amusing to see how grateful they were to have them for companions. The seals were now large, and would brook no familiarities from other members of the seal family that shared their quarters, but they immediately formed an attachment for the dogs really beautiful to see. The four slept together and ate from the same dishes; in fact, it was no uncommon thing to see one of the dogs seize and take from the seal a piece of food already in its mouth. The dogs would perch on their big friends' backs and bark at visitors, and often, in playfulness, would bite the seals; but these familiarities were not resented, and when the dogs made their way to another apartment, which they were able to do, the seals would try their utmost to follow, and betray great uneasiness until their little companions returned.

THE GREAT SEA-HORSE.

What I have written concerning seals applies generally to the several species, except my references to the domesticity of the animals, which has immediate reference to the common seals. The elephant-seal and the walrus, though belonging to the Phocæ family are so distinct in certain features and habits as entitles them to separate mention. I might also explain that the sea-lion proper is far different from the animal exhibited in menageries and zoological gardens as such, as we shall hereafter see, and I therefore prefer to treat them separately.

Of all the Phocine family none presents so terrible and grotesque an appearance as the gigantic Walrus, also known under the names of morse and sea-horse. The most striking feature of this great animal is its grizzly head, bristling muzzle and immense canine teeth, which are developed into mighty tusks, growing straight downward from the upper jaw. These fearful weapons attain a length of two feet, and measure at the base as much as seven inches in circumference; and sometimes weigh ten pounds. They are the finest quality of ivory, and constitute an article of considerable commercial value. By reason of the enormous size of these teeth, which are deeply imbedded in the upper jaw, the nose is abnormally enlarged, imparting to the beast much of its ferocious aspect.

"The Walrus," says Marmier, "is a shapeless, unwieldy beast, from twelve to fifteen feet long, and eight to ten in circumference. Its thick hide is covered with hair; under this skin stretches a thick layer of fat, which protects the animal against the rigors of winter. Frequently the walruses lie in great numbers along the banks of ice, motionless and piled pell-mell one upon another. Bnt one of them, during their repose, enacts the part of sentinel; at the slightest appearance of danger it precipitates itself into the waves. All the others immediately attempt to follow; but in this critical moment the slowness of their movements sometimes produces the most grotesque scenes. In the confused state in which they have been lying, it is with difficulty they disengage themselves from the masses of heavy flesh which enclose them on every side. Some roll awkwardly into the water; others crawl painfully along the ice. The weight of their bodies and the enormous disproportion of their limbs render all move-

WALRUS, SEA-LION AND SEALS.

ments upon the ice extremely difficult for them. But as soon as these ungainly animals are in the water, they resume all their vigor, and if attacked defend themselves with astonishing courage.

"At times they themselves begin to fight; they dart upon the fishermen's boats, seizing the gunwales with their long, hook-like teeth, and draw them furiously toward them. At times they glide under the skiff and endeavor to capsize it. Their hardy, scaly skin resists the blows of pike and spear, and it is neither without difficulty nor danger that the poor fishermen escape from such formidable adversaries. In these desperate combats the walruses are generally led by a chief, who is easily recognized by his great size and impetuous ardor. If the fishermen succeed in killing him, at that instant all his comrades abandon the struggle, gather round him, support him, by means of their teeth, on the surface of the water, and drag him in all haste far from the attacking boats and out of peril.

DESPERATE BRAVERY OF THE WALRUS.

But the most impressive and dramatic scene is when the walruses fight to secure their young. Generally they attempt to deposit them on a bank of ice, in order that they themselves may be left to fight more freely without injuring their young. If the mothers have not sufficient time to place their offspring in a remote place of safety, they take them under their paws, clasp them to their breast, and throw themselves with desperate audacity against the fishermen's boats. The young walruses exhibit a similar devotion and intrepidity when their parents are in peril. They have been known, when placed apart in security, boldly to quit the asylum chosen for them by anxious affection, and take their share in the struggle in which the mother was engaged, to sustain her efforts and participate in her dangers.

Captain Cook, who, by the way, was the first to give any correct account of the habits of the walrus, which previous to his time was regarded with no little superstition, thus describes an incident illustrative of the great affection which the walrus has for its young.

* * * "We hoisted out the boats and sent them in pursuit of the sea-horses that surrounded us. Our people were more successful than they had been before, returning with three large ones and a young one. On the approach of our boats toward the ice, they took all their cubs beneath their fins and endeavored to escape with them into the sea. Several, whose young ones were killed or wounded, and were left floating on the surface, rose again and carried them down, just as our people were upon the point of taking them into the boat, and they might be traced bearing them a great distance through the water,

which was colored with their blood. We afterward observed them bringing their young up at times above the surface, as if for air, and again diving under it with a dreadful bellowing. The female in particular, whose young had been destroyed and taken into the boat, became so enraged that she attacked the cutter and struck her teeth through the bottom of it."

The walrus is not without curiosity, but it never becomes imprudently so. Sailors who hunt the animal for its oil and ivory, tell wonderful stories of its remarkable sagacity. In approaching the animal in a boat it will sometimes manifest great surprise and gaze at the crew with wondering eyes, but in such cases the mothers will keep their young well in hand, so to speak, holding them carefully by their flippers, and when they anticipate danger will push their offspring under water, and hold it out of sight till their fears subside.

CUNNING OF THE POLAR-BEAR.

Aside from man the walrus has a dangerous enemy, and one, too, that gives him fair battle with results that vary; this bold desperado is the Polar-Bear, whose existence is maintained in the frozen regions, where his life is almost a continual battle. Knowing his power, the walrus regards the bear with great dread, so that in order to reach his elephantine prey, bruin resorts to some very cunning schemes, one of which is told in the following language:

"One sunshiny day one of these animals, about ten feet in length, rose in a pool of water not very far from us, and after looking round, drew his greasy carcass upon the ice, where he rolled about for a time, and at length laid himself down to sleep. A bear, which had probably been observing his movements, crawled carefully upon the ice on the opposite side of the pool, and began to roll about also, but apparently more from design than amusement, as he progressively lessened the distance between him and his prey. The walrus, suspicious of his advances, drew himself up preparatory to a precipitate retreat into the water, in case of a nearer acquaintance with his playful but treacherous visitor. On this the bear became instantly motionless as if in the act of sleep, but after a time began to lick his paws and clean himself, encroaching occasionally a little more on his intended prey. But even this artifice did not succeed; the wary walrus was far too cunning to allow himself to be entrapped, and suddenly plunged into the pool, which the bear no sooner observed than he threw off all disguise, rushed toward the spot, and followed him in an instant into the water, where he was as much disappointed in his meal as we were of the pleasure of witnessing a very interesting encounter."

FIGHTS BETWEEN THE WALRUS AND THE POLAR-BEAR

Although the polar-bear will attack the walrus with the view of making a meal of him, such attacks develop into combats that are by no means one-sided. The bear fights for food, while the walrus fights for life, and a desperate engagement it invariably proves to be. The tactics of the bear are to seize the walrus from behind and worry him to exhaustion, but, though clumsy, the walrus usually manages to keep its quarters well protected, until the bear becomes very much enraged and rushes in to fight at close quarters; it is now that the combat becomes interesting, but terrible. As the bear leaps toward the walrus, the latter tries to receive him on its two powerful teeth, which is frequently accomplished; but the bear is not easily killed, and survives the most astonishing wounds; the bodies of the two are soon covered with blood, and they become so maddened that neither will give up the contest until death ends the struggles of one. After killing a bear, the victorious walrus has been seen to drive its tusks into the dead body, as if it could not satisfy its bitter revenge. When the bear wins, he usually forthwith begins his feast, regardless of his numerous and sometimes fatal wounds, and eats up to the very moment that death claims him.

DREADFUL COMBAT WITH WALRUSES.

Owing to the difficulty of securing the body after the animal is shot, in the water, walrus hunters employ means to come up with their game and knock it in the head, or harpoon it. The dangers encountered in such sport are quite enough to deter any but those with stout hearts, as will be seen by frequent instances where men have lost their lives in pursuit of walruses, only one of which I have room here to record.

A large herd of walruses being discovered gamboling on an ice-floe, two boats were dispatched from the ship to go after them; each boat contained six men armed with harpoons and clubs, but no guns, as these weapons are not in favor with the hunters. After proceeding to within two hundred yards of the herd, a single walrus came up within a few feet of the bow of the advance boat, and offered such an excellent target, that a harpoon was thrown which struck it near the shoulder and remained fast. The animal made a noise indicative of

A BATTLE WITH WALRUSES.

great distress, and dived to a considerable depth, reappearing some distance away in company with three others. A singular thing now took place; there was apparently a council of war hastily held by the hundreds of walruses that were on the ice-floe, and in a few moments they all plunged into the water and made all possible speed for the

ESQUIMAU WALRUS HUNTER.

boats. Seeing an advancing host of such powerful creatures, the men became much alarmed, and would fain have put back for the ship, but their course was speedily intercepted, and one of the most terrible of all battles began. The walruses threw themselves with unexampled fury on the boats and received the blows that were showered on them without quailing for an instant. Every man felt that his life depended upon his ability to beat back an enemy far more powerful than he, under the circumstances against which he was contending. As the animals that attacked the boat were struck back by telling blows from the men, others would fairly climb over the sinking bodies, their gaping mouths, fiery eyes, dreadful tusks, ponderous bulks, and horrifying growls, inspiring a terror greater than words can express. The contest could not continue long, as the number of walruses constantly increased and a casualty to the boats was certain soon to occur, from some of the strokes made against them by the vicious and fury-driven animals. The men fought as never men fought before, plying their heavy cudgels with great effectiveness, but apparently in no wise diminishing the army that had attacked them.

That portion of the crew remaining with the ship saw the peril of their companions and quickly made ready two more boats, while the ship herself was moved up, so that from her decks the fight, which was now defensive, might be waged in greater safety. Before the other boats came up, however, a dreadful event had happened: the gunwale of one of the boats had been torn off and the water poured in so that it soon filled, and the poor unfortunate occupants were at the mercy of their tormentors. It was the work of a moment for the numberless walruses to fall upon the men and fairly rend them to pieces, like so many wolves set upon a stricken deer. Their fury was so concentrated upon the men in the water that they left the other boat and thus permitted it to row away, and the men in it were saved, but at the expense of their comrades' lives.

This painfully thrilling event occurred off the coast of Greenland in 1856, since which time there has been much greater caution used by walrus hunters, and such a serious casualty has not been repeated to my knowledge.

The usual mode of hunting the walrus now is with dogs, which are trained to attack them on the ice, and so disperse the herd that they cannot make a simultaneous charge upon the hunters. Such a chase is called a "cut," which is sometimes so successful that fifteen hundred or two thousand are killed out of a single herd.

THE SEA-ELEPHANT--A VERITABLE MONSTER.

Though not exactly a prototype of the land-elephant, the Sea-Elephant is well named and is a likely first-cousin of the greatest of land quadrupeds. Large specimens of this monstrous seal measure as much as thirty feet in length and eighteen feet in circumference, a prodigy much larger than the mightiest Jumbo, or the Mastodon of Petersburg.

The sea-elephant is an inhabitant of the southern hemisphere, where it is found over a wide range, and is extensively hunted on account of the vast amount of oil which its body yields. This animal not only resembles the land-elephant by its snout, which bears some analogy to the proboscis of the elephant, and from which it takes its name, but in habit there is also a marked similarity. Unlike all other members of the seal family, the sea-elephant is not confined to the sea, but is particularly fond of fresh water lakes and swampy

THE MONSTER SEA - ELEPHANT.

places, where it feeds on both fish and vegetables, though generally speaking, it is a carnivorous animal.

About June the females bear their young, during which time they retire inland and remain to nurse their offspring for two months. It is stated by naturalists as a fact that the males form a cordon about the females and compel them to care for the young, which they would otherwise desert, a statement which I can scarcely reconcile with female nature.

The sea-elephant is a polygamous animal, and takes his consorts by conquest. The season of courtship begins immediately after the young are brought to the sea, usually about two months after birth, and is a period of battle in which the males all participate until there is a settlement of the question as to which are strongest and which weakest. The former then proceed to select their several wives from the females that have been watching the fight; after the victors conclude their selections the vanquished are allowed to select from those "left over." The sea-elephant is a very tyrant over his harem; he has the virtue which many husbands lack; he will not obtrude upon another's family nor will he abandon his females in the hour of greatest danger. Knowing this fact, the seal hunters always direct their attacks against the females, being sure to capture the male afterward. If they were to kill the male first his harem would disperse like inconstant creatures detected in their guilt, or like bond-women to whom the door of freedom was accidentally opened.

Although these animals are of great dimensions and bodily strength, and are furnished with a very formidable set of teeth, they are not nearly such dangerous antagonists as the walrus. When roused from sleep they open their mouths in a threatening manner, but more for the purpose of frightening than attacking their enemies, for if the latter do not flee, the animal, more accommodating, will flee itself.

CURIOSITIES OF THE SEA-ELEPHANT.

Wood says: "The extraordinary development of the nose, which gives so weird-like a character to the aspect of the elephant-seal, is only found in the adult males, and even in them is not very perceptible unless the animal is alarmed or excited. While the creature is undisturbed, the nose only looks peculiarly large and heavy; as soon, however, as the animal becomes excited, it protrudes this proboscis-like nose, blows through it with great violence, and assumes a very formidable appearance. The female is entirely destitute of this structure, and except for its enormous dimensions might be mistaken for an ordinary seal. In the male it does not appear until the third year.

"The elephant-seal is easily tamed when taken young, and displays great affection toward a kind master. One of these animals was tamed by an English seaman, and would permit its master to mount upon its back, or to put his hand into its mouth without doing him any injury."

The trumpet-seal is also provided with a proboscis which is more elephantine than that of the elephant-seal itself. It derives its name from the trumpet-like sound of its voice, which is very sonorous and deep, and in the mating season may be heard for a distance of two miles.

THE SEA-BEAR.

The Ursine Seal, or Sea-Bear, is the most valuable, commercially, of the phocine family, and, strange enough, it is also the most numerous. In size it is not nearly so great as other species, but the limbs are much better developed and it can travel faster. It takes its name from a fancied resemblance to the bear, but the likeness is not noticeable to an ordinary observer. The color of its fur is very pleasing, the longj hairs being of a grayish-brown, while the thick, soft wool which lies next to the skin is a reddish-brown. When the skin is dressed the long hairs are removed and the wool only left, which constitutes the seal-skin of commerce.

THE TRUMPET-SEAL.

The sea-bear is a native of the cold regions, being found in greatest numbers on the coast of Kamtschatka and the Kurile Islands, where they congregate in such vast herds during summer as to fairly blacken the banks which they haunt. Like others of the family, the sea-bear is polygamous and a squatter sovereign, choosing his domain and suffering no encroachments thereon. As the number of females playing the part of consorts to the male is from forty to fifty, on an average, and the offspring of such family is usually more than one hundred, it will be seen that their reproduction is very rapid, partially justifying the great slaughter which is practiced by seal companies every year.

CHAPTER XVII.

THE MIGHTY POLAR-BEAR.

I HAVE preferred to include a description of the Polar, or Greenland Bear, in the first department of this book, because he is a sea-animal to the extent of living in the ocean a great portion of his life, and finding nearly all his subsistence by fishing. His natural home seems to be the ice, and his delight is greatest when surveying the landscape of driving floes, watching for his favorite prey, the seal. Three and even four hundred miles from the nearest land, he may frequently be seen riding on fields of ice, careless of threatening storms or approaching ice-bergs, that any minute may destroy his footing and leave him floundering in the sea; for he is almost equally at home in the water. Not only can the polar-bear swim without fatigue, but he can dart through the water and dive so deep, swiftly and unerring, that he is as perfect in fishing as the otter, and if left miles from land in the ocean, he could still find food abundant.

Nature has singularly endowed the polar-bear, making it one of the most remarkable of animals. In size it surpasses all others of the ursine family, possibly excepting the grizzly, while in activity its superiority must be acknowledged. Cast by nature in a rigorous district of the world, where the food supply must, from the very nature of things, at times become precarious, this animal has been given the power to subsist upon its own fat to a much greater extent than is seen in other hibernating animals. Sometimes raging storms sweep along the ice-ribbed shores for weeks, during which time the seals remain close within their caves, and the fish seek the quiet of great depths. Cut off from his supply of food, the polar-bear loses his appetite, as it were, and fasts without inconvenience until such time as his accustomed prey is again obtainable.

Of the habits of the polar-bear, Scoresby, the distinguished whaler and explorer, says:

"This formidable animal is, among quadrupeds, the sovereign of the Arctic countries. He is powerful and courageous; savage and sagacious; apparently clumsy, and yet not inactive. His senses are

THE POLAR-BEAR IN HIS CHOSEN HAUNTS.

extremely acute, especially his sight and smell. As he traverses extensive fields of ice, he mounts the hummocks and looks around for prey; or, rearing his head and snuffing the breeze, he perceives the scent of the carrion of the whale at an immense distance. A piece of kreng — fleshy part of the whale after the blubber is removed — thrown into the fire will draw him to a ship from the distance of miles. The kreng of the whale, however offensive to a human nose, is to him a banquet. Seals seem to be his most usual food; yet from the extreme watchfulness of these creatures he is often, it is believed, kept fasting for weeks together. He seems to be equally at home on the ice as on the land. He is found on field-ice over two hundred miles from the shore. He can swim with the velocity of three miles an hour, and can accomplish some leagues without much inconvenience. He dives to a considerable distance when in pursuit of his prey, but only when forced to. Near the east coast of Greenland they have been seen on the ice in such vast numbers as to appear like a large flock of sheep.

The extraordinary power of the polar-bear may be estimated by considering the following facts: The usual size of this animal is eight feet in length and nearly as much in circumference, while its height is from four to five feet, but Barentz, in 1596 — a long while ago — killed two bears, one of which measured twelve and the other thirteen feet in length, and their weight was nearly a ton each. Bears are not nearly so large now as they were three hundred years ago, judging by the size of those which Barentz killed, but they are still large enough to do infinite mischief. Those which measure eight feet in length have a paw seven inches broad, with claws two inches long, while their canine teeth, exclusive of the portion embedded in the jaw, are about an inch and a half in length. Having an amazing strength of jaw, they have been known to bite a lance in two, though made of iron, half an inch in diameter, or at least this fact is asserted by Scoresby.

DANGERS OF ATTACKING A POLAR-BEAR

The polar-bear may be captured in the water without subjecting one's self to great danger; but on the ice he has such powers of resistance that the experiment is extremely hazardous. When pursued and attacked he will invariably turn upon his enemies; and if struck with a lance he is apt to seize it in his mouth, and either bite it in two or wrest it from the hand. If shot with a ball, unless he is struck in the head or heart, or in the shoulder, he is enraged rather than depressed, and falls with increased fury upon his pursuers. When shot at a distance, and able to escape, he has been observed to retire to the shelter of an ice hummock, and, as if conscious of the styptical effect of cold, apply snow to the wound with his paws.

A curious fact concerning the bear is the palatableness of all its flesh, while the liver, usually a dainty morsel in other animals, is so deleterious that many sailors have died from the effects of eating it, while others have suffered the loss of the outer cuticle, which peels off as if blistered.

Scoresby relates several anecdotes of the polar-bear, some of which are worthy of transcription to these pages.

INTELLIGENCE OF THE POLAR-BEAR.

"The captain of one of the whalers being anxious to procure a bear without wounding the skin, made trial of the stratagem of laying the noose of a rope in the snow, and placing a piece of kreng within it. A bear ranging the neighboring ice was soon enticed to the spot by the smell of burning meat. He perceived the bait, approached and seized it in his mouth; but his foot, at the same moment, by a jerk of the rope, became entangled in the noose; he pushed it off with the other paw, and deliberately retired. After having eaten the piece he carried away with him, he returned. The noose, with another piece of kreng, being then replaced, he pushed the rope aside and again walked triumphantly off with the bait. A third time the noose was laid; but excited to caution by the evident observation of the bear, the sailors buried the rope beneath the snow, and laid the kreng in a deep hole dug in the center. The bear once more approached, and the sailors were assured of their success. But bruin, more sagacious than they expected, after snuffing about the place for a few moments, scraped the snow away with his paw, threw the rope aside, and again escaped unhurt with his prize.

"In the month of June, 1812, a female bear, with two cubs, approached the ship I commanded, and was shot. The cubs, not attempting to escape, were taken alive. These animals, though at first evidently very unhappy, became at length, in some measure, reconciled to their situation, and, being tolerable tame, were allowed occasionally to go at large about the deck. While the ship was moored to a floe, a few days after they were taken, one of them, having a rope fastened round its neck, was thrown overboard. It immediately swam to the ice, got upon it, and attempted to escape. Finding itself, however, detained by the rope, it endeavored to disengage itself in the following ingenious way: Near the edge of the floe was a crack in the ice, of a considerable length, but only eighteen inches or two feet wide, and three or four feet deep. To this spot the bear repaired; and when on crossing the chasm, the bight of the rope fell into it, he placed himself across the opening; then, suspending himself by his hind feet, with a leg on each side, he dropped his head and most of his body, into the chasm, and with a foot applied to each side of the neck, attempted for some moments

A HUNTER MANGLED BY A POLAR-BEAR.

to push the rope over his head. Finding this scheme ineffectual, he removed to the main ice, and running with great impetuosity from the ship, gave a remarkable pull on the rope; then going backward a few steps he repeated the jerk. At length, after repeated attempts to escape this way, every failure of which he announced by a significant growl, he yielded himself to his hard necessity, and lay down on the ice in angry and sullen silence."

MANGLED BY A POLAR-BEAR.

Continuing his remarks on the sagacity and ferocity of the polar-bear, Scoresby relates the following:

"Two of the crew of a vessel which had anchored near Nova Zembla, landed on an island at the mouth of the Weigats, and impelled by curiosity, wandered some distance from the beach; but while unconscious of danger, one of them was suddenly seized on the back by a bear, and brought to the earth. His companion ran off and gave the alarm, and a party of shipmates came to his assistance. The bear stood over its prey during their approach, without the least appearance of fear; and on their attack, sprung upon one of their number, and made him also a victim to its ferocity and power. The rest now fled in confusion, and could not be induced to renew the conflict. Three sailors only among the crew had sufficient courage to combat with this formidable animal; they attacked it, and after a dangerous struggle, killed it, and rescued the mangled bodies of their two unfortunate shipmates."

BATTLES WITH THE POLAR-BEAR.

Captain Cook, of the *Archangel*, landed on the coast of Spitzbergen, accompanied by his surgeon and mate. While traversing the shores a bear suddenly sprang up from a hummock, where it was concealed, and seized the captain between its powerful jaws. At this juncture, when a moment of hesitation must prove fatal, with rare presence of mind the captain shouted to his surgeon to fire, who, with admirable resolution so speedily obeyed the order, that he shot the bear through the brain before it had time to do the captain serious injury.

Captain Hawkins met with a similar danger, from which he as providentially escaped. Discovering a bear on a cake of ice, in Davis' Strait, he took a boat and rowed out to it. Upon reaching the bear, which appeared unconcerned for its safety, the captain struck his lance twice into its breast, but instead of the wounds intimidating or badly injuring the animal, they only served to enrage it, for in a trice it seized the weapon, and jumping into the boat, bit the captain savagely in the thigh, and then threw him over its head into the water. Singularly enough, the bear did not follow up the attack as is its custom, but leaping into the water itself, on the other side, made off while the other men in the boat were giving their attention to the rescue of their captain.

Captain Scoresby tells another curious story, illustrating the bear's insensibility to danger, from which I condense: A boat's crew attacked a bear in the Spitzbergen sea, with harpoons and lances, but

POLAR - BEAR AND WALRUS FIGHTING.

so far from disabling the animal, it turned savagely upon its enemies and continued to climb into the boat, whereupon the crew speedily betook themselves to the water, so that the tables were completely turned. To keep from drowning the poor fellows clung to the rings of the boat, from which chilling position bruin did not attempt to drive them, but contented itself with a seat in the stern of the boat, where it sat fairly laughing at its enemies' discomfiture. Another boat crew at length came to the rescue of their companions, and shot the bear as it sat staring at them.

WONDERFUL MATERNAL LOVE MANIFESTED BY A BEAR.

The female has her young in the month of March, and generally brings forth two at a time, which are remarkably small. The attachment she has for her young inspires her with a courage well worthy of admiration. The following occurrence was observed by the frigate on which the famous Nelson began his naval career. This frigate was in the polar regions, in 1773. At day-break, one morning, three bears were seen from the top of the mast coming very quickly over the ice toward the vessel. The men made out that it was a female accompanied by two young bears almost as strong as their mother. All three ran to a stove, into which some remains of a porpoise had been thrown; they drew out the pieces of flesh which the fire had not consumed. The mother distributed the pieces, giving the largest share to the young ones. The sailors seized this moment to fire at the two young bears, who remained at the stove, and also at the mother, whom they wounded without killing. Her despair would have touched the hardest heart. Without paying attention to her own wounds, or to the blood she was shedding, she only attended to her little ones; she called them with sorrowful cries, put before them her own share of food, and even broke it up for them. As they remained motionless, her groans became still more melancholy. She tried to lift them up, and finding her efforts useless, she went away a few steps and renewed her calls; then returning to the dead bodies, she licked the wounds, and would not leave them until convinced that life was gone; then, with frightful howlings toward the vessel, she seemed to accuse the murderers, and they answered with another discharge from their guns. Fatally wounded, the poor mother came to die by her young ones, licking their wounds to the last.

CHAPTER XVIII.

THE NARWHAL AND THE CROCODILE.

THE word *Narwhal* signifies in the Gothic, "beaked whale," which is not inappropriate, since it undoubtedly belongs to the whale family. *Sea Unicorn*, by which it is known, is a deserving title, given on account of the curious weapon of twisted ivory, which springs from the upper jaw and protrudes directly forward a distance of eight or ten feet.

The male narwhal, in which alone this polished weapon appears, uses it very dexterously, not only in charging his enemies, but also in breaking holes through the ice where great force is required; it is also employed to dig in the mud and around the rocks, where the animal's food is chiefly found, such as squids, shrimps and molluscs. Some persons maintain that the tusk is used to impale fish of considerable size, but this statement is hardly probable, being based on presumption rather than ocular evidence.

A narwhal has been known to encounter a ship and drive its tooth-spear through the sheathing, and deeply into the timbers, with all the power of a sword-fish. Occasionally these tusks are developed in the female, two specimens of which were captured and their heads still preserved, each of which had two tusks more than seven feet in length.

In former days an entire tusk of a narwhal was considered of inestimable value, for it was looked upon as the weapon of the veritable unicorn, reft from his forehead in despite of his supernatural strength and superhuman intellect. Setting aside the rarity of the thing, it derived a practical value from its supposed capability of disarming all poisons of their terrors, and of changing the deadliest draught into a wholesome beverage. These pleasing superstitious are perpetuated on England's coat-of-arms, whereon is a figure representing a horse with the unicorn's tusk growing out of his forehead.

The old superstition was that an antidotal potency was of vital consequence to the unicorn, whose residence was in the desert, among all kinds of loathsome beasts and poisonous reptiles, whose touch was death, and whose very look was contamination. The springs and pools at which such monsters quenched their thirst, were saturated

NARWHAL FISHING OFF GREENLAND.

with poison by their contact, and would pour a fiery death through the veins of any animal that partook of the same water. But the

WHALE ATTACKED BY A NARWHAL.

unicorn, by dipping the tip of his horn in the water, neutralized the venom and rendered the pool harmless. This admirable quality of the unicorn was a great recommendation in days when the poisoned chalice crept too frequently upon the festive board. Even a few shavings of the unicorn's horn were purchased at a high price, and the ready sale for such antidotes led to considerable adulteration — a fact which is piteously recorded by an old writer, who tells us that "some wicked persons do make a mingle-mangle thereof, as I saw among the Venetians, being, as I here say, compounded with lime and soap, or, peradventure, with earth or some stone (which things are apt to make bubbles arise), and afterward sell it for the unicorn's horn." The same writer, however, kindly furnishes an easy test, whereby the genuine may be distinguished from the counterfeit article. "For experience of the unicorn's horn, to know whether it be right or not, put silk upon a burning coal, and upon the silk the aforesaid horn, and if so be that it be true, the silk will not be a whit consumed."

The narwhal usually lives on terms of friendship with the Greenland whale, but it not infrequently occurs that the former becomes angered at his great fellow-cetacean, and dreadful combats ensue between them. An old whaler describes a fight which he once saw between a whale and a narwhal, as being the bloodiest and most terrible battle that he ever beheld, not excepting those which he had frequently seen before between the whale and grampus, and the whale and sword-fish. The narwhal, though fairly a mite compared with such a gigantic competitor, is extremely agile, and possesses a powerful weapon that it uses with an effect almost as terrible as the sword-fish. He darts about the whale, always avoiding punishment himself, while he thrusts his long, keen-pointed tusk into the whale's body, nor ceases his murderous onslaught until the mighty enemy lies dead upon the sea.

THE MAIL-CLAD CROCODILES.

The transition from seals to crocodiles is hardly violent, and when we consider that both are carnivorous, and can live equally in or out of water, and that they both haunt the shore a greater portion of the time, we must regard the change as natural, if not exactly according to natural history classification

The crocodile, owing to his colossal size, strength of muscle, voracity of appetite and terrible armature of sharp teeth, is the dread of the countries which he inhabits, ruling the rivers with a sway as despotic as is exercised by the lion and tiger on land, the eagle in the air, or the shark in the seas. There are not many different species, hardly more than three, in fact, that are distinct, viz.: the Gangetic (Ganges), Egyptian, and American, the latter being improperly called Alligator. The Gangetic crocodile, or gavial, is the largest and most curious of reptiles, frequently reaching a length of twenty-five feet, while the extraordinary projection of its muzzle gives it a weird and grotesque appearance. It is confined to India, where the Ganges River particularly swarms with them.

Since man worships force, the same disposition which prompts the Africans of Guinea to sacrifice little girls to the shark, as already related, influences the Indian mother to throw her child into the Ganges, the poor deluded woman believing that it will find the easiest road to

THE GAVIAL CROCODILE OF THE GANGES.

heaven through the stomach of a crocodile. A reference to such atrocious practices is enough to cause us to shudder, but our thirst for knowledge compels us to acquaint ourselves with many revolting facts.

SACRIFICES OF INFANTS TO CROCODILES.

In India, particularly before Great Britain began to exercise sway in the country, and, we may say, the original practices still continue about Benares and other interior places, it was common to see a mother bearing her child toward the Ganges, and with every demonstration of maternal love show how precious to her was the burden she bore away for sacrifice; the fond mother, believing she was preparing a flowery way to heaven for her child, would pause upon the river's bank and cover it with passionate kisses, fondle it in a thousand ways, as if deferring the dread act about to be committed, until a fairly bursting heart was overcome by religious devotion, when she would toss the innocent offspring to the cruel monsters that were waiting for the sacrificial feast. Never more than a single cry would fall upon her ears, for in an instant the little innocent would be torn to a hundred pieces, and only a bloody dye on the surface remain to show, for a few moments, where the tragedy occurred. Not only have such terrible sacrifices been made in years long since passed, but they are being made every day now, and are diminishing so slowly through public opinion, that we cannot prophesy when the infamous practice will cease.

BAKER'S ADVENTURES WITH CEYLON CROCODILES.

Sir Samuel Baker, aside from being one of the most distinguished explorers that has ever penetrated the world's wilderness, was an enthusiastic sportsman, fitted by all the qualifications that nature could bestow for conspicuous success in the field of adventure. But besides his vigorous constitution, courageous spirit and splendid acquirements, he had a large fortune at his command, so that he was thus, in all things, provided to follow the bent of his inclination and indulge every desire. He was an excellent linguist and profound scholar, and as a chronicler of stirring incident he has no equal, if we regard the interest excited in the masses. He wrote many books descriptive of his adventures in various lands, and in utilizing these, which are all filled with exciting escapades, I will have frequently to quote from him.

Though Baker spent several years in Africa, seeking the source of the Nile and in trying to suppress the slave-trade — the results of which labors and all his adventures there being recorded in my previous work, entitled "World's Wonders" — he was, for a still longer period, hunting and conducting business in Ceylon and India. In an admirable little book called "The Rifle and the Hound in Ceylon," he reports some thrilling incidents connected with his battles with elephants and other wild animals, but he does not overlook the crocodile, which in that country is as fierce in water as the tiger is on land. Of this animal he writes:

"Some of these vermin (?) grow to a very large size, attaining the length of more than twenty feet and eight feet in girth, but the common size is fourteen feet. They move slowly upon the land, but are wonderfully fast and active in the water. They commonly lie in wait for their prey under some hollow bank in a deep pool, and when the unsuspecting deer, or even buffalo, stoops his head to drink he is suddenly seized by the nose and dragged beneath the water. Here he is speedily drowned and consumed at leisure.

"It is a common opinion that the scales on the back of a crocodile will turn a ball; this is a vulgar error. The scales are very tough and hard, but a ball from a common fowling-piece will pass right through the body. I have even seen a hunting-knife driven, at one blow, deep into the hardest part of the back; and this was a crocodile of large size, about fourteen feet long, that I had shot at a place called Bolgodde, twenty-two miles from Colombo.

"A man had been setting nets for fish, and was in the act of swimming to the shore, when he was seized and drowned by a crocodile. The next morning two buffaloes were dragged into the water close to the spot, and it was supposed that these murders were committed by the same reptile. I was at Colombo at the time, and hearing of the accident, I rode off to Bolgodde to try my hand at catching him. Bolgodde was a very large lake, of many miles in circumference, abounding with crocodiles, widgeon, teal and ducks.

"On arrival that evening, the headman pointed out the spot where the man had been destroyed and where the buffaloes had been dragged in by the crocodile. One buffalo had been entirely consumed, but the other had merely lost his head, and his carcass was floating, in a horrible state of decomposition, near the bank. It was nearly dark, so I engaged a small canoe to be in readiness by break of day.

"Just as the light streaked the horizon I stepped into the canoe. This required some caution, as it was the smallest thing that can be conceived to support two men. It consisted of the hollow trunk of a tree, six feet in length and about one foot in diameter. A small outrigger prevented it from upsetting; but it was not an inch from the water when I took my narrow seat, and the native in the stern paddled carefully toward the carcass of the buffalo.

"Upon approaching within a hundred yards of the floating carcass, I counted five forms within a few feet of the flesh. These objects were not over nine inches square and appeared like detached pieces of rough bark. I knew them to be the foreheads of different crocodiles, and presently one moved toward the half devoured buffalo. His long head and shoulders projected from the water as he attempted to

SCENE ON THE MARGIN OF BOLGODDE LAKE.

fix his fore-claws into the putrid flesh ; this, however, rolled over toward him, and thus prevented him from getting a hold ; but the gaping jaws, nevertheless, made a wide breach in the buffalo's flank. I was now within thirty yards of them, and being observed, they all dived to the bottom.

"The carcass was lying within a few yards of the bank, where the water was extremely deep and clear. Several large trees grew close to the edge and formed a good hiding-place; I therefore landed, and sending the canoe to a distance, I watched the water.

DEATH OF THE MONSTER.

"I had not been five minutes in this position before I saw in the water at my feet, in a deep hole close to the bank, the immense form of a crocodile, as he was slowly rising from his hiding-place to the surface. He appeared to be about eighteen feet long, and he projected his horny head from the water, bubbled, and then floated with only his forehead and large eyes above the surface. He was a horrible looking monster, and from his size I hoped he was the villain that had committed the late depredations. He was within three yards of me; and although I stood upon the bank, his great round eyes gazed at me without a symptom of fear. The next moment I put a two-ounce ball exactly between them, and killed him stone-dead. He gave a convulsive slap with his tail, which made the water foam, and turning upon his back, he gradually sank, till at length I could only distinguish the long line of his white belly twenty feet below me.

"Not having any apparatus for bringing him to the surface, I again took to the canoe, as a light breeze that had sprung up was moving the carcass of the buffalo away. This I slowly followed, until it at length rested in a wide belt of rushes which grew upon the shallows near the shore. I pushed the canoe into the rushes within four yards of the carcass, keeping to windward to avoid the sickening smell.

"I had not been long in this position before the body suddenly rolled over, as though attacked by something beneath the water, and the next moment the tall reeds brushed against the sides of the canoe, being violently agitated in a long line, evidently by a crocodile at the bottom. The native in the stern grew as pale as a black can turn with fright, and instantly began to paddle the canoe away. This, however, I soon replaced in its former position, and then took his paddle away to prevent further accidents. There sat the captain of the fragile vessel in the most abject state of terror. We were close to the shore, and the water was not more than three feet deep, and yet he dared not jump out of the canoe, as the rushes were again brushing against its sides, being moved by the hidden beast at the bottom. There was no help for him, so, after vainly imploring me to shove the canoe into deep water, he at length sat still.

"In a few moments the body of the buffalo again moved, and the head and shoulders of a crocodile appeared above the water, and took a bite of some pounds of flesh. I could not get a shot at the head from his peculiar position, but I put a ball through his shoulders, and immediately shoved the canoe astern. Had I not done this, we should most likely have been upset, as the wounded brute began to lash out with his tail in all directions, till he at length retired to the bottom among the rushes. Here I could easily track him, as he slowly moved along, by the movement of the reeds. Giving the native the paddle, I now by threats induced him to keep the canoe over the very spot where the rushes were moving, and we slowly followed on the track, while I kept watch in the bow of the canoe with a rifle.

"Suddenly the movement in the rushes ceased, and the canoe stopped accordingly. I leaned slightly over the side to look into the water, when up came a large air-bubble, and directly afterward an apparition in the shape of some fifteen pounds of putrid flesh. The stench was frightful, but I knew my friend must be very bad down there to disgorge so sweet a morsel. I therefore took the paddle and poked for him; the water being shallow, I felt him immediately. Again the rushes moved; I felt the paddle twist as his scaly back glided under it, and a pair of gaping jaws appeared above the water, wide open and within two feet of the canoe. The next moment his head appeared, and the two-ounce ball shattered his brain. He sank to the bottom, the rushes moved slightly and were then still.

"I now put the canoe ashore, and cutting a stróng stick with a crook at one end, I again put out for the spot and dragged for him. He was quite dead; and, catching him under the fore-leg, I soon brought him gently to the surface of the water. I now made fast a line to his fore-leg, and we towed him to the village, the canoe being level with the water's edge.

"His weight in the water was a mere trifle, but on arrival at the village on the banks of the lake, the people turned out with great glee, and fastened ropes to different parts of his body to drag him out. This operation employed twenty men. The beast was fourteen feet long; and he was no sooner on shore, than the natives cut him to pieces with axes and threw the sections into the lake, to be devoured by his own species. This was a savage kind of revenge, which appeared to afford them great satisfaction."

A WOMAN CARRIED OFF AND DEVOURED BY A CROCODILE.

"I remember an accident," says Baker, "that occurred at Madampi, on the west coast of Ceylon, about seven years ago, the day before I passed through the village. A number of women were em-

A WOMAN CARRIED OFF BY A CROCODILE.

ployed in cutting rushes for mat-making, and were mid-deep in the water. The horny tail of a large crocodile was suddenly seen above the water among the group of women, and in another instant one of them was seized by the thigh and dragged toward a deeper part of the stream. In vain the terrified creature shrieked for assistance; the horror stricken group had rushed to the shore, and a crowd of spectators on the bank offered the little help that was in their power, which, however, was without avail. Three of the more daring natives followed the monster and thrust their spears into him, but he never relinquished his hold upon the victim. It was some distance before the water deepened, and the unfortunate woman was dragged for many yards, sometimes beneath the water, sometimes above the surface, rending the air with her screams, until at length the deep water hid her from their view. She was never again seen."

A SAFE PLACE OF DEPOSIT.

There are many queer things and beliefs in India, some of which tax our credulity, but yet we are prepared to hear much that is wonderful respecting the practices of that country without stamping it with improbability. People of India are not more honest, if they do affect more religion, than citizens of other countries, but they have some original ways of enforcing honesty hardly compatible with civilization. It is gravely asserted by travelers that the Government sinking fund in India, instead of being kept in iron vaults, protected by time locks and several walls, as in this country, is committed to a hollow log, the ends of which are sealed up. A hollow log would ordinarily prove a poor precaution against thieves, but as every man, high and low, is alike suspected in India, the money is entrusted to the keeping of no person. The log containing the treasure is thrown into a large pool, wherein are kept a large number of crocodiles, maintained at Government expense within the capitol walls. As these voracious creatures are forever hungry, and have such ferocious dispositions that no amount of studied blandishments will curb their appetite for human flesh, the sinking fund is not liable to any disturbance. When, at length, it is desirable that the money be recovered to meet the uses for which it was publicly intended, a proclamation to that effect is made, and the crocodiles of the pool are dragged out and killed; a machine, made for the purpose, then grapples the log and pulls it to the shore, where the seals are broken in the presence of certain functionaries.

THE EGYPTIAN MAN-EATING CROCODILE.

This terrible creature is found chiefly in the Nile, where it fairly swarms, and though the most dreaded and destructive animal of all Egypt, it has its uses; living exclusively on animal flesh, which it seizes with equal avidity whether fresh or putrid, it performs the part of an indispensable scavenger, and prevents the waters from becoming putrid. The crocodile is a dangerous foe to cattle and other beasts that come to the river-brink for water. The creature lies like a log upon the bank, watching for whatever prey may chance to come near, and cattle do not usually detect its presence until a stroke of its powerful tail knocks them into the water, where the unfortunate animal is seized and quickly torn to pieces.

Many instances are known where men have been surprised near the water's edge and captured by the monster. Mr. Petherick, a British consul in Egypt, relates an instance, where a man while drawing water, was attacked by a crocodile, and having his escape cut off was forced back into a recess behind the well-boxing. The crocodile followed after, but its body was too large to pass through the space and became wedged, with its gaping mouth scarcely one foot from the horrified man. Being unable to get forward or retreat, the crocodile fell a victim to several men who, hearing cries for assistance, ran to the prisoner's relief and dispatched it with bludgeons and spears.

HOW THE CROCODILE IS HUNTED.

As this reptile is so dangerous and costly a neighbor to the inhabitants of the river banks, many means have been adopted for its destruction. One such method, where a kind of harpoon is employed, is described by Dr. Ruppell: "The most favorable season is either the winter, when the animal usually sleeps on sand-banks, luxuriating in the rays of the sun, or the spring, after the pairing time, when the female regularly watches the sand islands, where she has buried her eggs. The natives find out the place, and on the south side of it, that is to the leeward, dig a hole in the sand, throwing the earth to the side which they expect the animal to take. Then they conceal themselves, and the crocodile comes to its accustomed spot and soon falls asleep. The hunters then dart their harpoons with all their force at the animal, for in order that the strokes may be successful, the harpoon head ought to penetrate to the depth of at least four inches, that the barb may be firmly fixed in the flesh. Upon being wounded the crocodile rushes for the water, and the hunters retreat to their canoes. A piece of wood, attached to the harpoon line, swims on the water and indicates the direction in which the crocodile is moving. The huntsmen, by pulling on the line, drag the beast to the surface of the water where it is struck with other harpoons until destroyed.

"When the animal is struck, it by no means remains inactive, on the contrary, it lashes with its tail and endeavors to bite the rope in two; to prevent this the line is composed of thirty separate small lines, not twisted together, but merely placed in juxtaposition, and bound together at intervals of every two feet. The thin lines get between the teeth and become entangled about them."

SCENE ON THE UPPER NILE.

In spite of the great strength of the animal, two expert men can drag it from the water, tie up its mouth, twist its legs over the back, and kill it by driving a sharp steel spike into the spinal cord, just at the back of the skull.

There are many other modes of capturing and killing the crocodile, such as a hook baited with meat, to which the voracious creatures are attracted by the cries of a captive pig, and the yelping of a dog will answer the same purpose. In some cases the negroes are bold enough to engage the crocodile in his own element, and to attack him with a long knife, with which they rip up its belly.

The margined crocodile is distinguishable from its Nile neighbor by the great concavity of its forehead and the strong keels of its back-plates. It is confined to the rivers of South Africa, and in boldness and ferocity equals the Egyptian and Indian species. Captain Drayson, author of "Sporting Scenes Among the Kaffirs," tells the following story to illustrate the voracity of this creature:

MAN TORN BY A CROCODILE.

"About two or three miles from the Bay of Natal there is a river called the Umganie; into this river a lake called the Sea Cow empties itself. The lake was, during my residence at Natal, the retreat of several hippopotami and crocodiles, which were in the habit of *treking* into the Umganie River. Often, when riding round the banks of this lake, I have disturbed two or three crocodiles, which were stealing among the reeds and long grass in hope of stalking a fat toad or a sleeping guana. Sometimes a scaly reptile might be awakened from his doze by the sound of my horse's feet, and would then rush through the long reeds toward his retreat. Their movement is much more rapid than one would suppose from their appearance, and they care nothing for a fall, head over tail, but almost fling themselves down the steep banks when alarmed.

"On the banks of the Umganie were several Kaffir kraals, in one of which resided a man who had been roughly treated by a crocodile. This man, seeing me pass his residence, called to me and asked, as a favor, that I would watch at a particular part of the river until I shot a rascally crocodile that had nearly killed him. The animal, he informed me, always made its appearance about sundown, and he hinted that a position might be selected so that the sun would dazzle the crocodile and prevent him from seeing me. Finding that I was willing to gratify his revenge, he limped out of the inclosure surrounding his huts, and offering me his snuff-gourd, at my request gave me the following account of his escape:

"He had so frequently crossed the stream below his huts, at all times of day, and had seen crocodiles of small dimensions, that he had become, as it were, familiarized to them, and did not imagine that there was any danger to be expected from them. One evening, at about sundown, he was wading across the river, the water of which reached above his waist. Suddenly he felt himself seized by the under side of his thigh, while he was at the same instant dragged under the water. His wife was following him, and seeing him fall, she scrambled forward to the place where he had disappeared, and thus caused considerable noise by splashing, which (or something else, perhaps the toughness or bad flavor of the Kaffir) had the effect of making the crocodile quit his hold, not, however, without tearing off a great portion of the under part of his thigh. The man with difficulty escaped to the shore, but he remained a cripple for life, unable to do more than put the toes of his foot to the ground."

EXCITING ADVENTURES IN KILLING THE CROCODILE.

In some of the rivers of Africa the natives are bold enough, and, indeed, skillful enough to combat with the crocodile in its own element; and, armed only with a sharp dagger, dive beneath it and rip the reptile open. It often happens, however, that the combat is fatal to the man, and frequently his only chance of escape is to force his dagger, or, if this be lost, his thumbs into the reptile's eyes with all his might, so as to produce great pain and blindness.

Waterton's account of catching a cayman, as the crocodile is sometimes called, is amusing. The creature had swallowed a large hook cast specially for it, and was being drawn toward the vessel, where the naturalist was waiting with a great rod in his hand intending to force it down the reptile's throat when occasion should offer. At this point of the proceeding Waterton says: "By this time the cayman was within a few yards of me; I saw he was in a state of great fear and perturbation. I instantly dropped the rod, sprang up, and jumped on his back, turning half round as I vaulted, so that I gained my seat with my face in a right position. I immediately seized his fore-legs, and by main force twisted them on his back; thus they served me for a bridle. He now seemed to have recovered from his surprise, and probably fancying himself in hostile company, he began to plunge furiously, and lashed the sand with his long and powerful tail. I was out of the reach of the strokes of it by being near his head. He continued to strike, and made my seat very uncomfortable."

This feat of riding a crocodile, as performed by Waterton, was not so wonderful when we consider that several persons were drawing the reptile by a rope, which prevented it effectually from doing the least harm to the rider.

In South Africa a similar feat was performed still more recently. A crocodile was shot at and wounded, but, though apparently not much hurt, he rose at once out of the water and attempted to reach a morass. At this juncture a native approached the reptile, and before it could retreat he threw himself upon the creature's back, snatched up its fore-paws in an instant and doubled them across its back. The crocodile, deprived of any support in front, was thus thrown upon his snout, and though able to move freely his hind feet and keep his tail in motion, he could not budge half-a-yard, though he made the most frantic exertions to move forward. The native bravely kept his seat and held the monster, which measured eighteen feet in length, until another shot could be fired into the reptile's brain.

A DISTINGUISHED ENGLISHMAN DEVOURED BY A CROCODILE.

The Teoge, or Zouga, River, in Southern Africa, is noted for the gigantic and ferocious crocodiles that swarm its banks and waters. Notwithstanding the well-known man-eating propensities of these reptiles, hundreds of natives, living in the vicinity of the stream and fishing in its waters, fall victims every year to these voracious creatures. But a particularly sad accident befell an English gentleman named Richardson, who, in company with another wealthy sportsman, named Manning, were shooting in Southern Africa. The circumstances attending the horrible death of Richardson were related by Mr. Manning, as follows:

While encamped on the Zouga, finding water-fowl somewhat scarce, the unfortunate gentleman shot a muscovy duck, which he was very anxious to secure, but could not for want of a boat. While looking for a canoe he observed a fine antelope approaching, and running quickly toward the wagon, which was hard by, he called out to his men to bring him a rifle. On his return to the river he found that the antelope had escaped. He then proceeded toward the spot from whence he had shot at the duck, which was still floating on the surface. Manning having by this time joined him, he expressed his determination to possess the bird at any cost, and that he would swim after it. He confessed, however, that he felt some doubt about the safety of such a proceeding, adding that he had once been a witness to the death of a man who was seized and destroyed by a shark alongside of his own boat. Notwithstanding this (his own) opinion of the risk he was about to incur, and the warning of his friend, he undressed and plunged into the stream. Having swum a little distance, he was observed to throw himself on his back, as if startled by some object beneath him, but in another moment he was pursuing his course. When, however, he was about to lay his hand on the bird, his body was violently convulsed, and, throwing his hands on high, he uttered a most piercing shriek, after which he was seen to be gradually drawn under the surface, never to reappear.

HORRIBLY MANGLED BY A CROCODILE.

Baker, in his "Nile Tributaries of Abyssinia," mentions the death of a celebrated Arab hunter, caused by being dreadfully mangled by a crocodile in the Atbara River. He says: "Accidents are continally occurring in this dangerous sport (hunting hippopotami), as the hunters are so constantly exposed, like baits, to the attacks of crocodiles. During the last season one of the sheik's party was killed. Several men were swimming the river supported by inflated skins, when one was suddenly seized by a crocodile. Retaining his hold upon the support, his comrades had time to clutch him by the hair and beneath the arms; thus the crocodile could not drag the buoyant skins beneath the surface. Once he was dragged from their grasp, but holding to his inflated skin, he regained the surface, and was again supported by his friends, who clung to him, while he implored them to hold him tight, as the crocodile still held him by the leg. In this way the hunters assisted him; at the same time they struck downward with their spears at the determined brute, until at last they drove it from its hold. Upon gaining the shore, they found that the flesh of the leg, from the knee to the foot, had been stripped from the bone, and the poor fellow shortly died."

NOBODY BUT A SLAVE; BUT OH! THE NECKLACE!

The Kafue River of South Africa is almost as famous as the Zouga for the huge reptiles that render its waters so dangerous to man or beast. The crocodiles in this stream are said to frequently attain a length of twenty-five feet. Lurking in the reeds along the banks, these mighty saurians succeed in capturing great quantities of game, not infrequently taking in the fierce cape buffalo, that is a fair match for the strongest lion. To effect the capture of these great animals, the crocodile hides himself in the reeds beside a frequented watering place, and when the buffalo stoops to drink, the wily reptile seizes the unsuspecting beast by the nose and drags it into the water; here, having all the advantage, the crocodile holds the head of its victim under the water until it is drowned, after which the carcass is removed to the bank, where it is allowed to remain until putrefaction begins, when the reptile enters upon its repast.

Women, who do all the menial labor in Africa, and their duties taking them most frequently to the river banks, fall victims to the crocodiles so often that accidents of this kind rarely occasion any excitement whatever among the tribes to which the victims belong. Bains mentions a case to illustrate this indifference upon the part of the natives to the loss of their women. He says that Chapman, his companion, upon reaching Victoria Falls, tried to obtain from a sheik some information respecting the Kafue and other rivers. In so doing he casually mentioned Green's accident on the river near Libebe, where, after the canoe had been capsized by a hippopotamus, Mr. Bonham and one or two natives were seized by crocodiles. "Yes," responded the sheik, "they are nasty beasts, those crocodiles; only last night one of them took one of my girls, and my *necklace, too! A fine bead necklace* I was letting her wear." He was utterly unconcerned about the death of the girl, but suffered the greatest grief over the loss of his necklace, which was much more difficult to replace.

TWO SLAVES EATEN BY CROCODILES.

Francisco Valdez, who spent six years in Africa, and has given us some very interesting descriptions of that country, writing of the River Barrado Bengo, says: "The crocodiles in this river are numerous, and of an enormous size. The natives have a novel way of destroying them; they take a small pig, and after killing it, drive through it a strong stick, each end of which has been made very sharp, and to the center of which they fasten a long rope. This bait being thrown in the way of the crocodile, that voracious animal immediately seizes it, and the sharp pointed stick piercing its jaws, the natives at once draw it on shore, where it is quickly dispatched."

Valdez, continuing his journey up the Bengo, came to some well cultivated farms, which he was invited to inspect, and while describing his visit, says: "While we were engaged in inspecting the various parts of the farms along the river, we were suddenly alarmed by the piercing cry, 'Uafu! Ay-u-e!' and a great movement toward the river. Soon afterward we were informed that it was

MANNER OF HUNTING THE CROCODILE BY BENGO NATIVES.

occasioned by two negroes, when about to enter their canoe, being attacked by the jarcares, or crocodiles, which succeeded in seizing the unfortunate men, who were drawn to the bottom of the river, and again raised to the surface for the purpose, as the people believe, of tantalizing them, and showing their triumph. It is said that the crocodiles never commence devouring their victims until quite dead, when they drag the bodies to some secluded place on the edge of the river, where they devour them.

"Soon afterward a number of the negroes came to the master and requested permission to go and revenge the death of their two comrades, both of whom were carpenters belonging to the estate. If I was amazed at the awful catastrophe, I was more so at the strange answer returned. 'No,' said he, 'the jacara is mine, and I ordered him expressly to kill every one whom he met, until the bridge I ordered you to build was completed.'"

EXTRAORDINARY TENACITY OF LIFE.

There are few, if any, creatures so difficult to destroy as the crocodile, as one or two instances will serve to show: A gentleman in Ceylon contrived to catch a crocodile by means of a large hook, and landing it, crushed its skull and otherwise mutilated the creature, until, to all outward appearances, life was extinct. Wishing to preserve the body until he could have it skinned, he opened the belly and removed all the viscera, and kept the aperture open by means of a stick placed across it, and turned the animal upon its back. What was his astonishment upon his return to the creature, after an hour's absence in search of some persons to do the skinning, to find that the dissected animal had recovered sufficiently to leave the bank and disappear in the water, where he was unable to find it again.

John Duncan, the Dahomy traveler, had an experience not wholly different from the above, which he relates in the following language: "Mr. Hanson, myself and a young Portugese, went up the lagoon to visit the Greejee market, and also to endeavor to kill an alligator-crocodile. We only saw two on our passage up; but on our return in the afternoon, we first observed one of small dimensions, about five feet and a half. It was close to the water's edge, under the boughs of a low shrub. I fired with a rifle and struck it, but it dropped instantly into the water, and we made no search after it. However, in ten minutes after we were more fortunate. One of the canoe-men observed a large one on the banks, several yards from the water, apparently fast asleep. After getting the canoe quite steady, I fired and shot it through the hardest part of its back, upon which it rushed into the water. After looking about some time, and being about to leave the spot, giving up the search, Mr. Hanson observed at a short distance, the enormous head of this monster resting on a broken stake of the fishing-hurdle across the river, its head only above the water. I fired a second shot, which knocked out its eye and carried away a large portion of its skull, upon which it sank into the water, but immediately rose again to the surface. I then took a sword, belonging to the young Portugese, and ran it into its belly, which was now uppermost, when it again sank to the bottom. Considering that the creature was now dead, I ordered the canoe-man to get into the water and secure it, but all at once we lost it, owing to the muddiness of the water caused by the men disturbing it. However, it is very fortunate that we did lose it at this time, as it proved to be only pretending death, for it was soon after perceived twenty yards higher up the stream, still strong, although in this mutilated state.

"We again commenced our hunt, but before we reached the wounded animal the old fisherman had lodged two harpoons in its back. As it still continued to struggle and appeared strong, I lodged another bullet in its head, which, being previously shattered, completely smashed it. After considerable more struggling, we secured the animal to the stern of the canoe with a rope borrowed from the fisherman.

"After our return to Ahguay we were obliged to give notice to the *caboceer* (chief) of our having killed this alligator; for, as the gall of the animal is a very virulent poison, notice is directed to be given on all such occasions to the head man or *caboceer*, in order to prevent its being used unlawfully. Men are then sent to take out the gall and throw it into the river, cutting the gall bladder first. The animal is then delivered to the person who kills it. The alligator is eaten in many parts of Africa, and is said to impart courage to the eater."

INTERESTING SUPERSTITIONS CONCERNING THE CROCODILE.

Egypt, while showing the earliest civilization and being the cradle of science, the source from whence Greece derived her knowledge of art and literature, yet she created and nursed more superstitions than any other country. The ibis was scarcely more sacred than the dung-beetle and crocodile. In Lower Egypt the latter was held especially sacred, where it was buried in the labyrinth with dead kings, being held too sacred in death even for Herodotus to see.

In the city of crocodiles, founded gratefully by King Menas, whom a crocodile ferried over lake Mœnis upon its back when the disloyal hunting hounds drove royalty into the water, was a crocodile so sacred, that it was kept separately in an especial lake, and suffered the touching of the priest. This was the crocodile Sachus, says Dr. Gardner, quoting Strabo—" one of our most distinguished citizens" in the city of crocodiles,—showed him and his friends as the sacred curiosity, conducting them to the brink of the lake, on whose bank the animal was extended. While some of the priests opened its mouth, one put in the cake and then the meat, after which the wine was poured. The crocodile would then dive to the other side of the lake, where a similar lunch would be given it. It has no tongue, says Plutarch, speaking through Sir Gardner, and is therefore regarded as an image of the deity itself, " the divine reason needing not speech but going through still and silent paths while it administers the world with justice."

BATTLE BETWEEN A CROCODILE AND TIGER.

The crocodile is not only master of the haunts wherein he dwells, but his survey of power extends to the shore also, where he delights to lurk and watch for his prey as it comes to drink. He has an omnivorous appetite, and fully conscious of his strong armature and the power of his well-armed jaws, he is little respecter of the character of his prey, whether it be the graceful pallah, innocent and defenseless, or the lordly tiger, whose fierce howls strike terror into the breasts of all quadrupeds, and whose teeth and claws are so terrible to cope with, the crocodile is totally indifferent; he attacks either with the same assurance when moved by hunger.

The tiger, like the crocodile, prefers the deep shadows of a dense copse, and he seldom strays far from water, as an ungovernable thirst invariably follows a hearty meal, and he madly plunges his head into the water up to his eyes to slake his desire. At this time the tiger becomes almost indifferent to his surroundings, and while thus drinking he frequently falls a victim to the deadly crocodile, that approaches with a stealth which is rarely discovered until he is fast in the reptile's jaws.

A hunter in India thus describes a combat which he once witnessed, and which took place on the edge of a small, stagnant creek that, in the spring-time, flows past a little village not far from Jabalpur.

BATTLE BETWEEN A CROCODILE AND TIGER.

"I had been hunting tigers for some months in the valleys of the Jabalpur country, and was fortunate in bagging eight without encountering any particular peril. In the month of September I got on the trail of another that had been committing much havoc among the flocks in the district of Ramgarh, but though I followed him with the greatest perseverance, and adopted every possible expedient to get a shot, I was unsuccessful. One day information came to me that the tiger had been seen in its favorite haunts, and, moreover, had captured another bullock which it had dragged into a thick copse, whence the natives were afraid to follow.

"Getting everything ready, I procured two gun-bearers, and following the directions of my informants, I proceeded in quest of the wily animal. An hour's walk brought us to a place where I felt sure the tiger had entered the jungle with his prey, and making my way slowly and cautiously I was not long in tracing him to the spot where he had made a hearty meal off the bullock, which I found was more than half eaten. The most careful examination, however, failed to discover the tiger, which I was now certain was not far off quenching his thirst at some pool of water. I knew there was a small creek less than half a mile distant, and thitherward I directed my steps, quite sure that I should find the bold depredator, and in a condition, too, that would make him an easy victim.

"I found the creek without trouble, and followed its shore only a few hundred yards, when around a sharp bend I heard a slight splashing, which led me at once to believe that I was very near the game. I had proceeded less than twenty steps further when my ears were thrilled by an agonizing roar, followed by a dreadful splashing in the waters and a half stifled growl. Rushing up, I was soon made acquainted with the cause of the tumult, for in the boiling, mud-covered waters I saw a crocodile and tiger in a terrible death struggle; at the same moment I caught sight of a female tiger as she was moving off, evidently little concerned about the dire extremity into which her male companion had fallen.

"The two combatants were too deeply engaged in the conflict to give any heed to my approach, while I was too much interested in the fight to end it by a shot from my rifle. I therefore let them fight it out, anxious to see the outcome. The crocodile had seized the tiger by the head, and evidently while the latter was drinking, for its hold was a terrible one, and placed the forest rover at a great disadvantage. Notwithstanding this, the tiger strove valiantly, and not entirely without avail, for with its left fore-claw it managed to tear up the scaly skin of the crocodile's head, and lacerate it dreadfully. Like a bull-dog, the crocodile maintained its powerful hold on its adversary's head, from which blood flowed freely, and soon the tiger's tongue was protruded between the two canine teeth, and it grew rapidly black from the grinding pressure exerted on the victim's windpipe. The struggles were truly appalling, and might have been heard for nearly a mile; the tiger seemed only anxious to escape its foe, and so tugged violently shoreward, while the crocodile exerted all its strength to draw its victim into the water. Thus was the tug of war continued, until, weakened from great pain and loss of blood, the tiger gradually gave way, until soon the crocodile had completed its triumph, and started across the creek to make a meal off the great beast it had vanquished. He, no doubt, well deserved the trophy of his victory, but I, nevertheless, put a ball behind his right fore-shoulder, which was so instantly fatal that the crocodile at once sank, carrying the tiger's body down with him, but both were recovered by my gun-bearers.

"After they were drawn ashore I examined the victims, and found that both the tiger's jaws had been crushed and its throat dreadfully mangled, while the brain of the crocodile had been laid bare in one place by the claws of its foe, but so great is the tenacity of life in the crocodile, that I doubt if this injury would have seriously disturbed it."

THE VORACIOUS ALLIGATOR.

The difference between the crocodile and alligator is difficult to distinguish, except that the former is larger than the latter; its teeth is also more formidable, and the head somewhat longer, but in habit there is a perfect similarity. One of the most marked characteristics of the alligator, entirely wanting in the crocodile, is its habit of bellowing at night-time, producing a horrible noise, somewhat between the croaking of a large bull-frog and the roar of a mad bull. It also avoids the salt water, and is seldom ever seen at the mouths of rivers, where the tide gives a brackish taste to the waters.

Like the crocodile, the alligator is a difficult animal to destroy, retaining life for some time even when mutilated in the head and body until the brain and viscera are destroyed; and so long as there is any evidence of life, it will try to bite. Fortunately, the creature can turn its head very slightly from side to side, on account of bony projections, but its tail is no less formidable than its mouth, a weapon which it uses quite as much.

In some parts of Florida, where alligators are particularly numerous, natives catch and kill them in the following curious manner: A grapnel is made of four strong sticks barbed at each end, and so bound together that the points radiate from each other. This singular apparatus is baited usually with a piece of pork, which is then suspended about one foot above the water by means of a rope. When the alligator seizes the bait, his efforts to dislodge it forces the sharp barbs into his throat, and makes it impossible for him to escape, so that he falls a victim to those who are thus trapping for him.

A MISSIONARY SEIZED BY AN ALLIGATOR.

Hearing so much of alligators in the bayous of our Southern coun-

A MISSIONARY SEIZED BY AN ALLIGATOR.

try, many suppose it to be an animal peculiar to the United States, but this is a decided mistake, for it is found in South America under the name of cayman, however, and is very plentiful in the rivers of South Africa.

Rev. Lewis Grout, for fifteen years a missionary in Zululand, describes an incident to which he was an eye-witness, as follows:

"* * * With reptiles, great and small, it is far otherwise in these our Zululand. With the alligator, the most formidable and most feared of this family, nearly all the deep, still waters of our larger rivers are infested. These ugly, fierce, scaly brutes, too well known to need description, are called by the natives *ingwenga*—a name which some make to mean, 'aquatic gorging tiger.' Basking upon the sand-banks, or among the reeds of the river's bank, or, scouring its deep pools, he is the dread of the traveler compelled to cross the stream. Mr. Butler, a member of our mission, narrowly escaped from one of these savage creatures with his life.

"In going to one of the stations it was necessary for him to cross the Umkomazi. No natives being at hand to manage the boat, he ventured to cross on horseback, though the water was deep and turbid. As he went over safely, when he returned the next day he again ventured into the river in the same way. When about two-thirds of the way across, his horse suddenly kicked and plunged as if to disengage himself from his rider, and the next moment an alligator seized Mr. Butler's thigh with its horrible jaws. The river at this place is about one hundred and fifty yards wide, if measured at right-angles with the current; but from the place we enter to the place we go out, the distance is three times as great. Mr. Butler, when he felt the sharp teeth of the alligator, clung to the mane of his horse with a death-hold; instantly he was dragged from the saddle, and both he and the horse were floundering in the water, often dragged entirely under, and rapidly going down the stream. At first the alligator drew them to the middle of the river, but at last the horse gained shallow water and approached the shore. As soon as he was within reach, the natives ran to his assistance and beat off the alligator with their spears.

"Mr. Butler was pierced with five deep gashes, and had lost much blood. He left all his garments except his shirt and coat on the opposite shore with a native, who was to follow him; but when the struggle commenced, the native returned and dared not venture into the water again. It was now dark, and without garments, and weak from the loss of blood, he had seven miles to ride before he could reach the station of a brother missionary. He borrowed a blanket of a native, and after two hours succeeded in reaching the station, more dead than alive. His horse was terribly mangled, a foot square of flesh and skin being torn from the flank. The animal, it is supposed, first seized the horse, and when shaken off it caught Mr. Butler first below the knee and then in the thigh, making five or six wounds from two to four inches long, and from one-half to two and one-half inches wide. After a severe illness, Mr. Butler recovered."

FIGHT BETWEEN AN ALLIGATOR AND BEAR

Hunting alligators in our country along the gulf-coast affords considerable sport, and is indulged in to a large extent. Although thousands are killed every year, their numbers do not perceptibly diminish, and the supply will no doubt be abundant for many years to come. They are very destructive to poultry and pigs, and will crawl out of the bayous at night-time and visit barnyards with all the stealth of foxes or bears.

FIGHT BETWEEN A BEAR AND ALLIGATOR.

A gentleman visiting in Florida, while penetrating the tangled forest upon one occasion heard a growling and wrestling which gave him much concern for his safety, but venturing to discover the cause observed a bear and crocodile in deadly conflict. Bruin was bleeding from several severe wounds, but he was now astride the saurian, which, in its struggles, had turned upon its back, holding one of its fore-feet in his mouth and evidently at great advantage. The alligator's struggles were terrible, lashing its tail with a force sufficient to kill almost any living thing, but its efforts now had no other effect than to break down the undergrowth and make a clear space for the combat. The bear never left his safe perch, but kept chewing his antagonist's leg and giving voice to low growls of vengeful satisfaction in answer to the horrible bellowing of the alligator.

The fight thus continued for the space of several minutes without change, until at length the alligator realized the futility of his efforts to shake off the bear, and wisely concluded to transfer the scene of battle to the water. Conceiving that he would be altogether better off in his proper element, the alligator dragged itself with great difficulty on three legs to the river bank, bruin riding his foe with no little grace in the meantime. When the brink was gained the alligator rolled into the water like a mud-turtle tumbling off a log; but so tenacious and dogged was the bear, that it maintained its hold and disappeared under the water with the alligator. But, though full of courage and the disposition to conquer or die, bruin could not fight under water, and was compelled to let go. As he rose to the surface, he looked anxiously around, but failing to discover his enemy, he returned to the shore, shook himself like a dog, and then ran off into the woods.

THE THALASSITES.

Associated with the seal and crocodile in their habit of spending a greater portion of the time on land, while yet being evidently water animals, are the *Thalassites*, which is a Greek term used by naturalists, meaning the sea, and applied to sea-turtles to distinguish them from the land-tortoise, marsh-tortoise and river-tortoise. It is maintained by some that the sea-turtle never quits the water except at breeding time, to deposit their eggs in the sand, where they are hatched by the heat of the sun. But this assertion is manifestly incorrect, for there are hundreds of trustworthy travelers who declare that a greater portion of the time is spent out of water by several sea species, some of which even climb high hills on the ocean shore to feed on certain plants. It is true, however, that the thalassites do not come on shore to sleep, like the tortoise or turtles of our rivers, but sleep profoundly out at sea, cradled by the waves; a habit which is taken advantage of by fishermen, who approach it so cautiously in boats as to be able to seize it by their hands.

The *Chelonidæ*, whose dorsal shell is covered with hard, horny plates, possessing peculiar properties, and which are well-known to everybody under the name of tortoise shell, is the most common of all the sea species. Its fecundity is amazing, as it lays no less than one hundred eggs at a time, and these are not destroyed by birds or animals, as are the eggs of crocodiles; neither are the young turtles

CATCHING A SLEEPING TURTLE IN THE MOZAMBIQUE.

pursued by any enemies. Notwithstanding its rapid increase, the chelonidæ are appreciably decreasing on account of man's incessant pursuit of them for the sake of their costly and beautiful shell. This substance is valued for its hardness, transparency, gleaming shades of color, the ease with which it is wrought and the fine polish of which it is susceptible.

CURIOSITIES OF SEA-TURTLES.

The edible, or green turtle, is one of the largest of the genus, sometimes attaining a length of seven feet and weighing nearly one thousand pounds. In shape it somewhat resembles a heart, or the shields worn by mediæval soldiers. Its flesh is peculiarly savory, on account of which it is vigorously hunted in its haunts about Ascension Island and the West Indies.

In the hot months of January, February, March and April, the females seek the land at night, and waddling over the sands in the various bays of the islands, far above high-water mark, they scrape up, by alternate scoops of their flippers, a hole deep enough to cover their bodies. Into this they get, sighing heavily, and deposit from one to two hundred eggs, cover them up and leave them for the sun to hatch, and then waddle back toward the sea again. Two hunters are, in the meantime, on the lookout, watching her movements, and running after her one of them seizes a fore-flipper, which he dexterously shoves under her to serve as a purchase; while the other, careful to avoid a stroke which might lame him for life, with a hook cants the turtle over on her back, where she lies helpless, being unable to turn herself again. Thus in a night two men will sometimes turn fifteen or twenty turtles, and in the morning drag the unfortunate creatures into their boats, whence they are taken to market.

The imbricated, or hawk-billed turtle, is so called from the fact that its scales lap over, like tiles on a roof, and its nose terminates in a beak, which bears a striking resemblance to a hawk's bill. It is a native of the warm seas, where it is hunted for its beautiful shell, which is semi-transparent, and finely checkered with cloudy undulations of a whitish, reddish, yellowish and brownish hue, so that when polished and carefully wrought, it is capable of adaptation to numerous ornamental purposes.

In the Mozambique Channel, where the imbricated turtle is found in considerable numbers, the natives capture it by employing the remora, or sucking-fish, in the following curious manner: This fish, which has already been described, is attached to a long line by means of a ring, so fixed around its tail as not to interfere with its swimming. The fish is thrown overboard, and as its nature is to attach itself to the first moving thing which it sees in the water, it usually encounters a large turtle, and so firmly adheres to it that both fish and turtle are drawn on board.

HOME OF THE LEATHER-BACK TURTLE.

The *Coriacious* turtle, so called on account of the leathery nature of its shell, is the largest of the turtle family, not infrequently weighing fifteen hundred pounds. Five strongly prominent tuberculated ridges traverse the entire length of its leathery cuirass. When caught or harpooned they give vent to a kind of cry or groan, horrible to hear; hence its scientific name, *Sphargis Coriacea*, which, in the Greek, signifies "noise in the throat." Its flesh is said to be poisonous to man.

THE SNAPPING TURTLE FIERCER THAN A TIGER.

The thalassite family are all remarkable for slothfulness, which indicates a humbleness that raises them scarcely above the worm, but the indication is deceitful, for among the genus is one species that, for voracity and ferocity, may be compared with the tiger on land and the shark in the sea. It is known under the double name of Fierce Trionyx, and snapping turtle, the former on account of its ugly disposition, and the latter from the manner in which it secures its prey or attacks its foe. This fierce and determined marauder not only inspires the smaller creatures about it with terror, but is also dreaded by man, upon whom it will make the most desperate attacks with serious consequences. Lurking on the banks, it snatches away many unfortunate animals as they come to drink, and commits great havoc among water-fowls, which it seizes from below without showing itself. When urged by hunger it will even seize alligators of considerable size, in combats with which it is invariably victorious.

The flesh of the snapping-turtle is esteemed for its delicacy and rich flavor, on which account it is industriously hunted, or rather fished for. So great is the voracity of this species that it will greedily seize any kind of bait composed of flesh, and by the use of large hooks attached to chains it is readily caught. Its captor's work, however, is not entirely confined to hooking and drawing it ashore, as this turtle when it finds itself being dragged through the water becomes possessed of a devilish ferocity, writhing its long flexible neck and darting its head furiously at the men with the rapidity of a serpent's stroke, and snapping sharply with its formidable jaws, one bite of which would cut away the fingers of a hand, or the toes from the feet, with the ease of a cleaver. Such misfortunes have not infrequently occurred. Mr. Bell records an instance where a snapping-turtle that was being conveyed to England contrived to reach the hand of a sailor, from which it bit a finger and swallowed it.

TENACITY OF LIFE.

The following curious account of this turtle's tenacity of life is given in Wood's Natural History: "As regards the tenacity of life of the snapping turtle, and the sympathy which seems to exist between its several limbs and body for some time after separation has taken place, I witnessed a very curious incident while stopping at a farm in Massachusetts.

"When I had brought the animal home, suspended by the tail, I killed it by chopping off its head, yet the mouth continued to open and shut and the eyes to roll intelligently about. When I held a stick between the open jaws, it closed them with violence; meanwhile the

THE SNAPPING, OR TIGER TURTLE.

headless body was crawling about on the ground. About an hour after severing the head, my mother got some boiling water, which I poured over the body, and then placed it in a tub, so as to separate the horny matter from the flesh. The moment this was done the back heaved and the sides were puffed out as if wind were blown between the skin and flesh, and instantaneously the head, which lay about three or four feet from the tub of hot water, on the ground, opened its mouth with a slight hissing sound, let go its hold on the stick, and the part of the neck adhering to the head expanded, as if also wind was blown into it, and both body and head lay motionless and dead. After having taken out of the body thirty-four eggs, I tore out the heart, which, strange to say, was still throbbing with life, contracting and expanding. I put it upon a plate, where it kept on beating until about noon the following day."

CHAPTER XIX.

BIRDS OF THE SEA.

THE curiosities of the sea are not confined to the monsters which live therein, nor to the quaint and strange forms that people its mighty waters, for there are other wonders to excite our interest in the singular natures bred in the ocean realm. How much too big appears the whale from the mammalia family, an animal unable to breathe in water, warm-blooded and suckling its young, and yet fish-like. We may say the same of seals and thalassites, which are conspicuous types of a double kingdom, since they are double-natured. But the anomalistic features of life in the sea extends still further, for there are aquatic birds so singularly allied to fish-nature that they are equally common to land or water, while the madreporic formations are the connecting link between the mineral and animal life; thus have we a universality, and representatives of all the divisions of natural history in the sea, which baffle our understanding to reconcile. If my readers have found entertainment in the foregoing pages devoted to life in the sea, they will find no little interest in the following descriptions of curious sea-birds, those ocean rovers whose sails are always spread and whose keels pass alike lightly over buffeting waves or deadly reefs.

THE GREAT DIVERS.

The largest species of water-birds, of which we have any distinct account, was the Great Auk, last found on the coast of Iceland some thirty years ago, and now believed to be extinct. It was apparently only an enlarged image of the millions of existing auks found on every coast of the Arctic and Antarctic regions, being in size scarcely inferior to the ostrich. Next to the great auk in size, among aquatic birds, is the great northern diver, found principally in the Arctic seas, where it is an indefatigable fisher, and where it is superstitiously regarded by sailors.

The great diver swims and dives with astonishing facility, and trusts so completely to this natural accomplishment that it very rarely takes wing, and is an indifferent flyer. It is possessed of a marvelous instinct for foretelling storms, and this same instinct admonishes him to seek the open sea, and there receive the tempest, where he rides the waves fearless of injury. Though it is common to find the dead bodies of auks and penguins on the beach after a storm, where they have been killed by waves dashing them against the rocks, such

THE GORFOU AND ITS NEST VILLAGE.

an accident never occurs to the diver, and his immunity from storm dangers and prescience for foretelling foul weather have raised him to the position of true prophet among sailors, who consider it a grave crime to kill the bird-augur.

The feet of the great diver are placed so far behind that they are almost utterly useless on land, except in pushing the bird forward on his breast, its progress on land being made by crawling. Though very timid and difficult to approach, when escape is cut off it fights most viciously with its long, dagger-like bill, which is a weapon of no little formidableness. It is occasionally caught in nets spread for fishes, and also on fish-hooks, where it has tried to take the bait.

THE JACKASS PENGUIN.

One of the most singular of birds, both for appearance and habit, is the penguin, a bird also frequenting Arctic seas, where it congregates in flocks numbering hundreds of thousands. Their feet are placed so far behind that the body rears bolt upright, when on shore, its tarsus, or lower portion of the leg, being flattened to act the part of a sole to stand on. The wings are rudimentary, so that it cannot rise, but, like the diver, trusts to its swimming powers, which are great. Singularly enough, though, the penguin seems insensible to fear, and will suffer itself to be approached and knocked over with a stick, particularly when the females are laying.

The Jackass Penguin is so-called on account of the strange noise it makes when on shore, which is very much like the braying of a donkey. When at sea its notes are quite deep and solemn. The king penguin is not unlike the other species, except in one or two habits, which are strikingly curious. When on shore, instead of a 'parade rest'' in promiscuous positions, they assume a military array, and whether lying or standing they keep in regular close rank, dressed, and eyes front. But they carry this military air still further than a mere review, for they are fastidious in the arrangement of classes so that each will be distinct, thus the young birds will occupy one position, the moulting birds another, the setting hens a third, and the clean birds a fourth; and so strictly do they observe these regulations that if a bird of one class trenches upon another it is at once ejected violently, and by a severe pecking is taught not to repeat the offense. The females lay only a single egg, which, instead of being committed to a nest is carried in a fold between the thighs, and never abandoned for a moment until it is hatched.

CITIES BUILT BY GORFOUS.

The Gorfous, which belong to the penguin family, are remarkable for their Meg Merriles appearance, which is enough to scare the soul out of a ghost, and also for the extraordinary manner in which they congregate together during the breeding season.

When they begin a camp, says Captain Delano, which is usually in connection with other species, they select a piece of ground situated in the neighborhood of the sea, as level and free of stones as possible, and arrange the earth in perfect squares, the lines crossing each other at right-angles as exactly as if drawn by a surveyor, forming squares just large enough for nests, with a compartment between them which serves as a passage-way. After having made ready their encampment each bird selects a square for its nest and takes possession of it. All the different species which breed in the rookeries, the albatross excepted, take care of their brood as a family, and are governed by one and the same law; they never abandon their nests even for a moment, until their little ones are old enough to care for themselves. The male bird hovers near the nest so long as the female sits upon it, and when the latter is about to retire he immediately glides into her place; for if the eggs were exposed for an instant the nearest neighbor would be certain to steal them. The royal gorfou was the first to make thefts of this kind, and never lost an opportunity of stealing the eggs which he found unprotected near him. Thus it sometimes happened that when the eggs were hatched, three or four kinds of birds were found in one nest.

The Great Crested Grebe is even homelier than the gorfou, a comparison which represents the former as about the ugliest and most wierd-looking creature nature ever designed. Its two horns might be likened to the devil, while its unkempt circular beard gives it the pronounced look of a nameless thing that drives through the brain of a dreamer when the stomach is disturbed by boiled cabbage and stale beer. This fright-inspiring creature is equally adapted to flying and swimming, though preferring the water, and will not take wing except when driven to it. The female grebe will bear her young upon her back when danger threatens, and so closely will they nestle under the maternal feathers that it is with difficulty they can be distinguished.

A SERPENTINE BIRD.

If naturalists did not maintain that it was impossible for a reptile to wear feathers I should be inclined to call the Black-Bellied Darter a serpent-bird; not that its appearance, when killed, resembles a snake, for it does not, but because its habits and movements in the water are singularly snake-like. This curious bird has a habit of stealing to the shore and secreting itself on a limb hidden by thick foliage which overhangs the water. Here it basks and watches for fish as they swim beneath, which it catches by darting its sharp head like a flash, swallowing the small prey almost as quickly. A person may watch a darter for hours and all the time believe it to be a snake, unless he is familiar with the bird; for its body lies so close to a limb that it can scarcely be distinguished, while the bird has a way of moving its head and long serpentine neck backward and forward that is an exact imitation of the action of an excited snake. To carry the delusion still further, when alarmed, the darter drops into the water head-first, and that, too, with as little noise as would be made by an eel; and when coming to the surface again it does not show any of its body, only a portion of the head and neck moving in a track exactly like a swimming snake would make.

THE CRESTED GREBE.

The darter seems to have been designed especially for rapid movement through the water under the surface, for its body is very slim and its wings are made to perform the part of powerful fins, so that it can shoot through the water with greater rapidity, I dare say, than any fish, with possibly, a very few exceptions.

BLACK-BREASTED DARTER, OR SERPENT-BIRD.

THE PELICAN AND SOME SUPERSTITIONS ABOUT IT.

The Pelican is a bird so common, even though its home is on the sea-coast, that it hardly merits a description here; nor do I need to say that it is chiefly remarkable for the dilatable pouch sustained by its lower mandible, which is capable of storing a half bushel of fish at a time. "This expansive pouch, whose elasticity is well-known to all who have witnessed the shapes into which it can be stretched, will hold a considerable number of fish, and thus enables the bird to dispose of the superfluous quantity which may be taken during fishing excursions, either for its own consumption or for the nourishment of its young. In feeding the nestlings — and the male is said to supply the female, when setting, in the same manner — the under mandible is pressed against the neck and breast to assist the bird in disgorging the contents of the capacious pouch, and during this action the red nail of the upper mandible would appear to come in contact with the breast, thus laying the foundation for the fable that the pelican nourishes her young with her blood, and for the attitude in which the imagination of painters has placed the bird in books of emblems, etc., with the blood spurting from the wounds made by the terminating nail of the upper mandible into the gaping mouths of her offspring."

Some of the means employed by the pelican in catching fish are so cunning as to appear like the result of reasoning, combined with a perfect knowledge of the habits of their prey. Sometimes, like the gulls, they will hover in the air until they discover a fish near the surface, when they pounce down upon it with almost unerring certainty; in so doing they flap the water with their wings violently, evidently to distract the fish from darting off sideways, or else to paralyze it, though the reason is not fully understood. One of their ingenious methods, however, is as follows: Discovering a shoal of fish, the first pelican that sees them turns back and communicates the intelligence to all the rest, if a flock be near. They now swim out from the bunch and form themselves into a large circle, surrounding the school; at a given signal from the leader each one begins to swim toward the center, thus contracting the circle, and by agitating the water driving the fish together into a small area. They thus continue to swim, picking up occasional prey that attempts to pass them, until the fish are packed so closely together they cannot swim; then the pelicans fall upon the writhing fish and glut themselves to the utmost, besides filling their pouches until their mouths are kept half open. They then return to the shore to sleep and eat again.

The greed of the pelican is so well understood that they are frequently kept by savage islanders and trained to fish, the keepers confining them by a string on the edge of ponds and taking the fish from them as fast as caught.

THE SWIFT-DIVING CORMORANTS.

The Cormorant is not less common than the pelican, being found in nearly all parts of the world, including fresh as well as salt water bodies. They are allied to the pelican, though not closely, for while the latter is on the wing a great portion of the time, the cormorant rarely soars, being a good swimmer and diver; but it is supplied with an æsophagian pouch, into which they store the fish not immediately needed for their food. For voracity the cormorant has no feathered equal, and so expert are they that two or three of them will soon depopulate a large lake of fish. During the summer of 1885 I had the opportunity of watching five cormorants that kept together in Spirit Lake, Iowa. They were not particularly wild, and yet wise enough to keep just beyond shot-gun range. Their gluttony quite astonished me; nearly every moment they would dive and seize a good-sized fish, which they would nearly always bring to the surface before swallowing. Frequently they would catch pickerel and wall-eyed pike-fish of as much as two pounds weight, which they had little difficulty in swallowing, and it appeared that digestion was accomplished almost instantly, for they never left off feeding.

The Chinese make excellent use of the cormorant, which they train with no little care to take fish in the following manner: A string is tied to the bird's leg, of sufficient length to allow it to swim to a distance from the boat, that it may gain confidence and forget that it is a captive; a ring is slipped over the neck that fits barely tight enough to prevent it from gorging a fish of any size. Thus prepared, the bird is taken out in a boat some distance from shore and put into the water; it swims rapidly from its captors until a hundred yards separate them, and now, feeling free, begins to fish. The owner watches his bird carefully, and the moment it captures a large fish he drags the bird toward him by the string; the bird will not loose its hold on the fish, but will continue its frantic efforts to swallow it until the prey is taken from its mouth; the bird is then given a small piece of fish and set back into the water again, where the same performance is repeated. After several days spent in this manner of training, the cormorant learns what is expected of it, and will catch fish and return with them to the boat to receive the small piece that is awarded for its services, apparently forgetting that it could swallow the entire fish.

MOTHER CAREY'S CHICKENS.

Far out at sea, and usually presaging rough weather, the stormy petrels, or Mother Carey's chickens, as they are most generally called, are met, skimming the waves and sometimes tapping their feet on the surface, hence the name Petrel, or Little Peter, from a fancied imitation of St. Peter walking on the water. These birds, when flying, very closely resemble our common bank swallows both in size and appearance. For many years it was believed that the petrel never visited land but carried her eggs under her wings through sunshine and tempest, until they were hatched, when the young immediately took wing, which it never quitted again while living. It is now known that they frequent headlands and islands not subject to disturbance, and there nestle in crevices of the rocks, holes in the turf, or under stones on the weedy shore, where the female lays a single large egg. Until able to fly the young do not quit their nest, and as the setting birds will not desert their young, however imminent the danger, they may be taken with the hand. Upon being seized they discharge the contents of their stomachs, which is generally a viscous fluid resembling oil.

"Up and down! up and down!
From the base of the wave to the billow's crown,
And amidst the flashing and feathery foam
The stormy petrel finds a home;
A home, if such a place there be
For her who lives on the wide, wide sea,
On the craggy ice, in the frozen air,
And only seeking her rocky lair
To warn her young, and teach them to spring
At once o'er the waves on their stormy wing."

It is not true that the petrel quits its flight only at breeding time, for I have seem them time and again resting on the water like gulls, which their webbed feet and thick coat of breast-feathers enables them to do with ease.

BIRDS OF TIRELESS WINGS.

Besides the sea-birds that haunt the coasts or dive through the waves as their natural element, there are others that live in the air, visiting land only to deposit their eggs, or to sleep a short time after great engorgement. Most familiar of these birds is the gull, of which there are a number of species, but all essentially of the same habits. They are decidedly sociable, and at times become so tame that they may be knocked down with clubs. Sailors regard them with considerable affection, and will invariably protect them, so that comparatively few are wantonly killed. One of the first evidences of an approach to land is the appearance of gulls about the ship; they come out several miles from shore to greet incoming vessels, and in hundreds troop about the stern, watching in the wake for any bits of food that may be thrown overboard. Amusement is sometimes afforded by dropping a line with baited hook in the wake of the vessel, which is sure soon to be seized by a greedy gull, and being caught by the hook a lively struggle ensues to land it, for the line and hook must both be very strong, or the bird will break away.

THE WANDERING ALBATROSS.

The least met with, and yet the best known bird that haunts the sea, is the Wandering Albatross, a bird of omen, and the subject of sailor superstitions, so exquisitely described in Coleridge's "Ancient Mariner." It is very large, having an expanse of wings sometimes of fourteen feet, and yet possesses the power of sailing along for days at a time without requiring rest or even flapping its wings. This power to cleave the air by merely extending the wings, is possessed also by the condor, buzzard, vulture, and a few others, and is a mystery which science does not attempt to explain. While walking in the footsteps of those who have gone before, and approaching the altars of science with a feeling of veneration, nevertheless, I cannot resist the temptation to offer my humble and crude opinion in explanation of this sailing power of certain birds:

The most striking difference in the structure of birds and creeping animals is found in their bones, which in the former are hollow, while in the latter they are filled with marrow. We know that marrow is the life principle of bone, for in case of fracture resulting in a loss of marrow, the bone, thus bereft of its life-imparting principle, dies, becomes rotted and disintegrates. If marrow is so essential to the bones of animals, why is it wanting in the bones of birds? The answer may be found in this: Nature, having designed birds for passage through the air, gave to them a structure wonderful for its lightness and strength, in doing which she made their bones hollow, and, instead of marrow, filled them with circulating air, which is an equally active life-principle. In the albatross and other birds which sail through space by the mere expansion of their wings, the air which circulates through their bones is supplied, not directly from the respiratory organs, but from the heart, which pumps the blood through the veins, and hot air at the same time through osseous ducts of the bones. This heated air acts to buoy the bird, in some much greater than in others, because the supply is not the same in all

THE WANDERING ALBATROSS.

species. Any one who is careful to examine the bones of the albatross will be astonished upon cracking them open to find how numerous are the minute osseous ducts which ramify the hollow, and, if the bird be recently killed, they will also be surprised at the great heat of the bones. The tendency of the bird, whose bones are thus filled with heated gases, is to rise or remain in suspension, as the will directs, and by placing its wings at the required angle it is enabled to move forward or sail in circles. Those who have watched these sailing birds know that in moving directly forward they never do so on the same plane, but gradually rise, then drop again, and thus continue alternately rising and falling; this illustrates the principle I have tried to explain, and serves to furnish a demonstration of the theory here advanced: that it is due to the circulation, through the bones, of air or gases, heated by the heart, certain birds are able to sail without flapping their wings.

ANGLING FOR ALBATROSS.

The Albatross is found only in Southern seas, its principal haunts being in the latitude of Patagonia, where it lives in great numbers. Like the petrel, it follows ships for the sake of obtaining food, and is such a glutton that it never knows when its appetite is satiated. A voyager around Cape Horn relates that he once saw an albatross seize a piece of whale's blubber weighing at least four pounds, which it swallowed entire; the bird was now unable to rise from the water, so gorged was its stomach, yet it eagerly seized another piece of equal size, which was thrown to it on a hook, and only escaped capture by the hook breaking in its mouth. Wood says:

"Angling for albatross is a favorite amusement, and the bird often gives good sport, sometimes rising into the air and being drawn down on deck like a boy's kite, but generally hanging back with all its might, and resisting the pull of the line by means of its wings squared in the water. It is no easy matter to haul in an albatross under such circumstances, and the bird often escapes by the hook tearing out or the line breaking. Nothing, however, teaches it wisdom, for in a few minutes it is quite as ready to take the bait again. Even those that have been captured, marked by a ribbon tied round their necks and set at liberty, will follow the vessel as soon as they recover themselves.

"When an albatross is hooked the others become very angry, thinking that their companion is monopolizing the tempting food. Down they sweep accordingly, pounce on the spot, and when settled on the water are very much astonished to see their companion towed away and themselves left sitting on the waves with nothing to eat. Should one of these birds be shot, the remainder pounce upon it at once, and soon entomb their late companion in their rapacious maws. These birds may, under some circumstances, be dangerous to human beings, as they have been observed to swoop upon the head of a man who had fallen overboard, and their long, powerful beaks are fearful weapons."

"I have read," says Mangin, "in a French paper, of the super-

THE SWIFT-WINGED FRIGATE-BIRD.

cargo of a French vessel, who having in bravado mounted on one of the yards and missed his footing fell into the waves. Unfortunately, the ship was not provided with any effective apparatus for the rescue of the drowning; but while a boat was being lowered to hasten to his assistance, he continued to keep afloat. But suddenly a flock of albatrosses threw themselves upon the unfortunate man, striking him with their heavy wings, and tearing his head and face with their cruel beaks. Unable to maintain this fierce combat against both the billows and his voracious enemies, he sank before the eyes of his approaching comrades."

THE SWIFT-WINGED FRIGATE-BIRD.

Nature seems to have created certain birds and animals only to rob others, withholding from them the instinct to procure food by innocent means, and thus licensing them to commit piracy through the operation of natural laws. An illustration of this curious fact is found in the Frigate-bird, whose life is devoted entirely to brigandage. This creature is little else than wings, having, we might say, the body of a sparrow and the pinions of an eagle. When the storm breaks it lifts itself to the serene heights where calm ever prevails. The poetical metaphor, false in relation to every other bird, is no mere figure of speech when applied to him. Literally, he sleeps upon the storm. When he wills to fly all distance vanishes; he may breakfast in China, and dine in America. Hè is the realization of Puck's boast to "put a girdle about the world in forty minutes." Though borne through the air at lightning speed the frigate-bird spends a lonely, nomadic existence, traversing fields which must soon grow monotonous, and, leading the life of a robber, he meets the robber's fate, satiated to-day, hungry to-morrow, mobbed by outraged victims the next.

Up and down the watery world speeds the frigate-bird, watching with piercing eyes the industrious fishing birds, which he attacks and compels to surrender to him their finny prey. He strikes the gull as it wings its way toward its nest with throat filled with food for the hungry young, and biting the poor bird's neck compels it to disgorge the fish, off which the robber then feeds.

CHAPTER XX.

SUPERSTITIONS AND LEGENDS OF THE SEA.

CAN we marvel at the strange beliefs, the faith in unseen things, the fanciful creations born of the sailor's brain, connected with the ocean? Reflect upon the terror and mystery with which the first man gazed upon the sea; the untutored mind that saw a spectre's face in every flash of lightning, and heard a monster's voice in every thunder peal. There, before his astonished gaze, lay the turbulent waters of an infinite empire over which mankind had laid no claim; a realm that stretched away to the beetling heavens, and mingled with the vault that o'erspread the world. He peopled the sky with gods, and fancied that the arch impinged upon the sea to give them pathway to the earth; he filled the ocean with monsters, and forthwith conceived their gateway to the skies; thus, far away to the horizon, were ascending and descending gods, and monsters who guarded their realm against the approach of man by mighty tempests and unfathomable depths, by whirlpools, water-spouts and supernatural hands.

> "Boundless, endless and sublime,
> The image of eternity, the throne
> Of th' invisible."

If man took up his primeval abode on the ocean coast, he felt that he was too near the domain of the spiritual, and withdrew himself afar from it, going into the interior to establish his kingdoms. But curiosity is a striking trait in human character, and though fear may hold its sovereignty for a time, curiosity will at last combat it. Mankind gradually spread over the interior and fructified the soil by well-directed labor, became familiar with rivers and lakes, ana, drawn on by his natural love for exploration, continued moving toward the sea. Here there was another pause, to contemplate the wonders which lay within the unknown depths which traversed the illimitable bosom, that haunted the rock-bound shore, and such as dwelt in the boiling clouds, or moved in the storm upon the seething surface.

LEGEND OF THE PILLARS OF HERCALES, OR HERCULES.

Though man stood upon the ocean beach and trembled before the mystery which the waters contained, his curiosity was stronger than his fears, and, following that natural bent for exploration, he at length builded small boats and ventured to ride upon the waves. From small vessels larger ones grew, and from oars sails developed, and man began to measure the littoral, to convey products, and to carry the munitions of war. This field of exploration was confined to the Mediterranean, however, and when the navigators came at last to the gates of Gibraltar, which led out into a boundless space of sea, here they halted again, before the great rocks that rose up on either side of the narrow strait, and said: "These are the pillars of Hercules," between which no ship dared tempt to sail. Beyond these pillars, to the benighted minds of the time, there was a region of impenetrable darkness, the home of frightful monsters possessing keen appetites for ships and their crews; worse than this was the hand of Satan, that rose up out of these waters to grasp any venturesome soul that dared to penetrate the domain of horrors.

But the Mediterranean had not yet lost its terrors, for there were Charybdis and Scylla, two frightful monsters near the island of Sicily, that allowed no vessel to pass near them without drawing it into their voracious maws and destroying both boat and crew. On the coast of Sicily also lived three dreadful cyclops, who, according to Hesoid, were especially fond of human flesh, and to obtain this it was their habit to lie in wait, concealed behind immense cliffs, for passing vessels, which they destroyed by heaving great stones at them, and then would wade out and secure the crew.

The Euxine, or Black Sea, also had its terrors for the sailors, thousands of whom, it is said, lost their lives in a vain effort to recover the golden fleece of the ram Chrysomallus, which was represented as being guarded by a sleepless dragon. And thus a hundred other superstitions of the ancients, preserved in the Greek and Roman mythology, might be given to show why progress in navigation was so slow.

SINGULAR ORIGIN OF OCEAN NAVIGATION.

The development of this now great industry, strange enough, is due, not to adventurous desire, as we might reasonably suppose, but to the enforcement of criminal laws in Egypt, by which several offenders were doomed, as a punishment, to sail beyond the Pillars of Hercules and accomplish the circumnavigation of Africa. Should they succeed in this they were to receive a full pardon for their crimes; but the sentence was supposed to be even worse than immediate capital punishment. Those who were thus sent upon the most perilous of voyages, after an absence of several months returned safely to Egypt; but it having been proved that they had not sailed around Africa, they were at once put to death. But a great advance had been made. A ship had gone out into what was considered the region of darkness and the domain of Satan, and the crew finding the ocean tranquil and the sun cheering, besides discovering the Canary Islands, these superstitious fears began to abate, and upon their return others volunteered to penetrate the ocean-world still further, and thus exploration continued.

Though there was thenceforth a stronger desire to sail the waste of waters, there was only a slight abatement of belief in sea monsters; indeed, I do not know that there was any less faith in the existence of frightful gods and dragons than before; but these unreal creatures had assumed different shapes in the minds of sailors, and, of course, lost some of their terrors.

THE FIRST SHIP AND SAILOR.

Sailors' traditions and songs always allude to Noah as the first sailor, and to his ark as the first that was ever made to float, though when the plans and dimensions of that vessel are explained, most of them shake their heads in solemn disapproval of the idea of going to sea in such a tub.

Many traditions concerning the Biblical Ark are reported. Berosus and Syncellus say fragments of it were preserved in the Georgian Mountains, and bitumen was taken from them, to be used as charms. El Kazwini says a temple constructed out of the planks of the Ark long covered the spot where it rested, enduring until the time of the Abassides. Epiphanius says the same. Josephus says pieces of it were reported as existing in his day, and El Macin tells us that the Emperor Heraclitus visited the remains of the ark on El Djudi. Benjamin of Tudela says Caliph Omar carried the Ark away in 640, and placed it in a temple on an island in the Tigris. I, Ben Abbas, commentator on the Koran, says Noah was bidden to build the Ark of the wood of a plane-tree which he had brought from India, and whose growth in twenty years furnished abundant material. Various times are stated in Mussulman legend as having been occupied in its construction, the term extending from ten to one hundred and twenty years. Oriental legends say the Ark made the tour of the world in six months. Jewish rabbis said it was miraculously lighted up by a shining stone. Many of the Christain fathers asserted that the wood of the Ark was to be seen in the Koord country, and Prevoux says a piece of it is shown in the town of Chemna, in Arabia. Rawlinson saw bits of wood brought from Jebel Joodee, the Ararat of the modern Armenians, by pilgrims. Marco Polo says there was a tradition in his time that the Ark still rested on a mountain in Armenia. In 1670, one John Stroan went up Ararat until he said he saw the Ark visible, a speck in the distance above him.

SUPERSTITIONS OF COLUMBUS' CREW.

When Columbus set sail for India his crew, though experienced sailors, were subject to great fears, which at one time became so intense that they threatened mutiny if a return was not at once made. How these anxieties were assuaged and the voyage continued is told in history. A portion of this history, however, is not generally known now, though it was freely given in several publications directly after Columbus returned to Spain.' I have already referred to the chronicles of Padre Philoponus, who accompanied Columbus, and who told such frightful stories of sea-gryphons, sea-dogs, and other marine monsters with which he had strange adventures, that it is a wonder Columbus could gather a crew to make a second voyage.

THE PHANTOM SHIP.

Though every wave of the sea has been tracked by some vessel until it is as familiar as the land, and though the natural history of the ocean is a science well understood, yet superstition has not wholly lost her grip upon those who, from constant familiarity with the sea, have least reason to be under her influence.

One of the most popular superstitions, shared generally by sailors, is an implicit belief in the appearance of a Phantom Ship, which is a sure precursor of fatal calamity. There is not wanting abundant evidence in attestation of this spiritual rover of the seas, and to read the affidavits of so many Jack-tars who swear that they have seen the phantom, confuses our belief until we marvel at man's credulity.

Sir Walter Scott has embalmed belief in the spectral ship in the following words:

"The phantom ship, whose form
Shoots like a meteor through the storm,
When the dark scud comes driving hard,
And lowered is my topsail yard,
And canvas wove in earthly looms
No more to brave the storm presumes;
Then 'mid the roar of sea and sky,
Top and top-gallant hoisted high,
Full spread and crowded every sail,
The demon frigate braves the gale,
And well the doom'd spectators know
The harbinger of wreck and woe."

During that period in American history when there was carried on an extensive, though infamous, traffic in captured slaves from Africa, the phantom ship was reported seen by several different vessels every month, until its haunts seemed to be established off the Cape of

THE PHANTOM SHIP.

Good Hope, a region quite dangerous enough to give rise to the superstition. The origin of this strange illusion is no doubt found in the fact that, under certain conditions of the atmosphere, objects on the surface of the sea loom up, so that a vessel so far distant that its masts are hidden by the sphericity of the earth, may yet be seen in an inverted position, apparently in the sky. Such a sight, witnessed by sailors totally unacquainted with the laws of refraction, would naturally impress them with a supernatural cause, and hence give rise to the belief in a phantom ship.

WITCHCRAFT ON THE SEA.

In Ingolsby's Legends, and Scott's Demonology, we will find a great many stories of witches whose powers prevail over the sea. An ancient chronicle, near the middle of the fifteenth century, when witches were particularly plentiful, records the following concerning an old woman named Sampson:

"* * * At that time His Majesty (James VI) was in Denmark, she took a cat and christened it, and afterwards bound to each part of that cat the chiefest parts of a dead man, and several joints of his body; on the night following this preparation the cat was conveyed into the midst of the sea, by herself and other witches sailing in their baskets, and so committed the said cat to the waves right before the town of Leith, in Scotland. Directly after this was done there arose such a tempest in the sea as a greater hath not been seen, which tempest was the cause of the perishing of a vessel wherein were sundry jewels and rich gifts, which should have been presented to the new Queen of Scotland, at Her Majesty's coming to Leith."

It may be proper to add that this is the record of the woman's confession. extorted, however, by toasting her over coals of fire.

Not only were ignorant sailors impressed by such ridiculous reports and beliefs, for kings and other great men industriously propagated the idle stories if they did not, indeed, believe them. King James even wrote a book on demonology, wherein he maintains with sober earnestness that "witches can raise stormes and tempestes in the aire, either on sea or land."

SINGULAR BELIEFS STILL PREVAILING.

The Doge of Venice, in early times, when that city was mistress of the maritime world, espoused the sea with all the ceremonial of a royal wedding. This custom was a recognition of the importance of the sea, and was believed to encourage the sea's favor into giving

Venetian vessels calm water and good winds. In later times the Greek metropolitan, at Constantinople, annually threw a small gold cross into the Bosphorus to secure the good offices of the sea. But even to this day the waters of the Neva River, at St. Petersburg, are blessed with lavish display of ceremony, in which all the priests of the city officiate. The original object of this strange church rite—which it has become—is lost, or at least upon inquiring among the priests while I was in St. Petersburg I was told that it was a mere ordinance of the church for the benefit of the poor. This, of course, does not explain the origin, but it is believed by the Russian lower classes that the water thus blessed is efficacious for the cure of every ill flesh is heir to.

Stones are used among several Pacific Island peoples to raise or abate the wind, and also to give good luck to fishermen. A certain kind of blue stones, resembling jade are very generally used for this purpose, and so sacredly are they regarded that a custodian is appointed to care for them; also, in administering an oath, the stone is placed in front of the witness, and is decidedly more impressive as an incentive to truth among the islanders than a Bible is in the presence of a Christian.

The Finlanders are very superstitious, carrying their rediculous credulity so far that they place implicit confidence in a line about five feet long, in which three knots are tied. This line is preserved through great lapses of time, as not every line is supposed to possess the same miraculous virtues. It is used wholly at sea, and to raise the wind. When a calm prevails one of the knots is unloosened, whereupon a good wind springs up; if rapid speed is necessary a second knot in untied, which always bring a favoring gale, and if the third be loosened a great storm breaks over the sea. They always carry a stone which the steersman rubs in order to make sure of his route; this stone prevents him from erring.

In the early days of navigation the French had an idea that the most effectual way of abating a storm was to offer a sacrifice, which always took place by tying a midshipman to the main-mast and flogging him cruelly. This it was thought would propitiate the storm-king.

The Normans of Dieppe, which is now French, entertained a very singular superstition concerning All Saint's Day, which they observed with religious fidelity. It was their custom to remain indoors on that day, believing that evil would befall all who ventured out, and that if an attempt to fish were made the fisherman would draw in only a net full of bones for his pains. The sailors of that port believed that at midnight a spectral funeral train passed through the streets, headed by a hearse drawn by eight white horses, and which contained the souls of all the sailors that had died within the year. Few dared to test the truth of this singular superstition, because it was veritably believed that anyone who even attempted to look upon the scene would die within a few days after; and, therefore, to avoid temptation the doors and windows of every sailor's house were closely barred on that dread night.

Fishermen, as a rule, are directed in nearly all their acts by some quaint belief, the origin of which, in most cases, they have forgotten. Those engaged in the Baltic fisheries never go to sea with their nets between All Saint's and St. Martin's Day, because such sacrilege would make them unlucky throughout the year. Easter and Palm Sundays are similarly observed, though generally given over to festivities. Fridays are considered as specially unlucky days, and no vessel will start out on a voyage on that day without unusual cause.

OFFERINGS TO SEA GODS.

An Eastern paper lately contained a narrative of an incident which took place on a sailing vessel bound from Liverpool to Australia. Meeting with head winds, the sailors conceived that the cause of the delay was the captain's dog, and took occasion, while the captain was asleep, to sacrifice the animal, after which the wind immediately changed. A similar occurrence is detailed by Bassett:

"An early traveler gives us an account of an offering made by sailors in the Black Sea. The ship had been long wind-bound near a rocky promontory, where a deity called Semes was supposed to reside, and the men said the vessel was charmed. The second mate declared that they would not get away without an offering. They were detained there four days, and after they got away the mate said: 'Ah, well, when I told you that you should propitiate Semes you laughed at me; but notwithstanding, if, during the night, I had not taken the resolution to climb secretly upon the rocks you would never have passed them. It was a custom in Germany during the fifteenth and sixteenth centuries to offer carp and pike to St. Ulrich, a fisherman's patron. Grimm shows from old documents that the Alemanni and Franks sacrificed horses at river crossings. Livonian fishermen, before putting to sea, propitiate the divinities by a libation of brandy poured on the waters. Norwegian sailors frequently made offerings to the water-spirits, as did Germans and Danes. A tradition exists that a man would offer a cake to the sea, but it was frozen over; he cut a hole in the ice, when a hand reached out and seized the cake. Fishermen of Folkstone formerly chose eight whitings out of each boat, and made a feast to a certain St. Rumbald at Christmas. In certain parts of Cornwall they used to set aside a certain portion of the catch, and leave it on the beach as an offering to Bucca, a spirit greatly feared."

DEITIES THAT PRESIDE OVER SHIPS.

The mythology of ancient times placed every enterprise under the care of deities, and according to this idea every ship had its guardian god, whose image was displayed prominently in some part of the vessel, generally at the prow. Hence comes the modern figure-head, of which many superstitions are narrated The general belief in demons which seek to harm, and in good spirits that strive to protect the sailors is very marked, and not a few curious features of this form of sailor superstition are recorded:

"Certain demons called landættir were believed in Denmark to threaten ships from the shore, and a law of *uleliote*, in the thirteenth century, required that the figure-heads then carried at the prow must be taken off on approaching shore, so as not to frighten these malevolent spirits. In the Issefiord, a part of Gattegat Strait, a sea-demon formerly dwelt who stopped each ship and demanded a man from it. But it was found by consulting the priests that he could be exorcised, and this was done by procuring the head of Pope Lucius, beheaded at Rome, and showing it to the demon. Three-winged fiends attacked the crew of one of Gorm's ships in his voyage to the Isle of the West, and were only appeased by the sacrifice of three men. In the romantic legends of William of Orange, Desrane's head is thrown into the sea, and demons so haunt the spot that sailors dare not approach it. There is an old legend that Satan got into the ark, and tried to sink it by cutting a hole. To these accounts of maritime demons in the middle ages, we may add a story of more tangible shape, believed to be demoniacal in character. The Abbe De Choisy tells the tale: 'Great noise among the sailors; some one suddenly cried, There is the devil! We must have him! Soon all is motion; every one took arm; naught is seen but spikes, harpoons and muskets. I ran myself to see the devil, and I saw a large fish which resembled a ray, except it had two horns, as a bull. It made several bounds, always accompanied by a white fish, which from time to time came to attack it, and then went under it. Between its two horns it carried a little gray fish, which one calls the pilot of the devil because it conducts it, and it sticks it when it sees a fish, and the devil goes like an arrow.' "

LAUNCHING AND CHRISTENING A SHIP.

The ship is the sailor's home, in the majority of cases all the home he has, and it is not at all remarkable that many sea superstitions should cluster about the vessel. His ship is always personified by the sailor, and he alludes to "her" frequently in terms of endearment, showing that to the marine mind a ship is something more than a mere aggregation of wood and iron. The safety of the sailors depending upon the staunchness of the vessel, the latter is watched with the most jealous care. The ceremonies at the launching of a ship are of no small consequence to sailors, and it is said to be remarkable how quickly the whole marine community becomes informed of incidents believed to be unlucky. Ceremonies at the laying of the keel, or at the launch of the new vessel into her destined element, have always been performed. Ancient authors state that the ship was launched with ceremonies, first decking it with flowers and a crown of leaves, and pouring out a libation. Similar practices prevailed during the middle ages. The vessel was decked with flowers, purified by a priest, anointed with egg and sulphur, consecrated and named for some saint, and then launched. When a modern ship of any size or importance is launched, it is frequently made a gala occasion, the vessel being gayly decked with flags, and a band of music stationed on board. The principal shores are removed, and but one or two left, to retain the cradle in which the ship is launched upon the ways. When ready, it is usual to break a bottle of wine over the vessel's bow, then the last shore is removed, and the vessel glides into her destined element amid the cheers of the beholders and the strains of music. It was always regarded as a bad omen should any accident happen or if the ship refused to move, or the wine was not spilled, or especially if any lives were lost. This must have occurred frequently during the middle ages, for we read that slaves or criminals were usually appointed to remove the last shores. In our day, this is done by electricity, the gentle finger of some favored maiden manipulating the key. In 1878 a large excursion steamer was launched at Norfolk, Va., in the presence of many invited guests. The wine was not broken over the bow, and many predicted disaster to the vessel, and regarded the omen as verified when the ship was lost while being towed to New York. Perhaps it will be remembered that when a big yacht was launched late as 1885, without the customary waste of a bottle of wine on her bow, the omission was telegraphed all over the world, because it showed a very remarkable temerity on the part of the owners.

MYSTERIOUS ISLANDS.

Among the odds and ends of superstitions found on board ships are some that have evidently had a basis of truth. Artificial floating islands are mentioned in several ancient histories, being really rafts covered with earth and vegetation, and the embodiment of these stories in tradition is still found among sailors of the present. "In the Speculum Regale we are tóld of an island that sometimes approached the Danish coast, on which grew herbs that could cure all ills, but no more than one person could land on it at a time, when it would disappear for seven years, and on bringing back its burden, it sank, and another island arose in its place similar to it. Giraldus tells us of an island that appeared and then vanished, but finally became fixed on some one landing on it. A French author, Pichot, says there were legends among northern sailors of floating islands, covered with grass, trees, etc., which sank in the sea at intervals. They regard them as the abode of malicious spirits, who cause them to rise and float about, so as to embarrass navigators. Gummers Ore, just in sight of Stockholm, was one of these islands, and it is figured in the charts of Bardeus, a geographer. Baron Grippenheim relates that he long sought it in vain, but finally saw it by chance, as he raised his head when fishing, it appearing as three points of land. The fishermen informed him what it was, and said that its appearance prognosticated storms and plenty of fish, and added that it was but a reef, inhabited by sea-trolls, or, perhaps, shapes assumed by the trolls. A floating island appears on Lake Derwentwater, in England. Some call it the Devil's Barge, and assert that it only appears in years of calamity, by this premise deducing the fact that England is about to be visited by the cholera. This prophecy is strengthened by the fact that it appeared in the last great cholera year. It matters not that it has also appeared since. Others (among them the oldest inhabitants) declare that it presages three months continual frost. Marco Polo tells us of islands inhabited by men alone, and of others inhabited by women alone. Colonel Yule says many ancient traditions of such islands were told. Mendoza heard of such in Japan, where there is still a legendary woman's island; and Columbus heard the same legend of Martinique. Near Formosa lies Mauriga Sima, said, in Japanese lore, to have been sunk for the crimes of its inhabitants, and yet peopled by their souls. Kempfer says the vessels and urns which the fishermen have brought from it are sold at an enormous price in China and Japan."

VIRTUES OF A CHILD'S CAUL.

One of the most extraordinary superstitions by which sailors are influenced is their belief in the marvelous efficacy of a child's caul. This is a very ancient superstition, frequently mentioned by the old writers. Grose says: "It is deemed lucky to be born with a *caul*, or membrane, over the face. This *caul* is esteemed an infallible preservative against drowning. * * * According to Crysostom, the midwives frequently sold it for magic use." Cæsar is said to have been brought into the world, unnaturally as he was, with a caul over his head, which presaged the greatness he was to attain.

Charles Dickens, referring to this quaint belief, in writing of himself, says: "I was born with a *caul*, which was advertised for sale in the newspapers at the low price of fifteen guineas"—seventy-five dollars. Similar advertisements may be occasionally seen in the English papers even to-day, though the caul is not nearly so highly esteemed as formerly.

Previous to the discovery of the compass, or rather before it became known to the mariners of Europe, there were some curious methods in vogue for guiding ships, not the least singular of which was the use of crows. These birds being considered wise beyond their nature were taken on board of every ship and loosed when the vessel got beyond the sight of land; the direction which they steered was taken as an infallible indication of the quarter in which the nearest land lay. If, perchance, the crow made a fatal mistake, his misery was pretty certain to meet with company, for the ship followed with a blind truthfulness.

Denis de Montfort, some of whose creations we have described in the chapter devoted to sea-serpents, delighted in putting in print the wild, weird fantasies which ever and anon disturbed his brain, and these phantasms were accepted by the people with a faith and solemnity which well illustrates the ignorance of the times. He told of a monster so immense that the largest whale was but a mere pigmy in comparison; this huge creature he represented as sometimes floating upon the surface of the sea, where, being covered with marine plants and barnacles, it was often mistaken for a floating island. Olaus Magnus not only confirmed these wonderful stories, but was particular in his description of the animal, which he pronounced to be a gigantic cetacean, to which ships not infrequently anchored under the false impression that its back was firm ground. He even went so far as to represent that sailors sometimes built fires upon the monster's back to cook their meals, without disturbing its slumbers.

MARVELOUS BIRD-BEARING TREES.

At first thought it would appear that human credulity could hardly compass more wonderful things than Magnus' cetacean, but a little reading convinces us that the faith of a sailor surpasses the conceptions even of Montfort and his colaborators of mysticism.

Sebastian Munster is the author of a treatise on cosmography, which, for extraordinary statements, transcends the Apocrypha. For a long time great mystery was attached to the origin of certain water-birds; for example, the petrel was supposed to be of tireless wing, and never to rest on shore. For these Munster conceived a theory at once original and wonderful, yet there were not wanting plenty of persons to accept it with implicit confidence. He maintained that all such birds as had not been discovered laying their eggs near the sea were the product of certain trees which grow in the marshes or on the coast of the ocean. Those who accepted this theory affirmed that there was a species of tree growing on the Orkney Islands which bore fruit resembling in size and shape a wild duck's egg; this fruit, they declared, opened at maturity, and from them escaped little ducks. In a description of this interesting product of the animal from the vegetable, Munster says:

"We find trees in Scotland which produce a fruit enveloped in leaves, and when it drops into the water at a suitable time, it takes life and is turned into a live bird, which they call a *tree-bird*."

Aldrovandus, the most learned ornithologist of the Renaissance, propagated these ridiculous fables in his great work, and not only so asserted, but even presented engravings, as did also his prototypes, Munster and Magnus, of the bird-bearing trees.

A writer mentions a singular ceremony which was performed a short time ago by some Scandinavian fishermen to bring good luck. The fishing chanced to be extremely poor during the season, which was then more than half spent, and, to change this evil condition, seized upon á cooper, whom they stripped of his clothes and then placed on him a heavy woolen shirt, which they stuck full of burrs. Thus scantily attired and presenting a ludicrous appearance, he was conveyed through the town in a hand-barrow, with all the people of the place at his heels shouting like so many bedlamites. It is not told whether or not this barbaric ceremony brought the fishermen good luck.

DEAD BODIES ON SHIP-BOARD.

A dead body in a ship is still considered to be a magnet which attracts calamity; this belief is not only shared by those who go before the mast, but exercises great influence even among captains of our ocean palaces. So prevalent is this base superstition that when a passenger dies at sea it is entirely discretionary with the captain whether the body be kept on board and carried to its destination, or immediately committed to the waves. So recent as the summer of 1885, a case illustrating this dread of dead bodies on ship-board was developed under the following circumstances: A gentleman in the last stages of consumption engaged passage, with his wife, on one of our finest ocean steamers from Liverpool to New York, this country being his home. When in mid-ocean the patient was seized with a hemorrhage which speedily terminated his life, and ministering friends at once prepared the body, at the widow's solicitation, by embalming, for the remainder of the journey. Scarcely had this been done when the captain learned of the man's death, and he immediately ordered it cast into the sea. The widow was shocked at this outrageous order, but her protestations availed nothing; being wealthy, she offered the captain a large sum of money to allow the body to remain, and then, with cries and heart-breaking entreaties, begged that she might keep her dead and consign it to the precious earth beside some of her children. The captain was inexorable, and even used some force in seizing the dead body and throwing it into the waves. This officer was hardly so brutal as he appeared, for he was really actuated by a superstitious fear that if the body were allowed to remain on board some dreadful calamity would befall the ship.

As a fitting conclusion to this brief description of some of the superstitions peculiar to seamen, I may mention a novel theory recently put forth by a man, sage, or lunatic, in New York. This marvelous genius maintains with much display of argument, that the world is a living body whose respiration is proved by the tides; the trees and vegetation are this creatures' hirsute adornment; the volcanoes are chronic ulcerations on its body, and the winds indicate the character of its exercise, being calm when the animal is quiet, and violent when it is performing some duty requiring much exercise of vigor. Silly as this theory is, it is not more so than a thousand other absurd superstitions which millions of credulous beings believe.

ANCIENT BELIEF IN THE MERMAID.

The verity of mermen and mermaids seems to have been thoroughly established in earlier centuries, if we accept the evidence of the most celebrated writers and naturalists of those ages, who, however, looked at nature through spectacles very different from those which are adopted to modern eyes.

Shakespeare, who gave fancy wings, alludes to these pleasing creatures in the following lines:

> "I heard a mermaid on a dolphin's back
> Uttering such dulcet and harmonious breath
> That the rude sea grew civil at her song."

And again:

> "Who would be a mermaid fair?
> Singing alone, combing her hair,
> Under the sea."

In a well known work entitled the "Speculum Regale," published in the twelfth century, which was regarded at the time as being one of the greatest scientific issues, occurs the following description of a mermaid, which was evidently given to set at rest all doubts on the subject:

"A monster is seen also near Greenland, like a woman as far down as the waist; long hands and soft hair, the neck and head in all respects like that of a human being. The hands seem to people to be long, and the fingers not to be parted, but united by a web like that on the feet of water-birds. From the waist downward this monster resembles a fish, with scales, tail and fin. This prodigy is supposed to show itself more especially before heavy storms. The habit of this creature is to dive frequently, and come up again to the surface with fishes in its hands. When sailors see it playing with the fish, or throwing them toward the ship, they fear they are doomed to lose several of the crew; but when it casts the fish, or, turning from the vessel, flings them away from her, the sailors take it as a good omen that they will not suffer loss in an impending storm. The monster has a very horrible face, with broad brow and piercing eyes, a wide mouth and a double chin."

More circumspect than this statement, however, appears a description recorded by the Jesuits of India, and made a part of their ecclesiastical proceedings, wherein it is asserted that seven of these wonderful creatures, both male and female, were captured on the Ceylon coast and thence taken to Goa, where the physician to the viceroy carefully dissected them. This learned man, it is claimed, found that "their internal structure was in all respects similar to that of the human."

FABLED MERMAID AND MERMAN.

In the light of a more ample knowledge of God's creatures, it may be said that a dissection of either the dolphin, dugong, lamantin or manatee will show that their internal parts are almost identical with those of a human. Another claim to the likeness which the dugong bears to a human is found in the fact that the animal gives expression to its grief in tears. The common people of Sumatra, where the dugong abounds, ascribe great virtue to the tears thus shed, and bottle them in the belief that they act as a charm to secure affection.

The remains of a species of Stellerus have been found which bear a much closer resemblance to a human than any that are at present known to exist. The creature is now supposed to be extinct, as no living specimen has been met with since about the middle of the last century.

Shakespeare alludes to the superstition which was at one time very general among sailors, that to see a mermaid swimming away from a vessel foreboded disaster, in the following line put in the mouth of Glocester, in "3d King Richard III:"

"I'll drown more sailors than the merman shall."

But in the "Comedy of Errors" the great poet pictures the beauty and divine grace of these exquisite creatures as follows:

"O, train me not, sweet mermaid, with thy note
To drown me in thy sister's flood of tears;
Sing, syren, for thyself, and I will dote.
Spread o'er the silver waves thy golden hairs,
And as a bed I'll take thee; and there lie;
And in that glorious supposition think
He gains by death, that hath such means to die."

In the reign of Queen Elizabeth all England went fairly mad over queer specimens brought up from the sea. There were more than a score of different entertainments going on at one time in London, the conspicuous features of which were sea-monsters, which the mountebanks were advertising as marine men. So great was this rage that Shakespeare has referred to it in his "Winter's Tale," where Autolycus, the ballad singer, is made to say:

"Here's another ballad of a fish that appeared upon the coast on Wednesday, the four-score of April, forty thousand fathoms above water, and sung this ballad against the hard hearts of maids. It is thought she was a woman, and was turned into a cold fish, for she would not exchange flesh with one that loved her. The ballad is very pitiful and as true."

PEOPLE OF THE SEA.

Lieutenant Bassett has collected together, in a book called "Legends and Superstitions of the Sea," the quaint stories, beliefs and customs of sailors and coast-dwelling people, that were current hundreds of years ago, as well as those now common, in which there is much to amuse the reader. He shows that the belief in mermaids, cities under the deep, water-cows, horses, sheep, dogs, fairies, trolls—and, in short, every phase of fact and fable on land has its counterpart in the sea—is not only implicit even in our day, but, from the very nature of things, is ineradicable.

On the subject of sea-humans Bassett says:

"The idea of creatures beneath the wave, possessed of a human form with fish-like extremities, is not a modern one. Aside from the many fish-gods of antiquity, we are told that a creature like a woman inhabits the Island of Ceylon, and Ælian assures us there are whales formed like satyrs. Tritons and sirens were also figured half fish in ancient representations. Demetrius says the Western islanders who died in hurricanes were mermaids. Pliny says they came on board ships at night and sunk them, and that Malos, making free with a sea-maiden, lost his head."

Pliny further says: "Several distinguished persons of equestrian rank have assured me that they themselves have seen, off the coast of Gades, a merman whose body was of a human form. He was accustomed to appear on board ships in the night time, and the part on which he stood gradually subsided, as if sunk down by his weight.

"The Nereids, daughters of the Oceanic Doris, and of Nereus, and mothers of many heroes, were at first imagined beautiful maidens. A mural painting in Pompeii shows such a one. Later they were given the fish-tail, thus becoming mermaids.

"Achelous, brother of Nereus, and Calliope, were parents of the sirens, and as we have seen, they, too, were gradually transformed from human-faced birds to fish-tailed maidens. So also with the Tritons, offspring of Neptune and Amphitrite, who, at first regarded as men in form, were afterward given the fish-tail and monstrous form usually seen in art.

"In the middle ages, stories of mermaids increased, and their characteristics were definitely settled.

"Arabian writers often speak of them. El-Kazwini says the Arabs believed that certain fish-men lived in the Indian Ocean, and ate drowned men. Abou Muzaine says a Siren named the Old Man of the Sea often spoke an unknown tongue. A similar animal caught a woman and married her, and their son spoke the language of both. Another similar animal, the Old Jew, came to the surface in the Mediterranean, on Friday night, and played about ships all the Jewish Sabbath. Ibnala Bialsaths says sailors in his time caught on foreign shores marine women, with brown skin and black eyes, speaking a strange tongue. Ibn-Batuta, an old Arab writer, says he saw fish in the Persian Gulf with a human head as large as that of a child.

"Theodore de Gaza saw several Sirens on board ship, in the Peloponnessian Sea, which were put back in the water, after being kept on board some time. They were beautiful maidens. George of Trebizonde saw one in the open sea. Gyllius says the skin of sea-men taken in Dalmatia is so tough that it is used to make saddle covers.

"In the Nibelungen Lieb, Hagen steals a mermaid's garments, but she foretold him good luck if he would give them back again. Another story is that a mermaid told Hagen's fortune, but he, dissatisfied with it, cut off her head, which mysteriously joined the body again, and a storm thereupon ensued."

WONDERFUL STORIES OF MERMAIDS.

Wieland, or Waylund, a mythical Vulcan of the middle ages, is said to have descended from a mermaid. So the French Counts of Lusignan, ancient kings of Cypress and Jerusalem, still claim as their ancestor and founder a water-maiden, Melusina, whom an ancestor saw bathing in a fountain, and whom he wedded.

"The romances of the middle age often speak of them. Such are the maidens of the Rheingold, celebrated in Wagner's melodious strains. In the romantic legends of William of Orange a mermaid is caught by a cavalier, but liberated. In gratitude therefor she saves her captor, when his ship is wrecked. When mermaids appeared 'then began they all to sing so high, so low, so sweet, and so clear, that the birds leave off flying, and fish leave off swimming.'

"The ballads of Chivalry extolled their beauty. Doolin says, of a beautiful woman, 'I thought she was an angel, or a sea-siren.'

"In a Sicilian tale, a maiden treacherously thrown into the sea, is carried off by a merman, and chained to his tail. A similar story is told by Gubernatis, but the mermaid is here liberated, her brother feeding the siren meat, while seven blacksmiths sever the chain.

"These mermaids particularly desire a human soul — a thing denied to them by the churchmen. Paracelsus says: 'So it follows that they woo men, to make them industrious and homelike, in the same way as a heathen wants baptism, to save his soul; and thus they create so great a love for men, that they are with men in the same union.' This of the maidens, but mermen were not so friendly, often dragging people down, like Nick.

In "The Eastern Travels of John of Hesse" (1389), we read: "We came to a smoky and stony mountain, where we heard sirens singing, *proprie* mermaids, who draw ships into danger by their songs. We saw there many horrible monsters, and were in great fear."

In 1187, a merman is said to have been taken near Suffolk, England. It resembled a man, but could not speak. It escaped one day, fled into the sea, and was not again seen.

"But the accounts of the early appearances of the mermaid are more circumstantial in northern countries. Here, where Nick dragged people down, where Rau sucked the breath of the drowned, and where the Stromkarl and the Kelpie flourished, the mermaid was often seen, sitting on the rocks, combing her hair, and predicting disasters to the mariner."

Icelandic chronicles relate that three sea-monsters were seen near Greenland. The first, seen by Norwegian sailors in the water, had the body of a man, with broad shoulders, stumps of arms, and a pointed head. Heavy storms succeeded its appearance. The second was like a woman to the waist, with large breasts, disheveled hair, and large hands on the stumpy arms, webbed like a duck's foot. It held fish in its hands and ate them.

We also read in the Chronicle of Storlaformus, of the Hafstrambr: "It resembles a man from the neck, in its head, its nose, and its throat, except that the head is extraordinarily high, and elongated in front. It had shoulders like a man, and attached to them two stumps of arms without hands. The body tapers below, but it has never been seen how it is formed below the waist." He also describes the *Marguguer*. "It is formed like a woman, as far as the waist. It has a large bosom, thick hair, large hands, with fingers webbed like the foot of a goose, attached to its stumpy arms."

This pleasing fiction of creatures half-human, living in the sea, is almost universal. Not only do we find it among people occupying the coast, but it is also common among barbarians, such as the tribes of Central Africa and the North American Indians. Those having never seen the ocean confine the mermaids of their belief to streams of water, spirits which we denominate Nereids and water-nymphs. This universality of belief, stretching round the world, is strikingly singular, and can possibly be explained by no other theory than that advanced by Donnelly, who accounts for the identity of superstitions among diverse people by fixing the seat of the beginning of mankind upon the Atlantis Continent, once a great and populous country, from whence the race radiated, after its submergence, which was gradual.

CROSSING THE LINE.

A singular ceremony, the origin of which has been lost in the great lapse of time since its first practices, takes place on board every ship that crosses the equatorial line. That it was originally intended as a propitiation to the god Neptune cannot be doubted, especially since, even at this day, a portion of the ceremony consists in calling upon the great sea-god. It has degenerated in these later days to a kind of buffoonery, or, to use a collegiate expression, "hazing," since the occasion is seized upon to initiate new sailors.

Little, in his "Twenty Years on the Ocean," refers to the ceremony of "crossing the line" on his first voyage as a sailor, in the following language:

"* * * After this the wind sprang up moderately from south-southeast, when we braced up our yards on the larboard tack, and as we expected to cross the line the next night, preparations were being made for the reception of old Neptune, such as dressing two of the oldest sailors to personate him and his wife, throwing over a tar-barrel on fire, and hailing the sea-god from on board. All this buffoonery was performed after dark, and so managed as to be kept secret from the green hands. And here I must not omit stating that this foolery was sanctioned by the captain and officers, very much to their mortification afterwards, as the scene of confusion which ensued had liked to have closed with a mutiny.

"On the next morning the play began; the green hands were confined to the forecastle, one at a time being sent up blind-folded, who was then received by his majesty of the sea, and the operation of shaving commenced. The lather consisted of slush mixed with the dirty water of the grindstone tub; the razor was a piece of old hoop-iron; the face being well besmeared with this lather, the shaving commenced, during which his majesty puts some interrogatories, such as, 'Do you intend to become a member of my family, and a faithful subject of my realm?' etc. When the mouth is opened to give answer, it is crammed full of odoriferous lather. This done, he is well scraped with the hoop and douched with salt-water, and then let off to enjoy the remainder of the farce.

"I recollect, when they were about to cram the delicious lather into my mouth, I struck the man who held it, and in the bustle the bandage fell from my eyes, and I discovered the whole trick. A scene of confusion here took place; the green hands all sided together, and determined not to submit to the operation, and the old sailors attempting to force us to yield, a riot took place, which was not without much difficulty quelled by the officers."

SYNOPSIS OF THE STORY OF THE ANCIENT MARINER.

Of all tales told by the sweet singers of the world, none exceed in exquisite beauty, sentiment and rhythm, that of the "Ancient Mariner," which has made the fame of its author, Samuel T. Coleridge, as perpetual as that of Shakespeare himself. My excuse for introducing it here is two-fold, viz. It describes one of the most general and tenacious superstitions connected with life on the sea, and, in addition to this peculiar relevancy to our subject, the poem is so full of sweetness and beauty that its republication always subserves an excellent purpose, because that which contributes to our happiness and culture cannot be too often repeated.

The story, so delightfully told in verse, may be briefly described as follows:

An old sailor, lately returned from a disastrous voyage, the incidents of which are the burden of his recital, meets three gentlemen who are on their way to a wedding-feast, one of whom he detains and compels to listen to his tale. The Ancient Mariner proceeds to tell his auditor how the ship on which he sailed was drawn by a storm toward the South Pole and into a region of ice and fearful sounds, where no life was to be seen, until an albatross appeared, which, being a bird of good omen, followed the ship as it returned northward. This bird was daily fed from the hands of the crew until the Ancient Mariner shot it with his cross-bow, believing that it was the cause of the fog and mist which continually surrounded the ship. His shipmates at first cried out against this fearful act, but as the fog soon after lifted, they justified the act, and thus became accomplices in the crime. A fair breeze continued with the ship until the equator was reached, when the wind suddenly ceased and the vessel lay becalmed.

A spirit had followed the ship from the time the albatross was shot, swimming in the wake of the luckless craft, "nine fathom deep," to bring vengeance upon the crew for their sacrilegious act. The shipmates now sought to throw all the guilt upon the Ancient Mariner, as a sign whereof, they hung the dead bird around his neck.

The crew were dying with thirst, when the Ancient Mariner beholds a sign afar off; as it approaches nearer he believes it to be a ship, and a burst of joy follows, but it is brief, for the wonder succeeds how a ship could move so rapidly without either wind or tide. As it approaches, the Ancient Mariner discovers that it is a phantom ship, on which are seen a spectre woman and her death-mate. The two spirits are seen casting dice for the ship's crew, and the one known as Life-in Death wins the Ancient Mariner. Soon after, the crew begin to die of thirst, one after another falling down, but the Ancient Mariner still survives, to suffer the pangs of a living death.

At this point in the old sailor's narrative the wedding-guest thinks it is a spirit that is talking, but he is assured that it is not so, and the Ancient Mariner proceeds to relate the horrors of his penance.

By the light of the moon the sailor beholds God's creatures of the great calm, their beauty and happiness, and he blesses them in his heart, whereat the spell which binds him begins to break. He tells how the rains came and refreshed him, where upon strange sights are seen in the sky, and portentious sounds break the weird stillness of the surrounding calm. These ominous manifestations proceed from a troop of angelic spirits which come to the call of the guardian saint.

The lonesome spirit from the South Pole propels the ship to the line in obedience to the angelic troop, but still requires vengeance. The Polar spirit's fellow demons, the invisible inhabitants of the element, take part in his wrong—which is the crime of killing the albatross, the sacred bird—and two of them relate that penance long and heavy for the Ancient Mariner has been accorded to the Polar Spirit who returned southward.

The Mariner is now cast into a trance, for the troop of angels cause the vessel to drive northward faster than human life can endure. But the supernatural motion is arrested; the Mariner awakes and his penance begins anew.

The curse is finally expiated, and the Ancient Mariner beholds his native country, whereupon the angelic spirits leave the dead bodies and appear in their own beautiful forms.

The hermit of the wood approaches the ship, when she suddenly sinks, but the Ancient Mariner is saved in the Pilot's boat. He entreats the hermit to shrieve him, but ever and anon throughout his future life an agony constrains him to go from land to land to tell his tale, and to teach, by his own example, love and reverence to all things that God has made.

BY THY LONG GREY BEARD AND GLITTERING EYE,
NOW WHEREFORE STOPP'ST THOU ME?

THE ANCIENT MARINER.

PART I.

IT is an ancient mariner,
And he stoppeth one of three,
"By thy long grey beard and glittering eye,
Now wherefore stopp'st thou me?

"The bridegroom's doors are opened wide,
And I am next of kin;
The guests are met, the feast is set:
Mayst hear the merry din."

He holds him with his skinny hand,
"There was a ship," quoth he.
Hold off! unhand me, grey-beard loon!"
Eftsoons his hand dropt he.

He holds him with his glittering eye—
The wedding-guest stood still,
And listens like a three-years' child:
The Mariner hath his will.

The wedding-guest sat on a stone;
He cannot choose but hear;
And thus spake on that ancient man,
The bright-eyed Mariner.

The ship was cheered, the harbour cleared,
Merrily did we drop
Below the kirk, below the hill,
Below the light-house top.

The sun came up upon the left,
Out of the sea came he;
And he shone bright, and on the right
Went down into the sea.

Higher and higher every day,
Till over the mast at noon—
The wedding-guest here beat his breast,
For he heard the loud bassoon.

THE WEDDING GUEST SAT ON A STONE:
HE CANNOT CHUSE BUT HEAR.

The bride hath paced into the ha',
Red as a rose is she;
Nodding their heads before her goes
The merry minstrelsy.

The wedding-guest he beat his breast,
Yet he cannot choose but hear;
And thus spake on that ancient man,
The bright-eyed Mariner.

And now the storm-blast came, and he
Was tyrannous and strong;
He struck with his o'ertaking wings,
And chased us south along.

With sloping masts, and dipping prow,
As who pursued with yell and blow
Still treads the shadow of his foe.

And forward bends his head,
The ship drove fast, loud roared the blast,
And southward aye we fled.

And now there came both mist and snow,
And it grew wond'rous cold;
And ice, mast high, came floating by,
As green as emerald.

And through the drifts, the snowy clifts
Did send a dismal sheen:
Nor shapes of men nor beasts we ken—
The ice was all between.

The ice was here, the ice was there,
The ice was all around;
It cracked and growled, and roared and howled,
Like noises in a swound.

At length did cross an albatross,
Through the fog it came;
As if it had been a Christian soul,
We hailed it in God's name.

It ate the food it ne'er had eat,
And round and round it flew,
The ice did split with a thunder-fit:
The helmsman steered us through!

AND NOW THERE CAME BOTH MIST AND SNOW,
AND IT GREW WONDROUS COLD.

And a good south-wind sprung up behind,
The albatross did follow,
And every day, for food or play,
Came to the mariners' hollo!

In mist or cloud, on mast or shroud,
It perched for vespers nine;
Whiles all the night, thro' fog-smoke white,
Glimmered the white moon-shine.

"God save thee, ancient mariner!
From the fiends that plague thee thus.—
Why look'st thou so?"—With my cross-bow
I shot the albatross!

PART II.

THE sun now rose upon the right,
Out of the sea came he,
Still hid in mist, and on the left
Went down into the sea.

And the good south-wind still blew behind,
But no sweet bird did follow,
Nor any day, for food or play,
Came to the mariners' hollo!

And I had done a hellish thing,
And it would work 'em woe;
For all averred, I had killed the bird
That made the breeze to blow;
Ah, wretch! said they, the bird to slay
That made the breeze to blow.

Nor dim nor red, like God's own head,
The glorious sun uprist;
Then all averred, I had killed the bird
That brought the fog and mist.
'Twas right, said they, such birds to slay
That bring the fog and mist.

The fair breeze blew, the white foam flew,
The furrow followed free;
We were the first that ever burst
Into that silent sea.

THE ICE WAS HERE, THE ICE WAS THERE,
THE ICE WAS ALL AROUND.

Down dropt the breeze, the sails dropt down,
'Twas sad as sad could be;
And we did speak only to break
The silence of the sea!

All in a hot and copper sky,
The bloody sun, at noon,
Right up above the mast did stand,
No bigger than the moon.

Day after day, day after day,
We stuck, nor breath nor motion;
As idle as a painted ship
Upon a painted ocean.

Water, water, every where,
And all the boards did shrink;
Water, water, every where,
Nor any drop to drink.

The very deep did rot: O Christ!
That ever this should be;
Yea, slimy things did crawl with legs
Upon the slimy sea.

About, about, in reel and rout,
The death-fires danced at night
The water, like a witch's oils,
Burnt green, and blue, and white.

And some in dreams assured were
Of the spirit that plagued so;
Nine fathom deep he had followed us
From the land of mist and snow.

And every tongue, through utter drought,
Was withered at the root;
We could not speak, no more than if
We had been choked with soot.

Ah! well-a-day! what evil looks
Had I from old and young!
Instead of the cross, the albatross
About my neck was hung.

IT ATE THE FOOD IT NE'ER HAD EAT.

PART III.

THERE passed a weary time. Each throat
Was parched, and glazed each eye,
A weary time! a weary time!
How glazed each weary eye,
When looking westward, I beheld
A something in the sky.

At first it seemed a little speck,
And then it seemed a mist;
It moved and moved, and took at last
A certain shape, I wist.

A speck, a mist, a shape I wist!
And still it neared and neared;
As if it dodged a water-sprite,
It plunged, and tacked, and veered.

With throats unslaked, with black lips baked,
We could nor laugh nor wail;
Through utter drought all dumb we stood,
I bit my arm, I sucked the blood,
And cried, A sail; a sail!

With throats unslaked, with black lips baked,
Agape they heard me call;
Gramercy! they for joy did grin,
And all at once their breath drew in,
As they were drinking all.

See! see! (I cried), she tacks no more!
Hither, to work us weal,
Without a breeze, without a tide,
She steadies with upright keel!

The western wave was all a-flame,
The day was well nigh done!
Almost upon the western wave
Rested the broad bright sun;
When that strange shape drove suddenly
Betwixt us and the sun.

And straight the sun was flecked with bars,
(Heaven's mother send us grace!)
As if through a dungeon-grate he peered
With broad and burning face.

* * * * WITH MY CROSS-BOW
I SHOT THE ALBATROSS.

Alas! (thought I, and my heart beat loud)
How fast she nears and nears!
Are those her sails that glance in the sun,
Like restless gossameres?

Are those her ribs through which the sun
Did peer, as through the grate?
And is that woman all her crew?
Is that a Death? and are there two?
Is Death that Woman's mate?

Her lips were red, her looks were free,
Her locks were yellow as gold:
Her skin was as white as leprosy,
The Night-mare Life-in-Death was she,
Who thicks men's blood with cold.

The naked hulk alongside came,
And the twain were casting dice;
'The game is done! I've won! I've won!"
Quoth she, and whistles thrice.

The sun's rim dips; the stars rush out:
At one stride comes the dark;
With far-heard whisper, o'er the sea,
Off shot the spectre-bark.

We listened and looked sideways up;
Fear at my heart, as at a cup,
My life blood seemed to sip;
The stars were dim, and thick the night,
The steersman's face by his lamp gleamed white,
From the sails the dew did drip—
Till clomb above the eastern bar
The horned moon, with one bright star
Within the nether tip.

One after one, by the star-dogged moon,
Too quick for groan or sigh,
Each turned his face with a ghastly pang,
And cursed me with his eye.

Four times fifty living men,
(And I heard nor sigh nor groan)
With heavy thump, a lifeless lump,
They dropped down one by one.

ABOUT, ABOUT, IN REEL AND ROUT,
THE DEATH-FIRES DANCED AT NIGHT.

The souls did from their bodies fly,
They fled to bliss or wo!
And every soul, it passed me by
Like the whizz of my cross-bow!

PART IV.

"I FEAR thee, Ancient Mariner!
I fear thy skinny hand,
And thou art long, and lank and brown,
As is the ribbed sea-sand!

I fear thee and thy glittering eye,
And thy skinny hand, so brown."—
Fear not, fear not, thou wedding guest!
This body drops not down.

Alone, alone, all, all alone,
Alone on a wide, wide sea!
And never a saint took pity on
My soul in agony.

The merry men so beautiful!
And they all dead did lie;
And a thousand thousand slimy things
Lived on: and so did I.

I looked upon the rotting sea,
And drew my eyes away:
I looked upon the rotting deck,
And there the dead men lay.

I looked to heaven, and tried to pray
But or ever a prayer had gush't,
A wicked whisper came and made
My heart as dry as dust.

I closed my lids, and kept them close,
And the balls like pulses beat,
For the sky and the sea, and the sea and the sky
Lay like a cloud on my weary eye,
And the dead were at my feet.

The cold sweat melted from their limbs,
Nor rot nor reek did they;
The look with which they looked on me
Had never passed away.

A SPECK, A MIST, A SHAPE I WEEN!
AND STILL IT NEARED AND NEARED.

An orphan's curse would drag to hell
A spirit from on high;
But oh! more horrible than that
Is the curse in a dead man's eye.
Seven days, seven nights, I saw that curse,
And yet I could not die.

The moving moon went up the sky,
And no where did abide;
Softly she was going up,
And a star or two beside.

Her beams bemocked the sultry main,
Like April hoar-frost spread;
But where the ship's huge shadow lay,
The charmed water burnt alway
A still and awful red.

Beyond the shadow of the ship,
I watched the water-snakes:
They moved in tracks of shining white,
And when they reared, the elfish light
Fell off in horny flakes.

Within the shadow of the ship
I watched their rich attire:
Blue, glossy green, and velvet black,
They coiled and swam; and every track
Was a flash of golden fire.

O happy living things! no tongue
Their beauty might declare:
A spring of love gushed from my heart,
And I blessed them unaware:
Sure my kind saint took pity on me,
And I blessed them unaware.

The self-same moment I could pray;
And from my neck so free
The albatross fell off, and sunk
Like lead into the sea.

PART V.

OH sleep! it is a gentle thing,
Beloved from pole to pole!
To Mary Queen the praise be given,
She sent the gentle sleep from Heaven,
That slid into my soul.

THE GAME IS DONE! I'VE WON, I'VE WON!
QUOTH SHE, AND WHISTLES THRICE.

The silly buckets on the deck,
That had so long remained,
I dreamt that they were filled with dew,
And when I woke it rained.

My lips were wet, my throat was cold,
My garments all were dank;
Sure I had drunken in my dreams,
And still my body drank.

I moved and could not feel my limbs
I was so light—almost
I thought that I had died in sleep,
And was a blessed ghost.

And soon I heard a roaring wind;
It did not come a-near;
But with its sound it shook the sails
That were so thin and sere.

The upper air burst into life,
And a hundred fire-flags sheen;
To and fro they were hurried about,
And to and fro, and in and out,
The wan stars danced between.

And the coming wind did roar more loud,
And the sails did sigh like sedge;
And the rain poured down from one black cloud,
The moon was at its edge.

The thick black cloud was cleft, and still
The moon was at its side;
Like waters shot from some high crag,
The lightning fell with never a jag,
A river steep and wide.

The loud wind never reached the ship
Yet now the ship moved on!
Beneath the lightning and the moon
The dead men gave a groan.

They groaned, they stirred, they all uprose,
Nor spake, nor moved their eyes;
It had been strange even in a dream,
To have seen these dead men rise.

I LOOKED UPON THE ROTTING SEA,
AND DREW MY EYES AWAY.

The helmsman steered, the ship moved on,
Yet never a zephyr upblew;
The mariners all 'gan work the ropes,
Where they were wont to do;
They raised their limbs like lifeless tools—
We were a ghastly crew.

The body of my brother's son
Stood by me knee to knee:
The body and I pulled at one rope,
But he said nought to me.

I fear thee, ancient Mariner!
Be calm, thou Wedding-Guest,
'Twas not those souls that fled in pain,
Which to their corses came again,
But a troop of spirits blest:

For when it dawned — they dropped their arms,
And clustered round the mast;
Sweet sounds rose slowly through their mouths,
And from their bodies passed.

Around, around, flew each sweet sound,
Then darted to the sun;
Slowly the sounds came back again,
Now mixed; now one by one.

And now 'twas like all instruments,
Now like a lonely flute,
And now it is an angel's song,
That makes the heavens be mute.

It ceased; yet still the sails made on
A pleasant noise till noon,
A noise like that of a hidden brook,
In the leafy month of June,
That to the sleeping woods all night
Singeth a quiet tune.

Till noon we quietly sailed on,
Yet never a breeze did breathe:
Slowly and smoothly went the ship,
Moved onward from beneath.

BEYOND THE SHADOW OF THE SHIP
I WATCHED THE WATER-SNAKES.

Under the keel nine fathom deep,
From the land of mist and snow,
The spirit slid; and it was he
That made the ship to go.
The sails at noon left off their tune,
And the ship stood still also.

The sun right above the mast,
Had fixed her to the ocean:
But in a minute she 'gan stir
With a short uneasy motion—
Backwards and forwards half her length,
With a short uneasy motion.

Then like a pawing horse let go,
She made a sudden bound;
It flung the blood into my head,
And I fell down in a swound.

How long in that same fit I lay,
I have not to declare;
But ere my living life returned,
I heard and in my soul discerned
Two voices in the air.

"Is it he?" quoth one, "Is this the man?
By him who died on cross,
With his cruel bow he laid full low
The harmless albatross.

"The spirit bideth by himself
In the land of mist and snow.
He loved the bird that loved the man,
Who shot him with his bow."

The other was a softer voice,
As soft as honey-dew:
Quoth he, "The man hath penance done,
And penance more will do."

PART VI.

FIRST VOICE.

BUT tell me, tell me! speak again,
Thy soft response renewing—
What makes that ship drive on so fast?
What is the Ocean doing?

THEY GROANED, THEY STIRRED, THEY ALL UPROSE,
NOR SPAKE, NOR MOVED THEIR EYES.

SECOND VOICE.

Still as a slave before his lord,
The Ocean hath no blast;
His great bright eye most silently
Up to the moon is cast.

If he may know which way to go,
For she guides him smooth or grim.
See, brother, see! how graciously
She looketh down on him.

FIRST VOICE.

But why drives on that ship so fast,
Without or wave or wind?

SECOND VOICE.

The air is cut away before,
And closes from behind.

Fly, brother, fly! more high, more high,
Or we shall be belated;
For slow and slow that ship will go,
When the Mariner's trance is abated.

I woke, and we were sailing on,
As in a gentle weather;
'Twas night, calm night, the moon was high
The dead men stood together.

All stood together on the deck,
For a charnel-dungeon fitter;
All fixed on me their stony eyes,
That in the moon did glitter.

The pang, the curse with which they died,
Had never passed away;
I could not draw my eyes from theirs,
Nor turn them up to pray.

And now this spell was snapt; once more
I viewed the ocean green,
And looked far forth, yet little saw
Of what had else been seen —

IT CEASED, YET STILL THE SAILS MADE ON
A PLEASANT NOISE TILL NOON.

Like one that on a lonesome road
Doth walk in fear and dread,
And having once turned round, walks on,
And turns no more his head;
Because he knows a frightful fiend
Doth close behind him tread.

But soon there breathed a wind on me,
Nor sound nor motion made;
Its path was not upon the sea
In ripple or in shade.

It raised my hair, it fanned my cheek
Like a meadow-gale of spring —
It mingled strangely with my fears,
Yet it felt like a welcoming.

Swiftly, swiftly flew the ship,
Yet she sailed softly too;
Sweetly, sweetly blew the breeze —
On me alone it blew.

Oh! dream of joy! is this, indeed,
The light-house top I see?
Is this the hill? is this the kirk;
Is this mine own countree?

We drifted o'er the harbour bar,
And I with sobs did pray —
O let me be awake, my God!
Or let me sleep alway.

The harbour-bay was clear as glass,
So smoothly it was strewn;
And on the bay the moonlight lay,
And the shadow of the moon.

The rock shone bright, the kirk no less,
That stands above the rock:
The moonlight steeped in silentness,
The steady weathercock.

And the bay was white with silent light,
Till rising from the same,
Full many shapes, that shadows were,
In crimson colours came.

UNDER THE KEEL NINE FATHOMS DEEP,
FROM THE LAND OF MIST AND SNOW,
THE SPIRIT SLID.

A little distance from the prow
Those crimson shadows were;
I turned my eyes upon the deck —
Oh, Christ! what saw I there!

Each corse lay flat, lifeless and flat,
And, by the holy rood,
A man all light, a seraph-man,
On every corse there stood.

This seraph-band each waved his hand
It was a heavenly sight;
They stood as signals to the land,
Each one a lovely light.

This seraph-band each waved his hand,
No voice did they impart —
No voice; but oh! the silence sunk
Like music on my heart.

But soon I heard the dash of oars,
I heard the Pilot's cheer;
My head was turned perforce away,
And I saw a boat appear.

The Pilot and the Pilot's boy,
I heard them coming fast;
Dear Lord in Heaven! it was a joy
The dead men could not blast.

I saw a third — I heard his voice,
It is the hermit good;
He singeth loud his godly hymns
That he makes in the wood,
He'll shrieve my soul, he'll wash away
The albatross's blood.

PART VII.

THIS Hermit good lives in that wood
Which slopes down to the sea.
How loudly his sweet voice he rears!
He loves to talk with marineres
That come from a far countree.

BUT WHY DRIVES ON THE SHIP SO FAST
WITHOUT OR WAVE OR WIND?

He kneels at morn, and noon and eve—
He hath a cushion plump,
It is the moss that wholly hides
The rotted old oak-stump.

The skiff-boat neared: I heard them talk,
"Why, this is strange, I trow!
Where are those lights so many and fair,
That signal made but now?"

"Strange, by my faith," the Hermit said—
"And they answered not our cheer;
The planks look warped; and see these sails
How thin they are and sere!
I never saw aught like to them
Unless perchance it were

"Brown skeletons of leaves that lag
My forest-brook along,
When the ivy-tod is heavy with snow,
And the owlet whoops to the wolf below,
That eats the she-wolf's young."

Dear Lord! it hath a fiendish look—
(The Pilot made reply)
I am a-feared"—"Push on, push on,"
Said the Hermit cheerily.

The boat came closer to the ship,
But I nor spake nor stirred;
The boat came close beneath the ship,
And straight a sound was heard.

Under the water it rumbled on,
Still louder and more dread:
It reached the ship, it split the bay;
The ship went down like lead.

Stunned by that loud and dreadful sound,
Which sky and ocean smote,
Like one that hath been seven days drowned
My body lay afloat;
But swift as dreams, myself I found
Within the Pilot's boat.

THIS SERAPH BAND, EACH WAVED HIS HAND;
IT WAS A HEAVENLY SIGHT

Upon the whirl, where sank the ship
The boat spun round and round;
And all was still, save that the hill
Was telling of the sound.

I moved my lips — the Pilot shrieked,
And fell down in a fit;
The Holy Hermit raised his eyes,
And prayed where he did sit.

I took the oars: the Pilot's boy,
Who now doth crazy go,
Laughed loud and long, and all the while
His eyes went to and fro.
"Ha! ha!" quoth he, "full plain I see,
The Devil knows how to row."

And now, all in my own countree,
I stood on the firm land!
The hermit stepped forth from the boat,
And scarcely he could stand.

"O shrieve me, shrieve me, holy man!"
The Hermit crossed his brow,
"Say quick," quoth he, "I bid thee say
What manner of man art thou?"

Forthwith this frame of mine was wrenched
With a woful agony,
Which forced me to begin my tale;
And then it left me free.

Since then at an uncertain hour,
That agony returns:
And till my ghastly tale is told
This heart within me burns.

I pass like night from land to land:
I have strange power of speech;
That moment that his face I see,
I know the man that must hear me:
To him my tale I teach.

What loud uproar bursts from that door!
The wedding-guests are there:
But in the garden bower the bride
And bridemaids singing are:
And hark the little vesper bell,
Which biddeth me to prayer.

I MOVED MY LIPS—THE PILOT SHRIEKED
AND FELL DOWN IN A FIT.

Oh Wedding Guest! this soul hath been
Alone on a wide, wide sea;
So lonely 'twas, that God himself
Scarce seemed there to be.

O sweeter than the marriage feast
'Tis sweeter far to me,
To walk together to the kirk
With a goodly company;

To walk together to the kirk,
And all together pray,
While each to his great Father bends,
Old men and babes, and loving friends.
And youths and maidens gay;

Farewell, farewell! but this I tell
To thee, thou Wedding Guest!
He prayeth well, who loveth well
Both man and bird and beast.

He prayeth best who loveth best
All things both great and small;
For the dear God that loveth us,
He made and loveth all.

The Mariner whose eye is bright,
Whose beard with age is hoar,
Is gone; and now the Wedding Guest
Turns from the bridegroom's door.

He went like one that hath been stunned,
And is of sense forlorn:
A sadder and a wiser man,
He rose the morrow morn.

PANORAMA OF NATURE.

THE WORLD ASHORE.

CHAPTER XXI.

THE UNFOLDING OF CREATION BY EVOLUTION.

IN the introductory chapter of this work I have given a very brief description of the theory of earth development, explaining how it grew up out of chaos and became bathed with the moisture that emanated from all the spheres; of how life first appeared in the moving waters of universal ocean, before land was anywhere upon the liquid globe, and referred, casually, to the argument of evolution, that theory which is the grandest conception of the greatest mind since Newton, and the peer of any age since the dawn of civilization. The extraordinary interest of the subject shall be my excuse for introducing to the reader again, not theories, but facts illustrative of the earth's growth from its primeval condition of disorder, through stages, or cycles, cataclysms, convulsions, eversions and gradual development, up to the grand climacteric aspect with which we now behold it.

> "Know ye how opens out the seed, and how the plant up-grows,
> How soft and green in sweet spring-tide, 'tis ripe ere summer's close?
> How in the downy covert of the swift-winged swallow's nest,
> Instinct to mother-love expands in the gentle creature's breast;
> And how, beneath the shelter of the fragile, ovate shell,
> A winged germ takes life one day to quit its narrow cell?"

As scientists, in their discussions of the earth's development, divided themselves into Plutonists and Neptunists, one believing that its formation was due to fire, while the other maintained that water was the agent, so, away back in the dark ages, before the clouds of ignorance had been lifted from man's brain, there were traditions of the earth's birth equally diametrical. For example, the Chinese, whose history long antedates Herodotus, represented Pan-kou-che as the Creator, who was a small man, even in their estimation, and withal feeble and nervous. Their traditions, however, tell them that this man, with hammer and chisel, hewed the globe out of chaos, broke away the granite spurs and huge inequalities of the crust, and carved highways through the wilderness and tunnels through mountains, until he reduced the earth to a habitable condition by the sheer force of his incomparable industry.

PAN KOU-CHE, THE CREATOR.—(FROM A PAINTING IN A CHINESE MANUSCRIPT.)

Opposed to the legends of the Chinese, we have the traditions of the Scandinavians, that race of free-born and war-like people who never slept under the arm of a conqueror, and whose rugged natures, bred to a rugged climate, made them glory in the power which they attained through struggles, viewed the whole world as a thing not understood and yet not so great but that they might rule it under the guidance of their god, Thor. As war was their ambition, so was their god a being of herculean might, with muscular arms and beetling brow, a mighty and valorous creator, who walked with a ponderous step, breathed like a cyclone, and crushed the things that opposed him like the lightning that splits up trees and bursts down the lofty crags. Thor—whose tones were thunder, is still remembered in that word, as he is also in Thursday—bore, also, a hammer, the first invention of mechanic genius, and while with this he broke his way through tumbled and chaotic nature, he forged thunderbolts and set in motion the mighty forces which impelled winds, rain and volcanoes.

THE WORLD BEFORE ORDER WAS ESTABLISHED.

The differences between the superstitious and the scientific in their theories respecting the world's origin, represent the difference between inductive and deductive reasoning, and since it is the province of the former to proceed from particulars to generals, or from a part to the whole, so have the facts, which will here be briefly set forth, been established.

The Neptunists and Plutonists were scientists in their day, both being on parallel tracks of truth while yet the great body of truth lay between. It is now known that fire and water have exercised the most potential effects upon the earth, the one acting by ignition to modify, and the other by dissolution to deposit. By chemical analysis we know that the globe was originally an incandescent mass; and, as Descartes has aptly observed, the earth now is only a sun crusted over and partially extinguished, the chilled skin of which hides the central furnace from view.

Swedenborg, I believe, is the author of the theory—though several others have promulgated the same—that originally every atom of solid matter was concentrated in one sun, which being intensely heated, revolved with such rapidity that centrifugal force rent it asunder—like a grind-stone sometimes splits when turned with great velocity—and the detached portions were hurled out into space, where they, too, became revolving bodies, one of which is our earth. If we could only account for this first and universal sun there would be an end to metaphysical speculation concerning the earth's origin, but, alas! we are in darkness on this momentous question, and must, therefore, venture out no further on this great speculative sea than a line will reach.

As the earth gradually cooled and formed a crust, the gases rising from the seething fires, which still raged within the fragile covering, burst from time to time and produced great convulsions, splitting the earth and upheaving mountains, covering some barren places with water, and in others raising islands and large bodies of land from the

THOR, THE NEPTUNE AND CREATOR OF THE SCANDINAVIANS, RECONSTRUCTING THE GLOBE.

bottom of the sea. No less than sixteen cataclysms have taken place, which have left evidences by which they can each be comprehended.

EFFECTS OF MIGHTY CONVULSIONS.

But the bursting of mighty internal forces has had other effects than the upheaving of continents, changing of ocean beds, and developing of mountain chains; for, besides remodeling the surface of the globe, these convulsions have changed the species of animals, since observation attests the fact that each telluric phase had its peculiar organic form. Respecting this fact Humboldt, the greatest of philosophic travelers, says: "Each upheaval of these mountain chains, of which we can determine the relative antiquity, has been signalized by the destruction of ancient species and the appearance of new organisms." Pouchet, who has painted in such elegant language the story of the world's development, observes: "The earth is only an immense cemetery, where each generation acquires life at the expense of the debris of that which has just expired; the particles of our corpses form new materials for the beings which will follow us. But we have now reached an epoch of transition; the exhausted creative powers are experiencing almost a period of arrest; they are waiting till new telluric perturbations awaken them from their torpor.

"The first compact crust which enveloped the globe was only formed by the cooling down and solidification of its superficial, once incandescent, layers. Hence the beds which compose it are called primitive, or plutonic, in order to indicate their antiquity or igneous origin. The strata which overlie the primitive rocks owe, on the contrary, their formation to deposits from the waters; and for this reason are called alluvial, or nepturian, strata."

Without attempting to follow the process of development, by which the earth was evolved from a fiery globe, thence a boundless sea, to its present condition of orderly separation of land and water, distribution of zones of climate, and profusion of life, I will merely say that when the cooling process had sufficiently advanced to admit the existence of plants and animals, an extremely low order of animate creation appeared. Among these, and most prominent, were the trilobites, so called from the arrangement of their articulated bodies, which consisted of three shells over-lapping and ranged side by side. A study of these crustaceans reveals to the scientist the condition of the seas at the time they existed, though for thousands of years these most ancient inhabitants of the seas have been stricken from the order of creation. They were abundant during the Silurian period, a name given to indicate the first appearance of molluscs, from *Silurus*, the earliest creatures of the sea, whose remains have been found in great quantities in Wales, where they have been chiefly studied.

THE FORESTS APPEAR.

The second age is called the Devonian, or age of fishes; the third the Carboniferous, or the age of coal; the fourth is the age of reptiles; and the fifth the age of Mammalia and of Man. As the earth was at one time a seething ball of fire, and at another covered with shoreless waves, so in the third, or carboniferous period, the land that had then been uncovered was fairly hidden by dense forests, so gigantic and dense that we can form no conception of its profuseness by looking upon the thickest growth in the jungles of Brazil. There was then, for example, the great Lycopodia, which reared its monster stems to a height of one hundred feet; to-day it is only a creeping, herbaceous plant. There was also the gigantic Lepidodendra, the body of which resembled a scaly cuirass, or the envelope of a

LABYRINTHODON RESTORED.

serpent; it has now disappeared from our forests; so, also, has the gigantic club-moss, whose tangled tendrils and immense stems covered the earth in places like an impenetrable pall of darkness.

These clusters of rank vegetation had their roots in marshy soil still surcharged with heat from the yet uncooled earth, and were further nourished by a great amount of carbonic acid, upon which plants feed. As an authority observes:

"At the present time the atmosphere contains only a thousandth part of carbonic gas, whereas, according to Mons. A. Brongniart, there was at the carboniferous period seven to eight parts in a hundred. This acid being an indispensable part of the food of plants, to which it gives up all its carbon, its presence easily explains the great development of the antediluvian forests of this period, and as such a quantity of acid in the air would clearly have been fatal to animals of a higher degree of development, such as mammals and birds, so none are met with at that time. Reptiles and animals only appeared when the plants and trees, by their absorption of the carbonic acid as food, had necessarily purified the atmosphere sufficiently to allow of animal life going on freely."

This impenetrable forest extended from pole to pole, for at this time modification of the temperature had not taken place, and all parts of the globe were equally heated; there was, therefore, a fairly unbroken forest waste, in the thick branches of which there was not a living thing, save possibly one small reptile, called the Archegosaurus, a few vestiges of which have been discovered; but even this lonesome creature was manifestly unborn in the early stages of the carboniferous period. Strangely enough, while life on land was confined to the vegetable, the sea was peopled by a multitude of moving animals, which I have described in one of the first chapters of this work.

But, ah! the marvelous change which time works; a transmutation more astonishing than the secret of the alchemist, more marvelous than genii ever conceived. Gradually the imposing forest, upon which nature seemed to have expended her resources, sank into the marshy loam that gave it sustenance, until the loftiest branches disappeared into the great laboratory where they were changed, by a marvelous process, into the coal fields which are a well-spring of almost indispensable usefulness to the present age.

THE BIRTH OF THE FAUNA—LAND MONSTERS.

We have seen, in earlier chapters on the sea, how, among the first inhabitants of the ocean, were mighty saurians, so gigantic that the lizards of our time are but the merest pigmies by comparison. The development of life on land was not dissimilar from that in the sea, for among the earliest land animals were veritable monsters, so colossal that there are none now in existence by which we might compare them.

The secondary epoch was as remarkable for the numerous and curious creatures which it brough forth on land, as the carboniferous was for the absence of fauna. Among the gigantic animals of the period was the immense Labyrinthodon, so named from the labyrinthine texture of its teeth. This creature, though uniting the form and many

THE MEGALOSAURUS AND IGUANODON.

characteristics of the frog with the scaly body of the saurian lizard, was in size equal to a large ox. The head was somewhat like that of a crocodile's, and its powerful jaws, armed with murderous looking teeth, made it a fit companion of the mosasauri, plesiosauri and ichthyosauri, which roamed the sea.

But equally terrible to behold, and more mighty in their vast proportions, were the Megalosauri and Iquanodons, whose reptilian lengths were forty-eight and fifty-two feet. The former is found in a fossil state in the Jurassic beds — named from certain rocks of the Jura Mountains,—where some of the remains are in an excellent state of preservation. This animal was a monster lizard, as its name implies, which crept about on four legs, so short that they scarcely served to keep its body from the ground, while its great tail must have dragged upon its extreme length. Cuvier says the megalosaurus resembled, in structure, both the iguana and monitors of the present day, and that it was undoubtedly terrestrial, though it was very similar in appearance to the amphibious saurians with which it was contemporaneous. Figuier observes that the complicated structure and marvelous arrangement of the teeth prove it to have been essentially carnivorous. It probably fed on serpents, crocodiles and turtles, all of which are found in a fossil state in the same cretaceous (chalky) beds with it. An examination of the lower jaw, an admirable specimen of which is in the British Museum, discloses the fact that its head terminated in a straight nozzle, like the India crocodile. The teeth, several of which adhere to the jaw, betray the destructive power which it possessed, partaking alike of the knife, saber and saw. Vertical at their junction with the jaw, they change as the animal ages, until they assume a backward curve resembling a pruning knife. Buckland says: "With teeth constructed so as to cut with the whole of their concave edge, each movement of the jaws produced the combined effect of a knife and a saw at the same time that the point made a first incision, like that made by the point of a double-cutting sword. The backward curvature taken by the teeth at their full growth render the escape of the prey, when once seized, impossible. We find here, then, the same arrangements which enable mankind to put in operation many of the instruments which they employ."

A MORE TERRIBLE MONSTER YET.

The Iguanodon (toothed lizard) was even more gigantic than the Megalosaurus, in fact the most colossal of all the saurians of the ancient world which research in paleontology has yet exposed. Professor Owen and Dr. Mantell have made a special study of this monstrous animal, but while they have succeeded in clearly defining its nature they are not agreed on the form of its tail; the former believing it to have had a short tail, while the latter stoutly maintains that it was long, proportionate to all others of the lizard species. This difference in opinion is important because it divides opinion on the length of the animal by fifty or sixty-feet. The largest femur (thigh) bone yet found measures four feet eight inches in length, which, when we consider how short are the legs in comparison with the body of all lizards, will give us a small idea of its extraordinary size.

The form of the feet, added to the existence of a horn, which grew on the upper part of the muzzle or snout, serve to identify it as a species of the Iguanidæ now existing, the only reptile which is

THE RAMPHORYNCHUS.

known to be provided with such a nasal weapon. But while the largest of the living Iguanidæ scarcely exceeds one yard in length, its fossil congener was probably fifty feet long, and large in proportion. The bone of the thigh of this animal surpasses that of the elephant, while the feet show that they were designed for terrestrial locomotion, and the formation of its teeth prove it to have been herbivorous.

In the period preceding the secondary there was another animal which deserves classification with the megalosaurus, by reason of a striking resemblance in appearance and equality of size; this was the *Hyleosaurus* (meaning lizard of the wood), a monster that was cuirassed like a knight and endowed with a muscular power almost immeasurable. So few of the bones of this animal have been found that, so far as I know, no scientist has undertaken to describe its characteristics.

A FIEND TOO DREADFUL TO LOOK UPON.

The *Ramphorynchus* (the meaning of which I do not know) was also contemporaneous with the hyleosaurus, and was a reptile strikingly congenerous to the pterodactylus, described among the ocean

DRAGON OF ANCIENT BELIEF.

creatures. This curious animal could not fly, though it possessed wings composed of a membrane connecting the fingers and body. Its mode of attacking its prey was to climb trees, or other elevations, and by making a sail, or parachute, of its wings, dart downward at whatever angle it chose. The ramphorynchus was a horrible appearing creature, but it was harmless, since it did not exceed a crow in size, and on the ground, where it spent much of its time, its progress was slow.

The most startling feature in the organization of this animal is the strange combination of two powerful wings attached to the body of a reptile. The imagination of the poets had long dwelt on such a combination; the *Dragon* was a creation of their fancy, and it had long played a great part in Pagan mythology. The dragon, or flying reptile, breathing fire and poisoning the air with its fiery breath, had, according to fable, disputed with man the possession of the earth. Gods and demi-gods claimed, among their most famous exploits, the glory of having vanquished this powerful and redoubtable monster. From pagan fictions the dragon passed into the poetry of the Greeks and Latins, and later still into that of the Renaissance, and to modern times. What a part did not the dragon play in the verses of Tasso and Ariosto! Consecrated by the superstitions of the earlier peoples, transferred from pagan mythology to Greek and Roman poesy, and finally into the poetic fictions of the middle ages, the dragon always has and always will belong to the supernatural. Indeed, does not the ramphorynchus and pterodactylus present a living embodiment of this poetic conception of the dragon? While the former was no larger than a crow, and the latter did not exceed a swan in size, yet the figure once impressed upon the mind may easily enlarge when out of sight. Thus several scientists have undertaken to prove by this analogy of reasoning that man lived contemporaneous with these two winged reptiles, a remembrance of which has been transmitted through successive generations until the one who first conceived a dragon borrowed the idea from the transmitted image.

BIRTH OF THE MAMMALIA.

The tertiary period, at which we have now arrived in the earth's development, shows as great changes as during any other age, and is remarkable for the appearance of that higher order of creation, the mammifera, which at once assumed a mastership over all animate things. We have seen how, in the transition or Devonian period, the animal kingdom was confined to crustaceans and fishes; that in the secondary age the rulership was transferred to the reptiles, whose decline, by some of the largest species becoming extinct, was succeeded by mammals, a great number of distinct types apparently appearing at the same time. Not only did the higher order of animal life appear during the tertiary epoch, but it is also a distinguished period from the fact that it was now that the earth's crust had become so thick

THE PALÆOTHERIUM AND ANOPLOTHERIA.

that the internal fires were losing their effect, and the solar rays began to show their influence on our planet; the poles were growing cold; lacustrine deposits of fresh water were formed in great numbers, and rivers, by their alluvial deposits, began to form new land. It is at the end of this period that continents and seas took their respective places as we now see them, and the surface of the earth received its actual form. Creation's hand had at last fashioned a habitation for animal life which showed the extraordinary development of species. Not only did monkeys, bats, mermots and pachyderms now appear on land, but the sea gave up its monsters, too, and cetaceans were born, which, though no less in size, were of harmless disposition and necessary in the preparation all nature was now making to receive the Master, the crowning work of creation, Man.

HUGE BEASTS OF THE TERTIARY PERIOD.

Most prominent among the animals of the tertiary epoch were the Palæotherium, Anoplotherium and the Xiphodon, all of which were herbivorous and gregarious in their habits Cuvier represents them as being intermediate between the rhinoceros, tapir and horse, since they possessed characteristics peculiar to all these. But more singular than this is the fact that in size they varied from that of a rabbit to an ox, indicating a wonderful variety of species. The *Palæotherium* (implying ancient beast) had heavy bodies, small, prehensile trunk, and generally resembled our tapirs. They congregated in vast herds along the river courses and lake coasts, where their bones may still be found in immense quantities, and particularly in the ancient basin of Paris. It is from this beast that our modern horse is supposed to have descended.

The *Anoplotheria* (meaning defenceless animal) has posterior molars analogous to those of the rhinoceros, and with hoofs divided like the ox. The most singular feature it possessed was a tail about three feet long and very thick at the junction with the body; this tail, it is supposed, served the animal as a rudder and propeller when swimming in lakes and rivers which it frequented.

"Judging from its habits of swimming and diving," says Cuvier, "the anoplotherium would have the hair smooth, like the otter; perhaps its skin was half naked. It is not likely either that it had long ears, which would be inconvenient in its aquatic kind of life; and I am inclined to think that, in this respect, it resembled the hippopotamus and other quadrupeds which frequent the water much."

In our own country the remains of equally wonderful animals are found, the cretaceous beds of New Jersey being particularly prolific with remains of extinct creatures much greater in size than any now existent. Among these mighty reptiles, that seemed to be confined

THE HADROSAUR AND CONTEMPORARY ANIMALS.

to American bayous, was the *Great Cimoliasaur* (chalk-lizard) and *Elasmosaur*, which presented forms like our conception of the modern sea-serpent. Their bodies equaled that of an ox, and they were provided with flippers, large as the whale's, to propel their forty feet of serpentine length through the water; so were there monster snapping-turtles, having heads a foot long and shells six feet in length.

THE FRIGHTFUL ALLIGATOR BIRD.

But the most remarkable animal that flourished on American soil, and perhaps the most wonderful in all creation, was the *Lœlops*, or eagle-beast, a carnivorous, kangaroo-like quadruped, twenty-three feet in length. Winchell describes it as a rude attempt of nature to realize the notion of a bird in the framework of an alligator. Its toes were long and slender, and very like those of a bird of prey. They were armed with flattened, hooked claws, which measured nearly a foot in length, and, like those of the eagle — from whence it takes its Latin name, *L. Aquilunguis* — were adapted for grabbing and tearing prey. The teeth were knife-shaped and serrate on the margin, so that when the upper and lower were brought together they cut like a pair of scissors. Such a creature could hardly be destroyed by modern sporting arms, and it might well terrify an army. The claws of the grizzly bear are scarcely three inches in length, and yet a lion can hardly stand before it; what, then, must have been the dreadful strength and fighting power of the lælops, with its claws a foot in length, and a body, no doubt, possessing the strong vitality of the alligator?

Another gigantic reptile, whose remains were found in Pennsylvania, was the *Hadrosaur*, which attained a length of thirty feet, but it was not furnished with such murderous claws as the lælops possessed. Its fore-limbs were less than half the length of the hind ones, thus proving it to be also of a kangaroo species. Its attitude when resting was upon its posterior extremities, and when feeding it reached upward and drew the branches down within reach of its grinding jaws, for it was an herbivorous animal. It is probable that this monstrous creature sometimes walked half erect upon its immense hind feet, in which attitude it must have presented a sight that would have frozen the blood of a courageous man, for it was more frightful than a nightmare.

In Ohio there has been exhumed the remains of an animal that was the very incarnation of horror. It is called the *Dinotheria* — meaning "terrible beast" — and in shape was analogus to the elephant, though very much larger and altogether of more forbidding aspect, yet its nature was comparatively harmless, since it fed chiefly upon herbaceous vegetables growing in flooded plains. It was provided with two tusks, which grew downward, like in the walrus, which it no

THE MONSTER DINOTHERIA.

doubt used to dig up feculent roots from the beds of rivers, while with the proboscis, which it also possessed, it could tear down the branches of trees and feast upon their foliage. Several bones of this creature have been dug up in Ohio, but in 1836 a head, nearly entire, was found in the already celebrated beds at Eppelsheim, Germany. Bones of the same animal have also been exhumed in Louisiana, so that its range seems to have been greater than that of any other animal of the tertiary age.

The *Mastodon* (meaning teat-like tooth) was next in size to the Dinotheria, which it somewhat resembled, but was more nearly analogous to the elephant. In fact, about the only distinction was in its heavy coat of coarse, bristly hair and the size of its tusks, which, in the mammoth, grew to a length of ten feet, and almost without any curve, while it was also provided with two shorter tusks, growing out of the lower jaw. The remains of this ponderous creature are quite numerous throughout the United States and Siberia, where they have been exhumed entire, and standing upright, as if suddenly overwhelmed and buried. Indeed, so perfect are some of these remains, that we still find in their stomachs the food they had just swallowed, and not yet digested.

The *Megatherium* (great beast) was larger then any elephant of the present period, standing more than twenty feet when in an erect position. It was allied to the sloths and ant-eaters, no representations of which now living exceed a common dog in size. Its remains seem to be confined to South America.

The *Sivatherium* (beast of Siva), found in India, is represented by Owen as having been one of the most gigantic and extraordinary of extinct quadrupeds. It was a stag as large as an elephant, and its head was armed with monstrous horns. The Irish deer, the largest of extinct animals found in Ireland, could not be compared with it, either in size or formidable appearance.

But besides gigantic saurians and other mastodonic beasts, which distinguished the tertiary period, there were other monsters, such as the *Glyptodons*, huge armadillos, that might have borne a house on their backs, so large and powerful were they. This also was the age of the great Salamander, which the dictum of a theological naturalist caused to be long considered as an incontestable relic from the hecatomb of the biblical deluge. There were also rhinoceros and hippopotami, though the fossil remains found of these animals do not show them to have been larger at that period than at present. Birds were also numerous, but not of extraordinary size, nor were there any monstrosities among the feathered creatures.

What I have written of the tertiary epoch has reference to that age as a whole, notwithstanding that it was divided into three sepa-

THE EARLIEST MAN AND HIS SURROUNDINGS.

rate periods, viz.: the *socene*, *miocene* and *pliocene*, each of which extended over a thousand years. This I have done for the sake of abreviation, as to have described these periods separately would have greatly enlarged this chapter, and extended it beyond the scope intended.

THE AGE OF MAN. AND TELLURIC DISTURBANCES.

The quaternary period follows the tertiary, merging one into the other, not by any distinct or marked act of nature, but like the gradual blending of light and shadow. During the tertiary age the earth was split and rent by mighty convulsions, but at its conclusion our planet assumed the shape which it still retains, save in some minor particulars, hardly of sufficient importance to describe. We now approach a period most remarkable for three important events, transcending all others in the earth's development, save alone its evolution out of original chaos; these three wonderful occurences were: The deluges, glacial invasions and the creation of man.

Those who have studied geology or paleontology, while reading of the animals which I have attempted briefly to describe in the foregoing, will be tempted to enquire how it is possible to restore a creature from only a bone that may be found, or a few bones, so that its appearance and habits while living may be known. To this I will make answer in the language of Prof. Winchell, who has anticipated me: "* * * Such is the unity and persistence of plan which runs through the different classes of the animal kingdom, that a single tooth, whether of a living or extinct species, will often suffice to enable an expert to disclose all the zoological relationships of the animal to which it belonged, to delineate its form, size and habits of life. Not less sublime than the work of the astronomer, who sits in his observatory and, by the use of a few figures, determines the existence and position in space of some far-off, unknown orb, is that of the paleontologist who, from the tooth of a reptile, or the long scale of a fish found thirty feet deep in the solid rock, declares the existence, ages ago, of an animal form which human eyes never beheld—a form passed totally out of being uncounted centuries before the first intelligent creature was placed upon our planet—and by laws as unerring and uniform as those of the mathematics, proceeds to give us the length and breadth of the extinct form; to tell us whether it lived upon dry land, or marshes, or in the sea; whether a breather of air or water, and whether subsisting upon vegetable or animal food."

The same laws by which animal creation is governed apply with equal naturalness to geologic formation; hence, as from the tooth of an extinct creature the paleontologist discovers it was a living thing brought to existence again; so the geologist, from the stones and shells which he may gather, pictures the whole panorama of change

THE MEGATHERIUM.

through which they have passed, and through these stones, as a Urim and Thummim, he sees the world as an infant, adult and aged.

CHAPTER XXII.

MONSTERS OF THE QUATERNARY PERIOD.

BEFORE describing the cataclysms which overwhelmed and destroyed the greatest works of creation, applied to animal life, let us consider some of the wonderful creatures which roamed the earth during the quaternary period, which is remarkable for the abundance of extraordinary monsters that were then distributed over the northern hemisphere. Europe and America were both the grazing grounds of enormous animals, now long extinct, but if we could penetrate the veil which hides from us the scenes of five thousand years ago, we might see upon the hillsides, river banks and coast bayous, creatures of such gigantic stature and terrible appearance as would fairly appal us. There were then elephants vastly larger than any now existent, and apes of proportions that render man insignificant by comparison.

In England, which was at that time a part of the European continent, there were serpents greater in size than any python that now renders the jungles of Africa terrible, while the turtles that sunned themselves upon the banks of her streams were almost equal to the elephants of our day. There also lived in the British forests tigers that exceeded any such as are now found in India, but even these ferocious and powerful beasts were unable to contend with another English native called the *Machairodus* (meaning dagger tooth), which, being carnivorous, sought its prey from among the formidable animals that lorded it over all others.

Over all Europe and Northern Asia there were countless hordes of ponderous creatures, whose bones now alone remain to remind us how wonderful are the changes which time has wrought. In the post-tertiary period, a division of the quaternary age, the rivers of Southern France and Italy were infested with hippopotami of gigantic size, while in the forest of all Europe there roamed by thousands the great hairy two-horned rhinoceros, bands of monster hyenas and herds of enormous bears, whose jaws were mighty enough to crush the bones of any contemporary animal. But the largest of creatures of that period was the huge Mammoth, which stood eighteen and twenty feet in height, with proportions like the elephant. It had tusks that measured fifteen feet in length, but these did not project straight outward, like the tusks of an elephant, but described a half-circle instead, so that their use does not so clearly appear. It presented other points of difference from the elephant, in that its body

THE MAMMOTH AND CONTEMPORARY ANIMALS.

was covered with a long, shaggy, reddish hair, while from its neck and back floated an immense mane; its legs, too, were shorter, so that, considering its great height, we may form some idea of the magnitude of its body.

RESURRECTION OF THE BONES OF GIANTS.

. Bones of gigantic quadrupeds underlie the surface of nearly all Europe, and the finding of them by the ancients gave rise to many curious speculations and superstitions. Theophrastus, who preceded Christ more than three hundred years, spoke of the fossil ivory in the soil of Greece, in which he gravely tells us that they "were both black and white, and born of the earth." It is a singular fact that some of the mammoth's bones bear a striking resemblance to those of man, and hence they were frequently mistaken for the bones of heroes and demi-gods. The Greeks for a long time sacredly preserved the patula of an elephant for the knee-bone of Ajax. Pliny was likewise deceived by some bones revealed by an earthquake, which he pronounced those of a giant man. To a similar origin we may assign the pretended body of Orestes, which was thirteen feet in length; those of Asterius, the son of Ajax, of eighteen feet, according to Pausanius, and also of the great bones found in the Isle of Rhodes, so elaborately described in Phlegon's "Subterranean World."

"In 1577," says Figuier, "a storm having uprooted an oak near the cloisters of Reyden, in the canton of Lucerne, some large bones were exposed to view. Seven years later a physician and professor of Basel, Felix Plater, being at Lucerne, examined these bones, and declared they could only proceed from a giant. The Council of Lucerne consented to send the bones to Basel for more minute examination, and Plater thought himself justified in attributing to the giant a hight of nineteen feet. In 1706 there only remained of these bones a portion of the scapula, and a fragment of the wrist-bone; the anatomist Blumenbach, who saw them at the beginning of the century, easily recognized them for the bones of an elephant. Let us not omit to add, as a complement to this bit of history, that the inhabitants adopted the image of this pretended giant as the supporter of the city arms.

Spanish history preserves many stories of giants. The tooth of St. Christopher, shown at Valence, in the church dedicated to the saint, was certainly the molar tooth of a fossil elephant, and in 1789 the canons of St. Vincent carried through the streets in public procession, to procure rain, the pretended arm of a saint, which was nothing more than the femur of an elephant.

In 1663, Otto Guericke, the illustrious inventor of the pneumatic machine, was witness to the discovery of the bones of an elephant, buried in shelly limestone. Along with it were found its enormous

THE MAMMOTH DURING THE AGE OF MAN.

tusks, which should have sufficed to establish its zoological origin. Nevertheless, they were taken for horns, and the great Leibnitz composed out of the remains a strange animal, carrying a horn in the middle of the forehead, and in each jaw a dozen molar teeth a foot

FOREST OF THE CARBONIFEROUS PERIOD.

long. Having fabricated this fantastic creature, he gave to it a name also, the *fossil unicorn*. During more than thirty years the unicorn of Leibnitz was universally accepted throughout Germany, and nothing less than the discovery of the entire skeleton of a mammoth was required to make them renounce their error. But though this people were at length convinced of their great mistake concerning the bones of Leibnitz's unicorn, they were just as ready to be deceived again; therefore, when some fossil bones of bears were exhumed in Germany only a short time after their enlightenment, they accepted with trusting faith the statement that they were the remains of the *dicorn fossil.* It had long before been asserted by the superstitious that the bones of the unicorn were a medicament of extraordinary virtue, and the people were therefore ready to believe that any bones dug out of the ground were the ones containing the sovereign properties for allaying ills. The court physician of Wurtemberg used the bones of this cave-bear to combat fever and cholic, under the mistaken idea that he was applying the great catholicon of the unicorn.

THE EARTH-MOLE, LARGE AS AN ELEPHANT.

It was in Prussia that the fossil elephant received the name of mammoth, and its tusks mammoth horns. Pallas asserts that the name is derived from mamma, which is the Tartar word for earth. Others incline to the belief that its origin is in *behemoth*, in the Book of Job, while yet others maintain that it comes from the Arabic epithet, *mehemot*, which they apply to the elephant when of extraordinary size.

There is a very ancient legend among the Russians of Northern Asia to the effect that many centuries ago Siberia was fairly overrun with enormous animals that lived underground like the mole, and which had such an affinity for darkness that they died at once upon being exposed to the light. Singular enough, this same belief is quite as current among the Chinese, as the following passage from an old and standard work on natural history, written by a Chinese naturalist in the sixteenth century, will serve to show: "The animal *tien-schu*, of which we have already spoken in the ancient work upon ceremonies, entitled '*Ly-ki*,' a work of the fifth century before Jesus Christ, is called also *tyn-schu*, or *yn-schu*, that is to say, the mouse which hides itself. It constantly confines itself to subterraneous caverns; it resembles a mouse, but is of the size of a buffalo or ox. It has no tail; its color is dark; it is very strong and excavates caverns in places full of roots and covered with forests." Another writer, quoting the same passage. thus expresses himself: "The *tyn-schu* haunts obscure places. It dies as soon as it is exposed to the rays of the sun or moon; its feet are short in proportion to its size. Its tail is as long as that of a

THE GREAT WOOLLY RHINOCEROS.

Chinese. Its eyes are small; its neck short. It is very stupid and sluggish. When the inundations of the river *Tam-schuanu-my* took place, in 1571, it often showed itself in the plain; it is nourished by the roots of the plant *fu-kia*."

THE CHINESE MOLE AND THE MEGATHERIUM IDENTICAL.

These legends, which are quoted in nearly every printed reference made to the mammoth, are somewhat confusing, for the reason that there is not the least application to the mammoth in the description, but there is a striking analogy between this Chinese mole, mouse or buffalo, as one may choose to call it, and the megatherium of South America, to which I have already referred, though so briefly that I may be pardoned for calling it again to mind, especially since it existed in both the tertiary and post-tertiary periods. This extraordinary creature, as has been said, has been placed by scientists between the sloths and ant-eaters, because its organization seemed to be equally adapted to climbing trees and burrowing in the ground. Some naturalists have been so bold as to declare that it climbed trees, back-downward, like the sloths of the present age, but this is pure fancy, since no tree could have borne branches large enough to sustain its enormous weight. But that the megatherium burrowed deep in the earth is well attested by the caves which it excavated as well as the adaptation of its physiology to digging and living underground. If the bones of this extinct monster had ever been found in Siberia or China, we could at once rest satisfied of the origin of the legend referred to, but since its fossil remains seem to be confined to Paraguay, it is difficult to understand how a belief so natural to the Paraguayans could have originated in Siberia.

THE MAMMOTH.

It is a most astonishing fact that in 1799 the remains of a mammoth were found intact, enclosed in a block of ice, near the mouth of the Lena River. This animal had been dead for thousands of years, and yet when found its flesh was in such a perfect state of preservation that wolves and bears made a feast off it, and the blood oozed from it as it would from fresh meat under a butcher's knife. It is known that flesh will not putrify when exposed to a temperature of zero, and it is to such exposure the preservation of this mammoth was due. The remains, much injured by wolves, were taken to St. Petersburg and properly mounted for the national museum. In 1882, while traveling through Russia, I had the pleasure of examining this skeleton, and also portions of the skin and hair, which had been preserved and placed on exhibition beside the skeleton and the restored remains of an elephant, that a comparison of the size of the two species might appear conspicuous.

ANCIENT ANIMALS OF THE THAMES.

Mammoths existed throughout Siberia in such vast numbers that their bones, washed down by the glacial drift, have accumulated in places about the Arctic coast in such quantity as to form islands. A valuable commerce has been carried on for years by the Tunguese and

CHEIROTHERIUM, OR HAND-ANIMAL.

Yakouts, who are engaged recovering the ivory from these island storehouses.

It was during the quaternary period that the horse appeared, both in North America and in Europe, though, curious enough, the species in Europe were very much smaller than those of our day, while the fossil remains of those found in North America show them to have been very much larger than our domestic horse.

MONSTER BRUTES AND GREAT BIRDS.

Among the strange reptiles of this period none exceeded in formidable aspect the *Glyptodon* (carved tooth), a species of armadillo found in South America. It was larger than an ox, and was covered with tessellated scales, including the head, giving it a cuirassed appearance invulnerable to any fowling-piece of to-day.

The *Cheirotherium* (hand-animal) flourished at this time, and has left its impressions in hand-like tracks found plentifully in ancient morasses, since turned into peat-beds. This animal bore a striking resemblance to our common toad-frog, though in size it equalled an ox.

Another strange creature was the *Mylodon robustus* (great millstone toothed), somewhat like the megatherium, though very much smaller, while its teeth and feet are different. President Jefferson found the bones of a mylodon on his farm in Western Virginia, to which he gave the name *Megalonyx* (great claw-nail), believing them to have belonged to a species of lion. The mylodon was furnished with a long, extensile tongue, like that of the giraffe, which, by one of those beautiful provisions of nature, thus reaches its leafy food.

During this period two gigantic birds existed, but most strange to relate, instead of being found upon a great continent, associated with immense animals, which would appear their most natural haunt, they were both confined to islands—one to New Zealand and the other to Madagascar.

The discovery of these wonderful specimens of feathered creation was made by the illustrious zoologists, Owen and Saint Hilaire, to whom we are indebted for a description. One of these, the *Dinornis* (terrible bird), a skeleton of which is in the London College of Surgeons, stood eighteen feet high. The bone of a man's leg is only a spindle compared with that of this colossal bird.

The disappearance of this monstrous bird dates from no distinct epoch, and everything attests that the first inhabitants of New Zealand were perfectly acquainted with it. The ancient legends of the island tell us that at the time of its discovery it was full of birds of appalling size. There are ancient poems still recited by the New

THE DINORNIS—(TERRIBLE BIRD).

Zealanders, in which the father teaches his son how to hunt the Moa, the name belonging of old to this species; in these are described the ceremonies which took place when one had been killed. The people feasted on the flesh and eggs, while the feathers were used for personal adornment. Some hills of the island are still strewn with the bones of the dinornis, the remains of the great feasts of the hunters.

The *Epiornis* (great bird) was even of greater size than the dinornis. Its remains have been found nowhere except in Madagascar; indeed, no bones of this bird have even been found there, but an egg of the bird has been discovered which is now in the museum at Paris. This egg is six times the size of an ostrich egg, and its shell more than three-fourths of an inch in thickness. No bones of this feathered giant having been discovered, science is unable, from its egg, to restore the skeleton, hence we can have no conception of its form.

A BIRD WITHOUT WINGS.

A single bone, found in a New Zealand water-course, was brought to England and sent to Professor Owen. It belonged, he said, to a wingless, tailless bird, which was at least twelve feet high! Other men of science thought this to be impossible, and tried to prevent him from making his opinion known. But Professor Owen was right, and a specimen of the *Apteryx* (that is, "wingless" bird) in due course arrived at the Zoological Gardens in London. This strange creature was nocturnal in its habits, and, if brought out into the light of day, it ran here and there in search of cover. Wingless and tailless it was, standing upon legs like those of an ostrich, and with a long bill that might belong to a stork. This long bill had more uses than in the case of most birds. When its ungainly owner leaned forward it was used as a support, and was also used to bore in the mud for worms, like our modern snipe. It is supposed to have be-

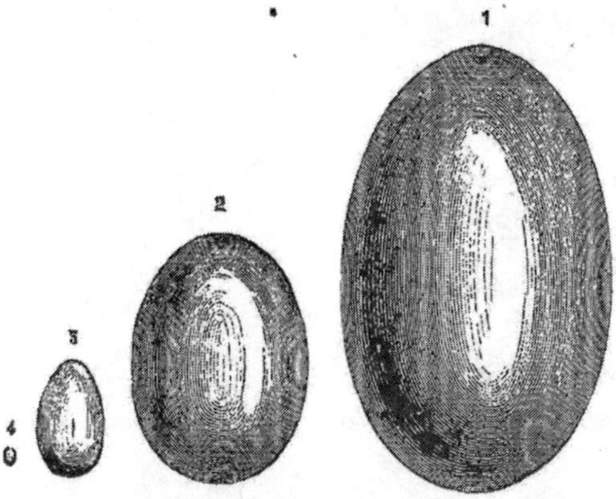

COMPARATIVE SIZE OF EGGS:

1. EGG OF EPIORNIS. 2. EGG OF OSTRICH.
3. EGG OF CHICKEN. 4. EGG OF HUMMING BIRD.

come extinct during the present century, but this is hardly a justifiable supposition, since there is nothing in the tradition of the native New Zealanders that concerns this strange creature. This fact leads to the more reasonable belief that the apteryx perished off the face

THE APTERYX, OR WINGLESS BIRD OF NEW ZEALAND.

of earth many centuries ago, perhaps at the time of the subsidence, into the sea, of that portion of the Asiatic continent of which New Zealand was a part. The traditions of man do not extend back to this probable event.

CHAPTER XXIII.

THE BIRTH OF MAN.

THE most important event in the world's history took place in the quaternary period, one which has proved to be the most wonderful climacteric unfolding of nature's scroll, pronouncing the completion of her greatest work. This wonderful mile-stone in the progress of evolution was the birth of man. What an ocean of mist rises before our vision when we attempt to look back through the vale of years to man in his infancy. Revelation does not satisfy the enquiry: "How came mankind upon the earth?" The Mosaic records, the oldest of our written history, whether of fable or fact, represent Western Asia as swarming with a population already somewhat advanced in the arts. Even the account of Genesis, in describing the creation of our first parents and their children, becomes confused by asserting that Cain, after killing Abel, went into the Land of Nod, where he took a wife and founded a great city; thereby implying that Adam and Eve were not, personally, the first man and woman. It is more probable, as their names imply, that they were only figuratively the first.

EVIDENCES OF OUR FIRST PARENTS.

The chief sources of our information respecting the earliest periods of human existence are: 1st. The remains of man himself, which have been found in caves, or buried in deposits of gravel or peat; 2d. Human works, of which we have the so-called Druidical monuments of unhewn stone, called *cromlechs*, which have been found in England and Ireland, and, I believe, also, in this country; 3rd. Implements, mounds and bones, the latter having evidently been crushed and even rudely carved by the unpracticed hand of primeval man. But from the first evidences we have of man's presence on the earth, we are bound to conclude that, though he was unclothed and unarmed by nature, yet he was at once the greatest power, the mind masterful of creation. Though he made his advent amid surroundings which would appear to be least favorable to his existence, beset by the most ferocious of animals, vastly larger than those of to-day and without means of escape or defense, yet nature had provided him with a reasoning power and thereby established him as king of all creation. But

PRIMEVAL MAN BATTLING WITH THE CAVE BEAR.

picture our rude forefathers living in the rugged wastes of fairly unorganized nature, hunting caves for shelter and subsisting upon roots, or, perchance, the flesh of some animal which accident threw in their way. Then, again, behold them when some genius from among their ranks devised their first weapon, the stone-hammer, and the ponderous club; with these they felt equipped to contend against beasts of prey, to attack the cave-bear, cave-lion, the hyena and other savage creatures with which the earth swarmed.

In the geological history of man we find him mounting from lower to higher manifestations in the progress of ages. The lower animals progressed, also, but it was a structural advance, while with man it was education: A contention, not only with animals, upon which he was largely dependent for food, but the evolution of genius, by which his condition was being constantly improved, until we behold this king of creation still crowned, and with none to dispute his sway.

WHERE WAS THE GARDEN OF EDEN?

Geology, archæology, or metaphysical speculation, do not properly belong within the scope of this work, but I am sure my readers will pardon me, for the sake of the great interest which is attached to the subject, if I pursue the matter touched upon in the last few pages a little farther.

For a long period of years men have been engaged in a search for the original site of Eden, and, like Troy, it has never been conclusively located. In 1882 there appeared a work entitled, "Atlantis; or, the Antediluvian World," by Mr. Donnelly, which, in my estimation, has shed more light upon this question than all the philosophers who have preceded him. Briefly, Mr. Donnelly adopts the unfinished story of Plato, who relates, through Critias, talking to Socrates, the history of Atlantis. This country of Atlantis once occupied a greater portion of what is now the Atlantic Ocean, from whence the name is derived, and it is here, Plato tells us, the old sages affirmed was the Garden of Eden. The proofs which Mr. Donnelly introduces to sustain the legend are numerous, and at times startling. He shows that there is more than mere coincidence in the similarity of civilization which prevailed coincident in Europe, Egypt and Western Asia, and North America, Mexico and Peru. This similarity consists in that the people of all these countries had the same traditions respecting their origin, the deluge and disappearance of Atlantis; a unity in their religious superstitions, worship of idols and of the sun, and, in addition to many other features of striking similitude, the very alphabets were alike, so nearly so in some of the letters that we

IMAGINARY SCENE OF THE BIBLICAL DELUGE.

cannot avoid the belief that they must have had a common origin.

Plato tells us that Atlantis was a mighty country lying beyond the pillars of Heracles (Hercules); that there our first parents were born; that a numerous people were there developed, who grew in art and civilization until they had become greater than any in Egypt or Greece had since grown; that it was ruled over by ten kings, each of whom was possessed of a divine nature; nevertheless, they builded the most sumptuous palaces, and of gold there was scarcely any limit, for it was a great commercial country, having thousands of ships, which brought from the seaports of the realm the produce which was raised out of the soil in great abundance. There were ten immense cities in Atlantis, over each of which ruled a king, but there was a king over these ten, whose name was Poseidon. His judgment was represented as being omniscient, and all his people virtuous. To sum up, there was never a country, before or since, where the people were so opulent, the cities so magnificent, the soil so rich, and everything so conducive to happiness as Atlantis. Amid all this prodigality of nature and incentives to contentment, the people became at length discontented and went to war among themselves. The country was finally destroyed by a mighty deluge, but the particulars are not given in Plato's story, which ends abruptly, for what reason we do not know.

The theory of Mr. Donnelly is, that ships went to and fro between Atlantis—which was a real country, as Plato describes—and the mainland of America, and not only by ships, but there was a land connection between the southern extremity of the country and South America, by which people passed between the two countries, and thus were carried, to America and Europe alike, the relics of Atlantean civilization. This wonderful island was destroyed by some mighty convulsion, as hundreds of other islands have been submerged within our own times, and the people were drowned, but Europe and Africa, as well as Mexico and Central America, were already inhabited by the descendants of the Atlanteans, and, though they possessed no written history, they remembered and transmitted the story of their island and preserved the traditions of their forefathers. Nearly all the names in Greek mythology were characters in this story of Plato's, and the same coincidence is true of the mythologic history of Central America.

THE GREAT DELUGE.

That there have been great cataclysms, by which not only cities but continents have been overwhelmed, is affirmed by innumerable evidences, so positive as to preclude argument. But as to the nature and effect of these deluges there is a wide range of speculation, usually

FUNERAL FEAST DURING THE GREAT BEAR AND MAMMOTH EPOCH.

taking the form of legends, some of which are very ancient but no less interesting.

Berosus, writing of the Chaldeans, says they held to the belief that the world is periodically destroyed by cataclysms and conflagrations; a belief, no doubt, founded upon the same evidences that were used in the compilation of the Pentateuch. But they even attempted to predict the periodicity of these disasters, fixing their alternate recurrence at twenty-one thousand and twenty-six thousand years, a period corresponding to the time occupied in the retrograde movement of the stars through one complete circumference — a phenomenon due to the precession of the equinoxes. This period was called the *annus magnus*, or great year. After the earth's destruction was complete, they believed it was renewed after the manner of its birth and evolution.

Plato says the Egyptians held that the heavens and earth were originally a chaotic pulp, from which the elements separated of their own accord; that fire sprang from the upper regions, and set the earth in motion, when life proceeded. The sun fructified the earth, and caused innumerable living creatures to come forth from the plastic mud, from whence they took their natural positions, whether in the air, water, or upon land. But man had no pre-eminence of birth, for he, too, sprang from the mud banks of the Nile. They also had a great year, which, according to Orpheus, was one hundred and twenty thousand years, but Cassander computed it at three hundred and sixty thousand years. At the end of this great cycle the Egyptians believed the world was destroyed by fire or water; but this destruction was more in the nature of regeneration, for, though all life was obliterated, there immediately came forth a purified order of creation again, so that the world was always being repeopled by creatures superior to those they succeeded.

HINDOO THEORY OF CREATION.

The Hindoo cosmogony — theory of creation — which contained the germ of the theory taught by western nations, makes prominent the doctrine of catastrophes and rejuvenation. The Institutes of Menu says: "The first sole cause thinks within himself, I will create worlds." Following the bidding of the celestial mandate, the waters are brought into being, over the surface of which moves Brahma, the creator. (Moses says: "And God moved upon the face of the waters," an expression and idea strikingly similar). Brahma next

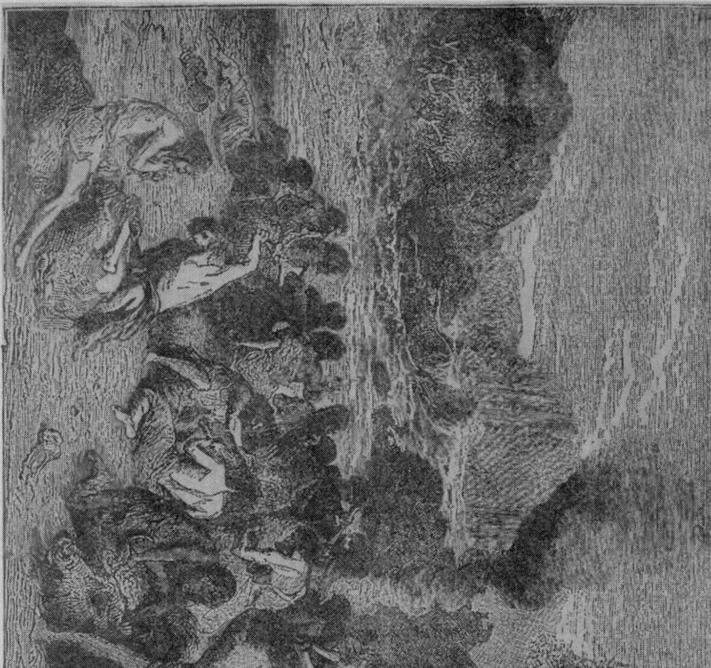

A FEAST DURING THE REINDEER EPOCH.

divides the land and water, and establishes a firmament over both. His next work is the vivification of earth, which is made to bring forth, in their order, plants, animals, celestial creatures, and, lastly, man. From Brahma spring forth all the elements; the sun from his eye, the air from his ear, fire from his mouth, while from his mouth, arm, thigh and foot proceed the founders of the chief Hindoo castes. After his period of energy expended in creating, Brahma seeks repose, and sleeps *one day*, but this one day corresponds to four thousand three hundred and twenty millions of years of our time, at the end of which period the world is destroyed by fire. The flames of the burning world are quenched by a torrent rainfall of one hundred years, when the waters overspread the earth and rise to the heavens. During this time the world is a waste of boundless waters and impenetrable darkness. Vishnu now appears, and with his breath drives away the clouds of darkness and pours a flood of light upon the liquid world, when Brahma is revealed reposing on his serpent couch upon the deep. As soon as the deity (Brahma) awakes from his slumber, he at once renews the world and all that it contained; thus at each period, called a *kalpa*, the world is destroyed and re-created, but at the end of one hundred years, each consisting of three hundred and sixty kalpas, and each kalpa of four thousand three hundred and twenty millions of years (1,555,200,000,000), Brahma himself, and all things with him, will cease to exist.

Among the Jews there has been extant, from time immemorial, a prophecy that the world was destined to endure 6,000 years—2,000 before the flood, 2,000 under the law, and 2,000 under the Messiah.

PERIODICAL DESTRUCTION OF THE EARTH.

From the East the doctrine of periodical destruction of the earth found its way, with the migration of man, into Europe. The Persians, Chaldeans, Egyptians and Phœnicians adopted it in Western Asia and in Africa, while the "Orphic Hymns" afford us the earliest germination of the Eastern faith in Greece. Orpheus and Menander, who flourished in the very twilight of Greek poetry and civilization, and who undoubtedly derived their philosophy from the Egyptians, reproduce the myth of the Great Year, and teach that the world is destined to be destroyed on the completion of that period.

In the Sibylline books (which Farquin, the proud, bought from a sibyl, under the belief thay they contained the prophecies foretelling the fate of Rome) whose origin, at least, antedates by 1,300 years

A FAMILY OF THE STONE AGE.

our present era, pronounce the same belief as expressed in the Institutes of Menu. In these mystic verses it is set forth that the world will endure only ten ages, the first of which is the Golden Age. The earth will be swallowed up by flames during this period, but forthwith will the Golden Age return again; the earth will be regenerated and produce her crops spontaneously; the lion and lamb will lie down together; grapes will grow upon thorn-bushes, and a royal vintage will be at hand.

The Stoics who, through Zeno, derived their doctrine of *passiveness* from the Phœnicians, and were its principal advocates among the Greeks, maintained that the earth would be destroyed by a conflagration. This calamity would occur, they said, "when the sun and stars shall have drunk up the sea." In speaking of the restoration of the world the Stoics make use of almost the identical terms used in the Bible, which is another coincidence we cannot overlook. Chrysippus calls it "Apocatastasis-restitution"—as St. Peter does in Acts. Marcus Antonius several times uses the term "Palingenesia"—regeneration—in the same connection as does our Saviour in Matthew and also Paul in his epistle to Titus.

The philosophy of Pythagoras was very similar to that of Zeno and the Phœnicians, which, like the latter, was also borrowed from Persia and India. The Epicureans entertained a similar belief respecting the periodical destruction of the earth. Plato, while not combatting the theories of older philosophers, was more progressive; he expresses the belief that the earth is subject to wonderful transformations due to conflagrations and deluges, but says the idea of God destroying so beautiful a creation as the world, as a whole, is repugnant to him.

Aristotle was the first philosopher to teach the indestructibility of matter, and in his discoveries and writings was proud of the distinction of being at variance with the unanimous belief of antiquity.

Among the Romans, Lucretius, Lucan, and even Ovid, laid aside his amorous verse to discourse upon the doctrine of periodical catastrophes. Cicero, the very echo cave of eloquence, and a man of profound erudition, declared that the remembrance of valorous deeds and great men can only exist for a measurable time, since conflagrations and deluges periodically destroy every record of human achievements. The Celts, if we are to believe Strabo, believed in the same traditions in the West of Europe, and the Druids were firm believers in the perpetuity of the earth through its periodic regeneration by fire and water.

The fable of the Phœnix, prevalent among the people of Arabia and India, is purely an allegory of the world's death and revivification. So is that of the fabled eagle, which in age soars so near the sun as to renew its youth. David refers to this belief in Psalms in the following passage: "Thy youth is renewed like the eagle's." The same is rendered by the Chaldee: "Thou shalt renew thy youth like the eagle in the world to come."

SIMILARITY IN THE AZTEC AND MOSAIC CHRONICLES.

It is somewhat singular that all the nations of the eastern hemisphere, from time immemorial, taught the destruction of the earth periodically by fire and water, as we have seen by the traditions and works referred to, but our surprise is very much increased when we learn that the same beliefs were entertained by the Aztecs, the most ancient people of Northern South America and Mexico. Humboldt first directed our attention to this marvelous coincidence of tradition. The following account of creation is taken from the Book of Quinches of Guatemala, also called the Popol Vuh. Its remarkable conformance to the style and description of the Mosaic account will at once appear:

"There was not yet a single man; not an animal; neither birds, nor fishes, nor crabs, nor wood, nor stone, nor ravines, nor herbs, nor forests; only the sky existed. The face of the land was not seen; there was only the silent sea and sky. * * * There was nothing that stood upright; nought there was but the peaceful sea;—the sea silent and solitary in its limits; for there was nothing that was. * * Those who fecundate, those who give being, are upon the waters like a glowing light. * * * While they consulted the day broke, and at the moment of dawn man appeared. * * * Thus they consulted while the earth grew. Thus verily the earth came into being. 'Earth,' said they, and the earth existed. Like a fog, like a cloud was its formation; as huge fishes rise in the waters, so rose the mountains; and in a moment the high mountains existed.

"Hear, now, when it was first thought of man, and of what man should be formed. At that time spake he who gives life, and he who gives form, the Maker and Moulder, named Tepau, Gucumatz: 'The day draws near; the work is done; the supporter, the servant is ennobled; he is the son of light, the child of whiteness; man is honored; the race of man is on the earth;' so they spoke. * * *

THE EARLIEST MANUFACTURE AND POLISHING OF FLINTS.

Immediately they began to speak of making our first mother and our father. Only of yellow corn and of white corn were their flesh, and the substance of the arms and legs of man. They were called simply *beings*, formed and fashioned; they had neither father nor mother; we call them simply *men*. Woman did not bring them forth, nor were they born of the Moulder or Builder, of Him who fecundates and of Him who gives being. But it was a miracle, an enchantment worked by the Maker and Moulder, by Him who fecundates and Him who gives being.

"Thought was in them; they saw; they looked around; their vision took in all things; they perceived the world; they cast their eyes from the sky to the earth. * * * Then they were asked by the Builder and Moulder, 'What think ye of your being? See ye not? Understand ye not? Your language, your limbs, are they not good? Look around beneath the heavens; see ye not the mountains and the plains?'

"Then they looked, and saw all that there was beneath the heavens and they gave thanks to the Maker and the Moulder, saying, 'Truly, twice and three times, thanks! We have being; we have been given a mouth and face; we speak; we understand; we think; we walk; we feel and we know that which is far and that which is near. All great things and small, on the earth and in the sky, do we see. Thanks to thee, O Maker, O Moulder, that we have been created, that we have our being. O our grandmother, O our grandfather.'"

In their other books, which I have not space to quote from, the Aztecs taught that eternity was not in continuity, but divided by mighty events which occurred periodically during every cycle of several thousands of years. One of these events they taught was a cataclysm that swept every thing from off the face of the earth; and another was the sun being blotted from the heavens only to be rekindled after all things had perished.

The unanimity in the belief of the doctrine of periodical catastrophes must proceed from one of two causes: 1st. A catastrophe such as the deluge, which Moses describes, must have taken place—not, however, universal—and the remembrance of it was preserved by traditions among people as they scattered to all quarters of the globe—such as is made probable by Donnelly's theory of the lost Atlantis; or, 2d., there have been similar catastrophes of flood and fire in all parts of the earth, but at each time only local. The probabilities are alto-

MAN OF THE REINDEER EPOCH.

gether favorable to the first theory, because the coincidence of traditions respecting the destruction of the earth is no more singular than the coincidence in the history of creation, fable, tradition, religion and civilization, as we find them related in the histories of the people of both hemispheres. All these evidences bespeak a common origin, and the theory advanced by Mr. Donnelly is, therefore, a very specious, not to say logical and satisfactory one.

CHAPTER XXIV.

HISTORICAL DELUGES.

GEOLOGISTS have conclusively established the fact of three deluges, two of which occurred before the appearance of man, and a third after his creation. The first was produced by the upheaval of the mountains of Norway, which flooded all Northern Europe. Occurring in an intensely cold region the sweeping waves carried with them enormous fields of ice which increased the terrors of their destructive force. The second deluge was caused by the upheaval of the Alps, and overwhelmed all of Southern Europe, but since the waves which washed over that portion of the earth carried no ice, the result was not nearly so powerful as the first deluge; yet its effects are seen in a wonderful change of the topography of all the land inundated. Both of these cataclysms were produced by the contraction of the earth's crust in cooling, and the explosion of confined gases, which rent the womb of the earth, and out of the sea-depths threw up the new birth of mighty mountains. A displacement of so much water would necessarily be followed by a terrible deluge.

THE GLACIAL DELUGE.

But the last of these two cataclysms was followed by a third, which far exceeded in destructiveness and awful terror both the others. Man was now upon the earth, but omnipotence did not extend a protecting arm even to him, and he was swept away like all other animate things wherever the mighty force was exerted.

This deluge was not of water, but of ice, a freezing cold that benumbed and overwhelmed every creeping thing wherever its influence extended. The Central and Northern parts of Europe and of Northern Asia, which had possessed a mild, if not warm climate, were suddenly enveloped with intense cold. Like the blizzard that visits the warm State of Texas, in a moment and without warning, so swept the frigid wave over the northern portions of the Eastern hemisphere, and, as many geologists maintain, it inundated a large portion of North America also, extending as far south as New York. It was during this awful visitation of nature's wrath, as it appeared, that the mammoth, woolly rhinoceros, cave-bear, and other gigantic animals, were crushed out of existence, to be known no more forever; man, too, suffered a like loss, though not extinction, for it is a peculiarity of human nature to exist in every section of the earth, whether hot or cold, moist or dry, so that his race endures and survives the catastrophes of sections.

But what caused this intense cold? Ah, there science even pauses, unable to make reply, though theories are not wanting, the most satisfactory of which is one advanced by the great French mathematician, M. Adhemar, whose reasonings are so specious that I am sure my readers will be interested in reading them, especially since it is not impossible that another glacial castrophe may visit us.

CAUSE OF THE GREAT GLACIAL CATASTROPHE.

Not a few scientists have urged that the sudden development of intense cold was due to the concussion of comets, whereby the sun lost for a time its calorific powers, or the earth was driven from its natural orbit and fell under influences which prevented the sun's heat from reaching it.

But M. Adhemar dismisses these theories as untenable, and boldly advances a new one, which has had the support of very competent writers. His theory, in brief, is this: We know that our planet is animated by two essential movements; one of rotation on its axis, which it accomplishes in twenty-four hours; the other of translation, which is performed in three hundred and sixty-five days. But besides these two prominent and generally observed motions, there is a third, and even a fourth, but with one of which, called *nutation*, we do not need to concern ourselves. The other motion is the one on which M. Adhemar bases his theory. Of this theory Mangin says:

"We know that the curve described by the earth in its annual revolution round the sun is not a circle, but an ellipse; that is, a circle slightly elongated, sometimes called a circle of two centers, one of which is occupied by the sun. This curve is called the ecliptic. We know, also, that in its movement of translation the earth preserves such a position that its axis of rotation is intersected at its center by the plane of the ecliptic. But in place of being perpendicular, or at right angles with this plane, it crosses it obliquely in such a manner as to form on one side an angle of one-fourth, and on the other an

A GLACIAL DELUGE.

angle of three-fourths of a right angle. This inclination is only altered in an insignificant degree by the movement of nutation. I need scarcely add that the earth, in its annual revolution, occupies periodically four principal positions on the ecliptic, which mark the limits of the four seasons. When its center is at the extremity most remote from the sun, or *aphelia*, it is the summer solstice for the northern hemisphere. When its center is at the other extremity, or *perihelia*, the same hemisphere is at the winter solstice. The two intermediate points mark the equinoxes of spring and autumn. The great circle of separation of light and shade passes, then, precisely through the poles, the day and night are equal, and the line of intersection of the plane of the equator and that of the ecliptic make part of the vector (radius vector, an ideal straight line joining the center of an attracting body with that of a body describing an orbit round it) ray from the center of the sun to the center of the earth — what we call the *equinoctial line*.

Thus placed, it is evident that if the terrestrial axis remained always parallel to itself, the equinoctial line would always pass through the point on the surface of the globe. But it is not absolutely thus. The parallelism of the axis of the earth is destroyed slowly, very slowly, by a movement which Arago ingeniously compares to the inclined turning of a top. This movement has the effect of making the equinoctial points on the surface of the earth retrogade toward the east from year to year, in such a manner that at the end of twenty-five thousand eight hundred years according to some astronomers, but twenty-one thousand years according to Adhemar,* the equinoctial point has literally made a tour of the globe, and has returned to the same position which it occupied at the beginning of this immense period, which has been called the Great Year. It is this retrogade revolution in which the terrestrial axis describes round its own center that revolution round a double conic surface, which is known as the *precession of the equinoxes*. It was observed two thousand years ago by Hipparchus; its cause was discovered by Newton, and its complete evolution explained by D'Alembert and Laplace.

CYCLE OF THE GREAT YEAR.

"Now, we know that the consequence of the inclination of the terrestrial axis upon the plane of the ecliptic is:

"1. That the seasons are inverse to the two hemispheres, that is to say, the northern hemisphere enjoys its spring and summer, while the southern hemisphere passes through autumn and winter.

"2. It is when the earth approaches nearest to the sun that our hemisphere has its autumn and winter, and that the regions near the

*This is a striking confirmation of the Chaldean belief in the periodic destruction of the earth, and even of the time they calculated that the cycle is accomplished.

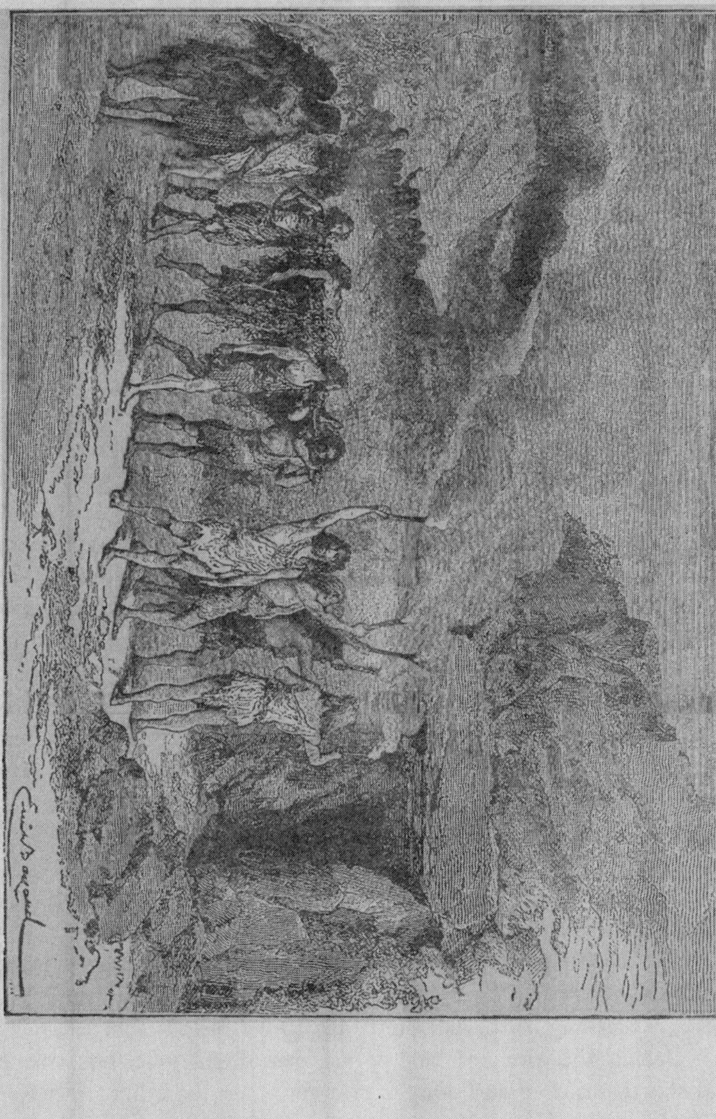

A FUNERAL CEREMONY DURING THE REINDEER EPOCH.

pole, receiving none of the solar rays, are plunged into darkness approaching that of night during six months.

"It is when the earth is most distant from the sun, when much the greater half of the ecliptic intervenes between it and the focus of light and heat, that the pole, being now turned toward the focus, constantly receives its rays, and when the rest of the northern hemisphere enjoys its long days of spring and summer.

"Bearing in mind that, in going from the equinox of spring to that of autumn of our hemisphere, the earth traverses a much longer curve than it does on its return; bearing in mind, also, the accelerated movement it experiences in its approach to the sun from the attraction, which increases in inverse proportion to the square of its distance, we arrive at the conclusion that our summer should be longer and our winter shorter than the summer and winter of our antipodes; and this is *actually* the case by about eight days.

"I say *actually*, because if we now look at the effects of the precession of the equinoxes, we shall see that in a time equal to half of the grand year, whether it be 12,900, according to the astronomers, or 10,500 years according to M. Adhemar, the conditions will be reversed; the terrestial axis, and consequently the poles, will have accomplished the half of their bi-conical revolution of the center of the earth. It will then be the northern hemisphere which will have the summers shorter and the winters longer, and the southern hemisphere exactly the reverse. In the year 1248 before the Christian era, according to M. Adhemar, the north pole attained its maximum summer duration. Since then, that is to say for the last 3112 years, it has begun to decrease; and this will continue till the year 7388 of our era before it attains its maximum winter duration.

"But the reader may ask, fatigued, perhaps, by these abstract considerations, what is there here in common with the deluges?

"The *grand year* is here divided for each hemisphere into two great seasons, which De Jouvencel calls the great summer and winter, which, according to M. Adhemar, are 10,500 years each.

"During the whole of this period one of the poles has constantly had shorter winters and longer summers than the other. It follows that the pole which submits to the long winters undergoes a gradual and continuous cooling, in consequence of which the quantities of ice and snow, which melt during the summer, are more than compensated by that which is again produced in the winter. The ice and snow go on accumulating from year to year, and finish at the end of the period, by forming, at the coldest pole, a sort of crust or cap, voluminous, thick and heavy enough to modify the spheroidal form of the earth. This modification, as a necessary consequence, produces a notable displacement of the center of gravity, or—for it amounts to the same thing—of the center of attraction, round which all the watery masses tend to restore it. The south pole, as we have seen, finished its great winter in 1248 B. C. The accumulated ice then added itself to the snow, and the snow to the ice, at the south pole, toward which the watery masses all tended until they covered nearly the whole of the southern hemisphere. But since that date our great winter has been in progress. Our pole, in its turn, goes on getting cooler continually; the ice is being heaped upon the snow, and snow upon ice, and in 7388 years the center of gravity of the earth will return to its normal position, which is the geometrical center of the spheroid. Following the immutable laws of central attraction, the southern waters accruing from the melted ice and snow of the south pole will return to invade and overwhelm once more the continents of the northern hemisphere, giving birth to new continents, in all probability, in the southern hemisphere."

SHALL THE EARTH BE AGAIN DESTROYED?

As cataclysms indicate the different stages of a ceaseless force, it is evident that others still menace us. Everything, indeed, seems to foretell that ages to come will see other plutonic phenomena display themselves, and new systems of mountains arise. Hence, as the upheavals follow a progressively ascending scale, we are quite led to expect new outbursts and more terrible convulsions. Man has, indeed, been enabled to verify these assertions, and himself to behold mountains issue from the bosom of the earth. In 1759 a catastrophe of this character occurred in the Jorullo district, about one hundred miles from the City of Mexico. In the month of June frightful earthquakes disturbed the soil, and continued increasingly for a period of two months. On the night of September 28th the earth was violently convulsed, and a region of thirty square miles was slowly raised until it attained a height of five hundred feet, still retaining its original shape of a plateau. During this time the earth undulated like the heavy seas in a tempest; thousands of small hills rose and fell again, and finally an immense gulf opened, from which smoke, fire, red-hot stones and ashes were violently discharged to prodigious heights. Six mountains surged up from the gaping gulf; among which the volcano of Jorullo, which rises two thousand one hundred and fifty feet above the ancient plain, is the most prominent.

At the moment when the earthquake commenced, the two rivers of Cuitimbo and San Pedro flowed backward, inundating all the plain now occupied by Jorullo; but in the upheaving region, while it continued to rise, a gulf opened and swallowed the rivers. They reappeared to the west, but at a point very distant from their ancient bed. This inundation reminds us of the phenomena — though on a small scale — which attended the Mosaic deluge.

In contemplating these mighty convulsions we realize how insignificant man is; he who wins eternal fame for the rearing of such structures as the pyramids, while the hand of God passes over the sea and dries it up; or, with a breath bursts the cinctures of earth, and as a child throws a ball into the air, so does the great hand of nature toss up mountains, break down the crags, and plough up ravines for river beds.

SHALL MAN BE SUCCEEDED BY A HIGHER ORDER OF CREATION?

To think of man compared with the elements by which he is surrounded, remembering at the time how species have developed, the curiously inclined cannot help inquiring, shall man be succeeded by a greater? Is the query not reasonable? M. Louis Figuier has written a beautiful passage on this subject which is worthy of repeated quotation: "Is it not possible," he says, "that man may be a step in the ascending and progressive scale of animated beings? The divine power which strewed on earth life, sensation and thought; which gave to the plant organization; to the animal movement, sensation and intelligence; to man, besides these manifold gifts, the faculty of reason, doubled by the power of aiming at the ideal, perhaps proposes to itself to create one day, along with man, or after him, a still superior being. This new creature, which modern religion and poetry appear to have foreseen in the etherial and radiant type of the Christian angel, would be provided with moral faculties, the nature and essence of which elude our understanding.

"We ought to satisfy ourselves with laying down this redoubtable problem without attempting to resolve it. This great mystery, to use the beautiful expression of Pliny, is concealed in the majesty of nature, or, better, in the thoughts and omnipotence of the Creator of worlds."

Bremser treats this inquiry with more seriousness, by saying: "It may still be presumed, supposing there should be a new radical change, that beings more perfect than those which resulted from preceding ones will be created. In man mind bears the same proportion to matter as fifty to fifty, with slight differences more or less, for sometimes mind and sometimes matter predominates. In a subsequent creation, supposing that in which man was formed not to be the last, there would probably be organizations in which the mind would act more freely, and where it would be in proportion of seventy-five to twenty-five. It results from these considerations, that man was formed at the most passive epoch of existence in our earth. Man is a sad middle state between the animal and the angel; he aspires to elevated knowledge and cannot reach it, albeit our modern philosophers fancy such is not the case. Man wishes to fathom the first cause of all that exists, and cannot attain to it; with fewer intellectual faculties he would not have the presumption to want to know these causes, which, on the other hand, would be quite clear to him if he were endowed with a more extended mind."

Winchell discusses the same inquiry at considerable length, in the negative, but he discourses too profoundly, though in elegant language. In the evolution of all animate things we perceive no such advancement among other animals as is observed in man, and his progressive state is so wonderful that, though we may not compute the time of his perfect development, the mind naturally turns to a contemplation of its final aggrandizement, and asks, shall man be forever excluded from the brotherhood of the celestial?

CHAPTER XXV.

WONDERS OF NATURE.

WE have briefly noticed some of the most important events which have transpired in the world's history, and the peculiar phases the earth has assumed in its evolution from out a nebulous and chaotic mass to the beautiful land which is now our heritage. It is a long bridge that spans the gulf which separates us from the infancy of man, and in that abyss of infinite years we behold titanic struggles, defeats and triumphs, which, however, are but the prototypes of the conflicts in every one's life. If there were mysteries in the handiwork of nature, so are there mysteries on every side of us now, for we are still walking in the valley of shadows, but jocund day stands tip-toe on the misty mountain top of civilization's hope, and the blessings of a propitious Providence lie in our way.

The beauties of nature are like the variable scenes in a kaleidoscope, ever unfolding new objects for our admiration and pleasure. With these it shall now be my pleasant duty to deal; to describe some of the innumerable wonderful things in creation; for, though many species of animal and plant life have been crushed into extinction by the display of destructive agencies in nature, yet others remain in abundance to remind us how marvelous are the designs, and how cunning is the handiwork of nature, for as she pulls down one noble structure she builds again upon the foundation a grander one, and thus do we perceive the way which leads from nature to nature's God.

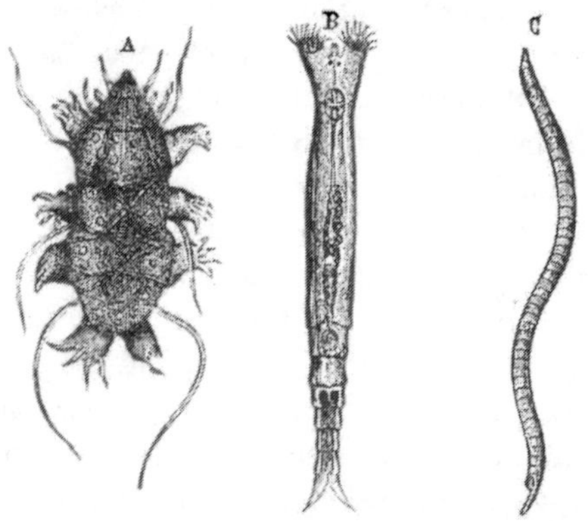

ANIMALS BELIEVED TO BE INDESTRUCTIBLE BY FIRE:
A. TARDIGRADE. B. ROTIFERA. C. ANGUILLULA.

In the olden days it was not only believed that the Phœnix bird renewed its youth through the ordeal of fire, but the salamander was considered a fire reptile by universal belief. These fables have had their day, and none are now so ignorant as to give them credence. But is the element of fire destitute of life? A great majority of scientists make answer in the affirmative, but there are not wanting many wise philosophers who assert the probability of existence even in the flames. In the early part of the year 1885, a subterranean body of water was discovered by some miners in Colorado; by the aid of torches it was also discovered that the lake—for such it was—was fairly swarming with fish, although the temperature of the water was nearly 200°, quite high enough to have cooked them. The fish, several of which were taken by means of dip-nets, were covered with dull scales, and with the exception of being slimmer, bore a close resemblance to our common carp. Upon being put into water of 60° temperature, they immediately died. I cannot state this wonderful thing as a fact of my own knowledge, but it was reported shortly after the discovery in many scientific journals, and I have never seen it disputed.

A number of years ago (1841) the question of universality of life was debated with such warmth in Paris, that a distinguished zoologist was induced to make an experiment with some infusoria which had been considered by a few as being practically indestructible by heat. He accordingly chose some microscopic tardigrades, rotiferæ and anguillulæ, and attaching them to a bulb of his thermometer, thrust them into a stove; here they were suffered to remain, subjected to a heat of 312° Fah. for a few moments, when, upon withdrawing them, they were found to be alive. It is only proper to state, however, that quite a number of scientists have also shown that desication of the tardigrades occurs at a temperature of 177° Fah. M. Pouchet, while discrediting the theory of existence in fire and of revivification, which many formerly maintained, says:

"It is true we are, in our day, obliged to erase the charming romance of palingenesis (regeneration), with which our forefathers amused themselves. Still, we must say that, although the rotiferæ cannot be resuscitated when they are once dead, their tenacity of life is one of the most extraordinary phenomena. Their resistance to cold is something marvelous, and we don't know even where it stops; the lowest temperature that we can obtain in our laboratories does not seem to have any effect upon them. I have seen these animals defy cold which would kill a man a hundred times over. Rotiferæ, placed in an apparatus where the temperature was 40° below zero, Fah., issue from it full of vitality. The natural history of the rotiferæ is a marvel from beginning to end. I have sometimes removed them quickly from the freezing apparatus and thrown them into a stove heated to 176° Fah. When they emerged from this they were seen to recover their animation and run about in full life. In this two-fold test and formidable transition from cold to heat, the Microzoa passed rapidly through a change of 216° Fah. without being in the least inconvenienced by it."

M. Broca expresses surprise that the rapid contraction and dilatation of the tissues of the animals, to which they were subjected, did not rupture them.

LANTERN INSECTS.

Whether there are animals so organized as to be indestructible by heat may remain a disputed question, but we do know that there are insects capable of producing light at will, and these are scarcely less wonderful than the rotiferæ.

Every one is acquainted with the *Lampyris*, our common glow-worm, or fire-fly, which make the summer nights so beautiful with their flashing lanterns. But there are other insects that produce a light far superior to our fire-fly. The great lantern-fly of India can supply a light which is quite strong enough to read by. In this instance the light emanates from the head, instead of from the lower body, as in the fire-fly. In the Antilles the *Coloeptera*, the fire-bug of that region, is of great use, being employed in place of lamps by the poorer people. In Cuba it is the custom of women to enclose

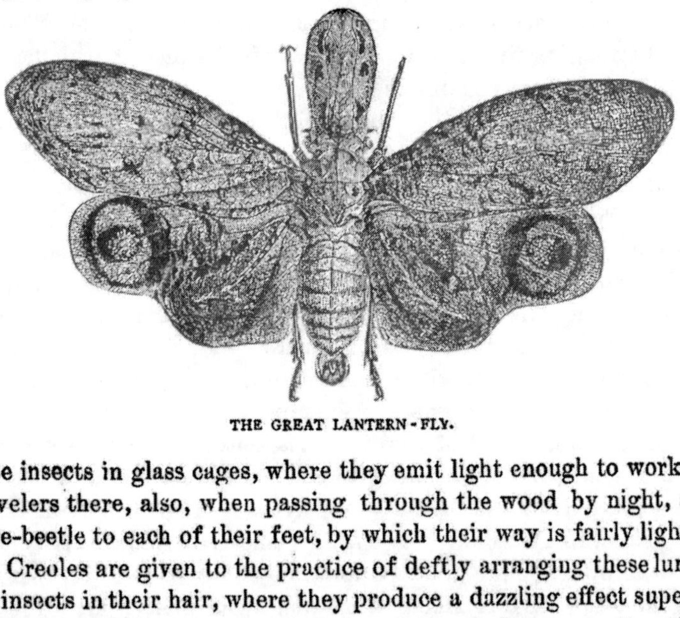

THE GREAT LANTERN-FLY.

these insects in glass cages, where they emit light enough to work by. Travelers there, also, when passing through the wood by night, affix a fire-beetle to each of their feet, by which their way is fairly lighted. The Creoles are given to the practice of deftly arranging these luminous insects in their hair, where they produce a dazzling effect superior to jewels. The negresses, at their nocturnal dances, scatter them over their airy garments, where, in their lascivious movements, their bodies assume the appearance of being robed in flames. How this natural light is provided, science is unable to tell us.

MARVELS OF INSECT LIFE—THE BOMBARDIER.

In considering the wonders of creation, we cannot overlook the little world of insects, for here we shall find the most remarkable things that nature has designed, creatures not alone of marvelous appearance and organizations, but of degrees of intelligence and adaptation quite as phenomenal. The handiwork of nature is nowhere more cunning than in the insect division of life, and when we consider the transformations which many of the little winged creatures undergo, the limit of extraordinary wonder seems to have been reached. The mosquito, butterfly, caterpillar, and other insects which are common to us, pass through stages of existence, sometimes emerging from one element to enter immediately another directly opposite, or gaining wings only to lose them again, and thus traveling through life as though endowed by some *geni* with the magical power of metamorphosis at will.

A CALOSOMA PURSUING A BOMBARDIER, WHO IS FIRING IN RETREAT.

But while these radical changes fairly bewilder us with surprise, we shall marvel none the less at the special providences which appear in many insects. How shall we find in all nature a more wonderful thing than the little insect properly called the *Bombardier*, a real soldier, with his arms always to hand and well loaded? They are provided with a novel means for vanquishing their enemies, against which only their artillery is directed. They belong to the class *Coleoptera* (case-winged). When excited they expel from their intestines an acid vapor, like smoke, which explodes with a slight detonation, like a true miniature gun loaded with a grain of powder. Its magazine is always well stored, so that it is able to fire as many as thirty-six discharges in quick succession, before having to renew its supply. Several of these curious insects, when collected together, will sometimes fire their guns together, and again in regular succession, like a file of soldiers firing from the left or right.

ASTOUNDING INTELLIGENCE OF BEES—EMBALMING.

So much has been written of the instinctive intelligence of bees that I shall not devote much space to describing their novel habits here, assuming that my readers are already familiar with most of the things I could write concerning them; nevertheless, I will present a few of the queer practices of bees that are not so generally known.

Every hive of bees, in addition to the workers, drones, neuters and queen, has several sentinels, whose duties are to apprise the hive of threatened dangers and to keep off intruders, for bees, like humans, are subjected to many annoyances, not the least of which are burglars. In case a bug, worm, snail, or other insect wanders into the hive, the sentinels first set upon it with their stings, and, after killing, eject it from their habitation without allowing the incident to interfere with the labors of the other bees. But where an insect too large for the sentinels to master invades the hive, all the bees are quickly notified and a general attack is made. Suppose the invader is a large slug, too weighty for removal; in this case the bees fall upon it with such fury that even retreat, if sought, is impossible, and it soon succumbs to the poisoned daggers thrust into its body. But so large a creature must not be suffered to remain in the hive, where, decaying, it would exhale a noxious odor which might develop a malady among the colony. The republic take counsel and speedily conclude, most sensibly, to embalm the body, which they proceed to do in the most expeditious manner possible. The laborers cease their gathering of honey and repair to the woods to collect a resinous substance called *propolis*, which is present in most trees, with which they envelope the body in a solid layer, more dexterously than the Egyptians ever applied their aloes and essences. By this means the slug is so perfectly embalmed that decay is arrested, and the body, if undisturbed, might remain fresh for endless years.

Sometimes it happens that snails find their way into hives, which, being protected by a cuirass of shell impervious to stings, are proceeded against in a no less intelligent and effective manner. The bees are not long in finding out the futility of an open attack by means of their natural weapons, so, flying away, they quickly gather each a quantity of resin, with which they speedily glue the snail fast to the hive. Not only is the cretaceous insect thus made a prisoner, but so effectually and perfectly is it glued to the spot that it remains there fairly embalmed, like the slug, since it will never putrify.

THE WONDERFUL PROCESS OF QUEEN MAKING.

I have read a great deal about queen bees, but nowhere have I seen so excellent a description of the process of queen making as is furnished by M. Pouchet, the eminent French naturalist, to whom I am indebted for the following:

By a singular anomaly in insects, it is the females which, though more delicate, take charge of the work; the males do absolutely nothing; they are the drones. But these females have none of the attributes of their sex; they are genuine neuters, in which the nurses have contrived scientifically to make every principle of fecundity abortive; in short, they are unsexed. These work-women, when young, have their bee-bread doled out to them in the most meager quantities; in vain do they cry for more to stay their hunger; the nurses are obdurate, and, when the proper time arrives, the larvæ are enclosed in their cells, so as to stop the process of development; when at last they mature and burst their prison, they come forth in full strength, but destitute of the organs of reproduction.

When by accident, or desertion, a hive of bees are deprived of their queen, they proceed directly to choose a new one, which is invariably effected without recourse to revolution or any change in the regular labor of the colony. One of the work-women is taken out of her small cell and carried to another, which has been prepared specially to receive her. These royal quarters are fifty times larger than the common cells, and are in every sense palatial. So soon as she is here established, though of plebeian blood, the nurses pay her the greatest deference by feeding her bountifully with the sweetest ambrosia, and so attending her needs that when she arrives at maturity she not only possesses the organs of fecundation, but her size is so affected by the stimulating treatment that she is much larger than any of her subjects, and thenceforth she rules with undisputed sway.

WONDERFUL HABITS OF ANTS—SLAVE-MAKERS.

In the bee we observe manifold evidences of a high order of intelligence, at times so remarkable as to appear like the product of reasoning power; but, great as the faculty of adaptation is in the bee, it is pre-eminently greater in the ant, as we shall see by considering some of its habits and designs.

Nearly all ants are war-like, though they also follow peaceful occupations, such as engineering, dairy-keeping, farming and other useful pursuits. In Texas observers have noticed the process of planting and reaping practiced by a species of small ant, found most numerously in that state. These insect farmers live in vast colonies and, like all others of the tribe, are communistic. Around the hill where they make their home, these industrious farmers clear away the weeds and prepare a considerable district for planting, and in due season sow the spot with the seed of a plant of which they are very fond, and from which they derive a principal subsistance. When harvest time arrives they cut down the plant and store it away in their granary, being always careful to preserve enough seed for the following season.

AN ARMY OF ANTS ON THE MARCH.

In South America the slave-making ants abound, though they may be also found in other tropical countries. Huber, who has made a life-long study of the habits of ants, tells us that the Amazon, or red ant, does no labor itself, but relies entirely upon the exertions of its slaves for everything save only the fighting. They execute their razzias invaribly at night, and usually upon the miner-ants, though the latter are stubborn warriors and do not yield without a desperate struggle. When they have issued from their abode, the amazons array themselves in serried columns and march in true military style to the nests which they have decided to spoliate. Their approach is always discovered by the videttes of the invaded colony, which give the alarm and forthwith every possible effort is put forth to bar the entrance against the despoilers. After a hard fought battle the amazons usually succeed in mastering the warriors, but these they do not attempt to enslave, since, being full-grown, it would be difficult to adapt them to the yoke of servitude; but pushing over the vanquished hordes the amazons penetrate to the center of the nest and there each one selects a larva, which they seize delicately and with it return to their abodes. When the young ants are thus brought to the nest of their enemies they are graciously received by the slaves already in captivity. These act a true maternal part, giving the larva food and nursing them with the tenderest care until they are capable of assuming the burden of workers.

DEPENDENCY OF MASTER UPON SLAVE.

It is an astonishing fact that the Amazon-ants are dependent upon their slaves not only for the care which a servant is expected to render its master, but for every morsel of food that they devour, and also for the raising of the larvæ. The amazon is good for nothing save fighting, and upon returning from battle they become so inert that the slaves must even convey food to their mouths, and otherwise attend them, as though they were paralyzed. Should it be necessary to abandon the nest on account of overflow or other destructive agencies, the amazon-ant is too helpless to save himself, but must rely upon the slaves to move him, which they, with wonderful faithfulness, always do, by carrying the masters between their mandibles.

Huber, anxious to discover how dependent the masters were upon their slaves, enclosed a number of the former by themselves, but surrounded them with an abundance of food, and also placed several larvæ among them, thinking this might stimulate them to action; he was astonished, however, to see that their apathy was so great that they would neither feed themselves nor pay the slightest attention to the larvæ; several of the ants actually died of starvation, when Huber placed a single slave among them, whereupon she fell to work instantly, apparently understanding the direful state of her charge, and gave all of the survivors food, and lavished the tenderest care upon the larvæ, by which exertions she saved those that were living when she was introduced among them.

In Switzerland Huber observed that the slave-ants constructed the dwellings of their masters, and that they also opened the outlets at day-break and closed them each evening, or when a storm was threatening.

ANTS THAT KEEP COWS.

The amazon-ants turn their attention to one other occupation besides fighting, which is dairy-keeping, thus entitling them to be called a pastoral species. They keep herds of cows, not such as we are accustomed to, but yet cows in the sense they use them. These cows are the *Aphides*, a little cricket-like insect, which distils a sweet liquor from two teats carried at the extremity of the back. We frequently find them scattered over the leaves of vegetables, where the ants are sucking them by means of their attennæ, as seen in the illustration. At other times, accompanied by their slaves, they carry off the aphides and keep them confined in their dwellings, in order to milk them at leisure, and there they are nourished exactly like we do stalled animals.

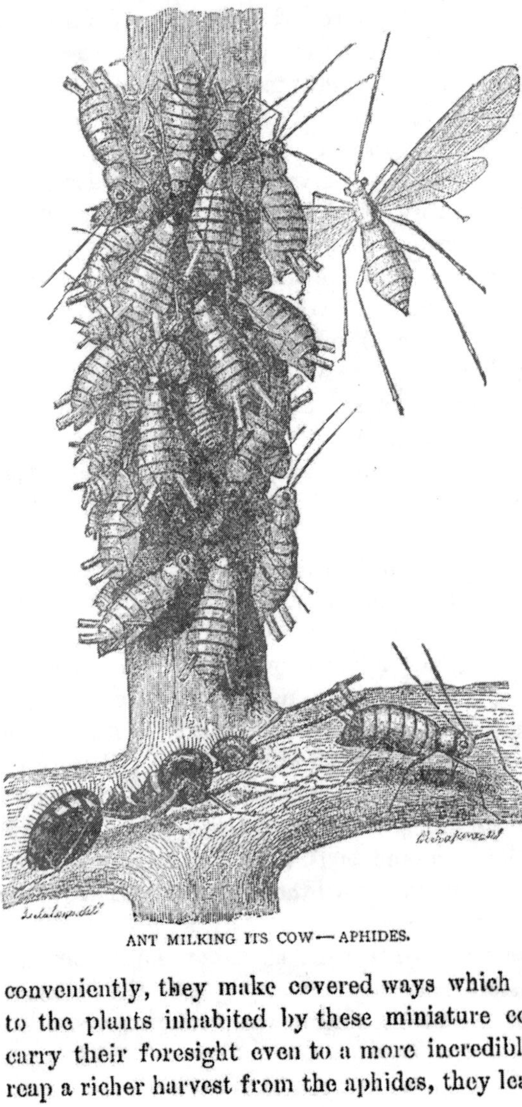

ANT MILKING ITS COW—APHIDES.

Huber further discovered that the ants are so greedy after this sweet fluid that, to procure it more conveniently, they make covered ways which lead from their nests to the plants inhabited by these miniature cows. Sometimes they carry their foresight even to a more incredible extent. In order to reap a richer harvest from the aphides, they leave them on the plants which they habitually feed upon, and with finely-tempered earth build there species of little stables, in which they imprison them. The naturalist just quoted discovered several of these surprising constructions, hence the fact is beyond doubt.

A BATTLE BETWEEN TWO ARMIES OF ANTS.

Huber describes a battle which he once had the pleasure of witnessing between two colonies of ants that had lived in harmony within a hundred yards of each other for a considerable time. The cause of this sudden rupture was not apparent, much to his regret, because it might have exhibited ant diplomacy, intrigue, or a keen sense of honor that would entitle the little creature to a higher position in the order of creation than it even now occupies by our classification.

"I shall not say," remarks Huber, "what lighted up discord between these two republics, the one as populous as the other; two empires do not possess a greater number of combatants. The two armies met midway between their respective residences. Their serried columns reached from the field of battle to the nest, and were two feet in width. An immense reserve therefore supported the fighting body, where thousands of ants, mounted on the smallest eminences, fought two and two, attacking each other by means of their jaws. Others carried off prisoners, but not without rough struggles, for they knew the cruel fate that awaited them as soon as ever they should reach the hostile nest.

"The field of battle, which extended over a space of from two to three square feet, was strewed with dead bodies and wounded; it was also covered with venom, and exhaled a penetrating odor. Here and there single combats were still maintained. The struggle began between two ants which locked themselves together with their mandibles, while they raised themselves upon their hind legs. They quickly grasped each other so tightly that they rolled over and over in the dust. Generally the two athletes were succored, and chains were seen of six and eight ants locked one with another, and dragging the two adversaries in different directions, until either one let go or was carried off by superior strength."

At the approach of night the two armies withdrew all their forces and retreated within their nests, but on the following morning they came out early and renewed the affray. So intent were they in fighting that they gave no heed to Huber, though he interposed his foot among them.

HOUSE EATERS AND ARCHITECTS.

One of the most wonderful, and at the same time most destructive, of insects is the *Termite*, or white ant, of South Africa. These creatures live in republics and are composed of soldiers, queens, workmen, males and females. The former are devoted entirely to defending the colony and enforcing the laws; they alone have wings. The queens are worshipped, and to them the most obsequious deference is paid. Most singular to relate, these queens are as unlike the ordinary ant as the latter is unlike an elephant, for they are estimated to be at certain periods two thousand times larger than any of their subjects. Like the queen bee, the queen termite lays all the eggs, and hence upon her alone depends the continuance of the race. When her fecundity is greatest her body is swollen to extraordinary proportions, so that she is unable to move, and must be fed by those that attend her. When laying, the eggs are delivered so rapidly that they issue as if by pulsations, at the rate of eighty thousand per diem.

The nests of these wonderful ants reveal an industry and intelligence truly astounding. They are not infrequently as much as twenty feet in height, and in such numbers as, when looking at them from a distance, to appear like a great city of sugar-loaf houses. But, though made of earth and pulverized wood, they are so strong that wild cattle may stand upon them without danger of breaking through. The interior reveals many chambers, some of which are quite large enough to contain a dozen men at a time. From these chambers galleries extend down into the ground several feet, and, though labyrinthine, they all connect in a free passage-way to the center of the nest, which is about six inches in diameter.

In constructing their nests the termite workmen make dreadful havoc upon the adjacent wood, which supplies the material they require. They do not confine themselves to the woods, but, using chiefly seasoned timber, they invade dwellings and penetrate the furniture and walls so insidiously that they reduce it speedily to a shell before their presence is detected. They never cut the outside of any wooden article, but penetrate the center and destroy all but the thinnest shell, so that houses and furniture so eaten will collapse, though still preserving an outer appearance of solidity. At times whole villages in South Africa are thus attacked and destroyed. Even in France, where the termite seems to have appeared in 1780, a great many houses have fallen from the effects of their depredations. In

South America their ravages at times are so terrible that cannon are used to batter down their nests, and gunpowder is then poured into the galleries so as to blow them up, root and branch.

CARPENTERS AND JOINERS.

There are as true artisans among insects as among men, and man may learn many useful lessons by observing the habits of little creatures which every day cross his path. The name *joiners* is given to that class of insects which divide and cut wood by means of their powerful mandibles, a most appropriate title, as we shall see.

The *Goat-Moth* is one of the largest wood-cutters, reaching the size of a man's great finger, and even longer. It is very much like our common wood-worm, which, while working, produces a noise that superstitious persons call the "death tick." This worm lives by eating wood, and in obtaining its livelihood it cuts tortuous galleries in the trunks of trees sometimes numerous enough to kill them. The metamorphosis of this insect is very admirably shown in the accompanying engraving.

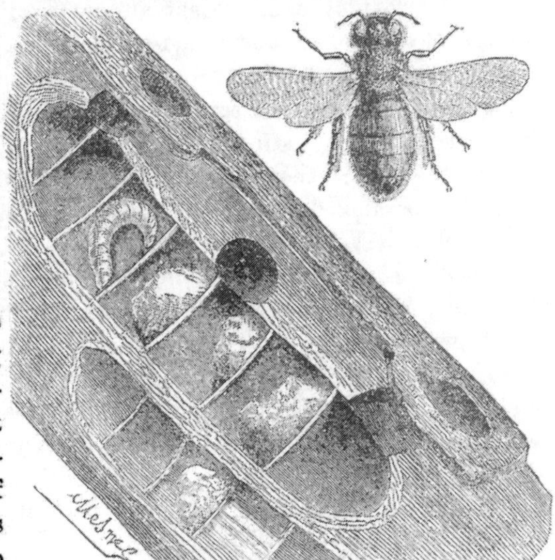

CARPENTER-BEE AND ITS LITTLE CHAMBERS.

But a more wonderfully ingenious artisan is the carpenter-bee and mud-mason, which are common enough throughout the United States. Though familiar to all, their habits are not so generally understood as to make a brief description of them uninteresting.

The *Carpenter-Bee* usually attacks very dry timbers, such as the sills, beams or rafters of a house, into which it bores its way and then excavates a channel several inches in length and of a width that will freely admit its body. Having completed the canal it now prepares it for its offspring. Into the end an egg is laid and beside it is deposited a quantity of bee-bread just sufficient to nourish the larva until it is able to eat its way out. Having thus provided for the offspring from the first egg, the bee constructs a partition, composed of pulverized wood agglutinated with saliva, and hermetically seals the egg up in a small cell to itself. She next lays another egg and repeats the same process of separating them until her complement is complete, when she leaves and gives no more concern to her offspring.

The *Mud-Mason* is even more remarkable than the carpenter bee, for while it displays a like skill in the construction of the cells for its larva, it provides nourishment altogether different. My readers have doubtless broken down mud-masons' nests time and again, and been surprised to find in the cells green spiders and bugs. Instead of leaving bee-bread with its egg, the mud-mason catches spiders and other insects, which it stings, not so as to produce death, but to so paralyze them that they continue in a state of coma indefinitely; having thus paralyzed a spider, it deposits it in the cell with its egg, and when the larva is developed it finds its natural food at hand as fresh as if just killed, and in precisely sufficient quantity for its subsistence, until it is ready to burst its prison and come forth the perfect insect.

Insects not only bore through wood, but some of them even attack metals, and seem to find nourishment in them. The *Giant Sirex* has been known to gnaw lead and deposit its larva in the excavations. M. Pouchet mentions the fact that, during the Crimean war, the balls in the soldiers' cartridges were sometimes so badly perforated by these insects as to be useless for shooting.

HOW THE DIVING-BELL CAME TO BE INVENTED.

It was from a little hydraulic engineer, commonly called the water-spider, that the idea of the diving-bell was obtained. This admirable work-fellow of the animal world is a genius so perfect in his way that even man cannot exactly imitate the completeness of his watery abode. His charming little house is made of silk, for he is a dainty creature, not above displaying a pride which borders on vanity. It is a veritable diving-bell in which he lives, and though extremely small, it is a work of marvelous perfection. This miniature bell is suspended by threads from a spear of grass, by which it is so firmly held that wind or wave is not likely to disturb it. They are expert swimmers, but cannot breath water as fishes do, so that they must keep their houses well supplied with fresh air. To do this the spider comes to the surface, and there gathers a bubble of air under his abdomen, with which he descends to his retreat, and by repeating this process soon fills his little home with respirable gas. Here he passes his winters in perfect ease, using barely enough exertion to seize the prey that strays near his retreat. Walckenær, who has made a special study of the water-spider, has given them the name of *Naiadeæ* (Naiads), and declares they are the most interesting and intelligent insects he has met with, an opinion in which scientists generally concur.

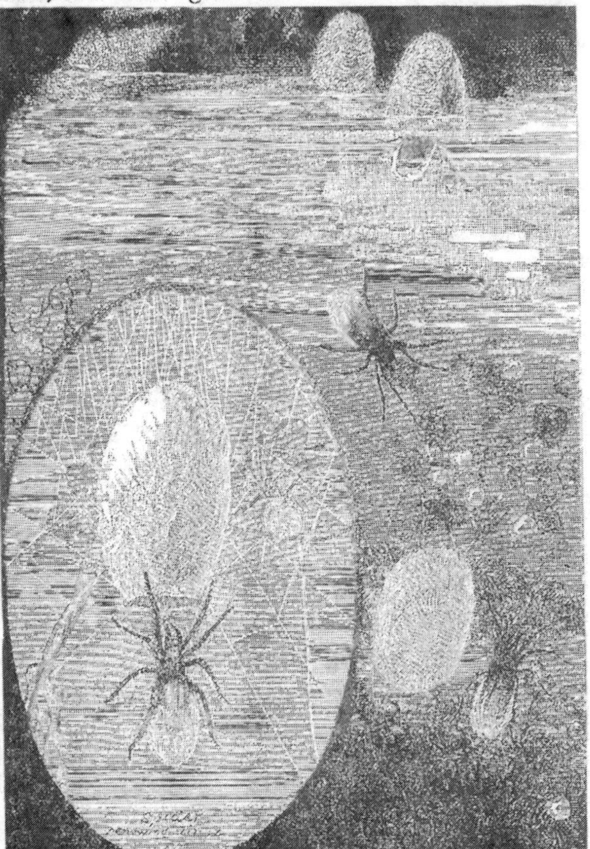

THE DIVING-BELL SPIDER.

THE PLAGUE OF LOCUSTS.

There is not much to be said of the intelligence exhibited by *Locusts*, but anything concerning them possesses interest from the fact that they ravage our fields and at times become the greatest plagues that nature has ever afflicted us with. Though the Western states have suffered immense loss from these insects their ravages in our country do not compare with that which they work in Asia and Africa. Frequently, when migrating through these countries, they resemble black clouds and darken the sun for hours at a time. Their track is marked by a waste as complete as if it had been swept by fire. Moses records the plague of locusts with which Egypt was afflicted, but his description of their destructiveness does not exceed that given by Pliny, who states that several districts of Africa have been entirely depopulated by these insects. St. Jerome, in his alarm, once exclaimed: "What is there stronger and more terrible than locusts? All human industry cannot withstand them. God alone regulates their march."

The army of Charles XII., when crossing Bessarabia, was arrested by a swarm of locusts; not only entirely obscuring the sun, but lighting upon the soldiers in such vast numbers as to blind them and threaten them with suffocation.

In the Island of Lemnos a law was enforced by which each person was compelled to bring to the magistrate a measure of locusts as annual tribute. In Cyrenaica, according to Pliny, every subject of the realm was required to make war on the locusts three days of the year. Those neglecting to obey this edict were punished as deserters.

Several times in Syria Roman soldiers were employed to destroy locusts to prevent famine in the country. Soldiers have been similarly engaged in Transylvania, reinforced by the entire population, yet, despite their combined exertions, many fertile districts were utterly ruined. Ibrahim Pasha, in Egypt, only a few years ago, summoned all the soldiery of the nation to his aid in staying the ravages of locusts, and to stimulate them in the work bared his head to the sun and fought with his men against the pest.

Although the migrating locust is one of the worst scourges with which agriculturists have to contend, it is not entirely destitute of value. As an article of food, we have the best of evidence to show that it possesses great merit. The Bible teaches us that the Jews ate it, and that four species were recommended by Moses as good to be eaten. John the Baptist, when he was in the wilderness of Judea, subsisted on locusts and honey, a diet not to be despised by even the most favored sons of God. Not only was it esteemed in ancient days, but there are still countries where the people appreciate it highly. In Bagdad the locust is exposed for sale alongside of the best meats, with which it has equal rank. In all Arabia these insects are dried and ground to a fine flour, when it is baked into wholesome and palatable bread. In 1693, Germany was so nearly desolated by reason of an invasion of locusts that, for the want of other food, the peasantry began eating them, when they acquired so much favor that a dish of locusts was found at nearly every table in the country for several years afterward. Livingstone was so partial to them that he declared they were a benefit conferred by Providence. Hon. C. V. Riley, the distinguished entomologist, in charge of that bureau in the United States, eats locusts with avidity, and pronounces them not only palatable and nutritious, but a *morceau* of almost unexampled deliciousness.

THE VORACIOUS ANT-LION.

A curious specimen of the voracious in insect life is the *Ant-Lion*, very appropriately named, because it is a carnivora of fearless character that lays its trap with wonderful cunning, and makes a dreadful carnage among ants and other creatures that fall in its power. The pit which the ant-lion constructs is always set in the driest and finest sand, where it scoops out a funnel-shaped basin beneath the surface level. In accomplishing this work it uses only the head, with which, by a dipping motion, it manages to throw the sand out so rapidly as to shower it in a continuous jet. When a depth of a foot or more is reached, the insect burrows itself at the bottom of the pit until nothing but its mandibles are uncovered. Here it lies quiescent awaiting the prey which will not be long in coming, for the place is selected with excellent judgment, near the pathway of an ant colony. Ants have great curiosity, and when they approach the pit they are almost certain to try to explore the hollow, which has suddenly appeared since their last journey by the place. But the moment it passes over the edge of the pit its doom is sealed, for the yielding sand prevents it from reascending, and every fresh exertion only serves to drive the unfortunate creature more speedily to the hungry jaws in waiting.

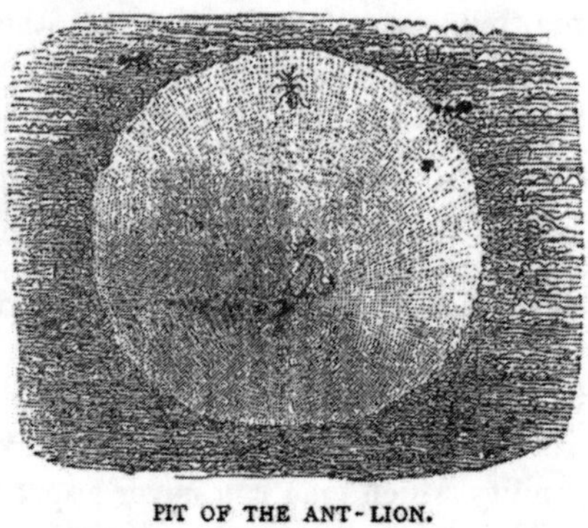

PIT OF THE ANT-LION.

Occasionally a large bug will, by chance adversity, fall into the treacherous hole, when in its struggles to surmount the slippery sides so much sand will fall down upon the ant-lion that, fearful of the escape of its prey, it will take a direct part in hastening the end. Issuing from his retreat, he launches in swift succession jets of sand upon the victim, and causes it to fall quickly to the bottom. Here no mercy is shown, no delay in the fell purpose of the destroyer, for, always thirsting for fresh blood, the ant-lion falls vigorously on the helpless bug, and in a trice has sucked the juices from its body.

But the ant-lion shows wisdom beyond its cunning for catching prey in so singular a trap. Since it lives entirely off the blood of insects its pit would soon become a charnel house of noxious vapors if the bodies were permitted to remain accumulating in the hollow; furthermore, passing insects might discover the fatal trap set for them when looking over the edge upon the skeletons of their compatriots, and being thus warned in time escape a like fate. The ant-lion is cunning enough to reason out all these probabilities, and, to guard against them, after destroying an insect he carefully balances its body on his head, then, with a spasmodic jerk, he throws it not only out of his den, but several inches beyond the border. After he has made a Golgotha of his surrounding, like a sensible fellow, he moves his habitation and renews the slaughter until new suspicions are created.

WONDERS OF THE SPIDER.

Of all artists and workers in animal creation the spider is the greatest, for he combines the acquirements of tailor, miner, carpenter, engineer, surveyor, and any number of other trades, in each of which he is an expert. We do not have to travel in foreign countries to find spiders that execute the most wonderful works, for every web is a study, being the product of an ingenuity which man can never approach. In a night he rears his gossamer structure, as airy as a sunbeam, and yet of cable cords of remarkable strength. Across paths in the wood we find his tensile threads, reaching from branch to branch like a suspension bridge, over which he travels; his ropes are always at hand and are made to serve him in the most wonderful ways. Should he desire to cross a stream, he has only to sit upon some tree or other elevated position, and there pay out his cable until the loose end floats on the breeze and catches to some object on the opposite shore. This constitutes his bridge, and on it he crosses safely over.

The spider's web is a mystery in construction, since it proceeds ready spun by nature from its body. This marvelous loom is situated in the abdominal extremity, and is composed of several teats. The thread issues, wonderful to state, from as many sieves, in each of which are more than a thousand holes, and out of each hole issues a tiny thread. As the threads are projected they agglutinate together into one thread, which is thus made up from six thousand strands. Scientists who have studied the spider's web by means of the microscope, affirm that it requires no less than four millions of strands to make a thread of the size of a hair. I refer to the product of garden spiders, for some species spin threads that are strong enough to be used in the manufacture of textile fabrics. In fact, Louis XIV had a suit of clothes made for himself from spider-webs, as did also some of the ladies of his court, but they were not durable. It is related, however, that Al. d' Orbigny had a pair of trousers made out of this filmy product which endured a long time of constant wear.

No less curious than his web is the tunnel which our common spider constructs, in which to hide while hunting, or to serve him for escape in case of danger. It is a cunning contrivance for the use to which it is put. Here, well enclosed from view, the spider sits, until a giddy fly, or other insect, dashes into the meshes he has skillfully set outside his den; then, in a trice, he issues forth and speedily binds his victim, off which he afterward dines by sucking its juices. But he carries his cunning still further; observation will show that he never suffers the blood of his prey to soil his web, nor does he allow the remains to lie long exposed in his net, but with admirable foresight, he drags them back through his den and ejects them through a lower opening, especially provided for the purpose. Thus he keeps his house in a cleanly and inviting condition, free from suspicious appearances, while below him are found the evidences of his voracity.

THE DREADFUL TARANTULA.

Most of the spiders found in the United States are harmless, but there is one whose bite is scarcely less to be dreaded than that of the rattlesnake; this is the *Tarantula*, first met with in the neighborhood of Tarentum, Italy, from whence its name comes. It is especially numerous in the Levant, but in our own country there are enough to make them interesting to Southerners. It was formerly believed that their bite produced a malady comparable to hydrophobia, and the credulity of the Italians extended to implicit faith in the sovereign remedy of music to effect a cure. The learned Boglivi even wrote a treatise, in which he gravely designated the particular airs to be played for every symptom exhibited by the person bitten. In Texas they substitute whisky for music, with more felicitous effects, though the bite of the whisky is sometimes worse than that of the tarantula.

The *Tarantula*, like the mason-spider, has its habitation in a neatly lined cylindrical hole in the ground, the entrance to which is covered by a lid that fits as snugly as the cork of a bottle. This lid is a master-piece of ingenuity, being composed of about forty alternate layers of earth and silk, and connected to the edge of the dwelling by means of a hinge so perfect that it may be opened and shut a thousand times without injury.

The poison apparatus of spiders is precisely analogous to that of serpents, only that it is extremely small. Poisonous spiders possess mobile teeth and hollow fangs which distil the noxious fluid into any

THE TARANTULA.

wound they make; this fluid is secreted by a small gland situated in the interior of the palpi (feelers), attached to the under jaw, which effect the bite.

It has been a subject of much dispute whether or not the tarantula's bite is ever attended by fatal results in a grown person; the best authorities say it is not, and cite many instances in proof. The tarantulas of Nassau grow to an enormous size, five inches long by four broad, and a gentleman whom I know, affirms that, while wintering at that famous resort, he killed one that was fully as large as the crown of a man's hat.

THE CHICKEN SPIDER.

Equalling, if not surpassing the tarantula in size is the *Chicken-Spider*, an inhabitant of South America. It is very poisonous and is said to employ its lethal fluid to destroy small birds and animals. Its favorite prey is humming-birds, which it manages to catch in a manner which scientists have not yet attempted to explain. The supposition, however, is that it surprises the bird when on her nest, and leaping upon her, like a lion does upon a deer, drives its mandibles into the feathered beauty, killing it almost upon the instant. But the chicken-spider does not limit its attacks to humming-birds; it is a barn-yard pest, also, committing, at times, great ravages among the poultry of Colombia. Its attack is usually made by springing upon the chicken and fastening upon its throat, where it speedily finds the jugular vein and sucks the blood until its victim expires. Pigeons are also objects of its voracity, as many as a dozen of these birds having been found dead in a single cote, all killed by one of these blood-thirsty creatures.

THE SCORPION—SOMETHING TRULY WONDERFUL.

The scorpion and spider belong to the same class of insect creation, called *Arachnida*, a Greek word used to denote a species wherein there is no distinction of head and thorax. The scorpion is to land creatures what the octopus is to those living in the water, a frightful appearing hybrid, whose proper sphere, it seems, ought to be in the dominions of Satan. It is devilish, or impish, not only in looks but character as well. They inhabit most warm countries, and are everywhere held in the greatest dread. All kinds of precautions must be taken to guard against them, for, loving darkness, they crawl into beds, creep under pillows, or into shoes, so that in countries where they abound they menace everybody. They are both active and savage, and perfectly aware of the terrible weapons with which they are armed. When alarmed the scorpion curls its tail over its body, flourishes the venomed weapon in a most threatening style, and, if its retreat be cut off, it boldly assumes the offensive and rushes to the attack.

However repulsive and venomous, the scorpion excites admiration for its wonderful attachment to its young. While yet young and feeble, they congregate upon the person of the mother, swarming over her back, forceps and limbs, and even cling to her tail, so as to completely conceal the outline of their parent.

A traveler has recently contributed an interesting paper on the scorpion, which was published in "Land and Water," in 1885, which

CHICKEN SPIDER OF SOUTH AMERICA.

has attracted much attention. From this account of the habits of the creature, I take the liberty of quoting as follows:

SOME ASTONISHING FACTS RESPECTING THE SCORPION.

"A few years ago, while in the Island of Jamaica, it was my fortunate chance to have an opportunity of observing some very curious facts in connection with the genus of the *arachnida* class commonly known as the scorpion, and the curious traits of character in these insects. Turning over some old paper in my office one day, I suddenly came upon a large black scorpion, which promptly tried to beat a precipitate retreat. Having read or heard somewhere that if you blow on a scorpion he will not move, I tried the experiment, and was greatly astonished to find that it had the desired effect. The scorpion stopped instantly, flattened himself close to the paper on which he had been running, and had all the appearance of 'holding on' for dear life. While I continued to blow, even lightly, he refused to move, though I pushed him with a pencil and shook the paper to which he clung so tenaciously. Directly I ceased blowing, he advanced cautiously, only to stop again at the slightest breath. I was thus able to secure him in a glass tumbler, which happened to be within reach, and then determined to try another experiment as to the suicidal tendencies which I had heard runs in the veins of the *pedipalpi* family.

"On the stone floor of the kitchen attached to my office I arranged a circle of burning sticks, about three yards in circumference, the sticks being so placed that, though there were no means of exit through the fire, it was not intense, but small and quite bearable as regards heat within a few inches, so that the central part of the circle was perfectly cool. Into this center I accordingly dropped my scorpion, who, on reaching *terra firma*, darted off in a great hurry, only to be quickly brought to a halt on reaching within a few inches of the periphery of the circle. After a short pause for reflection, he deviated to the right, and ran once completely around the circle, as near to the fire-sticks as it was prudent to venture. This he did three times, often approaching the burning sticks quite closely in his anxious endeavors to escape. In about a quarter of an hour, finding that his efforts were useless, he retired almost into the exact center of the circle, and there, in a tragic manner, raised his tail till the sting, or spur, was close to his head, gave himself two deliberate prods in the back of the neck, and thus miserably perished by his own hand. As I placed the body of the suicide in a bottle of spirits, I almost regretted that I had not let him escape before he had resorted to such an extreme measure.

"My last experience is even more curious than the preceding, as it shows a remarkable provision of nature that is almost incredible.

All I have ever read on the subject is contained in the following words:

"The young scorpions are produced at various intervals, and are carried by the parent for several days upon her back, during which time she never leaves her retreat.

"I was playing a game of billiards in a small village in the Blue Mountains; there was no ceiling to the room, the roof being covered, as is the usual custom in Jamaica, with cedar-wood shingles. My opponent was smoking a large pipe, and suddenly, just as I was about to make a stroke, what I thought was the contents of my friend's pipe, fell on the table close to the ball at which I was aiming. Instinctively I was on the point of brushing it off with my hand, when, to my amazement, I saw it was a moving mass which, on closer inspection, turned out to be a very large female specimen of a scorpion, from which ran away in every direction a number of perfectly formed little scorpions, about a quarter of an inch in length. The mother scorpion lay dying upon the billiard cloth, and soon ended her feeble struggle, the whole of her back being eaten out by her own offspring, of which, as they could not escape over the raised edge of the billiard table, we killed the astonishing number of thirty-eight. They had not only been carried by their parent, but they had lived on her, cleaning out her body from the shell of her back, so that she looked like an inverted cooked crab, from which the edible portions have been removed. She had clung to her retreat in the shingled roof until near the approach of death, when she had fallen and given us this curious spectacle. I was told by the attendant that the young scorpions always live thus at the expense of their mother's life, and that by the time her strength is exhausted the horrid offspring are ready to shift for themselves."

CHAPTER XXVI.

WONDERS OF THE VEGETABLE WORLD.

A FLORAL CLOCK.

BUT I must leave off further description of the loathsome creatures which so afflict the earth, and turn to a consideration of some of the equally wonderful things which a generous Providence has strewn with lavish hand throughout all creation. If we have homely and venomous insects against which it is our common duty to guard, so have we beautiful and delightful things to draw us to a contemplation of the goodness of nature and the bounty of Omnipotence.

Between animal and plant life there is only a step, in organization not so radically different but that we may see a connecting analogy between them, which seems to point to higher development as the dividing line. Let us follow this idea and note some of the marvelous facts connected with the vegetable world, facts which will excite as much surprise and admiration as we have felt in previous descriptions. Among the plants where inanimate activity holds sway, we will find a government directed by laws that have emanated from the master mind, and all these laws are directed towards the unfolding of new beauties and the adornment of earth. The invariableness of these laws has enabled men who have devoted themselves to a special study of the subject, to make wonderful calculations, to arrange calendars and time clocks, and to do a thousand other useful things.

It is known that Pliny, having noted with care the times at which plants flower, conceived the idea that we might make use of them to mark the different seasons of the year. Cuvier even asserts that the Roman naturalist proposed to arrange a complete floral calendar; but the idea was first consummated by Linneus, and it is one of the most delightful conceptions of his rare genius. According to his arrangement of flowers to mark the months of the year, we have: Through January's ice and snows first peeps the black hellebore. In February the stately alder shakes its catkins, and the mezereon appears in its acrid coat, scattering flowers to winter winds. The howling gusts of March whirl round the nodding golden corollas of the wall-flower, and bend low the pretty bells of the crown imperial. The periwinkle is the harbinger of spring, and greets April showers with its lofty net-work that loves all the forest. May comes tripping in fairly garlanded with lillies, lilacs and other perfume-laden flowerets that throw incense to the air. June and July are the months when Flora delights the world with poppies, pinks, fox-gloves, mint and a thousand others. The dahlias, heleanthus and asters come trooping in when August zephyrs shake the wood, and a blazing sun pours down to announce the return of dog-days. September introduces the purple calchium in our meadows, which comes to act as pall-bearer to all the northern flowers, for it is the last of Flora's train, save in southern climes, where the procession of bloom is endless.

Linneus not only made a floral calendar, but he extended his observations to all plants so critically that he at length arranged a clock of tolerable accuracy by marking the hour when certain plants open their flowers. His clock, unfortunately, was only serviceable in Sweden. Lamarck arranged one for France, but I know of none that we can use in the United States, though any well-versed botanist may easily construct one.

PEOPLE WHO LIVE IN PALM TREES.

M. Pouchet says: "The connection between man and the vegetable kingdom is not limited to these curious investigations; plants, living emblems of the rapid passage of hours and time itself, eternal lessons of wisdom, are associated with all our wants, our pleasures and our pains. The hardiest trees serve to build our dwellings with; other plants furnish our most natural food. Sometimes the existence of certain tribes depends on a single vegetable species. A palm which grows at the mouth of the Orinoco suffices for all the wants of some savage races, who, in company with the monkeys, live almost constantly perched, as it were, in the midst of its foliage. It yields them food, wine, and even cordage to swing their hammocks by, in which they suspend themselves during the inundations."

Speaking of these palm-tree dwellers, Humboldt, in his "Travels in Equatorial Regions," says: "At the time of the inundations the tufts of the fan-leaved *murichi* present the appearance of a forest issuing from the bosom of the waters. The navigator, traversing at night the branches of the Orinoco delta, sees with surprise the crowns of the palms lighted up by large fires. These are the habitations of the Guaranis suspended from the trunks of the trees. These people stretch mats in the air, fill them with earth, and on this bed of wet clay light what fires they require for household purposes. For ages they have owed their liberty and political independence to the treacherous and miry nature of their soil, which they traverse in seasons of drought, and over which they alone know how to pass in safety, to their isolation in the delta of the Orinoco, and to their living in trees."

THE BREAD-FRUIT TREE.

The wonders of the vegetable kingdom will grow as we proceed, but no book could contain all the marvelous things connected with plant life; we must, therefore, be content with only a few. Everyone has heard of the bread-fruit tree, which is found in great abundance in the Island of Tahiti (Otaheite). The fruit of this tree grows

BREAD-FRUIT TREE OF OTAHEITE.

to a size somewhat larger than a cocoanut, and weighs from two to five pounds, being solid like the pineapple. In preparing it for food the natives have only to cut the fruit in slices and cook them on a gridiron, when it becomes an excellent quality of bread, and would be so pronounced by an epicure.

But there are several other bread-yielding trees, or plants, from which a pith is obtained which may well answer the purpose of bread. Strabo tells us that the army of Alexander, while crossing a portion of Macedonia, being utterly destitute of provisions, sustained themselves for several weeks by eating the pith of a species of palm. If we are to believe Xenophon, the same thing happened during the famous retreat of the ten thousand Greeks.

In tropical countries the natives not only rely almost entirely upon the fruit of trees for food, but largely for clothing, also. Beneath the bark of certain trees there are thin layers called *libers*, so called from their resemblance to the leaves of a book. These may be separated without difficulty, and, since they are both pliable and strong, are easily wrought into valuable textile fabrics. The inhabitants of New Zealand convert the *liber* of some of their trees into most serviceable drapery, having first impressed it with ornamental patterns. In Cuba the negresses are much given to dressing in the soft *liber* of certain trees, on the score not only of cheapness, but also because clothes thus made are handsomer than if made from the cloths they are able to buy. On the Logetto, which is celebrated on this account, *liber* is found, the intertwined fabrics of which are as fine as our best muslins, on which account it is used very generally by ladies, who have given to it the name of lace-wood.

The inner layers of bark are sometimes found sufficiently flexible, smooth and compact to make a fairly good quality of writing material. The ancient Egyptians used this kind of paper, which is now called *papyrus*, in their records long before the civilization of Europe was begun. In fact, it was used anterior to history. Pliny relates that the Roman consul, Mucius, discovered a letter in the Temple of Lycia written on this material by Sarpedon, and dated from Troy. The existence of the sacred writings, the works of Homer and Hesiod, and the finding of the books of Numa in the tomb of that great legislator, all being recorded on *papyrus*, show how ancient was its use and how wonderful its durability.

THE WEEPING-TREE.

THE WEEPING TREE.

As previously stated, there is a surprising analogy between animal and vegetable life in several particulars. Plants breathe with the regularity of an animal, so have they circulation, sensibility, periods of waking and sleeping, and possibly a nervous system, which has been proven by the most delicate experiments. It has been shown that a man loses, on an average, two pounds and nearly a quarter every twenty-four hours, by the exhalation of watery vapor through the pores of his skin. A series of experiments, conducted by Hales, showed that through respiration the sunflower lost five-thirteenths as much as an average man. But the sunflower distils less water than most plants, some of which seem to pump water incessantly. An arum kept in the botanical garden at Amsterdam was observed by Ruysch to distil water drop by drop from its leaves in the proportion that it was watered. Musset discovered a plant of the same family, which distilled water so rapidly that little sprays might be seen, by very close observation, issuing from the pores of its leaves.

But the greatest marvel of plant respiration is seen in the Weeping Tree, which is indigenous to the Canary Islands, from whose tufted foliage there is a never ceasing and copious rainfall. At the foot of this wonderful tree is a pond, from which the natives obtain water, but should the pond become dry the tree would immediately show signs of languishing, since water is at once its breath and blood.

The leaves of other plants, more tenacious of the perspiration they distil, collect it in little cups, which are found at their ends, sometimes considerably open, sometimes closing and opening by means of a movable lid. Of these plants the *Nepenthes distillatoria*, more commonly known as the *pitcher-plant*, is most famous. Its leaves display a strong mid-rib, which extends beyond the blade and ends in an elegant cylindrical cup, provided with a hinged lid, which spontaneously opens and closes according to the state of the atmosphere. During the night this lid sinks down and hermetically closes the little vase, which then fills with limpid water exhaled by its walls. During the day the lid is raised, and the fluid evaporates more or less. The cooling liquid, properly called *nepenthe*, often quenches the thirst of Indians lost in the burning deserts.

THE WONDERFUL WINE TREE, MANNA TREE, AND WAX-PALM.

The Wine Tree, found in Mauritius Island, is only more wonderful than the pitcher-plant in that it distils an excellent quality of wine

THE WINE-TREE, OR WINE-BEARING SAGO-PALM.

instead of water, corresponding to old Concord. The natives are extremely fond of this natural intoxicant, and abuse its use like winebibbers throughout the world; but it is said that its effects are not so pernicious on the system as fermented wine.

We are told by Moses that manna fell from heaven to nourish the famishing Jews, but what is now called manna is the exudation of the flowering-ash, which is cultivated in Sicily. This waxy sugar runs and hardens on the tree-trunk in the shape of stalactites, which are scraped off by means of wooden knives, and are so pure that they may be used for all the purposes to which sugar is put without going through any process of refining.

MANNA, OR SUGAR-TREE OF SICILY.

In the western portion of South America, generally along the Andes, grows another wonderful tree, from which a wax is obtained that is strikingly similar to the product of the bee and may be used for the identical purposes, but it is chiefly employed for illuminating. This substance exudes from the trunk and collects in large balls, which are scraped off by the natives.

THE MARVELOUS MILK AND BUTTER TREES.

Still more remarkable than any of those just mentioned, is the *Butter-Tree*, which abounds in the forests lining the Niger River, in West Africa. Karl Muller, writing of this wonderful tree, says the slave merchants consider it very much more formidable than the restrictive measures sought to be imposed upon them by the English. "As the natives collect more butter than they require, the factors on the coast are uneasy as to what will happen should this butter become an article of commerce; and in order that nothing may divert the inhabitants from slave-hunting, they have induced the king of Dahomy to order the destruction of all the butter-trees in his kingdom. War is really declared against the tree; it is burned so soon as it springs up, and yet it reappears each year, as if constantly and energetically remonstrating with man for deliberately destroying a gift of nature." This butter is a secretion of the tree, and so profuse is it that as much as a hundred pounds may be gathered from one tree at once, to be renewed again in a few months. Its consistency is hardly equal to butter, but upon exposure to cold it hardens, and when salt is added it is next to impossible for a person to distinguish it from fresh, pure butter.

The butter-tree is one of nature's marvels, but it is equalled by the *Milk* or *Cow-Tree*, of South America. M. Boussingault, who, at Humboldt's request, analyzed the sap of the cow-tree, declares that its physical properties are exactly similar to those of cow's milk, except that it is a little more viscous. It is remarkable for containing an enormous quantity of wax, which constitutes fully one-half its entire weight. The natives regale themselves upon this nourishing lacteal by cutting the bark of the tree with an axe, when immediately the fluid issues out in a stream, which they collect in a cup and drink as we would fresh, cold milk.

STRANGE SUPERSTITIONS CONCERNING CORN.

It is with astonishment that we read of the superstitions prevalent among the ancient races of America concerning that most common of our products, *Maize*, or Indian corn. This plant is undoubtedly indiginous to American soil, else we should have heard of it through the writings of some of the poets or historians, such as Pliny, Dioscorides, Columella or Theophrastus, but no mention of it is made by any of these, while, on the other hand, after its discovery in America by the first voyagers succeeding Columbus, maize has been constantly referred to.

WAX-PALM OF THE ANDES.

"Joseph d'Acosta affirms that maize was one of the principal articles of food among the savages of the new continent long before it was conquered. At the time that Cortez reached Mexico this *grass* was sacred, being regarded as holy food. Montezuma sent leaves of it, steeped in human blood, to the celebrated conqueror. At certain public ceremonies the Mexicans made images of their gods in maize paste, and after carrying them through the streets, divided them among the people, so that every one might have a share in the sanctified food. When Pizarro made himself master of Peru similar practices still existed. The Incas offered as a sacrifice loaves made from this cereal, which the virgins consecrated to the worship of the sun, hardened with the blood of young infants, whose faces they lacerated in order to prepare this food." When the sacred plant failed in their gardens the Indians made imitations of the grain from gold and silver which they offered as sacrifice.

THE QUININE PLANT—ITS HISTORY.

"Nature offers us," says Pouchet, "in profusion, the greatest contrasts. On one side, with generous and beneficent hand she lavishes food and salutary remedies; on the other, she only distils poisons, as though in the laboratory of Medea. Here we see opium perspiring like a milky dew from the heads of our poppies, and becoming so indispensable to the art of medicine that Sydenham, the Hippocrates of modern times, said he would renounce his profession was he deprived of this powerful anodyne. There we behold the poisons of belladonna, datura and henbane, by turns useful and deadly. But no tree prepares in its invisible laboratories such precious crystals as the *Cinchona*; nature offers no other medicine which is so potent."

It is the belief of the medical profession, pretty generally, that quinine is the only positive specific remedy that is to be found in all *Materia Medica;* mercury comes next to it, but does not rank in the same sovereign character, for it will not always eliminate the virus which it is used against, while quinine is a certain specific against malaria. The history of the discovery of this marvelous remedial agent is an interesting one, as related by La Condamine, from whose account I take pleasure in extracting as follows:

"In 1638, Count Cinchon being vice-regent of Peru for the court of Spain, his august spouse was attacked with a severe fever. The corregidor of Loxa, filled with gallantry for the wife of his immediate superior, sent him word that the Indians of the neighborhood knew of a bark which cured their fevers, and might possibly have the same effect upon a person of so exalted a condition, and begged of him, should his resources fail, at all events to try this medicine of the savages. The vice-queen, getting worse and worse, the corregidor was called to Lima, in order himself to regulate the dose and mode of preparation of his medicine. But it may be easily imagined that no one was imprudent enough to administer so extraordinary a powder to the noble patient without some precautions; they therefore decided to try it on some of the common people, and it was only after they had cured with the corregidor's bark some poor Spanish beggars, shattered with fever, that the vice-queen took it and was cured.

"The inhabitants of the town of Lima, being astonished at this, sent a deputation to the convalescent, begging her to send to Loxa for a stock of the bark, a request which was complied with. The countess herself distributed the remedy to all who required it, and from this time it began to be known by the name of the Countess' Powder. Some months afterward she gave up the task, handing over what remained to the Jesuit fathers, who, to their praise be it said, continued to give it gratuitously, and hence it acquired the name of Jesuit Powder, which it long bore both in America and Europe."

This is a very pretty story, and may be true in part, but Humboldt has written some things concerning the cinchona-plant which cause us to doubt that the people accepted it as a gracious remedy, as La Condamine tells us. The great German scientist, who traveled in all parts of South America, assures us that the natives, so far from having any faith in the virtues of the plant, vigorously contemn it as poisonous and capable of producing gangrene.

THE SOAP AND CAMPHOR-TREE.

There are trees in China belonging to the genus *Dyallum*, from which a substance is gathered analogous to soap. The seeds of another tree in China serve the same purpose as soap, for which they are largely used. The seeds are first dried and mascerated, after which they are poured into hot water, where they quickly produce a strong suds, that will remove greese like magic.

The *Soapwort*, says Sowerby, was formerly used by mendicant friars for washing their clothes, for which purpose the leaves of the plant were admirably adapted, as a few of them steeped in water made a powerful saponine.

The *Camphor-Laurel* is a native of India and Java, where it is extensively cultivated for the resinous juices which it secretes, and which the natives convert into camphor by the simplest means. The

EXTRACTING MILK FROM THE COW-TREE.

tree, which grows to a great height, is cut up into small pieces and placed in a retort, where they are boiled for a short time. The essence is thus converted into a vapor, which condenses on the lid of the retort, where it is easily gathered, and is at once marketable.

THE DEADLY UPAS TREE.

Every person has heard of the *Upas Tree* of Java, a vegetable product of the devil's rearing. When a little boy I remember having seen a picture of an upas tree, in the temperance department of my father's library. It represented an allegoric tree, in which the trunk was composed of whisky barrels and the branches of snakes, the latter hanging head downward and vomiting their poison into cups held by drunkards, while on the ground were skulls and dying men. The picture made a great impression on me, and excited a horror for strong drink which may, in part, account for the radical temperance principles which I still adhere to.

As a matter of fact, the upas tree is one of the most deadly vegetable products of creation, though few things have been the subject of so many fabulous stories as the upas. A Dutch surgeon was the author of many of these fables, which were implicitly believed for a long time. He represented it as growing in a vast plain denuded of all other vegetation. Within three leagues of it no living thing could exist, for the vapors which it exhaled were certain death to animal, bird or insect life, so that the ground was strewn with skeletons of men and other creatures that had breathed its pestilential emanations. These exaggerations were not refuted until within the last few years, when Leschenault made a journey into Java, and there found the upas standing amid a thick forest growth, as innocent of noxious vapors as the sage and mimosa, while in the branches were lizards and birds of gorgeous hue. He had one of the trees cut down, and upon examination found that the waxy exudation issued from the broken and cut portions of the wood, some of which became accidentally smeared on his hands, but produced no ill results. Further observation, however, served to convince him that he had been dealing with one of the rankest poisons in nature, for had there been the smallest abrasion of the skin where the juice touched him, he would have probably forfeited his life to his inquiry. He discovered that a drop of the juice introduced through a pin puncture was sufficient to kill a dog within five minutes, while eight drops injected into the veins of a horse destroyed the poor animal in about the same time. Travelers relate that the natives punish their women guilty of adultery by pricking them on the bosom with a lancet dipped in upas juice, in which case death ensues generally in about six minutes.

Poisonous plants are specially numerous in India, and of such a deadly character that a distinguished botanist likens them to the venomous snakes of that country, and calls them, very appropriately, "the serpents of the vegetable kingdom."

There is a species of nettle, covered with hairs, which, coming in contact with the flesh of a human, will inoculate one with a poison so powerful that though the amount may not exceed the one-hundred-and-fifty-thousandth part of a grain, yet the symptoms produced are terrible. Each of the dainty hairs which cover this malignant plant is a veritable serpent's fang, being bent and armed identically, while to touch it ever so lightly is sure to receive its sting. Leschenault says he has seen the sting of this nettle bring on the most intense sufferings for a whole week.

Another species peculiar to Timour, an island north of Australia, which the natives call the *Devil's Leaf*, produces such wounds by the mere touch, that life is only preserved by an amputation of the afflicted part.

ANCIENT SUPERSTITIONS ABOUT PLANTS.

In the olden times, when there was either a god or devil in everything, including human beings as well, there were some singular beliefs respecting plants. Some learned men stoutly maintained that all plants had souls, and could distinguish between good and evil; like the mentors of conscience these vegetable souls were continually bent upon gratifying their inclinations, some by doing good and others so malevolent that they were always seeking some new evil thing to perform. No less distinguished a philosopher than Empedocles taught this silly superstition, though, at the same time, he aspired to be a god himself. But others took up the idea dropped by the sage of Agrigentum and carried it to yet more extravagant beliefs until the whole of vegetable creation was shrouded in the most absurd mystification.

The *mandrake* was a plant especially worthy of ancient veneration, for they not only attributed to it a human form, but also a human intelligence, though its soul was under the influence of Satan. They believed that when wounded, however slightly, the mandrake gave vent to the most gruesome groans. Those who gathered it were obliged to practice certain incantations, so as to make them proof against its devilish influence.

THE POISON-TREE, OR UPAS, OF JAVA, WITH FLOWER OF THE RAFFLESIA IN THE FORE-GROUND.

The *Solanea*, a species of night shade, was also in great repute among the ancients on account of its gloomy disposition and power to work great harm. In order to overcome it, certain ceremonies had to be performed, which Greece's most illustrious botanist, Theophrastus, gravely describes with all faith in their efficacy. The ceremony consisted in tracing three circles around the plant with the point of a sword, the exorcist all the while keeping his eyes steadily toward the east, while an assistant danced three times round the plant, repeating an obscene objurgation in the meantime.

Roots of the mandrake plant were used in enchantments, being first carved into semblance of men and women. They were also ground into powder and used as a philter by sorcerers. Special virtues were attributed to this plant, from the belief that it grew nowhere except on a spot over which a gibbet had once hung, and that it found nourishment only in the remains of murdered men. Mandragora philters were, therefore, as powerful as those of the enchanted Circe, and to add to this belief philosophers like Dioscorides, called them *Anthropomorphic powders*, meaning, literally, the ground body of a deity in human form.

There is a little plant called the *Dictamnus*, which grows on the slopes of Mount Ida, in Crete, to which the ancients ascribed the most miraculous powers for healing wounds. It was believed the gods themselves had first planted it, and then sent a messenger, who attended one of their feasts, to make known its marvelous virtues to mortals. When Æneas lay mortally wounded, Venus gathered the leaves of this plant and binding his hurts immediately restored him. Aristotle was not above the superstitions of his time, for he sincerely tells us that the goats which roamed wild over the Grecian mountains, when pierced by the arrow of the hunter, at once sought the dictamnus, which they ate, with the knowledge that by so doing the arrow would drop out and the wound be directly healed.

St. John's-wort was believed to preserve houses from lightning, provided it be gathered at a time designated by the legend and hung over the door. The *Thorn-Apple* was another cabalistic plant, from which a powerful poison was expressed, which witches used to intoxicate their victims and produce the spectacle of the Sabbath.

Camilla,Debaus, though hardly encouraging the belief, yet does not attempt to disprove the beautiful poetic legend to which he gives a place in his works; he therefore tells us of the rose from which rude winds have torn its leaves until, in agony, it sheds tears; and when murdered by frosts, he says the poor, sweet body is carried away by sorrowing gnomes to paradise.

CARNIVOROUS PLANTS

We are surprised to find in the vegetable kingdom plants which must have a solid food, such as animals alone are popularly supposed to thrive upon. In this, again, we find an apparent evidence of the animal life in plants, since the general classification of naturalists is based as much upon food as upon organization.

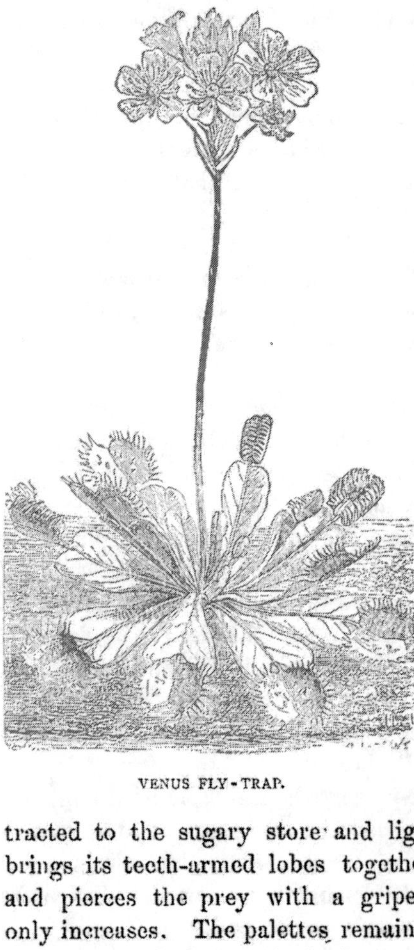

VENUS FLY-TRAP.

The *Venus Fly-Trap*, common in most large gardens, is an excellent example of carnivorous plants. Its leaves are so many insidious snares for entrapping insects, as will be seen by examination. Their expanded ends each present two small palettes armed with teeth set on the edges and all united by a longitudinal hinge. Each palette is also provided with three sharp spines about the middle, while at their base there is an exudation of a sweet fluid, which attracts flies and other insects. Now mark how astounding is the seeming intelligence displayed by the plant in catching its prey: When a small, winged creature is attracted to the sugary store and lights upon the leaf, it suddenly brings its teeth-armed lobes together, like the closing of a book, and pierces the prey with a gripe which its struggles to escape only increases. The palettes remain closed on the insect until all the juices are sucked from its body, nor can they be opened during the plant's feast without rupturing them. Animal food is so necessary to this kind of plant that if it be enclosed within a wire screen so that insects are excluded, it speedily languishes; on the other hand, if bits of meat are laid on the leaves from time to time it flourishes under the nourishment, and will even grow under a glass case.

The *Dog's-Bane*, of this country, is also carnivorous, feeding principally on flies, which it contrives to catch by their proboscis. So soon as the insect, attracted by the honey which is distilled on the expanded blossom, protrudes its proboscis in order to regale itself, the filaments close and seize it by the extremity of the organ with a grasp that is never relaxed until the fly dies from exhaustion. In this case it appears that the plant absorbs only the juices of the fly's head, and does not suck the body. The *round-leaved Drosera* is a fly-catcher also, but it is hardly so cunning as the two previously mentioned, since it secretes a glutinous fluid on its leaves so adhesive that when a fly once lights upon it there is no hope of its escape, for its feet are glued fast.

A MAN-EATING PLANT.

Travelers have told us of a plant, which they assert grows in Central Africa and also in South America, that is not contented with the myriad of large insects which it catches and consumes, but its voracity extends to making even humans its prey. This marvelous vegetable *Minotaur* is represented as having a short, thick trunk, from the top of which radiate giant spines, narrow and flexible, but of extraordinary tenaciousness, the edges of which are armed with barbs, or dagger-like teeth. Instead of growing upright, or at an inclined angle from the trunk, these spines lay their outer ends upon the ground, and so gracefully are they distributed that the trunk resembles an easy couch with green drapery around it. The unfortunate traveler, ignorant of the monstrous creation which lies in his way, and curious to examine the strange plant, or to rest himself upon its inviting stalk approaches without a suspicion of his certain doom. The moment his feet are set within the circle of the horrid spines, they rise up, like gigantic serpents, and entwine themselves about him until he is drawn upon the stump, when they speedily drive their daggers into his body and thus complete the massacre. The body is crushed until every drop of blood is squeezed out of it and becomes absorbed by the gore-loving plant, when the dry carcass is thrown out and the horrid trap set again.

A gentleman of my acquaintance, who, for a long time, resided in Central America, affirms the existence of such a plant as I have here

THE YA-TE-VEO, OR CARNIVOROUS PLANT.

briefly described, except that instead of the filaments, or spines, resting on the ground he says they move themselves constantly in the air, like so many huge serpents in an angry discussion, occasionally darting from side to side as if striking at an imaginary foe. When their prey comes within reach the spines reach out with wonderful sagacity (if I may be allowed to apply the expression to a vegetable creature), and grasp it in an unyielding embrace, from whence it issues only when all the substance of its body is yielded up. In its action of exerting pressure upon its prey, this dreadful plant resembles the instrument used in the dark ages for inflicting a torturous death. It was made of two long iron cylinders, on the inside of which were sharp, projecting pikes. The victim was placed inside, and the two cylinders then brought forcibly together, thus driving a hundred or more of the pointed pikes into all parts of his body and producing a frightful death. Generally this inquisitorial instrument was made, somewhat crudely, to represent a woman, hence the name applied to it was "The Maiden," by which it is still known.

Dr. Antonio Jose Marquez, a distinguished gentleman of the city of Barranguilla, in the United States of Colombia, in describing this wonderful plant to the author, affirms that when excited it violently agitates its long, tentacle-like stems, the edges of which, rasping upon each other, produce a hissing noise which resembles the Spanish expression, *ya-te-veo*, the literal translation of which is "*I see you.*" The plant is therefore known, in South America, by the name *Yateveo*. He further asserts that so poisonous are the stems that if the flesh of any animal be punctured by the sharp barbs, a rapidly-eating ulcer immediately forms, for which there is no known antidote, and death speedily ensues.

It is a singular thing, and much to be deplored, if such a voracious plant exists, that we can find no description of it in the most elaborate works on botany; and yet hundreds of responsible travelers declare they have frequently seen it, and not only watched it when in a normal condition, but one African explorer declares he once witnessed the destruction of a native who was accidentally caught by one. It has also been asserted that in the Fan country of Africa, criminals and those convicted of practicing witchcraft, are sometimes fed alive to this man-eating plant. All of which, however, I am inclined to doubt; not that there is no foundation for such statements as travelers sometimes make about this astonishing growth, but that the facts are greatly exaggerated.

CHAPEL OAK IN NORMANDY.

GIANTS OF THE FORESTS.

We have seen how curious are the habits of some plants, of which, however, I have only mentioned a few, while the whole world abounds with them; but the peculiarity of habit is no more curious than the surprises which are occasionally met with in the extraordinary size of vegetable growth, not alone in trees, either, but in flowers as well. For example, we have in the *Victoria Regina* a water-plant whose leaves are sometimes six feet in diameter, and capable of supporting a child, while the flower of the *Rafflesia* of Java and Sumatra is a colossus almost surpassing belief, being quite ten feet in circumference, and weighing as much as fifteen pounds. In appearance it resembles a puff-ball, while it exhales an extremely fœtid odor, so that it will hardly become popular as a lapel ornament. Still, the Javanese prostrates himself before this gigantic flower, clothes it with supernatural power, and makes a divinity of it.

In Africa there grows a still more extraordinary flowering plant, called the wonderful *Welnitochia*, which, astonishing to relate, is the very counterpart in shape of a *Polypus*, the most hideous creature in the ocean world. It has two leaves ten feet long, of a pale green color, which split up, under the influence of heat, into ribbons. In the center is a woody mass, having a cork-like surface rising a foot above ground, and bearing round its edges, just within the insertion of the leaves, an assemblage of small stems, about six inches long, dividing into smaller branches, each of which bears from three to five cones of a crimson color, with scalps like those of a fir-cone. The leaves are so straight grained that they can be torn from top to bottom without deviating a single line from the straight course. Rain rarely or never falls where this plant exists. The plant sometimes attains even greater size than mentioned above, some travelers asserting that they have seen the leaves eighteen feet in length, and the flower which it produces six feet in width and opening like two immense clam-shells, some eighteen inches across.

Giant trees are not confined to California, though little is written about gigantic growths in the forests of other countries, and a majority of persons are therefore in ignorance of many of the most wonderful products of vegetable creation.

Pliny, the Latin naturalist and author, whom I have so frequently referred to on account of his being the most intelligent observer of his time, says there was in Lycia a stout thriving plane-tree, in the trunk of which was seen a vast grotto, eighty-one feet in circumference, the whole extent of which had been tapestried by nature with a

GIGANTIC BAOBAB OF THE VIRGIN FORESTS OF AFRICA.

green and velvety hanging moss. Mutianus, who was governor of the province, made a merry feast upon a special occasion within the trunk, to which eighteen guests were invited. Here the night was spent in boisterous orgies, until toward morning, when the maudlin merry-makers went to bed on the natural floor without any remonstrances.

HISTORICAL TREES OF THE WORLD.

In the neighborhood of Constantinople there stands, or did a few years ago, according to De Caudolle, a lime-tree, the trunk of which is one hundred and fifty feet in circumference, while the circular hollow is nearly thirty feet in diameter.

In Normandy there is the most celebrated oak of all history, since for a hundred or more years it has been consecrated to religious services. It is called the "Chapel Oak of Allonville," and is very properly named, too, because it contains an altar dedicated to the virgin, where, on certain days, mass is said. Above the oratory there is a building, chapel-like in exterior, which serves as a sleeping-room for a pious anchorite, who thus elevates himself above the sordid cares of a sinful world. The trunk of this tree is thirty feet in circumference, and is held in great veneration by all the people.

In the vicinity of Smyrna, and also on the banks of the Bosphorus, there are plane-trees so ancient that they were even celebrated in antiquity. In size they are veritable giants, and have their trunks pierced with enormous cavities, being spread widely at the base, and representing three converging columns inclining toward each other, forming a kind of porch, beneath which a man may easily pass on horseback.

Of all trees, however, the great *Baobab*, on the banks of the Niger, takes precedence on account of its splendid luxuriance of growth, though it is not famed for gracefulness, for the branches are too thick and wide-spreading to be in harmony with its height. Almost always destitute of leaves, bearing them only during the short rainy season, its grayish, conical trunk, hardly twenty feet in height, is more than one hundred feet in circumference. This short and robust support is necessary to sustain its incredibly large dome of leaves, the bulk of which is sometimes so great that, seen from a distance, the baobab looks rather like a small forest than a single tree, its branches being sixty feet long.

In another part of Senegambia the natives have converted the hollow of a baobab tree into a grand council chamber, while another serves the purpose of a prison, as the interior of an oak once served the people of a town in Germany.

THE GREAT CHESTNUT-TREE OF MOUNT ÆTNA, CALLED OF A HUNDRED HORSES.

THE CHESTNUT TREE OF THE HUNDRED HORSES.

One of the most renowned and justly celebrated wonders of the vegetable kingdom is a gigantic chestnut tree which flourishes on the lower slopes of Ætna. An exact measurement of this tree, made by Count Borch some years ago, shows its trunk to be of a circumference of one hundred and ninety feet. Its trunk being hollow, as are the bodies of all great trees, a house was built inside, where a shepherd and his flock find splendid shelter. During the winter season he obtains his wood from its branches, and in the summer it affords him an abundance of fruit.

The "Chestnut of a Hundred Horses" owes its name not only to the vast extent of its branches, but rather to a circumstance told to the painter Houel to the effect that Jeanne of Aragon, when traveling from Spain to Naples, stopped at Sicily, and, accompanied by the nobility of Catania, paid a visit to Mount Ætna. She was on horseback, as were also her suite, and a storm coming up, she took shelter under this tree, the extensive foliage of which sufficed to protect the queen and her cavaliers from the rain. As a queen is expected to travel with a hundred horses, the circumstance is thus made memorable in the name of the tree.

The trees I have mentioned are notable for the circumference of their trunks, but in height any of them are exceeded by what we would regard as ordinary trees. In Palestine the cedars of Lebanon, which are so reverentially regarded from the fact that the Temple of Jerusalem was largely made of them, reach a height of one hundred and fifty feet, and are thought to be very majestic. The wax-palms of the Andes, to which I have already referred, wave their crested crowns in the clouds two hundred feet from the earth, and afford a gracefully beautiful sight.

But when we consider the lofty trees of the world, none will compare with the titanic products of California. One of the great cedars of that State measured one hundred and thirty feet in circumference, and reared its hoary head to a height of four hundred and ninety feet. Unfortunately, this mighty monarch of the world's forest was cast down by some unknown cause, and its trunk has been cut into sections and transported to various museums as curiosities. The hollow of the trunk was so large that a company of foot soldiers could manœuvre in it. Upon the stump of another a party of twenty diverted themselves in dancing, leaving plenty of room besides for a piano and three musicians. The age of these California mammoths, computed by the annual rings in a transverse section of the stumps, show them to be between three thousand and four thousand years old, or contemporaneous with biblical creation.

CONTEMPORARIES OF THE DELUGE STILL LIVING.

The great age accorded the giant trees of California suggests a very interesting subject, somewhat elaborated by Pouchet, to whom I am indebted for many of the facts here used. What are the oldest things on earth? Possibly the granitic hills, but even these do not show evidences of greater antiquity than some trees, the souls of which many philosophers assert are sentient and immortal.

The olive tree, so revered in ancient Greece, and which inspired such beautiful verses in the tragedy of "Ædipus" by Sophocles, according to a hoary myth, reached an immense age Pliny declares that in his time the celebrated olive which Minerva caused to spring from the ground, at the epoch of the foundation of the city of Cecrops, was still to be seen in the citadel of Athens.

The races of early history, struck with the noble and royal aspect of the oak, have in all ages invested it with curious legends, in nearly all of which the tree appears as a sentient thing. The great holm-oak, which in the days of Pliny stood near Rome, bore on its trunk an Etruscan inscription in letters of brass, stating that before the founding of the Eternal City it was already the object of popular veneration. The same Roman naturalist tells us that in the environs of Heraclea, in the kingdom of Pontus, there was a tradition that two oaks, which overshadowed the altar of Jupiter Stragius, had been planted by Hercules.

The imposing terror of the Hercynian forest has deeply impressed all those who have described Germany, and particularly Tacitus and Pliny. The aged oaks of its somber vales, where wandered the elk and aurochs, especially aroused the admiration of historians, and to which Tacitus refers as follows:

"The majestic grandeur of the oak in this forest surpasses all imaginable belief; this tree has never been touched with the axe; it is contemporary with the creation of the world, and appears to be the symbol of immortality."

IMMORTALITY IN TREES.

The idea of immortality in trees is often met with in the works of the ancients. Thus Josephus, in his history of the *Jewish War*, relates that in his time there was near the city of Ebron a turpentine-tree which was as old as the days of Adam.

"It is now a hundred years," says Pouchet, "since Adanson, by ingenious calculations, showed the learned that such ideas, though extraordinary, are yet facts of the most scrupulous exactitude. This naturalist, by a happy chance, found in the interior of the trunk of a *Baobab*, in one of the Cape Verd Islands, an inscription which had been traced on it by the English more than three hundred years previously. Starting from this point and comparing the diameters of the stems of many of these bulky trees, the French savant succeeded in proving that the most vigorous of these primitive inhabitants of the African forests might be at least five thousand years old.

"A bare-headed cypress, a venerable patriarch of the vegetable kingdom, has possibly traversed a still longer vista of ages. It is seen at the present day on the road from Vera Cruz to Mexico, and is celebrated for having sheltered the entire army of Fernando Cortez beneath its mighty shade. (The army of Cortez was composed of six hundred Spanish foot-soldiers, forty horsemen, and nine small pieces of artillery). The birth of this tree, according to some botanists, seems to date from an epoch so remote as to be almost beyond our ken. As its trunk, which is one hundred and seventeen feet in circumference, surpasses that of the baobabs, and as its growth is slower than theirs, De Candolle supposes this tree may be not less than six thousand years old, which carries back its origin to the time anterior to the Mosaic creation. Meanwhile we ought not to be astonished at seeing some botanists look upon trees as so many beings, the life of which is unlimited, and many of which, born amid the debris of former cataclysms, still vegetate full of sap and vigor."

The *Dragon's-Blood Tree*, of Teneriffe, is a still more singular and striking evidence of the extraordinary age some trees attain. We know that very anciently the Guanches, who were the original inhabitants of Teneriffe, worshipped it, and that in the fifteenth century mass was celebrated in the hollow of its trunk. So extremely slow is the growth of this tree, that since the first accurate measurement taken of its trunk, in 1402, by the companions of Bethencourt, it has not perceptibly increased in diameter. Humboldt, when he ascended the peak of Teneriffe, in 1799, measured the tree at a little above the ground, and found it forty-five feet in circumference, or the same

THE GUTTA-PERCHA TREE.

as Bethencourt ascertained it to be, nearly four hundred years before. Having attained such enormous dimensions, through a growth so slow as not to be perceptible in four hundred years, what must we conclude that its age is? The granite hills may be yet in their infancy by comparison. We even still find vestiges of the antediluvian flowers, which gave life to the first meadows on the earth.

CHAPTER XXVII.

CONFLICT BETWEEN MAN AND BRUTE.

NATURE is ingenious in all her works, but she is no less eccentric, viewed from the position which man occupies. While there is a marvelous adaptation invariably displayed, there is a sad lack of harmonious arrangement, which strikes even the least observant mind. Is this antagonism of animals a wise law, necessary to the development or regeneration of all creation? Possibly it is so, but the finite mind is hardly capable of reasoning out the justice of that inexorable mandate which declares that the weaker shall be a prey for the stronger. Tyndall's theory of a survival of the fittest finds ready elucidation in the harsh events which constantly transpire about us, but the fact is consistent with our own sense of justification as defined by the noblest instinct of our conscience. The lion will eat the lamb, because it is natural for it to do so, and nature, therefore, justifies it; but even so, yet we instinctively shudder at the cruel nature of the voracious beast; thus do we find a striking illustration of the inharmonious essence, or soul, of nature. Again, we subsist largely on the flesh of animals slaughtered for our especial use, and by patronizing the butcher we justify his vocation, yet it is a hard heart that can look, unmoved by sympathy, at the killing of a steer. The murderous axe and gore-steeped knife, or the weltering victim as it rolls its great eyes in a last imploring look as if begging for mercy, all appeal to our pity, and make us wonder why nature implants within us the disposition to kill, and, at the same time, the conscience to rebuke the act, thus rendering our lives twofold and paradoxical.

It is hardly fair to argue that but for this wise provision of Providence the world must soon be overrun with redundant populations, for it were just as reasonable to maintain that plagues serve the same purpose, and to attempt to arrest them is, accordingly, the contravening of a just law of nature. Without charging nature with the crime of inciting to murder among all animal creation, let us accept the anomalous fact and feel within ourselves that the reason therefor, though unrevealed to us, nevertheless rests in the bosom of the Creator.

HOW THE LION WINS HIS BRIDE.

Since we live in a world filled with struggles, where killing is an implanted propensity in both man and beast, whether as pastime, or the means of securing food, let us examine the habits of the more destructive brutes that terrorize the forests, and the expedients adopted by man in contending with them. In pursuing this subject I shall first consider the *Lion*, that fierce Sultan of Atlas, who roams in African wilds a veritable king, so powerful that man alone has courage to dispute his sway. Although made common by his exhibition in numerous menageries, and also by the stories which recite the perilous adventures encountered by bold spirits who hunt him in his native jungles, still, the lion is a creature whose habits few understand. To see him shorn of his freedom is to behold the lion under disadvantages which have robbed him of his royal mien and made a very cur out of the grandest beast nature ever designed.

The lion is peculiar to Africa, though it is also found in Asia, but not the ferocious beast that infests the dark continent. Formerly they were numerous in Algeria, but the march of civilization has driven them into the far interior, where they are now found in considerable numbers. Their habits are more like those of the cat than any others of the feline species, save in the particular of sexual association. In the February mating-time of birds, the lion seeks his consort, not by parading his beauty, but by exhibiting his prowess. It is a singular fact that there are more male than female lions, when the opposite seems to apply to all other animals. This preponderance of males leads to the most terriffic combats that imagination can conceive, for, while polygamy is common to many animals, polyandry seems to be impossible with the lion. Since all cannot, therefore, be provided with a spouse, the right of choosing must be determined by a resort to battle. Occasionally, at the mating season, a lioness will have three or four young suitors for her favors, and these may strive to win her affection by good natured purring and courtly fawning, with-

THE INTERRUPTED FEAST.

out fighting. In such cases, the coquette most generally leads her lovers distractedly about the forest, until they meet an old monarch, who chooses to wed the lioness himself. Hot-headed, as youths usually are, the pretendants will at once give battle to their new rival, piling on him in a concert of charges, reckless of consequences, until perhaps one has a jaw broken, another a leg crushed and the third an eye torn out, all happy at length for the good fortune which enabled them to escape without fatal injuries. The contest being concluded, the royal gladiator shakes the tangles from his bloody mane, and with a long, resonant, reverberating roar, he approaches the listless female and lays down at her feet, the very impersonation of obsequious devotion, which she probably notices by condescending to lick the blood from the wounds received as the price of her favors.

A TERRIBLE BATTLE BETWEEN TWO LIONS.

The incident of youths battling with an elder for the possession of a lioness is only occasional, but it is a common circumstance for two mighty monarchs to lay the wager of their hearts in terriffic combat for the espousal of a valor-loving dame. Such a fight is described by Gerard, the great lion-hunter, to whom the facts were related by a native, who, in company with his son, watched the battle from the branches of a tree. The account is as follows:

"It was in the stag's rutting season, and Mohammed, a great hunter of every kind of wild animal, perched himself at sunset in the boughs of an oak tree, to watch for a doe that had been seen wandering in the vicinity, accompanied by several stags. The tree which he had climbed was situated in the middle of a large clearing, and near a path that led into the neighboring forest. Toward midnight he saw a lioness enter the clearing, followed by a red lion with a full-grown mane, bearing the carcass of an ox, and soon after followed by another lion, lioness and three cubs. The lioness strolled from the path and came and laid herself down at the foot of the oak, while the lion remained in the path, and seemed to be listening to some noise, as yet inaudible to the hunter.

"Mohammed then heard a distant roaring in the forest, and immediately the lioness answered it. Then the lion commenced to roar with a voice so loud that the frightened hunter let fall his gun and held onto the branches with both hands, lest he might tumble from the tree.

"As the voice of the animal just heard in the distance gradually approached, the lioness welcomed him with renewed roarings, and the lion, restless, went and came from the path to the lioness, as though he wished her to keep silence, and from the lioness to the path, as though to say, 'let the vagabond come, he will find his match.'

"In about an hour a large lion, as black as a wild boar, stepped out of the forest and stood in the full moonlight on the other side of the clearing. The lioness raised herself to go to him, but the lion divined her intent, rushed before her and marched straight toward his adversary. With measured step and slow they approached to within a dozen paces of each other, their great heads high in air, their

THE BATTLE OF THE MONARCHS.

tails slowly sweeping down the grass that grew around them. They crouched to the earth—a moment's pause—and then bounded with a roar high in air, and rolled on the ground locked in their last embrace.

"The battle was long and fearful to the involuntary witness of this midnight duel. The bones of the two combatants cracked under their powerful jaws, their talons strewed the grass with entrails and painted it red with blood, and their roarings, now gutteral, now sharp and loud, told their rage and agony.

"At the beginning of the contest the lioness crouched herself on her belly, with her eyes fixed upon the gladiators, and all the while the battle raged manifested, by the slow, catlike motion of her tail, the pleasure she felt at the spectacle. When the scene closed, and all was silent and quiet in the moonlight glade, she cautiously approached the battle-ground, and, snuffing the dead bodies of her two lovers, walked leisurely away, without deigning to answer the gross, but appropriate, epithet Mohammed hurled at her instead of a bullet, as she went off."

COQUETRY OF THE LIONESS.

This example of conjugal coquetry and infidelity of the lioness is applicable to all her species. What she desires is a lover full grown and brave, who will drive away the young lions, whose beardless chins and constant quarrels offend her delicacy and disturb her repose. Such a lover she is sure to find, although she may not keep him, for the moment that a braver lion appears she gives him always a ready welcome. The lion, however, does not appear fickle in his matrimonial adventures, for having once won a spouse he remains not only monogamic, but so true to her that he never forsakes her for another, and all the while bestows the most lavish affection upon her, unworthy as she is.

When the royal couple leave their lair, both in going and coming, the lioness invariably leads the way, and when she pauses the lion stops until she is ready to proceed again. Upon arriving at a spot where they intend foraging for a meal, the lion now precedes his spouse, who lies down to await his adventure. He boldly dashes through the thicket or attacks the native kraal, and with deer or ox, or whatever his capture, he goes directly to the lioness and lays it down before her. Singularly enough, instead of regaling himself at once upon his prey, he patiently waits beside his consort until she has completed her repast, apparently taking great pleasure in witnessing her gratification.

The lioness usually becomes heavy with young in January, when she seeks a dense thicket and there prepares her lair in which to deposit them. The number of young produced at a birth is from one to three, but most commonly two, a male and female; but if only one is born, it is almost certain to be a male; so, in a litter of three, two of them are equally sure to be males, so that the preponderance of one sex over the other is due to the inequality in reproduction, and not to disproportionate fatality among the young, as we sometimes find it in other animals. The period of teething is the crisis in the lives of young lions, when nearly one-half die, but no more of one sex than of the other. The old lion provides all the meat needful for the sustenance of the lioness during her maternal watchfulness, though he sleeps in a separate lair, not so far away, however, but that his assistance may be readily summoned.

PERILS ENCOUNTERED BY YOUNG LION STEALERS.

When the young lions are about two months old the mother first leaves them to search for food, and during her temporary absence the cubs are sometimes taken by the natives, who are brave enough to undertake the deed for the reward their booty is sure to bring them. To accomplish this most hazardous enterprise much preliminary is necessary. The lioness is first seen in a condition indicative of early maturity, after which she is watched until her lair is discovered. In this dangerous business several men must engage, since the lioness is more likely to be frightened by the noise and appearance of a large party than of one or two, whose power she readily estimates, but, regardless of the number of persons employed, the perils are still very great, as the following incident will show:

"In a country of Africa called Zerdezah, a chief discovered a lioness almost ready to whelp and immediately conceived the idea of taking them when they should be born. After this event had occurred and more than a month elapsed, the chief called to his aid a neighboring sheik, and with sixty men from the two tribes they contrived to surprise the young lions, in the absence of the mother, and bear them away. This wonderful success delighted the native adventurers, and, after gaining a considerable distance from the lair, they retired carelessly within their rude tents thinking there was nothing more to fear. The chief was outside of his tent busying himself with official duties when, hearing a noise, he looked up just in time to see the lioness as she made a desparate spring for him. By a great leap he avoided the enraged animal, which, turning then from him, seized the chief's nephew. The young man was brave and faced the foe as best he could, and managed to bring his rifle into position, but, unfortunately, the gun failed to fire. Throwing aside his useless weapon he gave his left arm to the teeth of the brute, and without a cry from the pain of crunching bones, he drew his pistol with the right hand and lodged two bullets in her breast. Though badly wounded the lioness quitted her hold on the nephew's arm only to spring at another native, but as she was rushing towards him with wide distended jaws he fired a ball into her throat, which, however, did not stop her. He was seized by the shoulder and thrown down, his right hand ground to pieces, and he was sadly torn in other places, but his life was spared by reason of the lioness dying on his body. Though he was not killed he was rendered a sad cripple for life, while the nephew was so badly bitten that he died the following day."

Young lions begin foraging for food when about eight weeks old, but it is not until they are two years of age that they can strangle a horse, ox or camel, or leap hedges seven feet high. But having attained this period they become wantonly destructive, killing as much for the mere gratification of the deed as to procure food, and their ravages among cattle are sometimes terrible. They do not reach their full growth until the eighth year and run their natural course of life in from thirty to forty years, this being the limit.

The lion is essentially a nocturnal animal, procuring all his food during the night, and whiling away in sleepy indulgence the day.

A PECULIARLY SHOCKING INCIDENT—EATEN BY A LION.

I have frequently heard it said, and also seen it written, that the lion never attacks man except as a measure of defense or else when driven to it by excessive hunger. This impression obtains from the fact that, met with during the day, the lion is comparatively harmless, because he is drowsy and satiated, being indisposed at this time to even attack his favorite prey. But at night he is a terror to man, just as he is to cattle, for he would not hesitate to attack one as quickly as the other. This is proved by the large number of persons who are destroyed by lions; the number is not so great now, on account of the scarcity of the animals, but forty years ago it is estimated that ten thousand persons were killed every year by this terrible brute. The figures are no doubt the merest guess-work, and probably exaggerated, but the loss was certainly appalling enough.

As an illustration of the ferocity and daring of the lion before men, I will quote the following particulars of a shocking tragedy which occurred in the southern part of Algiers some years ago, indeed before the occupation of the country by French troops:

Two brothers, notorious bandits, whose renown had spread throughout all Algiers, were taken by a party of soldiers and thrown into prison. The Bey at once resolved upon their death, and to render their escape less probable, for they possessed extraordinary address and hardihood, he ordered that they be bound together by means of an

AN ESCAPING CRIMINAL EATEN BY A LION.

iron band welded around their legs, passing around the right ankle of one and the left of the other, the two bands being connected by a chain. This was accordingly done; nevertheless, when on the morrow the executioner came to their cell to behead them, he was astounded to find them missing, nor could anyone explain their extraordinary disappearance. The two brothers, as soon as they were free from the prison enclosure, made unavailing efforts to pry off their cumbersome shackles, but finding this impossible, fled across the country, avoiding as much as possible the frequented paths. When daylight came they hid themselves in the rocks, and only resumed their flight with the evening, being lighted on their way by the faint rays of a crescent moon and the bright hope of freedom. Thus they had traveled a long distance when, in the middle of the second night, one of the brothers, who chanced to be awake, discovered an approaching lion. His only weapon of defense was a spear, which he had picked up upon coming out of the prison ground, but this could avail him nothing against such an antagonist.

When the sleeping brother became aroused the two began throwing stones at the lion, and calling out as loud as they could, in order to make him flee, but the animal crouched down before them and did not move. Seeing that the stones and menaces were of no avail, the frightened men commenced their prayers; but before they were finished, the lion sprang upon them, and throwing them to the ground, devoured the elder while still chained to the body of his younger brother. The living man, as he heard the dying groans of his fated relative, and the crunching of the lion at his hideous meal, counterfeited death by swooning away into unconsciousness. When the lion had consumed the body down to the shackle, finding that he could not tear the iron, he contented himself with biting off the limb and leaving the other part still held in the iron band. Then, either from thirst or satiation, the animal left the still living man and walked to a brook a little distance off. No sooner had the lion disappeared than the man recovered from his faint, and springing to his feet, bounded off through the woods, dragging the mangled limb of his brother with him, until he reached a crevice between two large stones, in which he took refuge, and speedily barred the entrance with a rock, which, fortunately, lay convenient for the purpose. Scarcely had he thus defended his retreat when the lion, swiftly following on his track, arrived before the small cave and roared in thundering tones, enough to affright the senses of the most courageous. Finding he could not reach the man from below, the animal passed around and above the hole, and at last poked his nose down through a crevice and blew his hot breath upon the man, until a sense of suffocation overcame him. But daylight now appearing, the lion abandoned his intended victim, and took himself off to the woods.

The trembling fugitive, thus a third time saved, crowded out of his hiding-place and resumed his flight, but he was soon after apprehended by some horsemen sent after him by the Bey, who took him back to Constantine, where he was again thrown into prison. The Bey, astounded at the tale his soldiers brought back to him, ordered the culprit to be brought into his presence, that he might satisfy himself of its truthfulness. The man was produced, still dragging after him the leg of his unfortunate brother, and repeated the particulars of the tragedy in such a straightforward manner that the Bey was moved by compassion, and ordered that he be set at liberty.

DIFFERENT MODES OF KILLING THE LION.

The Arabs of Africa, though an autocratic race, and being fairly masters of the blacker tribes, are so cowardly that they rarely attempt the destruction of a lion save in some cunning manner by which they avoid all danger to themselves. The most common custom, therefore, is to dig a large, deep pit behind a thick hedge-row which encloses their village. The lion having already made several excursions upon the flock, the Arabs know where to locate the pit since, like the deer, the lion always jumps in the same place. The hedge is so thick that the animal cannot discover the pit beyond and, hearing the cattle near by, he leaps in expectation of a delicious meal, only to find himself imprisoned, and a howling mob of men and women overhead thirsting for his life. Unable to fight, the lion perceives his helplessness and stands defiant, receiving the bullets that are fired into him without a groan and dying like a victor at last.

The method which is next to the pit in popularity, and practiced by the Arabs, is that of preparing a hiding-place either in the ground or up in the trees. When they intend attacking the lion from the ground they first dig a hole about four feet square and of equal depth, which they cover with the trunks of trees and stones, leaving only a loophole at each end through which to point their guns, and a doorway that closes with a large stone. This blind is only constructed in the range that the lion takes every night, and in order to bring him to the spot and arrest his attention so that deadly aim may be taken, a hog is killed and laid in the path, within convenient range of the men in the blind. Though several balls may be fired into a lion's body, approached in this way, it is not often that the animal is killed outright, but comes charging at his foes, directed only by the sound of the guns, and unconscious of the fact that his enemies are beneath him. Stung with rage and pain he finally quits the spot and goes off into the woods either to die or recover from his wounds, for the Arabs are too regardful of their precious lives to follow him.

LION HUNTING ON FOOT, FACE TO FACE.

In Northwestern Nigrit, or what is now known as the Soudan, there is a mountain called Zerager, which is scantily wooded, but whose sides and peaks are covered with enormous rocks, piled up by some mighty convulsion, so that crevices and caves abound—the very best shelter for lions, which in former years were quite numerous. At the foot of this mountain is a rich and extensive plain occupied by a race called the *Cessi* and their vast herds of cattle. On these flocks it was the custom of the mountain lions to lay nightly tribute, so that the poor people were in constant harassment from these bold depredators, though they hunted the despoilers with great bravery and pertinacity.

When a lion first gave indication of his presence, either by a robbery of the cattle pens or by his deep roaring on the mountain at night, the news immediately spread from mouth to mouth, and preparations were made throughout the camp—for the Cessi lived in large kraals—to give the brute battle. The hunters congregated at an agreed spot, bringing with them such weapons as they could procure, but which were indifferent at best.

The moment of the arrival of the men, who have previously examined the woods for signs, is one of breathless interest, for they are not conspiring to make war upon a harmless game in which mere sport is the incentive, but the brute whose life they seek has the strength of fifty men, and the grinding grip of whose powerful jaws some one of the hunters is almost certain to feel, and a dozen may pay the extreme penalty for confronting the most dangerous of all animals.

The hunters, having arrived within gun-shot of the lion's lair, creep with great caution to a spot which overlooks the cover; the utmost quiet must be observed, for the lion has a wonderfully quick ear, and the cracking of a twig or rolling of a stone is certain to

METHOD OF HUNTING THE LION IN NORTHERN AFRICA.

arouse him, when, unlike most game, instead of taking alarm he boldly advances toward the place from whence the noise proceeded. By a well understood code of signals the advance, or skirmish hunters, communicate to those in the rear by moving their *burnous* — a kind of cloak — indicating by the various motions, when they see the animal, which direction he is taking, or whether motionless; but when the brute comes toward them they cry out, in Arabic, "*Aou likoum*" (Look out)! At this signal the hunters form in line of battle, if possible before some large rocks, so as to avoid being attacked from behind. Woe to the luckless wight who fails to hear the warning cry, and remains at a distance from his comrades. The moment the lion perceives him, whether he is fleeing or standing his ground boldly, the vicious brute charges with a bound, and, unless killed dead by a single shot, he is sure to tear the man as a cat does a bird.

DARING OF THE LION.

When the hunters have had the opportunity to unite their forces, with their backs to a rock, the lion will march majestically before them, with a menacing air, hoping by this means to throw their ranks into confusion, for he is a strategic warrior as well as brave. If he succeeds in thus inspiring the men with terror, so that they scatter in disorder like frightened sheep, as they sometimes do, he charges upon them right and left, and sometimes kills a dozen or more. But if the men are brave and remain steadfast in solid rank, the lion passes slowly and with a triumphant air directly before the leveled guns, uttering a low growl indicative of angry menace, and lashing his tail from side to side. This is the decisive moment! The word of command is given, by a chosen officer, to fire. Each one discharges his gun with such aim as can be taken, and then, dropping the discharged weapon, immediately draws his pistol and yatagan-sword.

It appears strange that thirty balls fired into the body of a lion at as many paces, do not instantly kill him, but it is a fact that this result does not occur more than twice out of five times. The animal is so tenacious of life, that he does not die at once under any number of balls, unless they should pierce his heart or brain. If, however, he falls under this leaden hail, the hunters spring upon him and a desperate fight ensues, until the last spark of life is fled from the royal beast. But the nearer the lion draws to death, the more dangerous he becomes. If, during an action of this kind, but before he is wounded, he overtakes a man, he merely overthrows him as an obstacle in the way, and gives the person a scratch of no serious character; but if the lion should be hit by one or more balls, he will kill or tear to pieces whomsoever he may catch, sometimes carrying the body in his mouth until he overtakes another, whom he in turn catches and drops his first prey.

But if badly wounded and still able to reach a man, he will draw him with his powerful claws, and after having turned up the face of his victim under his nose, will seem to delight in his agonies like a cat with a mouse. With his claws he slowly tears away the flesh of the unfortunate, while his burning, green eyes are fixed on those of the fallen hunter, who, under the fascination of their magnetism, is quite unable to utter the slightest cry. From time to time he will lick the face of the miserable man with his rasping, rough tongue, and then wrinkling his brows will bare his teeth in a threatening menace, as if conscious of the terror which the act inspires. This same vengeful and gloating disposition is manifested by the tiger, and occasionally by the leopard also.

THE COOLNESS THAT IS REQUIRED TO KILL A LION.

Gerard devotes a chapter in his interesting work on lion-hunting to advising amateur hunters how to attack their game with the greatest chances of success. Among other thrillingly exciting admonitions are the following:

"When you hear the roarings (of the lion) approach, and if you judge that the animal is on the same path with yourself, walk slowly toward him, until you find an open space, in which you can see your foe, and when you have found it, seat yourself and wait.

"Whether the lion, on leaving his den, walks with a rapid gait, or whether, having satisfied his hunger, he slowly strolls homeward, swaying his enormous head from side to side, as soon as he perceives you on his path he will not fail to stop. If you remain seated he will softly approach, stopping from time to time in order to paw the ground like a bull. Sometimes he will roar loud enough to make you fairly deaf, sometimes he will breathe diabolical sighs. Do not lose sight of him for a moment, and keep your eye fixed on his. If he leaves the path in order to sharpen his claws on a tree, be ready. Prudence and coolness are now especially needed, and the least haste will be fatal. He sees your arms, and none of your movements

SAVAGE SATISFACTION EXHIBITED BY THE TIGER OVER A FALLEN VICTIM.

escape him, though he will not attack you until the first shot is fired. When you aim he will crouch like a cat. In this position he will show nothing but the top of his head, and, on my word, however near you may be, I would advise you not to fire. With your gun to your shoulder and your eyes on those of the lion's, walk a few steps from the path, either to the right or left, according to the side the moon throws the best light over your enemy. If you turn too much he will think you are going to fire on his body, and will wheel round on his stomach, always keeping his face toward you. Take but two or three steps, and as soon as the side of his head seems to be opposite you, aim well between the ear and eye and pull the trigger. Of two things, either one or the other happens; either the lion is instantly killed, or, before being able to judge of the effect of your shot, you are stretched on your back under the wounded animal, whose head and fore-paws are on you, crushing you in the earth. But you are not dead for all that.

"If your ball has been well directed and not met any obstacle to turn it aside, you will escape with a dozen or more scratches from his claws, which you can cure, providing his teeth have not touched you, or if his agonies do not last longer than a few seconds, you may still get out of the scrape with your head on your shoulders. In any case, remember that you have a dagger, and if you have not lost it in the fall, strike quickly, firmly and in the right place. If the lion is killed on the spot, thank your God, and recommence the battle with the next one you meet.

"One word of advice. Whenever you find yourself opposite a full-grown lion, do not be too long in carrying out your manœuvres. If too much haste may cost you your life, too great slowness in the attack may be equally fatal. The lion, becoming impatient, has only to bound on you while you are aiming, and you will be disarmed and torn to pieces without having fired a single shot."

A LION MESMERIZES A LOVER.

The Arabs verily believe that the lion can mesmerize a man and in this condition compel him to follow it like a slave to its lair, and innumerable stories illustrating this peculiar power are told, one of which is as follows: Once upon a time, as all good stories are prefaced, a young man, of the Amemera tribe, loved most passionately a most brave girl whose affection was equally ardent, but who was restrained by a cruel father from wedding the amorous youth because, alas, he was poor. Though her liberty was curtailed, she contrived to communicate with her lover and to arrange a plan which required only the assistance of the young man to make successful and effect her liberty.

Ventursome and brave, the youth sought the goal of his betrothed and had the happiness of bearing her away; but as the twain fled over the hills by night, and neared the friendly camp of his own people, they were suddenly confronted by a lion which rose up directly in their path and roared so fiercely that they were both beside them selves with fear. The girl, however, shrieked so loud that the men in camp were aroused and rushed out to discover the cause. As they approached they were astounded by the sight which met their gaze. The burning youth was following the lion towards a dense growth despite the appeals and frantic efforts of the girl to draw him back. His reason apparently gone, he was saying to her: ‘ Come, dearest, our seignor calls us,'' and to the lion, "Don't listen to her, my seignor, she does not speak the truth ; I have no arms, and will follow you wherever you will.''

The ten men who had been attracted by the girl's screams attacked the lion with their guns, but at the first fire the animal, which was but slightly wounded, charged upon the mesmerized young man, and in a trice crushed his head between its powerful jaws ; having murdered the man, the furious beast caught the trembling girl and bore her off to the woods like a cat carries its kittens, where no trace of her was afterward seen.

A LION'S FEAST.

It is a singular fact that when once a lion tastes human flesh he always thereafter prefers it to any other food, and will take the most desperate chances to procure this favorite meat, in which respect the lion resembles the tiger of India, as we shall hereafter see.

A story is told by Madame Lakdar, which proves the propensity of the African lion as here charged. On the road from Constantine to Batua, in Algeria, there was in former days a large Mosque called *Jema-el-Bechiva*, the ruins of which now only remain. The priests of this holy place had procured a young lion, which they raised with great attention, until its full growth was attained, little reckoning how it would repay their kindness. One day the lion was missing, and its escape was considered only the exhibition of a nature which God has given to all wild beasts, so that no effort was made toward its recapture. Two days later, however, one of the priests was missing, nor did he present himself again on the succeeding day; on the other hand, instead of the first absentee reappearing, another priest was found absent. This was passing strange, but not so astonishing as the fact that each day for a period of forty days a priest of Jemael-Bechiva was lost, and so mysteriously that not the least clue to the cause could be surmised. There were yet ten priests remaining, but these, fearful lest the devil had taken up his abode in the neighborhood, departed, not being willing to wrestle with the cloven-hoofed demon who had vanquished so many of their brothers, so the mosque became deserted.

Finding that his daily allowance of a priest, whose body was the more succulent by reason of the good wines with which it was seasoned, had suddenly been discontinued, the lion, for such was the devourer, began to make his levies upon the laity, so that travelers fell into his capacious maw with astonishing frequency, until the route in which he had taken up his watches became entirely deserted.

AN EXCITING INCIDENT.

Gerard relates the particulars of a distressing accident, whereby one of his most faithful attendants was almost slain by a lion, in the following words: * * * "As we approached, the lion crouched down across the road, as though to bar our passage. I left Rostain at about thirty paces from him, and continued walking up. When within twenty paces I halted, where I could get a shot at his side, but like a cat at play, he wheeled about, lying close to the earth, and only showing me the oblique surface of his head. The attitude of the animal being so hostile and wary, I thought it unsafe to hazard a shot, which might merely glance along the skull without penetrating it, and therefore moved around to his side, keeping always at the same distance. When I attained a position that I thought was sufficiently good, I took aim again, but the lion, as before, wheeled around, calculating in his own mind whether he should spring upon me or not.

"Fully comprehending the extent of the danger in continuing these tactics, I slowly moved a little to one side, sighting the animal all the while over my rifle, and before he had time to wheel I fired at his shoulder. At the shot he attempted to spring forward; a broken shoulder prevented him, and he fell on his side, and while struggling to regain his feet, I gave him the other barrel.

GERARD'S ADVENTURE WITH A WOUNDED LION.

"Rostain, seeing the animal had fallen, ran forward towards where I was standing, but at the same moment that he came up, the lion raised himself on his left fore-leg and gave a roar that startled me by its fierceness. My gun was empty, and I seized the other gun from Rostain's hand, and walking forward two or three steps, fired just behind the shoulder, hoping to reach the heart. The lion fell, as before, but was immediately on his feet again. We were now without any means of defense, save my poniard, a feeble weapon against an animal that had not been killed by three balls.

"I had stood hand to hand with death so often that I did not fear for myself, but I thought it was all over with Rostain and me that night. I looked around for some place of retreat, and saw a large jujube-tree, or thicket, growing a little distance behind us, so I bade my comrade run, and we were fortunate enough to gain its protection. The jujube in question was about ten feet in diameter, and very close set, and the branches so studded with thorns that the lion did not attempt to force a passage through, but contented himself with following us around the bush, while we loaded as we ran. The wounded animal, after making one circuit, staggering all the while like a drunken man, laid himself down, expressing by growls his feelings towards us, in no very reassuring manner.

"We took advantage of this truce, and while Rostain kept watch, I finished reloading my gun, making as little noise as possible, and at the same time charging the gun carefully, that there might be no danger of a miss-fire in so desperate an emergency. When the last cap was placed on the cones, I felt relieved of an impending fate. We then moved back a short distance from the jujube, to avoid any surprise, and walked slowly towards the place where the lion had lain down, but he had left it, and there was nothing to be seen of him. Had the animal, not seeing or hearing us, gone to seek us? I thought it prudent not to wait to resolve the question. If he could get up and move out of sight in spite of our three balls, it was certain that in case we suddenly came upon him in the obscurity, he would make us pay dear for our fun. So we wisely drew off from further pursuit until after dawn of the following morning, when the search for the wounded animal was renewed by the addition of several Arabs to our party.

TORN BY A LION.

"Presently the trail led into a thicket of wild olive trees, that appeared a suitable cover for him to have taken refuge in, and the

Arabs stayed behind until I satisfied myself, by walking around the jungle, that the trail led no further, and that, dead or alive, the lion must be there. I then posted the Arabs in different groups around the thicket, and took my position where I judged he would most likely come out, relying upon his habit of charging a single individual rather than a number together. At a given signal the Arabs gave a loud hurrah, and, waving their burnous (cloaks), threw stones into the thicket, and urged on their dogs, that immediately disappeared in the underbrush.

"In a moment after I saw the lion coming cautiously out of the thicket, and taking the very path where Rostain was posted. I called to him, but before I could make him hear the animal was within ten steps of him, and losing his reason at the fierce bearing of his foe, he dropped his gun and fled, only instead of running up the hill, as the Arabs had done, he conceived the fatal idea of turning down the declivity to hide in the scattered woods at its base. The moment the lion caught sight of the fugitive he gave chase, with his mane ruffled and his tail in the air, while with every jump he roared with the full blast of his lungs. At each leap he staggered, but regaining his feet in an instant, he pursued his course with frightful earnestness.

"At the first glance at this chase I knew that it was all over with Rostain, though I ran with all my speed to his aid. As the animal crossed an opening in the woods, at forty paces from me, I fired a shot that struck him in the side and brought him to a halt. Had Rostain availed himself of this pause he would have been saved, but he must needs stop to see the effect of my shot. Seeing the lion recover himself and charging anew, he again endeavored to flee. His foot caught a root and he fell; before he could regain his feet the lion was upon him, and seizing him in its jaws the man and beast rolled down the hill together. In spite of the close woods that grew at the foot of the hill, I was at Rostain's side in a moment after he had been seized. He was lying motionless in a pool of blood, while the lion had disappeared, leaving him for dead. Nevertheless, he still breathed, and a hurried examination of the breast and shoulders showed that he was not hurt there. The four incisors of the angry lion had pierced his thigh like so many bullets, and sixteen deep long gashes from the animal's claws furrowed his back."

Continuing the narrative at some length, which I will not quote, Gerard states that Rostain was sent back to camp on a litter while the pursuit was continued. Soon after the lion was beat up again by the Arabs, into whom the animal fiercely charged and stretched two others upon the ground by strokes of his claws, so that three men were now desperately hurt, while the lion got away finally altogether, to die of his wounds without further molestation. Rostain recovered, but only after a loss of one leg and eight months of suffering in a hospital; the other wounded men also were restored, but wore the marks of their frightful wounds throughout their lives.

ADVENTURE WITH A FIERCE LIONESS.

Gordon Cummings, one of the most noted hunters that ever penetrated the jungles of Africa, met with a thrilling adventure, not long after his first introduction to the dark continent, which he describes as follows:

"Suddenly I observed a number of vultures seated on the plain about a quarter of a mile ahead of us, and close beside them stood a huge lioness, consuming a blesbok which she had killed; she was assisted in her repast by a dozen jackals, which were feasting along with her in the most friendly and confidential manner. Directing my followers' attention to the spot, I remarked, 'I see the lion!' to which they replied, 'Whar? Whar? Yah! Almagtig! dat is he!' and instantly reigning in their steeds and wheeling about, they pressed their heels to their horses' sides, and were preparing to take their flight. I asked them what they were going to do, to which they answered, 'We have not yet placed the caps on our rifles.' This was true, but while this short conversation was passing the lioness observed us. Raising her full, round face, she overhauled us for a few seconds, and then set off at a smart canter towards a range of mountains some miles to the northward; the whole troop of jackals also started off in another direction; there was, therefore, no time to think of caps. The first move was to bring her to bay, and not a second was to be lost. Spurring my good and lively steed, and shouting to my men to follow, I flew across the plain and, being fortunately mounted on Colesburg, the flower of my stud, I gained upon her at every stride. This was to me a joyful moment, and I made up my mind that either she or I must die.

"The lioness having had a long start of me, we went over a considerable extent of ground before I came up with her. She was a large, full-grown beast, and the bare and level nature of the plain added to her imposing appearance. Finding that I gained on her, she reduced her pace from a canter to a trot, carrying her tail stuck out behind, and slewed a little to one side. I shouted loudly to her to halt, as I wished to speak with her, upon which she suddenly pulled up, and sat on her haunches, like a dog, with her back toward me, not even deigning to look around. She then appeared to say to herself, 'Does this fellow know who he is after?' Having thus sat for half a minute, as if involved in thought, she sprang to her feet and, facing about, stood looking at me for a few seconds, moving her tail slowly from side to side, showing her teeth and growling fiercely. She next made a short run forward, making a loud, rumbling noise like thunder. This she did to intimidate me; but finding that I did not flinch an inch nor seem to heed her hostile demonstrations, she quietly stretched out her massive arms, and lay down on the grass. My Hottentots now coming up, we all three dismounted and, drawing our rifles from the holsters, we looked to see if the powder was in the nipples, and put on our caps. While this was doing the lioness sat up, and showed evident symptoms of uneasiness. She looked first at us, and then behind her, as if to see if the coast was clear, after which she made a short run towards us, uttering her deep-drawn, murderous growls.

"Having secured the three horses by their reins, we led them on as if we intended to pass her, in the hope of obtaining a broadside. But this she carefully avoided to expose, presenting only her full front. I had given Stofolus my Moore rifle, with orders to shoot her if she should spring upon me, but on no account to fire before me. Kleinboy was to stand ready to hand me my Purdy rifle in case the two-grooved Dixon should not prove sufficient. My men had as yet been steady, but they were in a precious stew, their faces having assumed a ghastly paleness, and I had a painful feeling that I could place no reliance on them.

"Now, then, for it, neck or nothing! She is within sixty yards of us, and she keeps advancing. We turned the horses tails to her. I knelt on one side, and taking a steady aim at her breast, let fly. The ball cracked loudly on her tawny hide, and crippled her in the shoulder, upon which she charged with an appalling roar, and in the twinkling of an eye she was in the midst of us. At this moment Stofulus's rifle exploded in his hand, and Kleinboy, whom I had ordered to stand ready by me, danced about like a duck in a gale of wind. The lioness sprang upon Colesburg and fearfully lacerated his ribs and haunches with her horrid teeth and claws; the worst wound was on his haunch, which exhibited a sickening, yawning gash, more than twelve inches long, almost laying bare the very bone. I was very cool and steady, and did not feel in the least degree nervous, having, fortunately, great confidence in my shooting; but I must confess, when the whole affair was over, I felt that it was a very awful situation, and attended with extreme peril, as I had no friend with me on whom I could rely.

"When the lioness sprang on Colesburg, I stood out from the horses, ready with my second barrel for the first chance she should give me for a clear shot. This she did quickly; for, seemingly satisfied with the revenge she had now taken, she quitted Colesburg, and slewing her tail to one side, trotted sulkily past within a few paces of me, taking one step to the left. I pitched my rifle to my shoulder, and in another second the lioness was stretched on the plain a lifeless corpse.

"Having skinned the lioness and cut off her head, we placed her trophies on Beauty — a horse — and held for camp. Before we had proceeded a hundred yards from the carcass, upward of sixty vultures, whom the lioness had often fed, were feasting on her remains. We led poor Colesburg home, where, having washed his wounds and carefully stitched them together, I ordered the cold water cure to be adopted. Under this treatment his wounds rapidly healed, and he eventually recovered."

A SHOCKING INCIDENT

The same distinguished sportsman and traveler tells the particulars of a ghastly tragedy which befell one of his most trusted servants, in the following language:

"The Hottentots, without any reason, made their fire about fifty yards from mine; they, according to their usual custom, being satisfied with the shelter of a large bush. The evening passed away cheerfully. Soon after it was dark we heard elephants breaking the trees in the forest across the river, and once or twice I strode away into the darkness some distance from the fireside, to stand and listen to them. I little, at that moment, dreamed of the imminent peril to which I was exposing my life, nor thought that a blood-thirsty man-eater lion was crouching near, and only watching his opportunity to spring into the kraal and consign one of us to a horrible death. About three hours after the sun went down I called to my men to come and take their coffee and supper, which was ready for them at my fire; and after supper three of them returned before their comrades to their own firesides and lay down; these were John Stofolus, Hendric and Ruyter. In a few minutes an ox came out by the gate of the kraal and walked round the back of it. Hendric and Ruyter lay on one side of the fire under one blanket, and Stofolus lay on the other. At this moment I was sitting taking some barley broth; our fire was very small, and the night was pitch dark and windy.

THE LION CARRYING OFF POOR HENDRIC.

"Suddenly the appalling and murderous voice of an angry, bloodthirsty lion burst on my ear within a few yards of us, followed by the shrieking of the Hottentots. Again and again the murderous roar of attack was repeated. We heard John and Ruyter shriek, 'The lion! the lion!' Still, for a few moments, we thought he was but chasing one of the dogs around the kraal; but the next instant Stofolus rushed into the midst of us, almost speechless with fear and terror, his eyes bursting from the sockets, and shrieked out: 'The lion! the lion! He has got Hendric; he dragged him away from the fire beside me. I struck him with the burning brands upon the head, but he would not let go his hold. Hendric is dead! Oh, God! Hendric is dead! Let us take fire and seek him.' The rest of my people rushed about, yelling as if they were mad. I was at once angry with them for their folly, and told them that if they did not stand still and be quiet the lion would have another of us, and that very likely there was a troop of them. I ordered the dogs, which were nearly all fast, to be made loose, and the fire to be increased as far as could be. I then shouted Hendric's name, but all was still. I told my men that Hendric was dead, and that a regiment of soldiers could not now help him; and, hunting my dogs forward, I had everything brought within the kraal, when we lighted our fire and closed the entrance as well as we could.

"My terrified people sat round the fire with guns in their hands till the day broke, still fancying that every moment the lion would return and spring into the midst of us. When the dogs were first let go, the stupid brutes, as dogs often prove when most required, instead of going at the lion, rushed fiercely on one another and fought desperately for some minutes. After this they got his wind, and, going at him, disclosed to us his position; they kept up a continual barking until day dawned, the lion occasionally springing at them and driving them in upon the kraal. The horrible monster lay all night within forty yards of us, consuming the wretched man whom he had chosen for his prey. He had dragged him into a little hollow at the back of the thick bush beside which the fire was kindled, and there he remained till the day dawned, careless of our proximity.

"It appeared that when the unfortunate Hendric rose to drive in the ox, the lion had watched him to his fireside, and he had scarcely lain down when the brute sprang upon him and Ruyter (for both lay under one blanket), with his appalling, murderous roar, and, roaring as he lay, grappled him with his fearful claws, and kept biting the poor man's breast and shoulder, all the while feeling for his neck, having got hold of which he at once dragged him away backward round the bush into the dense shade.

"As the lion lay upon the unfortunate man he faintly cried, 'Help me! help me! Oh God! men, help me!' After which the fearful beast got hold of his neck, and then all was still, except that his comrades heard the bones of his neck cracking between the jaws of the lion."

On the following morning Cummings went in search of the lion, which he had little trouble to find, since it had not yet abandoned the feast, but had very nearly consumed the body. The lion made off at speed through a heavy jungle, leaving only the lower portion of one of Hendric's legs, on the foot of which the shoe still remained, and a few tattered, blood-stained clothes to mark the spot where the poor fellow had been eaten. Turning from the dreadful scene, Cummings dashed on after the lion, which was soon brought to bay by the dogs. Bravely meeting his enemies, the lion rushed out of the covert and stood for a moment with head erect and lashing tail, as if defying the whole world; he thus presented an excellent target to Cummings, who, with two well-directed balls, brought him to the earth a fallen gladiator. Cutting off the lion's head, Cummings returned with it to the kraal, having been absent scarcely more than fifteen minutes.

A SOLDIER CARRIED OFF BY A LION.

Schweinfurth, in his work entitled "The Heart of Africa," mentions a sad accident which occurred in the immediate vicinity of his camp, on the river Tudyee. He says: "As we were preparing to continue our march, some people came to meet us with dismal intelligence from the neighboring village of Geegyee. They said that on the previous night a Nubian soldier, who had lain himself down at the door of his hut, about five paces from a thorn hedge, had been seized by a lion and, before he could raise an alarm, had been dragged off, no one knew whither." This incident is given by Schweinfurth merely as he would report an every-day occurrence in a diary, not deeming it sufficiently interesting to merit a circumstantial account, But further on he says:

"I learned that this district had for some years been infested with lions, and that lately the casualties had been so frequent that the greater part of the inhabitants of Geegyee had migrated in consequence. The entire village would have been transplanted long ago, but the lions had been always found to follow any change of position."

A MIRACULOUS ESCAPE FROM A LION.

Among the many daring lion-hunters of South Africa C. J. Andersson is prominent; a man who to reckless bravery combined the quality of a keen sportsman, besides being a graceful writer, who has left behind him the most interesting descriptions of his thrilling experiences and adventures among wild tribes and fierce animals. Among the many stirring incidents of his eventful life Mr. Andersson records the following, which he considers the narrowest escape from death that ever befell him:

While encamped at the forks of two small streams, some natives came to him and begged that his services be given them in destroying a large lion that was terrorizing the country and destroying great numbers of goats and oxen. Having already had some experience in lion-hunting, Andersson was glad of the opportunity thus offered to measure arms with the king of beasts, and he therefore lost no time in beginning the pursuit. The natives, armed with spears and assegais, and a few guns, guided him to a thick brake, where fresh spoor (tracks) showed that the lion was then concealed. But when this spot was reached the natives could not be induced to enter and beat up the game, so that Andersson had either to perform this most dangerous duty or else abandon the chase. Of the alternatives he chose the more serious one, although the risks involved were fairly desperate. Creeping with great caution through the dense growth, where any moment he might be pounced on by the dreadful beast, he had proceeded some distance without seeing his quarry when, suddenly, a shout sent up on the outside, told him that the lion had shown himself to the natives; a wild volley greeted the brute, but did no further damage than to drive him back again to his retreat. This performance was twice repeated without results, so that Andersson came out of the brake and pleaded with some of the natives to take his place as beater and allow him a chance to shoot the lion when it should again show itself, but none would go into the brake. I will give the concluding results of the attack in his own language:

"As the day, however, was now fast drawing to a close, I determined to make one other effort to destroy the lion, and should that prove unsuccessful, to give up the chase. Accordingly, accompanied by only a single native, I again entered the brake in question, which I examined for some time without seeing anything; but on arriving at that part of the cover we had first searched, and when in a spot comparatively free from bushes, up suddenly sprung the beast within a few paces of me. It was a black-maned lion, and one of the largest I ever remember to have encountered in Africa. But his movements were so rapid, so silent and smooth, that it was not until he partially entered the thick cover that I could fire. On receiving the ball he wheeled short about, and with a terrific roar bounded toward me. When within a few yards, he crouched as if to spring, having his head imbedded, so to say, between his forepaws.

"Drawing a large hunting-knife and slipping it over the wrist of my right hand, I dropped on one knee, and thus prepared, awaited his onset. It was an awful moment of suspense, and my situation was critical in the extreme. Still, my presence of mind never forsook me for a moment; indeed, I felt that nothing but the most perfect coolness and absolute self-command would be of any avail.

"I would now have become the assailant, but as — owing to the intertwining bushes and clouds of dust raised by the lion lashing his tail against the ground — I was unable to see his head, while to aim at any other part would have been madness, I refrained from firing. Whilst intently watching his every movement, he suddenly bounded toward me; but — whether it was owing to his not perceiving me, partially concealed as I was in the long grass, or to my in-

A HAIR-BREADTH ESCAPE.

stinctively throwing my body on one side, or to his miscalculating the distance — in making his last spring, he went clear over me and alighted on the ground three or four paces beyond. Instantly, and without rising, I wheeled round on my knee and discharged my second barrel, and as his broad side was then toward me, lodged a ball in his shoulder, which it completely smashed. On receiving my second fire he made another and more determined rush at me, but owing to his disabled condition I avoided him. It was, however, only by a hair's breadth, for he passed me within arm's length."

The probabilities are that the lion was crazed by the first shot, so that it was unable to distinguish its enemy, for it died almost immediately after making the leap.

HOW A BRAVE ARAB WAS TORN BY A LION.

During the several years that Gerard was hunting lions in Northern Africa he met with many narrow escapes himself, and was witness to several shocking tragedies committed by wounded animals.

Though previous to his exploits in their country the Arabs were slow to engage in a combat with the lion, Gerard's success as a hunter so inspired them with confidence that, when he had decided upon a campaign against the marauding brutes, he found even too many Arabs ready to join him.

On one occasion the Valley of Ourten was the scene of great slaughter among the cattle, perpetrated by a lion that was reputed to be uncommonly large, fierce and bold. This fact coming to the ears of Gerard, he immediately prepared to give battle to the forest monarch Of the many volunteers who offered their services, he accepted a half dozen, and with these he posted off to the grounds where the lion made his lair. Two days' search brought them to a brook called Tafrent, where signs were discovered, and soon after Amar-ben-Sigha, being somewhat in advance, saw the terrible animal cross the stream and enter a heavy copse, where he had made his lair.

It having now grown dark the hunt was abandoned until the morrow, when at early break of dawn it was resumed. By carefully picking their way through the cover they at length came up so closely with the lion that he broke away and appeared on the edge again lashing his tail in mad fury. Gerard had provided himself with a young kid for bait, and this he now tied to a tree and retired a short distance, knowing that its piteous bleatings would soon attract the hungry lion. Scarcely had this been done when the lion came stalking toward the bait with such ferocious looks that all the Arabs beat a hasty retreat, leaving Gerard alone to face the dreadful brute, which approached with a slow and majestic gait, never taking its piercing eyes from the sight of the hunter, until within fifty-yards, when it disappeared in the wood. Gerard well knew that the lion had withdrawn from sight only to creep nearer its prey, as is the habit of this dangerous animal. Nearly fifteen minutes had elapsed, and the silence was becoming oppressive, for not a sound disturbed the interval, before the lion showed himself again, but when he did appear it was within a few paces of the kid, which now suddenly ceased its bleating and began to tremble with a full knowledge, apparently, of its impending fate. The monstrous beast leisurely mounted the side of the gulch and halted at the edge of a clearing, not more than ten

A DISASTROUS FIGHT.

steps from Gerard, and there he faced the hunter, his broad head presenting an excellent target.

Though Gerard more than once drew aim, he did not fire, lest a front shot might produce no other effect than an invitation to charge. Presently the lion lay down, and pillowing his huge head on his paws continued to gaze intently upon the hunter, as if studying him, or contemplating the two feasts of kid and man, unable to decide which he should eat first. Several minutes thus elapsed when, at length, the lion arose and, as he presented his side for a moment, Gerard fired and sent two balls through his shoulders; with a terrific roar the great beast rolled down into the ravine, and, though dreadfully wounded, managed to conceal himself in some heavy growth.

The Arabs now ran up and being confident that the lion was dead, despite all of Gerard's protests, they followed down through the bushes stained with blood, eager to offer indignities to the dead monarch, as is their custom. As they were creeping through the brush, one of the Arabs, in his nervous excitement, discharged his musket, when, immediately, the lion gave a fierce roar and charged; all but one of the men ran towards Gerard, but Amar-ben-Sigha, a brave fellow, who was somewhat separated from the rest, stood his ground and fired, as did all the others, at the beast, not one of the shots, however, taking effect. In another moment the brave Arab was crushed to the earth, his gun was broken, his thigh stripped of the flesh, and when Gerard came to his succor Amar-ben-Sigha's head was in the lion's mouth, while the lion was lying on the prostrate form lashing his tail and breathing a bloody defiance to his foes. Fearing for the head of the man in aiming at that of the lion, Gerard fired for the heart, at which the lion released its hold and the man came rolling down to Gerard's feet, groaning from his lacerations and fatal wounds. The lion still kept his feet, by leaning against a tree, but another bullet gave him a final quietus, when he rolled down upon the body of Amar again.

Poor Amar paid the penalty of his rashness, for, after some days of excruciating agony, he expired, though such a death is esteemed among all African tribes an honor next to falling in battle for the Moslem faith.

MR. BALDWIN'S WONDERFUL LUCK.

Another great hunter, who has earned no little fame by reason of his intrepid daring in pursuit of the large game of South Africa, is Mr. Baldwin, whose fortune being ample, spent many years in African wilds for the sport that the life afforded. In an earlier period, say fifty years ago, the northern portion of Africa abounded with lions, but the mighty jungle monarch is now rarely found north of the equator, and, judging by the accounts we have of the animal, it would appear that as he approaches the hotter climate his disposition becomes more surley, and consequently the dangers that are encountered in hunting him are greater.

Mr. Baldwin, unlike Gerard, hunted on horseback, and generally with dogs, by which the peril is very much lessened, as the dogs, though never any considerable antagonist of the lion, yet serve to distract his attention from the hunter, while the horse is an admirable

MR. BALDWIN'S MARVELOUS ESCAPE.

means of escape; but even with these excellent aids the danger is not entirely avoided, as the following incident will show:

In the month of September, about the year 1862, though the date is not given in his account of the adventure, Mr. Baldwin was hunting in the Buchuana country which, at that time, was fairly infested with large game, such as lions, elephants, leopards and rhinoceri. He was splendidly mounted and had a considerable pack of dogs that were brought with him from England.

Early in the morning, after he had set out from a native village, the dogs struck the trail of some animal and swiftly followed it up until they brought the game to bay in an open space on the decline of a small eminence. Baldwin hurried forward, not yet knowing the character of game that the dogs were pursuing, until he approached within a hundred yards of the pack that was now barking with great energy. His horse betrayed so much excitement that Baldwin dismounted and crept forward until, as he gained the apex of the knoll, he discovered an immense lion standing at bay with the dogs at a respectable distance, one of which had been disemboweled by a stroke from the enraged lion's paw. This accident had taught the others prudence, and they were now contented to keep the game surrounded until their master could come to their aid.

As the lion stood still he afforded an excellent opportunity for a shot, and bringing his gun to the shoulder Baldwin fired, hoping to reach the monarch's heart; but his aim was bad, so that the lion received only a body shot, that in no wise disabled him. The lion quickly perceived from whence came this new attack, and breaking through the dogs, which were not slow to give him passage, he dashed directly after the hunter, bent on wreaking a desperate vengeance. Baldwin ran for his horse, after firing the second barrel of his gun, closely pursued, and would have succeeded in untethering the horse and getting away without accident except for the great restlessness of his animal, which prevented him from promptly mounting. When, finally, he gained the saddle the lion was so near that, as the horse dashed off, the enraged brute sprang squarely upon his rump, sinking one of its claws deep into the flesh, and at the same time tearing Baldwin's back with the left claw, almost pulling him from his seat. Fortunately, the attack did not arrest the motion of the horse, and the lion's hold broke, though not without cutting dreadful gashes in the poor steed and stripping Baldwin's coat from his back. Having made good his escape, though at such serious cost, Baldwin retired to the village from whence he had set out in the morning, and

A BROADSIDE SHOT.

procuring another horse he returned to renew the conflict. The lion was not again found until about the middle of the afternoon, when the dogs brought him to bay for the second time in open ground, near which was a ledge of rocks. Behind the rocky covert Baldwin took a favorable position, from whence he succeeded in killing the lion at the next fire, putting a bullet squarely through his heart.

WONDERFUL TENACITY OF LIFE IN A LIONESS.

The thrilling experience which Baldwin met with in his attack upon the fierce brute that had so nearly brought his sport to a tragic close, taught him a very useful lesson, to wit: the hunting of lions by the aid of a horse totally untrained to the purpose, is scarcely less dangerous than the pursuit on foot. He accordingly resolved to continue the eventful sport unmounted until such time as he could procure a horse that was broken to the hunt. He was not long kept thus unprovided, however, as a short time afterward Mr. Oswall and another Englishman, named Murray, came into the same country well mounted, and having spare horses, in quest of elephants. From these gentlemen Mr. Baldwin procured an excellent, thoroughly trained animal, from the back of which he hunted nearly two years afterward without again passing through so critical an experience as befell him on his first attack.

For nearly two weeks Baldwin, Oswall and Murray hunted together and met with great success, killing no less than ten lions and three rhinoceri. Among the former killed was an old lioness that exhibited a tenacity of life positively wonderful. Mr. Baldwin relates that while he was trailing the fresh spoor of two or three lions a large lioness was jumped which made through the grass to a bare ravine, where she passed in plain view at a distance of scarcely more than twenty-five yards. The three hunters quickly dismounted, to make their aim more certain, and each lodged two bullets in the fleeing animal without causing her to lessen her pace. She finally got away entirely, although it was seen that she had been badly wounded. On the following day Baldwin took two native gun-bearers and started out on the trail again, while Oswall and Murray got on to the track of a rhinoceros that they were very eager to bring down.

Several hours were spent by Baldwin in a useless search for the lioness, but about the middle of the afternoon she was discovered by the growls that she emitted as she lay well concealed in some high grass. The gun-bearers gathered several stones which they flung at

WONDERFUL TENACITY OF LIFE IN A LIONESS.

her until she issued forth in view, though she was too badly hurt to make a charge. Seeing her defenceless condition, Baldwin approached very near, hoping to speedily dispatch her and thus end her misery. But his good intentions he found difficult to put into execution for he declares that he fired no less than *twenty-one ounce balls* into the most vulnerable parts of her body before she finally expired.

HOW THE LION BRINGS DOWN A BUFFALO.

Although the lion will attack nearly any species of game when moved by hunger, his principal subsistence in South Africa is off cape buffaloes, which are very plentiful south of the Kalakari desert. These animals are not always an easy prey even to the strongest lion, while an old lion will seldom, if ever, attack them. The power of a three or four-year-old lion, however, is almost phenomenally great, while his courage is fully equal to his prowess.

In attacking a buffalo the lion uses no little stealth, for, since he is not a great runner, he must make up in cunning that which he lacks in speed. In searching for his prey the lion usually keeps close to the water courses, or pools, and there lies in some covert awaiting the approach of a victim. If a herd of buffaloes come to drink he abides his time until one becomes separated a little distance from the others, when he stalks this one until within a distance of four or five bounds. In making the attack he does not pounce upon his prey in a hap-hazard manner, but invariably strikes for the neck, seizing the unfortunate animal at the junction of the shoulder, when, with a desperate bite and a wrench sideways, he separates the vertebræ and causes almost instant death. Having secured his victim he does not at once begin his repast on the spot, but invariably drags the carcass a distance from where it first falls, though rarely into a thicket, apparently being content to move the body without regard to any particular place in which to make his meal.

A BRAVE SHEIK DESTROYED BY A LION.

It is with no little astonishment that we view the extraordinary bravery sometimes displayed by the native Africans, who hunt the most dangerous beasts that infest their country with no other weapons than the spear or assegai. We will presently see how the Abyssinian hunters pursue the elephant and rhinoceros, and meet these terrible animals face to face with only a sword. But the bravery which these experienced hunters manifest does not exceed that of a young sheik, whose desperate valor in the defence of a few of his followers

HOW THE LION SEIZES A BUFFALO.

caused him to lose his life. The story is told by Baker, who obtained the particulars from two eye-witnesses who escaped destruction by fleeing into the branches of a friendly tree. Briefly repeated the account is as follows:

A sheik and three followers were passing through a section of Nubia, enroute to a neighboring village, when they suddenly came upon a lion and lioness that stood directly in their way, nor deigned to step aside to let them pass. Usually a lion will retreat at the sight of a man, but on this occasion hunger must have made him bold, for he set up a dreadful roaring and otherwise showed his malicious spirit. The four men were greatly disconcerted by this bold spirit, for they perceived that the lion meant mischief. Being armed with no other weapons than some light assegais, they attempted to retreat, but the lion was determined that he would break his fast on the present opportunity, and pursued them so rapidly that the sheik saw one or more of his party must fall victims to the marauder, so bravely he determined to meet the lion's attack, trusting that by thus acting he could make escape for his followers possible. On rushed the growling brute, and heroically stood the sheik until he had hurled his weapon deeply into the lion, though the hurt it gave the creature did not even for a moment stay its attack. The lion leaped upon the poor fellow, and, bearing him swiftly to the earth, in a trice tore him limb from limb. The three companions succeeded in gaining the high branches of a tree, from which they were compelled to witness the horrible feast that followed. The lion dragged his victim a few feet away from where the attack was made, and then lay down beside the body and leisurely made his meal. The lioness, less bold than her consort, did not approach nearer, no doubt being afraid to participate in the feast on account of the men in the tree, but she patiently waited for her lord until he had finished his repast, when they both made off. The three men who had effected their escape through the sacrifice of their brave sheik, quitted their perch when the lions disappeared, and running to the village gave the alarm. A big hunting party was quickly made up and went in search of the lions, but the game was not found.

FACTS AND ARAB SUPERSTITIONS CONCERNING THE LION

The lion, as previously remarked, is chiefly confined to Africa, the tiger exclusively to India. Why this is so, no work on natural history, so far as my reading extends, undertakes to explain, and the fact is rendered more singular when we consider that the lion or tiger finds nothing in climate, provided it be torrid, injurious to its health,

A SHEIK'S BRAVE DEFENSE OF HIS FOLLOWERS.

or that interferes with their reproduction. In captivity they will thrive and breed, though taken from their natural haunts, but not so if given their freedom.

Those who know his habits best affirm that no animal can support hunger and thirst like the lion. When satiated he is fairly amiable, but during periods of hunger he is the most cruel and dangerous of beasts; not only will he attack man or beast, but he does not stop short of devouring even his own kind. In proof of this Andersson reports the following singular circumstance:

"Early one morning one of our herdsmen came running up to us in great fright, and announced that a lion was devouring a lioness! We thought, at first, that the man must be mistaken; but his story was perfectly true, and only her skull, the larger bones and the skin were left. On examining the ground more closely, the fresh remains of a young springbok were also discovered. We therefore conjectured that the lion and lioness, being very hungry, and the antelope not proving a sufficient meal for both, they had quarreled; and he, after killing his wife, had eaten her."

The Arabs entertain many amusing superstitions regarding the lions, some of which, taken from the popular works of the great writer, Abd-el-Merr, are as follows:

"He who rubs his body with the grease of a lion will cause every other animal to flee in dread.

"To cure a babe of any illness peculiar to the young, suspend a piece of the skin of a lion, with a morsel of hair, to the neck.

"To cure a person of paralysis, let him eat of lion's flesh.

"A piece of lion's skin put in a chest of clothing will preserve it from vermin.

"Rubbing the feet with lion's grease is recommended as an infallible cure for chilblains.

"He who carries about him the tail of a lion is proof against the wiles and deceits of the world, while the most virtuous amulets are those made from the hair or nails of a lion.

"Nothing is so quieting to the lion as the sound of musical instruments, or the singing of voices, by which he seems to be charmed.

"Though the lion is bravest of all animals, yet he will flee at the crowing of a cock or the ringing of metal, and a craving thirst will not even tempt him to drink from a pool in which a dog has first lapped."

A very remarkable trait with the lioness is, that when she leaves home to seek for food for her little ones, she covers over her tracks as she goes, that no one can find her young. When the old lion takes his offspring out to hunt, if he notices that one of them trembles at the sound of any voice or cry, he puts his mouth to its ear and gives a roar that renders the cub thereafter insensible to lesser sounds.

The Arabs believe that when Noah was taking two of every kind of animal into his ark, some objection was made to receiving the lion, on account of its vengeful disposition, whereupon God afflicted the leonine pair with a fever, which rendered them powerless; from this fever they never fully recovered, for the lion's body is yet very hot, while his breath is fœtid as if his blood were still ill-conditioned.

For every dream in which a lion figures the Arabs have an augury, and even the most intelligent classes impose great confidence in the predictions thus indicated.

Thus is the king of beasts hedged about with the marvelous romances which ever cling to royalty and the mighty.

The lion of Asia, though fierce as his congener of Africa, is still a poor beast by comparison, being almost destitute of mane, that seal of supreme sovereignty, and much smaller than the African species, which he but indifferently imitates.

It is a singular fact that though the lion is supposed to be a strictly carnivorous beast, he is nevertheless both insectivorous and frugivorous at times. In periods of scarcity, or when old age prevents it from capturing larger game, the lion will subsist on locusts and small lizards, nor does it even disdain to satisfy its hunger on beetles and a variety of other bugs. The water-melon of South Africa, which grows like a tuber, some feet under ground, is a favorite dish with the lion, especially during droughts, when he finds water difficult to obtain. These melons he finds by tracing the creeping vines and scratching them up like a dog.

CHAPTER XXVIII.

THE ROYAL TIGER.

IN Africa there is no animal that disputes the lion's sovereignty; he is there king, not by courtesy, but by might, and the striking dignity of his wonderful frame and ways. In Asia, however, there is one, if not a greater, still a peer, for in the Tiger we find all the attributes of a beastly monarch, with the natural strength, weapons and courage to enforce its rule over the animal kingdom, save alone that most wondrous animal, man.

The brilliant adornment of the tiger is familiar to all, and such beauty would appear to the casual observer to serve to make it conspicuous, and thus operate to its disadvantage, both in taking its prey and rendering it more likely of detection by the hunters, but, as Wood declares, "the vertical stripes of the body harmonize so well with the dry, dusky jungle-grass among which the creature loves to dwell, that the grass and fur are hardly distinguishable from each other except by a quick and experienced eye. A tiger may thus lie concealed so closely that even when crouching among low and scanty vegetation it may almost be trodden on without being seen."

The chief weapons of the tiger are his enormous feet, with their sharp, sickle-like claws, which cut like so many daggers. Besides the severity which lies in a stroke from the animal, there is a nervous effect produced that exceeds in intensity the injury that a blow or laceration generally occasions. Captain Williamson, an officer of twenty years' experience in Bengal, states that of the great number of persons he has known to be injured by tigers, not one of them died from wounds inflicted by a tiger's claws without suffering from lock-jaw previous to death ; and he adds, that those cases which appeared the least alarming were the most suddenly carried off.

VORACIOUS MAN-EATERS

Of all flesh upon which the tiger feeds, none seems to be so delicious to his horrid taste as that of human. He delights in striking down a buffalo, ox or deer, but when once he has tasted human flesh he leaves the wild haunts of abounding game and lurks about villages to steal man, woman or child, as chance may offer. With each victim he becomes bolder, until at last the tiger will even make his assaults in day-time, and take his human prey from the very streets, or even houses. Usually, however, he watches the road-sides, and when he discovers a person unattended, he stalks his victim in such a wary manner, creeping swiftly but softly, from bush to bush, that he is not seen or suspected, until his fatal spring is made. They have been known to leap onto a housetop and tear away the roof in order to get at the people within, but fortunately such adventures generally terminate disastrously to the invader, who, once getting inside is unable to get out, and though he may kill one or two of the occupants, is usually himself killed.

The measures adopted by the India Government, by which considerable rewards are paid for tiger scalps, has been of comparatively little benefit, as the scarcity of fire arms among the natives has prevented them from systematically hunting the dangerous beasts. In later years, however, English sportsmen have directed their attention to the tiger, particularly since the Prince of Wales made his famous

A STALKING TIGER KILLED BY A TOURIST.

hunt in India, and hundreds of these ferocious pests now fall every year before improved repeating rifles in the hands of these foreign hunters. In traveling the highways of that country, however, it is still important to be well armed, for tigers are yet quite common and their ravages very great. A story comes to us of a tourist with his wife, in 1886, having been stalked by a tiger on one of the most public roads, who saved his life by the fortunate circumstance of having a rifle with which he shot the beast.

The number of persons eaten by tigers every year, in Southern India is appalling, some authorities placing it as high as five thousand on an average; though this estimate is purely conjectural, it is by no means improbable, as several characteristic incidents which will hereafter be described will serve to show.

PECULIARITIES OF THE TIGER.

When about to bring forth her young the tigress retires to a dense jungle, taking special care to keep her retreat secret from the male, who, should he find the whelps, will eat them with the voraciousness he exhibits over the carcass of a buffalo. This propensity of the tiger to destroy his own progeny has the effect to keep down the population of these fierce marauders very materially, since it is estimated that fully one-half of those born fall victims to the gluttonous cannibalism of the male parent.

When the young are first brought forth they resemble nothing so much as bull-dog puppies, and are as helpless as young kittens during the first two weeks of their lives, but at the end of two months their ferocious instincts are so well developed that it would be dangerous for a man to attempt to handle them. During the period of whelphood they are very sportive with the mother and one another, whiling away the entire day in gamboling instead of sleeping, as do most animals of the feline species. The mother attends them with great care, providing for all their wants until they are about three months of age, when she takes them with her on the hunt and makes them lead the way. Should danger threaten, instead of braving it herself, the tigress compels her young to go before and bear the first attack, being apparently more regardful for her own safety than that of the cub, which she now seems to lose her affection for.

Though far from being an amphibious animal, and rarely taking the water except when forced to do so, the tiger is an expert swimmer, both in speed and endurance, and when cleaving the water it carries its shoulders very high, affording an excellent target for marksmen; but woe be unto any one who would approach it in a boat in the belief that it is powerless to do harm while swimming, for it can strike out of water with all the dreadful effectiveness it employs on land. Indeed, a story is related, on good authority, of a tiger which, being pressed by hunger, and seeing a schooner anchored not far from shore, boldly swam out to it and, despite a vigorous defense by the crew, contrived to board the vessel. The men, in affright, all jumped overboard, rather trusting themselves to the water than to stand before a fierce animal that was evidently bent on mischief. The tiger roamed about on board until he scented the larder, which he immediately tore open, and, after feasting to his content, leaped overboard again and returned to shore.

FIERCE COMBATS BETWEEN TIGERS AND LIONS.

In the early days of Rome, as every reader of ancient history knows, the populace were frequently entertained by gladiatorial com-

COMBAT OF THE JUNGLE MONARCHS.

bats and fights between wild animals, the favorite amusement being contests between lions and tigers. If the question be asked, which is the more powerful of these creatures, repeated battles between them show that the tiger is decidedly superior to the king of beasts.

A celebrated tiger, owned by the king of Oude, was brought to England some years ago, having been purchased for the sum of $2,000. It was called Jungla, and was kept for several years by the bestial potentate to furnish him with amusement in the gladiatorial ring. Time and again was it set upon the strongest lions that could be obtained, but in every contest it was victorious, having slain altogether nearly thirty lions. Shortly after its arrival in England, the keepers became spectators to a fierce battle between the new arrival and a favorite lion, resulting in the death of the latter inside of ten minutes.

The two creatures had been placed in a large iron cage, divided by a heavy partition in the center so as to separate the animals, but seeing his now common foe, the tiger was not long in tearing out the bars, and forcing his way into the lion's compartment. A desperate fight was at once begun, which no amount of beating and thrusting on the part of the attendants could stop, and they were thus forced to stand by and witness the fearful encounter. The lion wore a mane so heavy that his throat was well protected, and thus possessed an advantage very considerable, as the tiger had to confine its attack to its antagonist's legs and hindquarters. But a few minutes served to show the immense superiority of the tiger which, though lacerated somewhat about the neck, wounded the lion in such a horrid manner that in ten minutes the king of beasts was rendered helpless, while the tiger's injuries healed within two weeks.

In the combats referred to it was evidently the Asiatic lion that was engaged, for I am quite convinced that the African lion is superior to the tiger, as he is very much the superior of his Asiatic congener, as much so, indeed, as the African elephant is superior to the Asiatic species.

Though tigers, like lions, may be taken when young and so far tamed that they perform many amusing tricks and show considerable attachment for their keepers, yet they never entirely lose their fierce temper, and are very dangerous pets. The tragic death of a woman known as the "Lion Queen," which occurred some years ago, is an example of the untamable nature of the tiger. She was accustomed to perform twice every day with a tiger, going into his cage and making him leap over a whip, crouch, lift his paw, and run round her, until she regarded her employment as involving no more risks than were her great charge an affectionate dog, instead of a tiger who could deal death with one stroke of its paw, or a grasp of its murderous jaws. On one occasion the tiger seemed sullen and refused to obey its fair mistress, when she struck him a light blow with her whip, as was her custom; in a moment he sprang upon her, like the fiercest man-eater of India, forced her against the side of the cage and seized her throat. The horrified spectators rushed to her rescue and she was almost instantly extricated from the monster, but, alas, too late; that one grip of the tiger's jaws was enough; the woman was taken out of the cage dead.

HOW THE TIGER TAKES ITS PREY.

When seeking its prey the tiger never relies upon its strength or swiftness, both of which natural powers it possesses, but employs stealth, creeping cautiously toward its victim, availing itself of every cover, like the Indians who used to steal upon the settlers in the lonely West. More nearly like the Indian is the man-eating tiger that stalks his human prey, preferring defenseless women and children, and avoiding men, who, its cunning tells it, are usually armed. It is fond of lying in wait beside frequented roads, choosing some spot where there is the deepest shade and where water is near at hand, for, after eating, the tiger feels a great thirst that it must satisfy. From this dark covert he springs upon his victim with great precision, but it is a strange fact that should he miss his prey at the first leap, the tiger appears confused, and very rarely, if ever, returns to the attack, but makes off at great speed. It is said that the man-eating tigers are readily distinguishable from others by a darker hue of the skin and the redness of the eyes, this peculiarity of color being due, it is alleged, to the eating of human flesh. I very much doubt the assertion.

The places where there is the greatest probability of encountering a tiger are the crossing of nullahs—deep ravines—where water is found. Here he finds his two essentials, cover and water, without which he is a cowardly and helpless creature, neither given to attack nor standing to defend himself. But give him cover, and water near by, and the tiger will infest a locality so long as bullocks and people come his way.

Wood describes the following introduction which a deer-hunter had to a tiger in the *rhur* grasses of India: "He (the hunter) had crept up to a convenient spot, from whence he could command a clear view of the deer, which were lying asleep in the tall grass; he had taken aim at a fine buck which was only at twelve yards distance, and was just going to pull the trigger when his attention was aroused by a strange object which was waving above the grass, a few feet from the other side of the deer. It was the tail of a tiger, which had approached the deer from an opposite direction, and had singled out the very animal which was threatened by his rifle. Not exactly knowing what kind of an object it was that stirred the grass, the sportsman re-adjusted his piece, and was again going to fire, when a tiger sprang from his cover and leaped upon the very buck which had been marked out as his own. Under the circumstances he did not choose to dispute the matter, but retreated as quietly as possible, leaving the tiger in possession."

Another sportsman had a somewhat similar meeting, which he appreciated quite as little as the deer-hunter. Peacocks abound in the *rhur* grasses, their haunts being the same as the tiger's, so that peacock hunters are in constant danger of flushing the more serious game. On one occasion a hunter shot a peacock, but only wounded it in the wing, so that the bird made off through the grass with great rapidity, closely pursued by the excited sportsman; the chase was only for a few rods, when it was suddenly interrupted by a tiger, who roused up just in time to catch the wounded peacock and give the man a fright which he declares he never quite recovered from.

HUNTING THE TIGER.

There are several ways of destroying the fierce marauder of India, some of which I will briefly describe:

In one part of India the natives gather leaves of the *prauss* tree, which they bedaub with bird-lime and then deposit them over a considerable space of ground about the tiger's lair. The animal treads upon one of the leaves and finding that it sticks to his foot tries to pull it off, while at each exertion he picks up others, and by pawing and rolling over in his mad efforts to remove the leaves so besmears himself that he becomes blinded and helpless, and will not try to defend himself against the attacks of his human enemies.

A favorite way of capturing the tiger is by means of a large trap, made of heavy logs, at the entrance of which is a trap-door which drops the moment the animal puts its foot upon a set trigger. Inside the house is a small cage which confines a live dog or goat as an allurement for the tiger. The animal, hearing its favorite prey barking or bleating, goes into the trap, and in walking around trying to get at the bait steps on the trigger, and the next moment finds himself a prisoner.

The *Shikarrie* of southeast India, in hunting the tiger, takes more chances than his neighbors, whose devices I have just described, still his manner is far from sportsman-like, since it is somewhat cowardly.

When a tiger makes a raid on his cattle the Shikarrie watches the covert into which the bullock is dragged until he discovers the exact

TIGER HUNTING IN INDIA.

location of the carcass. The tiger, unless it be a man-eater, has no disposition to harm a human so long as opportunity offers for it to satisfy its hunger off domestic cattle; the Shikarrie, therefore, encounters little danger when watching the despoiler of his flocks, and, having located his lair, the hunter builds a strong platform upon a superstructure of large bamboo twenty feet high. Having completed this work he mounts to the summit of the scaffold with his gun and sword. Upon this safe retreat he watches for the tiger, which is near at hand, and manages to shoot the beast, occasionally, but the Shikarrie are never good sportsmen, and they more often wound than kill the tiger, in which latter event, though the hunter is out of reach, he is certain to be attacked. The tiger, perceiving the perch of its enemy, charges furiously up the hard bamboo stalks, into which it tries desperately to drive its claws; should the animal succeed in reaching the platform, as it sometimes does, the Shikarrie finds use for his sword, with which he cuts off the brute's fore-paws the moment they reach the edge of his retreat. Should the scaffolding fall under the tiger's assults, the hunter abandons himself at once, as well he might, to a horrid death which he is certain to suffer.

Should the tiger be killed, as it most frequently is, the neighbors are quickly attracted to the spot, with the hope of sharing the spoils, which are not inconsiderable. Besides the ordinary trophies, such as the skin, claws and teeth, there are other portions of the tiger more eagerly sought, such as the tongue and liver, which possess the greatest value. These organs are appropriated to the healing art, by first being cut into small cubes, after which they are dried and in this condition applied as remedies to perform all manner of cures.

Another mode of hunting the tiger, not much practiced now, but very popular in former days, is by the use of great nets into which the animal is driven by a large number of men and elephants. A tiger being first discovered is scared into the covert, where it remains until the nets are spread and everything is in readiness. The beaters now advance into the covert firing pistols, ringing bells, blowing horns and beating drums, making such a hideous din that the tiger is frightened and rushes out of its lair only to find that every avenue of escape is shut off save one, which leads to the nets; this latter it takes, only to find, at last, that it has chosen the most dangerous of all paths, for, becoming entangled in the net, the hunters quickly dispatch it with guns. Sometimes, even the noise of the beaters will not rouse the tiger, in which event rockets are set off which go ricocheting through the jungle, or just above it, like a monster fiery dragon.

This sight inspires the tiger with the most intense dread, and never fails to bring him quickly from his cover and in range of the guns of the hunters who have surrounded him.

POPULAR MODE OF HUNTING THE TIGER.

The most common manner of hunting the tiger now, since breach-loading and repeating rifles came into general use, is by bearding him

HIST! THE TIGER IS APPROACHING.

in his den, so to speak, as a genuine sportsman should. Two or three hunters usually go together, not so much for mutual protection as to make more certain of their game, as the hunt must be conducted in great fields of rhur grass or large tracts of jungles, from which the tiger might easily escape should any of the sides be left unguarded. The men proceed on foot, accompanied by beaters, whose duty it is, as just explained, to frighten the game so that it will come out and present itself a target for the hunters. This precaution is absolutely necessary, for the tiger loves to hide itself in as close a covert as it can find, and unless driven from its place of refuge by such frightful sounds, would lie closely crouched upon the ground, and either permit the hunters to pass by, or leap on them with a sudden spring, and so obtain a preliminary revenge for its own death.

There is a certain bushy shrub, called the *Korinda*, which is specially affected by tigers on account of the admirable cover which its branches afford. It does not grow to any great height, but its branches are thickly leaved, and droop over in such a manner that they form a dark arch of foliage, under which the animal may creep, and so lie hidden from prying eyes, and guarded from the unwelcome light and heat of the noon-day sun. So fond are the tigers of this mode of concealment that the hunters always direct their steps to the korinda bush, knowing well that if a tiger should be in the neighborhood, it would be tolerably certain to be lying under the sombre branches of the korinda shade.

If a tiger be fairly traced to its ordinary lair the sportsmen prefer to lie in wait at some convenient spot, and either to await the voluntary egress of the quarry or to send in the beaters and cause the animal to be driven out in the proper direction. When this mode is adopted it is found best to have, besides those which are held in hand, a whole battery of guns, eight or ten in number, which are laid on the ground, ready loaded and cocked, their muzzles all pointing toward the spot where the tiger is expected to make his appearance. The object of this expedient is twofold: firstly, to make sure of the animal in case the first shots fail to tell mortally; and, secondly, to be in readiness should a second or even a third tiger be driven from the bush. It is so usual an occurrence for two tigers to make their sudden appearance where only one was expected to lie, that the precaution is an absolutely necessary one.

Should the tiger not fall to the shot, but bound away, the hunters know whether the wound is a mortal one by inspecting the marks made in the ground by the feet of the retreating animal. It is a curious fact, that however hard a tiger may be hit, yet, if the wound be not a rapidly mortal one, the claws are kept retracted, and the footprints show no marks of the talons; but should the injury be one which will shortly cause death, the tiger flings out its limbs with the paws spread to their utmost, and at every leap tears up the ground with the protruding talons.

WONDERFUL BRAVERY OF THE GHOORKA TIGER HUNTERS.

The power and audacity of the tiger, which renders him the most dangerous of animals, is met with equal boldness by many native hunters who seek him in his fastnesses and make bold to attack him with the simplest of weapons. The best tiger hunters in India are the Ghoorka tribe, who occupy a considerable section in the mid-interior, where they keep a few domestic animals but rarely cultivate

GHOORKA HUNTER KILLING A TIGER.

the soil. They make the best of soldiers, and are famous for their daring and cunning. As there is a good reward paid by the government for tiger-scalps, and as the skins of the beautiful animals bring a fair price, the Ghoorkas spend much of their time in hunting, which is, indeed, their chief occupation. Previous to the general introduction of fire-arms into the country the natives hunted with no other weapons than the spear and sword, which could, of course, only be used in close quarters. The Ghoorka, however, relying upon his keen weapon and great dexterity, did not hesitate to enter the jungle, beat up the fiercest tiger, and invite his attack. One of these famous hunters, who died not long ago, is said to have killed more than a hundred tigers by skillfully cutting their throats as they charged him, which, if true, proves him to have been indeed a remarkable man.

WHY A SIMPLE WOUND PROVES MORTAL TO A TIGER.

The tiger has many weak points where a bullet does its work with great rapidity. The brain and heart are instantaneously mortal spots, and the lungs come next, though a tiger is capable of doing immense mischief with its lungs torn fairly out, but it soon succumbs. If struck in the liver, the tiger may live twenty minutes, and be able to fight furiously almost up to the moment of death.

"Perhaps of all animals," says Wood, "the tiger is one of the easiest to kill, although the wound may not be an instantaneous (I would say, direct) cause of death. Whether the cause may lie in the habits or diet of the creature is not certain, but true it is, that a wound inflicted on a tiger very soon assumes an angry appearance, becomes tainted, and affords a resting-place for the pestilent blow-flies, which take such a hold on the poor beast that even a slightly wounded tiger has been known to die, not from the immediate effects of the injury, but from the devouring maggots which swarmed in and about the wound." How doubly singular is it, therefore, that a very small wound inflicted by a tiger on a man will produce death, while that animal also dies from the effects of an equally trifling injury.

Hunting the tiger from the back of an elephant is anything but sport, and is only indulged in by those who are either destitute of courage or too effeminate to bear the fatigue of a march on foot and the weight of a gun. Royalty goes out in gay tinsel, perched in a gorgeously bedecked howdah, in quest of tigers, but the true sportsman disdains such advantage, for genuine honors of the chase can only be won by a display of courage and endurance, elements of man hood which weaklings do not possess.

CANNIBAL PROPENSITIES OF THE TIGER.

In the descriptions, contained in foregoing pages, of the lion, I re ferred to the occasional propensity displayed by that animal to feast upon its own species, giving an illustration in point from Andersson's adventures. A similar disposition is attributed to the tiger by Sanderson, though I do not remember having seen any confirmation of the charge in the writings of other sportsmen. In charging the tiger with cannibalism, Sanderson cites the following incident in proof:

"One of the strangest things I ever heard in connection with tigers, is an instance of three tigers devouring a fourth. This was also told me by Bommay Gouda and two Sholagas (his beaters, who were with him at the time of the occurrence). For my own part I believe the story. It was that a male tiger killed a buffalo late one evening; the carcass was found partially eaten next day; and the following, or second morning, when some low caste men, under Bom-

A TIGER'S DARING ATTACK ON AN INDIA OFFICER.

may Gouda's guidance, went to take whatever might be left, they found the head and shoulders of a large tiger, and some bones of the buffalo. The ground around bore traces of a savage fight, and it was found that a party of three tigers had disturbed the original slayer of the buffalo at supper, and the struggle which ensued for possession ended in his death."

Another occurrence somewhat similar is related by Walter Elliot, as follows: "Another instance was related by a celebrated sportsman in Khandeish, who, having killed a tigress, on his return to his tents sent a pad-elephant to bring it home. The messenger returned, reporting that on his arrival he found her alive. They went out next morning to the spot, and discovered that she had been dragged into a ravine by another tiger, and half the carcass devoured."

A MAN-EATING TIGER DESTROYS AN INDIAN OFFICER.

It is almost impossible to exaggerate the audacity of a man-eating tiger when roused to action by hunger. His thirst for human flesh seems to make him utterly insensible to danger, as the following incident will serve to show:

During the English conquest of India a company of native cavalry was conducting a reconnoissance in the vicinity of Lucknow when, in passing through a jungle rarely frequented by man, though in the immediate vicinity of a public highway, a most distressing accident occurred. The chief of the company was riding some twenty or thirty yards in advance of his men, utterly unconscious of any lurking danger, when suddenly, from out a thick clump, a large tiger sprang upon him with such impetuosity that both horse and rider were dashed to the ground. The advance of the company was within full sight of the occurrence, but neither their presence nor their cries served to beat off the desperate animal, which continued its fearful attack until shot by a dozen balls, and killed. The officer was so severely bitten in the breast that he died the following night.

DESPERATE RAVAGES OF A MAN-EATING TIGRESS.

In 1873, about September, as Sanderson, the hunter, relates, the town of Morley and surrounding neighborhood was in a state of intense excitement from the horrible ravages of a man-eating tigress. This animal's fits of man-eating appeared to be intermittent, for after killing three or four persons she would give over her horrid feasting on human flesh for a month or more. But at the time of Sanderson's arrival she had just killed two boys who were attending goats, preferring their bodies to that of either goats or bullocks.

On the 30th of November, when the work people had dispersed, news was brought in to the effect that a man, while returning to the village of Nagwully (six miles from Morley) with cattle, had been carried off the evening before. From an account of the place where the mishap had occurred, Sanderson knew it was useless to look for the tigress after the lapse of eighteen hours, as she would have retired to the dense jungle, and her tracks be lost. He therefore urged the people to bring news of further losses at the earliest possible moment.

On the 19th of December another man was carried off close to the village of Iyenpoor, five miles from Morley, but Sanderson was not notified until two days afterward. On Christmas day Sanderson took an elephant and some trackers with the intention of making a search in the jungles about Iyenpoor for tracks of the dreadful beast. Upon entering the village the widow of the tigress' last victim, followed by her three children, approached him with singular apathy and related what she knew concerning her husband's death. He gave her some money, as she would have to expend a small sum, in accordance with caste usage, to rid her of the devil by which she was supposed to be attended on account of her husband having been killed by a tiger, before she would be admitted into her caste's villages; and then, accompanied by the headman and others, went to the scene of the last disaster. A solitary tamarind tree grew on some rocks close to the village; there were no jungles within three hundred yards, only a few bushes in the crevices of the rocks; close by was the broad cattle-track into the village. The unfortunate man had been following the cattle home in the evening, and must have stopped to knock down some tamarinds with his stick, which, with his black blanket and a skin skull-cap, still lay where he was seized. The tigress had been hidden in the rocks, and in one bound seized him, dragged him to the edge of a small plateau of rocks, from which she jumped down into a field below, and there killed him. The place was still marked by a pool of dried blood. She had then dragged her victim half a mile, to a spot where were still found his leg bones.

Sanderson continued his search in the vicinity of Iyenpoor for about ten days without being able to get on to the track of the tigress, or to hear any word from the natives concerning her. At the expiration of this time, however, he was startled while eating his dinner by the cry of natives, who had come in from another village near by with the report that one of their people, while participating in a festival, had been seized and borne away by the man-eater. On the following day Sanderson again went in pursuit with his trackers, and was not long in coming upon the tigress' tracks. While examining these some crows attracted his attention, as they were hovering and cawing about a spot only a few hundred yards distant. Repairing to this place he found the remains of the man last taken, consisting only of the soles of his feet, palms of his hands, his head, and a few bones, over which the crows were disputing. Sanderson now followed fast on the tracks of the beast, only to find that the animal had crossed the river and made good her escape in the hills beyond, where it was useless to pursue her.

A PRIEST EATEN BY A TIGER.

About one week after this, the priest of a small temple ten miles due west of Morley, and in a comparatively open country, where a tiger had not been heard of for years, was jogging along on his riding bullock one morning, to sweep out and garnish the small jungle-temple in which he officiated, and to present to the god "Yeunay Hollay Koombappah" the offerings of the simple villagers whose faith was placed in that deity. Suddenly a tigress with her cub stepped into the path. The terrified bullock kicked off his rider and galloped back to the village, while the tigress—for it was the dreaded Iyenpoor man-eater, far out of her ordinary haunts—seized the bapless priest and carried him off to the bed of a deep ravine near.

The next death was of a horrible description. Several villagers of Ramasomoodrum were grazing their cattle in a swampy hollow in the jungle near the temple, when the tigress pounced upon one man who was separated from the others. She in some way missed her aim at his throat, seized the shoulder, and then, either in jerking him, or by a blow, threw him up into a thicket, several feet from the ground. Here the wounded and bleeding wretch was caught by thorny creepers, while the tigress, as generally happens when any *contretemps* takes place, relinquished the attack and made off. The other men and cattle had fled at the first alarm. The village was some distance away, and there was not time before night-fall for a party to search for the man, whose being still alive was not known.

Next morning the lacerated wretch was found. In his mangled state he had been unable to release himself; he was moaning and hanging almost head downwards among the creepers, and he died soon after he was taken down.

Sanderson left nothing undone to hunt down the beast that was so rapidly thinning out the Indian population, but though he had a hundred trackers with him scouring the country it was impossible to start the game, or even to come upon fresh tracks. No sooner were tracks discovered than it was found they were made by the animal returning from its forage and going back to the large hills, which were so densely covered with jungle that there was no possibility of a man penetrating them.

After the death of the Ramasamoodrum villager, nothing further was heard of the man-eater until the 14th of January, 1874, when the death-cry was raised at another village called Bussavanpoor, only two miles from Morley. This town was a small settlement, situated in the middle of open rice-fields, then bare. There was no jungle to cover the man-eater's advance, and a tiger had never hitherto been heard of near the village. This attack was therefore the more unlooked for and terrifying to the villagers. The attack had been most daring. At one end of the single street of the village stood a shady tree, round the base of which a raised terrace of stones and earth had been built as a public seat; within ten yards of this tree the houses began. From the marks that were left plain to be seen, the tigress had crouched upon this raised terrace, from which she commanded a view of the street. The nearest house on one side was occupied by an old woman; the one opposite by her married daughter, who, it appeared, sometimes slept in her own house, sometimes at her mother's. The night before she had been going to her mother's, and as she crossed the street, only a few feet wide, the tigress with one silent bound seized and carried her off. No one heard any noise, and the poor creature was not missed until morning.

HOW THE GREAT MAN-EATER WAS FINALLY SLAIN.

Sanderson, having come into the country for the purpose of destroying this most terrible of beasts, felt vexed beyond measure at his persistent yet futile efforts to come up with the tigress, which appeared, as the natives declared, to be in league with the devil, and therefore able to disappear at will. After the last fatal occurrence he resolved upon another mode of hunting this dreadful quarry, to which end he procured an elephant for his own use, and then divided his trackers into parties, each to pursue a different way and thus cover a large district of country. These parties were instructed to report to him, immediately, any news of the animal, so that he might be able to concentrate his men at points to cut off the beast's retreat.

Sanderson had started out his detachments early on the afternoon of the 15th day of January, and was rejoiced to learn in an hour afterwards, that four of his trackers had discovered the creature in a small hill hardly two miles distant. Fortunately this hill rose up about two hundred feet out of a level, cultivated plain, and its sides were so bare

A WOMAN CARRIED OFF BY A TIGRESS.

that a more favorable spot could not have been selected by the hunters to make their success more certain. There was no jungle in less than five hundred yards of this hill, so that, so long as the tigress remained here, she was perfectly isolated. Sanderson, at first, believed the tigress was still on the hill, so excited were the trackers in making their report, but he soon learned that it was on the hillside she had been discovered while dragging a bullock up its sides, and being frightened off she had sullenly retired to the jungle near by. He now arranged to receive her when she should return to her repast. On account of the barrenness of the country he had to cut branches and pile them upon a small shrub which stood in the plain, at least seventy-five yards from where the bullock lay, but, having completed his blind, he sent all the trackers away save one, and then settled down to watch for the tigress' coming.

Sanderson and his faithful companion sat through several weary hours and until twilight shadows began to steal over the landscape in a kind of mist, and they feared that their quarry would postpone her visit until it was too dark to shoot with any hope of precision. I will finish this description in Mr. Sanderson's language:

"We had been whispering quietly, as we were out of ear-shot of the cover, and Bommay Gouda had just said, after a glance at the setting sun, that it was the time, *par excellence*, for a tiger's return to its prey, when a pea-hen, which had been hidden among the boulders on the hillside to our right, rose with a startling clamor. This signal, well known as unmistakable, made us glance through the leafy screen, and there we saw the man-eater, a handsome but small tigress, her color doubly rich in the light of the sinking sun, walk from behind a rock across the side of the hill, here a barren sheet of blue granite, and come downwards towards the carcass. She halted now and again to look far out in the plain towards us. Was the beast dreaded by thousands, hunted by us so long, and which we had never even seen before, the guilty murderess, really before us? Could nothing but some untoward failure now avert her fate?

"I followed her so eagerly with my rifle that Bommay Gouda whispered to me to let her get to the carcass before I fired. When she reached the bullock she stopped, and at the same moment I fired at her shoulder, broadside on, with my express rifle. Bommay Gouda could contain himself no longer, and jumped up before I could stop him; I did so also, but could see no tigress. It was extraordinary certainly; we looked up the hillside but she was not there. Was she really a devil, as all believed, and had she vanished in air? Just then up went a tail on the far side of the bullock in a convulsive quiver; she had fallen exactly behind the carcass. I ran along the hillside to intercept her should she gain her feet; but it was all right; she was only opening her mouth in spasmodic gasps, and I settled her. On examing her we found she was in milk. She was in prime condition and had no apparent injury to account for her having taken to man killing. Her cub was heard calling its mother for several nights about Iyenpoor, but we never succeeded in killing it, and it is possible that the little thing died of starvation, else we must have sometime encountered it."

TERRIBLE ADVENTURE WITH A TIGER.

Sir Samuel Baker, in his "True Tales for My Grandsons," relates a very interesting story of a tiger hunt, ending in a thrilling adventure, from which I abstract the following: * * * * "Suddenly, but without sound, a magnificent black-striped head emerged from behind the thick bush into the bright sun-light, and slowly the form of an immense male tiger moved forward into the open space. As the head appeared, Everard had quietly raised his rifle to his shoulder, and waited for a few seconds, until as the tiger stepped slowly on, he took the sight exactly in a line with a fore-leg, and aimed at the center of the forehead. * * * He fired!

"The tiger sprang upon its hind legs, rearing to its full height, and with tremendous roars which rang in terrible notes through the forest, it fell backwards in several convulsive struggles beneath the dark green bush, where, after a series of loud growls which gradually relapsed into deep, low groans, it lay extended with its massive head beneath the shade of the evergreen.

"There was a thrill of satisfaction through Everard's frame; the tiger was dead, and he was about to raise a loud whistle upon his fingers as a signal, when two shots, in quick succession, were heard from the position occupied by Major Selwyn. 'That must be the tigress,' thought Everard, 'Selwyn is certain not to miss her.' * * * Half a minute later he was hurrying towards the station of his companion.

"'Take care!' shouted Selwyn, as he observed his approach, 'she's badly hit, and has rolled into those thick bushes. Don't go too near, but come up here until the beaters arrive, we must have the elephants to drive her out.'

"Nine accidents out of ten occur when animals have been wounded. It is impossible to be too careful in approaching a wounded beast; the tiger, lion, leopard, bear or buffalo that would have retreated when fresh, will assuredly attack if followed up when wounded.

"In a very short time anxious faces could be seen approaching, and it was quickly explained that one tiger was dead, while the other was severely wounded and concealed within the thick brush. A great number of men were quickly assembled and orders given that a messenger should be dispatched to summon the two elephants.

"In the meantime one of the shikarries ascended a tree within the thick jungle, and shouted to the other that he could see the tigress lying dead. A village shikarrie, who wished to exhibit his superior courage, collected several large stones and, advancing to the edge of the dense bush, threw one in the direction suggested by the man within the tree, who actually saw, or thought he saw, the tigress. No response was made to the first stone. Another was thrown with the same passive result. The tigress was declared to be dead, and the man forced his way into the jungle.

"Almost at the same moment a terrific roar was heard, and the tigress, with one bound, was upon him! Seizing the unfortunate man by the throat, she dragged him into the impervious thicket, where a succession of cruel roars and growls showed that she was tearing him to pieces. This had happened so instantaneously and unexpectedly that it had been impossible to render the slightest assistance. It was an agonizing moment, but hardly had the reality of the terrible event been impressed upon the bystanders when Everard, without a moment's hesitation, rushed to the spot, and throwing himself upon all fours, crept into the thorny jungle upon the track where the tigress had disappeared with her victim. With his rifle cocked and ready he lay flat beneath the bushes, and crept forward with caution but cool determination. He was not aware that the courageous shikarrie, armed only with his short spear, had followed close behind him, and was creeping on his hands and knees literally at his heels. A smothered cry from the native, mingled with the growls of the tigress, hurried the advance of Everard, who in a few seconds had crawled within view of the disastrous scene. Lying down upon the ground he distinctly saw the tigress holding the man by the back of his neck as she crouched upon the ground by his side; she was about four or five yards distant, and appeared to have given her whole attention to the destruction of her victim. Everard was in a distressing position. If he knelt he could not see the tigress through the dense thicket sufficiently well to insure a fatal shot; if he remained prostrate there would be a difficulty in taking aim, as the body of the man was dangerously exposed to his bullet.

"There was little time for consideration; the tigress suddenly discovered the approach of her new enemies, and without relaxing her grip of the neck, she changed her position and faced the coming attack. At that instant, with a cool and steady aim, Everard fired, hoping to reach the heart by striking her a little to the left in a line with her chin, as she crouched upon the ground. His bullet must have passed within an inch of the native's head, as the tigress pinned his neck firmly to the ground.

"At the report of the rifle, in the cloud of smoke, the tiger had bounded forward; Everard felt a heavy weight upon his legs, only for one moment, as he rolled quickly upon his side beneath the bushes, and then immediately sprang upon his feet! For an instant he turned round, being ready with his remaining barrel to meet the unknown danger, when, through the clearing smoke, he saw the body of the tigress at his feet, with the spear of the shikarrie buried at least three feet deep in her breast. The shikarrie was still holding the shaft of his weapon as he knelt upon the ground. The tigress was quite dead. Everard's bullet had passed through her heart, but her convulsive spring had carried her beyond his body as he lay close to the earth, and she had been fatally received upon the projected spear of the trusty shikarrie, who had brought his weapon to the ready on the same instant that he had observed Everard prepared to fire. She had completely impaled herself, and the spear had passed through heart and lung. The first impulse was to rescue the unfortunate native, whose body was now dragged from the thick bushes. Life was quite extinct; the bone of the neck had been dislocated by the wrench of the tigress' powerful jaws; deep gashes, inflicted by the claws, had cut the head and face to the bone, and a pool of blood was discovered where the tigress had first dragged the body."

FIGHTS BETWEEN THE ELEPHANT AND TIGER.

Every animal retires before the lordly elephant, whose mastery it is seldom that any creature, save man, attempts to dispute. The tiger will seek cover when it even winds an elephant, and at the sight it flees precipitately. This is true, generally speaking, and yet there are times when the tiger will brook no insolence from any creature, and, indeed, will attack the lordly monster without provocation. The time when the tiger grows boldest is the mating period, though he is subject to fits of anger at all times, when he will spend his madness upon any animal that crosses his path, regardless of the character of his antagonist. Those who have hunted the tiger by the aid of an elephant know that it not infrequently happens, in passing through the tall dry grass, where the animal is most generally found, that a tiger will rush out and attack the elephant, even though several hunters may be on his back. In making his onslaught the tiger generally attempts to seize the elephant's trunk, fully realizing the tenderness as well as use of that member. In the wild state the elephant makes a gallant defence and charges valorously, but with cat-like agility the tiger avoids his thrusts and efforts to trample, and usually manages to terribly mangle the giant's proboscis, or inflict such wounds on its flanks or legs as compel him to beat a retreat, the tiger rarely receiving any injuries himself.

Mr. Coryell, however, in a resent number of St. Nicholas, describes a fight between an elephant and a tiger in which the latter came off ingloriously, by sacrificing his life in an attempt to make a feast off a baby elephant. Describing this exciting contest Coryell writes, as follows:

"One of a party of hunters in India left camp one evening, intending to shoot one of the peacocks which were heard screaming in their discordant way not far from camp. He knew, from experience, that he might find a tiger in the neighborhood, though up to that time no traces of that animal had been seen. But the tiger is so fond of peacock that experienced hunters always go cautiously to shoot the birds.

"In this case the caution was wise, for when near the spot where the birds were, the hunter just saved himself from stumbling on a large tiger, which, fortunately, was so much taken up with stealing upon the birds that it did not notice the man. The latter, anticipating some interesting sport, watched the tiger move stealthily through the underbrush and come upon the noisy birds. Whoever has seen an ordinary cat crouch and spring can comprehend what the hunter saw. The spring was unsuccessful, however; and, as is its custom, the tiger, as if ashamed of his failure, was slinking away, when there came a noise of crashing underbrush, and the graceful creature crouched closely to the ground.

The noise, as the hunter had at once suspected, was caused by the approach of a herd of elephants. Again he waited silently for

BATTLE BETWEEN THE ELEPHANT AND TIGER.

further aevelopments. The huge creatures made their way straight toward the clearing where the peacocks had been feeding on the grain which grew there. At the head of the herd gamboled a baby elephant. Unconscious of the presence of the tiger, the little creature was almost upon it, when the great cat, as if unable to resist the temptation, darted toward it. Like magic the whole herd responded to the shrill cry of the mother, and the leader of the herd charged to the rescue.

The tiger seemed willing to retreat, but that the leader would not permit, and then began a fierce combat in which the tiger, with all its agility, strove to take the elephant anywhere but in front. To avoid this, the elephant moved about with astonishing celerity, and finally, with a quick plunge, caught the tiger under its ponderous foot, and with one terrible thrust pierced it with its tusks."

CHAPTER XXIX.

THE ELEPHANT.

FEW animals are more familiar, in a general way, to all people than the elephant, and of zoological curiosities he is the most common, yet familiarity in his case does not breed contempt, for eye will never tire viewing his colossal proportions and singular ways, nor will ear grow weary listening to stories of his sagacity and the stirring adventures in which he figures.

One of the strangest things, because utterly unaccountable, is the fact that, although elephants have been used as beasts of burden in India from time immemorial, no mention of them is made in Bible history, nor is there any evidence of them prior to the comparatively recent period of the Roman occupation. We know that it was the custom of Egyptians to portray the animals with which they were acquainted upon the walls of their temples and public buildings, and even upon the bricks of which their houses were constructed. But the most critical research fails to show any illustration of the elephant prior to the Christian era, though it is beyond doubt that vast herds of them existed in Africa and India.

Mention made in the Bible of "behemoth," if the term applies to the hippopotamus, clearly indicates a very significent fact, viz.: That the interior of Africa was not an utterly unknown region, even when Moses took his flight into Egypt, and since the elephant was found in

A HERD OF ELEPHANTS AT THE BATH.

Egypt since the date of its first discovery, a mention of the one great beast and not of the other greater one, is irreconcilable with any hypothesis that any naturalist has yet advanced, and is only equalled by the fact that of all domestic animals the camel is the only species that is not known to have at one time existed in a wild state.

There are two species of elephants, designated according to the countries to which they are peculiar, as the African and Asiatic. There are marked differences between the two, not, perhaps, in habit or disposition, but in physical features, chief of which may be mentioned, that the African species attains a much greater size, his ears and eyes are larger and his color darker than the Asiatic species; another disparity is found in the African possessing gigantic tusks, both male and female, while the Asiatic male elephant has small tusks and the female none whatever. The Ceylon elephant, though not regarded as being a distinct species, is different from both the African and Asiatic, in that it is much smaller and is of a gray color. I believe all native Ceylon elephants are destitute of tusks.

A very pleasing fiction is entertained by a large majority of people, whose information is received from the romances of superficial travelers who, in order to write something interesting, seize upon old stories that are veneered with orientalism. The fiction to which I refer is a belief in the existence of a white elephant, which, it is maintained, the Brahmins worship under a belief that it contains the soul of Buddha. Even some natural histories encourage this false idea; Wood says: "Sometimes an albino or white elephant is seen in the forests, the color of the animal being a pinky white, and aptly compared to the nose of a white horse." The American encyclopædia refers to this supposed freak of nature in this way: "Pure white albino elephants are very rarely seen;" giving the subject no further attention.

MY EXPERIENCE WITH A WHITE ELEPHANT.

During a visit which I made to Russia and Siberia, in 1882, I fell into a strange adventure with a white elephant, which has been described in the press of the country, but incorrectly. On an occasion, while wandering in the Alexander Zoological Garden of St. Petersburg, my attention was attracted by a very beautiful elephant, standing in its stall, beside which stood a number of people who were being amused by its tricks. I remarked, at once, to my guide, its extremely light color, which may be compared to the mark of a slate-pencil on a slate, and immediately made inquiry concerning its history. Through my guide I obtained an introduction to the keeper of the royal garden and from him soon learned that my first impression of the animal being a white elephant was correct, which greatly added to my curiosity. Further inquiry revealed the fact that the elephant, which was a superb female, had been presented to Alexander II. by the Emir of India, as a token of his royal appreciation for the recession of a large strip of territory, which the Czar had taken from Thibet, about 1859, and restored under treaty three years later. The animal was accompanied, at the time, by a castrate Singalese slave, who still attended it at the time of my visit. From this slave, who was a bright fellow, I learned a great deal concerning the so-called white elephant of India, Burmah and Siam, which fortified me against the fiction which nearly every one in a Christian country seems to accept implicitly.

THE WHITE ELEPHANT IS NEVER WORSHIPPED.

The white elephant is distinguished from his confreres by having a lighter skin, and pinkish splotches on the trunk, breast and fore-legs; but this peculiarity is not one of birth, since it is the result of a skin disease resembling mange. I may also add that these so-called white elephants are no more worshipped by Buddhists than is Maud S. and other fine stock of his noted stables worshipped by Bonner. It is frequently the case that the King of Burmah, for example, covers his elephants with gorgeous trappings and maintains certain officers who are called "keepers of the white elephants," but the term is not more significant than that of "Knight of the Bath." The flag of Burmah bears in its center the device of an elephant, but not a white one, being symbolical of power, similar to the lion of England, and the eagle of America. Gray, or pseudo white, elephants are rare, and are supposed to be more beautiful than the dark colored animals, hence the kings of certain Oriental countries hold them in great value and bestow upon them unusual attention. The same may be said of the Russian custom of estimating black horses, for the attention which Muscovites pay to their raven horses is akin to veneration.

But knowing how Americans and Europeans regard the supposititious white elephant of India, and the value of one for exhibition purposes, I at once set about making overtures to secure the animal for a tour of the United States. Having been previously presented to Count Tolstoi—who was closer to the Czar than any other official in the

Empire—by our minister extraordinary, Judge Hunt, I represented my project to him and requested his aid in obtaining the consent of the Czar, who was the owner of the elephant, to bring the animal to America for one or two seasons, proffering a bond of $50,000 for its safe return, stating at the same time that the American people would esteem the loan of the animal as another mark of his majesty's high regard for the Republic.

Two days thereafter I was delighted to hear from Count Tolstoi that the Czar had given his consent, together with a gracious reply to my communication, assuring me of his warm feeling for America. The news of the early removal of "Chin Chang"—the elephant's name—to America soon spread throughout St. Petersburg, and created the most profound excitement. Minister Hunt declared to me that he drove to the zoological garden, with his family, on three successive days to see the animal, but was unable to gain admission on account of the great crowds which thronged the place taking an affectionate leave of the elephant, which previous to this did not appear to receive much attention. The daily papers published whole pages of matter concerning the animal and its strange history, and universally deprecated the action of the Czar in consenting to its temporary removal. Indeed, the excitement was equally as intense as that displayed by Londoners over the removal of Jumbo to America.

A CONTRACT WITH BARNUM.

Having perfected my arrangements I returned to the United States, and immediately sought P. T. Barnum, with whom I entered into a contract to rent him the elephant for a period of two years for the sum of $25,000, he to pay all expenses of the animal's care and removal, and to also provide the bond that was required. This contract being signed, Mr. Barnum sent two men with me back to St. Petersburg to accept the elephant and bring it to America.

Upon arriving at the Russian Capital, in company with the agents sent by Mr. Barnum, I repaired to the garden for our charge and to arrange the bond with Emile Raust, the Czar's representative. I cannot avoid acknowledging the chagrin which I felt when the agent, after examining the animal, refused to accept it as a white elephant, because it was not as "white as milk," as he expressed it. The Czar's certificate, as well as that of our minister plenipotentiary, the well established history, the color so extraordinary, as he confessed, had no effect upon Mr. Barnum's agent; he took his stand that it was not as white as milk, which I never represented it to be, but on the other hand covered a slate with pencil marks, to show Mr. Barnum

THE SO-CALLED WHITE ELEPHANT.

its exact color, and thus supposed there could be no possibility of difference in the last moment. Suffice it to say, that this supreme ignorance of what a white elephant really is, upon the part of his agent, lost Mr. Barnum not less than one million dollars, and I had the consolation soon after of knowing that his chagrin was equal to my own because the elephant was not accepted. Overtures were again made to the Czar for the animal, but justly enough he refused to consider them, and to atone for the supremely great mistake, Mr. Barnum's partners insisted on bringing a small scrubby specimen of the Ceylon elephant to America and exhibiting it as a white elephant. This proved a most unprofitable venture, for the imposition was only too apparent. The animal thus exhibited bore no comparison either in size or color to Chin Chang, the former being dark, while Chin Chang was a beautiful and extremely light elephant, and besides being very large was the most docile and best trained animal that perhaps ever performed in public. But more than this, Chin Chang was a genuine, so-called, white elephant, and had been for years the property of the Emir of India, who had kept it in a stable filled with barbaric splendors, until he presented it with much ceremony, as a white elephant, to Alexander II., while the animal exhibited as a white elephant in this country could hardly be called a fair specimen of the species, and certainly could not rank above the commonest kind.

HUNTING THE ELEPHANT.

Although there is scarcely a peceptible difference in the adaptability and temperament of the African and Asiatic species, each being easily trained and made domestic, yet there is a wide variance in the uses to which they are put, which has given rise to the belief that the Asiatic is more tractable than the African elephant, or that it is quicker to learn, if not more sagacious, a belief that is without foundation in fact.

In India and Ceylon, where elephants are more commonly employed as work animals, the natives regard them exactly as we do horses. Men are employed to catch elephants and train them, a service which is almost as common as the rounding up of cattle for branding, and these animals constitute almost the sole reliance of certain classes who build houses, clear forests, and haul great loads, a service to which the elephant is quick to adapt himself. This makes him a domestic animal, and he takes the place of the horse with wonderful resignation and faithfulness.

In Africa we never see the elephant in service, not because he is less reliable than his Asiatic brother, but entirely because the Africans are never a laboring people, and chiefly because they are natural hunters, subsisting from day to day by the chase. Many of the tribes have large herds of cattle, which they are slow to slaughter even in times of food distress, because cattle constitute the African's measure of wealth; and even though they may go naked, they are, nevertheless, full of the pride which vaunts itself in a vulgar display of wealth. Every tribe in Africa regards the elephant as lawful prey, the flesh whereof they eat, while the ivory is gathered to trade with the Arabs for calicoes, beads, gew-gaws, etc.; consequently they never make the least attempt to domesticate this useful animal.

Hunting the elephant may be classed very properly among the royal sports, because, though the largest of beasts, it is also the most cunning, and a dangerous quarry at all times. All animals flee before man, and he therefore possesses an advantage which gives him a rulership, so to speak, over all. But the man who relies entirely upon this point of superiority, and makes his attacks on the elephant with impunity, will most likely be killed before he wins any great reputation as an elephant hunter. So naturally docile is this animal that a person may approach within a few yards without exciting its fears or anger; but when he once attacks he finds that a very fiend of vengeance is suddenly loosed from which he *may* escape if fortune favors him with sufficient speed.

CAPTURING THE ELEPHANT.

There are two modes of capturing the Asiatic elephant, each of a fairly gentle character, since rough means would either result in the animal's probable death or injury, or the embitterment of its nature so that it would always be dangerous. One of these modes is very simple, being nothing more than the driving of the animals, by a number of beaters, into a previously prepared pound, made of heavy timbers laid into a fence strongly braced. Once within this inclosure, the animals are fettered by means of rope-snares, so laid that they are certain to step into them.

The other method is more commonly employed, and is, at the same time, more exciting. The hunters, of which there are usually several, are aided by two or more trained female elephants, termed *koomkies*, which enter into the spirit of their duties with animation and cunning. When the koomkies perceive a wild male elephant they advance carelessly toward him, ridden by their drivers, called *mahouts*, to whom the wild animals are perfectly indifferent so long as they are on the back

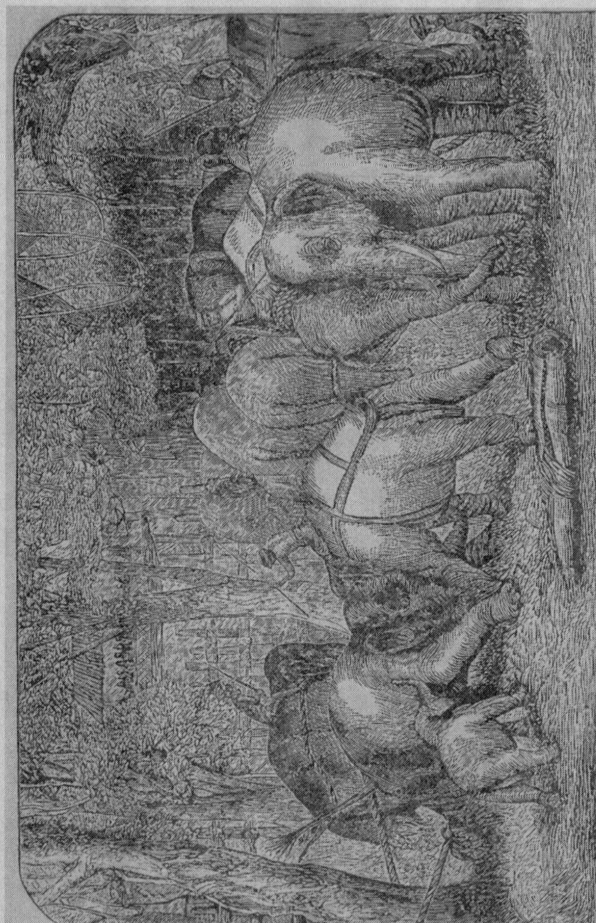

MANNER OF CAPTURING THE ASIATIC ELEPHANT.

of one of their kind. The male is soon attracted to the females, which, no sooner do they approach than they begin to lavish on him the most affectionate caresses, twining their trunks about his legs and rubbing up so closely that he feels ecstatic under their feminine influence. Being so happily engaged, the male takes no notice of the mahout, who now leaves his perch on the female's neck and, sliding down over her rump, he soon attaches ropes to the enormous elephant, and makes them also fast to neighboring trees. Should this affectionate meeting occur in a plain, the sagacious koomkies urge their victim toward the nearest trees that are strong enough for the purpose now soon to be employed. When the binding is thus completed the females move away in a cruelly indifferent manner, and leave their inveigled wild mate to his own resources.

Finding himself deserted and bound, he becomes fairly frenzied with rage and struggles with desperate energy to break his bonds. In these furious efforts the elephant displays a flexibility of body that is quite astonishing, and at utter variance with his clumsy aspect. He rolls on the ground, pitches, turns somersaults, and rends the air with piercing screams of rage. Again, he will rise and butt the trees to which he is bound with all his energy, trying to break them down; failing in this he again tumbles, sits on his haunches, then turns over, and sometimes stands on his head, with hind-legs elevated, straining in desperate might to part the thongs.

Formerly animals captured in this way were allowed to remain bound until they were reduced by hunger and exhaustion to subjection, but the growing scarcity of elephants has caused the hunters to treat them more carefully. Frequently, when long confined, the animals would injure their legs beyond recovery, and occasionally they died from exhaustion. Now the treatment is more humane. After a captive passes through his first paroxysms he is released and taken to a pen specially prepared; in doing this the koomkies are indispensable, for it is they that lead the captive away from the scene of his struggles and guide him into the pen.

So thoroughly do the trained female elephants enter into the sport of capturing males, that it is related by several naturalists, who claim to have confirmed the report, that a certain koomky, on one occasion, went into the forest, wholly unattended, and there captured a fine male, which she tied to a tree by means of some ropes which she carried for the purpose. If this story is true it is a striking demonstration of elephantine reason, and is only paralled by another equally intelligent action of a working elephant, which Wood relates: "The circumstances were these: Several elephants were engaged in the construction of a large log house, their duties being to carry the hewn logs and adjust them in place, which act alone requires a wonderful exhibition of instinct. Occasionally the logs would be improperly placed, in which cases the elephant so offending, was made to do his work over. At length, when the building was about half raised one of the animals was observed to be shirking, and as he stood up close against the logs he had laid, no amount of ordering to resume his labors had any effect, for he continued to stand immovable. Finally, by a vigorous use of pikes, he was driven away, when the cause of his obstinacy was immediately apparent. The elephant had performed his work improperly, and, knowing that he would have to do it over when the defects were discovered, he adopted this expedient of hiding the imperfect work by covering it with his body. In further proof of this I have only to add that the moment he was forced to expose the misplaced logs, without further orders he turned at once to relay them right."

HUNTING THE AFRICAN ELEPHANT.

Since the elephant is never used as a beast of burden in Africa, no efforts are ever made to take it alive, the natives being tempted to hunt it purely for its flesh and ivory, the latter being an article of great value and applied to a great variety of purposes. Formerly elephants were comparatively plentiful throughout that extensive range of country lying between the Soudan and Cape Colony. Its ruthless destruction by adventurers and Arabs, armed with repeating rifles and other modern enginery, has so far diminished the number that comparatively few are now seen save in the vicinity of the lakes of Central Africa. Although abundant in these localities it is not often seen by casual travelers, owing to its great vigilance, and the wonderful power it possesses of moving through the entangled forests with a tread as noiseless as that of the feline species. In spite of its enormous dimensions, it is one of the most difficult animals to discover that roams the forests. A herd of elephants eight and ten feet in height, may stand within a few yards of a hunter without being detected by him, even though he should be aware of their presence. The only sure means of ascertaining the proximity of elephants is by listening for one sound which they are continually giving forth, and which they are unable to control. This peculiar noise is caused by the movement of the large amount of water which is always kept stored in their stomachs, and which sloshes with every respiration, producing a gurgling sound somewhat resembling that of water escaping from a bottle, and is audible at some distance.

There are several different ways of hunting the African elephant, some of which I will briefly describe: The white hunters, who visit Africa for sport, usually take to the open country on horse-back, and rush on to the colossal game by sheer speed, trusting to their horses for escape in case the wounded elephant charges. This was Cummings' favorite mode, and he was one of the most successful hunters that has ever penetrated African jungles. Baker, Andersson and several other prominent travelers, who have been great elephant hunters, gave their preference to night shooting from small excavations in the earth, in which they would lie concealed beside some favorite drinking place and shoot the elephants as they approached for water. This mode is somewhat hazardous and many narrow escapes from wounded elephants serve to make more thrilling the interesting narratives of these great travelers, some of which I will relate in subsequent pages.

THE BRAVE HUNTERS OF AFRICA.

The *Bari* tribes of Africa, and the *Kaffirs* of South Africa, take even more desperate chances than white hunters, for they pursue elephants with no other weapon than the assegais and spear, and on foot. To approach the animal, which is so fierce and terrible when wounded, and drive a spear into its side, requires a degree of courage which very few civilized persons possess, yet the unlettered barbarians so little regard the danger thus incurred that they seem to find delight in tempting fate, for they not only attack the lordly elephant by hurling assagais at him, but rush upon him in the most reckless manner, trusting to their nimble limbs to escape the mad thrashes of the animal's trunk.

The death of a large elephant is an event for intense congratulation among the Kaffirs, who are thus provided with a liberal supply of food. Almost every portion of the animal is used by them, whose strong jaws are equal to any emergency of tough meat, while their stomachs do not become offended at the offer of the vilest portions. Indeed, it seems to be a rule among savages, that every part of an animal that is most repulsive to civilized tastes, is considered by them a luxury, in many cases too delicious to be spoiled by cooking. The flesh of the elephant is sometimes dried into what the Kaffirs call *biltongue*, which is only another name for jerked meat, while the fat is rendered out and the oil used for greasing the bodies of the natives, who do not consider themselves dressed unless they are copiously anointed with grease. To such an extent is this greasing of the body carried for ornamentation of person that butter, of which the Kaffirs and other tribes make vast quantities, is never used for any other purpose; eating it having never occurred to them.

KAFFIR HUNTERS.

Beneath the hard epidermis of the elephant is a thin skin, easily separable from the outer cuticle, which the natives make into most serviceable vessels for holding water and plantain wine.

CRUEL MEANS OF DESTROYING THE ELEPHANT.

The killing of elephants, which seem to possess a human intelligence, and a docility incompatible with their strength and wild habits, might be called cruel under any circumstances, but there are some methods of destroying the noble brute, compared with which the shooting of them appears humane.

The *Somali* hunters, who are tempted solely by the ivory which may be obtained, kill the elephant in a shockingly atrocious manner, though it involves no little risk of person. Having discovered the elephant reposing, the Somalian contrives to crawl upon his sleeping victim, and with a sharp sword severs the principle tendon in its hind leg. The animal, not realizing at first the character of its wound, and maddened with pain, rises and throws itself about, but is unable to move from the spot. Here the poor beast is allowed to remain until hunger and thirst completes the work which was begun by the hunter; after several days putrefaction sets in upon the carcass, so that the tusks may be easily drawn from the skull.

Another cruel mode of destroying the elephant is by means of pitfalls, in the center of which is placed a strong stake for the animal to impale itself on. These pitfalls are about twelve feet deep, and are dug tapering downward, so that if there is no stake in the center, as is sometimes the case, or if it prove defective, the fallen animal has its feet so forced together that it is helpless even to struggle, but must remain in agonizing pain until its tormentors see fit to destroy it. In case the elephant falls upon the sharp-pointed upright stake, his sufferings are still more terrible, as we may imagine, and thus impaled he sometimes spends two or more days before death comes to his relief.

On account of the extraordinary sagaciousness of the old elephants these pitfalls do not cause so great a number of deaths as might be expected, for, taught to be cautious by the many adventures which have befallen him, the old leader precedes the herd on their way to drink, along which path the pitfalls are dug and carefully concealed by a covering of dried sticks and leaves. As he moves along ahead, he keeps his trunk close to the ground and feels his way step by step, so that he is very certain to detect the snare laid for his species. Having discovered the pitfall, he stops until the others have come up, when he communicates his find to each member of his herd and then falls to and uncovers it completely.

The Abyssinians pursue the elephant with long spears and kill it with little less cruelty than do the Soumali tribes. They hunt always in couples and on horseback. When an animal is discovered they approach, and so enrage it, by tantalizing spear thrusts, that the elephant charges furiously after one of the hunters, who dashes off, keeping only far enough ahead to lure the quarry on in an expectation of soon catching him. While the elephant is thus in hot pursuit of the first hunter, the second one puts spurs to his horse and gallops up behind until he approaches near enough to deliver his thrust; he now drives his broad, steel-bladed spear into the animal at a point a few inches below the root of the tail, and pushes it so far in that the elephant's lungs are pierced. He now gallops away as the animal turns, leaving his spear sticking in the wound, which is sometimes eight or ten feet deep. The elephant has received his death-wound, and seems to understand that he can do no more, for, instead of charging on, he stops and stands still until his strength has departed from internal bleeding, and falls, at length, dead. So great is his vitality, however, that he will survive even such desperate wounds for several hours, but his rage is given over to a settled melancholy, and to see the poor beast standing so still, quivering with agony, while great tears roll down continually from his pity-inspiring eyes, is to look upon a picture that will melt the most callous heart.

Another method, rather commonly employed in Africa, to destroy elephants, is by driving large herds of such animals from the open country into jungles, where the larger forest trees have already been manned by several natives concealed in the branches, and armed with enormous lance-heads several feet in length, with a short handle, weighted with a heavy lump of hardened clay mixed with chopped straw. When the elephants are disturbed by the beaters, they generally retire to the jungle, and will congregate beneath the shade of the largest trees, from the branches of which the deadly spears are dropped perpendicularly by the concealed hunters. A spear-head of three feet in length thus dropped between the shoulders will inflict a fatal wound, as the short, weighted handle is struck by the dense and tangled branches as the animal rushes forward, and the blade is, therefore, in constant motion, cutting terrible gashes in the vitals of the elephant

AN ELEPHANT HUNT.

Thomas Bains, in his "Explorations in Southwest Africa," thus describes his first elephant hunt: * * * "We halted about eight and one-third miles of travel north by west, and Chapman, going down to the olei (water basin or gully) a quarter of a mile farther, found himself face to face with an elephant, with nothing but a charge of small shot in his gun. He returned at once for his rifle, and putting away my sketch half-dry, I took up mine. * * * Chapman, who runs faster than I, and has, besides, his guns carried by natives, was getting in advance, and as he descended into the next valley I

MANNER IN WHICH THE BARI HUNTERS ATTACK THE ELEPHANT.

heard three shots, in rapid succession, followed by a wild, shrill scream, and the baying of the dogs. I came forward double-quick, hoping that the elephant might come out my way, and give me a chance as well, but as I cleared the bush, I saw before me an open hollow, a very gem of the wilderness, with a broad olei in the center, and beyond it the huge broadside of the beast making off among the crackling bushes, while Chapman was trying to reload his rifle, and the rest of the people were gathering themselves up after their dispersion by the charge.

" * * * The elephant, I learned, on entering the hollow, was met by another coming, all unconscious of the chase, to refresh himself at the water, and Chapman, keeping back the people as much as possible, was obliged to fire at the second across the olei at between one and two hundred yards distance, although the ivory of the first, notwithstanding a broken tusks seemed to be forty pounds heavier than that of the intruder. At the second gun, the people had run past him and exposed themselves to a furious charge, Bill, after firing his shot, escaping with marvelous activity, but proving in the subsequent chase that he could run as fast after an elephant as he could away from him—following (so says report) almost between the legs of the beast, and firing with a boldness which, when assisted by skill in the use of his weapon, will make him a successful hunter.

"Returning towards the olei, the bushman pointed suddenly to some object, and handed Chapman's gun to him to shoot it; but another glance showed it to be the carcass of the elephant, lying within a few hundred yards of the spot where he had been first fired at.

"Traversing a length of hill and dale, which now seemed wearisome enough, we passed the olei, scarcely disturbing the wild fowl on its placid surface, and a few hundred yards beyond came in sight of the gigantic carcass looming like a boulder above the bush. Of course I have seen elephants, but it has always been at my home, and not in theirs, and neither picture nor well-groomed, black-skinned show specimen from India I had ever seen had quite prepared me to stand, for the first time, without a sensation of awe and wonder beside the mighty African, fallen in all his native grandeur in his domain."

This animal was 10 feet 9 inches in height, an uncommonly large one, though Bains claims to have killed one afterwards that measured 11 feet 8 1-2 inches, which is considerably taller than Jumbo was.

A MIRACULOUS ESCAPE FROM A HERD OF ELEPHANTS.

Of his many hair-breadth escapes from wild animals in the game regions of Africa, Andersson relates the following as one of the most curious:

"On another occasion, when the night was dark, I crept to within a short distance of seven bull-elephants, and was endeavoring to pick out the largest, when I was startled by a peculiar rumbling noise close behind me. Springing to my feet I perceived, to my surprise and alarm, a semi-circle of female elephants with their calves, bearing down upon me. My position was critical, being between two fires, so to say, and I had no other choice than either to plunge into the pool, which could only be crossed by swimming, in the face of the male elephants, or to break through the ranks of the females. I adopted the latter alternative, but first fired at the nearest of the seven bulls; and then, without a moment's delay, I rushed on the more open ranks of the female phalanx, uttering at the same time loud shouts. My cries caused a momentary panic amongst the animals, of which I took advantage, and slipped out between them, discharging my second barrel into the shoulder of the nearest as I passed her. No sooner, however, had I effected my escape, than the whole herd made a simultaneous rush at me, and trumpeted so shrilly as to cause every man at camp, as I learned afterwards, to start out of his sleep. Fortunately, the darkness prevented the beasts from following me; and, the jungle being close, I was soon in safety. In my precipitate flight however, I severely lacerated my feet; for, when stalking the elephants, I had taken off my shoes, that I might the better steal upon them.

"When, after awhile, I ventured out of my place of concealment, I found everthing quiet; only one solitary elephant remained. Having approached within a short distance, I could distinctly see him laving water onto his sides with his trunk. I immediately suspected that he belonged to the herd of seven bulls, and was the one that I had fired at. Seating myself right across his path, I quietly watched his proceedings. After a time I saw him, I thought, move off in an opposite direction. But I was mistaken; for in an instant his towering form loomed above me. It was too late to get out of his way; so, quickly raising myself on one knee, I took a steady aim at his foreleg. On receiving the ball he uttered the most plaintive cry, and, rushing past me, disappeared in the neighboring forest. The next afternoon he was discovered dead within rifle-shot of the water. It had been a successful night, for a fine female elephant had also fallen to my other shot."

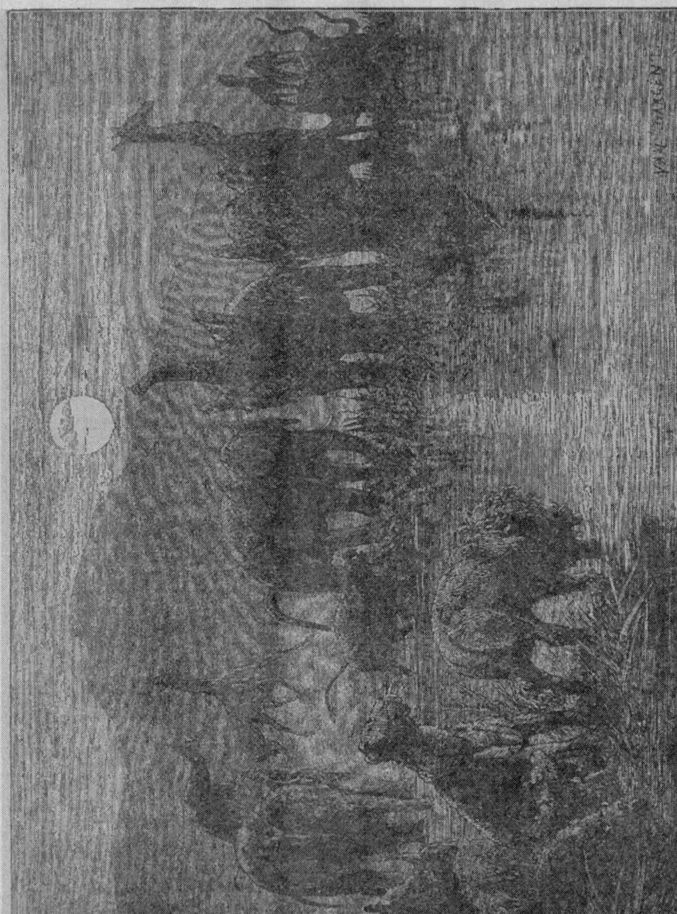

NIGHT SCENE ON LAKE NGAMI.

A THRILLING ADVENTURE, TERMINATING IN A MIRACLE.

The same author tells another still more wonderful story than the one just related, of how he escaped death from a wounded elephant by the interposition of an event little short of a miracle. He writes:

"Notwithstanding my anxious desire to reach the Ngami lake I determined, before finally leaving Kobis, to devote one more day, or, rather, night, to the destruction of the denizens of the forest. But the adventure nearly terminated fatally, and the night of the 15th of July will ever be remembered by me as one of the most eventful epochs of my life, for, in the course of it, I was three several times in the very jaws of death, and only escaped destruction by a miracle.

"From the constant persecution to which the larger game had of late been subjected at Kobis, it had become not only scarce, but wary; and hearing that elephants and rhinoceri still continued to resort to Abeghan, I forthwith proceeded there on the night in question. Somewhat incautiously I took up my position—alone, as usual—on a narrow neck of land dividing two small pools; the place on either side of my skarm—a small hiding-place made of stones—being only sufficient for a large animal to stand between me and the water. I was provided with a blanket and two or three spare guns.

"It was one of those magnificent tropical moonlight nights, when an indescribably soft and enchanting light is shed over the slumbering landscape; the moon was so bright and clear that I could discern even a small animal at a considerable distance.

"I had just completed my arrangements when a noise that I can liken only to the passage of a train of artillery, broke the stillness of the air; it evidently came from the direction of one of the numerous stony paths, or rather tracks, leading to the water, and I imagined it was caused by some wagons that might have crossed the kalakari. Raising myself partially from my recumbent posture, I fixed my eyes steadily on the part of the bush whence the strange sounds proceeded; but for some time I was unable to make out the cause. All at once, however, the mystery was explained by the appearance of an immense elephant, immediately followed by eighteen others. Their towering forms told me at a glance that they were males. It was a splendid sight to behold so many huge creatures approaching with a free, sweeping, unsuspecting and stately step. The somewhat elevated ground whence they emerged, and which gradually sloped toward the water, together with the misty night-air, gave an increased appearance of bulk and mightiness to their naturally giant structures.

"Crouching down as low as possible in the skarm, I waited with beating heart and ready rifle the approach of the leading male who, unconscious of peril, was making straight for my hiding-place. The position of his body, however, was unfavorable for a shot; and, knowing from experience that I had little more than a chance of obtaining more than a single good one, I waited for an opportunity to fire at his shoulder, which, as before said, is preferable to any other part when shooting at night. But this chance, unfortunately, was not offered till his enormous bulk towered above my head. The conse-

MIRACULOUS ESCAPE FROM A MAD ELEPHANT.

quence was that, while in the act of raising my gun over the skarm, my body caught his eye, and before I could place the piece to my shoulder, he swung himself round and, with trunk elevated and ears spread, desperately charged me. It was now too late too think of flight, much less slaying the savage beast. My own life was in imminent jeopardy; and seeing that, if I remained partially erect, he would inevitably seize me with his proboscis, I threw myself on my back with some violence; in which position, and without shouldering the rifle, I fired upwards at random towards his chest, uttering at the same time the most piercing shouts and cries. The change of position, in all human probability, saved my life; for, at the same instant, the trunk of the enraged animal descended precisely on the spot where I had been previously crouched, sweeping away the stones (many of a large size) that formed the fore part of my skarm, like so many pebbles. In another moment his broad fore-feet passed directly over my face.

"I now expected nothing short of being crushed to death. But imagine my relief when, instead of renewing the charge, he swerved to the left, and moved off with considerable rapidity, while I, most happily, received no other injuries than a few bruises, occasioned by the falling of the stones. Under Providence I attributed my extraordinary escape to the confusion of the animal caused by the wound I had inflicted on him, and to the cries elicited from me when in my utmost need."

SINGULAR ATTACHMENT OF A BABY ELEPHANT.

W. C. Harris, in a work describing his adventures, under the title of "Wild Sports in Southern Africa," gives several interesting accounts of battles with wild animals in which he was a participant. After killing several from out a herd of fully three hundred, as he declares, Mr. Harris tells the following story of the queer antics of a baby elephant, whose mother he had slain:

"Not an elephant was to be seen on the ground that was yesterday teeming with them; but on reaching the glen which had been the scene of our exploits during the early part of the action, a calf, about three and one-half feet high, walked forth from a bush, and saluted us with mournful, piping notes. We had observed the unhappy little wretch hovering about its mother after she fell, and having probably been unable to overtake the herd, it had passed a dreary night in the woods. Entwining its little proboscis about our legs, the sagacious creature, after demonstrating its delight at our arrival by a thousand ungainly antics, accompanied the party to the body of its dam, which, swollen to an enormous size, was surrounded by an inquest of vultures. Seated in gaunt array, with their shoulders shrugged, these loathsome fowls were awaiting its decomposition with forced resignation, the tough hide having defied all the efforts of their beaks, with which the eyes and softer parts had been vigorously assailed. The conduct of the calf now became quite affectionate and elicited the sympathy of every one. It ran round its mother's corpse, with touching demonstrations of grief, piping sorrowfully, and vainly attempting to raise her with its tiny trunk. I confess that I had felt compunctions in committing the murder the day before, and now half resolved never to assist in another."

LANGUAGE AND PECULIARITIES OF ELEPHANTS.

Of the many hundreds of books published on the large game of India and Africa, there was one issued in 1878 that immediately received the greatest attention, from the fact that its author, G. P. Sanderson, though an Englishman, had been for twenty years an officer in charge of the "Government elephant catching establishment in Mysore." The title of this standard work is, "Thirteen Years Among the Wild Beasts of India," which clearly indicates its character. Mr. Sanderson gives to the elephant the greatest attention, and his observations are particulary interesting, because often original. In treating of the habits of the elephant, he adds the following:

"In a herd of elephants the females with their calves form the advanced guard, whilst the tuskers follow leisurely behind; though, if terrified and put to flight, the order is reversed, the mothers and calves falling behind, as the unencumbered tuskers have no one to see to but themselves. I have never known of a tusker undertaking to cover the retreat of a herd. A herd is invariably led by a female, never a male, and the females with young ones are at all times dangerous if intruded upon. The necessity for the convenience of the mothers of the herd regulating its movements is evident, as they must accommodate the length and time of their marches, and the localities in which they rest and feed at different hours, to the requirements of their young ones.

"Elephants make use of a great variety of sounds in communicating with each other, and in expressing their wants and feelings. Some are uttered by the trunk, some by the throat. The conjectures in which either means of expression is employed cannot be strictly classified, as fear, pleasure, want, and other emotions are sometimes indicated by the trunk, sometimes by the throat. An elephant rushing upon an assailant trumpets shrilly with fury, but if enraged by wounds or other causes, and brooding by itself, it expresses its anger by a continual hoarse grumbling from the throat. Fear is similarly expressed in a shrill, brassy trumpet, or by a roar from the lungs. Pleasure by a continued low squeaking through the trunk, or an almost inaudible purring sound from the throat. A peculiar sound is made use of by elephants to express dislike or apprehension, and at the same time to intimidate, as when the cause of alarm has not been already ascertained, and the animals wish to deter an intruder. It is produced by rapping the end of the trunk smartly on the ground, a current of air, hitherto retained, being sharply emitted through the trunk, as from a valve, at the moment of impact. The sound made resembles that of a large sheet of tin being doubled.

"When a calf is born the herd remains with the mother two days; the calf is then capable of walking. Even at this tender age calves are no encumbrance to the herd's movements; the youngest climb hills and cross rivers, assisted by their dams. In swimming, very young calves are supported by their mothers' trunks, and held in front of them. When they are a few months old they scramble onto their mothers' shoulders, helping themselves by holding on with their legs, or they swim alone.

"Twice round an elephant's leg is his height, within one or two inches, more frequently it is exactly so. The age to which they live is, as must ever be the case with denizens of the jungle, uncertain. The general opinion of experienced natives is that it attains 120 years in exceptional cases, but more generally to about 80 years. This view, however, is based on observations of elephants in captivity; under the more favorable conditions of a natural life the elephant must attain a greater age than when confined. My own opinion is that it reaches at least 150 years."

STRANGE DISAPPEARANCE OF ELEPHANTS AFTER DEATH.

"One of the most remarkable facts in connection with elephants is the extreme rarity of any remains of dead ones being found in the jungles. This circumstance is so marked as to have given rise to the notion among the Sholagas of the Billig-rungan hills that elephants never die; while the Kurrabas of Kakaukote believe that there is a place, unseen by human eye, to which they retire to end their days. In my own wanderings for some years through elephant jungles I have only seen the remains of one female (that we knew had died in calving) and one drowned elephant brought down by a mountain torrent. Not only have I never myself seen the remains of any elephant that had died a natural death, but I have never met any one among the jungle tribes, or professional elephant hunters, who had seen a carcass. Bones would not decay for some years, and teeth and tusks would survive for some time, yet not a single pair of ivories has ever,

A HERD OF INDIA ELEPHANTS FEEDING AND SPORTING.

as far as I know, been found in the Mysore jungles during the time I have known them. A European gentleman, who, for thirty-six years, without intermission, had been living in the jungle, ascending to the summits of mountains in the prosecution of the trigometrical survey, and penetrating valleys in tracing roads and opening means of communication—one, too, who has made the habits of the wild elephant a subject of constant study and observation—has often expressed to me his astonishment that, after seeing many thousands of living elephants in all possible situations, he had never yet found a single skeleton of one, except of those that had fallen by the rifle. It may be supposed that in thick forests vultures do not attract attention to their carcasses, and monsoon rains and jungle fires soon dispose of them. Still, one would think that some carcasses, at least, would be found, whereas they never are; and though it is certain the animals die, I know of no reasonable explanation of what becomes of them."

IS THE ELEPHANT A SAGACIOUS ANIMAL?

We have been led to believe, by the wonderful stories told of its cunning intuition, that the elephant is the most sagacious of beasts, but Mr. Sanderson takes issue with this idea, and declares that there is no real reason for entertaining such a belief. Referring to this popular supposition, he says:

"Let us consider whether the elephant displays more intelligence in its wild state than other animals. Though possessed of a proboscis which is capable of guarding it against such dangers, it readily falls into pits dug for catching it, and only covered with a few sticks or leaves. Its fellows make no effort to assist the fallen one, as they might easily do by kicking in the earth around the pit, but flee in terror. It commonly happens that a young elephant falls into a pit, near which the mother will remain until the hunters come, without doing anything to assist it, not even feeding it by throwing in a few branches. This is, I have no doubt, more difficult of belief to most people than if they were told that the mother supplied it with grass, brought water in her trunk, or filled up the pit with fagots and procured its release. Whole herds of elephants are led into ill-concealed enclosures which no other wild animals could be got to enter, and single ones are caught by their hind-legs being tied together by men under cover of a couple of tame elephants. Elephants which happen to effect their escape are caught again without trouble; even experience does not bring them wisdom. I do not think I traduce the elephant when I say it is, in many things, a stupid animal."

HOW THE CARCASS OF AN ELEPHANT IS DISPOSED OF.

"I have seen the cream of trained elephants at work in the catching establishments in Mysore and Bengal; I have managed them myself, under all circumstances, and I can say that I have never seen one show any aptitude in dealing, undirected, with an unforseen emergency. I have a young riding-elephant at present, which is often my only hunting companion, that kneels, trumpets, hands up any thing from the ground, raises her trunk to break a branch, or passes under one in silence, stops, backs and does other things at understood hints as I sit on her pad; but no uninitiated looker-on would perceive that any intimation of what is required passes between us.

THE MUST, OR MAD ELEPHANTS.

"So much for the intelligence of the elephant. Let us now consider its temperament in captivity. I think all who have had to deal with elephants will agree in saying that their good qualities cannot be exaggerated, and that their vices are few, and only occur in exceptional animals. The not uncommon idea that elephants are treacherous and retentive of an injury is a groundless one. Male elephants are subject to periodical fits of *must* (mad) supposed to be of a sexual nature, of the approach of which, however, due warning is given, and during the continuance of which care is necessary in dealing with them, as they are quite irresponsible for their actions. But at all other times the male elephant is generally perfectly safe, rarely suddenly changeable in temper. Female elephants are, at all times, the most perfect tempered creatures in the world.

"Much misapprehension prevails regarding the uses and power of the elephant's trunk. This organ is chiefly used by the animal to procure its food, and to convey it, and water, to its mouth; also, to warn it of danger by the sense of smell and touch. It is a delicate and sensitive organ, never used for rough work. The idea that he can use it for any purpose, from picking up a needle to dragging a piece of ordnance from a bog is, like many others, founded entirely on imagination. An elephant might manage the former feat, though I doubt it, the latter he would not attempt. Elephants engaged in such work as dragging timber invariably take the rope between their teeth; they never attempt to pull a heavy weight with the trunk. In carrying a light log they hold it in the mouth, as a dog does a stick, receiving some little assistance in balancing it from the trunk. Tuskers generally use the tusks for this and similar purposes, and are more valuable than females for work. An elephant is powerful enough to extricate a cannon from a difficult situation, but he does it by pushing with his head or feet, or in harness—never by lifting or drawing with his trunk.

"An elephant rarely uses his trunk for striking other elephants or man. Newly-caught ones seldom attempt even to seize any one coming within reach of their trunks; they curl them up and rush at the intruder. Should any accident happen to an elephant's trunk to prevent in conveying water to its mouth, it drinks by wading into deep water and immersing the mouth in the manner common to most quadrupeds."

THE PERILS OF ELEPHANT SHOOTING.

On the authority of the greatest of ancient or modern Nimrods, Sir Samuel Baker, elephant shooting may be pronounced to be the most dangerous of all sports if fairly followed for a length of time. Many elephants may be killed without the sportsman being in any peril; but if an infuriated beast does attack, his charge is one of supreme danger. This danger, however, has this charm, that though so great unless steadily and skillfully met, it is within the sportsman's power, by coolness and good shooting, to end it and the assailant's career instantly by one well-planted ball.

"The wild elephant's attack," says Sanderson, "is one of the noblest sights of the chase. A grander animated object than a wild elephant in full charge can hardly be imagined. The cocked ears and broad forehead present an immense frontage; the head is held high, with the trunk curled between the tusks, to be uncoiled in the moment of attack; the massive fore-legs come down with the force and regularity of ponderous machinery; and the whole figure is rapidly foreshortened and appears to double in size with each advancing stride. The trunk being curled and unable to emit any sound, the attack is made in silence, after the usual premonitory shriek, which adds to its impressiveness. A tiger's charge is an undignified display of arms, legs and spluttering; the bison rushes blunderingly upon his foe; the bear's attack is despicable; but the wild elephant's onslaught is as dignified as it seems overwhelming—and a large tusker's charge, where he has had sufficient distance to get into full swing, can only be compared to a steady and rapid advance of an engine on a line of rail. With all this the sportsman, who understands his game, knows that there is a natural timidity in the elephant which often plays him tricks at the last moment. It is not difficult to turn or stop him with heavy metal, and if knocked down he very rarely, if ever, renews the attack."

When elephants are close at hand, standing in indecision, no one should shout to them. A charge by one or more of them is almost sure to be made if they are suddenly startled in this particular way. "I have seen," says Sanderson, "and myself experienced, several instances of the danger of this. In Chittagong, whilst driving wild animals into a stockade on one occasion, they approached the guiding-line of beaters too closely, when a man, who was behind a small bush, shouted at them within thirty yards. A female at once charged him; the man fell, and with the pressure of her foot on his chest she split him open, killing him on the spot. This elephant had a very young calf, and in her solicitude for it she became a perfect fury."

THE VENGEFUL ROGUE ELEPHANT.

Rogue elephants are occasionally met with which are distinguished by their fierce temper, and their affecting solitude. These animals are invariably dangerous, and not infrequently they way-lay roads for the purpose of killing any person who may chance to pass. The cause of this singular propensity, which is quite unnatural to elephants in general, has never been satisfactorily accounted for, but from wide reading, having no personal experience, I incline to the opinion that in every case the animal that manifests this ugly disposition is the victim of some painful disorder, either affecting his brain or racking his body with agony, and he becomes irritable and vengeful, just as men do under long suffering. Sanderson describes the killing of a rogue elephant which had destroyed several persons and rendered travel through the jungle roads so dangerous that none dared venture over them except in large parties and with servants engaged to beat symbols and gongs to frighten the beast.

After describing the manner of approach Sanderson says: "When the rogue trumpeted my men were greatly excited. Here we were face to face with the man-slayer. Old Poojarse, who was always ready for dangerous work, now took the lead. We pushed through dangerously thick stuff, where I expected to hear the elephant's war-trumpet every moment, and to have him burst out on us; but, fortunately, we had the wind, and the unconscious monster stood unaware of the fact that enemies were at hand.

"We were within ten yards of him before we could make him out, and he then only appeared as a dark mass in the young bamboo and grass in which he was standing. There was, fortunately, a good breeze blowing, which made sufficient noise amongst the branches to

SANDERSON AND THE ROGUE ELEPHANT.

cover our approach; but it was impossible to get near enough, even with this advantage, for the head-shot in such thick stuff. I therefore decided to give him the four-bore behind the shoulder, if I could only make out how he was standing; but there was a difficulty about this, as even his feet were hidden in the undergrowth so that, though we stooped and looked along the ground, we could get no clue to his position. As luck would have it, however, at this moment he raised his trunk to reach a bough overhead. I saw his temple and seized my twelve-bore, intending to reserve the four-ounce in case the first shot did not kill him; but before I could draw a sight on him, his head was again hidden. Fearing that if I delayed any longer a slant of wind might discover us, I took the four-ounce and fired at where I now knew his shoulder to be. The report and smoke from ten drams in such thick cover were tremendous. The elephant remained motionless for an instant after receiving the shot, when with a wild scream and awful crash away he went, fortunately not in our direction, as there was nothing thick enough to shelter us, and we might have been run over by accident. As soon as I could re-load the four-bore we raced after him. The grass and bushes on both sides of his track were covered with blood, and my hands, face and gun became sticky with it as we ran on through the grass. We had only gone about two hundred yards when the Kurrabas stopped short. There was the elephant standing about twenty-five yards from us in an open space amongst some grass up to his shoulders, facing us. The four-bore had taken him about half-way up the left shoulder, and his lungs must have been damaged, as blood was gushing from his mouth. He must have stopped through being choked by the bleeding, and hearing us running behind him, had faced round to receive us. As the Kurrabas vanished, he came a few steps forward with a grunt and again stopped.

"He certainly was a sight to give a novice in elephant-shooting a 'turn.' Blood was gushing from his mouth, covering his chest, fore-legs and trunk. His twinkling eye showed that he meant mischief; his head was held high, his trunk curled between his tusks, and one foot planted boldly in advance, ready for a forward movement. I and my gun-bearers were still within the cover and concealed; so taking immediate advantage of his halt for a steady shot, I aimed between his eyes, and dropped him dead with the four-bore."

CUMMING'S FIRST ADVENTURE WITH ELEPHANTS.

The feelings of a keen sportsman, at his first sight of elephants in their native wilds, can neither be imagined nor described, for it embodies an intensity that none may ever conceive except by actual experience. Cumming was a natural born hunter, and a man of strong nerve, who rarely grew excited, even in the face of the most disturbing circumstances; he had even killed more than one lion, and met with many narrow escapes without becoming nervous, yet when he first viewed a herd of elephants, even afar off, from a lofty ant-hill, cold chills ran over him, and a sensation of unutterable dread, or uneasiness, at least, took complete possession of him. These most uncomfortable feelings did not long disturb him, however, for as the elephants disappeared from sight the eagerness and impetuosity of the true sportsman overcame every other sensation, save that of a consuming desire to engage with the lordly game.

So much time had been occupied with reflections of an unpleasant character, not knowing the nature of elephants, that after the animals had stolen out of sight it was not until the following day that the herd was again discovered. Of the adventure which now occurred Cumming writes:

"We proceeded silently as might be for a few hundred yards, following the guide, when he suddenly pointed, exclaiming, 'Klow!' and before us stood the herd of mighty bull elephants, packed together beneath a shady grove, about one hundred and fifty yards in advance. I rode slowly towards them and, as soon as they observed me, they made a loud rumbling noise and, tossing their trunks, wheeled right about and made off in one direction, crashing through the forest and leaving a cloud of dust behind them.

"The distance I had come, and the difficulties I had undergone to behold these elephants, rose fresh before me. Dashing my spurs into 'Sunday's' ribs, I was very soon much too close in their rear for safety. The elephants now made an inclination to my left, whereby I obtained a good view of the ivory. The herd consisted of six bulls; four of them were full grown, first-rate elephants; the other two were fine fellows, but had not yet arrived at perfect stature. Of the four old fellows, two had much finer tusks than the rest, and for a few seconds I was undecided which of these two I would follow, when, suddenly, the one which I fancied had the stoutest tusks broke from his comrades, and I at once felt convinced that he was the patriarch of the herd, and I followed him accordingly.

CHARGED BY THE BULL ELEPHANT.

"Cantering alongside, I was about to fire, when he instantly turned and, uttering a trumpet so strong and shrill that the earth seemed to vibrate beneath my feet, charged furiously after me for several hundred yards in a direct line, not altering his course in the slightest degree for the trees of the forest, which he snapped and overthrew like reeds in his headlong career.

"When he pulled up in his charge I likewise halted; and as he slowly turned to retreat I let fly at his shoulders, 'Sunday' capering and prancing and giving me much trouble. On receiving the ball the elephant shrugged his shoulder and made off in a free, majestic walk. This shot brought several of the dogs to my assistance which had been following the other elephants, and on their coming up and bark-

CUMMING CHARGED BY AN ELEPHANT.

ing another headlong charge was the result, accompanied by the never-failing trumpet, as before. In his charge he passed close to me, when I saluted him with a second bullet in the shoulder, of which he did not take the slightest notice. I now determined not to fire again until I could make a steady shot; but, although the elephant turned repeatedly, 'Sunday' invariably disappointed me, capering so that it was impossible to fire. At length, exasperated, I became reckless of the danger and springing from the saddle, approached the elephant under cover of a tree and gave him a bullet in the side of the head, when, trumpeting so shrilly that the forest trembled, he charged among the dogs, from which he seemed to fancy that the blow had come; after which he took up a position in a grove of thorns, with his head towards me. I walked up very near, and as he was in the act of charging (being in those days under wrong impressions as to the impracticability of bringing down an elephant with a shot in the forehead), stood cooly in his path until he was within fifteen paces of me, and let drive at the hollow of his forehead, in the vain expectation that by so doing I should end his career. The shot only served to increase his fury—an effect which, I had remarked, a shot in the head invariably produced—and, continuing his charge with incredible quickness and impetuosity, he all but terminated my elephant hunting forever. A large party of Bechunas, who had come up, yelled out simultaneously, imagining I was killed, for the elephant was at one moment almost on top of me. I, however, escaped by my activity in doubling on him and running up hill as he came charging down, and by dodging round the bushy trees. As the elephant was charging, an enormous thorn ran deep into the sole of my foot, which caused me severe pain, laming me throughout the rest of the conflict."

Cumming now mounted his horse, and running alongside the already sorely wounded monarch, fired no less than fifteen ounce balls into his shoulder, each shot stimulating the brute to renewed charges from which, however, the rider easily escaped. At length, with nineteen large bullets in his vital parts, the elephant retreated to a heavy thicket where he stood tossing his huge trunk up and down and groaning so piteously as to excite compassion in the hunter's breast, for it was now plain to be seen that there were certain evidences of his rapidly approaching death, and that no more shooting was necessary to finish him. The great beast swayed backwards and forwards, trembling like an aspen leaf, while tears chased down his cheeks until, with a mighty lurch, he toppled over, dead. Thus ended the hunt and thus did Cumming kill his first elephant, while his heart was filled with exultation never before or since felt.

A SAVAGE SCENE.

It was quite late in the evening when the hunt terminated, so that the natives, who accompanied Cumming, did not begin the work of cutting up the elephant until the following morning. The Bechuanan process of butchering is one no less disgusting than it is exciting, presenting a scene which baffles all description. The natives, of which there are nearly a score, divest themselves of all covering and armed only with assagais they begin slashing the body. The rough outer-skin is first removed, in large sheets, from the side which lies uppermost. Beneath this outer-skin is a subcuticle, which the natives use for making water-bags, as it is a very pliable membrane, and so tough that it is not liable to rupture even from the roughest usage. They remove this inner skin with caution, using great care not to injure it with their assagais.

The flesh is next cut off in large sheets from the ribs, after which, by the use of hatchets, the ribs are taken out one by one.

A CLOSE CHARGE AND LUCKY ESCAPE.

The entrails are now laid bare and, in removing these, the most disgusting and bloody scenes occur. Surrounding the bowels are great layers of fat, which the Bechuanans prize above everything else. They use it largely in cooking their sun-dried biltongue—dried strips of elephant flesh—and they also eat it with their vegetables. Before this fat can be obtained, the bowels must be removed. To accomplish this, several men enter the immense cavity, now exposed, and with their assagais mine away at the fat, handing portions to those outside as fast as it is cut away. The natives have a horrid practice on these occasions of besmearing their bodies, from the crown of the head to the sole of the foot, with the black and clotted gore; and in this anointing they assist one another, each man taking up the fill in both hands, and spreading it over the back and shoulders of his friend. Throughout the entire proceeding an incessant and deafening clamor of voices is kept up, and violent jostlings and wrestlings are practiced by every man, all slippery with gore, as he endeavors to force his way to the venison through the dense intervening ranks, while the sharp and ready assagai gleams in every hand. The angry voices and gory appearances of so many naked savages, combined with their excited and frantic gestures and glistening arms, present an effect so wild and striking as will produce a thrill of horror in the bravest European who beholds it.

PERILOUS SITUATION OF AN ELEPHANT HUNTER.

The advantages which trained dogs give in hunting the elephant were strikingly illustrated on one occasion, when, but for their distracting running and barking, Cumming would have undoubtedly fallen a victim to an elephant's rage. The circumstances were peculiarly appalling. A herd of twelve cow elephants and their calves were discovered feeding on the side of a mountain, five hundred yards from the first observer, and the wind being favorable to the animals, they caught the scent of Cumming and his companions, and plunged into a dense jungle of wait-a-bit thorns, from which every effort to dislodge them, by shooting or shouting, was in vain. As a last recourse, Cumming made his way painfully into the jungle, reaching the center of which, at last, he found himself suddenly upon the elephants. The dogs then ran in barking, when a general trumpeting took place, followed quickly by a charging and crashing in all directions. Not knowing the direction from whence the charge was coming, being unable to see the animals, Cumming beat a hasty retreat until he could no longer hear them.

Everything having become quiet, and fearful lest he should lose them, Cumming pushed in again after the elephants, followed by his companions. They had found an elephant path and continued along this until crash! came another charge from the fierce brutes at his back, accompanied by the most deafening trumpeting. The elephants ran in upon them from different directions, and in a trice there was an inextricable confusion of elephants, dogs and men. As good fortune would have it, the barking dogs drew the entire attention of the elephants, which brushed by the horses without offering any violence to their riders, being wholly absorbed by a mad dash after the dogs. "I seldom remember," says Cumming, "a more startling or dangerous position; it was a decided case of 'Devil take the hind-most.' There was no time to select a path, so placing my head below my horse's neck and trusting to Providence, I charged through the thickest of the thorns, and presently found myself out of the way of the elephants. I know nothing which so effectually teaches a hunter the art of riding through a wait-a-bit jungle, in an artistical manner, as hearing the trumpet of an enraged elephant, which is following in about a spear's length in his wake."

TERRIBLE CHARGE OF A FEROCIOUS BULL-ELEPHANT.

Not long after the circumstance just related, when in the vicinity of Maugmakuky, Cumming was startled by a herd of immense bull elephants that were browsing within a thicket so near him that their heavy breathing was distinctly audible. Galloping down the hill and shouting at the same time, he succeeded in driving them out of the thicket, and shooting the largest bull in the herd. The animal wheeled immediately and charged with such impetuosity that he ran head-foremost into a large bushy tree, which he sent flying before him high in the air, coming down at the same moment on his knees. As the beast now turned off Cumming followed on his horse, loading and firing as fast as possible, sometimes at the head and then behind the shoulders; but it was not until he had opened fire with a Dutch sixteen-pounder, that he was able to bring down the huge beast.

COOKING AN ELEPHANT'S FOOT.

Several tribes of Africa eat nearly all parts of the elephant and esteem the flesh highly, but to the cultivated taste, or rather to an American, such food would be decidedly repulsive, since it is extremely tough and by no means juicy. There is one part of the elephant, however, to which this observation will not apply, since in the foot, when properly cooked, there is the succulence of a delicious dish which might well regale the most delicate taste.

The part used is the first joint below the knee, although we might well expect this portion to be the toughest of the animal. To prepare this joint properly, a hole of three feet depth is first dug in the earth into which large, hot coals are placed until the dirt surrounding is baked and raised to a very high temperature. Most of the coals are then taken out and replaced by the elephant's foot, which is then covered with a layer of earth, on top of which a hot fire is built and kept well replenished for several hours. By this means the foot is evenly baked, and when thoroughly done, instead of showing tough meat fibres, it is reduced to a gelatinous consistency so that it may be eaten with a spoon.

The Kaffirs are especially fond of elephant's foot, and cook it with a perfection never attained by other tribes. They usually make the preparation of an elephant's foot the occasion of a great feast at

COOKING AN ELEPHANT'S FOOT.

which many attend, and a merry-making takes place somewhat like the huskings and 'possum feasts of ante-slavery days.

HORRIBLE ACCIDENTS FROM ELEPHANT HUNTING.

From the many interesting accounts and narrow escapes given in the preceding pages, it would appear that fatalities in hunting the elephant are extremely rare, if not altogether wanting, but so far from this being true, the number of horrible accidents that occur in this wild sport are so great that they at once prove it to be one of the most hazardous pastimes in which adventurous men have ever engaged. Though a huge and inactive animal, the elephant is a courageous, cunning and desperate foe, being difficult to kill, and is aroused to a blind fury by wounds. Many hunters have faced the giant brute and fairly vanquished him, thereby winning rich honors and true sportsman renown, but hundreds of others have paid the greatest debt for their temerity, by being ground to dust beneath the ponderous feet of an enraged elephant.

Among the many spirited hunters who have fallen victims to this animal in the jungles of Africa was Lieutenant Arlett, of the English navy, a brave officer who was held in the highest regard by all his countrymen. A considerable party of Englishmen, among whom were Lieutenant Owen and Messrs. Major Jamison, Barrett and a dozen other seamen accompanied Arlett on a grand hunt on the east coast of Africa. The party had met with several adventures of a pleasant character, and had killed a large quantity of game, and particularly a large number of hippopotami with the skeletons of which they had almost loaded their schooner. Just before the day appointed for their departure from Africa, indeed they were at the time leaving the woods to regain their vessel, their attention was attracted by the spouting of a hippopotamus that was disporting among the reeds of a river. Arlett and Barrett, accompanied by two seamen, went in among the reeds to gain a shot, but they had proceeded only a short distance when Arlett, being in advance, cried out, "Here he is!" At this moment the shrill, angry scream of an elephant was heard by the party outside the reeds and Mr. Barrett rushed out, his face covered with blood, loudly calling for assistance, as Arlett was attacked and borne down by an elephant of the largest size.

The party were immediately on the alert and, though they had no shoes on to guard their feet from the reeds, actively commenced their search for the unfortunate officer. The elephant, alarmed at the increased number of his opponents, retreated as they advanced, leaving his victim on the ground, dreadfully mangled. When found he was stretched motionless on his back, covered with blood and mud, and his eyes were starting from their sockets in all the expressive horror of a violent death, the tragedy having been completed by the elephant trampling the body until nearly every bone was broken.

DEATH OF THE FAMOUS HUNTER, CARL KRIEGER.

Carl Krieger was, for many years, considered the greatest hunter in all Africa, his adventures being so numerous and of such thrilling character that his fame spread over all the civilized world. He was indefatigable, fearless and an excellent marksman, three of the essential qualifications of a good hunter. Hundreds of lions, rhinoceri, hippopotami and elephants had fallen by his rifle, and numerous successes had inspired him with a confidence in his abilities that rendered him imprudent, or rather, foolishly courageous. With all his experience and valor he was, nevertheless, doomed to meet his death from one of the animals he had for years so ruthlessly and suceessfully pursued.

One day, having with his party chased an elephant which he had wounded, Krieger ran ahead of his companions with the intention of killing the beast by a close shot. At the moment he was about to fire, the animal turned and received the bullet in its side, which did little injury, but so enraged it, that in a twinkling the elephant seized him with its trunk, and lifting him high in the air, dashed him with dreadful force to the ground. Krieger's companions, struck with horror, fled precipitately from the fatal scene, unable to turn their eyes to witness what might follow. But on the next day they returned to the spot and there collected the bones and flesh that could be found and buried them. The enraged animal had not only literally trampled the great hunter's body to pieces, but pounded the very flesh into dust.

GORED TO DEATH BY AN ELEPHANT.

The following story is related by Charles Williams as an incident of Boer daring, and at the same time as an illustration of the perils attending the hunting of elephants:

"On New Year's day a party of Boers became heated with liquor, when each began boastingly to tell of the feats of hardihood they had performed. One of them, who had been a great hunter of elephants, having killed in his day above forty of these gigantic animals, laid wager that he would go into the forest and pluck three hairs out of an elephant's tail. This feat he actually performed, and returned safely with the trophy to his comrades. But not satisfied with this daring act, he laid another bet that he would go back and shoot the the same animal on the instant. He went accordingly; approached the animal too incautiously, when his first shot not proving effective, the enraged animal rushed on him before he could reload, or make his escape, and having first thrust his tremendous tusks through his body, trampled him to pieces."

FRIGHTFUL DEATH OF OFFICER McCLANE.

An equally horrible death befell Captain McClane, an officer in a Cape regiment, who was hunting in the vicinity of the Great Fish

TRAGIC DEATH OF OFFICER M'CLANE.

river with Lieutenants Moodie and Chisholm, and two brothers named Knight. The party struck a herd of cow-elephants and each, in their eagerness to bag an animal, pursued different elephants and thus soon became separated.

Shortly after their first dash Moodie was thrown from his horse and so badly beset by a wounded cow that he loudly called for assistance. Lieutenant Chisholm and a Hottentot responded and came up only to see their companion beneath the feet of the enraged beast, which was worrying him with her feet and trunk. The hunters fired at her and caused her to retreat down the river bank; reaching their unfortunate comrade, what was their surprise, when expecting to find a crushed mass of flesh, they picked him up very little the worse for his perilous adventure, as he had managed to keep his body out of the way of the animal's great feet.

As Moodie, Chisholm and the Hottentot were returning to search for their brother officers they saw McClane racing at his topmost speed, on foot, across the plain, pursued by a large bull elephant that was shrilly trumpeting. The three were too far distant from him to offer the fated officer the least aid, and were, therefore, enforced spectators of the dreadful tragedy that was soon to be enacted. The ferocious beast soon caught McClane and lifting him high in the air carried the poor fellow more than a hundred yards back into the thick forest, whence his companions had retreated, then stopping and looking about, as if to fix upon the hardest spot, flung him violently upon the ground. The force with which he struck the earth no doubt produced instant death, but the elephant's rage was not appeased by this one vengeful act, for he trampled the body until not the least semblance of a human form was left. But even this wantonness did not abate the animal's fearful anger, for he gathered up the shapeless mass and carried it to an adjacent jungle, into the bushes of which he cast it.

By the time the elephant had spent his rage on McClane the others came up, and a shot was fired which broke the animal's left fore-leg, thus disabling him. He was now at the mercy of his foes, and speedily succumbed to their combined attack.

KILLING ELEPHANTS WITH THE SWORD.

The extreme perils which are encountered by every elephant-hunter, regardless of the weapon he may employ, appears to rather stimulate than discourage courageous hunters to participate in the sport. We may easily understand the inducements which draw the sportsman to the jungle when he is armed with the most powerful weapons devised by geniuses of the nineteenth century, but not more than one-tenth of the elephants slain fall before breech-loading rifles, the other nine-tenths being killed by courageous natives who attack the giant beast with no other weapon than a spear or sword.

I have already referred to the manner in which certain tribes hunt the elephant with assegais and swords, but I must again call attention to the wonderful acts of bravery displayed by skilled Abyssinians, called aggageers — sword-hunters — since their courage, hardihood and adroitness in the chase is phenomenal, to say the least. Sir Samuel Baker, the greatest of English sportsmen, travelled extensively in Abyssinia, exploring the Nile tributaries, and it was while thus engaged he fell in with a party of aggageers whose cunning in the chase he was very anxious to see tested. Opportunity was finally offered, and he describes the hunt in which he was an observer, rather than participant, as follows:

"We had ridden about a mile, and were beginning to despair, when suddenly we turned a sharp angle in the water-course, and Taher Sherrif (the chief hunter), who was leading, immediately reined in his horse, and backed him toward the party. I followed his example, and we were at once concealed by the sharp bend of the river. He now whispered that a bull elephant was drinking from a hole it had scooped in the sand, not far round the corner. Without the slightest confusion, the hunters fell into their respective places, Taher Sherrif leading, while I followed closely in the rear; we were a party of seven horses.

"Upon turning the corner, we at once perceived the elephant that was still drinking. It was a fine bull; the enormous ears were thrown forward, as the head was lowered in the act of drawing up the water through the trunk; these shaded the eyes, and with the wind favorable, we advanced noiselessly upon the sand to within twenty yards before we were perceived. The elephant then threw up its head, and with ears flapping forward, it raised its trunk for an instant, then slowly, but easily, ascended the steep bank and retreated. The aggageers now halted for a minute to confer together, and then followed in their original order up the crumbled bank We were now on most unfavorable ground; the fire that had cleared the country we had hitherto traversed had been stopped by the bed of the torrent. We were thus plunged at once into withered grass above our heads, unless we stood in the stirrups; the ground was strewed with fragments of rocks, and altogether it was ill-adapted for riding. However, Taher Sherrif broke into a trot, followed by the entire party, as the elephant was not in sight. We ascended a hill, and when near the summit, we perceived the elephant about eighty yards ahead. It was looking behind during its retreat, by swinging its huge head from side to side, and upon seeing us approach, it turned suddenly round and halted. 'Be ready, and take care of the rocks!' said Taher Sherrif, as I rode forward by his side. Hardly had he uttered these words of caution, when the bull gave a

ABYSSINIAN SWORD-HUNTERS DISTRACTING THE ELEPHANT'S ATTENTION.

vicious jerk of the head, and with a shrill scream it charged down upon us with the greatest fury. Away we all went, helter skelter, through the dry grass, which whistled in my ears, over the hidden rocks at full gallop, with the elephant tearing after us, for about a hundred and eighty yards at a tremendous pace. Tetel was a sure-footed horse, and, being unshod, he never slipped upon the stones. Thus, as we all scattered in different directions, the elephant became confused, and relinquished the chase; it had been very near me at the time, and in such ground I was not sorry when it gave up the hunt. We now quickly united, and again followed the elephant, that had once more retreated. Advancing at a canter, we shortly came in view. Upon seeing the horses, the bull deliberately entered a stronghold composed of rocky and uneven ground, in the cliffs of which grew, thinly, a few leafless trees, the thickness of a man's leg. It then turned boldly towards us, and stood determinedly at bay.

"Now came the tug of war! Taher Sherrif came close to me and said, 'You had better shoot the elephant, as we shall have great difficulty in this rocky ground;' this I declined, as I wished to end the fight as it had been commenced, with the sword; and I proposed that he should endeavor to drive the animal to more favorable ground. 'Never mind,' replied Taher, 'Inshallah (please God) he shall not beat us.' He now advised me to keep as close to him as possible, and look sharp for a charge.

"The elephant stood facing us like a statue; it did not move a muscle beyond a quick and restless action of the eyes, that were watching all sides. Taher Sherrif and his younger brother, Ibrahim, now separated, and each took opposite sides of the elephant, and then joined each other twenty yards behind it; I accompanied them, until Taher advised me to keep about the same distance on the left flank. In front of the elephant were aggageers, one of whom was the renowned Rodur Sherrif, with the withered arm. All being ready for action Rodur now rode slowly towards the head of the cunning old bull, who was quietly awaiting an opportunity to make certain of some one, who might give him a good chance.

"Rodur Sherrif rode a bay mare that, having been trained to these encounters, was perfect at her work. Slowly and surely she advanced towards her wary antagonist, until within about eight or nine yards of the elephant's head. The creature never moved, and the *mise en scene* was beautiful; not a word was spoken, and we kept our places amidst utter stillness, which was at length broken by a snort from the mare, who gazed intently at the elephant, as though watching for the moment of attack.

DOWN RUSHES THE CHARGING ELEPHANT.

"One more pace forward, and Rodur sat coolly upon his mare, with his eyes fixed upon those of the elephant. For an instant I saw the white of the eye nearest to me; 'Look out, Rodur! he's coming!' I exclaimed. With a shrill scream, the elephant dashed upon him like an avalanche.

"Round went the mare, as though upon a pivot, and away over rocks and stones, flying like a gazelle, with the monkey-like form of little Rodur Sherrif leaning forward, and looking over his left shoulder as the elephant rushed after him.

"For a moment I thought he must be caught. Had the mare stumbled, all were lost; but she gained in the race after a few bounding strides, and Rodur, still looking behind him, kept his distance so close to the elephant, that its outstretched trunk was within a few feet of the mare's tail.

"Taher Sherrif and his brother, Ibrahim, swept down, like falcons, in the rear. In full speed they dexterously avoided the trees, until they arrived upon open ground, when they dashed up close to the hindquarters of the furious elephant who, maddened with the excitement, heeded nothing but Rodur and his mare, that were almost within its grasp. When close to the tail of the elephant, Taher Sherrif's sword flashed from its sheath, as grasping his trusty blade he leaped nimbly to the ground, while Ibrahim caught the reins of his horse; two or three bounds on foot, with the sword clutched in both hands, and he was close behind the elephant; a bright glance shone like lightning, as the sun struck upon the descending steel; this was followed by a dull crack, as the sword cut through skin and sinews, and settled deep in the bone, about twelve inches above the foot. At the next stride the elephant halted dead short in the midst of its tremendous charge. Taher had jumped quickly on one side, and had vaulted into the saddle with his naked sword in hand; at the same moment Rodur, who had led the chase, turned sharp round, and again faced the elephant, as before; stooping quickly from his saddle, he picked up from the ground a handful of dirt, which he threw into the face of the vicious looking animal, that once more attempted to rush upon him. It was impossible! the foot was dislocated, and turned up in front like an old shoe. In an instant Taher was once more on foot, and again the sharp sword slashed the remaining leg. The great bull-elephant could not move! The first cut with the sword had utterly disabled it; the second was its death blow; the arteries of the leg were divided, and the blood spurted in jets from the wounds. I wished to terminate its misery by a bullet behind the ear, but Taher Sherrif begged me not to fire, as the elephant would quickly bleed to death without pain, and an unnecessary shot might attract the *Base* (a neighboring tribe), who would steal the flesh and ivory during our absence.

"The hunting of Taher Sherrif and his brothers was superlatively beautiful; with an immense amount of dash, there was a cool, sports-

WONDERFUL FEAT OF THE ABYSSINIAN ELEPHANT HUNTERS.

man-like manner in their mode of attack, that far excelled the impetuous and reckless onset of Abou Do; it was difficult to decide which to admire the most, whether the coolness and courage of him who led the elephant, or the extraordinary skill and activity of the aggageer who dealt the fatal blow."

STRANGE DEATH OF PROF. WAHLBERG.

One of the most renowned naturalists that has penetrated African wilds in pursuit of his interesting profession, was Professor Wahlberg, a Swede, who, in company with Chapman and Green, made an exploration of Southwest Africa as far as Victoria Falls and Lake Ngami. Professor Wahlberg entertained come singular beliefs, founded though they were entirely upon analogy, or, rather, assumptions which experience certainly contravenes. Among these fallacies was a belief, which he very strongly maintained, that in hunting elephants the safest plan to avoid the charge of an enraged animal was to stand still like a rock, as by so doing the elephant would be sure to swerve past the hunter without inflicting any injury, awed by the fearlessness and majesty of man. He even contended that in several instances he had demonstrated the fact. Green, who was at the time the boldest and most successful hunter in all Africa, maintained the discreetness of running away immediately upon firing at an elephant, without waiting to determine the result, and cited not a few occasions in which the wounded beast rushed forward and was standing in the very smoke of the gun when next seen.

A means of testing the question thus raised was soon offered for, though Green protested against the Professor placing himself in such imminent peril, which was little short of suicide, the naturalist was none the less eager to prove the correctness of his theory. Two days after the dispute was begun, the party, consisting of Green and brother, Chapman and Wahlberg, came upon a herd in which there were four bulls and six cows, all the latter having calves. As the animals were browsing near the edge of a jungle they were approached without trouble, the men having all dismounted and tied their horses some distance from the brutes. Green still continued to warn Wahlberg, and insisted on taking the lead himself, in order to prevent, if possible, an experiment which he felt certain must result in his friend's death. As the party approached within firing distance Green shot at the largest bull, but did not succeed in bringing him down. Wahlberg now rushed towards the bull and fired at his left shoulder, but his shot produced no other effect, apparently, than to further enrage the already unfuriated beast. The other elephants made off through the jungle, but the wounded bull, though quite able to travel swiftly, raised his head and trumpeted shrilly, as if challenging his foes to combat. All save Wahlberg so well understood the meaning of this act that they retreated precipitately, calling on the Professor to run for his life. In another moment the elephant came charging and trumpeting through the brush, having discovered Wahlberg, who was standing "like a rock" about ten yards from the edge of the jungle. In a trice the huge beast seized him in its trunk, and raising him very high in air dashed him violently on the ground. Horrified by the spectacle, Green and Chapman returned quickly and fired at the elephant right and left, whereupon it retreated again to the jungle, but not before one of its ponderous fore-feet had crushed in the breast of the naturalist. When his friends reached him the Professor was only a sickening spectacle of crushed bones and bleeding flesh, in which not a trace of life remained. He had settled the point in dispute, but in so doing science lost one of its ablest devotees.

BATTLES BETWEEN THE ELEPHANT AND RHINOCEROS.

The two most powerful animals that roam the jungles of Central Africa, or, indeed, that are to be met with in any region of the world, are the elephant and rhinoceros. The latter manifests greater timidity before man, but in his surly moods he does not disdain to engage in battle with the elephant and quite as frequently vanquishes his lordly adversary as he is himself beaten. The victory very much depends upon which has the better weapons, but when each is well provided in this respect the contest is nothing short of terrible. At times the rhinoceros is found almost destitute of the nasal horn, due, perhaps, to natural causes, usually his disposition to tear up young trees, excited by a parasite that frequently attacks his nostrils and causes him great pain. Age, also, affects the growth of the horn, which becomes worn so much as to be fairly useless as a weapon. The elephant, however, is hardly less fortunate, for sometimes we find him illy provided with tusks, and at others with no tusks at all, having broken them off in uprooting trees or in combat with those of his own species. Naturally the African rhinoceros is armed with a fearful weapon in the shape of a horn three or even four feet in length, terminating with a keen point, which he uses with desperate effect.

In waging the combat neither animal seems to exhibit much strategy, since they blindly rush upon each other and strike wherever opportunity offers. Should the elephant succeed in catching his adversary in the side he quickly impales him with his terrible tusks and is invariably victorious; but so great an advantage is uncommon. Most generally the rhinoceros is struck about the shoulders, and it often happens that his thick hide deflects the thrust, when he rushes on and plunges his horn either into his antagonist's abdomen or rips

COMBAT BETWEEN AN ELEPHANT AND RHINOCEROS.

his legs or breast. If the elephant turns to retreat he is certainly doomed, for then the rhinoceros attacks him in the rear or side and invariably tears him with his horn, nor ceases to ply this fearful weapon until the elephant is torn and gashed into an almost unrecognizable mass.

CHAPTER XXX.

THE RHINOCEROS.

ITS HABITS, FEROCITY AND DISPOSITION.

NEXT to the elephant in interest and curiosity, I unhesitatingly place the *Rhinoceros*. This animal would, no doubt, be king of the forest, but for his sluggish character, for he possesses a wonderful armature in the almost invulnerable coat with which nature clothes him, while his weapon is so formidable that no beast of his wild home can stand against him. The elephant is an acknowledged superior by reason of his ponderous bulk and majestic, awe-inspiring appearance, as well as for the great sagacity he manifests. But if the king of animals should be chosen from the most formidable of beasts, then the crown must surely be worn by the rhinoceros. It not infrequently happens that the mighty Titans of the forest, the elephant and rhinoceros, become engaged in terrible disputes, when the wonderful weapons with which they are endowed are wielded with an effect positively frightful to witness. The elephant thrusts with his tusks and attempts to trample, but the thick hide of the rhinoceros is fairly impervious to even these great pikes, and being extremely active for his immense size, the rhinoceros attacks his antagonist from beneath, and disembowels him with the dispatch with which a sportsman splits a fish. Of course, the contestant to which I refer is the large, black rhinoceros of Africa or India, the fierce autocrat of the jungle, and not the small, white species which roams the forests with his gigantic congeners.

DIFFERENT SPECIES AND WHERE FOUND.

The rhinoceros is peculiar to many countries, including Bengal, Siam, Ceylon, China, Java, Sumatra and Africa. But there is a broad distinction between those of Asia and of Africa. In the former country the animal is covered with an exceedingly coarse hide, which lies in folds, or creased, so as to somewhat resemble the large folds of the alligator. They have also only one horn, except the Java and Sumatra species, which have two horns, but these animals are small in size, and of so harmless a disposition that they never act, even on the defensive, against man, neither are they numerous.

Four distinct species of rhinoceri are known to exist in South Africa, two of which are of a dark color, and two of a whitish hue.

Hence, they are usually designated as the "black" and "white" rhinoceros. One of the two species of "black"—the *Borle*, as it is most commonly called—is the small, one-horned rhinoceros. The other—best known by the name *Keitloa*—is the large, two-horned animal, not only larger but much fiercer than the former. Both species, however, are extremely fierce and, excepting the buffalo, are perhaps the most dangerous of all beasts in Southern Africa.

Of the white species we have the *Koboaba*, or long-horned white rhinoceros. It is with regard to their horns that the two species chiefly differ from each other, for whilst the anterior horn of the one, called *monoohoo* by the Bechuanas, has an average length of two or three feet, curving backwards, that of the koboaba not unfrequently exceeds four feet, and inclines forward from the snout at an angle of nearly forty-five degrees.

The black and the white rhinoceros, though nearly allied to each other, differ widely in their mode of living and habits. The chief sustenance of the former consists of the roots of certain bushes, which it plows up with its strong horn, and the shoots and tender boughs of the "wait-a-bit" thorn; whilst the white rhinoceros feeds solely on grasses. In disposition, also, there is a marked distinction between them; the black is of a very savage nature, while the white, on the other hand, is of a comparatively mild disposition; and, unless in defense of its young, or when hotly pursued or wounded, will rarely attack a man.

The horn of the rhinoceros is the most curious feature, not only in appearance, but structure as well. The substance of which it is composed is not horn, but a mass of fine longitudinal threads resembling hair, attached not to the skull, but to a bony protuberance above the nostrils. It is believed by many, that when the animal is at rest, the so-called horns are soft and pliable, but when on the move they at once become hard and solid; moreover, that it can, at will, turn the posterior horn, the anterior one remaining meanwhile firm and erect. But this is merely an assertion without any reliable proof, therefore improbable. In former days the horn was supposed to bear an antipathy to poison, and to cause effervescence whenever liquid poison was poured upon it. Goblets were therefore cut from this material, and when gorgeously mounted in gold and precious stones, were employed by Eastern monarchs as a ready means for detecting any attempt to administer a deadly drug. The

Kaffirs make knob-kerries, or knob-headed sticks of the horn, which they use to kill birds and small game, and also in hand-to-hand conflicts. Ramrods are also made of the same material, for which purpose they are better than wood or steel.

In size, the African rhinoceros—the white species, at least—is only exceeded by the elephant. A full grown male measures from the snout to the extremity of the tail (which is about two feet) between fourteen and sixteen feet, and a circumference of ten to twelve feet, while the weight is probably from four to five thousand pounds.

A RHINOCEROS CHARGES A WAGON.

The general appearance of the African rhinoceros is somewhat like a shorn hog, for it is fairly destitute of hair. The eyes are extremely small, so that at a comparatively short distance they are imperceptible. Altogether, what with his huge body, mis-shapen head, ungainly legs and feet, trailing belly, and diminutive organs of vision, the rhinoceros is the very image of ugliness. Every indication points to the great longevity of the animal, though the extreme age to which it attains has not been fully determined. That it exceeds one hundred years, however, is a well established fact.

In strength the rhinoceros is scarcely inferior to the elephant, while the weapon with which it is provided enables it to do far greater mischief. It is on record, that a rhinoceros which Emanuel, King of Portugal, sent to the Pope in the year 1813, destroyed—in a paroxysm of fury, to which these animals seem to be frequently subjected—the vessel in which he was being transported, so that nearly all the crew were drowned. Mr. Bam, a traveler in South Africa, also relates an incident to show the extraordinary fury and power of this mighty animal. He says:

"As we entered the Swakop river one day we observed the tracks of a rhinoceros, and soon after unyoking our oxen the men requested to be allowed to go in search of the beast. This I readily granted, only reserving a native to assist me in kindling the fire and preparing our meal. While we were thus engaged we heard shouting and firing, and, on looking in the direction whence the noise proceeded, discovered, to our horror, a rhinoceros, rushing furiously at us at the top of his speed. Our only chance of escape was the wagon, into which we hurriedly flung ourselves. And it was high time that we should seek refuge, for the next instant the enraged brute struck his horn into the bottom boards with such force as to push the wagon several paces forward, although it was standing in very heavy sand. Most providentially, he attacked the vehicle from behind, for, if he had struck it on the side, he could hardly have failed to upset it, ponderous as it was. From the wagon he made a dash at the fire, overturning the pot we had placed along-side it, and scattering the burning brands in every direction. Then, without doing further damage, he proceeded on his wild career. Unfortunately, the men had taken with them all the guns, otherwise, I might easily have shot him dead on the spot. The Damara, however, threw his assegai at him, but the soft iron bent like a reed against his thick, tough and almost impenetrable hide."

A RHINOCEROS ATTACKING A WAGON.

Ungainly and heavy as the rhinoceros looks, it is, nevertheless, so exceedingly swift of foot, particularly the black species, "that a horse with a rider," to quote the words of Gordon Cumming, "can rarely manage to overtake it." The testimony of Captain Harris is to the like effect; for, when speaking of the chase of this animal, and after telling us that it is most difficult to kill, he says: "From its clumsy appearance one would never suppose it could dart about as it does, like lightning."

The rhinoceros is a very affectionate mother, and guards her offspring with the tenderest care. Little seems to be known of its breeding habits except that a single offspring is brought forth at a time. The young clings dotingly to its dam, and even a day or two after the latter has been killed the calf is frequently found beside the carcass.

The sense of hearing and of smell are very acute in the rhinoceros, but, on the other hand, his sight is very imperfect. From the peculiar position of his eyes — which are deep set in the head — and his large horns, he cannot see what is directly before him, nor does his range of vision extend much behind a line with his shoulder.

THE TERRIBLE FEROCITY OF AN INDIAN RHINOCEROS.

Seen in his native wilds, either when browsing at his leisure, or listlessly sauntering about, a person would be apt to regard the rhinoceros as the most stupid and inoffensive of creatures; yet, when his ire is aroused, he becomes the reverse, and is then the most agile and terrible of beasts.

Colonel Williamson writes of a rhinoceros in India whose ferocity was such as to render the roads impassable, by attacking travelers, or those who passed near its haunts. He relates the circumstances of an attack made by this animal upon a company of sportsmen who were not after such game. He says: "Two officers belonging to the troops cantoned at Dunapore, near Patua, went down the river toward Monghyr, to shoot and hunt. They had encamped in the vicinity of Derrzapore, and had heard some reports of a rhinoceros having attacked some travelers several miles off. One morning, just as they were rising, about day-break, to go in quest of game, they heard a violent uproar, and, on looking out, found that a rhinoceros was goring their horses, both of which, being fastened by their heads, and heels with ropes, were consequently unable to escape or resist. Their servants took to their heels, and concealed themselves in the neighboring jungle, and the gentlemen had just time to climb into a small tree not far distant, before the ferocious beast, having completed the destruction of the horses, turned his attention to their masters. They were barely out of his reach, and by no means exempt from danger, especially as he assumed a threatening appearance, and seemed intent on their downfall. After keeping them in dreadful suspense for some time, and using many efforts to dislodge them, seeing the sun rise, he retreated to his haunt, not, however, without occasionally casting an eye back, as with regret, at leaving what he wanted the power to destroy."

FIGHT BETWEEN FOUR BULL RHINOCERI.

The rhinoceros is not alone dangerous to man; all the beasts of the forest dread him, and none venture to attack this formidable monster. The lion, if he chances to meet a rhinoceros, slinks out of his way, not daring to suffer a near approach. The elephant, too, should they encounter, retreats, if possible, without hazarding an engagement.

A BATTLE OF GIANTS.

Major Lally described to the author of "Oriental Sports" a desperate battle, which he once witnessed from a neighboring hill, between a large male elephant and a rhinoceros. The combat was fierce beyond description, the huge animals contesting with a power that fairly shook the woods, and tearing up more than an acre of ground like a steam plow. The fight at length terminated in favor of the rhinoceros, who put his great antagonist to rout covered with frightful gashes which must have shortly afterwards proved fatal.

The rhinoceros not only measures strength with any animal of the forest, but will even court a combat with his own species, particularly during certain seasons when he appears to be in an irritable mood.

Andersson says: "One night, when at the skarm, I saw four huge beasts engage each other at the same time, and so furious was the strife, and their gruntings so horrible, that it caused the greatest consternation amongst my party, who were encamped a little way off. I succeded, after a while, in killing two of them, one of which was actually unfit for food, being literally covered with wounds received on previous occasions, and probably under similar circumstances."

HUNTING THE RHINOCEROS.

The rhinoceros is a favorite game with African sportsmen, notwithstanding its ferocious disposition and the difficulty in killing it. One of the most generally approved plans is to stalk the animal, either when feeding or reposing. If the hunter keeps well under the wind, and there be the least cover, he will have no difficulty in approaching the beast within an easy range when, if the ball is well-directed, the prey is usually killed on the spot. With proper precaution this kind of sport may be conducted without greatly endangering a person's safety.

But the least dangerous and most convenient way of destroying this animal is to shoot him from the skarm as he comes to the pool to quench his thirst. "In this manner," says Andersson, "I have killed many scores of rhinoceri." Occasionally the animal is taken in pitfalls, which are constructed in pretty much the same manner as those for the capture of the elephant and other large game.

DESPERATE SITUATION OF MR. OSWALL.

The rhinoceros is not often hunted on horseback, chiefly because his speed and endurance are such that it is very difficult to come up with and follow him—to say nothing of the danger attendant on such a course. Many a hunter, indeed, has thereby endangered his life. In proof of this Andersson relates the following harrowing incident, as it was told to him:

"'Once, as I was returning from an elephant chase,' said Mr. Oswall, in conversation with me one day, 'I observed a huge white rhinoceros, a short distance ahead. I was riding a most excellent hunter—the best and fleetest steed that I ever possessed during my shooting excursions in Africa—at that time; but it was a rule with me never to pursue a rhinoceros on horseback, simply because this animal is so much more easily approached and killed on foot. On this occasion, however, it seemed as if fate had interfered. Turning to my after-rider, I called out: 'By heaven, that fellow has a fine horn! I will have a shot at him.' With that I clapped spurs to my horse, who soon brought me alongside the huge beast, and the next instant I lodged a ball in his body, but, as it turned out, not with deadly effect. On receiving my shot, the rhinoceros, to my great surprise, instead of seeking safety in flight, as is the habit of this generally inoffensive animal, suddenly stopped short, then turned sharply round, and, having eyed me most curiously for a second or two, walked slowly towards me. I never dreamt of danger. Nevertheless, I instinctively turned my horse's head away; but, strange to say, this creature, usually so docile and gentle—which the slightest touch of the reins would be sufficient to guide—now absolutely refused to give me his head. When, at last, he did so it was too late; for, notwithstanding the rhinoceros had only been walking, the distance between us was so inconsiderable, that by this time I clearly saw contact was unavoidable. Indeed, in another moment, I observed the brute bend low his head, and, with a thrust upwards, struck his horn into the ribs of the horse with such force as to penetrate to the very saddle on the opposite side, where I felt its sharp point against my leg. The violence of the blow was so tremendous as to cause the horse to make a complete somersault in the air, coming heavily down on his back. With regard to myself, I was, as a matter of course, violently precipitated to the ground. Whilst thus prostrated, I actually saw the horn of the infuriated brute along-side of me; but, seemingly satisfied with his revenge, without attempting to do further mischief, he started off at a canter from the scene of action. My after-rider having by this time come up, I rushed upon him, and, almost pulling him off the horse, leaped into the saddle, and without a hat and my face streaming with blood, was quickly in pursuit of the retreating beast, which I soon had the satisfaction of seeing stretched lifeless at my feet.

"'My friend, Captain Vardon, by whom I was accompanied on this journey, soon after joined me, and seeing my head and face covered with blood, at first imagined me to be mortally wounded or dying. However, with the exception of a blow on the skull, occasioned by the stirrup-iron, which laid my head open a few inches, I received no further injury. But the horse was killed on the spot.'"

OSWALL BADLY WOUNDED BY A RHINOCEROS.

The good fortune which attended Mr. Oswall in the adventure just related entirely deserted him upon an occasion somewhat similar,

A GREAT HUNTER IN A PERILOUS POSITION.

which occurred soon after. Relating this story, at the same time, to Mr. Andersson, who records it, Oswall says:

"'On another occasion, as I was bending my steps towards my camp on foot, I espied, at no great distance, two rhinoceri of the species keitloa. They were feeding and slowly approaching me. I immediately crouched and quietly waited their arrival; but, though they soon came within range, from their constantly facing me I was unable to fire, well knowing the uselessness of a shot at the head. In a short time they had approached so close that, on account of the exposed nature of the ground, I could neither retreat nor advance, and my situation became highly critical. I was afraid to fire, for, had I even succeeded in killing one, the other would, in all likelihood, have run over and trampled me to death. In this dilemma the thought struck me, that on account of their bad sight I might possibly save myself by trying to run past them. No time was to be lost; and accordingly, just as the leading animal almost touched me, I stood up and dashed past it. The brute was, however, much too quick for me, and before I had made good many paces, I heard a violent snorting at my heels; and had only time to fire my gun at random into his head, when I felt myself impaled on his horn.

"'The shock stunned me completely. The first return to consciousness was, I recollect, finding myself seated on one of my ponies, and a Caffre leading it. I had an indistinct notion of having been hunting; and, on observing the man, I asked quickly why he was not following the animal, when he mumbled something to the effect that it was gone.

"'By accident I touched my right hip with my hand, and on withdrawing it, was astonished to find it clotted with blood. Yet my senses were still so confused, and the side so benumbed, that I actually kept feeling and working the wound with my fingers. Whilst trying to account for my strange position, I observed some of my men coming towards me with a cartel, and on asking them what they were about, they cried out that they had come to fetch my body, having been told that I was killed by some animal. The truth now, for the first time, broke upon me, and I was quickly made aware of my crippled condition. The wound I had received was of a serious character, and though it ultimately healed, it left scars behind which will remain with me to the day of my death.'"

THE VULNERABLENESS OF THE RHINOCEROS.

Andersson takes some pains in his work entitled "Lake Ngami," to disprove some of the popular errors entertained about the invulnerability of the rhinoceros. He says: "It is generally received as a fact that the hide of the rhinoceros is impenetrable to a bullet, or even to an 'iron ingot,' as a certain writer quaintly expresses it. But this is just as idle a notion, as regards the African species at least, as that entertained respecting the softness and pliability of the animal's horns; for a common leaden ball will find its way through the hide with the greatest facility. It is true, we should be near the brute; for, though I have known a rhinoceros killed at the distance of a hundred yards, it is an exception to the rule. Indeed, beyond thirty or forty paces one cannot make sure of the shot. Under all circumstances a double charge of powder is desirable, and a bullet made of two-thirds lead and one-third solder is most reliable.

"The most deadly part to aim at is just behind the shoulder; a ball through the center of the lobes of the lungs is certain to cause almost instantaneous death. From the very solid structure of the head, the great thickness of the hide on that part, the position of the horn, and the smallness of the brain, a shot in the head rarely or never proves fatal. The same may be said of the breast."

ANDERSSON'S PERILOUS ADVENTURE WITH A BLACK RHINOCEROS.

Andersson, the great hunter, claims to have killed nearly sixty rhinoceri during the first year of his travels in South Africa, which, considering the fact that these were slain while he was in pursuit of other game, furnishes an idea of the plentifulness of the animal in that region. It is not strange, therefore, that he should meet with remarkable adventures jeopardizing his life, and which may be fairly called "hair-breadth escapes." Among the perilous experiences which he records none are more thrilling than the following:

"One fine moon-light night, when snugly ensconced in my skarm, and contemplating the strange, but picturesque scene before me, my reverie was interrupted by the inharmonious grunting of a black rhinoceros. He was evidently in bad humor, for, as he emerged from amongst the trees into more open ground, I observed him madly charging anything and everything that he encountered, such as bushes, stones, etc. Even the whitened skulls and skeletons of his own species, lying scattered about on the ground, were attacked with inconceivable fury. I was much amused at his eccentric pastime; but, owing to the openness of the ground and the quantity of limestone thereabouts, which made objects more distinct, he was not easy to approach. However, after divesting myself of my shoes, and all the more conspicuous parts of my dress, I managed to crawl—pushing my gun before me—to within a short distance of the snorting beast. As he was advancing in a direct line toward me, I did not like to fire, because one has little chance of killing the rhinoceros when in that position. Having approached within a few feet of me, his attention was attracted, and suddenly uttering one of those strange 'blowing' noises, so peculiar to the beast when alarmed or enraged, he prepared to treat me in a similar manner to the stones and skulls he had just so mercilessly tossed about. Not a moment was to be lost; and, in self-defense, I fired at his head. I shall never forget the confusion of the animal on receiving the contents of my gun. Springing nearly perpendicularly into the air, and to the height of several feet, he came down again with a thump that seemed to make the earth tremble—then violently plunging forward (in doing which he all but trampled me), he ran round and round the spot for fully five minutes, enveloping every object in a cloud of dust. At last he dashed into the wood and was hidden from view. Not finding blood on his tracks, I had no reason to suppose that he was much hurt. My notion is, the bullet struck his horn, partially stunning him with its jarring violence. Had my gun missed fire when he charged, it is more than probable I would have been impaled."

A STILL MORE REMARKABLE ESCAPE.

"Having on a certain night," says Andersson, "stalked to within a few paces of a huge white rhinoceros (a female as it proved), I put a ball in her shoulder; but it nearly cost me dear, for, guided by the flash of the gun, she rushed upon me with such fury that I had only time to throw myself on my back, in which position I remained motionless. This saved my life, for, not observing me, she came to a sudden halt just as her feet were about to crush my body. She was so near to me that I felt the saliva from her mouth trickle on my face. I was in an agony of suspense, though, happily, only for a moment; for, having impatiently sniffed the air, she wheeled about and made off at her utmost speed. I then saw, for the first time, that her calf was in company, and at once recognized the pair as old acquaintances, and as especially vicious animals."

PERILOUS RIDE ON THE BACK OF A RHINOCEROS.

It is related by reliable travelers that on one occasion some *Namaquas* shot a rhinoceros as it was rising from its sleep, apparently killing it on the spot. Imagining that the beast was quite dead, one of the hunters, in a spirit of bravado, rushed up to it, and, seating himself astride the huge body, plunged his knife into it. The animal, however, had only been stunned, and being brought to his senses by the

PERILOUS RIDE OF A NAMAQUA.

thrust of the steel, jumped up and started off at full speed. This action was so instantaneous that the man had no time to dismount, and fairly paralyzed with fear he kept his seat while the mad beast went tearing away across the plain, presenting a scene at once comical and tragical. The other Namaquas started in pursuit, scarcely hoping, however, to save their companion from a frightful death. Good fortune did not abandon him in this sore extremity, for after running a short distance the rhinoceros stopped short, being now well spent by reason of the mortal wound he had received, and stood still until the hunters came up and fired another ball into his body, which ended its career. The rider was so frenzied with fear that he made no attempt to leap from the rhinoceros when it came to a halt, but maintained his seat until the animal dropped dead.

CHARGED AND LACERATED BY A RHINOCEROS.

In the preceding pages I quoted from Mr. Andersson's "Lake Ngami" an account which he gave of his marvelous escape from a huge bull-elephant that so nearly trampled on him that he had to scramble from between its legs. On the same night that this adventure befell him he passed through a yet more thrilling experience, which he relates as follows:

"Whilst pondering over my late wonderful escape, I observed at a little distance a huge white rhinoceros protrude his ponderous and misshapen head through the bushes, and presently afterwards he approached to within a dozen paces of my ambuscade. His broadside was then fully exposed to view, and, notwithstanding I still felt a little nervous from my conflict with the elephant, I lost no time in firing. The beast did not at once fall to the ground, but from appearances I had every reason to believe he would not live long.

"Scarcely had I reloaded when a black rhinoceros of the species *keitloa* (a female as it proved), stood drinking at the water; but her position, as with the elephant in the first instance, was unfavorable foı a good shot. As, however, she was very near me, I thought I was pretty sure of breaking her leg, and thereby disabling her, and in this I succeeded. My fire seemed to madden her; she rushed wildly forward on three legs, when I gave her a second shot, though apparently with little or no effect. I felt sorry at not being able to end her sufferings at once; but as I was too well acquainted with the habits of the rhinoceros to venture on pursuing her under the circumstances, I determined to wait patiently for daylight, and to destroy her with the aid of my dogs. But it was not to be.

"As no more elephants or other large game appeared, I thought after a time it might be well to go in search for the white rhinoceros, previously wounded, and I was not long finding her carcass; for my ball, as I supposed, had caused almost immediate death.

"In heading back to my *skarm* I accidentally took a turn in the direction pursued by the black rhinoceros, and by ill luck, as the event proved, at once encountered her. She was still on her legs, but her position, as before, was still unfavorable. Hoping, however, to

ANDERSSON IN HIS SKARM AT NIGHT, ON LAKE NGAMI.

make her change it for a better, and thus enable me to destroy her at once, I took up a stone and hurled it at her with all my force;

when, snorting horridly and erecting her tail, keeping her head close to the ground, and raising clouds of dust by her feet, she rushed at me with fearful fury. I had only just time to load my rifle and fire before she was upon me, and the next instant, while instinctively turning round for the purpose of retreating, she laid me prostrate. The shock was so violent as to send my rifle, powder-flask and ball-pouch, as also my cap, spinning in the air; the gun, indeed, as afterwards ascertained, to a distance of fully ten feet. On the beast charging me it crossed my mind that, unless gored by the horn, her impetus would be such (after knocking me down, which I took for granted would be the case) as to carry her beyond me, and I might thus be afforded a chance of escape. So, indeed, it happened; for, having tumbled me over (in doing which her head and the fore-part of her body, owing to the violence of the charge, were buried in the sand), and trampled on me with great violence, her fore-quarters passed over my body. Struggling for life, I seized my opportunity, and as she was recovering herself for a renewal of the charge, I scrambled out between her hind legs.

"But the enraged beast had not yet done with me. Scarcely had I regained my feet before she struck me down a second time, and with her horn ripped up my right thigh (though not very deeply) from near the knee to the hip; with her fore-feet, moreover, she hit me a terrific blow on the left shoulder near the back of the neck. My ribs bent under the enormous weight and pressure, and for a moment, I must, I believe, have lost consciousness — I have, at least, very indistinct notions of what afterwards took place. All I remember is, that when I raised my head, I heard a furious snorting and plunging among the neighboring bushes. I now arose, though with great difficulty, and made my way, in the best manner I was able, towards a large tree near at hand for shelter; but this precaution was needless; the beast, for the time at least, showed no inclination further to molest me. Either in the *melee*, or owing to the confusion caused by her wounds, she had lost sight of me, or she felt satisfied with the revenge she had taken. Be that as it may, I escaped with life, though sadly wounded and severely bruised, in which disabled state I had great difficulty in getting back to my skarm.

"GOOD GOD! THE BRUTE HAS ATTACKED THE LAD ALSO!"

"During the greater part of the conflict I preserved my presence of mind; but after the danger was over, and when I had leisure to collect my scattered and confused senses, I was seized with a nervous affection, causing a violent trembling. I have since killed many rhinoceri, as well for sport as food; but several weeks elapsed before I could again attack these animals with any coolness.

"About sunrise, Kamapyu, my half-caste boy, whom I had left on the preceding evening, about half a mile away, came to the skarm to convey my guns and other things to our encampment. In a few words I related to him the mishap that had befallen me. He listened with seeming incredulity, but the sight of my gashed thigh soon convinced him I was not joking.

"I afterwards directed him to take one of the guns and proceed in search of the wounded rhinoceros, cautioning him to be careful in approaching the beast, which I had reason to believe was not yet dead. He had only been absent a few minutes, when I heard a cry of distress. Striking my hand against my forehead, I exclaimed:— '*Good God! the brute has attacked the lad also!*'

"Seizing hold of my rifle, I scrambled through the bushes as fast as my crippled condition would permit; and when I had proceeded two or three hundred yards, a scene suddenly presented itself that I shall vividly remember to the last days of my existence. Amongst some bushes, and within a couple of yards of each other, stood the rhinoceros and the young savage; the former supporting herself on three legs, covered with blood and froth, and snorting in the most ferocious manner; the latter petrified with fear—spell-bound, as it were—and riveted to the spot. Creeping, therefore, to the side of the rhinoceros opposite to that on which the boy was standing, so as to draw her attention from him, I leveled and fired, on which the beast charged wildly to and fro without any distinct object. Whilst she was thus occupied, I poured in shot after shot, but thought she would never fall. At length, however, she sank slowly to the ground; and, imagining she was in her death agonies, and that all danger was over, I walked unhesitatingly close up to her, and was on the point of placing the muzzle of my gun to her ear to give her the *coup de grace*, when, to my horror, she once more rose to her legs. Taking a hurried aim I pulled the trigger, and instantly retreated, with the beast in full pursuit. The race, however, was a short one; for, just as I threw myself into a bush for safety, she fell dead at my feet, so near me, indeed, that I could have touched her with the muzzle of my rifle! Another moment and I should probably have been impaled on her murderous horn, which, though short, was sharp as a razor."

A THRILLINGLY EXCITING RHINOCEROS HUNT.

In a previous chapter I reproduced Sir Samuel Baker's description of the manner in which the aggageers (Abyssinian sword-hunters) killed a huge bull-elephant; I have now to introduce these famously courageous sportsmen again as hunters of the rhinoceros, quoting from Baker the following thrilling description of a chase after two fierce animals:

"We were thus leisurely returning home through alternate plains and low, open forests of mimosa, when Taher Sherrif, who was leading the party, suddenly reined up his horse and pointed to a thick bush, beneath which was a large gray, but shapeless, mass. He whispered, as I drew near, '*Oomgurrin*' (mother of the horn), their name for the rhinoceros. I immediately dismounted, and with the short No. 10 Totham rifle, I advanced as near as I could, followed by Suleiman, as I had sent all my gun-bearers direct home by the river when we had commenced this circuit. As I drew near, I discovered two rhinoceri asleep beneath a thick mass of bushes; they were lying like pigs, close together, so that at a distance I had been unable to distinguish any exact form. It was an awkward place, for if I were to take the wind fairly, I should have to fire through the thick bush, which would be useless; therefore, I was compelled to advance with the wind direct from me to them. The aggageers remained about a hundred yards distant, while I told Suleiman to return and hold my horse in readiness with his own. I then walked quietly to within about thirty yards of the rhinoceri, but so curiously were they lying that it was useless to attempt a shot. In their happy dreams they must have been suddenly disturbed by the scent of an enemy, for, without the least warning, they suddenly sprang to their feet with astonishing quickness, and with a loud and sharp whiff, whiff, whiff! one of them charged straight at me. I fired my right-hand barrel in his throat, as it was useless to aim at the head, protected by two horns at the nose. This turned him, but had no other effect, and the two animals thundered off together at a tremendous pace.

"'Now for a tally-ho!' Our stock of guns was scattered on the ground, and away went the aggageers in full speed after the rhinoceri without waiting to reload. I quickly remounted my horse, Tetel, and, with Suleiman in company, I spurred hard to overtake the flying

Arabs. Tetel was a good, strong cob, but not very fast; however, I believe he never went so well as upon that day, for, although an Abyssinian horse, I had a pair of English spurs which worked like missionaries, but with a more decided result. The ground was awkward for riding at full speed, as it was an open forest of mimosas, which, although wide apart, were very difficult to avoid, owing to the low crowns of spreading branches; these, being armed with fish-hook thorns, would have been serious in a collision. I kept the party in view, until in about a mile we arrived upon open ground. I again applied the spurs, and by degrees I crept up, always gaining, until I, at length, joined the aggageers.

A SIGHT FOR A SPORTSMAN.

"Here was a sight to drive a hunter wild! The two rhinoceri were running neck and neck, like a pair of horses in harness, but bounding along at tremendous speed within ten yards of the leading hamran. This was Taher Sherrif, who, with his sword drawn, and his long hair flying wildly behind him, urged his horse forward in the race, amidst a cloud of dust raised by the two huge but active beasts, that tried every sinew of the horses. Rodur Sherrif, with the withered arm, was second, with the reins hung upon the hawk-like claw that was all that remained of a hand, but, with his naked sword grasped in his right, he kept close to his brother, ready to second his blow. Abou Do was third; his hair flying in the wind—his heels dashing against the flanks of his horse, to which he shouted in his excitement to urge him to the front, while he leaned forward with his long sword, in the wild energy of the moment, as though hoping to reach the game against all possibility. Now for the spurs! and as these, vigorously applied, screwed an extra stride out of Tetel, I soon found myself in the ruck of men, horses and drawn swords. There were seven of us—and passing Abou Do, whose face wore an expression of agony at finding that his horse was failing, I quickly obtained a place between the two brothers, Taher and Rodur Sherrif. There had been a jealousy between the two parties of aggageers, and each was striving to outdo the other; thus Abou Do was driven almost to madness at the superiority of Taher's horse, while the latter, who was the renowned hunter of the tribe, was determined that his sword should be first to taste blood. I tried to pass the rhinoceros on my left, so as to fire close into the shoulder my remaining barrel with my right-hand, but it was impossible to overtake the animal, who bounded

BAKER'S WONDERFUL RHINOCEROS RIDE.

along with undiminished speed. With the greatest exertion of men and horses we could only retain our position within about three or four yards of their tails—just out of reach of the swords. The only chance in the race was to hold the pace until the rhinoceri should begin to flag. The horses were pressed to their utmost, but we had already run about two miles, and the game showed no signs of giving in. On they flew—sometimes over open ground, and then through low brush, which tried the horses severely; then through strips of open forest, until at length the party began to tail off, and only a select few kept their places. We arrived at the summit of a ridge, from which the ground sloped in a gentle inclination for about a mile towards the river; at the foot of this incline was a thick, thorny nabbuk jungle, for which impenetrable covert the rhinoceri pressed at their utmost speed. Never was there better ground for the finish of a race; the earth was sandy but firm, and as we saw the winning post in the jungle that must terminate the hunt, we redoubled our exertions to close with the unflagging game. Suleiman's horse gave in—we had been for about twenty minutes at a killing pace. Tetel, although not a fast horse, was good for a distance, and he now proved his power of endurance, as I was riding at least two stone (twenty-eight pounds) heavier than any of the party. Only four of the seven remained, and we swept down the incline, Taher Sherrif still leading, and Abou Do the last! His horse was done, but not the rider; for, springing to the ground while at full speed, sword in hand, he forsook his tired horse, and, preferring his own legs, he ran like an antelope and, for the first hundred yards, I thought he would really pass us, and win the honor of first blow. It was of no use; the pace was too severe and, though running wonderfully, he was obliged to give way to the horses. Only three now followed the rhinoceri—Taher Sherrif and his brother, Rodur, and myself. I had been obliged to give the second place to Rodur, as he was a mere monkey in weight; but I was a close third. The excitement was intense—we neared the jungle, and the rhinoceri began to show signs of flagging, as the dust puffed up before their nostrils, and, with noses close to the ground, they snorted as they still galloped on. Oh, for a fresh horse! 'A horse, a horse! my kingdom for a horse!' We were within two hundred yards of the jungle; but the horses were all done. Tetel reeled as I urged him forward, Rodur pushed ahead; we were close to the dense thorns, and the rhinoceri broke into a trot; they were done. 'Now, Taher, for-r-a-a-r-r-d! for-r-a-a-r-r-d Taher!!' Away he went — he was close to the very heels of the beasts; but his horse could do no more than his present pace; still he gained upon the nearest; he leaned forward with his sword raised for the blow — another moment and the jungle would be reached! One effort more, and the sword flashed in the sunshine, as the nearest rhinoceros disappeared in the thick screen of thorns, with a gash about four feet long upon his hindquarters. Taher Sherrif shook his bloody sword in triumph above his head; but the rhinoceri were gone. We were fairly beaten; regularly outpaced; but I believe another two hundred yards would have given us the victory. 'Bravo, Taher!' I shouted. He had ridden splendidly and his blow had been marvelously delivered at an extremely long reach, as he was nearly out of his saddle when he sprang forward to enable the blade to attain a cut at the last moment. He could not reach the hamstring, as his horse could not gain the proper position.

"Taher Sherrif explained that at all times the rhinoceros was the most difficult animal to saber, on account of his extraordinary swiftness, and, although he had killed many with the sword, it was always after a long and fatiguing hunt; at the close of which, the animal becoming tired, generally turned to bay, in which case one hunter occupied his attention, while another galloped up behind, and severed the ham-string. The rhinoceros, unlike the elephant, can go very well on three legs; which enhances the danger, as one cut will not utterly disable him."

FURIOUS DISPOSITION OF THE RHINOCEROS.

The two-horned black rhinoceros, as already observed, is an extremely fierce animal, apparently considering all creatures its enemies. It has been frequently observed by experienced hunters that this mad animal will nearly always charge down upon any object that it smells but does not see; thus, when the animal is concealed either in high grass or thick jungle, should it scent a man who may be passing unseen to windward, it will rush down furiously upon the object it has winded, with three loud whiffs resembling a jet of steam from a safety-valve. As it is most difficult, in fact next to impossible, to kill a rhinoceros when charging, he is a particularly unpleasant stranger to thus suddenly meet. Baker had an experience of this kind once which gave him a fright which he was a long time in recovering from.

While passing over some extremely rough country, covered with rocks and tall grass, Baker came upon the fresh tracks of a rhinoceros, which he was sure was still in the vicinity. While speculating with the aggageer-hunters as to its probable position, and thinking how extremely unpleasant an attack of the beast might prove in such a broken district, he was suddenly startled by the sharp whistling snort, whiff, whiff, and the great beast came thundering out of a thicket down upon him in a determined charge. There was no time left for giving battle, as the concern of getting away was all important. He dug the spurs into his horse's flanks, and clasping his steed round the neck he started the retreat, blindly trusting to providence. The poor horse scrambled with all his power over the huge boulders, through

VICIOUS CHARGE OF AN INFURIATED RHINOCEROS.

kettar thorns and grass ten feet high, stimulated not only by the spurs in his flanks but by the snorts of the vicious animal that threatened to rip him in the rear. The aggageers were all scattered and one of them was knocked over by the rhinoceros but not seriously hurt. All succeeded in making their escape, but they were so badly frightened that no attempt was afterwards made to bring the animal to bay.

THE NERVE REQUIRED TO SLAY A RHINOCEROS.

Sometimes, in fact often, it occurs that the rhinoceros will flee from a hunter, and thus become an innocent target for his sport, but the exception to this is by no means rare; indeed, no other animal charges so furiously nor so frequently as the rhinoceros, and since it is the most difficult of all brutes to kill, the hunter who follows rhinoceros shooting must possess most remarkable nerve, a quick sight and the activity of an acrobat. The hide of the rhinoceros is less than an inch in thickness, but it is so extremely tough that it requires an extraordinary force to penetrate it. The head, though large, may be perforated by an ordinary bullet, yet, owing to the remarkable smallness of the brain, which is largely protected by the horn, a head shot is perhaps the least likely to prove fatal.

When the game is dangerous and a perfect shot is necessary the greatest amount of nerve is required. The rhinoceros presents but one seriously vulnerable place — behind the shoulder — and to strike this spot fatally the hunter must be close to the animal. A wound is nearly always followed by a furious charge, and what on earth can be more terrible than a thrust from a horn four feet long and with a point as keen as a saber? Or, should the animal miss in striking his horrible weapon, there is the ponderous body thundering on like a locomotive on the down grade in front of a heavy freight train, most likely to grind the hunter into a mangled mass.

Few, if any men, have exhibited greater courage and coolness under desperate situations than Sir Samuel Baker, the greater part of his life being spent among savage people and in pursuit of the noblest game of the jungle. His adventures and hair-breadth escapes, fortunately published in many books, are an unending source of interest, and will be read with a thrill of delight by every one who admires pluck and daring, for centuries to come. For this reason I am continually tempted to quote from his marvelous records the thrilling experiences of his life. As an illustration of the nerve he possessed, the following incident, extracted from his "Nile Tributaries of Abyssinia," will serve admirably:

" * * * * To my astonishment there were the fresh tracks of a rhinoceros within a quarter of a mile of the camp; this animal must have concealed itself in the bed of the Royan during the fire, and had wandered forth when it had passed. I followed up the tracks with Bacheet and two of my *Tokrooris*. In less than half a mile from the spot, I found it lying down behind a bush. Creeping under cover of an ant-hill, I shot it through the shoulder with a Reilly No. 10; it immediately galloped off, but after running a couple of hundred yards it lay down on the edge of a thick, thorny jungle that bordered the margin of the Royan. I waited in the expectation

BAKER'S COOLNESS UNDER A TRYING SITUATION.

that it would shortly die, but it suddenly rose and walked slowly into the thorns. Determined to cut off his retreat, I pushed through the bushes, intending to reach the dry bed of the Royan and shoot the rhinoceros as it crossed from the narrow belt of the jungle, into which it had retreated; but I had hardly reached half way when I heard a sound in the bush upon my right, and I saw the wounded beast coming straight for our position, but evidently unconscious of our presence, as we were to leeward. I immediately crouched down, as did my men likewise, lest the animal should observe us. Slowly, but surely, it came on exactly towards us, until it was at last so near as to be unpleasant. I looked behind me and saw by the expression of my men that they were thinking of retreat. I merely shook my fist and frowned at them to give them confidence, and I waited patiently for my opportunity. It was becoming too ridiculous; the rhinoceros was within five or six yards, and was slowly but steadily advancing direct upon us; at the next step that he made I raised my rifle to my shoulder and whistled sharply; in an instant it tossed its head up, and seeing nothing in front, as my clothes matched with the leafless branches, it turned its head to the left, and I immediately pulled the trigger. It fell as though smitten by a sledge hammer and lay struggling on the ground. Bacheet sprang forward, and with an Arab sword cut the hamstring of one leg. To the astonishment of us all, the rhinoceros jumped up, and on three legs it sprang quickly round and charged Bacheet, who skipped into the bushes, while I ran alongside the rhinoceros as it attempted to follow him, and, with the Fletcher No. 24, I fired through the shoulder, by placing the muzzle within a yard of the animal. It fell dead to the shot, which was another feather in the cap of the good little rifle. This rhinoceros had no ears, they having been bitten off close to the head by another of the same species, while fighting. This mutilation is by no means uncommon."

AN EXCITING HUNT, AND TWO RHINOCERI CLEVERLY BAGGED.

A few days after the occurrence just related, Baker participated with the Arab hunters in another chase after rhinoceri, in which all the honor fell to him of bagging two monstrous brutes. The country in which he was hunting being covered with tall, rank grass, so thick as to obscure any animal that might be passing through it, Baker determined to render the surface bare by setting fire to the dry vegetation, which being carried into effect, a wonderful scene was at once presented. The smoke rolled away in tremendous waves, while from out the boiling clouds leaped lapping flames that spread with the rapidity of a slow-moving wind. The animals that were housed or browsing in the grass seeing the smoke and knowing what it portended, broke from the covert and sped away toward the hills; antelopes, blesboks, pallahs, hyenas, leopards, lions, rhinoceri and many other kinds of game, so that the scene constituted a panorama of extraordinary interest. Two days after the fire had spent itself, Baker went in search of the large game which he knew would soon return to the burned district, and taking up a position on a hill, round the base of which the grass had escaped the devouring flames, he obtained a perfect view of an immense tract of country. From his description I extract:

PREPARING FOR THE CHASE.

"I had been observing the country for some time from my high position, when suddenly I perceived two rhinoceri emerge from a ravine; they walked slowly through a patch of high grass, and skirted the base of the hill upon which we were standing; presently they winded something, and they trotted back and stood concealed in the patch of grass. Although I had a good view of them from my present position, I knew that I should not be able to see them in their covert, if on the same level; I therefore determined to send to the tent for my other horses, and to ride them down, if I could not shoot them on foot; accordingly I sent a man off, directing him to lead Tetel from the peak and to secure him to a tree at the foot of the hill, as I was afraid the rhinoceri might observe the horse on the sky-line. This he did, and we saw him tie the horse by the bridle to the branch of a tree below us, while he ran quickly toward the camp. In the meantime I watched the rhinoceri; both animals laid down in the yellow grass, resembling masses of stone. They had not been long in this position before we noticed two pigs wandering through the grass directly to windward, toward the sleeping rhinoceri; in an instant these animals winded the intruders, and starting up, looked in all directions, but could not see them, as they were concealed by the high grass. Having been thus disturbed, the rhinoceri moved their quarters, and walked slowly forward, occasionally halting, and listening; one was about a hundred yards in advance of the other. They were taking a direction at the base of the hill that would lead them directly on the spot where Tetel was tied to the tree. I observed this to Taher Noor, as I feared they would kill the horse. 'Oh, no,' he replied; 'they will lie down and sleep beneath the first tree, as they are seeking for shade — the sun is like fire.' However, they still continued their advance, and, upon reaching some rising ground, the leading rhinoceros halted, and I felt sure he had a clear view of the horse, that was now about five hundred yards distant, tied to a tree. A ridge descended from the hill, parallel with the course the animals were taking; upon this I ran as quickly as the stony slope permitted, keeping my eye fixed on the leading rhinoceros, who with his head raised, was advancing directly toward the horse. Tetel did not observe the rhinoceros, but was quietly standing beneath the tree. I ran as fast as I was able, and reached the bottom of the hill just as the willful brute was within fifty yards of the horse, which now for the first time saw the approaching danger; the rhinoceros had been advancing steadily at a walk, but he now lowered his head, and charged at the horse at full speed.

"I was about two hundred yards distant, and for the moment I was afraid of shooting the horse, but I fired one of the Reilly No. 10 rifles; the bullet, missing the rhinoceros, dashed the sand and stones into his face, as it struck the ground exactly before his nose, when he appeared to be just upon the unfortunate Tetel. The horse in the same instant reared and, breaking the bridle, dashed away in the direction of the camp, while the rhinoceros, astonished at the shot, and most likely half-blinded by the sand and splinters of rock, threw up his head, turned round, and trotted back upon the track by which he had arrived. He passed me at about a hundred yards distance, as I had run forward to a bush, by which he trotted with his head raised, seeking for the cause of his discomfiture. Crack! went a bullet against his side, as I fired my remaining barrel at his shoulder; he cocked his tail, and for a few yards he charged towards the shot; but he suddenly changed his course, and ran round several times in a small circle; he then halted, and reeling to and fro, he retreated very slowly, and laid down about a hundred yards off. Well done, Reilly! I knew that he had his *quietus*, but I was determined to bag his companion, who, in alarm, had now joined him, and stood looking in all quarters for the source of danger; but we were well concealed behind the bush. Presently, the wounded rhinoceros stood up, and walking very slowly, followed by his comrade, he crossed a portion of rising ground at the base of the hill, and both animals disappeared.

A RHINOCEROS CHARGING BAKER'S HORSE.

I at once started off Hassan, who could run like an antelope, in search of Tetel, while I dispatched another man to the summit of the peak to see if the rhinoceri were in view; if not, I knew they must be among the small trees and bushes at the foot of the hill. I thus waited a long time, until at length the two grays arrived with my messenger from the camp. I tightened the girths of the Arab saddle upon Aggahr, and had just mounted, cursing all Arab stirrups, that are only made for the naked big toe, when my eyes were gladdened by the sight of Hassan cantering towards me on Tetel, but from the exact direction the rhinoceri had taken. 'Quick! quick!' he cried, 'come along! one rhinoceros is lying dead close by, and the other is standing beneath a tree not far off.'

"I immediately jumped on Tetel, and, taking the little Fletcher rifle, as lighter and handier than the heavy No. 10, I ordered Taher Noor and Hassan to mount the other horses, and to follow me with spare rifles. I found the rhinoceros lying dead about two hundred yards from the spot where he had received the shot, and I immediately perceived the companion, that was standing beneath a small tree. The ground was firm and strong, all the grass had been burnt off, except in a few small patches; the trees were not so thick together as to form a regular jungle.

"The rhinoceros saw us directly, and he valiantly stood and faced me as I rode up within fifty yards of him. Tetel was worth his weight in gold, as a shooting horse; he stands like a rock, and would face the devil. I was unable to take a shot in this position, therefore, I ordered the men to ride round a half-circle, as I knew the rhinoceros would turn towards the gray horses, and thus expose his flank; this he did immediately, and firing exactly at his shoulder, I dropped him as though stone dead. Taher Noor shouted, 'Samme durrupto!' (well shot); the rhinoceros lay kicking upon the ground, and I thought he was bagged. Not a bit of it! the No. 24 bullet had not force to break the massive shoulder-bone, but had merely paralyzed it for a moment; up he jumped, and started off in full gallop. Now for a hunt! up the hill he started, obliquely; he chose a regular rhinoceros path, and scudded away, Tetel answering to the spurs and closing with him; through the trees, now down the hill over the loose rocks, where he gained considerably upon the horse. 'Easy down the hill, gently over the stones, Tetel,' and I took a pull at the reins until I reached the level ground beneath, which was firm and first-rate. I saw the rhinoceros pelting away about one hundred and twenty yards, when round he came with astonishing quickness, and charged straight at the horse. I was prepared for this, as was my horse also; we avoided him by a quick turn, and again renewed the chase, and regained our position within a few yards of the game. Thus the hunt continued for about one mile and a half, the rhinoceros occasionally charging, but always cleverly avoided by the horse. Tetel seemed to enjoy the fun, and hunted like a greyhound. Nevertheless I had not been able to pass the rhinoceros, who had thundered along at a tremendous pace whenever I had attempted to close; however, the pace began to tell upon his wounded shoulder; he evidently went lame, and, as I had observed at some distance before us the commencement of the dark-colored, rotten ground, I felt sure that it would shortly be a case of stand-still. In this I was correct, and, upon reaching the deep and crumbling sod, he turned sharp round, made a clumsy charge that I easily avoided, and he stood panting at bay. Taher Noor was riding Gazelle; this was a very timid horse, and was utterly useless as a hunter, but, as it reared and plunged upon seeing the rhinoceros, that animal immediately turned towards it, with the intention of charging. Riding Tetel closely to his flank, I fired both barrels of the little Fletcher into the shoulder. He fell to the shots, and stretching out his legs convulsively, he died immediately."

FURIOUS ONSLAUGHT OF A RHINOCEROS.

Bains relates the particulars of a charge made by a fierce rhinoceros among his dogs, and the desperate extremity to which he was put to save his own life, as follows:

"I had gone out the next morning soon after sunrise to look round the camp, when I saw several birds of a grayish color, about the size of a common thrush. Their notes, too, reminded me, as they sang their morning song, of a mistletoe thrush. Presently they flew off together some way up the stream, while I and my gunbearers and our pack of dogs followed after, feeling certain that the birds, which are found to generally attend the rhinoceros, would lead us to some big game. Directly after we saw the birds pitch behind a neighboring bush, and, getting to one side of it there, sure enough, was a large, black rhinoceros, on whose back were now perched the birds. These birds also occasionally follow the hippopotamus, and invariably give warning to their beast friend of approaching danger.

"At the moment of discovery the birds began flying up and uttering their familiar cry, when immediately the rhinoceros became startled and moved off without at first perceiving in what direction the danger lay. The dogs, at the same instant, saw the animal and started off with a bound, but their valor was hardly coupled with prudence, for as they closed in on the beast one of them was quickly hurled some yards, and badly wounded by the sharp horn of the rhinoceros, while the others immediately scattered to avoid a like fate. The rhinoceros now exhibited the most furious rage and came plunging at me; the rifle that I carried was unsuited for such large game, nor did the beast present a vantage shot, as he was coming head-on; nevertheless I fired, without effect, and to avoid a thrust from his cimeter-like horn,

A DISASTROUS CHARGE AMONG THE DOGS.

I plunged into the stream near the banks of which I was standing, and thus avoided him, as instead of pursuing me in the water he kept on after the dogs.

"As the rhinoceros was making in the direction of our wagon and cattle I had some misgivings that he might charge them, as he was evidently bent on glutting a savage revenge for our intrusion. I shouted with the hope of attracting the attention of those left in camp, but they were otherwise apprised of the charging rhinoceros soon enough, for the animal never stopped until he had attacked the wagon in the rear, and broke it up so badly that two days' hard work were required to repair it; following which, he made a fierce onslaught upon the horses, one of which, the leader, he killed by a single thrust of his terrible horn. But the brute's attack was promptly met by two of the servants, who fired their carbines into his shoulder with such precision that the monster fell dead fairly under the wagon."

THE RHINOCEROS-BIRD.

A very singular creature is the *Rhinoceros-Bird,* whose ministrations to the rhinoceros are like those of the *Trochilus-Bird* to the crocodile.

The faithfulness of the rhinoceros-bird is remarkable; it apparently never sleeps nor abandons its vigils over its great friend. "*Chukuroo,*" as the rhinoceros is called by the Bechuanas, may slumber with the serenity of a general who lies before an enemy with faithful sentinels on watch, for at the first intimation of danger the devoted bird flies up and utters his shrill cry of warning, and repeats it until his friend awakens, when, understanding the call, the beast immediately makes off.

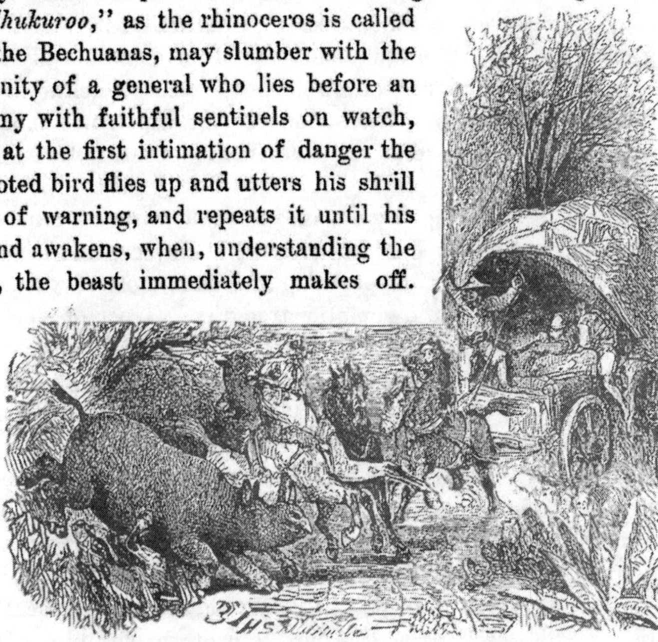

A RHINOCEROS' MAD CHARGE UPON A TEAM.

These birds may sometimes be seen sitting on the dead limb of a tree motionless for hours, in which case the observer may be certain that "chukuroo" is not far away, and is sleeping.

Cumming says: "I have often hunted a rhinoceros on horseback, which led me a chase of many miles, and required a number of shots before he fell, during which chase several of these birds remained by the rhinoceros to the last. They reminded me of mariners on the deck of some bark sailing on the ocean, for they perched along his back and sides; and as each of my bullets told on the shoulder of the rhinoceros, they ascended about six feet into the air, uttering their harsh cry of alarm, and then resumed their positions. It sometimes happened that the lower branches of a tree swept them from their living deck, but they always recovered their former station. They also adhere to the rhinoceros during the night. I have often shot these animals at midnight when drinking at the fountains, and the birds, imagining they were asleep, remained with them till morning, and on my approaching, before taking flight, they exerted themselves to the utmost to awaken chukuroo from his deep sleep."

CUMMING IS VANQUISHED BY A RHINOCEROS.

As great a hunter as Gordon Cumming, whose exploits fully entitle him to the distinguished reputation he bears, had to acknowledge a total defeat by a black rhinoceros, the fury of which was enough to terrify a battalion of hunters. His description of the rout he suffered is as follows:

"On the 22nd, ordering my men to move on toward a fountain in the center of the plain, I rode forth with Ruyter, and held east through a grove of lofty and spreading mimosas, most of which were more or less damaged by the gigantic strength of a troop of elephants, which had passed there twelve months before. Having proceeded about twelve miles with large herds of game on every side, I observed a crusty-looking old bull *borela*, or black rhinoceros, cocking his ears one hundred yards in advance. He had not noticed us; and soon after walked slowly toward our position and stood broadside, eating some wait-a-bit thorns within fifty yards of us. I fired from my saddle, and sent a bullet in behind his shoulder, upon which he rushed forward about one hundred yards in tremendous consternation, blowing like a grampus, and then stood looking about him. Presently he made off. I followed but found it hard to come up with him. When I finally overtook him, I saw that blood was running freely from his wound.

"The chase led through a large herd of blue wildebeests, zebras and springboks, which gazed at us in utter amazement. At length I fired my second barrel, but my horse was fidgety and I missed. I continued to ride alongside of him, expecting in my ignorance that at length he would come to bay, which rhinoceri never do; when suddenly he fell flat on his broadside on the ground, but recovering his feet, resumed his course as if nothing had happened. Becoming at length annoyed at the length of the chase, as I wished to keep my horses fresh for the elephants, and being indifferent whether I got the rhinoceros or not (?) as I observed that his horn was worn down with age *and the violence of his disposition*, I determined to bring matters to a crisis; so spurring my horse, I dashed ahead, and rode right in his path. Upon this the hideous monster charged me in the

THE HUNTER HUNTED.

most resolute manner, blowing loudly through his nostrils; and although I quickly wheeled about to my left, he followed me at such a furious pace for several hundred yards, with his horrid horny snout within a few yards of my horse's tail, that my little Bushman, who was looking on in great alarm, thought his master's destruction inevitable. It was certainly a very near thing; my horse was extremely afraid, and exerted his utmost energies on the occasion. The rhinoceros, however, wheeled about and continued his former course; and I, being perfectly satisfied with the interview, had no desire to cultivate his acquaintance any further."

CAPTURE OF A RHINOCEROS CALF.

W. C. Baldwin, another famous African hunter, whose work entitled "African Hunting from Natal to the Zambesi," is a popular addition to the adventurous literature descriptive of South Africa, has given us some very entertaining accounts of his exploits, from which I extract the following:

"We were plowing our way through long, heavy, wet grass and scrubby thorn trees, when an old rhinoceros cow got up slowly from behind a thorn tree, and, after giving me a good stare, advanced towards me. I had only my small rifle, my gun-carrier being about twenty yards behind with my No. 9. I beckoned frantically to him to come on, but he seemed very undecided. At last, however, being a plucky little fellow, he came up, threw the gun at me, case and all, and ran up a tree like a monkey. I lost no time in getting the gun out of the cover, and gave the rhinoceros a ball in the cheek. She turned round in double-quick time, panting like a porpoise. I followed, but a Kaffir cur prevented me from getting very near, so she got away.

"On climbing the top of the hill I saw two more, and sent my Kaffir below them, thinking they were sure to make down hill. I could not get near them; but just as they were about to make off, I shot one in the shoulder, but rather too low, and away they went. The dogs turned one and brought him back not fifteen yards from me at full trot, his head up and tail curled over his back, stepping out in splendid style, with fine, high action. He looked very much inclined to charge me; but a bullet behind his shoulders, which dropped him on his knees, made him alter his course. I felt convinced that I had killed him, and followed him. At last we saw a brute lying down in so natural a position that I never thought he could be dead, and shot him behind the shoulder; but he had lain down for the last time some hours before. It was the one I had shot first. After cutting out his horns, some *jamboks—koorbatches*—and his tongue, and hanging them up in a tree, we went off for water, and had not gone far when I saw another, about twenty yards off, looking at me, uneasy, and apparently trying to screen herself from being seen. I waited some time till she turned, and then shot her behind the shoulder, when she immediately came after me; but a ball in the center of her forehead stopped her progress, and she fell dead not ten yards from me; a lucky shot, as I hardly knew where to fire, and I had not an instant to lose. I must have been impaled on her very long horn if I had not been fortunate enough to kill her. She had a very young calf, with which the dogs were fighting, and he was squealing most lustily. I got them off, and wanted very much to take him to the wagon, and sent off my Kaffirs forthwith for half a dozen fellows to carry him. He was like a well-bred Chinese pig, pink-eared, very fine skinned and fat, and shone as if he had just been polished with black-lead; but while John and myself had gone to shoot a hartebeeste, to make something to carry him in, slung between two poles, the hyenas killed him, preferring him to his mother, though I had expressly cut a great portion of her hide off, that they might feed, as we were obliged to leave the calf all night to get water."

CHAPTER XXXI.

THE RIVER HORSE, SEA COW, OR HIPPOPOTAMUS.

AFRICA is noted for its gigantic animals. Being the only country that is still under the sway of barbarism, where savage life largely preponderates, it is here that we find remnants of species once numerous, but now long extinct in other countries. Once the lordly elephant, the ponderous rhinoceros, and the gigantic hippopotamus roamed all over Europe in immense numbers, as indicated by the vast amount of their bones still to be found imbedded in the clays of Italy, Germany and France, as well also along the coast of bleak Siberia. Cataclysms, glacial floods, changes of climate and the progress of the human race drove these animals from their long accustomed haunts, always back, back, like the receding Indian of to-day, until they finally disappeared, to be seen no more.

The march of civilization has passed only through the northeast and southern parts of Africa; elsewhere in that great country there remain benighted races whose ingenuity barely suffices for their existence, but which never enabled them to contend against the wild beasts, by which they are surrounded, with any greater success than our progenitors of the stone-age battled with the cave-bear and mammoth. Hence, we find in Africa the prototypes of great monsters that peopled the antediluvian world, and which can now be found in no other country. Among the wonderful creatures noted for their enormous size and prodigious strength is the *Hippopotamus,* from two Greek words signifying "river horse."

This leviathan is now found only in Africa, where it haunts the rivers, lakes and pools in large herds, being almost distinctively a water animal, and its place might therefore have been very properly

THE HIPPOPOTAMUS.

in that part of this book treating of the sea. Although the hippopotamus is a frequenter of fresh water it is by no means averse to the sea, and experiments even show that it prefers salt water to fresh. But being a pachydermatous animal belonging to the elephant, rhinoceros, tapir and the like families of quadrupeds, I have preferred to describe it in this connection.

The average height of a hippopotamus scarcely exceeds five feet, and its length twelve feet, but its bulk of body is fairly tremendous. The feet are very short, so that when walking on shore the belly almost touches the ground, giving it a very cumbrous and awkward appearance. Its skin is devoid of hair and is chiefly remarkable for extraordinary thickness, and an exudation through its pores of an oily liquid, which somewhat resembles blood. It has therefore been said by ignorant people that the hippopotamus sweats blood. But the most amazing feature of this animal is its enormous mouth, the oddity of its structure and the array of its gleaming tusks within. The nose is very blunt, and when its jaws are distended a more frightful sight was never seen than it affords. The incisor teeth of the lower jaw lie almost horizontally, with their points directed forward, and are used as crow-bars in tearing up aquatic roots off which it feeds. The canines are very monsters, being sometimes two feet in length, and curved like the fabled dragon's tooth. They are solid and will weigh as much as eight pounds each, and the value of which for ivory is rated at $5.00 per pound. With these wonderful teeth the animal can cut great swaths of grass as cleverly as though a scythe were used, nor do comparatively thick stems withstand its cutting grip.

DEVASTING HABITS OF THE HIPPOPOTAMUS.

Possessed of an enormous appetite, having a stomach capable of containing five or six bushels of nutriment, and furnished with such powerful instruments, the hippopotamus is a terrible nuisance to the owners of cultivated lands that happen to be near the river in which the animal has taken up its abode. During the day it is comfortably asleep in its chosen hiding place, but as soon as the shades of night deepen the hippopotamus issues from his lair and seeks the cultivated fields, where it begins its havoc among the crops. Not only does it devour vast quantities of grain and vegetables, but stalks so clumsily over the ground that it breaks down much more than it eats. A herd of these beasts is capable of destroying an immense crop in a single night.

The aggrieved cultivators resort to a variety of means to rid themselves of these nuisances. Among the more common plans is the digging of large pits about eight feet deep, at the bottom of which a sharp stake is fixed upright. The pit is then covered carefully with brush and leaves; the hippopotamus passes over his accustomed path and is precipitated into the pit, where he is fatally impaled. Another popular way the natives have of destroying the animal is by means of a harpoon attached to a heavy weight and suspended to the branch of a tree that overhangs the well-trodden path of the hippopotamus. The harpoon is held suspended by a trigger, which is sprung by a line that connects with the ground and is strung across the pathway. When the animal comes waddling over his usual route, his legs strike against the string, the trigger is thus sprung, and the poisoned point of the heavily weighted harpoon descends into his back, when, if the blow is not immediately fatal, death soon ensues from the wound and poison.

SPEAR-TRAP FOR KILLING HIPPOPOTAMI.

The hippopotamus is at home in the water for he can swim like a fish and dive like a loon. Before diving he inflates his lungs by a long respiration, and then sinks by a means which nature has given him, but which naturalists do not attempt to explain. He cannot remain under water for more than ten minutes at a time, but when anxious to avoid discovery he raises his nose barely above the surface, generally among some drift, and there remains secure, for the keenest eye is hardly able to detect him.

The female brings forth a single calf at a birth and guards it with most zealous care, though sometimes, especially in captivity, the mother becomes unnatural and destroys her young. In the *Jardin des Plantes*—zoological garden—of Paris, a hippopotamus viciously killed her new-born calf by tearing it to pieces, and upon a second birth, two years after, she killed her calf again, though it is supposed, this time, accidentally, while teaching it to swim.

The young hippopotamus is a comical appearing little thing, quite as thick as it is long; we may, therefore, expect it to be fairly helpless for the first few months of its life. Being unable to swim it is carried about on the mother's back, where it sits perched, the very personification of grotesqueness; never leaving its place while in the water, but on reaching the shore it gambols about on land like a Newfoundland dog puppy, or sleeps at the breast of its mother. As the calf is unable to remain long under water the dam rises frequently to the surface to give it air, at which times only the head of the little creature sometimes appears, its mother not being visible herself.

BAKER'S FIRST ADVENTURE WITH HIPPOPOTAMI.

Baker, the renowned African explorer and hunter, thus describes his first adventure with hippopotami, which he met with in the bed of the Atbara river, then nearly dry, as it was mid-summer:

"Early in the morning I procured an Arab guide to search for the reported hippopotami. My tents were among a grove of dome palm on the margin of the river; thus I had a clear view of the bed for a distance of half a mile on either side. This portion of the Atbara was about five hundred yards in width, and the banks were thirty feet in perpendicular depth, while the bed of the river had caused the formation of a deep hollow on the side opposite my position, which now formed a pool, every other part being dry. This pool occupied about one-third the breadth of the river, bounded by the sand upon one side, and by a perpendicular cliff upon the other, upon which grew a fringe of green bushes similar to willows.

"We descended the steep, sandy bank in a spot that the Arabs had broken down to reach the water, and, after trudging across about four hundred yards of deep sand, we reached the extreme and northwest end of the pool; here for the first time I saw the peculiar four-toed print of the hippopotamus' foot. A bed of melons had been planted there by the Arabs in the moist sand near the water, but the fruit had been entirely robbed by the hippopotami. A melon is exactly adapted for the mouth of this animal, as he can crunch the largest at one squeeze, and revel in the juice. Not contented with the simple fruits of the garden, a large bull-hippopotamus had recently killed the proprietor. The Arab wished to drive it from his plantation, but was immediately attacked by the animal, who caught him in his mouth and killed him by one crunch. This little incident had rendered the hippopotamus exceedingly daring, and it had upon several occasions charged out of the water, when the people had driven their goats to drink; therefore it would be the more satisfactory to obtain a shot, and to supply the hungry Arabs with meat at the expense of the enemy.

"At this early hour, 6 A. M., no one had descended to the pool, thus all the tracks upon the margin were fresh and undisturbed; there were the huge marks of crocodiles that had recently returned to the water, while many of great size were still lying upon the sand in the distance. The Arabs had dug small holes in the sand within a few yards of the water: these were the artificial drinking places for their goats and sheep, that would have been snapped up by the crocodiles had they ventured to drink in the pool of crowded monsters. The

HUNTING HIPPOPOTAMI IN THE ATBARA RIVER.

number and size of the fish, turtles and crocodiles were extraordinary; many beautiful gazelles approached from all sides for their morning draught; wild geese, generally in pairs, disturbed the wary crocodiles by their cry of alarm.

"I had killed several wild geese for breakfast in the absence of the hippopotami, when I suddenly heard the peculiar loud snorting neigh of these animals in my rear; we had passed them unperceived, as they had been beneath the surface. After a quick walk of about half a mile, during which time the cry of the hippopotami had been several times repeated, I observed six of these curious animals standing in the water shoulder-deep. There was no cover, therefore I could only advance upon the sand without a chance of stalking them; this caused them to retreat to deeper water, but upon my arrival within about eighty yards, they raised their heads well up, and snorted an impudent challenge. I had my old Ceylon No. 10, double rifle, and, taking a steady aim at the temple of one that appeared to be the largest, the ball cracked loudly upon its skull. Never had there been such a commotion in the pool as now! At the report of the rifle, five heads sank and disappeared like stones, but the sixth hippo leaped half out of the water, and, falling backwards, commenced a series of violent struggles; now upon its back, then upon one side, with all four legs frantically paddling, and raising a cloud of spray and foam; then waltzing round and round with its huge jaws wide open, raising gigantic swells in the hitherto calm surface of the water. A quick shot with the left-hand barrel produced no effect, as the movements of the animal were too rapid to allow a steady aim at the forehead; I accordingly took my trusty little Fletcher double rifle No. 24, and, running knee-deep into the water to obtain a close shot, I fired exactly between the eyes, near the crown of the head. At the report of the little Fletcher the hippo disappeared; the tiny waves raised by the commotion broke upon the sand, but the game was gone.

"This being my first *vis-a-vis* with a hippopotamus, I was not certain whether I could claim the victory; he was gone, but where? However, while I was speculating upon the case, I heard a tremendous rush of water, and saw five hippopotami tearing along in full trot through a portion of the pool that was not deep enough to cover them above the shoulder; this was the affair of about half a minute, as they quickly reached deep water and disappeared at one hundred and fifty yards distance.

"The fact of five hippos in retreat after I had counted six in the onset was conclusive that my waltzing friend was either dead or disabled; I accordingly lost no time in following the direction of the herd. Hardly had I arrived at the spot where they had disappeared, when first one and then another head popped up and again sank, until one, more hardy than the rest, ventured to appear within fifty yards, and to bellow as before. Once more the No. 10 crashed through his head, and again the waltzing and struggling commenced like the paddling of a steamer; this time, however, the stunned hippo in its convulsive efforts came so close to the shore that I killed it directly in shallow water, by a forehead shot with the little Fletcher. I concluded from this result that my first hippo must also be lying dead in deep water.

A BLOODY STRUGGLE.

"The Arabs, having heard the shots fired, had begun to gather towards the spot, and, upon my men shouting that a hippo was killed, crowds came running to the place with their knives and ropes, while others returned to their encampment to fetch camels and mat bags to convey the flesh. In half an hour at least three hundred Arabs were on the spot; the hippo had been hauled to shore by ropes, and, by the united efforts of the crowd, the heavy carcass had been rolled to the edge of the water. Here the attack commenced; no pack of hungry hyenas could have been more savage. I gave them permission to take the flesh, and in an instant a hundred knives were at work; they fought over the spoils like wolves. No sooner was the carcass flayed than the struggle commenced for the meat; the people were a mass of blood, as some stood thigh-deep in the reeking intestines wrestling for the fat, while many hacked at each other's hands for coveted portions that were striven for as a *bonne bouche*. I left the savage crowd in their ferocious enjoyment of flesh and blood, and returned to camp for breakfast, carrying some hippopotamus steaks.

"That morning my wife and I breakfasted upon our first hippopotamus, an animal that was destined to be our general food throughout our journey among the Abyssinian tributaries of the Nile."

The first hippopotamus, as Baker suspected, was killed by his second shot, and the body arose two hours afterwards, affording a second feast for the hungry Arabs whose joys were now unbounded as meat was thus provided sufficient to last three hundred gourmands for a week.

HARPOONING A BULL HIPPOPOTAMUS.

The Arabs of Abyssinia possess few guns, and even those who are supplied with fire-arms can use them only indifferently, consequently, since their country is the home of the largest and fiercest kinds of wild beasts, they must make up in daring what they lack in opportunity and the skillful use of the best improved arms.

The aggageers, of whom I have already written, are no more courageous in their attacks upon the elephants and rhinoceri than are the professional hippopotami hunters, whose sole weapon against the mighty behemoth is the harpoon. The following particulars of a hunt participated in by Baker, as related by himself, will serve to illustrate the skill and daring of these Arabs:

"After walking about two miles, we noticed a herd of hippopotami in a pool below a rapid, in the Settite river; this was surrounded by rocks, except upon one side, where the rush of waters had thrown up a bank of pebbles and sand. Our old Neptune (the Arab hunter) did not condescend to bestow the slightest attention when I pointed out these animals; they were too wide-awake; but he immediately quitted the river's bed, and we followed him quietly behind the fringe of bushes upon the border, from which we carefully examined the water. About half a mile below this spot, as we clambered over the intervening rocks, through a gorge which formed a powerful rapid, I observed, in a small pool just below the rapid, the immense head of a hippopotamus close to a perpendicular rock that formed a wall to the river, about six feet above the surface. I pointed out the hippo to old Abou Do, who had not seen it. At once the gravity of the old Arab disappeared, and the energy of the hunter was exhibited as he motioned us to remain, while he ran nimbly behind the thick screen of bushes for about one hundred and fifty yards below the spot where the hippo was unconsciously basking, with his ugly head above the surface. Plunging into the rapid torrent, the veteran hunter was carried some distance down the stream, but breasting the powerful current, he landed upon the rocks upon the opposite side, and retiring to some distance from the river, he quickly advanced towards the spot beneath which the hippopotamus was lying. I had a fine view of the scene, as I was lying concealed exactly opposite the hippo, who had disappeared beneath the water. Abou Do now stealthily approached the ledge of rocks beneath which he had expected to see the head of the animal; his long, sinewy arm was raised, with the harpoon ready to strike, as he carefully advanced. At length he reached the edge of the perpendicular rock; the hippo had vanished, but far from exhibiting surprise, the old Arab remained standing on the sharp ledge, unchanged in attitude. No figure of bronze could have been more rigid than that of the old river-king, as he stood erect upon the rock with the left foot advanced, and the harpoon poised in his ready right-hand above his head, while in his left he held the loose coils of rope attached to the ambatch buoy. I watched eagerly for the reappearance of the hippopotamus; the surface of the water was still barren, when suddenly the right arm of the statue descended like lightning, and the harpoon shot perpendicularly into the pool with the speed of an arrow. What river fiend answered to the summons? In an instant an enormous pair of open jaws appeared, followed by the ungainly head and form of the furious hippopotamus, who, springing half out of the water, lashed the river into foam, and, disdaining the concealment of the deep pool, he charged straight up the violent rapids. With extraordinary power he breasted the descending stream; gaining a footing in the rapids, about

ABOU DO ATTACKS THE HIPPOPOTAMUS.

five feet deep, he ploughed his way against the broken waves, sending them in showers of spray upon all sides, and upon gaining broader shallows he tore along through the water, with the buoyant float hopping behind him along the surface, until he landed from the river, started at full gallop along the dry, shingly bed, and at length disappeared in the thorny nabbuk jungle.

"I never could have imagined that so unwieldly an animal could have exhibited such speed; no man would have had a chance of escape, and it was fortunate for our old Neptune that he was secure upon the high ledge of rock. The old man plunged into the deep pool just quitted by the hippo, and landed by our side. I congratulated him upon his dexterity: but much remained to be done. I proposed to cross the river, and to follow upon the tracks of the hippopotamus, as I imagined that the buoy and rope would catch in the thick jungle, and that we should find him entangled in the bush; but the old hunter quietly laid his hand upon my arm, and pointed up the bed of the river, explaining that the hippo would certainly return to the water after a short interval.

"A few minutes later, at a distance of nearly half a mile, we observed the hippo emerge from the jungle, and descend at full trot to the bed of the river, making direct for the first rocky pool in which we had noticed the herd of hippopotami. Accompanied by the old howarti (hippo hunter), we walked quickly toward the spot. He explained to me that I must shoot the harpooned hippo, as we should not be able to secure him in the usual method by ropes, as nearly all our men were absent from camp, disposing of the dead elephants.

"Upon reaching the pool, which was about a hundred and thirty yards in diameter, we were immediately greeted by the hippo, who snorted and roared as we approached, but quickly dived, and the buoyant float ran along the surface, directing his course in the same manner as the cork of a trimmer with a pike upon the hook. Several times he appeared, but as he invariably faced us, I could not obtain a favorable shot; I therefore sent the old hunter round the pool, and he, swimming the river, advanced to the opposite side, and attracted the attention of the hippo, who immediately turned toward him. This afforded me a good chance, and I fired a steady shot behind the ear, at about seventy yards, with a single-barreled rifle. As usual with hippopotami, whether dead or alive, he disappeared beneath the water at the shot. The crack of the ball, and the absence of any splash from the bullet told me that he was hit; the ambatch float remained perfectly stationary upon the surface. I watched it for some minutes — it never moved; several heads of hippopotami appeared and vanished in different directions, but the float was still; it marked the spot where the grand old bull lay dead beneath."

After some hours of hard work the animal was finally drawn on shore, and being of such extraordinary proportions, Baker took some measurement of its body. He found its length, from the upper lip to the extremity of its tail, to be fourteen feet two inches. The head, measured from the front of the ear to the edge of the lip, was three feet one inch The harpoon was still sticking in the nape of the animal's neck, having penetrated two and one-half inches beneath the hide, which was one and three-quarters inches thick. Baker declares it one of the finest specimens he ever saw, while the tusks were very much larger than any others he ever met. The head of this gigantic beast now adorns Baker's hall in England.

FATAL ADVENTURE WITH A SAVAGE HIPPOPOTAMUS.

Baker mentions, only incidentally, however, a terrible accident by which the father of the Sheik of Sofi lost his life through his daring. The man was a famous hippopotamus hunter, who attacked the huge game with no other weapon than a harpoon, in the use of which he was marvelously adept. On this fatal occasion he was hunting hippos in company with his son, in the Atbara river. The two rowed out to an island in the stream in a small canoe, where several hippopotami were seen basking in the sun. So clever was the hunters' approach that the animals did not discover them until the two were landed and ready to hurl their harpoons. Father and son, however, were separated, each selecting his victim at opposite ends of the small island. The old man transfixed one very large bull, which appeared to be so badly wounded that it could not move, and to save the carcass from floating off he ran towards it for the purpose of cutting a strip in its hide, through which to pass a rope and thus anchor the body. The son, in the meantime, had also harpooned a smaller animal, which was engaging all his attention, when, suddenly, he heard a despairing cry, and turned just in time to see the great beast close its horrid jaws on his father. The animal had evidently been paralyzed for the moment by the harpoon, and recovered its senses, as the old hunter approached, in time to seize the unfortunate man, who was fairly bitten in two in an instant.

This dreadful accident did not lessen the Sheik's love for adventure, for afterwards he joined Baker and showed himself to be one of the most fearless of men in hunting the hippopotamus and all other large game.

FIERCENESS OF THE MALE HIPPOPOTAMUS.

Although the hippopotamus is generally harmless, the solitary old bulls are sometimes extremely vicious, especially when in the water. Baker says he has frequently known them to charge a boat, and that he has himself narrowly escaped being upset in a canoe by the attack of one of these creatures, without the slighest provocation. The females are extremely shy and they are most affectionate mothers; the only instances believed to be known of females attacking man have been in cases where their calves have been stolen. To the Arabs these animals are very valuable, yielding, as they do, in addition to a large quantity of excellent flesh, about two hundred pounds of fat, and a hide that will produce generally two hundred koorbatches.

Although the hippopotamus is amphibious, he requires a large and constant supply of air; the lungs are of enormous size, and the animal invariably inflates them before diving. From five to eight minutes is the time that he usually remains under water; he then comes to the surface and expends the air in his lungs by blowing; he again refills his lungs almost instantly, and if frightened he sinks at once. In places where they have become shy from being hunted or shot at, they seldom expose the head above the surface, but merely protrude the nose to breathe through the nostrils; it is then impossible to shoot them. Their food consists of aquatic plants and grasses of many kinds. Not only do they visit the margin of rivers, but they wander great distances from the water by night, if attracted by good pasturage, and, although clumsy and ungainly in appearance, they manage to clamber up steep banks and precipitous ravines with astounding celerity and ease; when undisturbed they enjoy basking in the sun beneath inviting shades, and they also lie upon the surface of the water like turtles, when they very much resemble old logs. Occasionally they may be found on high ledges or precipitous banks overlooking the sea; when suddenly alarmed they will leap headlong into the water, perhaps a distance of thirty feet, creating a splash that is audible for a mile or more.

Arabs attach little or no value to the tusks of the hippopotamus, though these are very much more valuable than elephant ivory, since they are less liable to crack and never change color. False teeth made of hippopotamus ivory are more perfect and beautiful than those from any other material.

AN EXCITING HOWARTIS HUNT OF HIPPOPOTAMI.

One of the most interesting hunts in which Baker participated during his sojourn in Africa, in which there was an extraordinary display of skill and daring, is thus described in his usual realistic and graphic manner:

"A little after sunrise I accompanied the howartis (Arab professional hippopotamus hunters) for a day's sport. There were numbers of hippos in this part of the river, and we were not long finding a herd. The hunters failed in several attempts to harpoon them, however, and we had to go further up the stream. At length we arrived at a large pool in which were several sand-bars covered with rushes, and many rocky islands. Among these rocks was a herd of hippopotami, consisting of an old bull and several cows; a young hippo was standing, like an ugly little statue, on a protruding rock, while another infant stood upon its mother's back that listlessly floated on the water.

"This was an admirable place for the hunters. They desired me to lie down, and they crept into the jungle, out of view of the river; I presently observed them stealthily descending the dry bed about two hundred paces above the spot where the hippos were basking behind the rocks. They entered the river, and swam down the center of the stream towards the rock. This was highly exciting — the hippos were quite unconscious of the approaching danger, as steadily and rapidly the hunters floated down the strong current; they neared the rock, and both heads disappeared as they purposely sank out of view; in a few seconds they reappeared at the edge of the rock upon which the young hippo stood. It would be difficult to say which started first, the astonished young hippo, into the water, or the harpoons from the hands of the howartis! It was the affair of a moment; the hunters dived directly they had hurled their harpoons, and, swimming for some distance under water, they came to the surface, and hastened to the shore lest an infuriated hippopotamus should follow them. One harpoon had missed; the other had fixed the bull of the herd, at which it had been surely aimed. This was grand sport! The bull was in the greatest fury, and rose to the surface, snorting and blowing in his impotent rage; but as the ambatch float was exceedingly large, and this naturally accompanied his movements, he tried to escape from his imaginary persecutor, and dived constantly, only to find his pertinacious attendant close to him upon

AN EXCITING HIPPOPOTAMUS HUNT.

regaining the surface. This was not to last long; the howartis were in earnest, and they at once called their party, who, with two of the aggageers, Abou Do and Suleiman, were near at hand. These men arrived with the long ropes that form a portion of the outfit for hippo hunting.

"The whole party now halted on the edge of the river, while two men swam across with one end of the long rope. Upon gaining the opposite bank, I observed that a second rope was made fast to the middle of the main line; thus upon our side we held the ends of two ropes, while on the opposite side they had only one; accordingly, the point of junction of the two ropes in the center formed an acute angle. The object of this was soon practically explained. Two men upon our side now each held a rope, and one of these walked about ten yards before the other. Upon both sides of the river the people now advanced, dragging the rope upon the surface of the water until they reached the ambatch float that was swimming to and fro, according to the hippopotamus below. By a dextrous jerk of the main line, the float was now placed between the two ropes, and it was immediately secured in the acute angle by bringing together the ends of the ropes on our side.

"The men on the opposite banks now dropped their line, and our men hauled in upon the ambatch float that was held fast between the ropes. Thus cleverly made sure, we quickly brought a strain upon the hippo, and, although I have had some experiences in handling big fish, I never knew one to pull so lustily as the amphibious animal that we now alternately coaxed and bullied. He sprang out of the water, gnashed his huge jaws, snorted with tremendous rage, and lashed the river into foam; he then dived, and foolishly approached us under water. We quickly gathered in the slack line, and took a round turn upon a large rock, within a few feet of the river. The hippo now arose to the surface, about ten yards from the hunters, and, jumping half out of the water, he snapped his great jaws together, endeavoring to catch the rope, but at the same instant two harpoons were launched into his side. Disdaining retreat, and maddened with rage, the furious animal charged from the depths of the river, and, gaining a footing, he reared his bulky form from the surface, came boldly upon the sand-bank, and attacked the hunters open-mouthed. He little knew his enemy; they were not the men to fear a pair of gaping jaws, armed with a deadly array of tusks, but half a dozen lances

TRYING TO DRAG THE MONSTER ON SHORE.

were hurled at him, some entering his mouth from a distance of five or six paces; at the same time several men threw handfuls of sand into his enormous eyes. This baffled him more than the lances; he crunched the shafts between his powerful jaws like straws, but he was beaten by the sand, and, shaking his huge head, he retreated to the river. During his sally upon the shore, two of the hunters had secured the ropes of the harpoons that had been fastened into his body just before his charge; he was now fixed with three of these deadly instruments, but suddenly one rope gave way, having been bitten through by the enraged beast, who was still beneath the water. Immediately after this he appeared on the surface, and, without a moment's hesitation, he once more charged furiously from the water straight at the hunters, with his huge mouth open to such an extent that he could have accommodated two inside passengers. Suleiman was wild with delight, and springing forward, lance in hand, he drove it against the head of the formidable beast, but without effect. At the same time Abou Do met the hippo, sword in hand, reminding one of Perseus slaying the sea-monster that would devour Andromeda, but the sword made a harmless gash, and the lance, already blunted against the rocks, refused to penetrate the tough hide; once more handfuls of sand were pelted upon his face, and again repulsed by this blinding attack, he was forced to retire to his deep hole and wash it from his eyes. Six times during the fight the valiant bull hippo quitted his watery fortress, and charged resolutely at his pursuers; he had broken several of their lances in his jaws, other lances had been hurled, and, falling upon the rocks, they were blunted and would not penetrate. The fight had continued for three hours, and the sun was about to set; accordingly, the hunters begged me to give him the *coup de grace*, as they had hauled him close to the shore, and they feared he would sever the rope with his teeth. I waited for a good opportunity, when he boldly raised his head from the water about three yards from the rifle, and a bullet from the little Fletcher between the eyes closed the last act."

HIPPOPOTAMUS FLESH AS A DELICACY.

Schweinfurth speaks of shooting hippopotami in the Dyvor river with a rifle that threw a light bullet; he says that though his range was rarely more than one hundred and fifty feet, yet of the hundreds he shot at only two appeared to be mortally wounded, and the body of only one was recovered, that had been hit behind the ear. Concerning the palatableness of hippopotamus flesh, which the natives devour with such avidity, he says:

"We were at work on the following day in turning the huge carcass of the hippopotamus to account for our domestic use. My people boiled down great flasks of the fat, which they took from the layers between the ribs, but what the entire produce of grease would have been I was unable to determine, as hundreds of natives had already cut off and appropriated pieces of the flesh. When boiled, hippopotamus-fat is very similar to pork-lard, though in the warm climate of Central Africa it never attains a consistency firmer than that of oil. Of all animal fats it appears to be the purest, or at any rate it never becomes rancid, and will keep for many years without requiring any special process of clarifying; it has, however, a slight flavor of train-oil, to which it is difficult for a European to become accustomed. It is stated in some books that hippopotamus-bacon is quite a delicacy, but I can by no means concur in this opinion; I always found it unfit for eating, and when cut into narrow strips and roasted it was as hard and tough as so much rope; the same may be said of the tongue, which I often had smoked and salted. The meat is remarkably fibrous, and is one continuous tissue of sinews.

KOORBATCHES USED FOR PUNISHING CRIMINALS.

"Several hundred Nile-whips or *koorbatches* can be made from the hide of a single hippopotamus, and afterwards, in Egypt, my servants made a profitable little market by selling the whips, for which they found a ready demand. By a proper application of oil, heat and friction, they may be made as flexible as gutta-percha. The flesh is easily cut cross-wise into long quadrilateral strips, and when half dry the edges are trimmed with a knife, and the strips are hammered into round whips as though they were iron hammered on an anvil."

The koorbatch is used throughout Africa as an instrument with which to punish criminals, and is also a common accessory of the slave-drivers, who make no sparing use of it.

A HIPPOPOTAMUS NEARLY KILLS A MISSIONARY.

Robert Moffat, agent of the London Missionary Society in South Africa, thus relates his narrow escape from a mad hippo: "The night before reaching home we had rather a narrow escape from a *Sea-Cow*. We were obliged to cross the river, which could only be effected by passing over two low islands, nearly covered with reeds and jungle. They were a great distance from each other, and it was now nearly dark. We had just reached the first, when a sea-cow came furiously up the stream, snorting so loud as to be echoed back from the overhanging precipices. Africaner shouted out to me to escape, and springing from his horse, which appeared petrified, he seized a large stone and hurled it at the monster, for our guns were both out of order. The enraged animal then made for the next ford, through which two of us were forcing our horses, up to the saddle, in a rapid torrent. A moment's delay on our part would have been fatal to one or both of us. The other three men remained till the infuriated animal had got again into the rear, when they also escaped to the second island, where, expecting another encounter, we made the best of our way to the mainland, effectually drenched with perspiration and water. The animals, in their undisturbed lakes and pools, are generally timid, and will flee at the approach of man; but when they have been hunted and wounded, from year to year, they become very dangerous, as the following fact will prove: A native, with his boy, went to the river to hunt sea-sows. Seeing one at a short distance below the island, the man passed through a narrow stream to get nearer the object of his pursuit. He fired, but missed; and the animal instantly made for the island, and the man, seeing his danger, ran to cross the bank of the river; but, before reaching it, the sea-cow seized him, and literally severed his body in two with its monstrous jaws."

NATIVE MODES OF HUNTING THE HIPPOPOTAMUS.

Throughout the entire range of the hippopotamus in Africa its flesh is highly esteemed, being very juicy, tender and having the taste of pork, the resemblance between the two meats being indeed remarkable, Schweinfurth's opinion to the contrary notwithstanding. On this account the natives devote much of their time in hunting the animal, and in the chase display no little skill and courage. The Makoba tribe, along the Zambesi river, are particularly successful hippopotamus hunters. Their weapons are harpoons and lances, but these they make almost as effective as the white man's best rifles. In preparing for the hunt they first ascertain the location of a herd in the river and then construct a considerable sized raft of reeds to which they moor two or more of their canoes, and upon which they float down among the unsuspecting animals.

Andersson, describing this novel manner of hunting, says: "As soon as the position of the hippopotami is ascertained, one or more of the most skillful and intrepid of the hunters stands prepared with the harpoons, whilst the rest make haste to launch the canoes, should the attack prove successful. The bustle and noise caused by these preparations gradually subside. Conversation is carried on in a whisper and every one is on the *qui vive*. The snorting and plunging become every moment more distinct; but a bend in the stream still hides the animals from view. The angle being passed, several dark objects are seen floating listlessly on the water, looking more like the crests of sunken rocks than living creatures. Ever and anon, one or other of the shapeless masses is submerged, but soon again makes its appearance on the surface. On, on, glides the raft with its sable crew, who are now worked up to the highest state of excitement. At last

MODE OF HUNTING THE HIPPOPOTAMUS BY THE MAKOBA TRIBE.

the raft is in the midst of the herd, who appear quite unconscious of danger. Presently one of the animals is in immediate contact with the raft. Now is the critical moment. The foremost harpooner now raises himself to his full height, to give the greater force to his blow, and the next moment the fatal rod descends with unerring accuracy into the body of the hippopotamus.

"The wounded animal plunges violently, and dives to the bottom; but all his efforts to escape are unavailing. The line or the shaft of the harpoon may break; but the cruel barb once imbedded in the flesh, the weapon (owing to the toughness and thickness of the beast's hide) cannot be withdrawn.

"As soon as the hippopotamus is struck, one or more of the men launch a canoe from off the raft, and hasten to the shore with the harpoon-line, and take a turn round with it about a tree, or bunch of reeds, so that the animal may either be 'brought up' at once, or, should there be too great a strain on the line, 'played' in the same manner as a salmon by a fisherman. But if time should not admit of a line being passed round a tree, or the like, both line and buoy are thrown into the water, and the animal goes where he chooses.

"The rest of the canoes are now all launched from off the raft, and chase is given to the poor brute, who, so soon as he comes to the surface to breathe, is saluted with a shower of light javelins. Again he descends, his track deeply crimsoned with gore. Presently—and perhaps at some little distance—he once more appears on the surface, when as before, missiles of all kinds are hurled at his head.

"When thus beset, the infuriated beast not unfrequently turns upon his assailants, and either with his formidable tusks, or with a blow from his enormous head, staves in or capsizes the canoes. At times, indeed, not satisfied with wreaking his vengeance on the craft, he will attack one or other of the crew, and with a single grasp of his horrid jaws either terribly mutilate the poor fellow, or, it may be, cut his body fairly in two.

"The chase often lasts a considerable time. So long as the line and the harpoon hold, the animal cannot escape, because the buoy always marks his whereabouts. At length, from loss of blood or exhaustion Behemoth succumbs to his pursuers."

ATTACK OF A HIPPOPOTAMUS AND CALF.

Several travelers testify to the harmless and timid disposition of the hippopotamus, but a majority of those best acquainted with the animal's habits declare it to be one of the most furious and vindictive of beasts, and this latter opinion I believe to be correct. Livingstone describes an unprovoked attack made upon a canoe, in which he was traveling, by a hippopotamus, and his experience with the beast led him to believe that it was dangerous at nearly all times. Baldwin mentions an instance where he was set upon, while in a canoe, by a female hippopotamus and her half-grown calf. They were moving along quietly over the water without a suspicion of harm when the animal bolted from the reeds and rushed upon them with the greatest fury, seizing the boat in her jaws and tearing it so that, but for a lucky shot he gave her, he must have been left floundering in the water. The calf appeared no less vicious, for he, too, sprang at the boat with open jaws and was bent on doing all the mischief in his power.

Another attack sustained by Baldwin he thus describes: "We mustered a strong party of fifteen, including the captain of the Kraal, and three fellows to carry beer. We took our blankets with us and walked a long way without seeing anything. At length an old buffalo jumped up close to me, and I gave him a bullet behind the shoulder which brought him to his knees, but he soon recovered himself and

BATTLE WITH A HIPPOPOTAMUS.

went off. Further on, I saw a large sea-bull lying asleep close inland, behind some reeds, and proceeded to crawl in on him; but just as I showed myself, half-way to my waist in water, he charged right at me at great speed. He stopped for a second about twenty yards off and I gave him a pill under the ear, which made him spin round and round like a top. I fired two more bullets into his body without effect, missed him with a third, and began to fear we were to lose him altogether, as he seemed recovering and was gradually getting further and further away into deep water, and giving very poor chances for a shot. The sun was shining so directly on him, that I could not see to shoot a bit; the footing was slippery, and I was half-way up to my middle in water and mud, when I got a last chance, and put the ball exactly between his ear and eye and killed him. The sun was fast setting; the Kaffirs got him nearly ashore, and we lighted three great fires with a cap and powder on the heel-plate of my gun, giving it a smart blow with a stone. We fed on the hippopotamus, but he was horribly tough."

A CLOSE CALL FROM A CHARGING HIPPOPOTAMUS.

Dr. Emil Holub, an Austrian, acting under an imperial commission from King Francis Joseph, made some explorations in South Africa during the years 1877-78-79, which were published in the German in 1881, though never translated, I believe, into our language. His book, in two volumes, possesses considerable interest, though it is more of a scientific character than given to the record of adventures. However, among the few thrilling incidents which he describes is a hunt in which he participated with some natives in a small stream in upper Zululand. The preparations made for this hunt included, among other things, the building of a double-prowed boat, after the European style, capable of carrying three or four men, with needful implements of the chase. In this boat the Doctor took his place with a native acting as guide and rower, while other natives were scattered along the shore to give notice of the vicinity of hippopotami, and to drive any that might be found, as occasion required, as the Doctor was to do all the shooting.

The first day's hunt was attended with no success, beyond the bagging of some inferior game, but on the second day, as the party proceeded in a different direction from that at first taken, several herd of hippopotami were found that afforded excellent sport, a half dozen being killed and their bodies secured. Towards evening of the same day, however, an incident befell the Doctor which came near ending his hunt disastrously. His native rower had beguiled the time on the first day telling the Doctor of his great prowess and courage, particularly on occasions when he had been brought face to face with the gravest dangers in hippo hunting. These assurances impressed the Doctor favorably, as they were intended, but, in fact, only increased the peril which he was soon after to encounter.

A herd of several hippos being discovered along the sedgy bank, the shore beaters drove them out by casting spears, some of which

DR. EMIL HOLUB'S THRILLING ADVENTURE WITH A HIPPOPOTAMUS.

struck two or three of the animals, one of which proved to be an extremely large bull. They moved out into the stream directly toward the Doctor, who fired with no other effect than to slightly wound the bull again, which now became so enraged that it made directly for the boat, half wading, as the water was too shallow to swim the beast. Another shot had no better effect than the first, for the hippo charged with a frenzy that took all the courage out of the native rower, who plunged precipitately out of the boat and scrambled with all haste to the shore, regardless of the fate of his companion. The Doctor fortunately did not lose his head, but with little excitement he awaited the close approach of the beast, into whose wide-gaping mouth he fired a third ball. This shot did not prove fatal, but so crazed the hippo that it rolled and thrashed around, until in its contortions it upset the boat and threw the Doctor out. All the while it gnashed its powerful jaws and exhibited a blind fury that was positively awful to witness. The Doctor did not abide long in the water, but hastened out, and with particular rapidity away from the beast, when, gaining dry land, he awaited the death or disappearance of the hippo, before attempting the recovery of his guns and munitions, which were now at the bottom of the shallow stream.

The beast succumbed to its wounds some hours afterwards, and the natives had little difficulty in fishing up two of the guns, but the other was lost, having been trampled deep into the mud by the animal in its desperate throes.

CHAPTER XXXII.

THE WILD DOGS OF AFRICA.

AMONG the many curious animals which abound in Africa there are but few that are more interesting to the student of natural history than the *Wild Dog*. These creatures are not alone singular in their hybrid appearance, but in their habits as well. They appear to be the result of an interbreeding between dog, hyena and wolf, since their nature partakes of all of these. It is a question whether the *Dingo*, or *Warragal*, of Australia, and the wild dog of Africa are not one and the same species. While they are classed separately, I am inclined to the belief, after reading many descriptions of the animals, that they are identical, for in appearance and habits I can discover no difference whatever. It is of the size of a common cur-dog, of a yellow color, sharp muzzle,

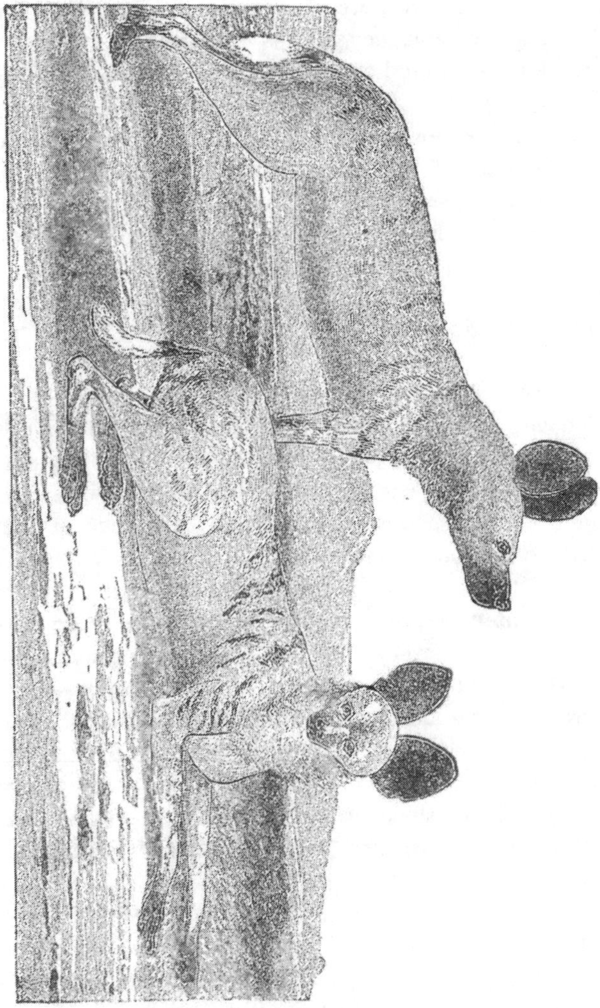

WILD DOGS OF AFRICA.

short, erected, pointed ears, bushy tail, small eyes and of a timid, wolfish countenance. A specimen which I saw in the zoological garden of St. Petersburg was nearly as large as a mastiff, but the keeper assured me that confinement and good feeding had made it much fatter, and, therefore, larger than it is found to be in its native state.

Wild dogs are gregarious, always associating together in large packs, for the double purpose of mutual defense and for hunting. A somewhat singular habit they possess is in their organization, for they appear to be under a kind of government, and are great sticklers for squatter sovereignty. Each pack is confined to respective districts, over which they exercise such control that if a dog chance to overstep the boundary of his own district, the pack which controls the territory thus trespassed upon falls upon and slaughters him without mercy. Should game become very difficult to obtain in any district the pack to which that portion of the country belonged migrates in a body to some section which is not already pre-empted, and thenceforth they maintain sovereignty thereon, which is very rarely disputed.

WONDERFUL TENACITY OF LIFE IN THE WILD DOG.

The tenacity of life which is exhibited in the wild dog is marvelous. It has more than fox-like cunning, for when close pressed, and finding itself unable to escape, it will feign death like the opossum, in which condition no amount of punishment will cause it to throw off the mask. It is related that one of these animals was overtaken and that it at length lay down as if dead. Knowing the peculiarity of the animals the hunters fell upon it with clubs and beat it so severely that it was supposed that every bone in its body was broken, and that it was dead beyond all possible doubt. After its supposed slayers had moved away to some distance they were astounded to see the creature get up, shake itself and hie away to the brush. Another apparently dead dingo had been brought to a hut for the purpose of being skinned, and actually suffered the operator to remove the skin from one side of its face before it permitted any symptoms of life or sensation to escape it.

As a general thing the wild dog is a timid creature, always prefering to run away rather than to fight. But when hard pressed by its foes it turns to bay with savage ferocity and then becomes a dangerous antagonist, especially to domesticated dogs, which appear to be its bitterest enemies. In captivity it is an extremely treacherous animal, never becoming tame, and, though timid, it is quick to make an attack upon either man or beast if it can do so unseen, but after such an onset it quickly retreats to the farthest recesses of its habitation and there crouches in fear and silence, whether it has failed or succeeded in its cowardly attempt. In other words, it is peculiarly wolfish, being at all times treacherous, even to those who treat it with the greatest kindness, for it will bite the hand that feeds it.

HOW THE WILD-DOGS HUNT.

As before remarked, wild dogs hunt in packs, but in a much more systematic manner than the deer and fox hounds we are accustomed to follow in the chase. Their game, which is generally of the antelope species, is very fleet of foot, and could easily distance the dogs and tire them down did they not resort to cunning, which shows a degree of intellectual resource, or a wonderful instinct.

The following account of the manner in which the dogs hunt, and the service they render some of the African natives, particularly the Bechuanas, is extracted from Mr. Moffat's "South Africa:"

"During our stay at this place a circumstance occurred which may throw some light on the habits of these people, and confirms the old adage, that 'one-half of the world does not know how the other half lives.' It was at noon-day when a fine large hartebeest (khama of the Bechuanas), the swiftest of the antelope species, darted close past the wagon, and descended toward the extensive valley. Startled by so unusual an occurrence, one of the natives called out, 'It is the wild dogs;' and presently the whole pack made their appearance, following their leader, which was pursuing the antelope. We seized our guns to attack them as beasts of prey. The poor people who were sitting around their flesh-pots started up and followed, begging of us most earnestly not to kill the wild dogs, for they were their providers. We, of course, laid down our guns again, and directed our attention to the khama, which was soon overtaken and seized by the hind leg. It turned round to defend itself and then started off till again seized by the wild dog. As we had in a measure retarded the speed of the pack, about thirty in number, the single dog who was engaged baiting the khama looked round and gave a piteous howl for his companions to come to his assistance. When they overtook the poor animal they fell upon it with one accord, and instantly brought it to the ground. One of my men ran off in order to secure a piece of the skin of which he wanted to make shoes, but by the time he reached the spot nothing remained but the bones, and those well picked. These the poor people afterwards collected for the sake of the marrow. On farther inquiry, I found that these people are in the habit, when they see an antelope, or even an ostrich, pursued by the wild dogs, of endeavoring to frighten them away, that they may come in for a share of the prey. One of the men, with much feeling for himself and companions, said, patting his hand on his stomach, 'Oh, I am glad you did not shoot the dogs, for they often find us a meal.'

"At another place the poor people were very glad, on the same account, that we had not killed the lion, which had been troublesome to us during the night. These children of the desert very promptly described the manner of the wild dog chase, which I have since had opportunities of witnessing. When the dogs approach a troop of antelopes they select one, no matter how it may mingle with others on the dusty plain; the dog that starts never loses scent, or, if he does, it is soon discovered by the pack, which follow after, as they spread themselves the more readily to regain it. While the single dog who takes the lead has occasion to make angles in pursuit of his prey, the others, who hear his cry or short howl, avoid a circuitous course, and by this means easily come up again, when a fresh dog resumes the chase, and the other turns into the pack. In this way they relieve each other till they have caught the animal, which they rarely fail to accomplish, though sometimes after a very long run. Should they, in their course, happen to pass other game much nearer than the one in pursuit, they take no notice of it. These dogs, of which there are two species, never attack man, but are very destructive to sheep and goats, and even to cows, when they come in their way."

WILD DOGS ATTACKING A LION.

Although the antelope and buffalo is the favorite game of wild dogs, when the supply is scarce they do not hesitate to attack any animal in the forest, not even excepting the lion. The leopard falls an easy prey to a pack of dogs, while baboons are their most powerful antagonists; indeed, nothing but sheer starvation will induce them to attack these cunning and ferocious creatures, for they, too, are always found in large numbers, so that an attack means a terrible battle, in which many on both sides are killed.

In bating a lion the dogs employ strategy, for they are fully conscious of his prodigious strength and dangerous claws; to rush in upon him would be the sheerest folly, and this they never do. Since the lion can go no where that the dogs cannot follow, they surround and drive him from covert to covert; when somewhat tired the lion comes to bay, whereupon the dogs sit upon their haunches, or lie down and rest, until he moves off again. The objective point of the dogs' attack is always in the rear of the lion, and by nimbleness they man-

A LEOPARD BESET BY WILD DOGS.

age to bite and worry him without receiving any injury from the victim. Thus the attack is continued until finally some one of the dogs emasculates the powerful brute, which so weakens him that he soon succumbs to his persistent foes.

WILD DOGS THAT KILL AND EAT TIGERS.

It is universally believed by natives of India that the tiger is occasionally killed by packs of wild dogs. These animals are not numerous. Their operations are of a character so destructive and harassing to game that no tract could support them in any considerable number. The wild dog is apparently a hybrid, or cross between the wolf and jackal; at least they bear somewhat of a resemblance to both, while they are intermediate in size; in color they are of a deep rusty brown above, paler on the belly and have a black, brushy tail. They run both by sight and scent, and their perseverance and endurance are such that they rarely fail to kill an animal on whose track they start. From their manner of hunting and of their power of lacerating there is no doubt of their ability to kill a tiger. Sanderson says: "I can call to mind two examples of their powers. One morning two dogs chased a spotted hind past my tent. One of them halted at sight of the encampment, the other, which was in springing distance, made two snatches at the exhausted creature's abdomen, and then drew off. The bites were inflicted with lightning speed; the deer went but a few paces when she fell with her entrails protuding. On another occasion I heard the yelping of jungle-dogs, and a noble spotted stag came racing down an open glade, his branching antlers laid along his back, and three wild dogs at his flanks. They had only time to make a snap or two when we interfered. The stag went but a few yards and fell, and was speared by one of my men. In the moment's biting it had been emasculated, and about four pounds of flesh torn from the inner part of the thigh.

"Similar injury might be easily inflicted on a tiger. I have seen more than one flee from a flock of curs—a very mangy one gallantly holding on to the royal beast's tail on one occasion—and it is probable a tiger would turn from wild dogs. The latters' habit of hunting almost exclusively during the day, would be in their favor in an encounter with a tiger. Their tactics are not to attack in front; they never expose themselves to the horns or hoofs of powerful deer. They would bite a tiger, should he run from them, in parts that might speedily cause his death. A Sholaga told me that he once saw a tiger, confronted by wild dogs, sitting on his haunches against a bamboo-clump. The dogs, ten or twelve in number, were making no active demonstrations, but walked close to him in a most impertinent and unconcerned manner. It is possible that in such a case, if the tiger maintained his position, the dogs would withdraw, as they could do nothing against him in a front attack."

Many African travelers assert that the wild dogs almost invariably emasculate their game when running it down, and that this cunning is so peculiar to them that they nearly always follow the male animal, which they are enabled thereby to bring down quicker. This declaration is subject to doubt, although confirmed by many reliable persons. It is no doubt true that they do sometimes destroy bull-buffaloes in this peculiar manner, but it is equally true that they capture their game by ham-stringing. So powerful are the jaws of these animals that they have many times been seen to tear away the entire flank of a hartebeeste, and at other times to seize the side of the poor creature and disembowel it. Whatever they have once begun to chase has little chance for escape, since, being always in large droves, they relieve each other and practice the most remarkable cunning.

The wild dog has an instinctive dread of its domesticated genus, and a small terrier will put to flight a thousand of these ferocious animals. That they have their origin from domestic dogs no one, I believe, doubts, but so thoroughly eradicated is the instinct which bound their progenitors to man, that there is no creature wilder, not even the hyena, than they. Yet they preserve many of the habits of the watch-dog. At night the wild dogs sit upon their haunches and bay the moon, and even in the day-time, they howl most mournfully, exactly like domestic dogs. They also manifest anger by barks and fierce growls, but their voice is sharper, and can be easily detected from that of the domestic dog.

CHAPTER XXXIII.

THE GORILLA—DOES HE EXIST?

NATURALISTS have for years been exercised over the question as to whether there is such an animal as the *Gorilla*. A singular point in dispute was with regard to the existence of such a creature as the *Unicorn*, which, many years ago, was fiercely debated by every learned person in Europe. It has at length been settled that the gorilla is a reality, while the unicorn is a myth; but there are not wanting persons who, if not still openly disputing the claim, do entertain grave doubts as to the existence of the gorilla, and their reasons for so believing are not without some force. It is a most astonishing fact that the only African traveler who so

THE GORILLA.

much as pretends to have seen the creature, or even to have heard of it through the wild tribes of that country, is Paul B. Du Chaillu. This explorer and writer may be the very best authority, especially since he brought several skeletons of the alleged animal to Boston and

London, where they may yet be seen. But, without throwing discredit on Du Chaillu's statements, it is plain that naturalists have too promptly accepted the evidences which he has produced. The skeletons, it is true, speak for themselves, as it were, but hardly conclusively. The principal point to decide is whether the *Orang Outan* and gorilla are not one and the same.

Du Chaillu claims to have found the gorilla in considerable numbers along the Gaboon River and throughout the lower Congo country; yet Livingstone, Moffat, Andersson, Oswall, Murray and a host of other noted travelers, who hunted for years through the same country, never so much as heard of the creature. This fact of itself is singular. Livingstone speaks frequently of an animal called the *Soko*, which, in shape, resembles the gorilla, but it is so much smaller that the two cannot be confounded. The other explorers describe their meetings with orang outans, some of which are declared to have been nearly seven feet in height, or nearly one foot taller than any of Du Chaillu's gorillas. Wallace also found the orang outan in Borneo, where he killed a specimen that measured six feet ten inches in height, and had a spread of arms of more than nine feet, evidently as powerful a creature as the so-called gorilla, but by no means so savage. The differences between the two animals seem to be very few. The gorilla, as Du Chaillu describes it, is at all times extremely fierce, and will attack a man, if pressed, with such extraordinary ferocity that, unless it be immediately killed by a well directed shot, the hunter is sure to fall a victim before it. He also claims that the gorilla seldom or never ascends trees, and that its haunts are in the deepest shades of the jungle. In these particulars it is quite unlike the orang outan, which rarely displays any courage, but will retreat even when wounded, and will not fight its pursuers unless driven to bay. Its home, too, is among the trees, where it climbs with great agility and sleeps at night.

The skeletons brought from Africa by Du Chaillu — only two in number, I believe — bear a striking resemblance to those of the orang outan, except the skulls, which exhibit a difference so radical as to incline naturalists to the belief that the two are distinct animals, and this single feature has fairly ended the dispute. I need not mention the fact that there is a wide range of dissimilarities in the skull of men of the same race; or, again, that there may be a striking likeness between the skulls of distant animals. An injury, disease, brain development, food, and a hundred other things, not to speak of malformations of birth, may account for the differences which we observe in the skulls of Du Chaillu's two specimens and those of the authenticated orang outan. I do not say that the gorilla is a myth, but until stronger evidences of its existence are produced we may expect that there will be doubts of its existence.

Mr. Bowditch, an African traveler, describes an animal which he called the *Ingheena*, that he heard frequent mention of by the natives in the vicinity of the Gaboon river. He says:

"It is in Equatorial Africa that the most powerful of all the quadrumana (four-handed animals) live, far exceeding the orang outan, and even the *Pongo* of Borneo."

Mrs. Lee, formerly Mrs. Bowditch, who was with her husband in Africa, adds the following: "Mr. Bowditch and myself were the first to revive and confirm a long-forgotten and vague report of the existence of such a creature, and many thought that, as we ourselves had not seen it, we had been deceived by the natives. They assured us that these huge creatures walk constantly upon their hind feet, and never yet were taken alive; that they watch the actions of men, and imitate them as nearly as possible. Like the ivory-hunters, they pick up the fallen tusks of elephants, but not knowing where to deposit them, they carry their burdens about until they themselves drop, and even die from fatigue; that they build huts nearly in the shape of those of men, but live on the outside; and that when one of their children dies, the mother carries it in her arms until it falls to pieces; that one blow of their paw will kill a man, and that nothing can exceed their ferocity."

The exaggeration of this description is apparent, not only because the assertions appear singular, but because they are in conflict with well-known physical facts. For example: None of the ape tribe are able to walk erect, for the reason that the spinal connection with the skull is so far back that the entire weight of the brain and skull is thrown forward and so overbalances the body. In man, the orifice —called the occipital foramen—where the spine enters the skull, is so nearly the center that a considerable portion of the brain lies behind, and the head is, therefore, perfectly balanced so that the easiest position is an erect one. A man is, accordingly, just as comfortable and natural while moving on "all fours" as an ape is when walking upright.

Du CHAILLU'S ADVENTURES WITH GORILLAS.

Since works on natural history treat the gorilla as a verity, I will not seek further to throw discredit on the belief, but add hereto some of the adventures recorded in pursuit of the monstrous Satyr-like creature. I have gone patiently through no less than eleven hundred different books on Africa and found nowhere, save in Du Chaillu's works, any description of the gorilla, if I may except Hanno's (the Carthagenian) account of a colony of the creatures he saw on the west coast of Africa, B. C. 350. I must, therefore, confine myself to excerpting from Du Chaillu, whose fame, however, I am glad to assist in spreading, for he was a great traveler. In a work I wrote a year ago, entitled "The World's Wonders," I gave many extracts from Du Chaillu's "Visit to Ashango Land," including a number of his adventures with gorillas, and among the Fan cannibals; I will now quote from his later work, "The Country of the Dwarfs," being an account of his visit to Africa in 1863. He writes:

"Gorillas were very plentiful near Nkongon-Boumba, and were committing great depredations among the plantain and banana trees; the patches of sugar-cane were also much devastated. I heard one afternoon, that the day before gorillas were in the forest not far from the village, and had already begun to play sad havoc with the plantain trees.

"The morning after the news, if you had been in the village, you would have seen me, just a little before day-break, getting ready to go after the gorillas. I was painting my face and hands with a mixture of powdered charcoal and oil. After my toilet was done, I put on my old, soiled panama hat, took one of my best guns, called Odanga, one of my boys, to accompany me, and off.

"It was a lovely morning; the sky was almost cloudless; everything was still, and one could only hear the slight rustling of the tree-tops moved by the gentle land breeze. Before reaching the grove of plantain-trees I had to pick my way through a maze of tree-stumps, half-burnt logs and dead, broken and half-burnt limbs of trees, where the land had been prepared for a new plantation. If gorillas are to be seen in a plantation near a village they most generally come in the early morning.

"By the side of the plantain trees was a field of cassada, and just as I was going by it I heard, suddenly, in the plantain grove, a great crashing noise, like the breaking of limbs. What could this be? I immediately hid myself behind a bush, and looked in the direction from which the sounds proceeded. What do I see? A gorilla, then a second gorilla, and a third one, coming out of a thick bush; then another one made his appearance—there were four altogether. Then I discovered that one of the females had a baby gorilla following her.

"So do not be astonished when I tell you that my eyes were wide open, and that I gazed on the scene before me with intense excitement. These gorillas looked so droll, walking in the most absurd way, on all fours, and now and then walking erect. How impish the creatures seemed! how intensely black their faces were! how hideous

FEMALE GORILLA WITH HER YOUNG.

their features! They looked like humans, but like wild men with shaggy hides, and their big, protuberant abdomens did not make them less ridiculous or repulsive.

"The gorillas went immediately at their work of destruction. I did not stop them, but merely looked on. Plantain-tree after plantain-tree came down; it seemed to me that they were trying to see which could down the greatest number of trees in the shortest space of time. In destroying a tree, they first grasped the base of the stem with one of their powerful, hand-like feet, and then with their prodigiously long arms pulled it down. Then they would set their big mouths upon the juicy heart of the tree, and devour it with great avidity; at another time they would give it one bite, or would simply demolish the tree without eating it. How strange sounded the chuckle they gave as if to express their contentment! Now and then they would sit still and look around—and such a look! Two or three times they looked in the direction where I was; but I lay so quiet, and was so concealed, that they could not see me, and as the wind was blowing from them to me, they could not smell me. How fiendish their looks were! a cold shiver ran through me several times, for, of all the malignant expressions I had ever seen, their's were the most diabolical. Several times they seemed to be on the point of running away, and appeared alarmed, but recovered their composure and began anew the work of destruction.

"The little baby gorilla followed his mother wherever she went. Gradually, without taking notice of it, they came to the edge of the dark forest, and all at once disappeared like a vision—like a dream. I went to the spot where they had made such havoc and counted over one hundred plantain-trees down on the ground which they had destroyed.

FACE TO FACE WITH A MONSTER.

"The next morning I went again with Odanga to the same spot, with no expectation of seeing gorillas again, for I did not think they would make another visit there, with their roving propensities, but I thought I might see an antelope, attracted by the young leaves of the cassada-tree, of which they are very fond. I carried a light double-barreled shot-gun, while Odanga carried my heavy double-barreled rifle to use in case we should see an elephant.

"The part of the plantation upon which we had come extended over two hills, with a deep hollow between, planted with sugar-cane. I was taking the lead in the narrow path, and just as I was going down the hill to cross over to the other side of the hollow, my eyes suddenly fell upon a monstrous gray-haired male gorilla standing erect and looking directly toward me. Without turning (for I dare not lose sight of the gorilla) I beckoned Odanga to come to me, so that I might get my rifle and shoot down the huge monster. But I beckoned all in vain. The huge beast stared at me and then moved off into the great forest on all fours. Then I looked round to see what was the matter with my boy, but no Odanga was to be seen. The fellow had bolted, gun and all; the gorilla had frightened him and he had fled. I was furiously angry, and promised myself to give Odanga such a punishment as he would not soon forget, that he might not play me such a trick a second time.

"On my return from Nkongon-Boumba, a great surprise awaited me — a *live* gorilla. An old chief, a friend of mine, named Akondogo, had just returned from the Ngobi country, situated south of Cape St. Catharine, and there, with some slaves of Olenga-Yombi, he had killed the mother, and captured the rascal before me. He was bigger than any gorilla I had captured, or that had ever been taken alive. Bigger he was than Fighting Joe, which many of you no doubt remember. (See World's Wonders.)

"Like Joe, this fellow showed the most ungovernable disposition, and to bite somebody seemed to be the object he was always aiming at. We had no chain with which to confine him, so that a long forked stick round his neck, was the only means we could employ to keep him at a safe distance.

CAPTURE OF ANOTHER GORILLA — A PITIABLE SPECTACLE.

"A few days after my return home one morning, a strange sight presented itself in front of my house — a sight which I firmly believe had never before been witnessed since the world began. There was a great commotion and tremendous excitement among the Commi people. There lay, in front of my bamboo house, a large female gorilla, bound hand and foot, alive, but frightfully wounded. There was a large gash in her scalp while her body was hacked and covered with blood. One of her arms had also been broken. Now and then the creature would give a sharp scream of pain, which lent horror to the darkness by which we were surrounded, the half-dozen lighted torches making the scene still more wild.

"This adult female gorilla had been mortally wounded in the morning, and lay on the ground senseless for a long time. A bullet from one of my hunters had fractured her skull, and while in a state of insensibility she had been securely tied to a strong stick, and in such an ingenious manner that there was no chance of her escaping. Her wrists and ankles had been tied strongly together, while the stick had been adjusted between her mouth and feet in such a way that she could not reach out to sever the cords with her teeth. Hanging from her breast was a baby gorilla (her child). The little creature was a female but a few months old, and now and then, after feeding from its mother's breast, it would give a plaintive wail. By the side of both stood a young live male gorilla, a fierce-looking fellow, which seemed afraid of nothing, and looked around with its deep, grayish, fiendish eyes as if to say, 'What does all this mean?' Not far off lay the corpse of a large female gorilla, quiet in the embrace of death, her face yet distorted by the death-agony.

"It was dark, and the scene was so strange and wild I will never forget it. The fiendish countenances of the living calibanish trio, one of them—the wounded one—with a face distorted with pain, were

DU CHAILLU'S CAPTIVES.

lit up by the ruddy glare of the natives' torches, and they seemed even more repulsive than their dead companion. What a commotion this sight would create, I said to myself, in a civilized land? There was no sleep for me that night; the terrific screams of the wounded mother kept me awake. Two or three times I got up and went out to see what was the matter, for I was in constant dread of the big gorilla untying the cords.

"The next morning I immediately prepared my photographic apparatus, and took an excellent photograph of the wounded mother with the young one in her lap. The night after I had taken the picture her moanings had became more frequent, and in the morning they gradually became weaker as her life ebbed out, and about ten o'clock she died. Her death was painfully like that of a human being, and her child clung to her to the last, and even tried to obtain milk after she was dead. How still was that fierce, scowling, black face! There was something so vindictive in it, and at the same time so human, that I almost shrank from the sight as I contemplated that wonderful creature which God has made almost in the image of man.

"Now, all I had to do was to take care of Tom and Minnie. Tom gave me no trouble, for he was quite old enough to feed upon the nuts and berries that were gathered for him, but with little Minnie it was a different thing, as she was too young to eat berries. Happily, I had a goat that gave milk, and I fed her as best I could, but she lived only three days after her mother's death; she died the fourth day towards noon, having taken an unconquerable dislike to goat's milk. She died gently; her tiny legs and arms had become shriveled, her ribs could all be seen, and her small hands had wasted to almost nothing. She died on the little bed of straw I had made for her as if she had gone to sleep without a struggle."

Du Chaillu had but little better luck with Tom, for he, too, died after a short captivity, though not in his native land. A ship having landed with supplies for Du Chaillu, he placed the gorilla in charge of the Captain and consigned him to Barring Bros., London. A quantity of plantains and bananas were sent to supply the precious creature with its natural food, but these were exhausted in five days after departure, and as his appetite could not be tempted by the offer of any other kind of food, the poor animal died of starvation on the seventh day.

ATTEMPTS TO DECEIVE THE PUBLIC.

Some years ago a young ape was sent to Berlin where it was placed in the Thiergarten and pronounced a young gorilla. The greatest interest was excited by this, as was alleged, the only gorilla that had ever been brought to Europe or exhibited in a civilized country; naturalists from many different countries paid the wonderful curiosity a visit, all of whom, I believe, were quite ready to acknowledge it as a veritable gorilla. As the animal increased in size, however, the typical features of the orang outan began to appear more positive, until at length it turned out to be, sure enough, one of those rather common creatures, when the naturalists laughed at each other for being "taken in" by the not very clever deception.

A deception even more glaring than the Berlin animal was perpetrated upon many naturalists by Barnum, who made up an impossible stuffed animal out of a variety of bear and wolf-skins, and exhibited it as a gorilla, to the great delight of thousands who accepted it without question. I saw the monstrous appearing thing myself, and being too young to form any correct judgment, I thought it must be a gorilla, because it was too ugly to be anything else.

Mermaids and unicorns have been on exhibition from time immemorial, and we have the evidence of thousands to the existence of such creatures, many of whom claim to have been eye-witnesses of the animals, while at one time there was not a person in all Europe who did not believe as implicitly in the marvelous medicinal virtue of unicorn bones as they did in saintly relics. I therefore repeat, that until a gorilla is brought under the examination of approved scientists who are familiar at least with the *Simian* family, cool-headed people, while not denying, will not conclude positively that there is in Africa, or in any other part of the world, such an animal.

TERRIFIC BATTLES BETWEEN MALE GORILLAS.

The extraordinary power and combativeness of the gorilla mark it as one or the most remarkable creatures, aside from its somewhat human analogy, that roams upon the face of the earth. It is much to be regretted, if such an animal really exists, that we have to depend upon a single authority for all the knowledge we possess concerning it, for of all the interesting products of creation surely none exceed the gorilla, and the naturalist is constantly thirsting for more information respecting it.

Since species are at war with each other we must assume that occasional battles take place between the mightiest monarchs of the jungle. Many witnesses have described terrible combats between elephants, lions, tigers and other powerful creatures of the jungle, but who shall depict a fight between gorillas, these giants with a human cunning, the prowess of man, and yet unarmed save with the weapons that God has given them? The gladiator in the arena presents no such possibilities of battle, even with sword and buckler, as does the gorilla, whose powerful limbs and frightfully armed jaws would seem to give force to his likeness of Satan.

A fight between two full grown gorillas must be a sight almost too terrible to witness, and certainly awful beyond description. Standing upon their hind legs, beating their breasts, and giving forth such hoarse, weird, guttural howls, gnashing their teeth and wrinkling their brows in a diabolical frenzy, the picture becomes so ghoulish and devilish that the strongest human courage must give place to the greatest fear, for in the monsters we behold images more frightful than a disordered brain has ever conjured up. Such battles are but

COMBAT BETWEEN TWO GORILLAS.

rarely witnessed, owing to the seclusion of the countries inhabited by gorillas, but the savage nature of the animal is sufficient evidence that these terrific contests are not infrequent.

Du Chaillu tells us that the gorilla and leopard are avowed enemies, and that between the two battles are not uncommon. Though he never claims to have seen such a fight himself, yet he says several natives of Africa, who have watched combats of this character, gave him the most realistic descriptions of the contests, and in each case assured him that the gorilla came off victorious. From accounts that we have been able to gather it appears that the gorilla is always more than willing to engage a leopard, since he uses no little strategy in coming upon this animal, most frequently hiding near the leopard's path, or stealing from tree to tree, keeping himself well out of sight until within springing distance. This caution does not appear fully justified, since it is asserted that the leopard rarely ever shows any disposition to avoid giving battle to the gorilla, even though the latter is much the more powerful. Conscious of the danger which lies within its adversary's claws the gorilla always makes the first attack, and endeavors to seize the leopard's fore-feet, which once within his dreadful grasp the beautiful animal is fairly helpless, and a moment after it lies dead from a bite of the gorilla, which wrenches and crushes the vertebræ of its neck. Satisfied with its victory the gorilla does not mangle its victim, but leaves the body the moment he is convinced that life is extinct, and moves away congratulating himself by making a noise which somewhat resembles both a grunt and a chuckle. Should he receive any wounds in the battle he seeks a certain plant which grows in some profusion in the Gaboon country, and makes a poultice by mascerating the leaves with his teeth, and then applies it with all the care that a human would, holding the grateful application on the hurt with his hand for several minutes, lifting it from time to time to note the effect, or to see if the juices are penetrating the wound. His actions while thus treating his injury are strikingly human.

THE ORANG OUTAN.

Having introduced some slight comparisons between the gorilla and orang outan, such as to throw some suspicion of doubt upon the existence of the former, I will now introduce descriptions of the latter animal obtained from the most authentic standard works of naturalists, by which it will appear the more probable that Du Chaillu has confounded the two animals. Some naturalists declare that the orang outan is not found in Africa, but is peculiar to South-east Asia, Borneo and Sumatra. This statement, however, is so far wrong that the animal is not only frequently met with in Africa, but in South America also, as well as in many of the Pacific islands.

The idea of the Satyr was obtained from the orang outan, and it is even now sometimes called *Satyrus*. The classic authors represented the Satyr as of a more intellectual countenance and as wearing hoofs of the goat instead of hands, but they preserved the reddish, chest-

GORILLA KILLING A LEOPARD.

nut hair with which it is colored. But the goat legs with which Satyrs are furnished are not indispensable, for some quaint illustrations found in 1530 represent the Satyr with true orang outan legs, and with all other features similar to that animal.

Dr. Lund has furnished us with descriptions of the Brazilian orang outan, which he calls the *Caypore,* obtained principally from the legends of the natives, which curiosly coincide with the gorilla of Du Chaillu and the *Ingheena* of Bowditch; so similar, indeed, that there is no doubting the identity of the three animals. By Lund it is represented as being equal to man in stature, to be in the habit of walking in the erect posture, and when aged to become fierce and dangerous, and to attack mankind with the formidable tusks that grow from its jaws. Among the legends is one which describes the caypore, "Dweller of the Wood," as being covered with long curling hair of a brown color, so thick as to be invulnerable, except in a single white spot on the abdomen. Its feet are each furnished with two heels by which it is enabled to foil its pursuers, since no one can determine by examining the tracks the direction in which the animal is traveling. It is declared to be the king of the wild hogs, and of such cunning and implacable disposition as to be certain to destroy any one who may kill its young. It is also represented as being half ape and half pig, and that it is most frequently seen in the midst of a herd of wild swine riding furiously on the back of the largest.

This same legend is told alike by the tribes of Western Africa, Borneo and Brazil, thus furnishing another proof of the identity already spoken of. The differences noted in the descriptions of the gorilla and orang outan may be accounted for by the fact that we have but one authority on the so-called gorilla, who was never able to study its habits in a domesticated condition, while the orang outan is perfectly well known, being familiar not only to many travelers, but fairly common in menageries.

In "The World's Wonders" I have given many adventures with the orang outan, or mias, of Borneo, chiefly extracted from Wallace's excellent work on the Malay Archipelago, so that I will here content myself with giving some of the habits and peculiarities of the animal.

POWER AND FEROCITY OF THE ORANG OUTAN.

The *Mias-Pappan,* as the orang outan is called in Borneo, where it seems to be best known, is the Satyr-like and terrible king of the jungles. Before man it is timid, and, as previously remarked, will try to escape until pressed to the last extremity, then its power and ferocity are wonderful, for it becomes more dangerous than the lion. Leading an arboreal life its arms are very long and muscular, enabling it to climb with facility, and to make rapid progress, swinging itself from branch to branch of the large forest trees, where it makes its home. It has a curious habit of constructing for itself a temporary resting-place in the trees by weaving together branches so as to form a rude platform, upon which it sleeps. Rajah Brooks narrates a tale of a female orang outan which, when severely wounded, ceased her attempts to escape, and binding together several branches she seated

NATIVES HUNTING THE ORANG OUTAN IN BORNEO.

herself on the scaffold so made and quietly awaited death. The entire process of weaving the branches together did not occupy her more than a minute, and when the hunters ascended the tree to throw down her dead body they found the platform upon which she rested strong enough to bear two or three men, and so level that they might have slept upon it comfortably.

The arms of the mias are so strong that they can bend with ease an iron rod half an inch in diameter, while the teeth and jaws are such that the animal will attack a leopard and kill it instantly by biting the neck. Although a vegetable feeder, the mias has need for the huge tusks with which it is provided, since cocoanuts constitute its principal food. Unlike others of the ape tribe who break the nuts by dashing them on the ground, the mias crushes the shell in its powerful jaws and drinks the milk as well as eats the meat inside.

The orang outan, when taken into captivity at an early period in its life, can be taught many amusing tricks but never develops much intelligence beyond that exhibited by other members of the monkey family. It has been taught to conduct itself with propriety at the table, to eat soup with a spoon and drink coffee from a saucer. Singularly enough, though in its native state it is a vegetable feeder, yet in captivity it becomes a voracious meat eater, taking the food offered it whether raw or cooked with equal relish. Another peculiarity is found in its readiness to adopt clothing, in which it affects such pride that the moment a new suit is given it the creature will tear up the old one in order to avoid having to wear it again. Another *civilized* trait it exhibits is a passion for beer, wine and stronger liquors. In other words it becomes a drunkard with all the naturalness of a society dude, and is happiest when full of grog. In his native woods the orang outan is slothful and solitary in his habits, spending much of his time in sleeping.

Generally speaking, the orang outan is both timid and inoffensive, and only upon the rarest of occasions does he engage in combat with other animals or those of his kind. However, if driven to extremities he will exercise the wonderful muscular strength with which he is endowed in the most ferocious and cruel manner. Should he succeed in grappling with his antagonist he uses both his claws and teeth to rend, nor ceases the attack until his enemy is entirely dismembered. Usually, when pursued, the orang outan ascends rapidly the tallest trees, and when further pressed he climbs from one tree to another, passing with great rapidity along the branches, at the same time giving voice to the most dolorous cries. He has also a habit of breaking off branches and throwing them down, not, however, hurling them at his pursuers, but rather, it would appear, merely to vent his rage. The Malay hunters take advantage of this curious habit, for, as the animal takes refuge in the thick foliage of the high trees, it might remain secure from observation by being quiet. The shouts of the

ORANG OUTAN KILLING A HUNTER.

pursuers below, however, cause it to strip off the branches by which it is surrounded, until the denuded limbs alone remain, when its body presents an excellent target for the native hunters, who shoot it to death with arrows.

DOES THE MIAS LOVE PRETTY WOMEN?

As previously asserted, the male mias attains an immense stature, more than six feet in height and having a reach of ten feet. When we consider the bulk of his body, large bones, tremendous muscles and enormous protuberant abdomen, we can readily conceive how monstrous a creature one six feet tall must be. No man, unarmed, can cope with such a mias a moment; one stroke of his great hand would prostrate an ox and he could tear a very Hercules limb from limb.

It is asserted, apparently on good authority, that the mias has strong predilections for pretty women, which he sometimes captures and bears away to his haunts in the jungle. In such cases he acts the part of a courteous bandit, never treating his lady-love with harshness, but holding her by a gentle, though none the less affectionate restraint. The *Dyak* women of Borneo are generally handsome, and living in a land where little traces of civilization are seen, they are hardy lovers of the chase and as adventurous as the men; hence, they are sometimes overtaken in the forest by crafty orang outans who seize them firmly in one arm and run off on three legs, so to speak, carrying the poor woman far into the dense recesses of the forest. Having reached a chosen spot the mias gathers leaves and small twigs with which he constructs a bed upon the ground for his mistress; should the captive attempt to escape the watchful mias quickly apprehends her and brings her back, not forgetting to bestow an admonition which is not all scolding. If she submits to his will the animal treats her with kindness, bringing her bountiful supplies of food each day, such as the woods afford, and allowing her to select and eat first from the store; should a storm take place he does everything in his power to afford her shelter. He will never relinquish his bride until compelled to do so by death, and in case he is attacked by hunters he places himself before the woman, as a protection, and fights to the last extremity.

THE FEROCIOUS MANDRILL.

More terrible than either the suppositious gorilla or the mias is an animal which belongs to the monkey race, a native of West Central Africa, where it is known under several names, but to zoologists

AN ORANG OUTAN ABDUCTING A WOMAN.

as the *Mandrill*. This wonderful creature exceeds all others in ferocity as well as in devilish appearance, and so great is its power that every other animal, including the elephant, flies before it. In sagacity it is inferior to all others of the ape family, but it is not without some cunning.

With all its hideous, hobgoblin-like aspect, the mandrill is singularly marked with wonderful colors, rivaling the plumage of sunbirds, but these embellishments of nature are most strangely placed, and only serve to really increase the creature's ghoulish appearance. "A bright azure," says Wood, "glows not in its 'eyes of heavenly blue,' but on each side of its nose, where the snout is widely expanded, and swollen into two enormous masses. Lines of brilliant scarlet and deep purple alternate with the blue, and the extremity of the muzzle blazes with a fiery red. That all things should be equally balanced, the opposite end of the body is also radiant with a chromatic effect, being plenteously charged with a ruddy violet, that is permitted to give its full effect by the pert, upright carriage of the tail."

The mandrill not infrequently attains a height of five feet and is as muscularly proportioned as the orang outan, while its tusks and jaws are equally as powerful; but added to these the mandrill possesses a hopelessly savage disposition, and is subject to the most violent bursts of passion, in which it becomes fairly insane with fury. In such desperate moods it knows no such thing as fear and will attack any living thing. It has been known to become so infuriated that it has worked itself into such paroxysms as to cause death.

A writer says of this animal: "Sudden and quick in passion as is the mandrill, it bears no short-lived anger, after the manner of most quick-tempered creatures, but cherishes a rancorous and deeply-rooted vengeance against any one who may be unfortunate enough to irritate its froward temper. It will often call into aid its natural cunning, and will pretend to have forgotten the offense, in order to decoy the offender within reach of its grasp."

A MANDRILL ATTACKS A MAN.

I was once a witness to the fury of a mandrill, which attempted to expend its unprovoked anger upon a friend who, with me, paid a visit to Cole's menagerie which was at the time in winter quarters in St. Louis. Several cages of wild animals were arranged around a large space within a barn and, with the keeper, we were looking at the several wild captives. Within a corner of the building, and next to a cage containing several lions, was a well-ironed pen, which was so dark within that we had not noticed the occupant. My friend chanced to approach very near the bars of this cage, when in an instant a huge arm was shot out from between the iron rods and a monstrous hand grabbed him with great violence by the coat-sleeve near the shoulder. At the same moment the impish creature screamed so horribly that my friend nearly fainted from fright. Although he was a strong man, the prodigious mandrill, for such it was, drew him against the bars and must have done him serious injury but for the prompt aid of the keeper, who beat off the furious creature with an iron bar which he carried. The mandrill now exhibited a fury I never saw equalled; it shook the cage, tried to break the rods; jumped violently against the sides of its prison, screamed most fiendishly and could not be made to abate its violence though punished severely by the keeper, and until we left it continued its frightful demonstrations, provoking all the other animals to anger until thé place fairly became a very pandemonium.

WATCHING VILLAGES FOR VICTIMS—THEIR LOVE FOR WOMEN.

It is affirmed of these animals, which live in large societies, that they frequently keep watch over native villages, and when the male population is dispersed to field labor, the mandrills issue from the woods in great numbers, and enter the defenceless homes which they proceed to plunder, despite the terrified women. It is further asserted that they do not stop at plunder, but also carry off the women like the chimpanzee and mias. Wood says this assertion is not improbable since it is strengthened by much collateral evidence. The large baboons, when in captivity, always make a great distinction between their visitors of the two sexes, always preferring the ladies to the gentlemen. Sometimes they are so jealous in their disposition that they throw themselves into a transport of rage if any attentions be paid to a lady within their sight.

I once saw an illustration of this propensity exhibited by a large *Chacma* ape in the zoological garden of St. Louis, which struck me at the time as extremely curious. The specimen, which is in the garden, is a very large animal, and old enough to be very sedate in his manner, so that he is quiet and taciturn, and so tame that he will permit any one to caress him. On the occasion referred to the animal was sitting in the rear part of its cage, apparently in a brown study, only occasionally opening its eyes to furtively glance at the crowds which were passing before him. Presently a very pretty girl, handsomely dressed, came by and paused to look at the half-sleeping animal. In an instant the creature jumped up, ran to the bars and, fixing its gaze intently on the girl, began chattering, smacking his lips and thrusting out his hands towards her in the most affectionate and appealing manner; his every action was clearly indicative of the feeling which had so suddenly smote him. The girl saw she was selected from the crowd as the object of his attention, but, of course, did not surmise that the ugly, dog-faced creature had fallen in love with her. When she moved away the chacma followed her with his eyes, straining his utmost to view her as long as possible, and when she vanished he seeemed to be as utterly inconsolable as a love-lorn callow youth who realizes that his affection is not reciprocated. The poor, heart-broken animal cried most piteously for hours afterwards, and never left the bars the remainder of the day, watching most eagerly in the hope that the girl might return again.

Wood also relates a somewhat similar incident which served to recapture a large chacma that had escaped from its cage in Paris. He says:

"It had already baffled many attempts to entice it to its home, and when force was tried, repelled the assailants, severely wounding several of the keepers. At last a ready-witted keeper hit upon a plan which proved eminently successful. There was a little window at the back of the cage, and when the keeper saw the chacma in front of the open door he brought a young lady to the window, and pretended to kiss her. The sight of this proceeding was too much for the jealous feelings of the baboon, which flew into the cage for the purpose of exterminating the offending keeper. Another keeper was stationed in ambush near the cage, and the moment the infuriated animal entered the den, he shut and fastened the door."

THE HUMAN APE, OR CHIMPANZEE.

We now come to a creature which is separated from man by a single missing link, but for which we might trace our ancestors back to a protoplasm—or something else. At first thought it appears that the gulf between the simian, or monkey tribe, and human family is so great that the idea of an identical origin could not be conceived in a rational brain, but such a conclusion is the product of the most superficial inquiry. The differences of appearance, thought, action and character between an American of to-day and the Bushmen of Australia, or the troglodytes of South Africa, are so striking as to apparently controvert the idea of the two belonging to the same species. Yet the anthropologist can plainly trace the cultured man and the savage back to a common ancestry. The link, however, which connects us with the monkey is entirely wanting, and when we consider that the ape, as he is to-day, was one of the antediluvian animals, we are not encouraged to believe that it will ever be found. If we pass the line of separation between man and monkey we meet our nearest relation in the *Chimpanzee*, an animal which, though far inferior to man, is superior to all other animals, while his structure bears a closer analogy to that of man than either the so-called gorilla or orang outan.

The chimpanzee is found occupying a very small district, being confined to Equatorial West Africa, in the section where Du Chaillu claims to have met with so many gorillas. Its range is about ten degrees on each side of the equator, but hardly more than one degree inland, being, apparently, a coast animal. Zoologists formerly maintained that the chimpanzee and gorilla were one and the same, but it is now held otherwise and the two are classed as belonging to different families, although the distinction is by no means radical.

The tint of the hair is almost identically the same as that of the gorilla, which is a brownish black; and, as in the gorilla, the hair of the fore-arm is turned toward the elbow, where it meets the hair of the upper arm and forms a pointed tuft, while in other respects there is a similar resemblance. The chimpanzee, however, lives in a social state, while the gorilla is represented as being solitary in his habits, though Du Chaillu mentions having frequently seen as many as seven together.

According to information obtained from the natives of West Africa, chimpanzees build huts for themselves in which they live; this statement is denied by others, however, who maintain that only the female and their young inhabit these huts, while the male takes up his position on the roof. The probability is that neither statement is correct. The chimpanzee spends most of his time on the ground, it is true, but his habits, when in captivity, show that he contents himself with a simple bed and never makes any effort to erect a roof to protect him from exposure.

HOW THE CHIMPANZEE FIGHTS WITH A CLUB.

One of the most remarkable habits of the chimpanzee, and one which indicates the proximity of reasoning power, if not its actual possession, is the manner in which it defends itself when attacked. All animals rely upon instinct and their natural weapons to defend themselves, save alone man and the chimpanzee, which create artificial and more powerful ones by exercising an intelligence which other creatures do not possess. The chimpanzee is armed with great tusks — the incisor teeth — with which it can tear large plantain trees and cut down bushes of considerable size, but it does not fight with its natural and powerful weapons until brought to close quarters. Instead, it seizes a large club and attacks with great ferocity, wielding the weapon with such force that a dozen men could do nothing against one if unprovided with guns or spears. The animal, when rendered desperate, has been known to snap, with a single effort, branches so thick that the united strength of two men could scarcely bend them. Their muscular strength is, therefore, enormous and their power for mischief with a large club must be terrible. Nor is the strength which lies in their hind-legs scarcely inferior; a large, adult chimpanzee, in the zoological gardens of London, frequently hangs head downwards from a cross-bar in his cage by a single foot, and after remaining in this suspended position for some time will draw himself up again onto the bar without the aid of his hands or the other foot.

The degree of intelligence in the chimpanzee is small and its reasoning power seems to be limited to the use of clubs, though it is a wonderful mimic. It loves the warmth of a fire, and will sit by the grateful blaze until the fuel is entirely consumed, never once thinking to renew it, but will cry for some one else to do so, or, perhaps, merely because the fire has expired. He loves pretty clothes, too, but will never learn to dress himself. He seems to comprehend, when in the wild state, that the danger which threatens him from the hunter does not reside in the man but in the weapon, consequently if an attack be made by the hunter and he flees before the combined assault of a herd of chimpanzees, as is often the case, he may save his life by casting away his weapon. The animals will stop and seize the gun or spear and expend all their anger upon it, thus enabling the hunter to make good his escape.

HUMAN-LIKE HABITS OF THE CHIMPANZEE.

George Thompson, author of several works on Africa, in one of his publications entitled "Palm-Land," writes as follows of the Chimpanzee:

"It is said to be the nearest approximation to the *human* in the animal creation — and it certainly acts much like mankind. I have seen persons who had the features and expression almost precisely; at any rate a sight of one will immediately remind the beholder of some person he knows. Some have been seen as tall as a man — from five to seven feet high, and very powerful. It is said of them that they build a kind of rude house of sticks, in their wild state, and fill it with leaves; and I doubt it not, for when domesticated they always want some good bed, and 'make it up' regularly. If left to themselves they will gather a pile of clothes beneath and around them to make a warm and soft bed. And when they sleep they are entirely different from the monkey tribes, which sleep in clusters, sitting up, enfolded in each others' arms; for the chimpanzee always *lies down*, as regularly as a man, on the side, and at times on the back, or in other positions; and thus will sleep and snore and cough (if it has a cold) and wheeze as naturally as a child; and groan, whine and cry so as often to be mistaken for a person. If the creature is crossed or vexed it will manifest excited passion by screaming, pounding the floor with its hands, holding its breath, throwing itself on the floor, etc., like a 'spoiled child.' If pleased, by giving it what it likes, it shows all the joy amaginable, by thanking you, shaking the hand, and kissing it, and by a peculiar ha, ha, ha, which shows its thankfulness. It eats the same as a man, taking very small mouthfuls and chewing slowly and thoroughly. Its front teeth are similar to human, but the 'eye teeth' are short *tusks* from a half to one inch long.

"It has been taught to wash itself, to sit in a chair, and eat at a table with plate, spoon, etc.; and to go to the brook and *wash* its dishes when done, and put them in their place; to *beat rice*, clean and prepare it for cooking; to bring water; and to think as much of fine clothes as any other proud man. If allowed it will help itself to any article on a table it likes best, as readily as any of us. It smells of every thing before tasting of it, and is very particular what it eats — is fond of bread, crackers, meat, cakes, fruits and almost everything that we eat. When sick, it shows it in the countenance and actions as quickly as any person. When *shaved* (as I saw one), they hold as still and act as properly as if they had been shaved a thousand times. They can not *talk* our language, or be taught to read it, though they seem to understand as quick as any body, on many points. This is truly a wonderful animal. One brought from Africa sold for $900 some years ago; but they do not live long in cold countries."

CHIMPANZEES ABDUCTING WOMEN.

The natives of the lower Congo country positively declare that the chimpanzee is guilty of abducting women for immoral purposes, and that occasionally it seizes a man or boy, but its treatment of the two sexes is very different. When the animal carries off a woman his attentions are so constant and brutal that, unless rescued, she dies for want of sleep; but a man pays an equally dear penalty, for he is generally bitten to death and his bowels torn out. Whether these reports are true or not we have no means of knowing, but they are rendered probable by a circumstance which Wood reports as having actually occurred some years ago in the vicinity of Sierre Leone. He states that a particularly fine specimen was tamed and domesticated in its native country, where it lived with its captor for twenty-one years. On one occasion a soldier came near and commenced playing with it, when suddenly the creature seized and bore him with perfect ease, despite his struggles, half-way up the tree to which it was chained, when help came and he was rescued none the worse for his novel experience. The circumstance was important as showing both the power and the disposition of the animal, and certainly renders the stories of the natives, as to its habit of carrying people off, not only possible but probable.

The chimpanzee, gorilla and orang outan all belong to the baboon family, though the real baboon, as we understand that specific animal, is much smaller than the three named; its habits, however, are very similar. They live in large colonies and will not hesitate to attack travelers who intrude upon their domain, especially after one of their number has been wounded, and they are very ferocious antagonists.

CURIOUS HABITS OF THE BABOON.

Sir Samuel Baker thus describes some of the curious habits of the baboon as he saw them along the Settite river in Abyssinia:

"Troops of baboons are now exceedingly numerous—along the Settite river—as the country being entirely dried up, they are forced to the river for water, and the shady banks, covered with berry-bearing shrubs, induce them to remain. It is very amusing to watch these great male baboons stalking majestically along, followed by a large herd of all ages, the mothers carrying their little ones upon their

A CHIMPANZEE CAPTURING A WOMAN.

backs, the latter with a regular jocky seat, riding most comfortably, while at other times they relieve the monotony of the position by sprawling at full length and holding upon their mothers' back hair. Suddenly a sharp-eyed young ape discovers a bush well-covered with berries, and his greedy munching being quickly observed, a general rush of youngsters takes place, and much squabbling for the best places ensues among the boys; this ends in great uproar, when down comes a large male, who cuffs one, pulls another by the hair, bites another on the hindquarters just as he thinks he has escaped, drags back a would-be deserter by his tail, and shakes him thoroughly, and thus he shortly restores order, preventing all further disputes by sitting under the bush and quietly enjoying the berries by himself. These baboons have a great variety of expressions that may, perhaps, represent their vocabulary; a few of these I begin to understand, such as their notes of alarm, and the cry to attract attention; thus, when I am sitting alone beneath the shade of a tree to watch their habits, they are not at first quite certain what kind of a creature I may be, and they give a peculiar cry to induce me to move and show myself more distinctly."

A LUDICROUS WAY OF CAPTURING AND SUBDUING A BABOON.

In another part of his "Nile Tributaries of Abyssinia," Baker describes a curious hunt for baboons, as follows:

"We had several times disturbed antelopes during the early portion of the march, and we had just ascended from the rugged slopes of the valley, when we observed a troop of about a hundred baboons, who were gathering gum arabic from the mimosas; upon seeing us they at once waddled off. 'Would the lady (Mrs. Baker) like to have a *Girrit* (baboon)?' exclaimed the ever excited Jali; being answered in the affirmative, away dashed the three hunters in full gallop after the astonished apes, who, finding themselves pursued, went off at their best speed. The ground was rough, being full of broken hollows, covered scantily with mimosas, and the stupid baboons, instead of turning to the right into the rugged and steep valley of the Settite, where they would have been secure from the aggageers, kept a straight course before the horses. It was a curious hunt; some of the very young baboons were riding on their mothers' backs; these were now going at their best pace, holding on to their maternal steeds, and looking absurdly human; but, in a few minutes, as we closely followed the Arabs, we were all in the midst of the herd, and with great dexterity two of the aggageers, while at full speed, stooped like falcons from their saddles and seized each a half-grown ape by the back of the neck, and hoisted them upon their horses. Instead of biting, as I had expected, the astonished captives sat astride of their horses, and clung tenaciously with both arms to the necks of their steeds, screaming with fear. The hunt was over, and we halted to secure the prisoners. Dismounting, to my surprise, the Arabs immediately stripped from a mimosa several thongs of bark, and, having tied the baboons by the neck, they gave them a merciless whipping with their powerful koorbatches of hippopotamus hide. The little creatures cried most pitifully, and at the same time looked so appealingly into the eyes of their captors, that my keenest sympathies were excited, and I tried to prevent the further whipping of the helpless captives, which now more than before appeared so child-like. It was in vain that I remonstrated, they persisted in the punishment, otherwise they declared the baboons would bite, but if well whipped they would become humble. At length my wife insisted upon mercy, and the unfortunate captives wore an expression like prisoners about to be led to execution, and they looked imploringly at our faces, in which they evidently discovered some sympathy with their fate. They were quickly placed on horseback before their captors, and once more we continued our journey."

BABOONS AND GIBBONS OF SOUTH AFRICA.

THE HOWLING AND PREACHER MONKEYS.

The strikingly-human characteristics which we find in the gorilla (?), chimpanzee and orang outan are discoverable also in some of the smaller simian species. Indeed, at times, the similarity is so great that the most impassive hunters of these curious animals acknowledge that they have never been able to conquer a painful remorse which invariably is excited when witnessing the human-like agonies of their victims.

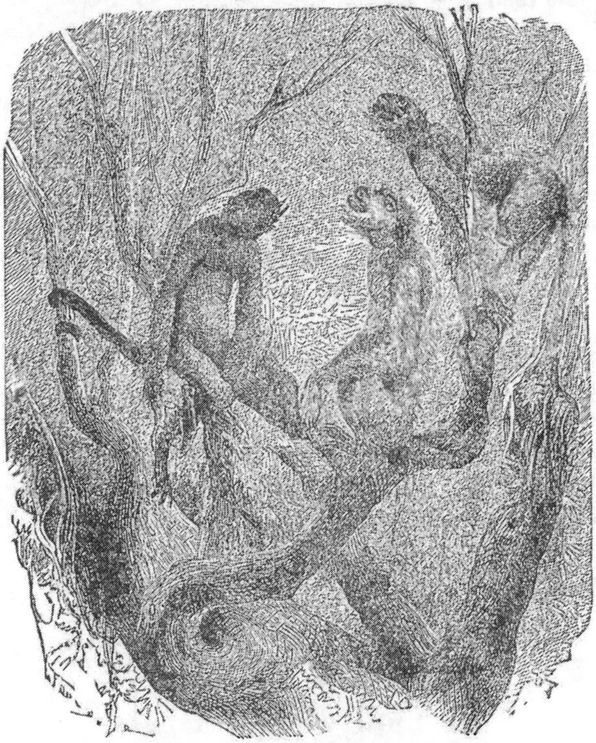

HOWLING MONKEYS OF SOUTH AMERICA.

Devoid of the fierceness and power of the orang outan, though more singular in its habits, is the *Howling Monkey* of South America. This astonishingly uncouth little creature is provided with a long tail and the most reverend cut of whiskers, while its solemn cast of countenance is mirth-provoking to a degree. The quaint aspect of its funereal features is hardly so curious, however, as the habit which it almost continuously indulges, of *howling*. From this circumstance the monkey takes its very appropriate name. In their native forest it is more common for three or four of the species to go together, and in the tops of the trees they sit for hours at a time giving vent to their dolorous cries. The cause of their making such strange noises is not understood. Some naturalists have thought it was to intimidate their enemies, but while horrible enough perhaps to accomplish this purpose, this can hardly be the real prompting, since in captivity they howl no less than when free.

The *Preacher Monkey* is also a species of the howlers, though it is considerably larger than the kind just referred to. This latter is about the size of a common fox, has long black hair and a beard very much like the former. It is also a native of South America and has received its name from the extremely curious preaching habit in which it indulges. They are gregarious and seem to be governed by a leader who, upon frequent occasions, ascends to the low branches of a tree, where he addresses an assembly of his species which sit around on the ground below him exactly like a congregation listening to their pastor. His preaching is not by chattering, as one might suppose, but by howling in a voice so shrill and loud that he may be heard a long distance. After thus emitting two or three screams, or howls, he pauses a moment and then signals to his auditors, whereupon they join in a deafening chorus which is prolonged for several minutes. These quaint exercises take place usually early in the morning and late in the evening, never, I believe, during the middle of the day.

CHAPTER XXXIV.

THE MIGHTY GRIZZLY BEAR.

THE lion, tiger, elephant, rhinoceros and gorilla are often regarded as being the most powerful and dangerous animals that are hunted, but so far from this being true, it is much to be doubted if either of the five named are so ferocious and difficult to kill as is our own North American *Grizzly Bear*, and, so far as my own experience extends, I am frank to say that I would rather meet any other monster that roams the wilds of any region, than to face a grizzly bear. No other animal manifests so little fear of man, and while other beasts flee before the first scent of the hunter, the grizzly is often attracted by it and frequently attacks without even the incentive of hunger.

The grizzly bear is almost omnivorous and never dainty. His preference may be for fresh meat, but he appears quite content when eating nuts like a hog, shaking down persimmons, digging up succulent roots, or even — though very seldom — browsing like an ox. His haunts are invariably in mountain fastnesses, from whence he sallies forth at all seasons of the year either to hunt wild game or conduct a predacious excursion among domestic stock.

GRIZZLY BEAR CARRYING OFF A DEER.

The Sierra Nevada mountains are still the home of many grizzlies, but they are not so much hunted now as formerly, and the sight of the carcass of the mountain monster has become a rare one.

The grizzly is an excellent hunter, and as the black-tailed deer affects the same haunts as himself, he more frequently dines off venison than any other kind of meat. As he is a poor runner, while his quarry is remarkably swift of foot, the grizzly resorts to a strategy that is very cunning and none the less effective. When upon the hunt he throws his head aloft frequently to sniff the air for a scent of the game; when he discovers that a deer is somewhere in the vicinity, he soon learns the direction, and, trailing the scent, so to speak, he moves cautiously, his nose never failing to indicate the distance the deer may be from him. As he approaches closer his caution is increased until he may be observed creeping along from one tree or rock to another, always keeping some object between himself and the game, occasionally stopping and lying so flat and motionless on the ground as to appear as a stump. He carefully marks the direction in which the deer is feeding, and manages to get the animal's wind, when he carefully conceals himself behind some shelter, not, however, obstructing his sharp look-out, where he waits until the deer approaches close enough for him to spring upon it. Though extremely wary and quick, the black-tailed deer seems to be easily caught by the grizzly, for venison may be said to constitute its most common food.

After securing his prey the grizzly seldom begins an immediate feast, preferring, it would appear, to first bury it and to dig it up a day or two afterwards, when the body is permeated with the moldy flavor of the soil. Nor does he bury the body on the spot where the capture is made, but carries it in his arms to some place, not, however, far distant, that may suit his fancy, where he digs a shallow hole, into which he carefully lays the deer, and then covers it with sticks and leaves as carefully and intelligently as a man would.

PERILS OF HUNTING THE GRIZZLY.

More men have been killed by grizzly bears than were ever slain by lions, and of the two animals the former is very much more to be dreaded. The lion, though desperate in an encounter, is a coward before man; besides, it is not very difficult to kill. On the other hand, the grizzly is aggressive and quite as tenacious of life as the crocodile. Indeed, they have been known to continue to battle furiously and pursue their hunters with great persistency, when pierced with twenty rifle balls. A gentleman of my acquaintance was killed by a grizzly that had been shot as many as seventeen times, but which still continued active and able to outrun a fleet hunter. The incident may be briefly described as follows:

The friend who thus met such a horrible death, was visiting some relatives in Sacramento, intending to spend the winter in that delightful region. Being a great lover of hunting, he accepted the invitation of some acquaintances to go upon a bear hunt up in the Sierras.

SAD RESULT OF A GRIZZLY BEAR HUNT.

The party was composed of four gentlemen, none of whom, however, had ever before penetrated the haunts of the grizzly or knew anything of its habits. They took with them a complete camping outfit, intending to cast their tent in the country which they thought most promising for their expected sport. In addition to the tent, they had a half-dozen excellent dogs that were loaned them by a gentleman living in the vicinity of Devil's Peak, and which had several times before given chase to grizzlies. Being armed with repeating rifles, the hunters anticipated no accidents, and were anxious to give battle to the great kings of the mountain fastnesses.

It was in the winter season when they started and the snow lay several feet deep in the gorges which they penetrated. The first day's hunt resulted in the killing of only a single deer, but they had discovered the tracks of a grizzly which, however, were not fresh. On the following day they arose early and traveled as rapidly as possible along the trail, and toward evening their dogs gave tongue which told plainly they had come up with the game. The gentleman who afterwards fell a victim to the animal he was hunting, being somewhat in advance of his companions, was first to sight the bear, which he discovered sitting on a rock bayed by the dogs. Much excited by this discovery he did not wait for his associates to come up, but immediately opened fire and succeeded in wounding the animal several times, but it nevertheless made off up a canon where, owing to the great rocks and dense growth of pine, it was impossible for the hunters to follow.

The gentlemen returned to their camp much disappointed, but not discouraged, for at break of day they renewed the hunt, separating, however, so as to cover a greater extent of country and thus increase their chances of falling in with the first one or another grizzly. Toward noon three of the party heard the dogs barking a considerable distance off and apparently down in a deep valley; shortly after several shots were heard, and being now convinced that their friend was engaging some kind of game they hastened with all possible speed toward the spot from whence the sounds proceeded. The dogs continued their barking with increased violence, but as no more shooting followed fears were excited that some accident had happened. Nor were their misgivings without cause, for as the first of the three came in view of the place where the noisy combat was waging, his blood was fairly frozen with horror as he discovered the dead body of his friend lying half-covered in the snow, while a monster grizzly was standing over it fighting off the dogs. The other two came up speedily, when the three opened fire and after discharging a score or more of shots succeeded in killing the ferocious animal. The poor fellow who had fallen a victim to his impetuosity was horribly mangled, so that his body could hardly have been identified except for the knowledge of the circumstances which his companions had.

CATTLE ATTACKED BY A GRIZZLY BEAR.

When the body of the bear was examined no less than twenty-three wounds were discovered, sixteen of which they believed were made by shots from the dead man's rifle, so that the bear had evidently overtaken and torn the hunter, though wounded so frequently as must have speedily killed any other animal.

HOW THE GRIZZLY BEAR ATTACKS CATTLE.

It quite frequently happens that excessively cold weather and scarcity of food drives the grizzly out of his accustomed haunts, and prompts him to forage among domestic flocks. His depredations are nearly always committed at night, for he is a cunning fellow, and quite wise enough to know that discovery would pretty certainly lead to a chase by dogs or a physic of lead. In his forays upon the cow-yard he conducts himself with great caution, and lacks only the wisdom of knowing that his attacks must cause enough noise to awaken the soundest sleeper. He creeps with soft tread and slow motion, and mounts whatever fence may interpose with the utmost care, coming down backwards on the inside. The cows are very liable to give the alarm before the attack is made, for the grizzly gives off a strong scent that inspires terror in all domestic quadrupeds. As they rush round the lot he watches his opportunity and springs upon his victim in a manner almost identical with the lion; that is to say, he nearly always seizes the unfortunate bullock at the apex of the neck and bites through or disjoints the vertebræ, bearing the animal to the earth and speedily dispatching it.

Should the grizzly catch a cow or ox in the open he drags it away a short distance, and then, if not disturbed, begins his meal, never attempting to bury it as he does the body of the deer. He seems to reason that his depredation must soon become known, and to appear before the carcass a second time would be like inviting the farmer to attack him; hence, as soon as his feast is made he scampers off, not to appear in the same vicinity again. If he kills his prey in a barn-yard he never attempts to eat it, for, knowing that he cannot drag the body out of the enclosure, he makes off with every evidence of great fear and without attempting to satisfy his hunger.

BATTLES BETWEEN GRIZZLIES AND BUFFALOES.

In the early days of California, when the amusements of the miners were generally of the most exciting character, it was a common thing to introduce a grizzly and a buffalo into a strong enclosure, about which an amphitheatre was erected for spectators, and goad the animals into a terrific combat, which invariably meant death to one or the other. It may appear, at first consideration, that a buffalo would have little chance for his life penned up with a strong grizzly bear, but it is a fact that the former more frequently proves the master than the latter, though his fighting abilities rest in his power to butt rather than to gore.

Frequent encounters have been witnessed between the two monarchs of the plains in unrestrained wildness, where one was prompted by hunger and the other by self-defense. The grizzly is extremely fond of young buffalo meat, and to obtain this, his favorite *bon mot*, he has

FIGHT BETWEEN A GRIZZLY BEAR AND BUFFALO.

often been known to attack herds in his efforts to get at the calves, but not always with success. Upon the appearance of a grizzly before a herd of buffalo, the bulls are first to give the alarm, when the cows and calves at once gather themselves into a compact mass while the bulls take up a position in front, and by pawing the earth and bellowing seem to bid defiance to the enemy. The grizzly does not make an immediate attack, but slowly circles about the herd trying to find a weak place to break through the line, which he sometimes succeeds in doing, for if he once seizes upon a calf the herd immediately stampedes, and flies swiftly over the plains in a mad effort to escape further harm. He is more frequently met, however, by some powerful and courageous bull that rushes upon him with the force of a catapult and ingloriously rolls him over the ground with broken ribs or other bones. The attack is then followed up, often aided by other bulls, until the marauder is killed. While the contest is going on the cows gaze, like meek-eyed spectators, and betray far less concern than they evidently feel.

THE FEROCITY OF A CAPTIVE GRIZZLY.

Of all animals I believe the grizzly bear alone resists all efforts at domestication. Lions, tigers and even hyenas have been raised to such familiarity with man that they would follow their masters like dogs and never manifest any treachery. The grizzly, however, always remains the sullen and ferocious beast that we find him when in his natural home. I once saw a baby grizzly, perhaps two months old, that would suck a person's finger and play on the carpet like a little kitten. This same bear, six years afterwards (though in the meantime it had been constantly in the care of a kind master) killed a man, who chanced to come near it, by a powerful stroke of its great paw, and that, too, without the least provocation.

In the year 1878, while on a visit to California, I noticed an uncommonly large grizzly that was kept confined in a cage at the railroad depot in Lathrop, where the Central Pacific trains stopped for passengers to take their meals. Two years afterwards, when on another similar trip, I saw the same bear and noticed children feeding it with peanuts, cakes and pop-corn. There was no railing about the cage, so that anyone might venture as close to the animal as desired. I remarked at the time, that a serious accident would one day occur, to prove that the bear was still extremely dangerous though evidently long in captivity. It was only a few months after this visit that I learned, through the press, that this bear had seized a little girl and torn her arm off at the shoulder, so badly mutilating her that death speedily resulted.

CHAPTER XXXV.

WILD RACES OF MANKIND.

THE WONDERFUL PIGMIES OF AFRICA.

HAVING described some of the more remarkable animals, whose haunts are in the wilderness of the world, it is but natural that we turn to a consideration of the wild races of men, whose lives are spent amid scenes and surroundings which are peculiarly savage, where the battles continue between brute and barbarian almost as in the days of primeval man.

As Africa is the field whereon the most wonderful animals disport, so is it the chosen ground of more curious people than any other portion of the earth can lay claim to; hence, it is rich with quaint specimens and surprises, a study of which holds us fairly spell-bound with interest.

In olden times, it is maintained, there existed a race of giants in Africa, whose strength and prowess enabled them to cope with the mastodonic forms of life in the forest; but if these once existed they are now long since buried in extinction, and live only in legend or superstition. But, although the giants have disappeared, their antithetical congeners still continue in the *Pigmies*, the quaint little humanities that roam the forests in miniature batallions fighting cranes, as in the Homeric story, and battling for life against the lords of the benighted wilderness. Some call them *Dwarfs*, but only because there is in the name something gnomish, a suggestion of goblin or wood-spirit to harrow up our thoughts; but they are not dwarfs, nor unrealities, but a distinct race or races, whose habits of life are no less curious than their diminutive stature. In fact, of all the numerous singular creatures to be met with in Africa, these little beings are the quaintest, but they have received more attention in nursery history than in the works of naturalists, whose silence would seem to indicate that they regarded them as mythical personages.

EVIDENCES OF PIGMY RACES.

While Schweinfurth was traveling up the Nile on his way to the dark interior of the unexplored continent, he was astonished to hear his servants talk day after day about the pigmies and their fights with the cranes. Had the stories of Homer been told to them, or was it the traditions of a long past age that prompted such reflections?

When he asked these ignorant Arabs from whence they had learned of the pigmies, his astonishment was greatly increased to hear several of them declare that they had seen dwarfs, and ere their return would prove that little people with long beards were frequently to be met with in African woods. On this interesting subject Schweinfurth writes:

"It was a fascinating thing to hear them confidently relate that in the land to the south of the Niam-niam country there dwelt people who never grew to be more than three feet in height, and who wore beards so long that they reached to the knees. It was affirmed of them that, armed with strong lances, 'they would creep underneath the belly of an elephant and dextrously kill the beast, managing their own movements so adroitly that they could not be reached by the creature's trunk. Their services in this way were asserted to contribute largely to the resources of the ivory traders.

"I listened on. The more, however, that I pondered silently over the stories that they involuntarily disclosed—the more I studied the traditions to which they referred—so much the more was I perplexed to explain what must be either the creative faculty or the derived impressions of the Nubians. Whence came it that they could have gained any knowledge at all of what Homer had sung? How did it happen that they were familiar at all with the material which Ovid and Juvenal, and Nonnus and Statius worked into their verse, giving victory at one time to the cranes, and at another to the pigmies themselves.

"My own ideas of pigmies were gathered, originally, only from books, but the time seemed now to have come when their existence should be demonstrated in actual life. Legends of pigmies had mingled themselves already with the earliest surviving literature of the Greeks, and the Iliad, it will be remembered, mentions them as a race that had long been known. But not the classic *poets* alone; sober historians and precise geographers have either adopted the poetic substance of the tradition or have endeavored, by every kind of conjecture, to confirm its accuracy. Nothing, for instance, can be more definite than the statement of Herodotus about the *Nasamonians* after they had crossed the Libyan deserts: 'They, at length, saw some trees growing on a plain, and having approached they began to gather the fruit that grew on the trees; and while they were gathering it some diminutive men, less than men of middle stature, came up and seized them and carried them away.' The testimony of Aristotle is yet more precise, when he says, plainly: 'The cranes fly to the lakes above Egypt, from which flows the Nile; there dwell the pigmies, and this is no fable but the pure truth; there, just as we are told, do men and horses of diminutive size dwell in caves.'"

Pauer attempts to prove that the story of cranes battling with pigmies is no more than an Egyptian allegory representing the cranes battling with the falling waters of the Nile, along the banks of which these birds congregate in great numbers. But Pauer's efforts in this direction are not unlike Gladstone's sophomoric attempt to locate Troy and the birth-place of Homer.

Three or four centuries before the Christian era the Greeks certainly knew of a race of people inhabiting a district near the reputed source of the Nile which were remarkable for their stunted growth. The indefiniteness of this location is not so inconsistent with the facts as we might, at first, be inclined to suppose, when it is considered that while the source of the Nile is, or was until Speke's discoveries, a problem unsolved, there is the very best of evidence to show that some thousand or more years ago all of Central Africa was almost perfectly known. We may, therefore, reasonably conclude that Homer and Aristotle, when they wrote of pigmies, were treating of a subject with which they were quite, if not thoroughly, familiar.

POSITIVE PROOF OF A PIGMY RACE.

Many alleged scientists, hearing their servants speak of what they regarded as marvelous things, would have lightly regarded the testimony such as was contained in the Arabs' stories of dwarfs, but Schweinfurth, though a wise man, did not consider himself omniscient and had the good judgment to institute a careful inquiry into the interesting subject so strangely brought to his attention. He recalled to mind the story told by Speke of a celebrated dwarf which he had the pleasure of seeing at the court of Kamrasi, but until now he had supposed that this specimen was no other than a freak of nature such as may be found in all countries, and common in museums, but the fact that there was a *dwarf* now caused Schweinfurth to become greatly interested in the subject and to make inquiries as he proceeded. It was not long before his curiosity was gratified, for, shortly after his arrival at the palace of the Monbutto king, in Nubia, he learned that the dwarf country was not far distant, while one or more of these peculiar creatures was at that time in the village, which they were accustomed to visit for purposes of barter.

Schweinfurth was intensely delighted to learn that he was in the dwarf country and forthwith applied to Munza, the King, for his assistance in obtaining an interview with the pigmies, for though Schweinfurth's servants had already seen several, they were so frightened at the sight of a white man that they made off in great alarm. Munza promised his aid and sent some of his men to bring in one of the dwarfs, but before they returned Mohammed, who was one of Schweinfurth's party, chanced to observe one when on his way to the King and by swiftly running captured him. A great shout was immediately raised in the village, which brought Schweinfurth from his tent in time to see Mohammed approaching with the wonderful dwarf seated on his right shoulder, nervously hugging his neck and betraying signs of intense fear.

SCHWEINFURTH'S INTERVIEW WITH A PIGMY.

The quaint specimen of miniature manhood was taken to Schweinfurth's tent and there deposited on a chair, while an interpreter was sent for who soon appeared. At first the little fellow was so dreadfully frightened that he could not be induced to talk, but gradually his confidence returned, under the influence of innumerable gifts, until he at length suffered himself to be measured, sketched, and plied with a great number of questions. The dwarf's replies to the inquiries addressed to him elicited the following interesting facts:

His name was Adimokoo, and the name of the nation to which he belonged was Akka. The meaning of these words Schweinfurth neglected to obtain. This nation of pigmies occupied a large district south of Monbutto, and was composed of nine tribes, ruled by as many kings — most probably chiefs. Several families of the pigmies had settled in the vicinity of Monbutto, since it was the desire of the king, and he had given them many inducements to remain near him.

The principal portion of the Akka people resided in a district the borders of which were only two days' journey from Monbutto, and the dwarf assured his questioner that the Akkas were extremely numerous. Before departing, by the offer of many additional presents, Adimokoo was induced to go through the evolutions of his war-dances, in which, being dressed in a rokko-coat, plumed hat, and armed with bow and arrow and lance, he created no little amusement.

The height of this dwarf was four feet and ten inches, and he was, as he declared, an average size of his race. It is singular that this pigmy knew nothing whatever of any race similar to his own, especially when there is the best of evidence in proof of Lauture's assertion that a numerous nation of pigmies live to the south of Baghirmy; nor did he know of the existence of the Kenkob or Betsan tribes mentioned by Kolle. It was evident, though perhaps he was as intelligent as any of his people, that he had not traveled, nor were his people given to traveling, so that their knowledge was restricted to their immediate locality.

ADIMOKOO, THE AKKA PIGMY.

THE DANCING DWARF.

Speaking of Adimokoo's agility, Schweinfurth writes: "Although, I had been repeatedly astonished at witnessing the war-dances of the Niam-niam, I confess that my amazement was greater than ever when I looked upon the exhibition which the pigmy afforded. In spite of his large, bloated belly and short, bandy legs—in spite of his age, which, by the way, was considerable—Adimokoo's agility was perfectly marvelous, and I could not help wondering whether cranes would ever be likely to contend with such creatures. The little man's leaps and attitudes were accompanied by such lively and grotesque varieties of expression that the spectators shook again and held their sides with laughter. The interpreter explained to the Niam-niam that the Akka jump about in the grass like grass-hoppers, and that they are so nimble that they shoot their arrows into an elephant's eye and drive their lances into their bellies.

"On the following day I had the pleasure of a visit from two of the younger men. After they got over their alarm some of the Akka came to me every day. As exceptional cases, I observed that some individuals were of a taller stature; but, upon investigation, I always ascertained that this was the result of intermarriage with the Monbutto amongst whom they resided. I regret that I never chanced to see any of the Akka women, and still more that my visit to their dwellings was postponed from day to day until the opportunity was lost altogether."

Schweinfurth induced an Akka boy to accompany him on his travels, not, however, without the most extravagant inducements. This boy remained with him ten months, and the explorer hoped to bring him to Europe, but the little fellow was taken with dysentery and died, despite every exertion to save him.

CONFIRMATORY EVIDENCES OF PIGMIES.

Not only has Schweinfurth given considerable attention to the dwarfs of Africa, in which he is an enthusiastic believer, but nearly every traveler through that dark region of the earth has given more or less testimony to the existence of pigmy races. Readers of Du Chaillu's works will remember his descriptions of a wandering tribe of hunters called *Obongo*, whose height rarely exceeded four feet seven inches, and in several respects, Schweinfurth affirms, the Obongo greatly resembled the Akka. Battel, who traveled through Ashango land subsequent to Du Chaillu, reports having met considerable parties of the Obongo race and confirms all that the great gorilla hunter has said of them. The Portuguese, who trade in that part of the world, have also given considerable confirmatory evidence of the dwarf people, whom they call *Bakka-bakka*, which is a designation for the country rather than the race itself. Dapper, however, gives us a very entertaining account of a race called the *Yogas*, who, he declares, in olden times spread fear and destruction as far as the town of Loango, a hundred miles away. This coast town was a Portuguese trading and outfitting post, from whence large caravans were despatched into the interior to bring back ivory collected by trading with the natives. These caravans suffered dreadfully from the attacks of the Yogas, whose malicious propensities were never gratified, and whose fierce and murderous aggressions were only arrested by vigorous onslaughts of large parties of well-armed Portuguese who were employed at length to guard the caravans. The Yogos were a diminutive race, hardly so large as the Akka of whom Schweinfurth writes, but the Bakka-bakka, which were a neighboring race, and who sometimes affiliated with the Yogos, were much smaller than the latter, and also much fiercer. "The little men," says Dapper, "are stated by the Yogas to have the power of making themselves invisible, and can consequently slay an elephant without trouble."

In another place, in describing the court of Loango and the dwarfs who took up their positions before the throne, he writes: "The negroes affirm that there is a wilderness inhabited by these dwarfs and where there are many elephants; they are generally called Bakke-bakke, but sometimes Mimos. These small creatures, whose size he neglects to give, carried on the greater part of the ivory trade of the kingdom."

Escayrac du Lauture, in an article contributed to the Bulletin of the Geographical Society of Paris, and published in 1855, announced his discovery of a race called *Mala-gilaget* (literally men with tails) who were of singularly stunted stature. The idea of these dwarfs having tails no doubt arose from a custom common among the Bongo tribe of wearing an ox-tail suspended at one end from a girdle round the waist, leaving the brush end pending.

Kolle, a distinguished African explorer, affirms with great earnestness that there is a tribe residing on the Leeba river called the *Kenkob*, who are only two or three feet in height. It is only proper to add that Kolle, notwithstanding his declaration, does not claim to have seen any specimens of these people, but is quite content with the testimony of those who assured him that they had often seen and traded with them.

Another witness, in whom Kolle placed implicit confidence, told him of a race living along the Shary lake, or river, called *Betsan*, whose height varied from three to five feet, and whose hair and beard trailed upon the ground. Notwithstanding this hirsute encumbrance, these dwarfs, Kolle's informant declared, supported themselves entirely by the products of the chase. In this connection let me say, that the Niam-niams, of East Africa speak of a tribe to the west of them that are of small stature and great beards.

Krapf, who has given much study to the races of South Africa, mentions the *Doko*, on the Upper Juba river, as a tribe of dwarfs, whose stature does not exceed that of an ordinary European boy ten years of age. Considerable trade is carried on between the Doko people and the Mohammedans of Somali, who speak of them as the *Berikeemo*, *i. e.*, people two feet high.

Stanley has not failed to add his testimony to that of a hundred other explorers confirmatory of the existence of races of pigmies in Africa. The numerous evidences thus supplied lead to a general conclusion that the fact is well established; but it is singular no specimens of these curious people have ever been brought to Europe or America, and beyond the attempt made by Schweinfurth, I have heard of no effort, upon the part of any one, to carry a specimen of the pigmies out of Africa to any country, though the exportation of slaves for centuries has scarcely been interrupted. I incline to the opinion that an African pigmy would prove as great a curiosity as any wild animal, so that here is an opportunity for some enterprising showman.

DU CHAILLU'S HUNT FOR DWARFS.

It is with some hesitation that I call, in support of the proof that there are races of pigmies in Africa, the well-known traveler, Du Chaillu, since readers of his works cannot fail to note the somewhat singular fact that, invariably, whenever this explorer went in search of a curious or apocryphal thing he not only found it, but met with some adventure which enabled him to write something extremely interesting about the discovery. Thus, he not only met with the gorilla, the *ipi ant-eater*, the Fan cannibals, but also the pigmies, though a hundred other observing travelers who carefully explored the same countries could discover no traces of these curiosities. But I cannot, nor am I disposed to, throw discredit on Du Chaillu's discoveries, for Africa is full of surprises, and I know that experienced miners sometimes overlook large beds of precious ore which are afterwards opened by the "tender-footed pilgrim," and Du Chaillu may be the lucky prospector. At any rate, his account of the Obongo pigmies, which he claims to have visited, is so interesting that it is eminently entitled to be added to the other proofs already submitted. In truth, of all Du Chaillu's writings, I do not believe that any are so interesting as his descriptions of the dwarfs, and for this excellent reason I will include the material parts of his novel experiences:

Du Chaillu sailed from London in 1863, for the express purpose of visiting the country of the dwarfs; he took, in a vessel chartered for the purpose, a large supply of goods, gew-gaws of every description, guns, ammunition, medicines, scientific instruments, etc., and landed near Cape Lopez without incident. He immediately sent off presents to the Commi people, with whom he already had considerable acquaintance, and procuring guides he plunged into the wilderness in search of the little people of the wood. After many months' traveling toward the interior, and numerous narrow escapes from native tribes that beset his path, all obstacles were overcome and his perseverance was rewarded most bounteously. He relates the particulars of his discovery, and wonderful adventures with the pigmies, as follows:

DU CHAILLU'S DISCOVERY OF A PIGMY VILLAGE.

"Early the next morning we started again on our journey through the great forest, passing many hills and several rivulets with queer names. Suddenly we came upon twelve strange little houses scattered at random, and I stopped and asked Kombila (the guide) for what use these shelters were built. He answered, 'Spirit, those are the houses of a small people called Obongos.'

"'What?' said I, thinking that I had not understood him.

"'Yes,' repeated Kombila, 'the people who live in such a shelter can talk and they build fires.'

"'Kombila,' I replied, 'why do you tell me a story? How can people live in such small places? These little houses have been built for idols. Look!' said I, 'at these little doors. Even a child must crawl on the ground to get into them.'

"'No,' said Kombila,' 'the dwarfs have built them.'

"'How can that be?' I asked; 'for where are the dwarfs now? There are no plantain trees around; there are no fires, no cooking-pots, no water jugs.'

"'Oh,' said Kombila, 'these Obongos are strange people. They never stay long in the same place. They cook on charcoal. They drink with their hands, or with large leaves.'

"'Then,' I answered, 'do you mean to say that we are in the country of the dwarfs?'

"'Yes,' said Kombila, 'we are in the country of the dwarfs. They are scattered in the forest. Their little villages, like the one you see before you, are far apart. They are as wild as the antelope, and roam in the forest from place to place. They are like the beasts of the fields. They feed on serpents, rats and mice, and on the nuts and berries of the forest.'

"How strange the houses of the dwarfs seemed! The length of each house was about that of a man, and the height was just enough to keep the head of a man from touching the roof when he was seated. The material used in building were the branches of trees bent in the form of a bow, the ends put into the ground, and the middle branches being highest. The shape of each house was very much like that of an orange cut in two. The framework was covered with large leaves, and there were little doors which did not seem to be more than eighteen inches high, and about twelve or fifteen inches broad. Even the dwarfs must have lain almost flat on the ground in order to pass through. When I say door, I mean simply an opening, a hole to go through. It was only a tiny doorway, but I managed to get inside one of these strange little houses, and found there two beds, which were as curious as everything else about the premises. Three or four

AN OBONGO DWARF VILLAGE.

sticks on each side of the hut were the beds. Each bed was about eight inches, or, at the most, ten inches in width. One was for the wife, the other for the husband. A little piece of wood on each bed made the pillows. Between the two beds were the remains of a fire, judging by the ashes and pieces of burnt wood."

Being unable to see any of the dwarfs, who had evidently abandoned their village on his approach, Du Chaillu continued on to an *Ishogo* village, several leagues farther in the interior. Here he met the king, who received him cordially. To his inquiries concerning the dwarfs he was told that they inhabited a neighboring district, and that one of their villages was only a few miles from his present lodgings. "But," said the King, "if you want to see them you must not go to them with a large number of attendants. You must go in a small party. Take one of your Commi men, and I will give you my nephew, who knows the dwarfs, to go with you. You must walk as cautiously as possible in the forest, for those dwarfs are like antelopes and gazelles; they are shy and easily frightened. To see them you must take them by surprise. If you are careful to-morrow you shall see them."

On the following day Du Chaillu set out with four men for the dwarf village, and in a few hours came within view of a cluster of twelve small huts, but, despite the carefulness with which they traveled, the little creatures had discovered the white man's approach and made off before any of them were seen. This was a sore disappointment, but with the hope of winning their confidence, and to prove his friendly intentions, Du Chaillu hung several strings of beads and three-quarters of a goat upon the trees surrounding the dwarf village, and then returned to his quarters in the Ishogo settlement.

DU CHAILLU AT LENGTH MEETS THE DWARFS.

His anxiety to see the pigmies caused Du Chaillu to start again the next morning in search of the human curiosities. He says: "We continued to walk very carefully, and after a while we came near another settlement of the dwarfs, which was situated in the densest part of the forest. I see the huts; we cross the little stream from which the dwarfs drew their water to drink. How careful we are as we walk towards the habitations, our bodies bent almost double, in order not to be easily discovered. I am excited—oh, I would give so much to see the dwarfs, to speak to them! How craftily we advance! how cautious we are for fear of alarming the shy inmates! My Ashango guides held bunches of beads. I see that the beads we hung on the trees have been taken away. All our caution was in vain. The dwarfs saw us and ran away into the woods. We rushed, but it was too late; they had gone. But as we came into the settlement I thought I saw three creatures lying flat on the ground, and crawling through small doors into their houses. When we were in the very midst of the village I shouted, 'Is there anybody here?' No answer. The Ashangos shouted, 'Is there anybody here?' No answer. I said to the Ashangos, 'I am certain that I saw some of the dwarfs go into their huts.' Then I shouted again, but still no answer was returned. Turning towards me, my guides said, 'Oguizi, your eyes have deceived you; there is no one here, they have fled. They are afraid of you.' 'I am not mistaken,' I answered. I went towards one of the huts where I thought I had seen one of the dwarfs go inside to hide, and, as I came to the little door, I shouted again, but there was no answer. It did seem queer to me that I should have suffered an optical delusion. I was perfectly sure that I had seen the dwarfs get inside of their huts. 'Perhaps they have broken through the back part, and have escaped,' said I; so I walked round their little houses, but everything was right — nothing had gone outside through the walls.

CATCHING A DWARF WOMAN.

"In order to make sure, I came again to the door, and shouted, 'Nobody here?' The same silence. I now lay flat on the ground, and again shouted, 'Nobody here?' It was so dark inside that, coming from the light, I could not see, so I stretched my arm in order to feel if there was any one within. Sweeping my arm from left to right, at first, I touched an empty bed, composed of three sticks; then, feeling carefully, I moved my arm gradually towards the right, when — hello! what do I feel? A leg! which I immediately grabbed above the ankle, and a piercing shriek startled me. It was the leg of a human being, and that human being a dwarf! I had got hold of a dwarf!

"'Don't be afraid, the spirit will do you no harm,' said my Ashango guide.

"'Don't be afraid,' I said, in the Ashango language, and I immediately pulled the creature I had seized by the leg through the door, in the midst of great excitement among my Commi men.

"'A dwarf!' I shouted, as the little creature came out. 'A woman!' I shouted again — 'a pigmy!' The little creature shrieked, looking at me. 'Nchende! nchende!' said she. 'Oh! oh! oh! Yo! yo! yo!' and her piercing wail rent the air.

"What a sight! I had never seen the like. 'What!' said I, 'now I do see the dwarfs of Equatorial Africa — the dwarfs of Homer, Herodotus — the dwarfs of the ancients.

"How queer the little old woman looked! How frightened she was! She trembled all over. She was neither white nor black; she was of a yellow, or a mulatto color. 'What a little head! What a little body! What a little hand and foot!' I exclaimed. 'Oh, what queer looking hair!' said I, bewildered. The hair grew on the head in little tufts apart from each other, and the face was wrinkled as a baked apple. I cannot tell you how delighted I was at the discovery.

THE CAPTURE OF TWO MORE DWARF WOMEN.

"So, giving my little prize to one of the Ashangos, and ordering my Commi men to catch her should she try to run away, I went to the other little dwelling where I thought I had seen another of the dwarfs hide. The two huts stood close together. I shouted, 'Nobody here?' No answer. Then I did what I had done before, and, getting my head inside the hut through the door, again shouted, 'Nobody here?' No answer. I moved my right hand to see if I could feel anybody, when, lo! I seized a leg and immediately heard a shriek. I pulled another strange little dwarf out of the door. It was also a woman, not quite so old as the first, but having exactly the same appearance. The two dwarf women looked at each other, and began to cry and sing mournful songs, as if they expected to be killed. I said to them, 'Be not frightened.'

"Then the Ashangos called to the last dwarf who had hid to come out, that it was no use, I had seen them all. They had hardly spoken, when I saw a little head peep out of the door, and my Ashangos made the creature come out. It was a woman also, who began crying, and the trio shrieked and cried, wringing their hands until they were tired. They thought their last day had come. 'Don't be afraid,' said the Ashango, 'the Oguizi is a good Oguïzi!' 'Don't be afraid,' said my Commi men. After a while they stopped crying and began to look at me more quietly.

"For the first time I was able to look carefully at these little dwarfs. They had prominent cheek-bones, and were yellow, their faces being exactly the same color as the chimpanzee; the palms of their hands were almost as white as those of white people; they seemed well proportioned, but their eyes had an untamable wildness that struck me at once; they had thick lips and noses like the negroes; their foreheads were low and narrow, and their hair, which grew in tufts, was black, with a reddish tinge.

"After awhile I thought I heard a rustling in one of the little houses, so I went there, and looking inside saw it filled with the tiniest children. They were exceedingly shy. When they saw me they hid their heads, just as young dogs or kittens would do, and got into a huddle and kept still. These were the little dwarf children who had remained in the village under the care of the women, while the other dwarfs had gone into the forest to collect their evening meal — that is to say, nuts, berries and fruits — and to see if the traps they had set had killed any game.

"I put beads around the necks of the women, gave them a leg of wild boar and some plantains, and told them to tell their people to remain and not to be afraid. I gave some meat to the little children which they seized and ran away with.

"I waited in vain — the other inhabitants did not come back. They were afraid of me. I told the women that the next day I should return and bring them meat (for they are said to be very fond of it), and plenty of bread."

THE DWARFS BECOME FRIENDLY WITH DU CHAILLU.

Several visits were paid by Du Chaillu to the dwarf village and great quantities of beads and meat were left each time, before the pigmies would suffer themselves to be approached. The old woman first captured by Du Chaillu, soon became friendly and it was through her influence that the curious little people at length accepted the traveler as a friend and were persuaded to sit with him in the village.

Du Chaillu was anxious to possess a skeleton of a pigmy to bring home with him as a specimen, and therefore asked his guides the burying ground of the dwarfs. They replied that such a question propounded to the pigmies would cause them to disappear at once, for nothing could induce them to reveal their most sacred secret.

In order to encourage them to greater confidence Du Chaillu brought to the dwarf village two legs of goats, a leg of wild boar, ten house rats, a large dead snake and two land turtles, which he had cooked and served up in a grand feast, to which fifty-nine of the curious little creatures were invited.

A WONDERFUL ASSEMBLY OF PIGMIES.

Continuing his narrative of the dwarfs, and particulars of the feast, Du Chaillu writes:

"'Obongos,' said I, 'we have come to have a good time. First, I am going to give every one of you beads.' Then the Ashangos brought before them a basket containing the beads, and I asked who was the chief. I could not find him, and they would not tell me. The dwarfs were now eager for beads, and surrounded me, and though I am a man of short stature, I seemed a giant in the

DU CHAILLU AMONG THE PIGMIES.

midst of them; and as for Rebouka and Igalo (the guides), they appeared to be colossal. 'Ya! ya! yo! yo! ye! qui! quo! oh! ah! ri! ri! ke! ki! ke! ki!' seemed to be the only sounds they could make in their excitement. Their appearance was singular indeed, the larger number of them being of a dirty yellow color. A few of them were not more than four feet in height. But if they were short in size, they were stoutly built; like chimpanzees, they had big, broad chests, and, though their legs were small, they were muscular and strong. Their arms were also strong in proportion to their size. There were gray-headed men, and gray-headed, wrinkled old women among them, and very hideous the old dwarfs were. Their features resembled very closely those of the chimpanzee. Some had gray, others hazel eyes, while the eyes of a few were black.

"As I have said before, their hair was not like that of the negroes among whom the dwarfs live, but grew in little short tufts apart from each other, and the hair, after attaining a certain length, could not grow longer. These little tufts looked like so many balls of wool. Many of the men had their chests and legs covered with these little tufts of wooly hair. The women's hair was no longer than that of the men, and it grew in the same manner.

"After I had given them beads, I took out a looking-glass, which I had hidden, and put it in front of them. Immediately they trembled with fright, and said, 'Spirit, don't kill us!' and turned their heads away. Then the musical box was shown, and when I had set it playing the dwarfs lay down on the ground, frightened by the music, and by turns looked at me and at the box. Some of them ran away into their little huts. After this little by-play I ordered the feast to begin.

"When they had finished eating, the Obongos seemed more sociable than I had ever seen them before. I seated myself on the dead limb of a tree and they came around me and asked me to talk to them as the spirits talk. One of them asked me if I lived in the moon, then another if I lived in a star, and another if I had been long in the forest; and did I make the fine things I gave them during the night."

A DANCE, AND THE PIGMIES THEN TELL THEIR STORY.

After a somewhat lengthy conversation, in which their curiosity was partly relieved, at Du Chaillu's request, the dwarfs entertained him with a dance, in which, to the music of a drum, they leaped, gesticulated, kicked backwards and forwards, and shook their heads from side to side, making no effort to keep time but rather displaying their abilities to act like crazy people.

Du Chaillu fired two guns which greatly alarmed the pigmies, but their fears gave place to astonishment when he explained to them that by the aid of such a report as they had just heard, he could kill an elephant, gorilla, leopard or other large game, which statement he demonstrated by firing again and bringing down a bird out of the top of a neighboring tree.

The dwarfs, in response to Du Chaillu's questions, said they never tarried long in one place because the fruits and berries were soon exhausted in one locality, and they had, therefore, to move to another for new supplies; that they built small houses because they did not occupy them long, and, therefore, did not want to spend their time in labor. Fire, they explained, was made by striking two flints together, and causing the sparks to fall on a species of oakum that grows on the palm tree. They marry among themselves, never between tribes; in fact, each tribe is careful not to trench upon the territory of another, since a battle is certain to result.

HOW THE PIGMIES BURY THEIR DEAD—STRANGE SUPERSTITIONS.

Du Chaillu had now learned very much about the habits of the pigmies, but his anxiety to obtain a skeleton so increased that he was upon the point of asking the dwarfs where they bury their dead. His Ashango guide begged him not to make such a request, as the dwarfs would not only refuse to tell him, but that they would immediately become his enemies. Pressed for a reason, the Ashango guide said that the fear of the dwarfs was always great lest the skull of one of their tribe should fall into the hands of a stranger, in which event they believed it would be used as a fetich to tell the owner where the village of the Obongos might always be found. When an Obongo dies, the Ashango guide further explained, there is great sorrow among the dwarfs, and some of their men are sent into every part of the forest to find a tall tree which has a hollow at the top. If they find one, they come back to the settlement and say, "We have found a tree with a hollow." Then the tribe travel together into the forest, bearing the dead body on a litter, preceded by the man who found the tree. Upon reaching the spot, two or more ascend the tree, carrying with them creepers by which the body is afterwards drawn up and deposited in the hollow and covered with earth and dry leaves.

Sometimes a hollow tree, such as will supply the purpose, cannot be readily found, in which case the Obongos go in search of a stream of running water. This being found, however great the labor, it is diverted from its bed, a grave is then dug in the land thus exposed, in which the body of the dwarf is deposited and buried; the obstructions in the stream are then removed so that it returns to its natural bed, and thus hides from possible detection the body and bones of their dead.

Du Chaillu contented himself with the explanations of his Ashango guide, and though his attendants offered to capture one of the dwarfs he forbade them, and thus left the Obongos without a single evidence that he had, indeed, ever seen a dwarf.

Just before this volume was sent to press, a remarkable verification of the truth of Du Chaillu's statements, with regard to the dwarfs, was received in the following cable dispatch from the city of Brussels:

"The explorer, Ludwig Wolff, just returned from the Congo, reports having met in the Sankouron region many tribes of dwarfs, generally measuring less than four feet, beardless, and with short and wooly hair. They live by hunting, and are wonderfully agile and good-tempered. Many thousands of them are dispersed over this wild region, and are known under the name of *Batonas*. They mix very little with the full-grown population. 'This,' says Wolff, 'confirms the ancient conjectures of Herodotus and Aristotle as to the existence of a race of pigmies in Africa. These African Lilliputians received me very hospitably.'"

CHAPTER XXXVI.

BARBARIC NATIONS OF THE EARTH—CANNIBALS.

FROM the higher quadruminous—four handed—animals, it is but two steps to the lower species of human life; the first step leads to a chasm, which is unbridged, as already explained, but the line of separation, though well marked, is not so great but that progressive evolutionists are still investigating and hoping, if not believing, that future discoveries will furnish a complete chain connecting man with the lower animals.

The question, "What race or tribe is the lowest in the scale of human creation?" is, by no means, a settled one. Some maintain that the troglodytes, or earth-dwellers, of Africa, are the lowest; others as stoutly declare that the Terra del Fuegians occupy the most despised position; but if Du Chaillu's description of the African pigmies is a faithful and true one, we must award them the unenviable place, not alone because of their inferiority in size but for their habits as well. The pigmies are next to the beasts in many things; their houses are the rudest, temporary shelters; they never abide long in any one place, they wear no clothes, so to speak; they flee before every other race; have no forms of government; and, lastly, subsist upon bugs, snakes, lizards, centipedes and fruits. But questions of scientific dispute do not properly belong to this work; all uncivilized races have curious customs that are of very great interest to the highly favored people of our own heaven-kissed land, and in treating of the rather wonderful animal life of the world, I cannot afford to omit mention of some, at least, of the singular human creatures whose homes are made in the jungle of tropical heat, or the weird wilderness of perpetual snow. As in previous chapters the order of treatment has been from a lower to a higher plane of life, I will not depart from that plan now; but, as nearly as possible, consider the wild races in an ascending scale, as measured by the barometer of civilization.

It is a strange fact, which seriously interrupts the classification of races, that, while cannibalism is an evidence of degradation, the limit of which may not be exceeded, yet many tribes are guilty of this most abominable of all infamous habits who, in other respects, manifest many marks of intelligence, admirable government, industry, ingenuity and homogeneity such as civilization is wont to boast of. But since this disgusting custom is an index of the most extreme barbarism, I shall first notice some of the remarkable cannibal tribes of the world.

THE MONBUTTO CANNIBALS.

The *Monbuttos* of Nubia are a strange tribe even among the wild races of all the world, none others apparently combining so many peculiar and anomalous features. Having never come in contact with civilizing influences, they are wild by nature and yet exhibit no little ingenuity and an intelligence quite incompatible with their surroundings. In all respects it may be said that they maintain an isolation not exceeded by the troglodytes or anthropomorphic apes. They cultivate, however, the sweet potato, cassava, plantain, fig-tree, and are experts in extracting oils for cooking, lighting and drinking purposes. They know nothing of the art of weaving, but continue to make fabrics, strings, and hut coverings from the bark of the fig tree. They never make clothing from the skins of animals, though few, if any tribes, excel them in hunting, their principal game being elephants, buffaloes, wild boars and antelopes, which afford them an abundance of meat at all times.

The Monbuttos are intense lovers of grease, and not only consume large quantities of oil expressed from palm pods, earth nuts, sesame, and the fruit of forest trees, but they gather quantities of a certain plant, from which they extract a greasy substance by boiling, and this they drink with great relish. But of most universal use among them is human fat, the climax of their culinary practices.

A KING THAT DINES OFF BABIES.

The cannibalism of the Monbutto is the most pronounced of all the nations of Africa. Surrounded as they are by a number of people who are blacker than themselves, and who, being inferior to them in culture, are consequently held in great contempt, they have just the opportunity which they want for carrying on expeditions of war or plunder, which result in the acquisition of a booty that is especially coveted by them, consisting of human flesh. The carcasses of all who fall in battle are distributed upon the battle-field, and are prepared by drying for transport to the homes of the conquerors. They drive their prisoners before them without remorse, as butchers would drive sheep to the shambles, and these are only reserved to fall victims, on a later day, to their horrible and sickening greediness. Schweinfurth says that during his stay at the court of Munza—the Monbutto King—the general rumor was quite current that nearly every day some little child was sacrificed to supply his meal. "It would hardly be expected," he writes, "that many opportunities should be afforded to strangers of witnessing the natives at their repast, and to myself there occurred only two instances when I came upon any of them whilst they were actually engaged in preparing human flesh for consumption. The first of these happened by my coming unexpectedly upon a number of young women who had a supply of boiling water upon the clay floor in front of the doorway of a hut, and were engaged in the task of scalding the hair off the lower half of a human body. The operation, as far as it was effected, had changed the black skin into a fawny gray, and the disgusting sight could not fail to make me think of the soddening and scouring of our fatted swine. On another occasion I was in a hut and observed a human arm hanging over the fire, obviously with the design of being at once dried and smoked.

"Incontrovertible tokens and indirect evidences of the prevalence of cannibalism were constantly turning up at every step we took. On one occasion Mohammed and myself were in Munza's company, and Mohammed designedly turned the conversation to the topic of human flesh, and put the direct question to the King how it happened that just at this precise time, while we were in the country, there was no consumption of human food. Munza expressly said that being aware that such a practice was held in aversion by us, he had taken care that it should only be carried on in secret."

THE MONBUTTO A SUPERIOR RACE.

"As I have said, there was no opportunity for strangers to observe the habits of the Monbutto at their meals; the Bongo and Mittoo of our caravan were carefully excluded by them as being uncircumcised and, therefore, reckoned as savages, whilst the religious scruples of the Nubians prevented them from partaking of any food in common with cannibals. Nevertheless, the instances I have mentioned are in themselves sufficient to show that the Monbuttos are far more addicted to cannibalism than their hunting neighbors, the Niam-niam. They do not constitute the first example of the anthropophagi—human flesh eaters—who are in a far higher grade of culture than many savages who persistently repudiate the enjoyment of human flesh (for example the Fiji Islanders and the Caraibs). It is needless for me to recount the personal experiences of the Nubian mercenaries who have accompanied the Monbutto on their marauding expeditions, or to describe how these people obtain their human fat, or again to detail the process of cutting the flesh into long strips and drying it over the fire in its preparation for consumption. The numerous skulls now in the Anatomical Museum of Berlin are simply the remains of their repasts, which I purchased one after another for bits of copper, and go far to prove that the cannibalism of the Monbutto is unsurpassed by any nation of the world. But, with it all, the Monbutto are a noble race of men; men who display a certain national pride, and are endowed with an intellect and judgment such as few natives of the African wilderness can boast; men to whom one may put a reasonable question, and who will return a reasonable reply. The Nubians can never say enough in praise of their faithfulness in friendly intercourse, and of the order and stability of their national life. According to the Nubians, too, the Monbutto were their superiors in the arts of war, and I often heard the resident soldiers contending with their companions and saying, 'Well, perhaps you are not afraid of the Monbutto, but I confess that I am, and I can tell you they are something to be afraid of.'"

NIAM-NIAM WARRIORS.

Some years before Schweinfurth's visit to Africa the Khartoom traders had a trial at arms with the Monbutto, of which he heard frequent confirmatory accounts, and particularly of the heroism displayed by a famous Amazon, the sister of King Munza. Eye witnesses of her wonderful skill and bravery relate that she was equipped in full armor and armed with shield and lance, and girded with the rokko apron of a man. Thus caparisoned she led on the troops of her father against Aboo Guroon, whose large force of

Arabs, that was well supplied with firearms, she put to utter rout, though the army which she led bore nothing but spears and lances. This noted battle occurred in the year 1866, since which time no other trader has had the temerity to hostilely invade the Monbutto kingdom.

OLD WOMEN EATEN BY NIAM-NIAMS.

Schweinfurth, like all African explorers who enter the country by way of the Nile or Zanzibar, was dependent almost entirely upon his Mohammedan guides and assistants who, besides the duty of attending him, looked as much after their own interests in procuring ivory and slaves. He therefore tells of an incident which he would gladly have prevented, but was powerless to do anything, owing to this self-interest of the Mohammedans: During his passage through Nubia, Mohammed, the leader, represented to Schweinfurth that his supply of corn was nearly exhausted and that famine threatened the caravan unless a store of this necessary provision was obtained. To replenish his stock he proposed a raid upon a tribe called the *Babuckur*, who occupied a district near by and bordering the Niam-niam country. Schweinfurth objected, but this protest did not prevail with Mohammed, who, to accomplish his purpose, without appearing openly insubordinate, sent his lieutenant, Surroor, to the Niam-niams and with promises of aid had no difficulty in inciting them to lead an attack against the Babuckur. The raid which followed was accompanied by the most shocking brutalities, as the Babuckurs were taken so completely by surprise that they scarcely made an effort to defend themselves. A large number of slaves were captured, together with a great quantity of corn. The Niam-niams paid particular attention to the female Babuckurs, the youngest of whom they destined for their houses, the middle-aged for their agriculture, and the oldest for their caldrons. Of their horrible atrocities perpetrated in this raid, Schweinfurth writes but little, but leads the reader to infer a great deal by mentioning the fact that a few days after the attack some natives came to him with the heads of three women freshly boiled; they had heard that he gave rings of copper in exchange for skulls and offered to sell the ghastly trophies of their raid.

FEASTING OFF AN INFANT.

"Some days after the raid on the Babuckurs," says Schweinfurth, "I was witness of a scene that can never be erased from my memory. During one of my rambles I found myself in one of the native farmsteads. Before the door of the first hut I came to, an old woman was sitting surrounded by a group of boys and girls, all busily engaged in cutting up gourds and preparing them for eating; at the door of the opposite hut a man was sitting composedly playing on his mandolin. Midway between the two huts a mat was spread; upon this mat, exposed to the full glare of the noon-day sun, feebly gasping, lay a new-born infant; I doubt whether it was more than a day old. In answer to my inquiries I learnt that the child was the offspring of one of the slaves who had been captured in the late raid, and who had now been driven off to a distant quarter, compelled to leave her infant behind, because its nurture would interfere with her properly fulfilling her domestic duties. The ill-fated little creature, doomed to so transient an existence, was destined to form a dainty dish; and the savage group was calmly engaged in their ordinary occupations until the poor little thing should have breathed its last and be ready to be consigned to the seething caldron! I profess that for a moment I was furious. I felt ready to shoot the old hog who sat by without displaying a particle of pity or concern. I was prompted to do something rash to give vent to my sensation of abhorrence; but I was swayed by the protestations of the Nubians ringing in my ears that they were powerless in the matter, and that they had not come to be law-givers to the Niam-niams."

CHAPTER XXXVII.

THE FANS AND THEIR DREADFUL HABITS.

NEXT to the Monbutto tribe of cannibals, if not indeed equaling them in bloody propensities, are the *Fans* of Southwest Africa. In "The World's Wonders" I devoted considerable space to these people, and will, therefore, only add a few pages of additional information here, gleaned from several travelers who sojourned in the Fan country.

Of all barbarians none are more cruel and rapacious than the Fans; their delight is in war, which they wage upon weaker tribes without the slightest provocation, and invariably conduct their campaigns with the view of totally annihilating those whom they attack.

Du Chaillu describes a scene, which occurred during his visit to Ashango land, in which the Fans attacked an Mpongwe village that was incapable of offering any defense, and remorselessly murdered all the inhabitants. After completing their murderous work, they set in to plundering the huts, and when these were emptied the monsters invaded the burial-grounds, where they dug up the festering or decayed bodies for the sake of the ornaments that had been buried with them. Their spoils filled two canoes, but still the victorious Fans lingered about the ruins of the village until they came to a newly-made grave. This they opened, like a pack of hyenas, exhumed the fresh

FAN CANNIBALS ATTACKING AN MPONGWE VILLAGE.

body and, after carrying it to a clump of mangroves near by, built a fire and cooked the body in the very pots they had found buried in the same grave. The feast which followed was revolting in the extreme, as they tore away the crisp flesh with their teeth, not taking the time even to cut it into pieces with their knives.

Some tribes which practice cannibalism are ashamed of the custom and will invariably deny it, but the Fans seem to look upon it with a feeling of pride and justification. Occasionally, when missionaries protest against such inhuman habits, the Fans will acknowledge that *some* of their tribes do eat human flesh, but not those whom the missionaries are questioning; that those of the neighboring villages are human flesh-eaters, but not they.

Knowing this peculiarity, Mr. W. Reade, the explorer, took care to ask no questions on the subject until he had passed through all the places previously visited by white men, and then questioned an old and very polite cannibal. His answers were plain enough. Of course they all ate men. He ate men himself. Man's flesh was very good, and was "like monkey, all fat." He mostly ate prisoners of war, but some of his friends ate the bodies of executed wizards, a food of which he was rather afraid, thinking that it might disagree with him.

He would not admit that he ate his own relations when they died, although such a statement is made, and has not yet been disproved. Some travelers say that the Fans do not eat people of their own village, but live on terms of barter with neighboring villages, amicably exchanging their dead for culinary purposes. The *Oshebas*, another cannibal tribe of the same country, keep up friendly relations with the Fans, and exchange the bodies of the dead with them. The bodies of slaves are also sold for the pot, and are tolerably cheap, a dead slave costing, on an average, one small elephant's tusk.

The friendly Fan above mentioned held, in common with many of his dark countrymen, the belief that all white men were cannibals. "These," said a Bakalai slave, on first beholding a white man, "are the men that eat us!" So he asked Mr. Reade why the white men take the trouble to send to Africa for negroes, when they could eat as many white men as they liked in their own land. His interlocutor, having an eye to the possible future, discreetly answered that they were obliged to do so, *because the flesh of white men was deadly poison*, with which answer the worthy cannibal was perfectly satisfied.

DAUGHTERS A BLESSING TO FAN FATHERS.

Nearly all the tribes of Africa increase very slowly, notwithstanding the fact that polygamy is general. The Fans, however, seem to be an exception, though their habits are different from other tribes only in marrying their children off at a later age than is the custom with other races in Africa. A daughter is an unmixed blessing to a Fan father, for, until she becomes of a marriageable age—about sixteen years—she assists her mother in performing all the hard work, and when she at length marrys she brings her father an excellent return. There is no such thing as courtship among the Fans. Frequently the daughters are sold for wives in infancy, not to be taken, however, until they reach what is considered a marriageable age. In case the girl grows up without a suitor, the father offers her at "public vendue" to the highest bidder; if she is pretty, there is no lack of bidders, at which time the "old man" extols her merits, beauty and value, while the bidders in loud voices decry her charms, until at last a sale is made.

After a girl has been sold, the marriage ceremony has to be performed before she fairly becomes wife to her purchaser, and this ceremony is more expensive, as a rule, than the girl herself. A great

A FAN FATHER AUCTIONING OFF HIS DAUGHTER.

feast must be prepared, and presents given to all the relatives, the cost of which must be borne by the husband. As the feast is expected to last several days and is attended by scores of people, this item of expense is sometimes so great that the groom is utterly impoverished, and he therefore becomes, literally, what our grandparents used to call "a new beginner."

THE NIAM-NIAM CANNIBALS.

Immediately south of the Equator, and near the Nile basin, is a large and fertile territory held by a tribe of extremely fierce cannibals called the *Niam-niams*, or *Neam-nam*. Our information respecting these curious people is almost wholly obtained from Mr. Petherick, the English consul at Khartoum, who visited them about 1860. They are not blacks, but in color are a light brown, or olive tint, and wear their hair so long that it flows down over their shoulders. Though they have never had any relations with even Arab traders, and know nothing whatever of civilization, they clothe themselves in a cloth woven of the fibers of certain barks, and they wear a very pretty sandal having a leather sole. The women and men wear numerous ornaments made from shells, ivory and hippopotamus hide, and for bodily cleanliness they are positively remarkable. But for all this they are voracious cannibals, and so war-like in disposition that they strike terror into all neighboring tribes.

When Mr. Petherick passed through their country, many of his porters could not be induced to enter the territory of such a terrible tribe, even though protected by the white man's weapons. Several of them deserted on the way, and at last, when they had come in sight of the first village, the rest flung down their loads and ran away, only the interpreter being secured.

As they neared the village, the menacing sound of the alarm drum was heard, and out came the Niam-niams in full battle array, their lances in their right hands and their large shields covering their bodies. They drew up in line, and seemed disposed to dispute the passage; but as the party marched quietly and unconcernedly onward, they opened their ranks and allowed them to enter the village, from which the women and children had already been removed. They then seated themselves under the shade of a large sycamore tree, deposited the baggage, and sat in a circle round it, keeping on all sides a front to the armed natives, who now began to come rather nearer than was agreeable, some actually seating themselves on the travelers' feet. They were all very merry and jocose, pointing at their visitors continually, and then bursting into shouts of approving laughter. There was evidently some joke which tickled their fancy, and by means of the intepreter it was soon discovered.

The fact was, that the Niam-niam were cannibals, and meant to eat the strangers who had so foolishly trusted themselves in the country without either spears, swords, or shields, but they did not like to kill them before their chief arrived. When this pleasant joke was explained, the astonished visitors were nearly as amused as the Niam-

niams, knowing perfectly well that their weapons were sufficient to drive off ten times the number of such foes.

Presently the chief arrived — an old, gray-headed man, who, by his sagacity certainly showed himself worthy of the post which he held. After a colloquy with the interpreter, he turned to his people, and the following extraordinary discourse took place:

"Niam-niam, do not insult these strange men. Do you know whence they come?"

"No! but we will feast on them," was the rejoinder. Then the old man, holding up his spear, and commanding silence, proceeded thus:

"Do you know of any tribe that would dare to approach our village in such small numbers as these men have done?"

"No!" was again vociferated.

"Very well; you know not whence they come, nor do I, who am greatly your senior, and whose voice you ought to respect. Their country must indeed be distant, and to traverse the many tribes between their country and ours ought to be a proof to you of their valor. Look at the things they hold in their hands; they are neither spears, clubs nor bows and arrows, but inexplicable bits of iron mounted on wood. Neither have they shields to defend their bodies from our weapons. Therefore, to have traveled thus far, depend upon it their means of resistance must be as puzzling to us, and far superior to any arms that any tribe, aye, even our own, can oppose to them. Therefore, Niam-niam, I, who have led you to many a fight, and whose counsels you have often followed, say, shed not your blood in vain, nor bring disgrace upon your fathers, who have never been vanquished. Touch them not, but prove yourselves worthy of the friendship of such a handful of brave men, and do yourselves honor by entertaining them, rather than degrade them by the continuance of your insults."

It is impossible not to admire the penetration of this chief, who was wise enough to deduce the strength of his visitors from their apparent weakness, and to fear them for those very reasons that caused his more ignorant and impetuous people to despise them.

Having thus calmed the excitement, he asked to inspect the strange weapons of his guests. A gun was handed to him — the cap having been removed — and very much it puzzled him. From the manner in which it was held, it was evidently not a club; and yet it could not be a knife, as it had no edge; nor a spear, as it had no point. Indeed, the fact of the barrel being hollow puzzled him exceedingly. At last he poked his finger down the muzzle, and looked inquiringly at his guests, as if to ask what could be the use of such an article. By way of answer, Mr. Petherick took a gun, and, pointing to a vulture that was hovering over their heads, fired, and brought it down.

But before the bird touched the ground, the crowd were prostrate, and grovelling in the dust, as if every man of them had been shot. The old man's head, with his hands on his ears, was at Mr. Petherick's feet; and when he raised him, his appearance was ghastly, and his eyes were fixed on him with a meaningless expression. Mr. Petherick thought that the chief had lost his senses.

"After shaking him several times," says Mr. Petherick, "I at length succeeded in attracting his attention to the fallen bird, quivering in its last agonies between two of his men. The first sign of returning animation he gave was putting his hand to his head, and examining himself as if in search of a wound. He gradually recovered, and, as soon as he could regain his voice, called to the crowd, who one after another first raised their heads, and then again dropped them at the sight of their apparently lifeless comrades. After the repeated calls of the old man, they ventured to rise, and a general inspection of imaginary wounds commenced."

THE WONDERFUL WEAPONS OF THE NIAM-NIAMS.

When the Niam-niam warrior goes out to battle, he takes with him a curious series of weapons. He has, of course, his lance, which is well and strongly put together, the blade being leaf-shaped, like that of a hog spear, only very much longer. On his left arm he bears his shield, which is made of bark fibre, woven very closely together, and very thick. The maker displays his taste in the patterns of the work, and in those which he traces upon it with various colored dyes. Within the shield he has a sort of wooden handle, to which are attached one or two most remarkable weapons.

One of these is wholly flat, the handle included, and is about the thickness of an ordinary sword-blade. The projecting portions are all edged, and kept extremely sharp, while the handle is rather thicker than the blade, and is rounded and toughened, so as to afford a firm grip to the hand.

When the Niam-niam comes near his enemy, and before he is within range of a spear thrust, he snatches one of these strange weapons from his shield, and hurls it at the foe, much as an Australian flings his boomerang, an American Indian his tomahawk, and a Sikh his chakra, giving it a revolving motion as he throws it. Owing to this mode of flinging, the weapon covers a considerable space, and if the projecting blades come in contact with the enemy's person, they are sure to disable, if not to kill, him on the spot. And as several of these are hurled in rapid succession, it is evident that the Niam-niam warrior is no ordinary foe, and that even the possessor of fire-arms might, in reality, be overcome if taken by surprise, for, as the "boomerangs" are concealed within the shield, the first intimation of their existence would be given by their sharp blades whirling successively through the air with deadly aim.

HUNTERS OF GAME AND YET FEEDERS ON HUMAN FLESH.

The same weapons which the Niam-niam use with such deadly effect against their enemies are employed with equal success in hunting the elephant, hippopotamus, antelopes, leopard, lion, and other game with which his country abounds. So brave and expert are these hunters that they will pursue and kill an elephant quite as quickly as any of the white men who have hunted in Africa with the best improved rifles of to-day.

It is a singular thing that, game being so plentiful in their territory, the Niam-niams do not content themselves with the natural food thus provided, particularly since they lead the life of hunters almost, if not quite, as much for the pleasure the pursuit affords, as for the flesh it yields. The argument which has been universally advanced by theorists to excuse the anthropophagous habits of barbaric man do not apply with the least relevancy to the Niam-niams, nor can the custom be accounted for upon any other theory than that they eat their fellows purely because they prefer it to other food.

The Niam-niams are gluttons of human flesh, who not only devour their enemies but are ready to appease their horrid appetites on any victim who may fall in their way. They even admitted to Mr. Petherick that when their own people became too old and feeble for further service, they were put to death and their bodies eaten. So, also, when any of their slaves attempt to run away and are captured they are eaten, rather as a warning to others, however, than for the feast which their bodies afford.

CHAPTER XXXVIII.

THE BONNY CANNIBALS.

OF all the savage tribes of Africa, and there are many, there are none that can rival the *Bonnys* in ferocity, blood-thirstyness, cannibalism and infamous practices generally. These impish and fiendish people inhabit a rather small district near the west coast of Africa, and their chief city, or capital, which is also called Bonny, is situated on the river bearing the same name, a stream of water so murky, foul and fœtid that when Burton ascended it in a canoe, he was obliged to stop his nostrils with camphorated cotton.

The history of Pepper, Piemento, or Peppel, as he is variously called, King of Bonny, is a wonderful one. This remarkable potentate was accustomed to dine every day off the palms of young men's hands, for which he had a passionate liking. His bloody propensities were such that he hesitated at no crime, but, at length, he murdered a popular chief named Manilla, and also shot his wife because she displeased him, which base crimes so incensed his subjects that he was deposed and sent to Ascension, while the government was handed over to four regents.

Peppel, though a savage, was not without much cunning, by the exercise of which he contrived to be taken to England, in 1857, and there adopted English manners, became religious, was baptized, and then he set about to perfect a scheme for re-establishing himself on the throne of Bonny. The church people of England took the liveliest interest in him, not only showing him such attentions as he was utterly unfit to receive, but they very willingly subscribed to his great scheme for Christianizing his countrymen. To this end they contributed the sum of $100,000 towards establishing a missionary station, and the old reprobate, not satisfied with this princely assistance, induced several Englishmen to return with him to Bonny as his suite, to whom he promised ministerial positions in his court and splendid salaries.

When the deluded followers of Peppel arrived with him at Bonny their surprise may be imagined when, instead of finding a sumptuous palace abounding with every conceivable luxury, they saw only a collection of the most miserable hovels surrounded by a mud-wall, while the whole town occupied a mud flat from which emanated such vile odors and vapors as no civilized nature could long withstand. And as to the royal salaries and luxurious apartments in the palace, they were found to be as imaginary as all the other representations of the old scoundrel, the king presenting each of the officials with a couple of yams as an equivalent for pay and lodging. They had to make the best of their terrible position, which, however, did not long continue, for they speedily succumbed to the deadly climate and more deadly filth of their surroundings.

THE SACRED JU-JU HOUSES.

Peppel had no sooner regained the throne than he threw off every semblance of civilization and returned again to the beastly customs which characterized his first administration.

The architecture of the Bonny tribe, as described by Burton and Reade, is by no means elaborate, the houses being composed of swish and wattle supported on posts, while the floors and walls are of mud, perhaps because that article is ready to hand in inexhaustible quantities, to be had for the scooping up. The ordinary houses, which somewhat resemble Swiss cottages in their outward appearance, consist of three rooms, to-wit: a living room, a kitchen, and a ju-ju, or chapel room. This latter is an indispensable adjunct to every Bonny house, for within it is invariably kept the fetish, or ju-ju, which is the guardian of the house and its inmates. Into this room are also crowded nearly all the valuables of the family, which, owing to its sacred character, is in no danger of being robbed by covetous, though superstitious, neighbors. As to the ju-ju itself, anything answers the purpose, such as an illustration, a peg, pill-box, a tooth, an old shoe, or any discarded article that the fancy of the owner may hit upon.

The public ju-ju house of the town is a truly ghastly-appearing edifice because of its well-known associations with hideous crimes. It is built of swish — interlaced branches — and in shape is oblong, of forty or fifty feet in length, and is roofless. An altar is placed in the end over which is a covering to keep the rain off the priests. Under the eaves of this covering are nailed rows of human skulls painted different colors, and one of which is conspicuous by reason of a large black beard which still adheres to it. There are also several goat skulls arranged between the human, while many skinless heads look grinningly down on the altar from upright poles fixed in the ground. Under the altar is a circular hole having a raised rim made of clay, in which is received the blood of victims, together with the sacred libations. Within this ju-ju house are buried the bodies of Bonny kings, since it is meet that they should lie amid the bloody scenes they had in their lifetime so frequently provoked.

BLOOD AND TORTURE.

The ju-ju house admirably illustrates the character of the people —a race which takes a positive pleasure in the sight of blood, and in inflicting and witnessing pain. All over the country the traveler comes upon scenes of blood and torture. Animals are bound in various positions calculated to cause them the greatest suffering; goats and fowls, for no other reason than malignancy on the part of the natives, are found everywhere tied to posts head downward, dogs hung up by their ears or one leg, and all left to die in that position, after which they are eaten. Even the children of prisoners taken in war — which is usually waged merely for the purpose of plunder — are hung by the middle on tall poles while the parents are reserved to be sacrificed and eaten.

As to this last report, the Bonnys declare it to be false, but the facts cannot be doubted, since we have the confirmation of several white travelers who have witnessed the act. For example, King Peppel gave a grand banquet in honor of a victory which he had gained over Calabar, and in which Amakree, the King of that district, was taken prisoner. The European traders were invited to the feast, and were most hospitably entertained. They were, however, horrified to see the principal dish which was placed before Peppel. It was the bleeding heart of Amakree, warm and palpitating as it was torn from the body. Peppel devoured the heart with the greatest eagerness, exclaiming at the same time, "This is the way I serve my enemies."

HORRIBLE SCENES WITNESSED BY DR. HUTCHINSON.

More recently than the event just mentioned, Dr. Hutchinson was a witness to Bonny cannibalism. He had heard that something of the kind was contemplated, although it was kept very quiet. On the appointed morning he had himself rowed to the shore at some distance from the ju-ju house, near which he concealed himself, and waited for the result. The scene which he soon witnessed he thus describes:

"I know not of what kind are the sensations felt by those around

Newgate, waiting for an execution in the very heart of London's great city; but I know that on the banks of an African river, in the gray dawn of morning, when the stillness was of that oppressive nature which is calculated to produce the most gloomy impressions, with dense vapors and foul smells arising from decomposing mangroves and other causes of malaria floating about, with a heaviness of atmosphere that depressed the spirits, amidst a community of cannibals, I *do* know that, although under the protection of a man-of-war, I felt on this occasion a combined sensation of suspense, anxiety, horror, and indefinable dread of I cannot tell what, that I pray God it may never be my fate to endure again.

"Day broke, and, nearly simultaneous with its breaking, the sun shone out. As I looked through the slit in the wall on the space between my place of concealment and the ju-ju house, I observed no change from its appearance the evening before. No gibbet, nor axe, nor gallows, nor rope — no kind of preparation, nothing significant of death, save the skulls on the pillars of the ju-ju house, that seemed leering at me with an expression at once strange and vacant. It would have been a relief in the awful stillness of the place to have heard something of what I had read of the preparations for an execution in Liverpool or London — of the hammering suggestive of driving nails into scaffold, drop, or coffin, of a crowd gathering round the place before early dawn, and of the solemn tolling of the bell that chimed another soul into eternity. Everything seemed as if nothing beyond the routine of daily life were to take place.

"Could it be that I had been misinformed; that the ceremony was adjourned to another time, or was to be carried out elsewhere? No, a distant murmur of gabbling voices was heard approaching nearer and nearer, till, passing the corner house on my left, I saw a group of negroes — an indiscriminate crowd of all ages and both sexes — so huddled together that no person whom I could particularly distinguish as either an executioner or a culprit was visible among them. But above their clattering talk came the sound of a clanking chain that made one shudder.

"They stopped in the middle of the square opposite the ju-ju house, and ceased talking. One commanding voice uttered a single word, and down they sat upon the grass, forming a circle round two figures, standing upright in the center — the executioner and the man about to be killed. The former was remarkable only for the black skull-cap which he had on him, and by a common cutlass which he held in his hand. The latter had chains round his neck, his wrists and his ankles. There was no sign of fear or cowardice about *him* — no seeming consciousness of the dreadful fate before him — no evidence even upon his face of that dogged stubbornness which is said to be exhibited by some persons about to undergo an ignominous death. Save that he stood upright, one would scarcely have known that he was alive. Amongst the spectators, too, there was a silent impassiveness which was appalling. Not a word, nor gesture, nor glance of sympathy, that could make me believe I looked at human beings who had a vestige of humanity among them.

THE SLAUGHTER.

"As the ju-ju butcher stepped back and measured his distance to make an effectual swoop at his victim's neck, the man moved not a muscle, but stood as if he were unconscious — till ——

"Chop! The first blow felled him to the ground. The noise of a chopper falling on meat is familiar to most people. No other sound was here — none from the man; not a whisper nor a murmur from those who were seated about! I was nearly crying out in mental agony, and the sound of that first stroke will haunt my ears to my dying day. How I wished some one to talk or scream, to destroy the impression of that fearful *hough*, and the still more awful silence that followed it?

"Again the weapon was raised to continue the decapitation — another blow as the man lay prostrate, and then a sound broke the silence! But, O Father of mercy! of what a kind was that noise — a gurgle and a gasp, accompanying the dying spasm of the struck-down man!

"Once more the weapon was lifted — I saw the blood flow in gory horror down the blade to the butcher's hand, and there it was visible, in God's bright sunshine, to the whole host of heaven. Not a word had yet been uttered by the crowd. More chopping and cleaving, and the head, severed from the body, was put by the ju-ju executioner into a calabash, which was carried off by one of his women to be cooked. He then repeated another cabalistic word, or perhaps the same as at first, and directly all who were seated rose up whilst he walked away.

"A yell, such as reminded me of a company of tigers, arose from the multitude — cutlasses were flourished as they crowded round the body of the dead man — sounds of cutting and chopping arose amidst the clamor of the voices, and I began to question myself whether, if I were on the other side of the river Styx, I should see what I was looking at here through the little slit in the wall of my hiding-place: a crowd of human vultures gloating over the headless corpse of a murdered brother negro — boys and girls walking away from the crowd, holding pieces of bleeding flesh in their hands, while the dripping life-fluid marked their road as they went along; and one woman snapping from the hands of another — both of them raising their voices in clamor — a part of the body of that poor man, in whom the breath of life was vigorous not a quarter of an hour ago.

"The whole of the body was at length divided, and nothing left behind but the blood. The intestines were taken away to be given to an iguana — the Bonny man's tutelary guardian. But the blood was still there, in glistening pools, though no more notice was taken of it by the gradually dispersing crowd than if it were a thing as common in that town as heaven's bright dew is elsewhere. A few dogs were on the spot, who devoured the fragments. Two men arrived to spread sand over the place, and there was no interruption to the familiar sound of coopers' hammering just beginning in the cask-houses, or to the daily work of hoisting palm-oil puncheons on board the ships."

On passing the ju-ju house afterward, Dr. Hutchinson saw the relics of this sacrifice. They consisted of the larger bones of the body and limbs, which had evidently been cooked, and every particle of flesh eaten from them. The head is the perquisite of the executioner, as has already been mentioned. Some months afterward, Dr. Hutchinson met the executioner, who was said to have exercised his office again a few days previously, and to have eaten the head of his victim. Being upbraided with having committed so horrible an act, he replied that he had not eaten the head—his cook having spoiled it by not having put enough pepper on it.

CHAPTER XXXIX.

THE DAHOME AND ASHANTI PEOPLE.

ON what is known as the slave coast of Africa, whose shores are washed by the Bight of Benin, live the *Dahome* and *Ashanti* races. Though maintaining separate governments they are the same people, both in race and habits. I believe they have never been classed among the cannibal tribes, but their horrible customs fall little short of this infamous practice, for their cruelty and blood-loving propensities are carried to the greatest extremes. The rulership of the two kingdoms is confined to a king and caboceers; these latter are men of wealth rather than hereditary rank, corresponding somewhat to the lords of England, though their power is greater.

Eminently a practical people, both the Dahomeans and Ashantees are very particular about the royal blood of their rulers, as is evidenced by the law of succession. Instead of succession in a direct line, the throne passes to the brother or nephew of the deceased monarch; the nephew, however, must be the son of the king's sister, and not his brother. The reason for this is, that the people are sure that their future king has some royal blood in his veins, whereas, according to their belief, no one can be quite certain that the son of the queen is also the son of the king, and, as the king's wives are never royal blood, their offspring might be purely plebeian. Therefore, the son of the king's sister may be chosen; but this singular idea is carried still further, viz.: The sister in question need not be married, provided that the father of her child be strong, good-looking, and of tolerable position.

SHOCKING SACRIFICES.

In both countries are practiced a horrible rite called the "customs," at which there is a shocking sacrifice of human victims. These rites take place at the celebration of the Yam and Adai festivals, the former occurring in September and the latter every three weeks.

At the Yam festivals hundreds of people are slain, not because they are objectionable malefactors, but for the sole reason that the people delight in the sight of blood and murder and must be *amused*. It is the same sentiment as actuated the Romans to provide entertainments in which slaughter was the chief feature of the show. Should the Yam festival fall upon the king's birth-day the number of human sacrifices is increased to thousands. It is said, though with what truth I cannot positively decide, that when an addition to the king's palace, or a new one is built, that the mud, of which it is chiefly composed, is mixed with the blood of slaughtered victims. This may be an exaggeration, though it is next to impossible to magnify the horrible excesses of these bloody-minded people.

The Adai custom cannot be compared with the Yam festival, though it is atrocious enough. On these occasions, which occur so frequently, generally only those apprehended for offences are murdered; but these offences may be as well imaginary as real, for they rest entirely upon mere accusations, the accused being allowed no trial, or to submit any evidence of an exculpatory character. When the slaughter is ready to begin the victims are brought out from a house where they have been previously confined, and, amid the distracting din of the fetish trumpet and drum, they are decapitated before the delighted crowd which has assembled. The Ashantees are somewhat more given to this abominable custom than the Dahomeans, though both people sacrifice so many victims that their populations have frightfully decreased.

PURPOSES OF THE DAHOME SACRIFICES.

It is stated by travelers that the sacrifices offered by the Ashantees are not the result of any religious obligation, but are essentially the product of the irresponsible rulership of the king, whose inexcusable warrants for executing those objectionable to him have so wrought upon the naturally brutal people that now they love the very sight of murder.

The Dahomeans, however, while their practices are almost identical with those of the Ashantees, offer a *quasi* excuse for their periodical blood-lettings, by declaring that those whom they execute at the customs are messengers sent to their deceased kings in the spirit world. When a Dahome king dies five hundred males and females are immediately despatched to serve him as slaves in the other world. As some of these may afterwards desert him, the king is sent other slaves in the same way, and also messengers to carry to him the news of the kingdom and to request his advice. Whatever the living king does must be reported to his dead predecessor through a messenger who is killed for the purpose. "No matter how trivial the occasion may be," says Burton, "if a white man visits him, if he has a new drum, or if he moves from one house into another—a messenger is sent to tell the departed king." If, after the execution, the king should find that he had forgotten something, away goes another messenger, like the postscript of a letter.

Captain Burton says that he never saw the most repulsive parts of the sacrificial ceremonies of the Dahomeans, but states that there is only one approach to cannibalism in Dahome. This is in connection with the worship of the thunder god.

This deity is supposed to preside over the heavens and to hold in his hands the lightnings which are the weapons with which he destroys those who incur his displeasure. Thus, if a person be killed by lightning, they consider his death due to the thunder-god's vengeance, and his body, therefore, must be execrated; it is accordingly refused burial, and, in lieu thereof, is laid on a board where certain women are appointed to cut it up into small bits, these pieces of flesh the women hold in their mouths and pretend to eat, but in reality do not.

HORRIBLE CELEBRATION OF THE GRAND CUSTOM.

The Ashantees and Dahomeans both celebrate their annual Customs, as before stated, but the latter people have also another "festival" which they call the Grand Custom, which occurs only in commemoration of the decease of a king, and is carried out by his successor. As it has been the pride of each king to outvie his predecessor, by inventing some more novel or revolting mode of performing the sacrifice, each in turn has been more bloody than the previous celebration. To obtain victims for the frightful ceremony it is customary to reserve the criminals for a considerable length of time until their number is quite large, or else make war upon neighboring tribes, and sacrifice the prisoners taken.

On the great day of the Grand Custom, the king appears on a platform, decorated, according to Dahomean ideas, in gorgeous raiment on which are painted the figures of various animals. Around him are his favorite wives and principal officers, the latter being designated by the umbrellas they carry. Below him is an immense crowd of his subjects waiting for the royal favors which he distributes among them in the shape of cowries, rolls of cloth and strings of beads, over which they fight and scramble, like so many hyenas over a carcass.

After the favors are distributed the crowd now shout, "We are hungry, oh king!" "Feed us, oh king!" and this cry is repeated until the mob becomes infuriated and demand blood, which they are sure to get in abundance. The victims are now brought forward, each being gagged in order to prevent him from crying out to the king for mercy, in which case he must be immediately released, and they are firmly secured by being lashed inside baskets, so that they can move neither head, hand nor foot. At the sight of their victims the yells of the crowd below redouble, and the air is rent with the cry, "We are hungry! Feed us, oh king!"

Presently the deafening yells are hushed into a death-like silence, as the king rises, and with his own hand, or foot, pushes one of the victims off the platform into the midst of the crowd below. The helpless wretch falls into the outstretched arms of the eager crowd, the basket is rent to atoms by a hundred hands; and in a shorter time than it has taken to write this sentence, the man has been torn limb from limb, while around each portion of the still quivering body a mass of infuriated negroes are fighting like so many starved dogs over a bone.

Gelele, the present king, following the habits of his ancestors, introduced an improvement on this practice, and, instead of merely pushing the victims off the platform, built a circular tower some thirty feet in height, decorated after the same grotesque manner as the platform, and ordered that the victims should be flung from the top of this tower. Should the kingdom of Dahome last long enough for Galele to have a successor, some new variation will probably be introduced into the Grand Custom.

"After Galele had finished his gift throwing," says a writer who witnessed the ceremonies, "a strange procession wound its way to the tower—the procession of blood. First came a number of men, each carrying a pole, to the end of which was tied a living cock; and after them marched another string of men, each bearing on his head a living goat tied up in a flexible basket, so that the poor animals could not move a limb. Next came a bull, borne by a number of negroes; and, lastly, came the human victims, each tied in a basket, and carried, like the goats, horizontally on a man's head.

Three men now mounted to the top of the tower, and received the victims in succession, as they were handed up to them. Just below the tower an open space was left, in which was a block of wood, on the edge of a hole, attended by the executioners. The fowls were first flung from the top of the tower, still attached to the poles; and it seemed to be requisite that every creature which was then sacrificed should be tied in some extraordinary manner. As soon as they

CELEBRATING THE GRAND CUSTOM IN DAHOME.

touched the ground, they were seized, dragged to the block, and their heads chopped off, so that the blood might be poured into the hole. The goats were thrown down after the fowls, the bull after the goats, and, lastly, the unfortunate men shared the same fate. The mingled blood of these victims was allowed to remain in the hole, which was left uncovered all night, the blood-stained block standing beside it."

The illustration on the preceding page depicts the last feature of this terrible scene. On the right hand is the king, seated under his royal umbrella, surmounted with a leopard, the emblem of royalty, and around him are his wives and great men. In the center rises the cloth-covered tower, from which a human victim has just been hurled, while another is being carried to his fate. Below is one of the executioners standing by the block, and clustering in front of the tower is the mob of infuriated savages.

Just below the king is seen the band, the most prominent instrument of which is the great drum carried on a man's head, and beaten by the drummer who stands behind him, and one of the king's banners is displayed behind the band, and guarded by a body of armed Amazons. In front are several fishermen, their heads adorned with the conical cap, their bodies fantastically painted, and the inevitable skull in their hands. The house which is supposed to contain the spirit of the deceased king is seen on the left.

THE AMAZON SOLDIERY.

The *Amazons*, or female soldiers of Dahome, constitute an institution found no where else in the world, I believe, to-day, though ages ago they were common in the trans-Caucasus, also in parts of Central Africa, and in South America. But though the African amazons have always been fierce soldiers, as I have described them in "The World's Wonders," in no other country have they constituted such a strong, disciplined, fighting force as in Dahome.

The king of Dahome maintains a standing army, composed entirely of women, five thousand strong, which are called the "king's wives," and also, "our mothers," though in neither case is the title appropriate, for they are never wives and are rarely mothers, since they are not permitted to marry. They hold a high position at court and each one possesses at least one slave, while others hold as many as fifty.

Bloodthirsty and savage as are the Dahomeans naturally, the amazons take the lead in both qualities, seeming to avenge themselves, as it were, for the privations to which they are doomed. The spinster soldiers are women who have been selected by the king from the families of his subjects, he having the choice of them when they arrive at marriageable age; and the once married soldiers are women who have been detected in infidelity, and are enlisted instead of executed, or wives who are too vixenish toward their husbands, and so are appropriately drafted into the army, where their combative dispositions may find a more legitimate object.

In order to increase their bloodthirsty spirit, and inspire a feeling of emulation, those who have killed an enemy are allowed to exhibit a symbol of their prowess. They remove the scalp, and preserve it for exhibition on all reviews and grand occasions. They have also another decoration, equivalent to the Victoria Cross of England, namely, a cowrie shell fastened to the butt of the musket. After the battle is over, the victorious amazon smears part of the rifle butt with the blood of the fallen enemy, and just before it dries spreads another layer. This is done until a thick, soft paste is formed, into which the cowrie is pressed. The musket is then laid in the sun, and when properly dry the shell is firmly glued to the weapon.

The possession of this trophy is eagerly coveted by the amazons, and after a battle, those who have not slain an enemy with their own hand are half-maddened with envious jealousy when they see their more successful sisters assuming the coveted decoration. One cowrie is allowed for each dead man, and some of the boldest and fiercest of the amazons have their musket butts completely covered with cowries arranged in circles, stars, and similar patterns.

How recklessly these amazons can fight is evident from their performances at a review. In this part of the country the simple fortifications are made of the acacia bushes, which are furnished with thorns of great length and sharpness, and are indeed formidable obstacles. At a review witnessed by Mr. Duncan, model forts were constructed of these thorns, which were heaped up into walls of some sixty or seventy feet in thickness and eight in height. It may well be imagined that to cross such ramparts as these would be no easy task, even to European soldiers, whose feet are defended by thick-soled boots, and that to a barefooted soldiery they must be simply impregnable. Within the forts were built strong pens seven feet in height, inside of which were cooped up a vast number of male and female slaves belonging to the king.

The review began by the amazons forming, with shouldered arms, about two hundred feet in front of the strong fort, and waiting for the word of command. As soon as it was given, they rushed forward, charged the solid fence as though thorns were powerless against their bare feet, dashed over it, tore down the fence, and returned to the king in triumph, leading with them the captured slaves, and exhibiting also the scalps of warriors who had fallen in previous battles, but who were conventionally supposed to have perished on the present occasion. So rapid and fierce was the attack, that scarcely a minute had elapsed after the word of command was given and when the women were seen returning with their captives.

The women of most acknowledged courage are gathered into the

AN AMAZON REVIEW.

Elephant company, their special business being to hunt the elephant for the sake of its tusks, a task which they perform with great courage and success, often bringing down an elephant with a single volley from their imperfect weapons.

FETISH CUSTOMS OF THE CONGO PEOPLE.

Since Stanley's explorations in Africa, and particularly his journeys and investigations in the Congo land, great attention has been attracted to the Congo country, a district of territory extending along the western coast between the equator and 20° south latitude. Efforts are now being made to resolve this territory into an independent state, which is so far successful that it is already recognized by the great powers, and a system of extensive internal improvement is expected to begin very soon, while a large immigration is already pouring in.

There is little doubt that the Congo possesses many wonderful natural advantages, and that it will speedily develop into a grand country of vast commercial advantage; but these advancements can only be hoped for through the exertions of white immigrants, for the native population, large as it is, is one of the least progressive, most ignorant and superstitious people on earth. In some particulars they resemble the Ashantees and Dahomeans, and in all things are no more intelligent. Their religion is polytheism, but so imperfect that practically it is fetishism.

The fetish priests of Congo possess greater power than the king, and their rule is antagonistic to the last degree, especially that of the chief, who is called *Chitombe*, and ranks as a god. He is maintained in luxury by annual contributions of the first fruits of the harvest, which are given with great ceremony.

A sacred fire burns constantly in his house, and the embers are sold at enormous prices to the people, who believe that they possess marvelous medicinal virtues. Once each year he visits all the subordinate priests, during which time every wife and husband must separate, under pain of death. This singular law is the product of a belief that children begotten during the tour of the Chitombe become messengers of evil, very devils indeed.

The Chitombe is regarded as being so holy that he is not allowed to die a natural death, since such an event would immediately precipitate the destruction of the world. Consequently, so soon as he is seized with a serious illness, the Chitombe elect calls at the holy residence and saves the universe from destruction by knocking the sick chief's brains out with a club, or kills him by strangling, as the Chitombe may prefer.

Next to the Chitombe is a priest called *Nghombo*, who preserves his superiority by reversing his position whenever he walks. To walk erect like other men would make him their equal, so he always walks on his hands, with his feet in the air, by which astonishing work of godliness he impresses the laity with his supernatural endowments. Some of the lower priests are rain-makers, who perform the duties of their important office by scraping up the earth into little mounds, in the center of which they place fetishes. By means of certain incantations a nameless bug is called forth from one of the mounds, which at once mounts to the sky and turns the stop-cock, which lets pour the pent-up waters of heaven. However, only so much rain is let fall as the priests are paid for, and the credit system is not in vogue among them, either. Dwarfs, hunchbacks and albinos are considered to be the best rain-makers, since they are supposed to bear the marks of a consecrated priesthood.

The priests have, as usual, an ordeal through which they must pass before assuming the sacerdotal power. The common test to prove godly power is the drinking of poison, and the rarest is the application of a red-hot iron to the skin. These same tests are applied to persons accused of crimes, by which to determine whether or not they are guilty. If a person drinks the poison and dies from the effect, of course he is guilty, or if the iron burns, the accused must be guilty. But the Congo people, like the civilized tribes of the United States, easily defeat these laws by the payment of a proper sum to those who apply the test. No man there need be punished for crime if he is wealthy enough to buy his acquittal.

HOW WOMEN HAVE CONTROLLED THE DESTINIES OF CONGO.

The wives in Congo are tolerably well off, except that they are severely beaten with the heavy hippopotamus-hide whip. The women do not resent this treatment, and, indeed, unless a woman is soundly flogged occasionally, she thinks that her husband is neglecting her, and feels offended accordingly. The king has the power of taking any woman for his wife, whether married or not, and, when she goes to the royal harem, her husband is judiciously executed.

The people of Congo are—probably on account of the enervating climate—a very indolent and lethargic race, the women being made to do all the work, while the men lie in the shade and smoke their pipes and drink their palm wine, which they make remarkably well, though not so well as the Bube tribe of Fernando Po. Their houses are merely huts of the simplest description; a few posts with a roof over them, and twigs woven between them in wicker-work fashion by way of walls, are all that a Congo man cares for in a house. His clothing is as simple as his lodging, a piece of native cloth, tied round his middle, being all that he cares for; so that the ample clothes and handsome furs worn by the king must have had a very strong effect on the almost naked populace.

According to traditional history, Congo was in old times one of the African kingdoms. Twice it rose to this eminence, and both times by the energy of a woman, who, in spite of the low opinion in which women are held, contrived to ascend the throne.

Somewhere about 1520—it is impossible in such history to obtain precision of dates—a great chief, named Zimbo, swept over a large part of Africa, taking every country to which he came, and establishing his own dominion in it. Among other kingdoms, Congo was taken by him, and rendered tributary, and so powerful did he at last become, that his army outgrew his territory, and he had the audacity to send a division to ravage Abyssinia and Mozambique. The division reached the eastern sea in safety, but the army there met the Portuguese, who routed them with great loss. Messengers conveyed the tidings to Zimbo, who put himself at the head of his remaining troops, went against the Portuguese, beat them, killed their general, and carried off a great number of prisoners, with whose skulls he paved the ground in front of his house.

CHAPTER XL.

THE DYAKS OF BORNEO.

THOUGH Africa is peopled almost exclusively by wild and savage tribes, especially all the central portion, and while nearly every form of superstition and bestiality is practiced in that great division of the earth, yet we find in other parts of the globe uncivilized races distinct from the Africans in character, color, religion, habits and all that goes to make up the attributes of humanity. This fact itself is remarkable only when we consider the races of man and the line of separation between the savage and the civilized; or, rather, the evolutions of man socially and morally. In other words, assuming that all races had a common origin, and that shades of skin are due to climatic influence, it apparently ought to follow that, in the absence of civilizing means, a similiarity of character would be manifest in races occupying similar climates, or identical lines of latitude. So far from this being true, the differences are so great that they exhibit all the evidences of varied origin. Between the Fuegians of the extreme south and the Esquimaux of the

Artic, though there be an identical climate, there is as wide distinction in character as there is distance which separates them, as we shall see in a future chapter.

Passing from the equatorial region of Africa eastwards, to the Malay Archipelago, we find other barbaric tribes, races perhaps, which are subject to almost the very same natural influences, and yet who exhibit such marked peculiarities as to dispute, apparently, at least, the principles held by ethnographers, that climate and topography exert the greatest influence in race development. No one can imagine a greater difference between any two races than exists between the Central Africans and the *Dyaks* of Borneo. The former are remarkable for their savagery, brutality, thievishness, superstition, selfishness, polygamy, treachery and lewdness; the Dyaks, on the other hand, are more than civilized, so far as their moral character is concerned, for they are hospitable, sympathetic, honest above all other people, steadfast in friendship, utterly without religious sentiments, for they have no idea of a God, never given to slavery, monogamists who are devoted to their families, while lewdness is almost unknown among them. These attributes belong to the Dyak in his natural life, when uninfluenced by the Malays and other interlopers who so corrupted him, at one time, that his nature was completely changed from a moral being to a savage creature that stopped short of no excess, as will be shortly explained.

HISTORY OF THE DYAKS.

The Dyaks now occupy the interior of Borneo, having been driven from the coast, except on the south, by the Malays, Javanese, Chinese and Europeans. When the Malays first set foot on the island, they found the Dyaks not only peaceable and contented, but so hospitable in their nature that the new-comers were treated with every mark of kindness. These first visitors, however, were pirates, who not only made their quarters in the unexplored rivers and indentations of the Bornean coast, where, for a long period, they remained safe, but when piracy, at length, became extremely hazardous, the Malays turned their hands to the equally profitable occupation of slave-trading, which they practiced for many years, unmolested, throughout the island.

Insinuating themselves into the favor of the Dyaks by presents of fire-arms, swords, calicoes and gew-gaws, the Malays next instigated tribal wars and then profited largely by purchasing the prisoners taken by either side, by which means they were enabled to carry away thousands of the poor Borneans annually.

THE HEAD HUNTERS OF BORNEO.

Previous to the coming of the Malays, it is asserted by travelers who have visited the island, and also by Sir James Brooks, the governor of the British Commercial possession of North Borneo for many years, that war between the Dyak tribes was almost unknown, but that the slave trade developed by the Malays led, not only to incessant internecine wars, but also created a disposition in the Dyak to murder, which he never before displayed. He was taught to believe that bravery was the greatest quality of the human heart, and that to be brave it was necessary to incite war, fight desperately, and take prisoners to be sold into slavery. This propensity, thus created and stimulated, grew until a Dyak was not considered eligible for matrimony until he had a human head dangling from his waistband to prove his valor. As a man was appreciated by the number of heads he had taken, head-hunting soon became a rage among the male population. The Malays further taught the simple-minded Dyaks that famine, plague or disease, was caused by some offended god who would soon bring them plenty, or abate the disease if he be propitiated by an offering of heads.

This practice of head-hunting was at one time so common, so Sir Stanford Raffles informs us, that the depopulation of the island was seriously threatened. Every hut became fairly festooned with bleached skulls and no Dyak had the least standing among his people who had not these ghastly proofs of his valor hung to his waist or suspended before his door.

RELIGIOUS SACRIFICES.

The Kyans come the nearest to having a religious belief, or, rather, system of formulated superstitions, of all the Dyaks. The Baram Kyans believe in a future existence, and their heaven and hell are divided into various compartments for the proper accommodation of all according to the circumstances under which they die. They pay much attention to the carving of wooden images and charms, to all of which more or less meaning is attached; still, their ideas of a Supreme Being and a future state are very vague, and they have no religious rites or outward observances.

The Trings have a well-defined belief in a tribal heaven, and a purgatory of toiling and enduring which must be passed through before the heaven can be reached. Yet the Trings practice cannibalism in war, and offer human sacrifices at the *tiwahs* (death feasts) which are made upon the return of an expedition. Mr. Perelaer describes such an event, held on the Upper Kahajan river by a Kyan clan (of

A DYAK VILLAGE.

which the Trings are a branch), at which forty slave debtors were put to death by torture, or by flesh wounds inflicted by the men and boys of the tribe. This species of savagery was unknown before the Malays visited the island, aud must therefore be regarded as one of the results of their influence.

The houses of the Kyans are, in general, very similar to the long-houses of the Sea Dyaks, each of which accommodates a number of families, but very often a number of these long-houses are grouped together in regular village style.

THE MORALS OF THE HILL DYAKS.

The Sea Dyaks are very like the Kyans in habits and disposition; both are warriors by preference, and have been noted for their head-taking propensities, and other savage customs. They also live alike, in long houses, built on posts, ten, and sometimes fifteen feet above the ground. Each house is composed of many rooms, and each room is occupied by a family. For furniture they are content with a mat to lie upon, and the fire they warm and cook by is built on a pile of baked clay which lies in the center of the room. Even now, skulls, blacked by smoke and begrimed by dirt, may be seen hanging over the doors of the Sea Dyaks' houses, but the custom of head-taking has about become obsolete.

The Hill Dyaks more nearly retain their primitive manners than any others of the Bornean tribes. Living remote from the coast, in the mountainous regions of the island, they escaped the influence of the Malays, and are to-day nearly what they were before the slave traffic was inaugurated; hence, a description of their present habits will represent the aborigines, or, at least, the Dyaks in their original simplicity. To W. T. Hornaday, author of "Two Years in the Jungles," I am indebted for most of the information here given of the Hill Dyaks.

The people of this tribe are morally the most highly developed of any in the island of Borneo, if not in the whole archipelago, which, in view of the extent of the influence Hindooism formerly exerted over them, is all the more surprising. Although they are, as a tribe, wholly without religion or any of its restraining influences, their moral principles would put to the blush the children of Israel in their best days.

To the other virtues of the Dyak must be added that of strict honesty and profound respect for the rights of property. Whether they steal from each other I cannot say; I suppose they do sometimes, although it must be very seldom. It is positively asserted, however, that they never pilfer from Europeans, nor even Malays and Chinese, from whom they would have a right to take something in remembrance of past oppression and extortion in the one case, and sharp practice with false weights and measures in the other.

Strangely enough, some of the Hill Dyaks burn their dead, a custom which they have clearly adopted from the Hindoos who flourished in Western Borneo several centuries ago. I believe all the people of this tribe in Sarawak Territory practise cremation, excepting those who live on the Sadong. The Sadong River Dyaks bury their dead, and bury with them various articles belonging to the deceased, especially his betel box with fresh sirih leaves (black pepper), some old clothes of no value, and perhaps his spear. His land is then divided equally among his children, without discrimination for or against either sex.

The Hill Dyaks have dim ideas regarding a future state and a Supreme Spirit named *Tupa* or *Jowata*, both Hindoo names. They believe the good Dyaks go to a place under the earth, called *Sabyan*, where they are happy, and that the bad go to another place, also called *Sabyan*, where they are not happy. A few believe that sometimes their ancestors take the form of a deer after death, for which reason, like the Hindoos from whom the idea was probably derived, they will neither kill deer nor eat of their flesh.

Some believe that certain of their warriors become "wood-spirits," or wood-devils (antus), after death, and remain on earth to plague such of their survivors as have offended or injured them. They have no religious ceremonies or observances whatever, nor any conception of a God who controls the destinies of men for good or ill.

Marriage among the Hill Dyaks is not a solemn event, but the wife is honored for all that. The ceremony is not always the same; sometimes it is effected by the mere exchange of presents, or by the killing of a fowl between them, or the eating of rice together; simple as this is it answers the purpose admirably; a public avowal of the marriage is invariably made, and thenceforth the parties live together in great harmony, save in very rare instances. As the curse of strong drink is not known to them they, of course, live happily, as every other people would if there were no such thing as intoxicants. In case of death the property is equally divided among the children, without regard to sex; so, if a man dies leaving a widow, all his property immediately passes to her, without the annoyance of executors; she is bound for his debts and always manages to pay them.

Says Hornaday: "Once more I assert, with the certainty of being disbelieved, that the Dyaks actually do not steal. I have an account of one who did once steal some gutta from a companion, but he is dead now—hanged, 'in the usual manner.'

"Their most wonderful trait, however, is their faithfulness in pay-

DYAK GIRLS AND HOUSE.

ing their debts. If the people of the village want goods, a trader will give them his whole cargo, if he can get them to accept it, in exchange for jungle produce *to be collected*. The day for full settlement is named by the head man, and by that day the debts are all paid. What a glorious country for an honest merchant to start business in!

A PEOPLE WITHOUT RELIGION.

"Like their neighbors of the hills, the Sea Dyaks are without priests and creeds or even the faintest notion of religious observances. Their moral laws are the product of their own evolution, for we see in them no reflection of the religious customs of any of the people who have thus far come in contact with them, either Hindoos, Javanese, Chinese, Malays or Europeans. Savage nations usually acquire all the vices, and but very few of the virtues, of the civilization which touches them, but so far the Dyaks of Northern Borneo have gone through the fire unscathed. They are yet free from the groveling idolatry and abominable religious fanaticism of the Hindoos, the sordid avarice of the Chinese, the deceit, treachery and licentiousness of the Malays, and the brandy-and-sodaism of the Europeans."

The Dyaks, as may be supposed, are subject to very few diseases, and insanity is so rare that many of the people never saw a case; deformity of person is almost unknown, and the diseases so common to women of America are unheard of among the Dyaks.

Hornaday concludes his description of the Dyaks, as follows:

"Thus ends our brief survey of the Hill and Sea Dyaks, and what does it teach us? In these strange children of nature we see all the cardinal virtues without a ray of religion, morality without ministers, the Christian graces without Christ or gospel. They keep no Sabbaths, pray no prayers, build no temples, worship nothing and nobody, and acknowledge no higher tribunal than the bar of public opinion on one hand, and the Sarawak government court on the other.

"The Dyak is perhaps the most happy and contented human being under the sun. His wants are few, and his native jungle supplies nearly all of them. Thanks to his state of savagery, he has not developed one-tenth of the diseases which so often make the lives of civilized people a burden. His children do not have scarlet fever, diphtheria, croup, or whooping cough, nor does he or his wife have the consumption, pneumonia, dyspepsia, rheumatism or gout. But for the rascally Chinaman, who years ago taught him to make toddy from the palm tree, and who even now supplies him with arrack, he might to-day be without the means of getting drunk. As is the case with nearly all savages who drink intoxicating liquors, this vice is the gift of civilization.

"In hospitality, human sympathy, and charity, the Dyaks are not outranked by any people living, so far as I know, and their morals are as much superior to ours as our intelligence is beyond theirs. If happiness is the goal of human existence, they are much nearer it than we. In this instance, at least, the highest civilization has not evolved the most perfect state of society, and to this extent the fundamental theories of theology, of sociology, and human evolution are utterly at fault. Borneo is no field for the missionary, for no religion can give the Dyaks aught that will benefit him, or increase the balance of his happiness in the least."

THE HORRIBLE BATTAS OF SUMATRA.

While the contrast between the natives of Equatorial Africa and the Dyaks of Borneo is wonderfully great, our surprise is doubly increased when we come to compare the Dyaks with the *Battas* of Sumatra. The comparison lies in the identity of climate, surroundings and topography, the equator passing through the center of both Sumatra and Borneo, while both are apparently of common origin and alike subject to Malayan influence; yet in contrasting the Dyaks with the Battas we are struck with the almost marvelous differences in character which they present. As the Dyaks are noted for their good qualities so are the Battas distinguished for their turpitude; the latter have been acquainted with civilization for hundreds of years, but these influences have seemingly operated to multiply their crimes and increase their savagery, until we may safely assert that of all the tribes and races of the earth the Battas are the most barbarous.

The Battas occupy the northern half of Sumatra and carry on a considerable commerce with the Chinese and people of the Malay peninsula; but this intercourse has not served to in the least destroy their aged customs and atrocious habits. They learned to take heads, like the Dyaks, but never followed the practice persistently, perhaps for the reason that they prefer the bodies of prisoners, or dead people generally, to trophies such as the Dyaks were content with. In other words, the Battas are cannibals whose propensities lead them to practice this horrid feature of savagery in its most repulsive form.

THE GOVERNMENT OF THE BATTAS.

When Sir Stanford Raffles arrived on the island as governor of Bencoolen, a division of Sumatra, he found the wreck of a great empire scarcely known to Europeans. He was astounded to find the Battas a fairly governed race, having a written language which very few of them could not write. They had deliberative assemblies and formulated laws, though not a code, and justice was impartially administered. They also possessed a religion, but it was a mixture of Buddhism, Christianity and paganism, and therefore difficult to describe.

Though the Battas are excellent agriculturists and their island yields an abundance of fruits and vegetables, and abounds with wild game, yet they are confirmed cannibals, relishing the flesh of a human body more than any other product which their cultivation can produce. So great is their greed for human bodies that many of their laws are framed with the view of providing victims to gratify their horrid taste. Not only do they eat all prisoners taken in war, but their own people are sacrificed, when charged with certain offenses, and thus the supply of human meat is usually quite plentiful in every Batta village.

CHILDREN EATING THEIR PARENTS.

From information chiefly supplied by Raffles, it appears that in olden times the flesh of human bodies was regarded by the Battas as a luxury which only those of high official standing or wealth could afford; but the common people were not wholly without means for regaling their appetites on this precious meat. While the functionaries of the government and those able to buy victims dined off prisoners and culprits, the poor had occasional feasts, when their parents died or became too old for further service. "It is a truly astonishing fact," says Sir Stanford, "that when it was decided to sacrifice their parents, the greedy children would suspend the old people by the hands to the branch of a tree, and, inviting their friends to the feast, a circle was formed round the swinging bodies and the merry-making began. As the crowd danced round their victims they would cry out from time to time, 'When the fruit is ripe, then it will fall!' This sacrifice nearly always took place when the limes ripened, though sometimes it occurred after a supply of salt and pepper, which the Battas are very fond of, but only obtain in trade with the Malays."

That this peculiarly horrid feature of cannibalism prevailed down to quite recent times, we have the evidence of many authorities who have visited the Battas and made themselves familiar with their customs. A certain writer who spent some time in Sumatra calculated that in 1817 no less than one hundred old people were thus sacrificed in a comparatively small district, reports of which were brought to him by natives.

OTHER SACRIFICES FOR PURPOSES OF CANNIBALISM.

The great traveler, Marco Polo, who visited Sumatra in the thirteenth century, describing the Battas, says: "Whenever an individ-

HORRIBLE FEAST OF THE BATTA CANNIBALS.

ual was stricken with sickness, his relatives immediately inquired of the priests or magicians whether he would recover; if the answer was in the negative the patient was at once strangled, cut in pieces and devoured, even to the very marrow of the bones. This, they alleged, was to prevent the generation of worms in the body, which, if allowed to infest it, would, by gnawing, deface and torture the soul of the dead." The absurdity of this excuse is immaterial in the face of the fact that strangers were eaten from the same humane motive.

The evidence of cannibalism, as now practiced by the Battas, is not alone confined to the statements made by Raffles and Marsden, of the British Government, but the facts are further confirmed by the missionaries Ward, Burton, Jacks and Prince, who for a long time resided and preached among them. The practice of sacrificing old people, which was once very common, has been abandoned, not because the tastes of the people have changed, but entirely because the execution of later laws has served to so greatly increase the supply of human bodies that it is no longer necessary to kill the old, and therefore very tough people, for even the poor Battas may now feast on so-called stall-fed victims.

Their present laws declare that four offences, called the four high crimes, subject the criminal to death, whose body shall be eaten, to the end that revenge for the violation shall be enjoyed by the people among whom the crime was perpetrated. These crimes are: murder, treason to the king, notorious adultery, and aggravated theft. This last named offence is doubtless highway robbery, in which the victim is seriously injured, or burglary. It is also ordained that all prisoners taken in war—when it is waged with the people of another district—shall be eaten, and it is also lawful to eat the dead bodies left on the field of battle, or the bodies of any of the enemy that may be buried.

Persons who are accused of the offenses above named are arrested and brought before a tribunal, over which two chiefs preside. These judges patiently listen to all the evidence, and at the conclusion either order the accused released or pronounce him guilty. After announcing the verdict of the court the two judges stand up facing each other and drink together a cup of palm-wine, which act is equivalent to confirming the sentence imposed.

In cases of adultery it is not allowed to carry the sentence of death and eating into effect unless the relatives of the wife appear and partake of the feast. The condemned is then brought forward and bound to a stake, with his hands extended. The husband or party most aggrieved by the offense then approaches the victim and, having the privilege of first choice, usually cuts off his ears. The next degree of relation takes the second choice, and so on, each relative cutting the portion he may select from the condemned. After the relatives have thus maimed and most cruelly cut up the victim, the chief who has condemned him next advances and cuts off the man's head, which he carries home for his own feast. The brains, however, are not eaten, but are carefully extracted and preserved in a bottle for fetish purposes.

It is generally customary to devour the body of a culprit on the spot where his crime was committed, and usually the flesh is eaten raw, but in later days it is not uncommon for the feasters to grill the flesh, seasoned with lime juice, pepper and salt. Intoxicants are prohibited during these ghastly feasts, but, in lieu of wine, many of the feasters fill sections of bamboo with the blood of the victim and drink it off with the relish of veritable vampires. The flesh of man is denied women, and none of the sex are allowed to even be present at the cannibal banquet, but travelers assert that that which is lawfully denied them many of the women obtain by stealth, so ingrained into the whole people is their taste for human flesh.

HORRORS IMPOSSIBLE TO DESCRIBE.

Dr. Jacks tells us that frequently, at the execution of criminals, so blood-thirsty are the Battas that they are not content with *cutting* off parts of the living victim, but will tear him with their teeth and eat the pieces thus bitten out raw until the poor fellow is literally devoured alive. He further relates that a British resident, on one occasion, while walking through the woods, came upon the remains of a British soldier who had been about one-half eaten. The Battas had evidently been surprised at their feast, for a fire was burning beside the remains, and a finger of the soldier was found half-cooked upon a fork that had been left by the cannibals in their hasty flight.

The following description of the execution and eating of a Batta criminal is abridged from a report made by a British officer and addressed to the Court of Direction of the East India Company, which may aptly conclude this tale of Batta horrors:

A few years ago a man was found guilty, after due trial, of an offense which came under the head of high crime, though the writer asserts that the man was really guilty of a mere petty offense. But he was sentenced to be eaten, according to the law providing for the punishment of adulterers. The execution took place close to a British post called *Tappanooly* and was witnessed by the writer and two other British residents.

Upon reaching the scene of execution, the gentleman making the report found a large assemblage of Battas all in a hilarious frame of mind over the feast that was about to be prepared. The criminal was soon produced and bound to a stake, around which the people formed in a circle. The minister of justice, if I may call him such, came forward, holding in his right hand a long, cruel-looking knife which he flourished for a moment as he approached the victim. Close behind him followed a man who carried a dish containing a condiment made of limes, chillies and salt, and called, by the natives, *Sambul.* The justice raised his knife before the culprit and called to the injured husband to come forward and select his part of the doomed man. In this case the husband chose the right ear, which the judge immediately severed from the victim and passed the bloody member to the husband, who, at once, rolled it in the sambul and ate it raw. The others in the asemblage next fell upon the bound criminal from whom they cut such morsels of flesh as they chose and dipped them into the sambul, after which they were eaten.

When the poor offender had lost nearly half of his body by the human vultures who were thus devouring him peacemeal, despite his despairing cries of anguish, a second officer rushed up and stabbed him to the heart, more out of respect to the wishes of the British spectators, however, than any disposition to end the unfortunate man's sufferings, for the Battas rejoiced in these.

As I have before said, the Battas of Sumatra are the most savage people in the world, and yet their form of government, religion, commerce, written language, arms and houses, show them to be far in advance of all other barbarous tribes, and if it were not for their cannibal and brutal propensities they would undoubtedly rank with the Malays, their nearest neighbors.

CIVILIZED PEOPLE WHO PRACTICE CANNIBALISM.

We know that there are a score or more of races and tribes who practice cannibalism, a number of which I have not thought it of interest to describe, since there is a marked similarity in the ceremonies attending the sacrifice and eating of victims. The general belief that the practice is confined to savage tribes of Africa and the Pacific islands is one which is so far wrong that the facts should be commonly known, and a few of which I will attempt to give.

The republic of Hayti, which is almost at our door and the most fruitful member of the West Indies, possesses "a government modeled on that of France, with president, senate and house of representatives; with secretaries of state, prefects, judges, and all the paraphernalia of courts of justice and of police; with a press more or less free, and an archbishop, bishops and clergy nearly all Frenchmen." In this connection Hayti must not be confounded with its sister republic of Santo Domingo, inhabited by Spanish-speaking negroes and occupying the largest part of the island. Santo Domingo is said to be far more enlightened than Hayti.

Sir Spenser St. John, now British Minister to Mexico, was twelve years, beginning with 1863, minister resident and consul general from Great Britain to Hayti. In his recently published book, called "Hayti, or the Black Republic," he has a chapter on "Voudou Worship and Cannibalism," and his testimony is so strong and direct that the horrible facts which he exposes can hardly be refuted. Cannibalism in Hayti is an accompaniment of the barbarous voudou worship brought from Africa. The evil is so widespread in Hayti that the government has never dared to grapple with it, with the exceptions of the administrations of Presidents Geffrard and Boisrond Canal, and it is probable that they, in some measure, owe their fall to this action. The Emperor Soulouque was a firm believer in the voudou, the mulatto, Governor Therlonge, was one of its high priests, and a late prime minister was said to be a chief priest of the sect. A believer in voudouism is, however, not necessarily tainted with cannibalism, there being two sects who follow the worship, one consisting of those who only delight in the blood and flesh of white cocks, and spotless white goats at their ceremonials, and the second comprising those who are not only devoted to these, but on great occasions call for the flesh and blood of the "goat without horns," or human victims.

A VOUDOU CEREMONY.

At a dinner Sir Spenser heard the Archbishop of Port-au-Prince give an account of the occurrences at a voudou ceremony held the preceding week in the district of Arcahaye (in 1869). A French priest in charge of the district had a curiosity to witness the ceremonies, and he persuaded some of his parishioners to take him to the forest where a meeting was to be held. They were very unwilling, saying that if they were discovered he and they would be killed, but he promised faithfully that, whatever happened, he would not speak a word. So he was taken with them, disguised as a peasant. After the usual ceremonies of killing a white cock and white goat, those present being marked with the blood, the priest said that presently an athletic young negro came and knelt before the priestess of the occasion and said, "O, maman, I have a favor to ask." "What is it, my son?" "Give us, to complete the sacrifices, the goat without horns." She gave a sign of assent; the crowd in the shed separated, and there was a child sitting with its feet bound. In an instant a rope, already passed through a block, was tightened, the child's feet flew up toward the roof, and the priest approached it with a knife. The loud shriek given by the victim aroused the Frenchman to the truth of what was going on. He shouted, "O, spare the child!" and would have darted forward, but he was seized by his friends around him and literally carried from the spot. He got safely back to the town and tried to arouse the police, but they would do nothing until the morning, when they accompanied him to the scene. They found the remains of the feast, and near the shed was the boiled skull of the child. The authorities were exceedingly incensed at the priest for his interference, and, under the pretense that they could not answer for his safety, shipped him off to Port-au-Prince, where he made his report to the archbishop.

Sir Spenser says that, in general, when incidents relating to voudou worship are spoken of in society, the Haytien gentlemen endeavor to turn the conversation, or they say you have been imposed on, or the events have been exaggerated. He tells in detail, however, the story of a trial which he witnessed in a criminal court, a detailed account of which is given in the official journal of the day. It occurred during the Presidency of Gen. Geffrard, whom the author calls the most enlightened ruler since the days of President Boyer. A man named Conge Pelle lived a couple of miles to the west of Port-au-Prince, in the village of Bizoton. He had been a laborer, a gentleman's servant, an idler, who was anxious to improve his position without an exertion on his own part. In his dilemma, he addressed himself to his sister, Jeanne, who had long been connected with the voudou, and was, in fact, the daughter of a priestess, and herself a well known mamanloi. (They call their priests and priestesses respectfully papalois and mamanlois, corruptions of papa roi and maman roi, royal father and royal mother.) It was agreed that about the new year some sacrifice should be offered to propitiate the serpent whom they worshipped. It was thought better to offer a more important sacrifice than the customary white cock or goat. A consultation was held with two papalois, Julien Nicolas and Floreal Appollon; it was decided to sacrifice a female child, and the choice fell on Claircine, the niece of Jeanne and Conge. This was the account given in court; but it appears to be an undoubted fact that human sacrifices are offered at Easter, Christmas eve, New Year's eve, and more particularly on Twelfth Night.

A CANNIBALISTIC DEBAUCH.

The mother was induced to go to Port-au-Prince for an afternoon, when the child was kidnaped and hidden under the altar of a voudou temple. The mother was deceived on her return, and on New Year's eve a select company assembled at the house of Jeanne to partake of a savory feast. The child was horribly butchered, carved up, and the flesh placed in wooden dishes. After various ceremonials, the flesh was cooked with Congo beans, and the head was put into a pot with yams to make some soup. One of their women present, urged by the fearful appetite of a cannibal, cut from the child's palm a piece of flesh and ate it raw. The night was passed in eating, dancing, drinking and debauchery. The next morning the remains of the flesh were warmed up for breakfast. Fourteen persons were arrested, and sufficient evidence was found against eight, who were tried, condemned and executed. Sir Spenser asked the public prosecutor if he thought that the mother had been really ignorant of the fate reserved for her child. He replied: "We have not thought proper to press the inquiry too closely, for fear that we should discover that she partook of the feast; we required her testimony at the trial." After a pause he added: "If full justice were done, there would be fifty on those benches instead of eight." During the trial, proofs were adduced that the devotees of voudou worship associate it with the ceremonies of the Catholic religion. Crosses and pictures of the Virgin are strangely mingled on their altars with the objects of their superstition. In 1862 the delegates of the Pope left the country in disgust on account of the prevailing corruption, the dearth of religion among the secretaries of the voudou, and the opposition which he met with in what in Hayti is called civilized society.

The Spanish minister reported to his government the case of an unknown youth of about twenty years, found dead in the streets of

Port-au-Prince, his heart pierced by a weapon attached to which was a thin, hollow cane. It was supposed that he was assassinated in order to suck his blood. The power of the voudou priests, according to the report made by the Spanish minister, Mr. Alvarez, was something tremendous in its influence on the people. "They produce death,—apparent, slow or instantaneous — madness, paralysis, impotence, idiocy, riches or poverty, according to their will. * * * If it be doubted that these individuals, without even common sense, can understand so thoroughly the properties of herbs and their combinations, so as to be able to apply them to the injury of their fellow-creatures, I can only say that tradition is a great book, and that they receive these instructions as a sacred deposit from one generation to another, with the further advantage that in the hills and mountains of this island grow in abundance similar herbs to those which in Africa they employ in their incantations."

HUMAN FLESH AS REGULAR FOOD.

Beside human sacrifices connected with religion, there is another phase — cannibalism practiced for the sake of the food which the slaughtering of human beings affords to a vile section of the community. A lady, the wife of a missionary, forced to stay in the interior on account of civil war in the surrounding districts, related some horrible incidents of her own knowledge. She declared that human sacrifices were constant; that human flesh was openly sold in the market. A high government official told Sir Spenser the following: A man traveling with his wife was obliged to seek shelter in a cottage on account of a storm. The latter was ill, and becoming worse, the man went to seek help, leaving his wife with the occupants, two men and one woman. It was a long time before he could find any one, and on his return his wife was gone. They told him she had followed him, becoming uneasy at his long absence. He rode away and induced the police to follow him. The three inmates were arrested, and the body of the woman, already dismembered, was found in a cask in an outhouse, covered with a thick layer of salt. The only punishment the assassins received was that administered by the clubs of the police as they were taken to prison. The practice of midwives slaying children to eat them is an old one in Hayti. As late as 1878, two women were arrested in a hut near Port-au-Prince, caught eating the raw flesh of a child. It was found that all the blood had been sucked from the body, and part of the flesh had been salted down for future use. A woman arrested for cannibalism was asked by a priest: "How could you eat the flesh of your own children?" She answered coolly, "And who had a better right?"

There is in Hayti a class of human monsters called *loup garous*, who make it a practice to prowl about lonely houses at night to carry off the children. They are employed by the papalois to secure children for sacrifice in case the neighborhood does not furnish a suitable subject, and they are naturally the bugbears of the country. In closing this frightful record, Sir Spenser says that, except during one year of Geffrard's Presidency, no Government has ever cared to grapple with the evil. If they have not encouraged it, they have ignored it, in order not to lose the favor of the masses.

THE TERRA DEL FUEGIANS.

As the Battas are the most cruel, so are the Fuegians the most singular of all people. They are an anomaly in nature, a very freak of physical laws, setting nearly every standard of physiology at defiance, and becoming at once a *lusus naturæ*, and yet a race, typical, of human beings. We can understand why men live in caves, or in trees, why others are continually emigrating, why some live on insects, and others subsist upon the spoils taken from their neighbors or enemies. But we cannot understand the law of nature that would protect persons living in the fire, because the conditions would appear, and are, impossible.

But what are we to say of the Fuegians, a somewhat populous race, who maintain the most miserable of existences on a barren island, projecting almost into the Antarctic circle, where in midsummer the voice of winter is never silent. Even here, as with the Esquimaux in the far north, we might expect a hardy race, but it is an astonishing fact that we find here a race who persist in nudity, to whom clothing is a greater burden than to the tribes of Central Africa! A race of humans in whom the sensation of cold seems to be entirely absent, for in their nakedness they exhibit less suffering from the severity of climate than does the polar bear in his great, cold-defying robe.

In his "Uncivilized Races of the World," J. G. Wood, describing the marvels of the Fuegians, says:

"One of the strangest phenomena connected with the Fuegians is their lack of clothing. In a climate so cold that in the middle of summer people have been frozen to death at no great elevation above the level of the sea, it might well be imagined that the natives would follow the same course as that adopted by the Esquimaux, and make for themselves garments out of the thickest and warmest furs that can be procured.'

"They might do so if they chose. In some parts of their country they have the thick-wooled guanaco (probably an importation from the mainland), and in others are deer and foxes, not to mention the dogs which they keep in a domesticated state. Besides, there are few furs warmer than those of the seal, and seals of various kinds abound on the Fuegian coasts, some, such as the sea-lion, being of very large size. Then there are various water birds, whose skins would make dresses equally light and warm, such as the penguin, the duck, the albatross, and the like.

TYPES OF THE FUEGIAN RACE.

"It is evident, therefore, that if the Fuegian is not warmly and thickly clothed, it is not from want of material, and that he is naked not from necessity but choice. And he chooses nudity, neither sex wearing any description of clothes except a piece of seal or deer skin about eighteen inches square hung over one shoulder. No other covering is worn except this patch of skin, which is shifted from one side of the body to another according to the direction of the wind, the Fuegian appearing to be perfectly indifferent to frost, rain or snow. For example, a Fuegian mother has been seen with her child in her arms, wearing nothing but the little piece of seal-skin on the windward side, and yet standing unconcernedly in the snow, which fell not only on her naked shoulder, but was heaped between her child and her breast, neither mother nor infant seeming to be more than ordinarily cold. During mild weather, or when the Fuegian is paddling or otherwise engaged in work, he thinks that even the piece of seal-skin is too much for him, and throws it off."

THE RUDENESS OF FUEGIAN HUTS.

As the Fuegian neglects to protect his body against icy blasts, so in his rude hut, which serves him as a habitation, he avoids any attempt to make it a comfortable shelter, using it rather to break the wind from the fire at which he cooks his meat, but around which he seldom sits for warmth. These huts are of the simplest construction, consisting of a number of long poles, with the thicker ends sharpened and stuck into the ground in a circle, so that the tops may be bent over and fastened at a common center. This completes the framework, which is then covered with small branches woven into the interstices between the poles, and the whole is afterwards covered with grass. The inside is furnished with a bed of grass, upon which the miserable people lie, and they do their cooking at a fire built in a small place scooped out of the earth in the center; quite as often, however, the fire is built outside the huts, opposite the wind.

Their cooking is of the rudest character, and generally consists in putting the food into hot ashes, and allowing it to remain until it is only fairly warmed. Cooking in vessels of any kind is unknown to them, and the first lessons given them in cooking mussels in a tin pan were scarcely more successful than those in sewing, when the women invariably made a hole in the fabric with the needle, then pulled the thread out of the eye of the needle and inserted it through the puncture. They were repeatedly taught the use of the eye in carrying the thread, but to little purpose, as they always returned to their primitive way of sewing with a fish-bone and fibre of sinew.

WEAPONS AND PROWESS OF THE FUEGIANS.

The Fuegians are a quarrelsome people and war is almost continually prevailing between different tribes, though the number killed is never great. Their weapons are the bow and arrow, the spear, and the sling; though capable of doing great execution, these arms are not generally employed in war *for fear some one may be killed*, but are reserved for use in hunting seals, guanacos, deer, fish and birds. In the use of all these weapons the Fuegians are marvelously expert. The shafts of the spears are generally about ten feet in length, and instead of being round, are octagonal in shape. The heads are made of bone, six or eight inches long and have a barb near the junction with the shaft.

WONDERFUL STONE-THROWING BY THE FUEGIANS.

The sling of the Fuegian is made of a cup of seal or guanaco skin, to which are attached two cords similar in material to the bow-strings, thus combining apparent delicacy with great strength. The cords of the sling are more than three feet in length. The skill which the Fuegians possess with this weapon is worthy of the reputation attained by the Balearic islanders. Captain King has seen them strike with a sling-stone a cap placed on a stump fifty or sixty yards distant, and on one occasion he witnessed a really wonderful display of dexterity. He asked a Fuegian to show him the use of the weapon. The man immediately picked up a stone about as large as a pigeon's egg, placed it in the sling, and pointed to a canoe as his mark. He then turned his back, and flung the stone in exactly the opposite direction, so that it struck the trunk of a tree, and rebounded to the canoe. The men seem to think the sling a necessity of life, and it is very seldom that a Fuegian is seen without it either hung over his back or tied round his waist.

FISH-CATCHING DOGS AND CANNIBALISM.

Dogs are regarded with very mingled feelings by the Fuegians, who neglect and illtreat them, scarcely ever taking the trouble to feed them, so that if they depended on the food given them by their masters they would starve. However, their aquatic training gives these most useful servants the power of foraging for themselves, and, when not required by their masters, they can catch fish on their own account. They are odd, sharp-nosed, bushy-tailed animals, with large, pointed, erect ears, and usually with dark rough hair, though a few among them have the fur nearly white. They are watchful and faithful to their masters, and the sight of a stranger, much more of a clothed stranger, sets them barking furiously.

Although the Fuegian neglects his dog, he has a great respect and even affection for the animal. It often happens that the mussels and limpets fail, that the weather is too tempestuous for fishing, and that in consequence the people are reduced to the brink of starvation. It might be presumed that, having their dogs at hand, they would avail themselves of so obvious a source of food. This, however, they never do, except when reduced to the last extremity, and, instead of eating their dogs, they eat their old women, who, as they think, are worn out and can do no good, while the dogs, if suffered to live, will assist in catching fish and guanacos.

The Fuegian's great feast, however, takes place when a whale is stranded on the shore. All the people within reach flock to the spot, while fleets of canoes surround the stranded monster, and its body is covered with little copper-colored men carving away the blubber with their shell knives. Each cuts as much as he can get, and when he has torn and carved off a large piece of blubber, he makes a hole in the middle, puts his head through the aperture, and thus leaves his

FUEGIANS FEASTING OFF A WHALE CAST ASHORE.

hands free to carry more of the dainty food. It is immaterial whether the flesh be putrid or not, perhaps they like it better if it is; anyhow, Mr. Darwin, who visited them during his journey round the world in the ship *Beagle*, declares that the Fuegians eat the flesh of the whale when in the very last stages of decomposition; and what they can't eat at once they bury in the sand for future occasion.

FILTHY HABITS AND IMITATIVE POWERS OF THE FUEGIANS.

Though much of their time is spent in and about water, especially the sea, it is a strange fact that the Fuegians never wash themselves, the idea of cleanliness having never been conceived by them. They have a most disgusting habit of bedaubing themselves with grease and mud, until their natural color is quite concealed, and as this cosmetic is never removed, while new applications are continually being made, their bodies smell with an odor more mephitic than unaccustomed noses can possibly endure.

Generally, the Fuegians are ill-disposed towards strangers, and have murdered many boat crews that have landed among them; Captain Parker Snow, however, seems to have met with a hospitable reception during his visit to the island, and succeeded in obtaining their confidence to such an extent that crowds daily came on board his ship, and one of them willingly accompanied him to England. It was hoped that, giving him the advantages of civilization, he would be the means, upon returning to the island, of redeeming some of his people. After several years spent in England, during which time this Fuegian received a very good education, and was trained in the Christian faith, he was sent back to Terra del Fuego. A few years afterwards some voyagers met him on the island, when, to their astonishment, they found he had almost forgotten everything learned in England, and had relapsed into barbarism, so far as habits were concerned, though he had not forgotten to be polite.

The faculty of acquiring language is singularly developed in the Fuegian. A very absurd example of this curious facility of tongue occurred to some sailors who went ashore, and taught the natives to drink coffee. One of the Fuegians, after drinking his coffee, contrived to conceal the tin pot, with the intention of stealing it. The sailor demanded the restoration of his property, and was greatly annoyed that every word which he uttered was instantly repeated by the Fuegian. Thinking at last, that the man must be mocking him, and forgetting for the instant that he did not understand one word of English, the sailor assumed a menacing attitude, and bawled out, "You copper-colored rascal, where is my tin pot?" As it turned out, "the copper-colored rascal" had the pot tucked under his arm.

The natives evidently seemed to think that their white visitors were very foolish for failing to comprehend their language, and tried to make them understand by bawling at the top of their voices.

THE PATAGONIANS COMPARED WITH THE FUEGIANS.

Separated from the Fuegians, by the very narrow Strait of Magellan, are the *Patagonians*, to whom I will merely call attention to

PATAGONIANS HUNTING WITH THE BOLAS.

illustrate the remarkable differences which exist between races so closely situated that it would appear their habits, or manners of life, ought to approximate each other.

The Patagonians are noted for habits directly opposite to those of their southern neighbors. While the Fuegians have no horses, and never even employ dogs for draught purposes, the Patagonians are as essentially horsemen as were the ancient people of Thessaly. Their very infancy is almost cradled in the saddle, and the depth of poverty among them is to be without a horse. Though their climate is not nearly so cold as that of the Fuegians, they wear a superabundance of clothing, made of furs, and build their houses in a fairly substantial manner. So, in all their customs, whether domestic, social, governmental or religious, they are the very opposite of the Fuegians. But that this contrariety may be further increased, nature has given her assistance by making the Patagonian of extraordinary stature—the tallest race in the world. Formerly it was believed they not infrequently attained a height of ten and even twelve feet, but it has since been proven by many travelers, that their general height is about six feet, for both men and women, but seven feet is very common, so that the average is, perhaps, an inch or two above six feet.

No race exceeds the Patagonians in enthusiasm in the chase. They are great hunters, though seldom fishermen, in which respect they are again directly the opposite of the Fuegians. Their principal, and nearly sole, weapon is the *bolas*, a simple, but most effective agency in their hands. This is made by covering three round stones—sometimes iron and copper—the size of a man's fist, with guanaco skin, and connecting them with as many thongs, of unequal length, from three to nine feet. In throwing this weapon they exhibit truly marvelous expertness, and at a distance of fifty yards they can hurl it with the precision of a rifle-bullet. The game chiefly hunted is the guanaco, a very fleet animal, which abounds in Patagonia in great numbers, and supplies the people with nearly all their food and clothing.

THE ESQUIMAUX—THEIR LOVE FOR A FROZEN WILDERNESS.

A description, or history, of any of the several races which I have briefly noticed is always interesting, but I doubt if there is any tribe, or phase of human existence, so singularly attractive to either the student of nature or casual reader, which presents so much that is fascinating to lovers of the phonomenal, as the *Esquimaux* (more properly called *Innuits*). These wonderful people appear to us like beings who belong to another world than ours, some sphere where the sun sinks and rests his blazing face, and where the brilliant lances of Ithuriel are forged to drive away the black specters of night. They are the folk of fable, the people of the snow and ice, a race peculiar to wonder-land.

How, by what law of nature, can human beings subsist in a perpetually frozen wilderness, where the landscape is devoid of verdure and naught but icy peak and hoary plain, beetling crags of frost and whistling winds, vary the dull monotony of a scene grand in death-like slumber, the funeral scene of nature? Aye, not only subsist, but subvert the elements of cold to their own purposes, and pass as happy lives in their inclement country as do the apparently more favored inhabitants of sunny climes.

APPEARANCE, DRESS AND HABITS.

The Esquimaux are a short, and by no means strong race, their average stature being about five feet. Whence they descended no one knows, and few have even conjectured. Their eyes are set obliquely like the Chinese, whom they also resemble in complexion, but in all other respects they present the appearance of Indians, especially the high cheek-bones, hair, and facial features. Living in an excessively cold climate where any exposure of body is followed by frost-bite, we cannot wonder at the fact that the Esquimaux never wash. Such a thing is unknown to them and, I may add, is unnecessary. But we do wonder that they are equally ignorant of such vigorous exercise as running and jumping, the very practices which it would appear their condition would develop. The young people have games of ball and *shinny*, but while playing they never exercise violently.

The Esquimau women use the tattoo quite liberally, covering a greater portion of their faces and bodies with queer designs. The process of tattooing is an extremely painful one, which none would submit to except for fashion's sake, whose votaries never stop at anything, either painful or ridiculous. It is accomplished by means of a bone-needle and a thread of deer's sinew; with these rude implements the artist sews through the skin of the victim by short stitches, the thread being blacked with soot from time to time, which leaves its color under the skin, as it is drawn through the wounds. The suffering entailed by this operation must be terrible.

THE WONDERFUL KYAK BOAT AND ITS MANAGEMENT.

The means of transportation used by the Esquimaux are of two kinds, viz: by sledges and boats. There are two kinds of boats, called the *kyack* (or kia), or man's boat, and the *oomiak*, which is used by the women. This latter is employed exclusively for transporting large quantities of baggage, or a number of persons, at a time. They are generally twenty-five feet in length and of three feet depth, and, being made of skins, have a wonderful carrying capacity. The kyack is a remarkable piece of workmanship. It is shuttle shaped, both ends being sharply pointed.

It is made of a very slight framework of wood and whale-bone, over which is stretched a covering of skin. In the middle there is a hole just large enough to admit the body of the rower, and when he takes his seat, he gathers the skin together round his waist, so that the boat is absolutely impervious to water. The average length is twenty-five feet, and so light are the materials of which it is made, that a man can carry his kyack on his head from the house to the water.

These slight canoes have no keel, and sit so lightly on the water that they can be propelled over, rather than through it, with wonderful speed. The paddle is a double one, held in the middle, and used in a manner which is now rendered familiar to us by the canoes which have so largely taken the place of skiffs.

There is one feat which is sometimes performed in order to show the wonderful command which an Esquimau has over his little vessel. He does not, however, attempt it unless another kyack is close at hand. After seeing that the skin cover is firmly tied round his waist, and that his neck and wrists are well secured, the man suddenly flings himself violently to one side, thus capsizing the boat, and burying himself under water. With a powerful stroke of his paddle he turns himself and canoe completely over, and brings himself upright again. A skillful canoe-man will thus turn over and over some twenty times or so, almost as fast as the eye can follow him, and yet only his face will be in the least wet.

SINGULAR SUPERSTITIONS OF THE INNUITS.

As may be expected among a people wholly in a condition of barbarism, the Innuits—Esquimaux—have many strange superstitions, though religious belief, as respects the worship of a deity, is entirely wanting. Marriage is a recognized institution, but it is not preceded by any ceremony with them, consisting of no other form than a mere consent to live together. Polygamy is common, but there is always a favorite wife, generally the first one, who assumes the responsibility of the igloo, and in turn has the best bed, food and attention in the household. When an Esquimau wife is about to become a mother she retires apart from all her family to an igloo built especially for her. Here she is suffered to remain without a single companion, caring for herself until her child is about two weeks old, when she comes out of the igloo for the first time, throws away all her old clothes, which no one may afterwards wear, invests herself in new

ESQUIMAUX IN THEIR KYACK BOATS.

furs, and then visits every family that may be in her village. This ceremony completes her purification and she resumes her place with her family.

Death is a matter of small concern, apparently, among the Innuits, judging by the indifference they manifest. When an Esquimau falls ill he, or she, as the case may be, is carried to a new igloo and, being supplied with food and drink near at hand, is left to perish or survive as fate may decree. In taking the patient into an igloo, however, it is never by way of the door, but through a breach made in the wall, but why, no one has attempted to explain.

In case of death the body is carried to an adjacent rise in the ground and laid upon the summit, and then covered with snow, where the wolves or dogs soon devour it. But the place of deposit is called a grave, to which the friends of the deceased pay frequent visits and talk to the spirit, which is supposed to be always present, just as they would converse with a living body.

CHAPTER XLI.

CURIOSITIES OF THE HUMAN RACE.

RIVER DWELLERS OF THE ORINOCO.

IN the preceding pages I have cursorily described some of the most interesting races of the world, and, while omitting mention of many others, I have not neglected to select a sufficient number of races to fairly include the most important customs that are to be met with throughout the world. Therefore, to describe them all would necessarily cause much repetition, which, in a book of this general character, it is desirable should be avoided. Before dismissing the subject entirely, however, some further interesting information may be found in the curious phases which some races have developed, whose habits are so phenomenal as to rank them with certain animals, or at least to destroy the strongest ties that bind them to tribes of man. Though human creatures in form, intelligence and attributes, we may justly call them freaks of nature, or subjects of curious development, at utter variance with all other human creatures.

Among these aberrant people is a race of amphibious men whose houses are on the Orinoco river; not strictly within the water, but whose habits are common to both land and water. These are the *Warau* and *Carib* tribes, not so numerous now, but once as powerful, perhaps, as any race of South America. These singular people are inoffensive, extremely ignorant and intensely superstitious. One of the beings which they most dread is the water mamma, or *Orehu*. This is an unfortunate being who inhabits the water, and occasionally shows herself, though in different forms, sometimes even assuming that of the horse, but often taking that of the manati. The Orehu is a female spirit, and is generally, though not always, malicious, and, when she is in a bad temper, is apt to rise close to the canoes and drag them and their crews under water.

HERODOTUS' MENTION OF LAKE DWELLERS.

In the fifth book of Herodotus occurs a passage which, until discoveries were made of the remains of dwellings in the lakes of Switzerland, once occupied by a people who made their homes above the surface of the water, was believed to be a mere invention of the historian. After enumerating the various nations that Megabazes subdued, he states that the Persian monarch also attempted to conquer "those who live upon the Lake Prasias in dwellings."

"They live in the following manner: Every man has a hut on the planks, in which he dwells, with a trap-door closely fitted in the planks, and leading down to the lake. They tie the young children with a cord round the feet, fearing lest they should fall into the lake beneath. To their horses and beasts of burden they give fish for fodder, of which there is such abundance, that when a man has opened his trap-door, he lets down an empty basket by a cord into the lake, and, after waiting a short time, draws it up full of fish."

THE WONDERFUL ITA PALM.

The Waurus construct their dwellings of the *Ita* palm, as seen in the engraving, the tree being to them food, drink and covering.

When full-grown the Ita palm resembles a tall, cylindrical pillar, with a fan of ten or twelve vast leaves spreading from its extreme top. Each leaf is some ten feet in width, and is supported upon a huge stem about twelve feet in length, looking more like a branch than a leaf-stem. Indeed, a complete leaf is a heavy load for a man. At regular intervals the whole fan of leaves falls off, and is replaced by another, the tree adding to its height at every change of leaf, until the stem is nearly a hundred feet high, and fifteen in circumference.

Food is supplied by the tree in various forms. First, there is the fruit, which, when ripe, is as large as an ordinary apple, many hundreds of which are developed on the single branch produced by this tree. Next, there is the trunk of the tree and its contents. If it be split longitudinally at the time when the flower branch is just about to burst from the enveloping spathe, a large quantity of soft, pith-like substance is found within it. This is treated like the cassava, and furnishes a sort of bread called *vuruma*.

Drink is also obtained from the ita palm. From the trunk is drawn a sap, which, like that of the maguey or great American aloe, can be fermented, and then it becomes intoxicating in quality. Another kind of drink is procured from the fruit of the ita, which is bruised, thrown into water, and allowed to ferment for a while. When fermented, the liquor is strained through a sieve made of ita fiber, and is thus ready for consumption.

THE MARACAIBO LAKE DWELLERS.

Besides the Waurus there are the *Maracaibo Lake Dwellers*, a race not inferior in numbers to the Waurus, perhaps; indeed, more numerous. There are four large villages on the lake, besides numerous detached dwellings in the various bays which indent the shores. Instead of using the ita palm, however, the Maracaibos construct

THE WAURU LAKE DWELLERS OF SOUTH AMERICA.

their habitations on piles made from the iron-wood tree. How they manage to cut these trees into proper length, when the wood is so hard that it will turn the edge of an axe, I have not been able to learn; nor do I know how they contrive to drive the piles into the bottom of the lake, as travelers in that region have neglected to describe the process. But the fact remains, and is a very interesting one. On these piles cross-beams are laid for the support of planks of light wood, and when the roof is added, and sometimes flimsy walls, the house is complete.

When the Spaniards first entered the Gulf of Maracaibo, and came within view of the lake, they were struck with amazement at these curious habitations, and called the place Venezuela — *i. e.*, Little Venice — a name which has since been extended to the whole of the large province.

THE WONDERFUL LAKE DWELLERS OF SWITZERLAND.

Having even thus casually referred to the Waurus, and merely incidentally mentioned their prototypes of Switzerland, further notice of the latter is rendered necessary, especially as in all the phenomena of tribal existence, none are so surprising as the habits and attainments of the *Swiss Lake Dwellers*. In the years 1853–54, great drought prevailed in nearly all Switzerland, and the winters were so cold that the little water that remained in the rivers was frozen, which cut off all supply from the lakes, until in many places their dry beds began to appear. Such a scarcity of water was never before known to the people then residing near the lakes, and great distress was felt in consequence. But this drought did not prove altogether unfortunate, for by disclosing, as it did, several lake beds, a most remarkable discovery was made, viz: the relics of a race or tribe not previously known to exist; a people whose habits were identical with those of the Maracaibo Lake Dwellers, whom I have just mentioned.

The houses which this ancient people inhabited were built on piles driven into the Swiss lakes, and they had walls wattled and plastered with clay, so as to make them comfortable at a time when Europe was no doubt passing through the glacial period. Not only were the piles upon which the houses were built, and fragments of the walls, discovered, but also numerous specimens of the weapons, ornaments, cooking utensils, and even food used by the inhabitants were brought to light after centuries of inhumation below the waters.

The resemblance, indeed identity, between many articles found in the beds of the Swiss lakes and those still in common use among several savage tribes of the Americas, is more than remarkable; but more wonderful still is the fact that among these resurrected relics are found not a few that are identical with inventions of modern times, upon which the period of exclusive right had not expired, when the discoveries referred to were made.

Learned archæologists tell us that these lake habitations were evidently in use during the stone age, prior to the time when fire became known. This is proved by the quantity of stone weapons and domestic implements which have been found in the lakes. A long period of occupation is also established by the differences shown in the architecture of these lake dwellings, by which we know that these people were progressive, each generation, perhaps, exhibiting new development by the aid of new invention.

From the relics that have been discovered, the character of these lake-dwellings is easily understood. They were built upon piles, driven by some powerful machinery into the bed of the lake. These piles were connected by cross-beams on which a flooring was laid, fastened with thongs, and on this the circular superstructure was reared tall enough inside to allow a man to stand up straight; the roof was peaked to a common center, and thatched so as to turn rain.

The reason for building these edifices is analogous to that which prompts military engineers to surround their forts with moats filled with water. In those primitive times, man waged a continual war with wild beasts, such as the cave-bear, wolf-bear and larger animals, so that these lacustrine habitations proved to be strongholds which such enemies could not assault. While original man was no doubt a hunter, he was also hunted by many fierce creatures from which his intelligence alone protected him.

CURIOSITIES FOUND IN THE SWISS LAKES.

A vast quantity of relics of this extinct race have been recovered from the lakes, which possess extraordinary interest for the anthropologist. The original piles have, in many instances, been found standing, and several were drawn for the purpose of determining the depth to which they had been driven. Portions of the wattled walls of the huts have also been found, together with great numbers of stone implements made at a very early age. Great quantities of pottery have also been found, the crescent being a favorite ornament, and a number of utensils of crescentic shape have likewise been discovered.

These relics were the remains left by the earliest occupants of the lake dwellings; then, as time went on, succeeding generations of these people improved upon the earlier work of their progenitors, and substituted metal for stone, a new discovery, but the manner in which they smelted the ore is not known. Examples of their handiwork, are, however, abundant, such as axes, spears, arrow-heads, necklaces, bracelets and hairpins, and — what is strangely remarkable — there are specimens of the identical article now of nearly universal use in nurseries, *the safety-pin.*

We have abundant evidence of the kind of food which these lake-people subsisted on, in the way of bones of various animals gnawed and cut by them, and also, singular to relate, the kind of bread they ate. As may be supposed, their bread was of the coarsest character, being made from grains of corn that were first roasted, then pounded with a stone and pressed into cakes. Even fruits have been found ready cut and prepared for consumption, the apple being quite common among the petrified specimens. There have also been found seeds of the plum, raspberry and blackberry, also hazel and beech-nuts, all of which were used for food. Of the people themselves! Where are they? From whence descended, and whither have they passed? Nothing but the age-covered relics mentioned remain to tell us that such a singular people ever existed.

THE TREE DWELLERS.

As races of men are found dwelling in lakes, rivers and caverns, so do we find others making their habitations among the trees, as if to prove that mankind, in his undeveloped state, adopts the ways of animals among which he maintains a struggle for existence. Sometimes the ravages of beasts, with which he is unable to contend, drive him from a natural condition and serve to impart to him the most singular ideas, leading to the adoption of equally curious modes of living. The same results may arise from oppressions imposed by a more powerful race; and yet again, in the wildernesses of the world, where there is no stimulant to ambition, we occasionally find man living as he did at the dawn of creation—in shape a human, in condition a beast.

More than one tribe of equatorial savages are noted for their singular mode of life in constructing their dwellings high up upon the branches of lofty and gigantic trees, where they not only build isolated houses, but villages as well. Among these strange people the *Bakones*, of South Central Africa, are best known, because they are more universally tree dwellers than any other tribe of whom we have any reliable information. Mr. Moffat, the well-known missionary, who has given us so many interesting descriptions of the African tribes among whom he labored for nearly twenty-five years, writes as follows of the tree dwellers:

THE HOUSES OF THE BAKONES.

"* * * On reaching the topmost hut, about thirty feet from the ground, I entered, and sat down. Its only furniture was the hay which

ARABS ATTACKING THE BAKONE TREE DWELLERS.

covered the floor, a spear, a spoon, and a bowlful of locusts. Not having eaten anything that day, and from the novelty of my situation, not wishing to return immediately to the wagons, I asked a woman who sat at the door with a babe at her breast, permission to eat. This she granted with pleasure, and soon brought me more in a powdered state. Several more females came from the neighboring roosts, stepping from branch to branch, to see the stranger, who was to them as great a curiosity as the tree was to him. I then visited the different abodes, which were on several principal branches. The structure of these houses was very simple. An oblong scaffold, about seven feet wide, is formed of straight sticks. On one end of this platform a small cone is formed, also of straight sticks, and thatched with grass. A person can nearly stand upright in it; the diameter of the floor is about six feet. The house stands on the end of the oblong, so as to leave a little square space before the door."

BARBARIC DESTRUCTION OF CHILDREN.

The Bakones are not a numerous tribe now, though believed to have been once populous; their timidity and infamous practices have done much to diminish their numbers. The Arabs, knowing them to be a cowardly people, have captured thousands and sold them into slavery, and even to this day occasionally attack the Bakone villages, not so much to make them slaves as to plunder them of the ivory they may possess.

The Bakones are extremely superstitious, and carry their barbaric ignorance to the point of sacrificing infants to the gods they worship. It is also their custom to kill their children for the most frivolous causes, so that comparatively few are suffered to attain their majority. If a child turns from one side to another during sleep it is murdered, because the Bakones believe an evil spirit has influenced the act, and therefore will continue control of the child if it be allowed to live. All deformed children are at once put to death; so are all infants that cut the upper teeth before the lower ones appear.

The Bakones have few weapons and rely chiefly on the bow and arrow, with which they hunt the antelope species and smaller animals. They also use a strange weapon made like a two-pronged hoe, with short handle, which is of great service to them in digging out ground-animals such as mice, moles, ipis, ants, small snakes, etc., all of which they eat with avidity.

THE MONKEY MEN OF NEW GUINEA.

There is also a race of blacks peculiar to Dourga strait, on the coast of New Guinea, that spend much of their time among the branches of trees. Their huts are built upon the ground, where a clearing is made for the purpose, but they are nearly always found, as are the monkeys, with which their territory is thickly populated, either resting on the limbs of trees or making their way by leaping from branch to branch, by which they travel for miles without once touching the ground.

MONKEY-MEN OF NEW GUINEA.

The tribes of this part of New Guinea are by no means agreeable specimens of the *Papuan* race. They are barely of middle size and lightly built. Their skin is decidedly black, and they ornament their bodies with red ochre, paying special attention to their faces, which are made as scarlet as ochre can make them. They are a dirty set of people, and are subject to diseases of the skin, which give them a very repulsive appearance.

Dress is not used by the men, who, however, wear plenty of ornaments. They mostly have a belt made of plaited leaves or rushes, about five inches wide, and so long that, when tied together behind, the ends hang down for a foot or so. Some of them adorn this belt with a large white shell, placed exactly in the middle. Ear-rings of plaited rattan, necklaces and bracelets are worn by nearly all. Some of them have a very ingenious armlet, several inches in width. It is made of plaited rattan, and fitted so tightly to the limb that, when a native wishes to take it off for sale, he is obliged to smear his arm with mud, and have the ornament drawn off by another person.

The agility of these Papuans is really astonishing. Along the water's edge there run wide belts of mangroves, which extend for many miles in length with scarcely a break in them. The ground is a thick, deep and soft mud, from which the mangrove-roots spring in such numbers that no one could pass through them, even at low water, without the constant use of an axe, while at high water all passage is utterly impossible.

As the natives, who are essentially maritime in their mode of life, have to cross this belt several times daily in passing from their canoes to their houses, and *vice versa*, they prefer doing so by means of the upper branches, among which they run and leap, by constant practice from childhood, as easily as monkeys.

The familiarity of these people with the trees causes them to look upon a tree as a natural fortress, and as soon as explorers succeeded in reaching the villages, the natives invariably made off, and climbed into the trees that surrounded their miserable little huts. Seen among the branches, whither they had taken refuge, their resemblance to monkeys was so striking that they were given the very appropriate title of *Monkey-men*, by which they are now known among ethnologists.